# A GOOD TOWN CONTINUES

N'S HOTEL

# A GOOD TOWN CONTINUES

## BRACEBRIDGE 1915 TO 1999

BRACEBRIDGE 125TH ANNIVERSARY BOOK COMMITTEE

EDITED BY NANCY R. THOMPSON

*Published by the Town of Bracebridge, 125th Anniversary Committee*

FRONT COVER *Steamers at the wharf, Bracebridge Bay, 1932. See page 97 for additional information.* COURTESY OF THE BRACEBRIDGE PUBLIC LIBRARY

BACK COVER AND TITLE PAGE *Downtown Bracebridge, 1999. The old post office building with its clock tower opened in 1915.* COURTESY OF GARY LONG

OPENING PAGE AND ABOVE *The quintessential Bracebridge scene for a century (1950 on opening page, 1985 above).* COURTESY OF THE TOWN OF BRACEBRIDGE

FRONTISPIECE *Downtown Bracebridge in the 1920s. Many of the buildings still stand, although functions and facades have changed. Automobile styling has certainly evolved! See page 77 for additional information about this scene.* COURTESY OF IAN TURNBULL



Published by the Town of Bracebridge
125th Anniversary Committee
23 Dominion Street, Bracebridge, Ontario P1L 1R6
Telephone (705) 645-5264 Fax (705) 645-1262

*Cover and interior design* Lorrie Szekat
*Typesetting and production* Fox Meadow Creations
*Printing and binding* Transcontinental Printing
*Set in Monotype Octavian*
*Printed in Canada on acid-free paper* ∞

*Canadian Cataloguing in Publication Data*

Main entry under title:

A good town continues : Bracebridge 1915 to 1999

Includes bibliographical references and index.
ISBN 0-9686003-0-1

1. Bracebridge (Ont.) – History.
I. Thompson, Nancy R. (Nancy Rose), 1946- .
II. Bracebridge (Ont.). 125th Anniversary Book Committee.
III. Bracebridge (Ont.). 125th Anniversary Committee.

FC3099.B73G66 1999 971.3'16 C99-932389-X
F1059.5.B722G66 1999

# DEDICATION

*this book is dedicated to*

The fine people who unselfishly volunteer their time and energy to help make Bracebridge a splendid place to live, to work, and to enjoy

The volunteers who donate their care and attention to the patients, visitors, and staff at the South Muskoka Memorial Hospital

The volunteers who are found helping the children, the old, and the less fortunate

The volunteers who work with the police, the fire brigade, and the service clubs

The volunteers who worked on the 125th celebrations

The volunteers who researched and wrote this book

# "We Never Sleep."

**Take a drive in one of our**

**CLASSY NEW TURN-OUTS,**
**LUXURIOUS CARRIAGES,**
**BEAUTIFULLY GROOMED HORSES**

**Show your visitors Muskoka's scenic wonders in either of our two comfortable cars,-- the ones that always get back.**

## McNeice Bros.

*"Bracebridge's Leading Horse and Car Livery"*

**Telephone 94** **Opposite Picture Show**

*An early advertisement for the McNeice Brothers, about 1915. Tourists wishing to enjoy the scenery of the Bracebridge area did not lack options for transportation – although the possibility that a car might not make it home obviously weighed upon the minds of many!* COURTESY OF THE BRACEBRIDGE PUBLIC LIBRARY, REDMOND THOMAS COLLECTION

# CONTENTS

*This picture in the summer of 1999 was taken from the sidewalk that climbs the steep hill east of the bridge at the top of the falls. The very first road to Bracebridge, the Muskoka Road, descended this hill and crossed an ancestor of the present bridge. Early visitors arriving by this route got their initial view of the frontier settlement as their wagon or stagecoach lurched down the precipitous incline.* COURTESY OF GARY LONG

# PREFACE

BRACEBRIDGE is the central town of Muskoka District, Ontario, and is located on the 45th parallel of latitude – halfway between the Equator and the North Pole. It is today an area municipality within the District Municipality of Muskoka created in 1970, so that it now consists of the former town, the former townships of Draper, Macaulay, and Oakley, and parts of the former townships of McLean, Muskoka, and Monck, with a year-round population of 14,000 and many more during the summer.

This book covers the major events in and around Bracebridge from 1915 to 1999; it is intended as a sequel to Robert J. Boyer's 1975 book, *A Good Town Grew Here*, and to bring our history to near the beginning of the 21st century and the 125th anniversary of municipal incorporation (1875 to 2000).

The material on which this book is based comes largely from the minute books of the Town of Bracebridge, the minute books and pictorial history of the fire department, the newspapers on microfilm at the Bracebridge Public Library, and from newspapers not on microfilm.

The book was researched and written by Nancy R. Thompson (who also edited the material), Judith Ruan, Donna Ivey, Gary Denniss, Barb McMurray, Ken Veitch, Lyle Longhurst, Libby Brownlee, Brenda Cox, Nancy Cox-Godfrey, Libby Clarke, and Murray Clarke, with extra help from Heather Coupland and Brian Thompson. The authors are indebted to the staff of the Bracebridge Public Library for their able assistance, and to the town's chief administrative officer and clerk Murray Clarke and his staff for their friendly encouragement and administrative support. Thank-you to all who loaned photographs for the project. Credits appear with each picture.

*Looking northwest towards downtown Bracebridge, early 1900s, from approximately the same spot as the 1999 view on the previous spread (notably no trees obscuring the view!). Though clearly of an earlier era, the town with its numerous brick buildings, iron bridges, and hydro poles has obviously become established as an important and prosperous community. The Bird Woollen Mill and the town's water-pumping station (the latter originally the hydroelectric plant) occupy the river bank between the road and railway bridges; beyond the railway is the lower end of Manitoba Street. The impressive British Lion Hotel stands at the corner of Ontario and Dominion streets, upper left, with the courthouse to the right and the Town Hall a little farther along skyline.* COURTESY OF THE ARCHIVES OF ONTARIO

# INTRODUCTION

## *by Robert J. Boyer*

FOR THE 125TH ANNIVERSARY of Bracebridge municipal incorporation, the committee which worked on a history book for the Town has honoured me by asking that I write an introduction for the book. They want to link my book of 1975, *A Good Town Grew Here*, with their 1915 to 1999 report of major events of more recent decades.

*A Good Town Grew Here* told the story of Bracebridge development from 1861 to 1914, almost every year a year of growth, 40 of the years with village then town status. It told of industrial growth, tanneries located here for the plentiful red hemlock "tan" bark from sale of which land owners prospered, sawmills that operated with superior equipment, the woollen mill which encouraged Muskoka sheep farming, and saddlery made and delivered across the country.

As one of the leading ports on the Muskoka Lakes navigation system and centre for the District's principal roads, Bracebridge was a town recognized for the number and quality of merchant establishments. Always Muskoka's judicial centre, the courthouse, registry office and several law offices were here, not to mention in that period the district jail. Churches had attractive new buildings. The principal parks were Jubilee to honour Queen Victoria and Memorial for two young men from Bracebridge killed in the South African War.

In 1894 Bracebridge became the first municipality in Canada to own and operate its own hydroelectric power generation system, at Bracebridge Falls, and the town also installed a water distribution plant.

The government at Ottawa did things helpful to Bracebridge such as constructing a wharf adequate for steamboat service and deep-dredging the river approaches as well as building an access road, opening a customs office and a downtown post office building.

Behind all evidence of progress was what Captain L.R. Fraser called "the dynamic, driving spirit of the Old Timers who built up the Town." In this new book on Bracebridge are recorded slowdown times and even a loss of people resulting from war conditions and the big Depression. Removal of the Beardmore tannery to Acton in 1923 took paying jobs away, then in 1930 the large Anglo-Canadian leather tannery, producing only for the U.S. market, closed when tariff duties applying to shoe leather were increased by the Americans from 27 to 50 percent. After a few years the population had declined by 600 but gradually was restored. Better news for the period was the opening of the high school newly built in 1925, the hospital in 1928, streets paved, and several church additions built.

Forming a leading part always in Muskoka's economy and always benefiting Bracebridge has been the tourist resort industry. From the early days one shoreline wooden hotel after another was built on lakes and rivers and prospered for many years. About 1950 and since, hotels became fewer when several were bought by individuals to turn them into private residences, keeping the shoreline strictly private. This has not happened to certain historically established hotels whose future seems assured.

Bracebridge with its river location for dozens of years was one of Muskoka's boat-building centres, and power pleasure launches made in Bracebridge boat works, if

*Bracebridge Bay was a natural harbour for steamboats in an era when water transportation was vital to any Muskoka community aspiring to a prominent economic role in the district. For many years the wharf was near the outlet of the bay, by the present beach, where in this picture, about 1900, several steamers (including the* Muskoka, Kenozha, *and* Oriole*) are moored. On the opposite shore stands the huge tannery complex of the Anglo-Canadian Leather Company.*

COURTESY OF THE NATIONAL ARCHIVES OF CANADA PA157711

they survived fibreglass, are honoured as examples of Muskoka classic wooden craft.

In 1960 and in succeeding years Bracebridge and the two other towns of Muskoka benefited with a new interest in locating industry in the District. The first of several was called Canadian Motor Lamp, at Bracebridge, now Meritor Automotive Canada. Others followed. At the time of this book it may be said that Bracebridge, and also Huntsville and Gravenhurst, never had so many employees in industry. To keep up with the needs of such expansion, Bracebridge's water supply was substantially increased, benefiting also new householders.

By the 1960s Muskoka land sales reached such a number that no provincial land registry office outside the cities had a volume equal to that of Muskoka. Problems of land use and the outdated road system in an unorganized District plus other weaknesses in municipal government led to new District government administration in 1971 with District's own Council able to act in many matters in a united manner with six local area municipalities.

When the province required a District Board of Education in 1970, Muskoka was ready since the District was the first in Ontario to have schools under the Township School Area system instead of small school sections. By the 1960s each of the 25 municipalities had new school construction, with central schools in townships. As new residents moved here, then came a demand for separate schools and Bracebridge has now the Monsignor O'Leary Elementary School and St. Dominic Secondary School.

My book told of the unsuccessful efforts to gain support for the District to build a Home for elderly persons who needed care. Finally, when Muskoka District became the last district or county in Ontario lacking a home for the aged, most town, village. and township councils approved the plan and in 1960 The Pines Home for the Aged was built, to be increased in size in the 1980s. Since then a number of private retirement homes and long-term care facilities have been established in Muskoka.

My book *A Good Town Grew Here*, but for 14 years, had to do with the 19th century, a century which introduced railways, steamships, electric power and light, telegraph, and telephone. Greater benefits came in the 20th century – air travel, motor vehicles, radio, television, computers, Internet.

The new century will have its own surprises. The anniversary year, because it leads into a new century and a new millennium, tends to make it an occasion of special awe. Yet the days will pass normally with the promise that our "Good Town" will keep growing here in its scenic beauty and with friendly residents, its advance sustained by the dynamic driving spirit that has characterized this town's most prosperous periods.

*Bracebridge in 1873, shortly before its incorporation as a village. This photograph was taken from the Muskoka Road as it descended into the village at the top of the falls – almost the same vantage point again as the photographs on pages 10 and 12. Barely 13 years old, the community still retains a rough, frontier flavour. The bridge is the original one built in 1860 when the Ontario government pushed the Muskoka colonization road north into the wilderness. At lower left stands the Bird Woollen Mill, powered by the falls. By providing a convenient bridge point, a source of power for early industry, and forming the head of navigation above Lake Muskoka, Bracebridge Falls made this a natural location for an important community to grow.* COURTESY OF THE BRACEBRIDGE PUBLIC LIBRARY

# EARLY YEARS

## *Summary of Events 1860 to 1914*

IN PREPARING this volume to commemorate the 125th anniversary of municipal organization in Bracebridge, the committee felt it would be helpful to include a summary of the material published in 1975 by Robert J. Boyer. *A Good Town Grew Here* was prepared to help celebrate Bracebridge Centennial Year.

The highlights of those formative years, as taken from *A Good Town Grew Here*, are now reviewed to provide the reader with knowledge of the historical events that preceded those about to be covered in the pages of this present book.

1859 – the first settler, John Beal, followed soon after by David Leith and the Cooper brothers

1861 – the Muskoka Road reached North Falls, bridge was built to replace the log crosser – stage services provided by John Harvie – Wesleyan Methodist religious services begun by Rev. J.L. Kerr, a circuit rider from Orillia

1862 – the first resident minister, Rev. Gillman Willson of the Methodist Episcopals

1863 – the first white child born, Mary Liddard – lots surveyed by William Holditch and James Cooper

1864 – a flour and grist mill established by Alexander Bailey – Bracebridge post office opened by postmaster Alexander Bailey

1865 – United Townships of Morrison and Muskoka organized – Norwood Mills lumber business of Gillman Willson established at Wilson's Falls

1866 – Anglican services began in a log chapel north of the village – the Loyal Orange Lodge began – first wedding ceremony performed: William Holditch married Elizabeth

Willson – teenager Robert A. Barron privately organized the first school – the *Wenonah* (first steamboat) arrived

1867 – Confederation celebrated with a picnic, sports, and games – Orange Hall built and the Twelfth of July commemorated – Alexander P. Cockburn elected as Liberal MPP – the first fall fair – The District Exchange, first really substantial store, established by John Teviotdale – Alexander Bailey's business interests purchased by Thomas Myers and Robert Perry – tavern and store built by Hiram James McDonald (year approximate)

1868 – Free Grant and Homesteads Act spurred settlement in Muskoka – Presbyterian Church built on King Street (year approximate) – United Townships of Draper, Macaulay, Stephenson and Ryde organized, the growing Bracebridge village being located in the southwest corner of Macaulay – settlement recognized as District seat with a division court, registry office, and Crown lands agent established and a public building erected on the corner of Dominion and Ontario streets – school section No. 1 Macaulay set up to include Bracebridge with a two-room school eventually built on the "school lot"

1869 – County Orange Lodge of Muskoka formed with Bracebridge businessman George F. Gow as County Master – seven lodges in existence in Muskoka – Monck Township organized with J.B. Browning as reeve and William Payne as clerk – Muskoka Township incorporated

1870 – the first newspaper, *The Northern Advocate*, was published by Thomas McMurray – first medical doctor, J.N. Byers – Wesleyan Methodist Church on Dominion Street opened – the Winter Evening Amusement Association presented dramatic plays

1871 – mass was celebrated in area homes during the 1870s – Macaulay Township incorporated with George Gow as reeve and James Boyer as clerk

1872 – the *Free Grant Gazette* was established by E.F. Stephenson, publisher – St. Thomas Anglican frame church opened on the corner of James and Mary streets – Henry J. Bird established a woollen mill – baseball club was organized

1874 – the original bridge at "the forks" completed – visit of the Governor General and his wife Lord and Lady Dufferin – on June 5 a bylaw was passed to erect the Village of Bracebridge to an incorporated village apart from Macaulay Township – the Mechanic's Institute (library) was established

1875 – the first village elections – Robert E. Perry, reeve; James Boyer, clerk; Alfred Hunt, treasurer; Robert H. White, assessor and tax collector; John Dobbin, constable; and John Haw, first fire warden – five tavern licences granted

1876 – first wooden plank sidewalks laid – Bracebridge fire brigade formed with the purchase of a fire engine, hose, and ladders – fencing and shade tree planting encouraged – dedication of frame building for Knox Presbyterian Church on corner of Quebec and McMurray streets

1877 – William Kirk became assessor when Robert White resigned; Robert Oaten collector – Beardmore Tannery built on land in Monck Township which was annexed by the village – Jonas Bowman and David Barber agreed to establish a tannery where Northern Planing is now – Masonic Lodge No. 360 formed, Isaac Huber first Worshipful Master – brick registry office built on Dominion Street

1878 – *The Muskoka Herald* newspaper first published by F.T. Graffe and Harry Oaten – Beardmore Tannery enlarged to employ 30 men – Teacher's Association for Muskoka formed

1879 – McMurray Street school property and Dominion Street municipal office property purchased – dog licence bylaw passed, also bylaw to license and regulate transient peddlers – first macadamized street cost $800 – main street first called Manitoba Street officially – District jail with five cells built – St. Joseph's Roman Catholic Church erected and consecrated – fire destroyed four stores and damaged others – Cricket Club organized.

1880 – Bracebridge Public School built – Henry Boyer's tombstone factory opened

1881 – Town Hall completed – Village divided into two polling divisions – H.S. Bowyer became chief engineer of fire-fighting apparatus

1882 – tough times in the area, many in tax arrears – Beardmore Tannery sold to C.W. Tillson, renamed The Muskoka Leather Company

1883 – first lacrosse match played August10; Bracebridge beat Gravenhurst 5-3 – mother and child burned to death in house fire – bowling alley bylaw

1884 – Village lost costly lawsuit over illegal seizure of steamer *Flora Barnes* – H.J. Bird allowed his mill pumps to run waterworks system for fire protection – land set aside for railway station and siding – first night watchman, Robert Howard, appointed – first Board of Health organized with Dr. Shaw as medical officer of health

1885 – railway survey completed and station built – Baptists organized as a congregation

1886 – W.C. Mahaffy appointed first judge in District – first passenger train arrived in Bracebridge June 28 – Odd Fellows Lodge No. 251 instituted – "Tanbark Street" opened to Amosville or "The Hollow" – Peter and Robert Hutchison opened their grocery store – Dowler match factory exempted from taxes for five years – Huntsville incorporated as a village

1887 – fire destroyed five businesses; fire killed two and destroyed home – "fire ward" bylaw limited construction of wooden frame buildings – Warren & Copeland opened an iron foundry – Baptists purchased Temperance Hall for their church.

1888 – Bracebridge continued as government seat for new Provisional District of Muskoka – large fall fair building erected on new fair grounds (later Jubilee Park) – iron lamp posts installed along some streets – many brick buildings replaced those burned previous year – Bird Woollen Mill enlarged to provide a warehouse and shop – first Court of Assizes for Muskoka opened in Bracebridge – bylaw for store closing between 6:00 p.m. and 5:00 a.m. with exceptions – several children died of diphtheria

1889 – Bracebridge incorporated as a town March 23 – first snowplow purchased – new brick Methodist (now United) Church dedicated – another major Manitoba Street fire – examination for qualifications for teachers conducted here twice a year

*Bracebridge from Woodchester Villa about 1890. A 240-metre slide, built in 1883, allowed lumbermen to bypass the treacherous rocks of the falls on the annual log drives to their mills.* COURTESY OF THE ONTARIO ARCHIVES 15963-16

1890 – fairgrounds taken over as town park – Dominion flag purchased for use by the town

1891 – new tannery built near J.D. Shier lumber mill – town extended to Ward 4 – Women's Christian Temperance Union branch formed March 10 – Messrs. Topp & Anderson opened dry goods, grocery business – Robert Hoffman opened flour, feed, and grocery store – *Muskoka Herald* moved to new building next to Town Hall (upstairs room, the Herald Hall, popular for lodge meetings)

1892 – W.S. Shaw installed a power plant on the upper falls to provide electricity to the new tannery; Town arranged to get lighting for Town Hall and some streets – Young Men's Reform Club formed – Baptist Church bricked – Alloway Kirk Camp, Sons of Scotland instituted September 23 – much migration to western Canada

1893 – the town bell was purchased for $183.50 and hung in a tower at Town Hall; used to indicate work hours as well as sounding curfew times for children under 14 – steel bridge over the falls completed – large brick residence of J.L. Fenn completed, later became Memorial Hospital – telephone system established by Automatic Telephone and Electric Co. (later taken over by Bell Company) – Alfred Hunt had a private bank in Bracebridge, the only bank in Muskoka at the time – a "tent" of the Order of the Knights of the Macabees was instituted

1894 – Bracebridge became the first municipality in Ontario to own and operate a hydroelectric generating station as a public utility (purchased W.S. Shaw's 80-HP plant) – a system of water mains was constructed – original Anglican rectory destroyed by fire, replaced by a brick building – George W. Sibbett opened a liquor store

1895 – new, larger, 2,000-light-capacity generator installed – Barron spring property in Macaulay purchased to augment water supply – bylaw passed to prohibit riding of bicycles and tricycles on sidewalks – fire chief appointed at $30 a year – decided it was not in the best interest of the town that cows should run at large – horse stable erected on fair grounds

1896 – new brick Anglican Church opened December 6 – market site provided on location of current Memorial Park

1897 – Diamond Jubilee of Queen Victoria celebrated with community service and fair in Jubilee Park – Alfred Hunt's private bank robbed – new post office building completed (near Chancery Lane) – roads repaired – first gravel pit purchased – telephone central in Thomson's Drug Store

1898 – Monck school section No. 7 opened a one-room school – Hunt's private bank failed – Bank of Ottawa to open a branch – Grand Trunk Railway installed a switch and track behind the station – William J. Hammond hung for the murder of his wife – first cheese factory established (Cheese Factory Hill, north Wellington) – Shier's sawmill and shingle mill destroyed by fire – curling club organized with 45 members – summer of severe frosts then intense heat and drought – Muskoka set up as provisional judicial district separate from Parry Sound

1899 – Board of Trade formed – Boer War began October 11 – water service extended, sidewalks improved – Town gave $100 to Bell Telephone Company to assist telephone link to other communities – main streets watered for first time

1900 – Memorial Park established and trees planted in honour of Fred Wasdell and J.H. Finlay, killed in Boer War – Market Street renamed Kimberley Avenue (South African battle) – request made for one or two cannons for the park – secured services of a Victorian Order of Nurses – courthouse completed – William Spencer appointed police magistrate for $200 a year – new long distance switchboard – new Bank of Ottawa building – Town purchased a team of horses, wagons, sleighs, watering cart and equipment (continued to keep a work team until 1933) – B.W. Tillson hired as bandmaster at $200 a year for Citizen's Band; weekly outdoor concerts June to September

1901 – held many memorial services for Queen Victoria's death – addition for a high school built on public school – first library board appointed and one-half mill granted to library – contract let for powerhouse with a 300-kW generator at lower Bracebridge Falls – several cases of smallpox – Shier Avenue opened – G.W. Ecclestone and J. Pratt both erected large brick buildings on Manitoba Street – J.A. McCargar took over Bracebridge Flour Mill and also did gristing and chopping – Ladies' Literary Society formed – population 2,480 – John

*The powerhouse at the bottom of the falls as it looked in 1903. Today, the plant is not only one of the most picturesque hydroelectric stations in Canada, but also one of the oldest still in operation. The turreted house on the hill, originally built for Judge Mahaffy, later became Holiday House.* COURTESY OF THE BRACEBRIDGE PUBLIC LIBRARY

Anticknap, tonsorial artist, opened shop – first South Muskoka Woman's Institute District meeting held – Bracebridge Juniors lacrosse team won Canadian Lacrosse Association championship (first major sports championship by a local club) – scow bridge in place for the winter

1902 – J.D. Shier rebuilt with the first double-cutting band mill in Canada – Muskoka Foundry established by Mungo Park McKay – Bracebridge Furniture Factory started – 12 to 15 steamers a day – teacher strike – Wilson's Falls bridge removed – four downtown businesses destroyed by fire – Kirk's store burned later as did Tennant's mill – three-storey brick building erected by H.J. Bird – two new railway switches added – Holiness Movement Church opened a chapel on Ontario Street – Knox Church re-bricked and two-storey addition added – first storm sewer (built on Dominion Street)

1903 – five-storey building of Hess Furniture Company began operation, had own railway switch – Bracebridge Brick Co.(later Watson) established yard and kiln at end of Milton Street – more sidewalks – skinny dipping declared illegal within town limits – many Italian families brought in by the tanneries – R.M. Browning Memorial Hall, a gift from his widow, replaced old frame Anglican Church – illustrated booklet about town published by Board of Trade

1904 – Dominion Linen Mills in operation – John Baker got Dominion government contract to build wharf – new "stone cottage" lock-up built behind Town Hall – IOOF Hall built – steamer *Oriole* sank– Crown Bank of Canada opened a branch on July 18 – Ecclestone-Wasley curling trophy donated

1905 – new wharf completed – two cannons received for Memorial Park – construction started on new Thomas Street (now Taylor Road) bridge – first cement sidewalks laid along Manitoba, James, Victoria, Dill, and

Holditch streets – Bracebridge Tannery renamed Anglo-Canadian Leather Co. – second unit installed at No. 2 powerhouse to develop 400 HP – William McConnell engaged as police chief and H.R. Ferrier night watchman – W.C. Simmons hired as town engineer for $900 a year with free light and water – H.R. Scovell new school principal – IOOF lodge rooms dedicated – Town agreed to take over Citizen's Band instruments and pay debt – *The Gazette* sold to L.B. Williams – Excelsior Life Assurance Company trophy donated to intermediate hockey – cheese factory closed – Salvation Army showed a moving picture at the Town Hall

1906 – Thomas Street bridge opened – two freight trains crashed at station – Lacrosse Club won Junior Championship of Canada – more sidewalks and drains – new approach to wharf constructed – accidental dynamite explosion smashed windows across town – completed installation of second 300-kW generating unit at powerhouse – original powerhouse used solely for pumping water – accepted Mr. Carnegie's plan for a library building – furniture factory faded out – Grand Trunk improved main line and strengthened bridges over falls – *The Gazette* sold to G.H.O. Thomas – Phillip J. Marrin started a barber shop, later evolved into present-day wholesale business

1907 – cannons installed in Memorial Park – H.R. Scovell became resident inspector of schools in Muskoka – Town granted power rights to High Falls and Wilson's Falls after failing in bid for South Falls – four wells sunk at Barron springs more than doubled the water flow – Ward 4 school built (now Legion Hall) – new poultry house at fair grounds – Poultry & Pet Association formed – Muskoka Lakes and Bracebridge Telephone Co. formed and line constructed to Port Carling – 100 telephones in town so Bell granted continuous service – addition to British Lion Hotel – McCargar flour mill sold to W.A. Press

1908 – sixty Anglo-Canadian workers went on strike;

*A view down Queen's Hill, Manitoba Street, in the early 1900s. The town's business section boasts substantial, sometimes even impressive, brick buildings and wide sidewalks, but the street itself is yet unpaved and horses still provide the motive power for vehicles.* COURTESY OF BRENDA COX

40 left for Italy and the company brought in 50 people from Poland – public library and Ward 4 school opened – voted to establish a Muskoka House of Refuge – work started in August to dredge the entrance to the Bay below the falls as well as the river mouth and the cut – ladies formed a Relief Committee to assist poor families – most serious fire in history on December 28; all stores from Thomas Street (now Taylor Road) to south side of Sibbett block destroyed – two moving picture shows opened, Wonderland and Lyceum – Crown Bank became Northern Crown Bank – won Junior Canadian Lacrosse Association championship again.

1909 – flour mill (oldest industry in town) burned, also destroying Grand Trunk water-pumping station – new Free Methodist Church opened – motion to develop Wilson's Falls power plant passed and tenders awarded – Ecclestone hardware burned but rebuilt with third storey added – one-acre site for garbage dump purchased and fenced – School Board extended continuation school to Fourth Form work (Grade 12) – summer school for teachers held in Bracebridge – several boathouses built on Bracebridge Bay – Amateur Athletic Association formed to promote sports training – Juniors won CLA championship fourth time in a row – new cattle sheds for fair

1910 – railway switch to Muskoka Leather Co. proposed – bylaw requiring owners and tenants of property to remove snow from sidewalks – J.H. Elliott started stationery and jewelry store – Bracebridge Launch Works new industry – new 8,000-gallon water tank for railway – more dredging – Clef Club and Canadian Club of Bracebridge formed – 1,800 Orangemen in 12th of July parade from 50 clubs – three-week strike at Grand Trunk Railway – Halley's Comet visible – cannon fired on Halloween – Wilson's Falls power plant opened December 29, had 600-kW capacity – Queen's Hotel burned – Children's Aid started – Bracebridge Tennis Club formed

1911 – first Water, Light and Power Commission elected – local option vote turned town "dry," closed four bars and the liquor store – customs office opened April 1 with R.A. Findlay in charge – Rev. Michael O'Leary came to town (later to become Monsignor) – Town one of eight model teacher training school locations – two groups of Boy Scouts formed – Minett Boat Works started in old furniture factory – first navigation lights placed to mark channel at mouth of river – Mahaffy Bros. purchased the first motorcar in town – isolation hospital established

1912 – linen mill closed – Bracebridge branch of Women's Institute formed and rest room building built in Jubilee Park – Town shocked by *Titanic* disaster – Arthur A. Mahaffy appointed District Judge after death of Judge W.C. Mahaffy – many disastrous fires – extension of town water system

1913 – construction of new Dominion government building for post office and customs commenced (opened 1915) – WCTU iron water fountain donated for use in front of the newly constructed post office – Toboggan Club formed with slide built behind school – first children's fair – improvements to Muskoka Leather Co. and Watson Brick Co. – Peter MacNaughtan opened grocery store

1914 – clock was installed in post office tower by J.H. Elliott – enrollment of 669 in public schools, 93 in high school – 800-gallon-per-minute pumping equipment installed for waterworks system – channel opened into Alport Lake from Muskoka River – Tillson Egg Farm began – new system of street lighting plus 20 lights on Bracebridge Bay – earthquake felt here in February – War was declared August 4 – 24 Bracebridge men of Company C of the 23rd Regiment, Canadian Volunteers, joined their unit for formation of the First Canadian Contingent – 23rd Northern Pioneers Regiment sent three officers and 100 men in the second contingent.

*Bracebridge's 5th decade opened with the country embroiled in the First World War. The Grand Trunk Railway station was the point of departure for the young men of town who had enlisted – some, unfortunately, never to return. Here in 1916 the boys of the 122nd Battalion wait to embark for Camp Borden.* COURTESY OF THE TOWN OF BRACEBRIDGE

# 1915–1924

## *Our 5th Decade: A Terrible War, and Recovery*

THE WAR was affecting all segments of life in Bracebridge in 1915.

Town officials were appointed the same as 1914. As requested by the townships of McLean, Ridout, and Sherborne, a resolution was passed asking for government assistance to build a hydroelectric line from Dorset to Baysville.

The new post office opened May 6 with Mr. John Cain in charge of the Dominion government building. A war tax of one cent was imposed on each letter and postcard mailed in Canada.

Members of the Public School Board were chairman Harry Linney, Dr. P.B. McGibbon, J.W. Reid, C.H. Bailey, Robert Whaley, Geo. R. Simmons, A.E. Fawcett, Alfred Rowan, and secretary A.C. Salmon.

The 1914 Minister of Education report stated that in Muskoka there were 108 teachers (95 of them women), the average female salary $389 "with that of men a little higher." There were 106 school buildings (23 brick, 1 concrete, 2 stone, 69 frame, 11 log). Bracebridge had 987 school-age children of whom 655 were pupils. Total expenditure in Bracebridge was $8,576.4 with $5,920 in salaries. Bracebridge also had three teachers in high school work with salaries of $3,135. Four new teachers that year were Miss Lulu Edmonds and Miss Ada Found, BA, for the high school, and Miss Ida Higgins and Miss Elsie Scholey for the public system. There was record school attendance in September with the average being 530 pupils. The Gospel Hall was being used for the primary department.

The annual meeting of the South Muskoka Agricultural Society found that the 1914 fair had cleared about $400. The president was H.L. Goltz, the vice presidents Herb Beaumont and A. Barron, and the directors George Yearley, A.E. Fawcett, A.J. Goltz, W.J. Fitzmaurice, J.B. Kaye, Chas. Faires, G.W. Miller, L.J. Taylor, and Chas. Peake. A committee of ladies to assist the directors was chosen which included Mrs. Barron, Mrs. Goltz, Mrs. McGibbon, Mrs. Williams, and Mrs. W.J. Fitzmaurice. Mr. G.W. Boyer was re-appointed secretary-treasurer and Mr. A.C. Salmon auditor.

Census figures of agriculture in Muskoka showed about 2,500 farmers and 75,000 acres of improved land. There were over 300,000 acres of unimproved land, 223,000 acres of forest, and 60,000 acres of marsh. For livestock, the 1910 census showed 4,803 horses, 6,439 cows and 8,602 other cattle, 11,325 sheep, 5,593 swine, 1,363 turkeys, 419 geese, 838 ducks, 78,966 hens and chickens, and 223 hives of bees. The District was much below the average of other districts and counties of the province.

The South Muskoka Farmers' Institute president was H.E. Beaumont, with vice president Byron Kaye, secretary-treasurer G.W. Miller, and directors Alex Brown, Thos. Lovatt, George Yearley, R.J. Campbell, Wilt Cross, Albert Goltz, Thos. Stephens, Henry Speedie, and Wm. Spong. Hay, grain, and root crops were considerably above average in 1915.

Although the fall fair was held for two days instead of three this year there was an immense crowd between 3,500 and 4,000 people with total gate receipts of about $700. Soldiers attended from the Niagara Camp Signaling Corps, and a machine gun section with two officers and 63 soldiers. There was also a concert by the Anglo-Canadian Italian Band. Failure of the fruit crop in Muskoka that season, due to severe early June frosts, cut down on the entries in the cookery department and in the fruits exhibits. About 900 children, led by the band, marched in the children's fair which was again organized by the Women's Institute (president, Mrs. Arnold). Gate receipts went to the war effort.

The Minister of Agriculture established the office of Mr. F.C. Paterson, District representative, permanently at Huntsville. The work done by this office had an important relationship to the development of our greatest industry – agriculture.

"Despite hard times and threatening weather" there was a fair crowd at the Labour Day celebration under the auspices of the Catholic Men's Society. The Citizen's Band was present and gave a good program of music during the afternoon. The judges of the horse racing and the other events were S.H. Armstrong, MPP, Mayor Smith, and A.J. Gavin.

Muskoka farmers made nearly a clean sweep in entries at the Winter Fair. Messrs. H.L. Goltz and Wm. Naismith won 22 prizes. Mr. Goltz made 15 entries and won 14 prizes including eight firsts. Mr. Naismith won four firsts and three seconds.

A free distribution of superior sorts of grains and potatoes was made this year to Canadian farmers by instructions of the Minister of Agriculture. It was hoped to increase yields and improve quality.

The Ecclestone Hardware Store was badly gutted by fire and the stock destroyed in January. Mr. Ecclestone set up a temporary store in the Russell Block, opposite the public library. His insurance included $2,000 on the store building, $1,700 on elevator and stairs, $300 on plate glass, $3,000 on the store building in the Mercantile, and $2,000 on the stock with each of the Caledonian, Yorkshire, Western, Union, British American, and Atlas companies.

The small isolation hospital at the upper end of town burned to the ground. A man with a suspected case of smallpox was in the building and did not know of the fire until some burning pieces of the ceiling fell on his bed. He escaped through a window and went down town to report to the medical health officer.

Mrs. Phillip Leeder's house was a total loss to fire although her family was able to carry out a few articles of furniture. The shop of the Misses MacMillan (milliners) lost its stock to fire and the subsequent water damage.

The following men from Bracebridge were among those in attendance at the camp of the Third Contingent in Parry Sound: Thomas Dryland, Herbert Redman, Isadore Arbic, William Prentiss, Fred Wright, James Gibbons, and Ben Drew.

Dr. McGibbon received a call from the Royal Army Medical Corps to report for service in France.

Professor Square, Toronto University, gave an address in the Town Hall, under the auspices of the Women's Institute , titled "The Trail of the Destroyer." He was thoroughly familiar with Belgium and northern France and was able to show what devastation had been caused by the destroying German armies.

Bracebridge was one of the few Ontario towns that had not organized a home guard.

It was decided to form a branch of the Canadian Patriotic Fund here. Officers elected were president Judge Mahaffy, vice president H.B. Bridgland, secretary I. Huber, and treasurer Wm. Kingsmill. The committee of finance consisted of Sheriff Bastedo, G.W. Ecclestone, A. Hunt, Dr. Williams, G.H.O. Thomas, and the relief committee of Dr. McGibbon, Dr. Speers, Dr. McIlmoyle, Mayor Smith, John Thomson, P. Hutchison, and H.J. Bird. The fund was to provide for the families of Canadian soldiers at the war. It was planned that in every instance the allowance of the wife and family be brought up to $45 a month. The Canadian government paid $20 a month of this, the soldier sent home money from his allowance, and the Patriotic Fund added sufficient to make up the total amount. So far Bracebridge had made no payment to the fund (except what private citizens may have sent) and was one of but four towns of its size in the province that had been thus dilatory.

Mr. A.E. Ames, MP, of Ottawa, gave his celebrated lecture on the British navy to inaugurate the campaign in April. The committee of the Patriotic Fund arranged a whirlwind campaign to use automobiles in an endeavour to cover the whole town in one afternoon and by June $3,787 had been raised.

A patriotic linen shower was held by Mrs. George Ecclestone under the auspices of the Bracebridge Women's Institute for the University of Toronto Base Hospital.

The Women's Patriotic League was formed with president Mrs. Kingsmill, vice presidents Mrs. McGibbon and Mrs. P.A. Smith, secretary Mrs. T.N. Bird, associate secretary Miss Bridgland, and treasurer Miss Pearl Smith. They decided to work for the fund already started by the Clef Club, the object being a motor ambulance. The operetta *Bulbul* was to be performed by the youth in

*On July 1, 1915, a patriotic parade makes its way along Manitoba Street. Many of the floats have a military flavour. The new post office building with its clock tower had just recently opened.* COURTESY OF BRENDA COX

the Clef Club at the Town Hall to raise money for the motor ambulance. On July 1 the Gala Day proved a big success with over $1,000 raised.

The Women's League was able to order a $1,500 fully equipped four-stretcher motor ambulance from the McLaughlin Carriage Co. of Oshawa. The Red Cross expressed their pleasure in accepting the ambulance, and gave instructions to the McLaughlin Co. for its shipment directly overseas. The balance of the funds would be used to do further Red Cross work, and knitting and sewing.

Summer train service started two weeks earlier that year and in order to provide the additional accommodation it was reported that "two of the largest hotels in this District have already booked over five hundred reservations each."

The new transcontinental train to run between Montreal and Winnipeg via the Grand Trunk, Temiskaming and Northern Ontario, and Grand Trunk Pacific started. Train No. 9 ran north passing Bracebridge at 3:15 a.m. on Wednesdays, Fridays, and Sundays, and No. 10 south on Tuesdays, Thursdays, and Saturdays at 7:40 a.m. Only six stops were made between Toronto and North Bay.

The steamer *Algoma*, owned Mr. Wes Archer, was first up the river while the steamers of the Navigation Co. started running April 24.

One of the busiest manufacturing plants in Town was the Minett Launch Works, where 10 vessels were under way for early delivery in the summer. There were two 35 by 7 feet, one 88 by 6½ feet, and some 16-foot punts. Mr. Minett had several more orders for completion that summer.

*The town's street-watering wagon on Quebec Street, 1915. Drunks detained overnight in the town jail had to fill it in the morning, hence the term "on the [water] wagon."* COURTESY OF IAN TURNBULL

Mr. A.T. Wattie sold the retail part of his butcher business to Mr. Pelletier. Mr. Wattie and his brother continued their wholesale trade with branches in Port Carling and Barrie ... the telephone line was extended to Raymond in June ... a bylaw closing all businesses on Thursday afternoon during July and August at 3 p.m. was passed ... Mr. Frank Slingerland passed his final examinations with the Canadian School of Embalming and went to work for Mr. W.W. White ... Justice Clute presided over the Fall Assizes ... In August, Port Carling raised $1,100 to purchase a machine gun.

Grand Trunk Railway detectives were in town watching for trespassers on the railway bridges ... a Reserve Militia was authorized for those over 35 years and physically fit.

Mr. J.W. Oakes organized "The Committee of 100" with the object of a dry Ontario by July 1,1916. H.A, Rogers was elected president, with vice president George Tennant and secretary George E. Denniss.

Many thousands farm labourers were wanted for harvesting in western Canada. Train fare going west was offered at $12 to Winnipeg with the return trip at $18.

Several new cars were seen around town. Mr. Wm. Galbraith purchased a Studebaker five-passenger car, Mr. Henry Richards had a new Overland, Mr. Dixon of Fraserburg a Ford, Mr. Thos. Pelletier a Ford, Mr. J.H. Burton an Overland, and Charlie Leeder a Studebaker.

The Dominion June election saw a race between Dr. McDonald, Liberal, from Huntsville, and Mr. William Wright, Conservative.

Summer school was held with 153 teachers under the charge of Mr. Plewes of Chatham. The teachers and students were guests of Mayor Smith and Council on an excursion aboard the *Medora*. The band was in attendance.

An inquest was held into the death of Archibald Post, 34, of Ryde Township, who died in the District jail, where he had been confined as a dangerous lunatic. Associate coroner Dr. McQuay called the inquest and Crown Attorney Johnson conducted the examination of the witnesses, those giving evidence being Mr. McDonald, the jailer, Dr. Speers, Rev. L. Slingerland, and Mrs. Post (an aunt of the deceased). Mr. Post had been placed in jail awaiting examination for entry into a provincial institution where he could be properly cared for. During the night he was almost continually in convulsions. It was shown that the jailer and jail surgeon had given him every possible care and attention. The coroner's jury brought in a verdict of death from exhaustion following an epileptic convulsion.

Bracebridge collected $1,300 on Trafalgar Day, which was devoted to the collection of money for the British Red Cross Society. The Grafanola, donated by Mr. G.W. Ecclestone for a drawing contest, brought in $423.

Livery bylaw charges were as follows: for one horse, trip not exceeding 16 miles and return, $2.00; for one horse driving around town, three hours or less, $1.50; for driver per hour, $0.15; for automobiles, $1.50 an hour while running, or $0.50 an hour standing.

Mr. Harry Martin of Port Carling donated wool to Mrs. H.L. Goltz for the knitting of 76 pairs of socks to be distributed to our enlisted Muskoka boys.

Bracebridge had raised over $8,000 for patriotic purposes or about $2.95 for each man, woman, and child. When the first contingent went away we raised $1,100 as a present for the boys. Then there was a contribution of $250 towards the Red Cross hospital ship and on Dominion Day the ladies raised $1,600, (including the proceeds of the *Bulbul* entertainment). Another $4,000 was subscribed and had been paid or was being paid in installments towards the Patriotic Fund, and the Red Cross appeal brought in $1,300. Besides these cash amounts, numerous bundles of clothing, boxes of fruit, etc. were sent overseas.

In November, 20 or more Italians left Bracebridge on their way to join the colours of their native land in her fight against Austria. These men had mostly been employed with the Anglo-Canadian Tannery Co. and had proven themselves good citizens. The Citizen's Band paraded them to the station where they were given a good send-off.

Captain Cade was conducting a vigorous campaign for recruits in his territory which extended from Burk's Falls to Severn. Bracebridge enlisted about three dozen men in a month, which was as good a record as any town of its size in Canada. We had nearly 200 men in khaki, but "if the present course of action [of basing men in Parry Sound, not here] is persisted in it will mean either no recruits from this section or a separate company for Muskoka." General Sir Samuel Hughes was granted permission in September to have a squad based in Bracebridge.

The Knox Church Guild presented a bright little play entitled *The Minister's Bride* with Miss Zaida Fraser and Mr. Laurie Ryan playing the bride and groom, and Mr. James Morrison the part of the minister. Proceeds went to the Red Cross Fund.

The year 1915 saw the death Mr. Aubrey White, 69, Deputy Minister of Lands, Forests and Mines of Ontario. He died on Chief Island, Lake Muskoka, of a stroke. He had been out rowing, swimming, and fishing. Mr. White was twice married, his first wife being Miss Emily Bridgland and the second Miss Mary Bridgland, sisters of the late Dr. Bridgland, MPP, and of Mr. H.B. Bridgland of Bracebridge. The funeral took place at St. Thomas Church with interment following at the St. Thomas Cemetery. The body was brought from Chief Island by the steamer *Islander* and was met at the dock by many friends from the town and district. A long cortege of autos and carriages formed and proceeded to St. Thomas Anglican Church.

Other deaths in 1915 included James Dawson Shier, founder of the J.D. Shier Lumber Company ... Thomas E. Hunt, 50, who came about 1888 and took a prominent role in public affairs including the Board of Health and Town Council ... Mr. William Henry Spencer, police magistrate ... Elizabeth Langford, 90, wife of the late Isaac Langford ... Mr. William McBride, 79, an early settler in Draper ... Mr. Jos. Yeoman, killed in action ... John Hollingworth, Beatrice, who went with the first contingent from Bracebridge and was killed in France ... Miss Gertrude Eileen Andison, 27, daughter of Mr. and Mrs. John Andison of Fraserburg, of meningitis and typhoid ... Samuel Richardson, one of Bracebridge's earliest citizens ... Bert Bailey, son of Mr. Edward Bailey,

*The 122nd Battalion camps in Jubilee Park while on manoeuvers. The old exhibition hall stands at left. In this picture local residents watch some kind of match in progress. The houses in the background are on Dill Street.* COURTESY OF BRENDA COX

crushed to death by one of the large wooden wheels while replacing broken staves at the Anglo-Canadian tannery.

There were 65 births and 14 deaths during 1915. The total number of dogs was 105.

**1916** G.H.O. Thomas defeated George Mahaffy by a vote of 280 to 217 in the race for mayor. Muskoka received grants of $5,400 for roads, $11,400 for bridges, and $300 for drainage on the Muskoka District Road ... The assessor reported a population of 2,803, down 134 from 1915. Assessment increased by $5,000 and now stood at $832,768 ... A new amusement tax regulation affected the "moving picture house" with the admission fee becoming 11 cents, one cent going to the government ... There were 595 children of school age.

Council instructed Chief McConnell to stop the practice of riding bicycles on the sidewalks. A cement walk was constructed on the east side of Muskoka Road from Edward Street to King Street and a cinder walk down the hill from King Street. The tax rate was 30.5 mills for municipal purposes with an additional 1 mill Provincial War Tax.

The School Board with Harry Linney, chairman, decided to abolish the high school fee system for resident pupils, that is, $2.50, $5.00, and $7.50 yearly from pupils in Forms I, II and III, respectively. Non-resident fees were left unchanged.

The Peter Duff store closed in the Sibbett block; Mr. John Thomson leased their premises ... Mr. J.H. Hines of Toronto, nephew of our Mr. Geo. A. Hines, was appointed express agent ... Mr. G.W. Ecclestone was appointed agent for the Chevrolet car for south Muskoka ... Mr. L.J. Lacey leased the Humphries store and continued to carry groceries, flour, and feed ... G.W. Boyer resigned as editor of the *Herald* to be replaced by Mr. Burleigh Bastedo. G.W. Boyer was appointed paymaster of the 122nd Battalion ... 60 employees of the Anglo-Canadian Tannery went on strike for an extra 30 cents a day … Lee Bing, the laundry man, left for Hong Kong. He owned a row of houses in Toronto and had a big interest in a Chinese steamship line … The Queen's Hotel was granted a licence as a place of accommodation for the traveling public, and was subject to government inspection at any time … the Dominion Hotel was fined $250 for selling liquor on Fair day … Mr. Alfred Hunt, deputy sheriff for over 10 years, resigned due to ill health. He was replaced by Mr. I.B. Aulph.

The public library reported having 626 borrowers of their 5,064 books, with 181 books purchased in the past year.

The Committee of 100 received 300 signatures on a petition asking for prohibition by July 1, which was 72 percent of the vote at the last election. They also had the support of 520 others who did not have the franchise – women and boys.

The Bracebridge Women's Institute set aside a fund of more than $50 for sanitary improvements in the school and sent the Belgians a bale valued at $86.45. Mrs. Salmon, president, was succeeded by Mrs. Fryer.

A letter arrived from May M. Bird in Alexandria, Egypt, to Mrs. Galbraith with thanks to the Institute.

Skating on the river was splendid in the winter. The lights at the wharf and bay were turned on, and with a large arc light by the Anglo-Canadian Leather Co., added much to the enjoyment of the hundreds of skaters.

The Bracebridge Women's Patriotic League shipped to the Red Cross Society 18 khaki flannel shirts valued $54, 30 hospital shirts at $10.80, 70 pairs of socks at $56, two elbow rests, eight surgical kits, 20 dozen compresses, 200 gauze sponges, 19 dozen small pads, 50 large wipes, 450 small linen mouth wipes, two dozen hot water bottle covers, and 30 dozen bandages. The League sponsored a concert by the Anglo-Canadian Italian Band from Huntsville which included 40 bandsmen: nine coronets, six alto horns, four trombones, two euphoniums, four basses, six clarinets, four saxophones, four drums, and the cymbals.

A Citizen's Recruiting League was formed with president W.W. Kinsey, vice president Wm. Lowe, and secretary-treasurer H.J. Bird. Information given included: "During mobilization the wife of a married man, not billeted at home, will receive $0.65 per day and when the battalion is established in barracks she will instead receive $20 per month. In every case clothing is supplied to the men and there is a good system of pension and disability funds if a man returns injured. In a short time there will be fifty or more families in and around Brace-

*Another view of the 122nd Battalion encampment at Jubilee Park. Houses along Church Street line the hilltop in the background. Note the lack of trees.* COURTESY OF BRENDA COX

*The motor ambulance purchased with funds raised by the Women's Patriotic League and the Clef Club, parked in front of the courthouse.* COURTESY OF THE TOWN OF BRACEBRIDGE

bridge drawing from the Fund." A single private received $1.75 a day seven days a week out of which he paid his own board. A married private received $1.95 a day and if he lived at home his board was paid to his wife.

A Muskoka District Recruiting League was formed in March, proposing to add four mills to the year's taxes for patriotic purposes. The vote was 185 for, 126 opposed. In 1915 Bracebridge gave $4,200 to the fund but did not reach the average giving. The District league requested that Bracebridge provide one tent, one field kitchen, a team and transport wagon, and certain mess supplies to a total value of $2,000 for the 122nd. The Women's Patriotic League provided the tent, Judge Mahaffy $100, G.W. Ecclestone $100, and the Bird Woollen Mills Co. $100.

The local company of the 122nd Battalion route-marched to Falkenburg where the ladies invited them into the store of Mr. E.W. Hay for milk and cake before the men marched home (Hay's store is now at Muskoka Pioneer Village in Huntsville).

During the worst storm of the winter, fire broke out in the dwelling occupied by Mrs. Fred Wright, and in a half hour the place was burned to the ground. Mrs. Wright had barely time to escape with her six little children. Her husband has been at the front serving his country and was lying wounded in a hospital. Mrs. Wright has been making the payments on the property to Mr. John Gibbs. The Bird Woollen Mills Co. and employees took up a subscription as had many others.

The old wharf store house burned to the ground and considerable damage was done to the covering of the wharf at the old dock.

About 2,500 people gathered for the Winter Carnival of Sports in March which gave the town and schools a half holiday and raised $226.35. A monster military parade of 300 visiting soldiers, who came by special troop trains, paraded until noon, when they were fed by the Women's Patriotic League. This was followed by a football match, tug-of-war, snowshoe races, cross-cut sawing competition, grand military demonstration, and a fancy dress carnival.

The *H.M.S. Pinafore* drew big houses for the Canadian Patriotic and Red Cross funds. It was directed by Mrs. Wm. Kingsmill. The musical conductor was Mr. B.W. Tillson, and the accompanist Miss Bridgland.

There were nearly 500 little chicks at the Tillson Egg Farm, a 35-acre farm situated just north of the station. The incubator room contained a steam hatchery with a 3,000-egg capacity. They shipped eggs all over Canada.

News from overseas reported the deaths of Private George Clark, son of Mr. and Mrs. Charles Clark of Fraserburg and a member of the 2nd Battalion, in France … Private Alexander Mathieson who was killed in action near Ypres in 1915 … Corporal Donald M. Jeffrey was killed in action. He had worked in Mr. G.W. Ecclestone's hardware store … Private James Barrett was killed at St. Julien … Postmaster R. P. Perry's eldest son, Lieutenant Claude Perry, was killed. He had been serving with a British regiment at the front.

K.A. Mahaffy was promoted to captain in the 5th Battalion at the front … Lance-Corporal Don Jeffrey was on the casualty list. Donald was in some heavy fighting with the Perth Co. of the 18th Battalion … Private Frederick Wright returned home, having spent seven months in the trenches. He was not wounded but took sick of nephritis due to exposure … Private Verne Failes, son of Mr. and Mrs. Harry Failes, was again wounded and was at No. 2 Canadian Stationary Hospital, Boulogne … Lieutenant Dr. P.B. McGibbon was awarded a military cross for faithful service and saving of life in a gas attack, and bravery in the field ... Captain Kenneth Mahaffy was wounded again ... Sergeant Isadore Arbic was wounded in action ... Private Howard Vincente returned to Bracebridge after spending 11 months in hospital in England.

Eight machine guns arrived in town, each valued at $1,000.

A reception was held to welcome home Private Howard Vincent, DCM, Private Percy Cutler, and Private Fred Wright. Each was presented with a $50 cheque.

Mr. Joseph Oakes of the Dominion Fish Hatchery, Point Edward, was loaned to the Muskoka Lakes Trade Bureau to operate the fish hatchery at Port Carling. They placed 8,000,000 pickerel fry in the lakes during the year.

Mr. Ecclestone and Mr. George Mahaffy ran for election as the Conservative candidate to replace the deceased S.H. Armstrong. Mr. Ecclestone won and was acclaimed Member of Parliament.

There were not enough young men left in town to make a formidable team of either lacrosse or soccer.

Summer school began again with about 150 in attendance under the direction of Mr. J.A. Plewis.

About 60 boys of the 122nd Battalion came home from Camp Borden on a one-month furlough for the haying and harvesting. Labour hands had been very scarce all summer. The 122nd Battalion was lacrosse champion of Camp Borden.

Probably the most devastating forest fire in Canada's history started in late July in the regions of Matheson and Cochrane. The toll of the dead was estimated between 350 and 400 and the loss of property in the neighbourhood of $3,000,000. The area covered by the conflagration was about 50 miles deep and 130 miles long. Kelso, Matheson, Homer, Nushka, and Monteith were wiped out. Many families from Bracebridge had settled in the area. Among those included in the death toll were George Little, Mrs. Arthur Small and children, Mr. and Mrs. Ed Robinson and family, Mr. and Mrs. Joseph Elvin and family, Mr. and Mrs. Ed Schmidt and his father. Mrs. Schmidt was a daughter of Mr. and Mrs. Thos. Little. Many settlers from all of the villages were unaccounted for.

The Firemen's Tournament and Band Competition was held at Parry Sound. As Gravenhurst and Huntsville were unable to secure suitable transportation to run excursions, their teams and supporters came to Bracebridge and accompanied the local brigade which ran on the steamer *Cherokee* to Bala, thence to Parry Sound by CPR. The Bracebridge team of Herb Ireland, Jas. Gohm, Geo. Mitchell, Thos. Ball, Charlie Yeoman, Roland Dyer, Jos. Coleman, Bob Tennant, and Aboil Leishman won the hose-wagon contest and captured the banner. Council presented the winners each with a $5 gold piece and a suitable address of congratulations.

*While Bracebridge got its electricity from its own hydro plants at Bracebridge and Wilson's Falls, as of 1916 both Huntsville and Gravenhurst received theirs from Ontario Hydro's new 1,000-kW South Falls station, a completely remodelled version of the old Gravenhurst plant here.*
COURTESY OF ONTARIO HYDRO

On August 15 the Hydro-Electric Power Commission of Ontario turned on the power at the new plant at South Falls. The Commission has acquired the plant from the Town of Gravenhurst, enlarged it, and added a second generator.

At the winter fair in Guelph, Mr. W.E. Nasmyth took

all the first prizes but one in potatoes, Mr. H.L. Goltz sent 13 exhibits and received 12 prizes, including two seconds in potatoes, third in oats from the field crop, and the championship in beans.

Deaths during the year included Mr. Samuel Henry Armstrong, councillor, reeve, and the first mayor of Bracebridge (he remained in that office until 1890). On October 18, 1912, he was elected by acclamation to represent the District in the Ontario Legislature, in the by-election occasioned by the appointment of Mr. A.A. Mahaffy as judge of Muskoka. In the general election of June 29, 1914, he was sustained in the seat by an 850 majority over Mr. G.W. Lankin, the Liberal nominee ... Mr. Joseph Caisse, barber, came to Bracebridge in 1882 ... Mrs. Mary Julie Blackburn, 85 (widow of the late Edward Colley), came to Muskoka in 1876 ... Mrs. Fred Walsh's year-old son Asina Kitchener, who died from a severe attack of measles, followed by pneumonia. A detachment of soldiers under Corporal Harvey Mayes attended the funeral as pallbearers ... Mrs. Richard Lance, mother of postmaster Lance of Beatrice ... Mr. R.N. Thompson, a Town employee killed in a dynamite explosion ... Mr. Donald Fraser, 86, who lived in Draper for 31 years then moved to town.

## 1917

Muskoka boys went overseas, the emphasis was on production, coal was in short supply, and the bill on conscription became law.

The 1916 Council returned for 1917. The tax rate was struck at 35 mills on the dollar exclusive of the Provincial War Tax. The clerk began to publish minutes of council meetings in both local papers, at a cost of $25 each a year. Assessment for 1917 was $834,5497, the population 2,476 with 548 males between the ages of 21 and 60.

The new road sprinkler arrived and was used to sprinkle clear water or a mixture of water and oil. Mr. I.B. Aulph, deputy sheriff, was given the added job of division court clerk.

A bylaw was passed to change the Bracebridge Con-

*The congregation of Knox Presbyterian Church gathered out front after the farewell service of Rev. J.A. Pue-Gilchrist on September 9, 1917.* COURTESY OF VICKY BILLINGSLEY FROM THE R.J.BOYER COLLECTION

tinuation School into a high school and, after the approval of the Minister of Education, provide for the appointment of high school trustees. Principal Shannon reported that the total number of pupils enrolled for April was 558 with 29 non-residents.

There was a closing-out sale for W.W. Kinney … W.J. Tozer had a bankruptcy sale … Mr. Jos. Bird purchased McKay Bros. Mill in Draper … Mr. Thos. J. Ball took over Robert Holden's dairy … Shier Lumber lost a team in Hollow Lake. The horses broke through the seven inches of ice, and although another team was employed to help rescue them, it could not pull them out … Mr. Wm. Swanson reopened the harness depot formerly occupied by H.S. Bowyer … Dr. Grant, from Alberta, moved to Bracebridge and occupied a portion of Mrs. S.H. Armstrong's residence … Mr. H.B. Bridgland retired after 35 years as druggist. He succeeded the late Dr. Bridgland and was followed by Mr. D'Alton Campbell … Messrs Isaac Huber, I.B. Aulph, and J.B. Bastedo all had new cars … the Bracebridge Launch Works closed … businesses closed at 1:00 p.m. on Thursday for the summer … Kirk Bros. on Manitoba Street closed … Dr. P.B. McGibbon had a fine addition built to his residence for use as his office … Charlie Lem of Toronto purchased Young's Cafe and Chop Suey … The Muskoka Foundry Co. purchased the Linen Mills Building in Ward 4 and installed considerable machinery to double their capacity … John Burke reopened his cleaning and pressing business … Mr. Albert Tibbett sold his interest in the Tibbett Bros. Livery business to Mr. Arthur Tibbett. Mr. Albert Tibbett resumed the carting business.

A new order-in-council proclaimed Tuesdays and Fridays as meatless days. These were observed by the Queen's and the Albion, both replacing the usual meat with fish.

Methodist union services were quite harmonious in Bracebridge. There was a general exchange of pulpits and each evening a union meeting was held.

The South Muskoka Agricultural Society elected H.E. Beaumont president, Alex Barron and A.E. Fawcett as vice presidents, and Jerry Dickie as secretary-treasurer. Membership was 114.

A recruiting depot for the newly organized 257th Battalion was established in town with Major R. Herron of North Bay in charge. The 122nd Battalion was also recruiting for 200 men for the Forestry Branch. It accepted a lower physical standard and paid the same as infantry. Maximum age was 48, minimum height 4 feet 11 inches; men missing two fingers or two toes or either or both feet could be accepted; ordinary flat feet, blindness of one eye, or deafness of one ear would not hinder.

A farewell banquet for the boys of the 122nd Battalion was held at the Queen's Hotel, arranged by the Women's Patriotic League. His Honour Judge Mahaffy presided. Each soldier received a handsome leather case for writing materials, and a pocket searchlight. The boys sang their favourite marching song to the tune of *John Brown*:

Our Battalion number is
One hundred and twenty-two;
We're from old Muskoka,
Who the h--- are you?
We'll dress you up in khaki
And surely put you through
As we go marching on.
*chorus – Glory, Glory etc.*
We are the brave Muskoka boys
You've heard so much about;
We'll make the Germans tremble
When they hear our battle shout;
We captivate the pretty girls
As we go marching out. As we go marching on.

The 122nd Battalion was delayed at Galt due to an outbreak of mumps.

Private Alex Bell, 17, sustained a gunshot wound in his left arm at the battle of Vimy Ridge … A civic reception was held in the honour of the return of Captain Dr. McGibbon, Mrs. McGibbon, and Miss Grace Mahaffy from Europe … Private Robert Moreland, 29, was killed in action … Dr. A.F. Bastedo was called into service with the Canadian Medical Corps. He enlisted shortly after the outbreak of the war but at that time there were 900 doctors available for 250 positions … Captain F.N. Reid, who had been recruiting men for the Forestry, was called overseas … Lieutenant Lawrence B. Tillson was awarded the Military Cross for bravery in the fields of France ... Returned from France were Private Stanley A. Dickie, suffering pleurisy and his right leg numbed or paralyzed, and Lance-Corporal Frank Fuller to recover from three bullet and shell wounds.

When the 122nd Battalion passed through Toronto, town residents met them at Union Station and presented the Battalion Colours donated by the Women's Patriotic League of Muskoka. The Battalion arrived safely in England having travelled on the White Star liner *Olympic*.

The Colours of the 122nd Overseas Battalion of the Canadian Expeditionary Force, under the command of Lieutenant Colonel D. Mackenzie Grant, were deposited in the choir of St. George's Chapel, Windsor Castle. The banners were first consecrated outside of the south door of the chapel and afterwards borne into the choir with some ceremony.

By summer, the 122nd Battalion was no more, all having been transferred to the Forestry Branch. Men from all Ontario Battalions where lumbering occurred were taken into the Forestry Department to run sawmills and to plank roads at the front to make possible the quick bringing up of the batteries. At Vimy Ridge nearly all the roadways had been planked.

Six weeks after arriving, our Muskoka boys established a record cut for a Scots mill of any forestry company in England or France. The previous record was 34,000 feet for 10 hours work. Our boys cut a total of 61,100 feet for 10 hours work.

The scarcity of coal was keenly felt in the unusually severe, cold winter. From every quarter the Railway Commission was being asked to relieve congestion of freight by reducing passenger service, so that the necessary quantity of fuel could be obtained.

There was no Orange celebration in Muskoka due to inability to secure efficient railway or boat transportation and the absence of so many members (nearly 40 of local Lodge 218 were in the military service).

Steps were taken to organize a new band as there had not been one for a year.

A south-bound freight train collided with passenger train No. 41 near Utterson. The passenger train was travelling at such a speed that the light mail car was crushed, killing the mail clerk, A.L. Barclay, the fireman, Albert Thornbury, and fatally injuring the engineer, Zeke Firman of Allendale. Dr. McLeay of Gravenhurst, coroner, conducted the inquest. The jury found "that a mistake had been made by Conductor McLennan and the agent of Utterson, Wm. Leitchield by neglecting orders issued to them."

The ice was clear and thick for the ice harvest. By late March, Arthur Fielding and Wes Brooks disposed of 30,000 blocks to Bracebridge customers and had several outside contracts still to be filled.

A large advertisement was run in our papers: "Britain calls to Canada, the nearest producer of staple foods for these farm products: wheat, oats, beef, bacon, cheese, eggs, butter, poultry, beans and peas, wool, flax and flax fibres, and dried vegetables." Martin Burrell, Minister of Agriculture, said it was "the supreme duty of every man on the land is to use every thought and every energy in the direction of producing more – and still more." "Recruits wanted for production" was the advertisement from the Department of Agriculture. The farmers of Ontario urgently needed help. There was an appeal to those unfit for military service to enlist in the farm help campaign, particularly in seed time and harvest. There was also a call to sign the Food Service Pledge to substitute other foods for white bread, beef, and bacon, and to prevent waste of a single ounce of food in homes.

Our sawmills had an exceptionally large cut during the year.

Roads throughout the District broke up faster than normal making them absolutely bottomless and impossible to travel on. Several horses were lost and stage drivers were unable to get through with the mail.

Fire badly damaged Corrigan and Campbell's blacksmith shop and spread quickly to Mr. Fred Sander's livery stable. A new livery stable about double in size was built on the site of the old building.

A Junior Patriotic League was organized with president Miss Bird, vice president Miss O. Bastedo, treasurer Miss G. Salmon, and secretary Miss A. Fulton.

Mr. G.H.O. Thomas appealed to electors to support him as an "Independent" candidate. The Union convention of the Liberal and Conservative electors of the Dis-

*The fine old homes in the older sections of Bracebridge were built for the town's leading business and professional men. Above is the Kimberley Avenue residence of G.H.O. Thomas, businessman, newspaper publisher, and community leader. Mrs. Thomas sits on the front steps. The house is now the Thirsty Judge restaurant.* COURTESY OF BRENDA COX

trict in favour of the win-the-war government selected Dr. McGibbon as Union candidate for the Dominion election.

The Jubilee Celebration was a grand success and netted $1,800 for the treasury of the Patriotic League. The grand parade consisted of 10 floats, three automobiles, and five bicycles, all very prettily decorated. There were drawing contests, two bicycle races, a shooting gallery, fortune-telling booths, and a baseball game; the local firemen gave exhibitions of reel, hose,and ladder drill. Thirteen automobiles from Huntsville conveyed visitors to the celebration. The Anglo-Canadian Band added greatly to the pleasure of the celebration.

Deaths in Town included Alfred E. Hunt, 57, who owned the first bank in Bracebridge. He was a former councillor and mayor, an avid sportsman and a splendid citizen ... Mr. Walter W. Kinsey, 61. He ran Kinsey's Harness Emporium, was also a former councillor and mayor, and had served as president of the Board of Trade and the Bracebridge and Lake of Bays Railway Co., and as chairman of the Bracebridge Recruiting League ... Dr. W.D. McIlmoyle, a physician here for seven years ... Mr. W.J. Hallett, principal of the Bracebridge school about 1877, married Miss Carrie Sibbett, summered at his cottage at St. Elmo ... Mrs. Samuel Taylor, 74 ... Mr. Fletcher Phillips, 76 ... Mrs. Joseph R. Bastedo, 85, mother of Sheriff Bastedo ... Mr. Archie Devine, an employee of the local Water and Light Commission, electrocuted ... Mrs. William Fish, 73 ... Mr. George Yearley, 69 ... Mr. James H. Ptolemy, 69, moved to town in 1892 ... Miss Jessie Brotherston, 61,well-known dressmaker ... Mrs. John T. Shier, 36, formerly Margaret Toshack Marshall. Mr. Shier was in charge of the planing factory of the Shier Lumber Co. ... Mrs. George Bailey, 58, one of the earliest members of the Knox Presbyterian Church Ladies' Aid. In 1876 she married Captain Bailey, who became Commodore of the Muskoka Navigation and Hotel Company.

The assessed population for Bracebridge in 1917 was 2,506 with a total assessment in 1916 of $883,733, a municipal debenture debt of $168,202, and a school debenture debt of $7,575.

## 1918

Bracebridge had 72 births, 24 marriages, and 32 deaths in 1918. The population was 2,261, compared to 2,135 in Huntsville and 1,600 in Gravenhurst. The decrease in population was unquestionably because no war industries had been established here, while many had gone to other centres to engage in munitions work.

The 1918 estimates from the provincial government indicated grants of $19,275 and $11,400 for colonization roads and public works.

An adding machine was installed in the town clerk's office.

Mayor T. Jas. Anderson was defeated by Alex. Walker with a 62 majority ... A bylaw was passed to compel the tying up of all dogs from April 1 to October 31 to prevent them from worrying local sheep. Ten dogs were poisoned with strychnine in January ... A bylaw granting a fixed assessment at $7,500 for 10 years for the Muskoka Foundry Co. was passed.

Council asked that anyone with vacant land suitable for gardening and willing to let it be used, should contact the clerk and have it ploughed for free, then seeded.

The previous fall the Town Council had purchased a quantity of street oil and found after using it several times to be very satisfactory; however, when the supply was gone it could not be replaced as all oil had to go to munitions. The government allowance to an overseer of roads being built from the Colonization Road Grant was $3.00 a day, and some municipalities could not secure the services of the most efficient men at that pay.

The bridge over the North Branch of the Muskoka River was closed for cementing of the roadway in June.

John H. Burton was elected chairman of the School Board with Alex Salmon re-appointed clerk and treasurer. Attendance at the Continuation School was high at between 100 and 125. Another room and the employment of an additional teacher was necessary. On a visit, Inspector Hogg stated that the large attendance, coupled with the fact that there were four first-class teachers on the staff, made it necessary to establish a regular high school here. He also remarked that no other continuation school in Ontario had a staff of four teachers.

Mr. Elliott Fulton was appointed janitor of the Central School and Gospel Hall.

Officers of the Fire Department were chief Albert E. Ecclestone, 1st lieutenant W.M. Ross, 2nd lieutenant Jas. Gohm, captain of hook and ladder Geo. F. Gibson, foreman of hose Jos. Coleman, 1st hydrant Wm. Ross, 2nd hydrant Clifford Gibbs, 1st branch Oscar Simmons, 2nd branch Herb Ireland, 3rd branch Job. L. Casse, 4th branch Thos. Foster, assistant foreman hose Jas. Green, hook and ladder Gilbert Gibes, W. Waite, W.K. Hare, and Will Ramset, auditor Job. Casse, caretaker Oscar Simons, and secretary W.M. Ross.

A 10-piece band was organized for the winter months to provide music for skaters at the rink. Mr. Herbert L. Clarke, noted American cornet soloist, was engaged to play for the Anglo-Canadian Band and became director and manager. Mr. George R. Simons continued as assistant conductor.

Rev. A.B. Irwin, BA, was inducted to the pastorate of Knox Church congregation.

In the Dominion election there were 6,641 voters in Muskoka, 68 percent of whom voted for and elected Dr. McGibbon over Thomas.

A.E. Fawcett replaced H.E. Beaumont as president of the South Muskoka Agricultural Society, with vice presidents J.B. Kaye and H. Richards, and secretary-treasurer Jerry Dickie. It was noted from the old minute book that at the 13th annual meeting held in the British Lion Hotel in 1888 there were 144 members, same as at present, and fall fair expenses totalled about $500. The society arranged with the Ministry of Agriculture to put on a motion picture show about agriculture in the Town Hall. A grant of $100 was made to the South Muskoka Agricultural Society and permission given them to erect permanent pens for sheep and pigs, and posts for tying cattle.

Disagreeable weather caused poor attendance at the fall fair; however, there were 29 entries alone for the prize offered by the Bird Woollen Mill Co. for the best loaf of war bread (made of 50 percent standard flour and 50 percent wheat substitute flour). The erection of the new pens for sheep and swine induced the farmers to exhibit some of their best animals.

In sports, Bracebridge won the Ecclestone-Wasley Cup in the annual contest with Gravenhurst. The first hockey match of the season was played in February between Bracebridge and Orillia; neither town was represented in the OHA that winter but both had good teams. Bracebridge won. A committee organized a town baseball league with three teams. Officers included president George Parlett, vice presidents A.E. Fawcett, Dunc McDonald, and Geo. Gibson, with secretary-treasurer Gordon Wells.

Mr. S.G. Morse of Leamington bought the dry goods business of Mr. W.J. Tozer ... The brick veneered residence on East Dominion St., built in 1809 and known as the Brophy residence, was torn down by Messrs. Ernest and Albert Gibes. The owner, Mr. John Gibes, sold to the Bank of Ottawa ... Mr. Wm. Shier purchased the home of Mr. Harry Failles in the Fourth Ward ... The Shier Lumber Co. mills started on April 30 and had an excellent cut ... Mr. William Swanson moved his stock of harness from the old Bowyer stand on the Queen's Hill to the stand recently occupied by the Modern Taylor Co. opposite the Whitten Co. store ... One merchant adopted the cash and carry system instead of delivery of goods. It was estimated that delivery cost the merchant from $18 to $20 a week for each delivery wagon on the road ... Mr. Geo. Tennant's mill had a very busy season.

Mr. H.J. Bird Sr. had six acres of his grove ploughed, harrowed, and well prepared for gardening. He let plots to citizens of the town at a nominal figure. Mr. Bird said he was too old to fight but not too old to help increase production.

A one-storey concrete building, 90 feet long and 30 feet wide, was built for the Bird Woollen Mill Co. Ltd. as a store house. There was a basement room 60 feet long and the full width of the building ... Mr. H.G. Everett of Simcoe purchased the drug business of D'Alton Campbell.

Fifteen thousand boys between the ages of 15 and 19 were organized as "soldiers of the soil" to work on Ontario farms.

In January, the first draftees, five in number, left to join the Colours in Ottawa. Another urgent call was put out for unmarried men between the ages of 20 and 23 who were physically fit. Young men of 19 were required to register.

On June 29 a registration of man-power and women-power of Canada between the ages of 16 and 60 was taken. Registration was compulsory and the election machinery was used to complete the work on one day. Mr. John Thomson, Bracebridge, was appointed registrar for the Muskoka District.

Tragedies of the war included Private T. Allen, killed in action ... Sergeant D.G. Cameron, wounded ... Private Stanley B. Kaye, injured while working with the Forestry in France and temporarily blinded. He was exposed to poisonous gas ... Corporal Hilton Miller, son of Mr. and Mrs. G.W. Miller of Muskoka Township, died of wounds received in France ... Private Douglas Johnson, 21-year-old son of Crown Attorney Johnson, was killed in France ... Signaller James "Albert" Rutherford was killed in action ... Private Charles Wormeld Sr., was killed in action in France, leaving his wife and two small daughters ... Private Archie McDonald died of wounds in France. Lieutenant Colonel McCrae, author of *In Flanders Fields*, died January 28 in France.

Mayor Walker asked citizens to contribute sporting goods such as footballs, baseballs, bats, mitts, etc., for the 122nd boys overseas. A Muskoka Boys' Club Room was established in London, England, by the Bird Woollen Mill Co. Ltd. for our soldiers on leave in that city.

The Women's Patriotic League reported raising $3,093.40 for the year. It shipped to the Red Cross 4,925 articles valued at $2,981.20. At Christmas 169 boxes were sent to the boys overseas. The president was Mrs. Kingsmill, the vice presidents Mrs. Jas. Thomson and Mrs. McLean, the secretary Mrs. Thomas Bird, and the treasurer Miss Sibbett.

Mr. G.W. Ecclestone, MP, persuaded the government to

*The Bracebridge Fire Brigade poses in front of its quarters at the Town Hall, having just won a fire department competition. Chief A.E. Ecclestone sits on the right on the wagon. The brigade is framed by Mayor G.H.O. Thomas on the left and G.W. Ecclestone, MPP, on the right.* COURTESY OF VICKY BILLINGSLEY FROM THE R.J. BOYER COLLECTION

take over the operation of the fish hatchery for the year with Mr. Duke of Port Carling in charge.

The steamer *Alporto*, one of the supply boats belonging to J.J. Beaumont & Son, sank at its dock. It was the second loss of that nature they had experienced, the *Nyquist* having sunk in Lake Muskoka six years earlier.

Captain C.W. Archer acquired the steamer *Llano* from Wm. Irwin of Windermere and placed it on the route between Bracebridge and Browning Island, carrying daily mail and passengers. No less than 400 people were served by him, and merchants appreciated his efforts in developing trade on Muskoka Lake that looked to Bracebridge as the shopping centre. The 70-foot *Llano* was built of white oak with a steel frame, and could seat 50 passengers ... The Muskoka Navigation Co. suffered a heavy loss when the steamer *Kenozha*, commanded by Captain R. Lee, burned at the head of Lake Joseph.

The Spanish influenza hit Bracebridge mid-October. The Board of Health closed the churches, the schools, the library, the theatre, and all public buildings until the "flu" abated. The postmaster kept the outer doors of the post office building locked while the mail was being sorted in order to avoid the usual crowding in the lobby. Armstrong's Meat Market was closed as the flu got them all at the same time. The post office staff was hardest hit in town. Local subscribers to the Bell Telephone were requested to use their phones as little as possible owing to sickness of staff. The British Lion Hotel was converted into an emergency hospital. There were about 400 cases in town and the Board of Health wanted as many flu patients as possible at the hospital where constant attention was available.

Every effort was made to keep the epidemic in check. By November 10, the churches could resume their services, but the schools, theatre, and other public places remained closed for an extra week.

The ringing of bells and blowing of whistles signalled that the war was over. When the clamour of bells had subsided, a gathering took place at Memorial Park where Councillor J.G. Myers read the official bulletin announcing the signing of the armistice and called upon the citizens to give thanksgiving. His address was followed by the singing of the Doxology and the Lord's Prayer. Meanwhile the "band boys" gathered and played up and down the street. All this was accompanied by the noise of fire crackers, tin pails, cow bells, tin horns, etc., and the citizens showed no restraint in expressing their joy. About 7:30 p.m. a large procession was formed, and led by the band and an array of torches, proceeded to Jubilee Park. There a large bonfire had been built with two effigies of the Kaiser placed on the summit of the heap. The fire, a few shots from a rifle, and "infernal combustion" made a complete job of the "Potsdam gentleman." There followed impromptu speeches by G.W. Ecclestone, MPP, Dr. McGibbon, MP, and Lieutenant L.B. Tillson. The national anthem was sung and the crowd dispersed to a dance in the new Bird Woollen Mill building.

The citizens of Muskoka invested $854,300 in Victory Bonds. Bracebridge led the way with $333,750, Huntsville raised $157,650, and Gravenhurst $80,850.

Civilian deaths during the year included H.B. Bridgland, 61, sheriff of Muskoka 1903-1906. He purchased the drug store from his brother Dr. S. Bridgland and ran it until his retirement in 1917; he was also a president of the Board of Trade ... Henry T. Hey, 66, resident for 40 years and an expert gardener ... Mrs. Thos. Richards, 66, well known in town and Baysville ... W.N. Clark, 64, a skilled carpenter and builder ... Mr. T. Jackson, 67, a well known and respected farmer ... Mr. Isaac Huber, 76, ran a book, stationery, and jewelry store, then was clerk of the District and surrogate courts for about 30 years ... Mrs. Wm. Ferguson, leaving six little children (including Arthur, who later was on the board of the Children's Aid Society for many years) without mother or father, Mr. Ferguson having been killed in a runaway accident a year earlier ... Ambrose W. Mandley, 57, carpenter, builder, and contractor by trade ... Mrs. Carter Wilson, 30, formerly Mrs. Frank Hunt, daughter of George Johnson, died with her twin baby boys ... Mrs. D.E. Bastedo, wife of Sheriff Bastedo and mother of editor Burleigh Bastedo of the *Herald* ... Mr. Arthur Fielding, 50, of influenza and pneumonia. He had conducted a successful carting business in Bracebridge ... Mrs. John Bailey, 73, resident in Bracebridge since 1868 ... 6-year-old Ruth Tozer, daughter of Mr. and Mrs. W.J. Tozer, drowned during a picnic outing at High Falls ... Mrs. W.C. Fryer, suddenly of a heart attack, leaving three small children and a fond husband ... Mr. Thos. Boyes, one of the pioneers of the District ... Yaing Wood, a Chinaman who conducted a laundry business, drowned. His wife and family were living in China so the laundry business was taken over by his brother from Toronto.

## 1919

This was the busiest and most profitable season we had ever had in Muskoka. Train service was the best since 1914. Vital statistics for the year: births 64, marriages 33, deaths 21.

Council fixed the taxation rate for the year at 38 mills, four mills lower than in 1918. A bylaw was passed for the purpose of raising $4,000 by debentures for the erection of a stable and hose tower in connection with the fire hall. Plans had been prepared for enlarging the old Town Hall, built in 1881, and Council was going to ask the ratepayers to vote on a debenture bylaw for $4,000 ... Mr. Ausborne Hewitt was appointed road overseer for the town in place of Mr. Jas Green ... Meatless days were cancelled and the use of butter no longer prohibited ... Petitions were presented to Council for and against daylight saving. With those in favour ahead by 2-1, the town adopted it at 2 a.m. on Monday, March 31, 1919.

Council had an "arch of welcome" erected on Thomas Street to greet the Bracebridge boys returning from overseas. The arch was illuminated with electric lights and decorated with bunting and evergreen boughs, with the words "Welcome Home" inscribed thereon. Messrs. Ed Hunt, Lyman Perkins, and Geo. Brown did the work. The welcome committee of the Soldiers' Aid Commission arranged to have a large sleigh meet the returning soldiers at the station. Sergeant Everett Draper, DCM, had the honour of being the first Bracebridge soldier returning home and to pass under the "Welcome Home" arch.

Boys of 122nd Battalion arriving home were Edward Perry, Fred Couture, Robert Bell, Wm. Brazier, Herb Dyer, D'Arcy Armstrong, E. Strong, Fred Strong, and Lance Corporal Verne Failes, one of the first Bracebridge boys to enlist.

Major Kenneth A. Mahaffy of the 5th Battalion received a bar to his Military Cross from King George at a Buckingham Palace investiture.

The picturesque ceremony of handing back the Colours to the 122nd Overseas Battalion Canadian Expeditionary force took place. The Colours had been deposited in St. George's Chapel in July 1917 for safe custody during the time the battalion was engaged on active service in the field. An escort of 100 men of the 2nd Battalion Coldstream Guards was provided under the command of Captain Viscount Marsham.

Ten thousand dollars worth of work on the Baysville Road started in charge of Messrs. Richard Zimmerman and Richard Piper. About 10 feet was to be blasted off the crest of the Devil's Gap and the road greatly improved with a new bridge over Outlet Creek. By summer, tourists from the south to the Lake of Bays would be able to make the trip by motorcar through to their cottages.

Work resumed on the trunk road from Sudbury to Toronto as soon as labour could be procured.

The South Muskoka Agricultural Society erected a fine new bandstand in Jubilee Park and wired it for lighting.

Redmond Thomas was called to the bar … The Moore brothers, who had been running the Crystal Theatre, leased the Dominion Hotel to make a theatre and purchased Mr. John Hill's pool room … Mr. and Mrs. W. Fisher, managers of the Queen's Hotel, were succeeded by Mr. and Mrs. W.A. Howard from Peterborough … Mr. Geo. Marshall bought the cartage business of Mr. Thos. Morrow … Mr. Albert Ball of Utterson took over the confectionery business of Mr. Geo. Jotham … Mr. Fred Sander sold his livery stable to Messrs. Clarence and Jack McNiece of Reay. The business was established by Mr. Sander about 30 years previously … Mr. Ed Freure of Beamsville leased the poultry farm of Mr. Bert Brown of Manitoba Street, to specialize in White Wyandottes … The central sample room at the Queen's Hotel was turned into a reading room … Dr. Melville Anderson, captain of the Canadian Dental Corps, opened a new dental parlour above the Misses MacMillan store … Rev. F.H. Hincks left for Haileybury … Mr. D'Alton Armstrong sold his meat market to Messrs. Thos. and Jos. Pelletier.

The Bank of Nova Scotia absorbed the Bank of Ottawa … Mr. Harry Lockhart opened a grocery store in the premises formerly occupied by the Hare Bros … The Dominion Bank opened a branch with temporary quarters in the Queen's Hotel with Mr. Henry Warren as manager … William Bennett purchased the Mundy store from George Tennant; James McKay opened a blacksmith shop at the rear … The local branch of the Bell Telephone Co. moved into new quarters in the building formerly occupied by Wasdell's Butcher Shop. The interior of the shop was completely renovated and nicely decorated. The new switchboard was equipped with two local and two long distance positions … Mr. Jack Hill purchased the livery and sales business from Mr. Jack Beaumont … Messrs. Williams and Ross opened a new business college in town, in Armstrong's hall on the corner of Manitoba Street and Chancery Lane. Williams and Ross already conducted the North Bay Business College, the Haileybury Business College, and the Northern Correspondence Schools.

Lacrosse was reorganized for the first time since 1913 with president W.C. Simmons, vice presidents Geo. Tennant and Bun. Wasdell, secretary Dr. Mel Anderson, treasurer Ed West, time-keeper Alex C. Salmon, and temporary captain Sam Boyer. The committee of management comprised Chas. Bailey, Charles Arnott, Phil Marrin, Dunc Mcdonald, Geo. Thomas, and I.B. Aulph. Bracebridge was the Intermediate OALA champion in 1919.

Mr. Art Tibbett was selected manager of the hockey team which would play Huntsville, Burk's Falls, Gravenhurst, and Orillia.

In May, the Muskoka Motor Club formed in affiliation with the Ontario Motor League. The president was Geo. Tennant, the vice president Peter Hutchison, and the secretary-treasurer Mel Ross. Membership cost $5.

This season promised to be the best yet in the motorboat business. Makers of launches in town and around the lakes were busy installing engines in hulls that had lain idle owing to the war. There was an increasing demand for family motorboats of medium speed and also a good market for the extra-fast variety.

The Dominion Chautauqua Festival was held July 11-17 under the big tent with seating for 1,500 in Jubilee Park. They presented five concert companies, seven lectures, and one play.

It was quite a task for motorboats to wend their way up the river during the summer owing to the logs and bark. It would have been a great thing for Bracebridge if the river could be kept clear for July and August. One could not blame the tourists for not coming to town when the river was full of treacherous logs.

A day's sport was arranged in honour of the returned men with a lacrosse match and aeroplane rides. Over 40 people took trips above the town on this first opportunity to have an aeroplane ride in Bracebridge. Margaret Bird accompanied the pilot to Toronto, being the first Bracebridge person to make this trip by plane.

In the provincial election on October 20, H.E. Rice of Huntsville ran for the Liberal Party against Mr. G.W. Ecclestone, Liberal-Conservative. Mr. Ecclestone won, as did Premier E.C. Drury. The temperance referendum was held the same day. Ontario would be dry – a large majority voted "No." This was the first election in Ontario when women could vote. According to the enumerator's list there were 350 voters in Bracebridge, more than double the number on the last one, due to the women's right to vote.

Deaths in 1919 year included Lieutenant Scott Waldie, 40, who went overseas as captain of the 122nd Battalion and died of pneumonia on the way home ... David Wright, 62 ... Sir Wilfred Laurier, 77 ... Mrs. George Parlett, 59 ... Mrs. York , in her 104th year ... Mrs. Wm. Bennett, 86 ... Samuel Jacques, 74, employee of the Muskoka Leather Co. ... Benjamin McDonald, 60 ... Mr. J.J. Beaumont of Alport Farm, Muskoka Township.

## 1920

The population of Bracebridge was 2,424, the assessment $951,598, and there were 609 children between the ages of 5 and 16. There were 85 dogs licensed. The tax rate for 1920 was set at 42 mills with the school rate up five mills and the Town rate down one mill.

The town clerk was instructed to inform the Mickle, Dyment Co. that "if the river is not free of logs by the date set by the statute governing same, legal proceedings will be taken by the Corporation." Police chief McConnell was asked to rigidly enforce the bylaw regarding speeding automobiles, and to see that traffic regulations for cars were enforced. No car was to be parked in the business section (between the Free Methodist Church and the south end of Memorial Park).

Mayor Wattie and councillor Fawcett were appointed to purchase a team of horses for the town. They bought a handsome span of dappled greys at $625, bred by Mr. Chas. Carley of Milton.

The Public School Board elected Mr. J.H. Burton as chairman. Salaries were fixed as follows: Miss Parlett, Miss Johnson, and Miss Mainprize $850, Miss Veitch, Miss Richards, Miss U. Murphy, Miss Perkins, Miss I. Murphy, and Miss Boyer $800, and Miss Creasor $825. The secretary was instructed to notify the teachers and ask for their reply. In the case non-compliance the education committee was empowered to engage a substitute.

The High School Board elected Mr. T.N. Bird as chairman. Five applications were received for the position of high school principal at a salary of $2,000 a year. Mr. A.B. Steer, BA, of Watford was hired. It was decided to re-engage Miss Hood at $1,400, Miss Logan at $1,300, and Miss Ferguson at $1,300. Fees for non-residents were doubled.

A vote of the ratepayers in August approved the request to form one Board of Education. The first board would be elected at the next year's elections (1921).

Over 100 attended the annual meeting of the Muskoka Teachers' Institute held in Memorial Hall with president Scovell in the chair.

The 20 members present at the annual meeting of the Board of Trade elected president Alex Walker, vice president W.A. Howard, and secretary-treasurer D.T. Hodgson. A 32-page folder containing 60 illustrations advertising Bracebridge as a summer resort was issued by Mr. D.J. Armstrong.

The Anglo-Canadian Leather Co. placed a group insurance policy with the Canada Life Assurance Co., giving each employee protection of $1,000. It was understood that office staff and general employees at Montreal, Toronto, Huntsville, and Bracebridge would be included, and also the employees of the Navigation Co. and the Bigwin Inn Co. – in all about 400 employees [it was the Huntsville navigation company which was referred to, controlled along with the Bigwin Inn by C.O. Shaw of the tannery].

The Bracebridge hockey team won the District series but lost out to Collingwood in the OHA semi-final. Our lacrosse team won the intermediate championship. A Bracebridge Athletic Association was formed with president G.H.O. Thomas, vice president George Parlett, William S. Simmons, and secretary G.W. Boyer.

The South Muskoka Agricultural Society elected F.M. Higgins president, J. Bryon Kaye and H. Richards vice presidents, and Jerry Dickie secretary-treasurer. Mr. Wm. Naismith of Falkenburg entered 10 exhibits in the potato competition of the Ottawa Fair and received eight firsts, one second, and one fourth. The 46th Annual Fall Fair had 1,713 entries and fine weather but perhaps a shade too warm for the butter exhibits and horse racing.

Dr. McGibbon, MP, arranged to have a captured three-inch German gun, taken by the 2nd Division Canadians in August 1918, presented to Bracebridge.

A flu epidemic disrupted town life to the extent of cancelling the skating carnival, closing the public and high schools for two weeks, and causing as few public meetings as possible to be held.

The Annual Report of the Public Library stated that 715 people used the library's 5,680 books, an increase of 86 over the year previous. Circulation was 13,688. The library subscribed to two daily papers, 12 weekly papers, and 14 monthly periodicals. The Library Board for 1920 consisted of Judge Mahaffy, Mayor A.T. Wattie, Rev. W.E. Morrow, and Messrs. Thos. Johnson, M.J. Dickie, Elliott Fulton, and W. Reginald Kirk. Mr. Dickie was the secretary-treasurer and Miss Dickie the librarian.

About 4,000 visitors came to town for the celebration of Orangeman's Day under the direction of Bracebridge Orange Lodge No. 218. Special trains from Washago and Burk's Falls brought nearly a thousand people while the steamers *Cherokee* and *Islander* brought more. Others came on regular trains, private boats, and in a stream of cars. All places of business reported an excellent day's sales.

Mr. R.M. Best, formerly of Toronto, purchased the law practice of the late Geo. Mahaffy and occupied the same offices in the Sibbett block ... Mr. C.W. Archer formed a limited liability company, of which he and his chief engineer, Mr. Heintz, were the principal shareholders, to be known as the Archer-Heintz Lake Service Co. Ltd. It would operate the passenger and freight steamers *Llano* and *Mildred* ... Captain L.R. Fraser purchased *Queen of the Isles* from the Muskoka Leather Company.

About 200 members of the Michigan Pikers Association came in 80 cars and 15 trucks complete with a 55-piece band as part of their International Good Roads Tour. They were dined at the Queen's and British Lion hotels. The committee set up for arrangements included H.J. Bird (chairman), W. A. Howard, George Tennant, and C. Barnes (billeting), Milton Bechtel and W.C. Simmons (gasoline and oil supply), Peter Smith (finance), and G.W. Boyer and D.T. Hodgson (advertising). The visitors were met by the Bracebridge Motor League and escorted through the streets to Jubilee Park where they camped and attended a monster rally and good roads meeting with music, singing, and speakers. On Sunday, the citizens of the town gave the visitors a trip on the steamer *Medora*. On leaving, each guest received a picture souvenir of their visit.

The Bracebridge Driving Club elected president George Tennant, secretary-treasurer William Kingsmill, clerk of the course B. Bechtel, and timer Ernest Boyd.

Town Council passed a bylaw requiring all places of business close at 10:30 p.m. on Saturday nights ... Mr. D'Alton Armstrong purchased the store premises next to the Bracebridge Garage and had it changed to a storage room for cars ... Carl Brown, formerly of Utterson, opened a billiard and pool room in the Burton premises, with new tables and fixtures ... Messrs. Will Towns and

*Construction of the railway through Bracebridge required substantial bridges over both branches of the river, as well as a deep rock cut at Queen Street. Here a passenger train steams across the 20-metre-high south branch bridge. The river was used by lumbermen for driving logs until the 1930s.* COURTESY OF BRENDA COX

Horace Parlett purchased the grocery and provision business of Mr. Art Tibbett ... Bracebridge stores commenced closing Thursday afternoons ... Mr. S.L. Kirby of Newmarket purchased the moving picture theatre, The Crystal Theatre, from Mr. Jos. Moreau. He also leased the upper room of the Town Hall and had it converted into a first class picture show ... Messrs. C. Maura and Co. discontinued business. The store, owned by Mr. Sibbett, was taken over by the Chinese café. The Dominion Hotel occupied the former café location ... Mr. F.H. Higgins was named president of the Navy League of Canada, a position rendered vacant by the death of Mr. H.B. Bridgland, and Mr. H. Warren took over that of secretary, previously held by Rev. F.H. Hincks ... Mr. J.H. Elliott purchased the Thorneloe business block.

Main Street behind the Grand Trunk Railway station was raised, graded, and given proper drainage. A building was erected at the railway station for use by the Canadian Express Company ... There were 187 telephone subscribers in Bracebridge, including 82 business phones and 151 connections for outside calls handled through the local exchange. There were 10 employees and a monthly payroll of $508.70. The company paid the town $210.86 in taxes the year before.

The Bracebridge Business College leased the Herald Hall with plans to reopen about September 1 in the new premises, which were being redecorated and painted.

Rev. and Mrs. Morrow left the Baptist Church for a new charge in Peterborough.

Chief McConnell arrested Frederick Dunn, George Fereon, and William Runoff in the Anglican cemetery in Beatrice. Mr. McConnell received word in the morning that the lunch belonging to the road gang working near Moore's mill had been stolen and that three strangers had been seen in the neighbourhood. The chief investigated and found that the three men had tried to sell a car in Utterson for $150. The car was found abandoned on the road near Beatrice and the men were discovered at the rear of the building in the graveyard. One of them carried a revolver loaded in all chambers. The chief brought the men back to Bracebridge and further inquiry found that the car belonged to Mr. E. Featherstone, a farmer near

*Bracebridge Bay from the Grand Trunk Railway tracks. The old wharf (top left) and the new wharf (bottom right) had separate road access until a connecting road was built around the bay behind the boathouses in 1921.*
COURTESY OF IAN TURNBULL

Oakville. Chief McConnell took the men to Oakville where they were later sentenced to one year each at Burwash farm. They had been confined in separate cells in the county jail at Milton as they were considered dangerous men. (Imagine one police officer arresting three suspects, one armed!)

Mr. Bert Thompson of Uffington was killed by lightning while sitting in his living room. Everyone in the room was stunned, as was his father in a workshop nearby. Bert regained consciousness, said he was all right, then died. Both shoes were torn from his feet and one side of his body was marked. Their dog was instantly killed.

An accident at the level train crossing at Moore's mill killed Mr. E.K. Hagerman of Toronto, a passenger in a car. The car was travelling about 15 miles an hour up the grade to the track when the train suddenly appeared. The engine struck it with such force that the cowcatcher was badly damaged and the car was demolished. Mr. Hagerman was thrown 70 feet and expired almost immediately. An inquest found the railway negligent.

Other deaths during the year included Mr. Alex Barron, former councillor and reeve of Macaulay Township, and later clerk ... Mr. George Mahaffy, 41, son of the late Judge William Cosby Mahaffy. He was a lawyer and active in real estate ... Mrs. Ann Grant, 97, widow of the late Charles Grant ... Mr. Peter Duff, 53, former businessman in dry goods and ladies furnishings until 1916 ... Jacob W. Dill, 80. He had been in partnership with Mr. Wm. Kirk, was a former reeve of Bracebridge, and in 1885 was elected to the Legislature ... Mr. Isaac Bridgeman, 59, after being kicked in the stomach by a horse ... Mr. George Spence, 79, 13 years reeve of Draper.

The District Municipal Association was formed in September with membership composed of the heads of the municipalities and clerks or other two delegates. The membership fee was set at $5 annually. Officers were president Capt. L.R. Fraser, Monck, vice president Edward Speers, Ridout, and secretary-treasurer. J.H. Forbes, Medora and Wood.

The trial of Mr. Joseph Willoughby, former station agent in Bracebridge, was held by His Honour Judge Mahaffy. Crown Attorney Johnson prosecuted and Mr. Redmond Thomas appeared for the defence. Mr. Coulter, the auditor for the Grand Trunk Railway Company, produced documents showing a shortage in Mr. Willoughby's accounts of something over $5,000. The defence sought to show absence of criminal intent, urging that the funds had been misapplied in error and largely as a result of overwork. His Honour in judgment briefly reviewed the evidence, which he said clearly established the guilt of the accused, and sentenced him to three years at Kingston.

In compliance with the King's proclamation, Bracebridge citizens ceased all activity for two minutes at 11 o'clock on the morning of November 11 in remembrance of those killed in the Great War. The Town Hall flag was flown at half mast in honour of the day.

The Women's Patriotic League received a service flag bearing the names of the Bracebridge men who served so valiantly overseas, and placed it in the public library.

The first meeting of the Mothers' Pension Board was held in Bracebridge in November with chairman Mrs. H.L. Goltz, Bardsville, vice-chairman Mr. Archie Sloan, Gravenhurst, and secretary Mr. D.T. Hodgson, Bracebridge. The Mothers' Allowance Act provided for a monthly payment toward the support of dependent children under the age of 14 years. Applications were to be considered only when the mother was a widow, the wife of an inmate of a hospital for the insane in Ontario, or whose husband was permanently disabled and incapable of contributing to the support of the family. All applications went to the local board.

## 1921

Vital statistics showed 72 births, 39 deaths, and 38 marriages ... The municipal election was quiet with only half the vote polled. Mr. A. Wattie was elected mayor, Mr. T.N. Bird re-elected chairman on the high school board, and Geo. Tennant chairman of the Water, Light and Power Commission.

The filling of ice houses began late January, later than usual, but the ice was a foot to a foot and a half thick, and clear. The lake opened on April 6, the earliest in 40 years.

The heaviest rain storm to visit Muskoka in many years fell in March with four inches of water coming in a few hours. This caused great floods with culverts being torn away and damage done to the streets. Nearly all the cellars in town were flooded, meaning considerable loss in many cases, where fruit and other provisions were damaged. Probably the most serious damage was to the machines at the Wilson's Falls hydroelectric plant. The waterwheel at the Bird Woollen Mills became blocked and the plant closed down. The wheel was about six feet under water and it was impossible to make repairs until the water level fell. A hot dry summer followed, which was good for tourists but bad for crops.

The budget for 1921 was set at $68,245, making a tax rate of 40 mills including a 22-mill school rate. Council passed bylaws to raise $5,000 for the repair of streets necessitated by the recent floods, and to provide for the opening of a roadway from the new wharf to connect with the old wharf. The purchase of the adjoining land from Mrs. Mahaffy made the proposal possible.

Council sold the existing bridge over Bracebridge Falls to the Minister of Public Works for $5,000 and placed an order with the Dominion Bridge Co. for a standard government bridge to accommodate 15-ton trucks for a contract price of $6,500. The new bridge had two spans, one 50 and the other 80 feet, with sidewalks at each side and the entire flooring of cement. The old bridge was rebuilt by the government and used over the river at the Macaulay-Stephenson town line.

Ladies were present for the first time at the annual Board of Trade banquet held in the Queen's Hotel. The 1921 folder of Bracebridge and vicinity contained a complete map of the town, showing business places, manufacturing places, churches, public buildings, and residences. Persons wishing their names placed on the map on their property could have this done for the sum of one dollar each.

The Adolescent School Attendance Act came into force in September, requiring the attendance at school of all children 14 years of age and under, who would be expected to remain in full attendance until they reached 16 years. Those already employed would be allowed to remain, but a certificate of employment or a home permit had to be produced. Non-resident school fees for high school were raised to $70 (cost per pupil exceeded $72.50). The highest fee charged in the past was $30.

Mr. Ralph Landen resigned as principal of the Public School and was replaced by Mr. B.G. Minns of Port Carling at a salary of $1,400. Mr. E.E. Ingall of Peterborough was in charge of Summer School this year.

Captain Duncan Forrest, Inspector for the Children's Aid Department for the District of Muskoka, reported 160 calls made on 70 wards of the society, 37 complaints dealt with involving 52 children, three crippled children placed in the home for incurables, 14 homes visited and reported on regarding the placing of children, and temporary aid secured effecting 21 children. A total of 2,136 miles were traveled, 822 letters received and sent out, five court cases heard, 26 warnings given, and 565 interviews conducted ... The Mothers' Pension Board met and nine applications were passed, making the total to date 27. Only three women received cheques this year.

In March both tanneries reported increasing output and employing more men. There was little unemployment in Bracebridge.

Of the 4,777 students at the provincial university in Toronto, Muskoka District had 144 in attendance, a number exceeded only by Toronto, Simcoe, Wentworth, and York counties. Parry Sound had only 12 in attendance.

Accidents during the year included the disappearance of Mr. William Stubbs, book-keeper for Geo. W. Ecclestone, in late March. He had been out of hospital only a few days and it was feared he may have tried to cross the scows and fallen into the river. The entire community helped with the search but his body was not found until May 5. Master Will Gohm, 16, eldest son of Mr. and Mrs. Thos. Gohm of Macaulay, drowned in Doley's Creek, which ran through his father's farm.

In April, arrangements were made with Lieutenant Colonel D.M. Grant to deposit the Colours of the 122nd Battalion in the courthouse.

Rev. R. and Mrs. McEachern came to Knox Presbyterian Church to replace Rev. A.B. Irwin and Mrs. Irwin, who left for Thessalon. A recital by Miss Frances Nickawa, the Cree Indian elocutionist, was held at the Methodist Church. It included a mixture of humorous numbers and selections from the writings of Pauline Johnson.

Changes during the year included: the Foster Meat Co. started to use a covered motor truck for delivery purposes ... A.T. Wattie Cold Storage installed a cooling plant which did away with the necessity for using ice ... Mr. Thomas Ball introduced the use of bottles altogether in his milk delivery. It was a nicer way to handle this commodity and appreciated by his customers ... Messrs. Williams and Ross sold their interests in the Bracebridge Business College to Mr. Leonard A. Blayley, former principal of the North Bay College ... Messrs. G. Draper and Albert Buck started business in town as electricians ... The price of bread decreased to 20 cents for a large loaf ... A Chevrolet touring car cost $895 and a roadster $880 ... Mr. Thos. Bruce took the agency for the Massey-Harris Implement Co. and opened an office and sales room in the British Lion Hotel ... Mr. A.A. Ball purchased a confectionery and restaurant business in Huntsville and intended moving to that town ... Mr. and Mrs. Jas. Buckler and Miss Buckler of Uffington moved to town, occupying the Leeder residence on Hunt's Hill, where Mr. Buckler intended to open an art studio. Upon completion of Mr. J.H. Elliott's building , he would occupy it for his stationery and jewelry store and Mrs. Burton would move her dry goods stock into the premises then occupied by Mr. Elliott ... The Telegraph Co. moved to the Burton store ... Mr. R. Hepplestone of Barrie opened a butcher shop in the Caisse building ... Mr. Bert Brown took over the Metropolitan Life Insurance Co. agency formerly held by Mr. Skinner.

The fall federal election brought much political activity to Bracebridge. In August, the Hon E.C. Drury, Ontario premier, spoke at the "Great Field Day." In October, for the first time in the history of Bracebridge, the town was honoured by a visit of a Prime Minister of Canada. The Rt. Hon. Arthur Meighen and the Hon. Hugh Guthrie were met at the station by civic officials, a large concourse of people, and the students of the high school. Large audiences greeted the prime minister when he spoke at the Town Hall and at the Regent Theatre.

Candidates for the election were incumbent Dr. Peter McGibbon, Liberal-Conservative, Mr. G.H.O. Thomas, Liberal-Progressive, and Dr. J.D. McDonald, United Farmers of Ontario. The Liberals swept the country, soundly defeating the Meighen government. There were 1,900 names on the voters list in Bracebridge.

The fall fair was again a success with 2,184 entries (1,995 the year before). Highlights included horse races, an exhibit from the experimental station at Kapuskasing, a demonstration of fighting fires with firefoam, and over 800 participants in the children's parade.

Stanley House, on Lake Joseph, was destroyed by fire caused by a defective fireplace. One hundred guests were in residence but there were no casualties. Damage estimated at $50,000 was partially covered by insurance.

The Board of Health advised parents to have their children inoculated with antitoxin prior to the opening of school. In cases where parents were unable to pay, children could be taken to Mrs. Goggin's private hospital, where Nurse Arnott administered the same free, the cost being borne by the Board of Health.

The Bracebridge Choral Society was formed with president Mrs. H. Bird, vice president Mr. J.W. Reid, secretary Mr. Allan Hines, treasurer Mr. A.E. Whitton, and conductor Mr. B. Tillson.

Canadian Authors' Week took place across Canada in November for the first time and a large number of books by Canadian authors were on exhibit at the library.

Deaths in the year included Mrs. William Simmons, wife of the superintendent of the Water, Light and Power Commission ... Mrs. Annie Thompson, widow of John W. Thompson, the last charter member of the Baptist Church ... Mr. Frederick Leeder, 83 ... Mrs. John Linney, 78 ... Mrs. Burleigh Bastedo.

## 1922

At the first meeting of Council, newly elected Mayor Smith resigned due to his move with the Beardmore Leather Company to Acton. He was presented with a gold-headed cane on a farewell excursion aboard the *Cherokee*. Mr. Smith had served as mayor 1904-6 and 1914-15, and as a councillor. Henry J. Bird Jr. was appointed mayor in his stead.

A.C. Salmon was re-appointed clerk-treasurer with a salary of $950, T.A. Hewitt as road overseer for $1,500, Wm. McConnell as constable, tax collector, fire warden, and bread and sanitary inspector for $1,200, Dr. Peter McGibbon medical health officer for $10 and fees, and A.E. Ecclestone fire chief. Mr. I.B. Aulph, deputy sheriff, was appointed Justice of the Peace for Muskoka ... The fire hall bylaw which was endorsed by the ratepayers, passed, and work commenced on the stables and fire tower at the Town Hall in August. The tax rate was set at 46 mills. A new furnace was installed in the Town Hall.

Council accepted a policy with the Globe Indemnity Co. of Canada covering employer's liability at $160 a year and also a policy covering a public liability at a rate of 4½ cents per capita of population. This latter policy insured the town against payment for damages in case of accident on public streets up to $5,000 for one accident or $10,000 in the case of two accidents.

Captain L.R. Fraser retired as president of the Muskoka Municipal Association to be succeeded by Mr. Alfred Judd of Juddhaven, with Mr. J.H. Forbes as secretary-treasurer.

The Bracebridge Board of Trade under president W.A. Howard, then H.G. Everett, passed a resolution of appreciation of Mr. Harry Linney's endeavours to advertise and promote the interests of the district. Both the Canadian Pacific and Grand Trunk railways issued handsome folders advertising the Muskoka Lakes, in which much information accurately and interestingly prepared was furnished with hotel directory and maps.

Mr. Ecclestone, MPP, advised Council that part of the "Scenic Highway" through Muskoka via Baysville, Dorset, and Haliburton would be built during the year, an appropriation of $15,000 having been made.

The Bracebridge Board of Education came into effect early in the year with Mr. C. Spreadborough elected as chairman and A.C. Salmon as secretary-treasurer. It decided to abolish non-resident high school fees on the understanding that the Department of Education would pay 80 percent of the cost of the high school. They also asked Council to raise $1,200 for the erection of a temporary schoolroom for a kindergarten. In September a bylaw passed to raise $3,600 by debenture to erect a two-storey brick-veneered addition to the main building of the Central School. By October the primary class moved from the Gospel Hall into the new addition.

The Muskoka Board for Mother's Allowance, with chairman Mrs. H.L. Goltz, approved seven applications, one each from Bala, Huntsville, and Gravenhurst, and two each from Watt Township and Dorset. There were 23 widows receiving pensions totaling $730 a month. In the province there were 2,882 recipients receiving a total of $102,550 a month.

The Public Library Annual Report indicated a circulation 14,720 volumes with 175 volumes purchased, 42 volumes donated. The number of borrowers stood at 813.

The steel work of the new bridge was lowered in place and riveting completed in early February with a temporary plank floor. In March a bylaw was passed for $7,500 to pay for cement paving and painting. Mr. Geo. Tennant secured the contract for moving the steel of the old bridge to the Macaulay-Stephenson town line where it would be erected. The new bridge was opened May 23.

A bylaw limiting the speed of motor-driven cars to five miles an hour on the town bridges and a bylaw for the collection of a special tax rate in order to put oil on Manitoba Street were both passed.

The rest room committee of the Women's Institute engaged rooms over Miss Jackson's confectionery store on Manitoba Street to be used as a women's rest room. They were opened to the public in early March.

Sixty-five members of the Anglo-Canadian Band under conductor Herbert L. Clarke gave a splendid program at Jubilee Park.

Mr. Earl Dunn of Fenn, Anderson & Co. won the $75 second prize in the Pictorial Review Company window dressing contest. Many competed from Canada and the U.S. Eight hundred people attended a horse race held at Jubilee Park in August, with $900 in prizes. William Kingshott was president and E.E. Boyd secretary-treasurer for the organizing committee. Horses came from Port Hope, Orangeville, Cookstown, Coldwater, Penetang, and of course Bracebridge.

Muskoka crop statistics for 1921 (acres under cultivation): fall wheat 30, spring wheat 214, barley 617, oats 17,458, rye 185, buckwheat 174, peas 551, beans 22, flax 8, mixed grains 909, corn 167, fodder corn 383, potatoes 1,123, turnips 416, mangels 46, sugar beets 30, carrots 44, alfalfa 22, hay and clover 28,215. Horses totalled 3,579, sheep and lambs 12,617, cattle 16,734, swine 3,458, turkeys 763, geese 618, ducks 844, and other fowl 51,290.

It was announced in March that the Muskoka Leather Co. was leaving town and the Anglo-Canadian closing down for an indefinite period – a hard blow for Bracebridge. There was not enough business for the Anglo-Canadian Co. to keep both its Huntsville and Bracebridge tanneries running or Muskoka Leather to keep both Acton and Bracebridge going.

Mr. and Mrs. Howard, who had charge of the Queen's Hotel for the preceding three years, left, and Mr. John Thomson took over the management.

A bylaw to grant assistance to the Maple Leaf Hosiery Co. Ltd., which would employ about 30 workers, was passed in a vote held July 3. The company would get $3,000 and a fixed assessment rate of $5,000 for 10 years.

*The closure of the Beardmore tannery (known as the Muskoka Leather Company for much of its existence) obviously dealt a blow to the local economy, as it employed a considerable workforce. Tannery manager Peter A. Smith was active in the community and served as mayor.* COURTESY OF VICKY BILLINGSLEY FROM THE R.J. BOYER COLLECTION

*In 1877 the Beardmore Company erected a leather tannery on the north bank of the Muskoka River at the foot of Wellington Street, to take advantage of Muskoka's abundant supplies of hemlock (hemlock bark was a source of tannin for the tanning process). In 1922 the firm closed the extensive plant and consolidated operations in Acton, Ontario, due to dwindling supplies of cheap bark and the availability of alternative tanning agents.* COURTESY OF BRENDA COX

An Industrial Committee was appointed consisting of two members of Council, two members of the Board of Trade, and the chairman of the Water, Light and Power Commission, to make an energetic canvass with a view to securing new industries for Bracebridge and otherwise to promote the interests of the town.

Lawrence Ryan, DDS, opened a dental office … Mr. Ivan Bickmore completed installation of his radio receiving set and was able to hear concerts from New York and other distant points … Entertainment included *The Eloquent Dempsey*, a pleasing Irish comedy presented by St. Joseph's Dramatic Club in the Town Hall with Miss Eleanor Fenn, Patrick Murphy, Mr. Thomas Montague, and Mr. John McCann in the cast.

It was not likely that Bracebridge would have a weekly half holiday in the summer. The tourist season meant the busiest season for the Bracebridge merchants, several of whom were opposed to closing their places of business one whole afternoon each week. The proposal had been made, and favourably received, to close the stores at five o'clock each evening except Saturday during the summer.

At 4:40 a.m. on May 17, the execution of George Cyr took place by hanging, for the December 1921 murder of George Wethers of Chaffey Township. The proceedings were of as private a character as possible, there being present only the jail officials, the physician, the deputy sheriff, and the spiritual adviser of the prisoner, besides Mr. A. Ellis, the official employed for this purpose.

The entire plant of the Muskoka Wood Manufacturing Co., one of Huntsville's largest and most important industries, was destroyed by fire.

The special government committee investigating the hotel and tourist business visited town in August. The Ontario Temperance Act had hit the hotels hard, as had the change in the traffic conditions. More people were travelling on the roads than on the railways and this would be accentuated as roads improved. Railways provided lavatories, etc., for their patrons, but motorcars had none of these and they had to be provided chiefly by the hotels. The question for the committee to consider was, "What can the Government do to develop the hotel accommodation of the Province?"

*In operation from 1872 until the 1950s, the Bird Woollen Mill enjoyed a national reputation for its high-quality products. It reached its zenith during World War 1 and into the 1920s, employing as many as 60 men and women. The staff here poses on Muskoka Road in front of the mill complex, which had been significantly expanded in 1912.* FROM "PICTORIAL HISTORY OF WOODCHESTER VILLA"

Many Canadian authors were present the first week in August at the Canadian Chautauqua, and an all-Canadian library was opened and a four-year reading course on Canadian literature inaugurated.

The Dominion Railway Board sent representatives to Bracebridge to decide what protection or further protection should be given on account of the level railway crossing within the municipality. The three crossings were inspected, at Thomas Street, at Bird's Woollen Mill, and on Shier Street beside the Muskoka Foundry. The commissioners suggested as a primary measure of safety the placing of a speed limit of 10 miles an hour within the town limits, and this was put into effect. Before leaving town the members of the party were given a trip to the lake in the *Bobolink* by Mr. and Mrs. T.M. Bird.

Twenty years earlier Mr. T.B. Rosewarne, of Macaulay and Bracebridge, started growing strawberries and that year had eight quarts for sale. In 1922 he expected to market 6,000 boxes. Mr. Elliott Fulton showed baskets of red plums from his trees, grown from shoots of a wild plum found in Macaulay Township.

Owing to the scarcity of coal it was found necessary by the Navigation Co. to withdraw the steamer *Oriole* from passenger service and use her for securing wood. The *Cherokee* was put on the Bracebridge trip, coming into town at noon. The No. 42 train south and No. 45 north were temporarily laid off because of the shortage.

The Bracebridge Business College opened again on August 28 in the charge of Miss Erminie A. Williams.

Haileybury and much of Temiskaming District was destroyed by fire in late September. It was decided to make an appeal for funds and supplies with a goal of

$1,000 in cash and a big car full of clothing, food, and other supplies. Part of the Kinney Co. store was loaned for use as a depot for the reception and dispatch of all supplies, except potatoes and other vegetables, which Mr. John Keeler volunteered to look after at his restaurant. A public meeting was held October 22 in the Town Hall, called by the president of the Board of Trade and the mayor. By October 27 a large refrigerator car well filled with clothing, food, bedding, and other supplies was shipped from Bracebridge to the chairman of the Northern Relief Committee, with cash donations over $1,000.

Deaths in the year included Mr. Wm. McKay, 84. A stone cutter and builder by trade, he supervised the erection of the Albion Hotel, the Empire Hotel, the public school and high school and the Town Hall in Gravenhurst, as well as the frame schoolhouse at Uffington and the church at Aspdin ... Mr. Jas. Johnston, 83, former reeve of Oakley ... Mrs. William Parker, 85, pioneer of Parkersville ... Mrs. William Archer, homesteaded on Stephens Bay in the 1870s, then moved to Bracebridge ... Mr. John Hammell Sr., 64, brother of W.J. Hammell, MP. He came in 1866, and married Miss Catherine Mitchell of Raymond ... William Albert Ireland, 29, youngest son of Mr. and Mrs. George Ireland, died of appendicitis. He came to Bracebridge in 1895 and had been a member of the machine gun section of the 3rd Battalion ... Mrs. Fitzmaurice, 75, of Monck ... John Hutton Sr., 73, farmer, Ontario government scaler, and proprietor of Hutton House. He married Miss Jane E. Bruce of Bracebridge ... Mrs. C.S. Hare, wife of the Royal Bank manager, who came in 1913. She left her husband with two small children ... Miss Lorna Boyes, 22, of Vankoughnet, died of the measles after having trained as a nurse.

## 1923

Henry J. Bird Jr. was elected mayor in place of Peter A. Smith ... H.E. Rice was selected as Liberal candidate ... The Board of Trade elected a new president, D.G. Hodgson, with vice president Coldham Spreadborough and secretary-treasurer J.T. Andrews.

Bracebridge "notables" this year included:

*A "Bird" sits in the Mayor's chair*
*A "Steer" is guardian of our school*
*A "Dickie" runs the great big fair*
*A "Minns" brings out the rule*
*A "Tennant" is in our power and light*
*A "Salmon" in the Hall*
*A "Hare" sits on the library Board*
*The electrician is a "Ball."*

The Bracebridge Water, Light and Power Commission and G.W. Ecclestone, MPP, had long tried to have the government control the feeders of the North Muskoka River by a system of dams. It was fully expected that in this way a steady flow could be maintained over Wilson's Falls and Bracebridge Falls that would keep the power supply regular during wet and dry seasons.

The estate of the Maple Leaf Hosiery Co. Ltd and inventory of assets was offered at auction March 23, 1923, in Toronto. It was purchased at a very low figure by Mr. G.W. Ecclestone, who wanted to interest one or more ambitious young men with a knowledge of the industry.

The Bracebridge High School won the district hockey championship and brought home the Oshawa Rotary Club Cup in the Central Ontario Interscholastic Hockey League. The Bracebridge Intermediates won the McGibbon Cup against Gravenhurst.

A Baseball Club was formed with president Redmond Thomas, vice presidents George Gibson and Duncan McDonald, and secretary-treasurer Clarence Salmon.

The second annual concert by the Bracebridge Choral Society was presented in the Town Hall February 28 with the Anglo-Canadian orchestra.

In December Mr. J.J. Matthias of Uffington was appointed magistrate and Justice of the Peace for Muskoka.

A terrible tragedy occurred at the Anglo-Canadian tannery in March. As a result, Mr. James Prentiss lost his life and Messrs. Louis Braida and Bert Banks sustained injuries. The unfortunate men were at work at a pile of "hog feed" (wood that had been ground into small pieces by machinery) when they were buried by a sudden movement of the stuff. It took 20 minutes of hard work before Messrs. Prentiss and Braida were extricated. Bert Banks was not completely covered but was buried up to the hips. When willing workers got to Messrs. Prentiss and

Braida, the former was dead and the latter was blue in the face from suffocation, and unconscious. The deceased was survived by his wife and five children.

A horse owned by Mickle, Dyment & Sons was killed by a train while hay was being unloaded from rail cars.

In a June provincial election George W. Ecclestone, Liberal-Conservative candidate, ran against H.E. Rice, the Liberal candidate. Ecclestone carried Muskoka by a majority of about 1,935. The Conservatives won in a landslide in Ontario, with 75 seats. The United Farmers got 17, the Liberals 14, Labour 4, and one independent.

Gravenhurst Public School was destroyed by fire.

Eleven lives were lost when the Wawa Hotel on Lake of Bays burned down in late July. A fire that started in the baggage room raced up the elevator shaft to the second floor bedrooms. The inquest jury deprecated the absence of systematic inspection of public buildings for the purpose of testing fire-fighting appliances, and also made a number of recommendations. "There being at present no government supervision, inspection [must] be enforced to provide adequate fire escapes, efficient fire-fighting equipment, the organization of a watchman service, and for a general alarm system, either by means of powerhouse whistle or the electric gongs within the buildings or for both." It further recommended that all elevator or hoist shafts in such buildings be of fire-proof construction, and that in the case of the building of new hotels or lodging houses, construction of a fire-retarding nature be used within reason, and that where possible segregated units be erected, instead of one large building.

A fire started in the basement and fourth form of the high school and only the prompt action of the brigade saved the whole building from destruction, although damage to the school was quite heavy.

A committee was appointed to re-organize the Citizen's Band: Dr. McGibbon, Messrs Bruce Minns, Coldham Spreadborough, and William Towns, with Mr. John Thomson as chairman. It was decided that only the band leader should receive pay and that "it is a privilege, a great privilege, to get musical instruction from a good teacher without cost. Each member of the band should feel a patriotic desire to be a useful public member of the community."

A citizens' memorial service was held in the Town Hall, when a crowded house turned out to pay tribute to Armistice Day in remembrance of five years of peace.

On June 8, 1879, the cornerstone of St. Joseph's Church was laid by His Grace, Archbishop Lynch. In October 1923 that cornerstone was removed and a small tin box containing newspapers removed from it. The Toronto and Bracebridge papers contained therein were of Friday, June 6, 1879. St. Joseph's was being raised from its foundation three feet and placed on a new foundation with a basement beneath. The building was temporarily free from a foundation and supported on jacks. The Bracebridge papers were the *Muskoka Herald* and the *Free Grant Press*. There were also the *Globe*, *Mail*, *Tribune*, and the *True Witness*, a weekly edition of the *Montreal Post*.

A bylaw was considered to levy 1½ mills of the dollar on the total assessment of the town for 1924 and to pay the amount so raised to aid the band, and in each succeeding year one mill for the same purpose.

Deaths included Holland Rockwell Scovell, president of the Muskoka Teachers' Association in 1920 and for many years inspector of public schools ... Rev. Arthur T. Lowe, 77, moved to Acton Island with his parents in 1870 (the island was named for his eldest brother). Mr. Lowe built the *Lady of the Lake*, the first private steamboat on the lakes, and later entered the ministry ... Mrs. Laughlin McEachern, 77, one of Muskoka's earliest settlers. She married Mr. David Gray and came to Bracebridge in 1868, then homesteaded in Oakley. After the death of her first husband, she married Mr. McEachen; she raised 10 children ... Mr. Robert Doley, 49, a bachelor, came to the High Falls area as a small boy, then moved to Toronto Street ... Mrs. A.T. Corbett, 47, nee Bertha Archer, eldest daughter of Mr. William Archer, sister of Mrs. George Boyer ... Mr. George Smith, 77, of Beatrice. He came in 1862, married Isabel Grant of Windermere ... David McFadden, 21, graduated from the Bracebridge Business College and worked for the Whitten Company ... Richard Walter Ryan, 69, came abut 1883 and opened a photography gallery next to the Muskoka Garage ... George W. Sibbett, 70, moved into Bracebridge in the 1880s, served on the school board for many years, and

*Members of the Bracebridge Citizen's Band pose in front of a house on Main Street (now part of Hiram) across from the railway station.* COURTESY OF BRENDA COX

married Miss Agnes Gertrude Angell ... William H. Matthias, 64, one of seven small children who came with his parents to Draper about 1870.

## 1924

This was a red-letter year marked by the visit of Lord Byng, Governor General of Canada. Bracebridge had not been so honoured since Lord Dufferin visited in 1874. Other notable events were the 50th anniversary of Bracebridge Fall Fair, the first public appearance of the Bracebridge Citizen's Band, and the completion of the power line linking Bracebridge with Ontario Hydro.

Henry Bird Jr. was acclaimed mayor. A 180-88 plebiscite vote gave a one mill tax to the Citizen's Band. David Kirkness was appointed road overseer at $960 a year. Alex Hamilton of Fraserburg was appointed inspector of colonization roads. R.H. Thompson, the town assessor, reported 1924 total assessment of $991,297 with 2,367 people and 103 dogs. The 1925 figures were $995,240 with 2,419 people and 98 dogs. The Registrar General of Ontario reported Muskoka's population at 19,098 with 457 births, 142 marriages, and 228 deaths.

Ontario's population was 2,981,182.

A vote on a bylaw to grant a fixed rate of taxation to the Anglo-Canadian Leather Co. of $40,000 was 173 for, 13 opposed. On the same ballot was a question for a bylaw to raise $8,000 for waterworks extension. This one passed 172-23, one of largest votes ever recorded for a bylaw. The upper room and stairs of the Town Hall were renovated by Mr. Will Adamson; we now had opera chair seating and could reserve for 228. Debentures to pay for extended waterworks along Woodchester Avenue and River Road were issued.

The crib shifted and cracked the cement at end of the breakwater that was put in by the Dominion government the year before. The Ontario government dredge worked to widen Bracebridge Bay.

In December, Council ordered the police chief to erect signs to keep delivery sleighs off the walk on Front Street. Bylaw 455 was passed to raise $85,000 for the purpose of acquiring property for building and equipping a high school. Bylaw 458 was passed to repeal Bylaw 271 providing for the election of commissioners for the waterworks and electric light and power plants.

The Shier Lumber Company usually drove some 5,000 logs of pine and hemlock down the river but in 1923 they also made a test drive of hardwood logs from near Hollow

Lake to their Bracebridge plant. This proved so successful they did it in subsequent years.

Miss H.A. Dickie, librarian, reported 16,083 books circulated in 1923, 144 books purchased, and six donated. The library now had 5,669 books.

The Children's Aid Society had 37 applications for children, 287 children involved, and three made wards. There were167 investigations and 16 court attendances.

Two hundred men were employed constructing the Ontario Hydro plant at Hanna's Chutes, Muskoka Falls, with Mr. T.J. Berger in charge, assisted by Mr. Vogen. Another 50 men were employed at the hydroelectric works with Mr. Wm. Wallace in charge during the absence of Mr. Berger. Electric power was now in use from the Bracebridge plant.

The motor league president, C. Spreadborough, and the vice president, John Reid, purchased the Motor Park property from Mr. Mungo Park McKay. They had had the use of it for several years. A new cement floor was put in the cookery. They had nearly 1,000 tourists registered in 1924. The second annual Bracebridge Water Sports Regatta was held at the Motor Park with a large crowd. Games included a tug-of-war, married couples canoe races, log burling, canoe races, and a swim-with-egg race, all to the music of the Citizen's Band.

Baron, Lord Byng of Vimy, Governor General, and Lady Byng visited Bracebridge on September 5. A Guard of Honour of veterans, the Citizen's Band, and the Boy Scouts ushered them in procession from the train station to Memorial Park. The next morning Lord and Lady Byng visited Muskoka Falls and embarked aboard the *Wenonah* for trip to Port Carling.

Mr. and Mrs. Chas. Bard celebrated 60 years of marriage. Mr. and Mrs. Alfred Hunt celebrated their golden wedding anniversary, as did Mr. and Mrs. Henry Boyer, and Mr. and Mrs. John Donally, Bardsville, who came to Muskoka in 1868.

The Bracebridge Citizen's Band, conducted by Mr. B.W. Tillson, made its first public appearance in concert at the Town Hall in June. Mr. John Thomson was chairman of the band committee. Band members comprised: cornets, J.T. Andrews, Gus Thomson, George Beggs, Lorne Scoville and Cecil Bruce; clarinets, G.R. Simmons and Raymond Simmons; tenors: E.A. Whitten, C. White, and H. Kennedy; basses, Ben Smith and Clarence Bird; saxophone, Allan Hutchinson; drums, B. Wasdell and Vernon Corbett. The first band concerts were at Memorial Park on Mondays, but at the Motor Park in summer.

Mr. Frank S. Weisman, director of the Toronto Conservatory of Music, was in charge of the Anglo-Canadian Band again for the summer.

In 1922 and 1923 the Methodist Conference and the Presbyterian Assembly, respectively, and the the Congregational Union of Canada approved the basis of union between the three churches after over 20 years of consultation and discussion. A bill to create a United Church of Canada passed by the private bills committee of the House of Commons May 23 with the amendment to delay at least two years.

The Baptist Church held services in the Town Hall while repair work was done to the church. Dedication of the new pipe organ in the Methodist Church took place in October. Mr. Arthur Lye of Messrs. Edward Lye & Sons, Toronto, who designed and built the organ, gave a splendid recital and concert. The organ had a chestnut case finished with dark oak, 15 feet 6 inches wide, 18 feet high, and 10 feet deep. Rev. W. Barker, 80, former pastor, preached ... The Women's Aid of St. Thomas Church held a two-day bazaar with booths, decorations, and costumes, with proceeds of $1,000 ... The Women's Christian Temperance Union medal in elocution was won by Miss Constance Winters.

Fire started at the rear of "The Pines" home of Mr. and Mrs. McVittie on the outskirts of town. The fire brigade took ladders, chemical extinguishers, and a tank of water as it was too great a distance for use of the hose. The firemen were assisted by many willing helpers who used all the well water and brought more water in barrels from Barron's springs on Mr. Hutchison's truck. Flames quickly consumed the shed, wood piles, a young pine stand, and the back of the house. The valiant workers saved the rest of house with water, sand, even tea leaves and the morning's milk.

A night fire was discovered by watchman Mr. M. Wenham in the wool drying room of Bird's Woollen Mill. Fire apparatus at the plant together with the town fire

*The branches of the Muskoka River served as water highways for lumbermen to float logs to their sawmills. Although the south branch was more extensively used for this purpose, the north branch also saw its share of spring "drives" and was still being used in the 1920s particularly to supply the Tennant mill at Bracebridge. In this view of Wilson's Falls the log slide bypassing the headpond dam is visible to the right of the powerhouse.* COURTESY OF BARBARA MCMURRAY

brigade confined the fire to one room but the wood walls and ceilings were destroyed with slight damage to the drying machine. All the wool in the room (worth $3,500) was lost, as well as the dyes. Mr. Bird gave $100 to the fire brigade in thanks for their prompt action.

The rear south wing at the Central School was destroyed with much damage to the interior. A water main burst on the main street near Fryer's store, reducing pressure to a slow running stream so that pails also had to be used. The town reservoir was emptied for the first time in 10 years. A town crew opened the emergency valve to force river water into mains and managed to repair the broken main overnight, but people were told to boil their drinking water for a week. The loss at the school was estimated at $13,000 plus much personal equipment of principal A.B. Steer. The Board of Education later donated $100 to the fire brigade and gave $500 to principal Steer for his losses.

Fire destroyed the barn, stable, hen house, other outbuildings and contents belonging to George McNeil at South Falls. Horses and cattle were saved but chickens were lost, as well as two cars, the summer's feed of hay and grain, seed grain, and most of the farm implements.

Morinus House, built about 1894 on Lake Rosseau, was destroyed by fire in August. It was owned by Mrs. MacNaughtan and under the management of Mr. Eugene Jocques.

Six thousand people paid admission for the Golden Jubilee Fall Fair. There were throngs of automobiles, motorboats, carriages, trains, and steamers ,and a record 2,295 entries. It was the greatest ever school parade. It included the Boy Scouts and was led by the Rama Indian Band which made a splendid impression playing on the streets and almost non-stop throughout the fairgrounds. The postal display booth run by postal inspector Hartley of Toronto had many interesting displays and gave out informative booklets and blotters. The largest family on the ground was won by Mr. and Mrs. H.L. Goltz with

*From a vantage point on the hill overlooking the top of the falls, you can see straight up Manitoba Street in the centre of the picture in this 1920s photograph. The overall impression is of a well-established and prosperous community.*
COURTESY OF BARBARA MCMURRAY

their 12 children. Mr. John Spencer of Bardsville won the "Oldest Resident" – 64 years in Muskoka.

Mr. John Askin, Raymond, had a record yield of oats at 1,000 bushels from 12 acres. H.L. Goltz had wonderful success at the Royal Winter Fair, winning a dozen prizes. It was the biggest hay crop in Muskoka for many years.

The CNR offered special harvest trains at $15 from Toronto to Winnipeg to transport the 18,000 men needed for the harvest in western Canada.

People were now required to have a $200 licence to act as a guide for hire, obtainable from Mr. B. Gooderham.

Mr. Arthur H. Richardson, Ontario Professional Forester, Toronto, was in town to visit Dr. Williams' property in Oakley where he had planted red pine

Four MPP's conducted an agricultural inquiry meeting in town to advocate the practice of reforestation with systematically planted pine as well as systematic security against wolves who were killing many sheep and dogs. They also discussed the need for more provincial roads to entice tourists, more fish stocking, and the very high reputation of Muskoka's lamb.

During 1924, 6,397,500 fry were released into Muskoka's lakes and rivers. A 23-inch, 7½-pound pickerel was caught in the river.

There were some accidental deaths. A Barnardo Home boy, John Wilson, living with Mr. and Mrs. Harry Mather at Matthiasville, drowned in the river. The body was not found. Lake Muskoka claimed two victims. Earl Lemyre of Gravenhurst fell off the *Medora* just after leaving Beaumaris and was pulled under by the suction of the boat while handling the gang plank. Henry Fisher, 18, drowned when he upset while fishing near Beaumaris.

Mr. Oliver Tyron was killed at Tennant's mill in October. He was an expert setter and was just to start at this mill after the J.D. Shier mill closed for the season. He was riding the carriage by the big circular saw when he slipped. He was killed instantly when the huge saw nearly severed the back of his head and shoulders. An inquest was presided over by Dr. McGibbon, coroner. Mr. Tyron was a very popular, highly esteemed young man from Ryde Township. He enlisted in January 1915 in the Canadian Expeditionary Force where he served in France and rose to the rank of sergeant. He married Miss Sadie Mathieson of Bracebridge in December 1919, whom he left a widow with four children and a home on Ontario Street.

Other deaths included Mr. James Whitten, 81, an invalid in his Kimberley home for 10 years. He came from Ireland to Kingston with his parents in 1847. They died of cholera. He was the only one of the family to survive to maturity. He moved from the Eastern Townships of Quebec when hemlock got scarce for tanneries there, becoming manager of the Muskoka Leather Co. tannery in 1883. Subsequently he left to form a partnership with Mr. B.W. Tillson. They bought out the hardware business of J.L. Fenn Sr. at the corner of Manitoba and Thomas streets. The partnership dissolved in 1900, and Mr. Whitten controlled the business until the disastrous fire of 1908 when the store and its contents were destroyed. He then bought the hardware business of J.L. Fenn & Sons & Co. in April 1909, and incorporated as The Whitten Company Ltd. in 1914. He served on municipal council 1911-13 and was chairman of the roads and bridges committee.

Mr. Charles Smith, 87, then his wife, 79, 57 years married, died after losing everything in the destruction of their Macaulay home by fire. They had stayed at the Royal Hotel in Bracebridge on their way to their land on lot 25, concession 9, McLean. He carried a heavy pack of provisions and bedding while she carried their infant daughter and personal belongings. They lost their home on three different occasions to fire. They had nine children, 33 grandchildren, and 11 great-grandchildren. Mr. Smith was a popular violinist at dances. Mrs. Smith was the first assistant to Dr. S. Bridgland and Dr. Thos. Byers.

Other deaths in 1924 included Mr. Archibald Mitchell, 70, eldest son of Donald, pioneer of Raymond. He married Miss May Glass in 1887, drove the stage from Point Kaye to Bracebridge ... George A. Hall, 63, had both legs amputated by a shunter at Shier's mill in 1900, started a small store on Ontario Street ... Nathaniel Bogart, Ufford, engaged in lumber milling with his father, Jack, and older brother James, spent his summers at the Windermere boat livery and refreshment rooms ... Mrs. Wm. McVittie, nee Laura Phillips, mother of John, died of tuberculosis at The Pines ... James Rusk, 86, came to Muskoka in 1860, cleared land for a farm, married Adele Jackson of Severn Falls.

The Dominion Restaurant was sold to V. Dupuis by Dan McPhee. Mr. Jas Green added a verandah and balcony. W.A.J. Brown had Geo. Waltenbury brick veneer his house. Alex Milne leased his garage to Don Gary to carry on a general garage business. Abel Denniss purchased the livery stable from John Lloyd.

The school board reported 450 students enrolled in public school with all available space full. Mr. J.C. Strothers was appointed school inspector and Mr. George S. Johnson, Monteith, was hired as the new high school principal for salary of $2,500. The school board also hired Mr. J.B. Bastedo, Miss Luella Broad, and Miss McQuarrie. Miss Orma Snider was appointed teacher at Muskoka Falls. Summer teacher training school opened in Bracebridge, taught by Messrs. Ingall and Patterson and Miss Andrew.

The vote for the Ontario Temperance Act went 4,000 in favour over those supporting a government liquor store. Prohibition was started by the Hearst government but allowed importation of spirits. After importation was cut off in 1921 everybody took to the dandelion patch or into the rhubarb. Black cherries could scarcely get ripe before someone had them in the mash. Since 1921 people looked to bootleggers for regular supplies.

*Although the Great Depression would cast a shadow on the town's sixth decade, in 1925 an important step in the municipality's development occurred with the construction of a new high school. Here town dignitaries and community leaders attend the laying of the cornerstone.* COURTESY OF VICKY BILLINGSLEY FROM THE R.J. BOYER COLLECTION

# 1925–1934

## *Our 6th Decade: Progress, then the Great Depression*

THE YEAR 1925 is remembered particularly for construction of the high school building, the church union, and the arrival on her maiden voyage of the steamship *Segwun*.

George W. Boyer was elected mayor in the first mayoralty contest in 10 years, other mayors having been acclaimed. Reeves elected in nearby townships were James Glass, Monck; J.W. McNiece, Draper; John G. Sloper, Macaulay; and R. McKay, Muskoka.

Bracebridge Council appointed A.C. Salmon as clerk- treasurer for $950 (he also received remuneration as secretary of the Board of Education and of the Water, Light and Power Commission); David Kirkness as road overseer and caretaker of Jubilee Park for $1,000; William McConnell as chief of police for $1,200; Robert H. Thompson as assessor for $250; John Cole as caretaker of the Town Hall for $936; Aboil Leishman as teamster for $900. Dr. Peter McGibbon was medical officer of health, Albert E. Ecclestone the fire chief, and William Galbraith the town engineer. A.A. Watt was appointed to the Library Board. Coldham Spreadborough was chairman of the Board of Education.

It was decided to expropriate the Lount property on McMurray Street for the new high school. The board offered $6,000 but a board of arbitration consisting of Dr. Francis Williams, Peter A. Smith, and George Tennant set compensation at $8,500. It was found that $85,000 would be required to be placed in debentures (Bylaw 455). Under the direction of George Brooks, work began April 14 tearing down the house, which was originally built by Thomas McMurray.

Laying of the cornerstone took place on June 3, the King's birthday. Speakers included I.H. Levan, high school inspector; board chairman Coldham Spreadborough, G.W. Ecclestone, MPP, Mayor Boyer, principal Johnson, H.J. Bird Jr., and G.H.O. Thomas. On this occasion the young people were encouraged to write their names on a brick and during the afternoon bricklayers received these and placed them in a wall. An open house was held December 26 with all the classrooms ready for occupancy.

The union of the Methodist Church and the Presbyterian Church took place in June. The Methodist Church, having voted on the matter several years before, entered the union as a unit but in each Presbyterian congregation a vote took place. Knox Presbyterian Church, Bracebridge voted not to enter the union by a vote of two. Sixty unionist members left to join the United Church. Rev. R.C. Ballard resigned from Knox Church to become the associate minister with Rev. Archie McNeill in the United.

The first combined service took place Easter Sunday. The first communion for the new United Church was held Sunday, May 3 with 173 members attending. In the meantime those remaining at Knox Church decided to continue all organizations with Rev. J. McConnell of Hensall as their minister.

The Muskoka Lakes Navigation and Hotel Company announced that the hull of the steamer *Nipissing* would be overhauled, new cabins and decks built, and two new twin screw engines installed to make her the fastest of the fleet. This was, of course, the steamer *Segwun*. She made her maiden voyage under Captain L.A. Larsen to Bracebridge on July 9, being met by a large crowd, the Citizen's Band, and Mayor Boyer at the Bracebridge wharf. Later in the day St. Thomas Anglican Church took an excursion to Mortimer's Point and back.

In the November federal election the new riding of Muskoka-Northern Ontario came into being. Dr. Peter McGibbon was elected Member of Parliament by a majority of 3,576 votes over R.H. Halbert, Liberal-Progressive.

The returning officer for the district was Mr. H.E. Rice of Huntsville. Registrars for the election were A.C. Salmon (Ward 1), D.T. Hodgson (Ward 2), H.A. Rogers (Ward 3), and R.H. Thomson (Ward 4).

The former Hess furniture factory was destroyed in a spectacular fire. The building was owned and used by George Tennant and J.T. Shier for their newly established Northern Planing Mills Company Ltd. The fire also took the Whitten Company warehouse and the stable of the former Dominion Hotel. Northeast winds kept the flames from the Tennant lumber piles. Small fires at John Dunn's home and at the rear of the British Lion Hotel were controlled. The estimated loss was $20,000 and many employees lost their carpenter tools. Splendid work by the fire brigade using 12 streams of water gained control. The Gravenhurst fire brigade arrived within 30 minutes to give splendid assistance but the Huntsville brigade was delayed in a breakdown north of Utterson and did not make it.

In September, the upper works of the steamer *Sagamo* were destroyed by fire at Muskoka Wharf, Gravenhurst. In May, the steamer *Llano* burned at the Archer boathouse on Bracebridge Bay. The fire spread rapidly to adjoining boathouses and burned half a dozen or more, destroying four motorboats and several rowboats as well as the Archer-Heintz Lake Services steamer and boathouse. Losing boathouses were J. Parker, L. Olivero, Thomas Woodhouse, William C. Denniss Jr., and the Ontario government, which also lost its launch. There was $2,000 insurance on the *Llano* but the loss was twice that much plus the loss of the season's business. Captain Archer said they would put the *Mildred*, then stored at Browning Island, into service immediately. The steel frame of the *Llano* was all that was left and at a later time it was purchased and moved to the Huntsville Lakes where it was rebuilt.

Earl Rosewarne's garage burned down the night of April 29 with four cars and much stock and equipment lost. Mr. Craig's Albion Hotel stable burned September 25 but the horses were all saved.

In Macaulay, on August 6, the barn on the S.R. Mills farm was struck by lightning and destroyed with all contents except horses, pigs, and some implements which were saved. A heavy rain saved the farmhouse.

The Bracebridge fire brigade took prizes at the annual firemen's tournament in Parry Sound. Seven brigades participated in the event, from Gravenhurst, Huntsville, Parry Sound, Orillia, Bracebridge, Burk's Falls, and MacTier.

During the year Mr. Peter Hutchison bought the

*The splendid new brick Bracebridge High School on McMurray Street saw its first students in 1925. Outwardly, this structure remains relatively unchanged in 1999, although it now comprises only a small part of the sprawling Bracebridge and Muskoka Lakes Secondary School.* COURTESY OF THE BRACEBRIDGE PUBLIC LIBRARY

Horner property south of the public school, originally the home of sheriff Bettes, on McMurray Street, where he erected three residences.

D Company of the Northern Pioneers Regiment, a unit of the Canadian Militia, occupied the Armories part of the Dominion post office building and held a six-week course of military instruction for officers and non-commissioned officers. A drum head service was held at Memorial Park by D Company together with the Boy Scouts. Chaplain Captain the Rev. F.G. Sherring was assisted by local church choirs.

On July 12 an Orange celebration, in Bracebridge, was attended by an estimated crowd of 8,000, special trains having arrived from Orillia and Huntsville and special trips being made by the steamers *Cherokee*, *Segwun*, and *Mildred*. With many fife and drum bands, including Bracebridge's own band under Nelson Baynton, 23 lodges took part in the parade. The Bracebridge lodge did an enormous amount of work meeting trains and boats. T.A. Hewitt and Robert Whaley were parade marshals.

The 25th anniversary district annual meeting of the South Muskoka Women's Institute branches was held with 73 members attending. Over the preceding three years $3,000 had been raised for the rest room. Douglas Thomas won the $5 gold piece for the highest standing in entrance exams in Bracebridge as well as in all of Muskoka.

Kelvin Grove Park was the site of the third annual regatta put on by the Muskoka Motor League. Music by the Bracebridge Band accompanied contests for log rolling, long diving, double canoe, double skiff, war canoe, ladies and gents tandem canoe races, swimming, greasy pole, etc.

In early September there were serious forest fires near Bala, Torrance, and Leonard Lake. At one time 500 men were fighting to save the CNR bridge.

On Lake Muskoka, Rossclair House summer resort burned down with a loss of $20,000. It was built by the late W.T. North but was sold to J.H. Jackson in 1920.

A successful South Muskoka Agricultural Society fall fair was held at Jubilee Park with an estimated 4,000 in attendance. One of the most popular events was "speeding in the ring" with horses from Muskoka, New Liskeard, Sturgeon Falls, North Bay, Coldwater, and Toronto. New cattle sheds enticed more cattlemen to show their stock. The school children's parade was as always a feature. Receipts totaled $1,585.60, over a hundred dollars more than the previous year.

A number of entertainments took place at the Town Hall with rush seats 35 cents and reserved seats 50 cents. These included the Methodist choir drama in three acts titled *Home Acres* and the young people of St. Joseph's church performing *My Wild Irish Rose*. The Bracebridge orchestra played several selections at intermission, with songs by Miss Mary Fenn and Mr. Severeno Didero. April 30 saw a production of *Here Comes the Bride* put on by the Citizen's Band directed by Mr. John Thomson, with proceeds to buy band uniforms. The Clef Club staged *The Tyrolean Queen*, a four-act operetta in June with Mrs. McGibbon and Mrs. George Johnson as leads and Mrs. Wilbur Anderson as accompanist. Two hundred dollars was collected for the band fund.

The Bracebridge Water, Light and Power Commission along with town superintendent W.C. Simmons reported that with the Barron springs on the Peake property, 300,000 gallons a day would be available – enough for a town of 6,000 or 7,000 people.

Farming in Muskoka was booming. The Ontario Department of Agriculture, through their Muskoka-Parry Sound representative, arranged several demonstrations including sheep and wool, sheep dipping, and poultry culling. In December, Roy and Adair Goltz, Victor and Wilfred Creasor, Monte Kay, and Harry Jackson from Ziska were among the 70 boys attending a three-day educational class in swine at the Union Stock Yards in Toronto. H.L. Goltz won top prizes in eight categories in Ottawa and Toronto. His Irish Cobbler potatoes received the highest sale price of any at the Toronto National Fair.

Notable physical phenomena this year included an eclipse of the sun on January 24, which could be seen from Bracebridge, and an earthquake that rattled china and stopped clocks in town at 9:22 on Sunday evening, February 28. The winter of 1925 was mild right from the beginning, making for poor travelling on both lakes and roads. Indeed, two horses were lost through the ice. March saw the worst floods since 1876 throughout Ontario. Spring started early but May 24 was the coldest on record in 76 years. Dry weather required water conservation in Bracebridge in June. There were tremendous forest fires in the district by August. Fall was wet with the roads nearly impassable by November.

The two daughters of Mr. and Mrs. William Campbell, Muskoka Falls, drowned in the south branch of the Muskoka River July 4. The 8-year-old daughter got into difficulty while swimming. The 13-year-old went to save her and both drowned. Ivan Magee, 8, drowned when he slipped on a log in Sharpe's Creek. Miss Alice Martin drowned after fainting and falling into Lake Vernon. Alex Barton, 20, drowned in a boating accident on Lake Rosseau.

James W. Bettes, Liberal member for Muskoka in 1878 and later sheriff of Muskoka 1888-1902, died.

The first Crown attorney of Muskoka in 1888-1890, Mr. A.A. Adair, died at his home in Riverside, California.

The third sheriff of Muskoka, appointed in 1906, was David Edgar Bastedo, 65, who in 1872 came to Bracebridge to learn the printing trade at the *Northern Advocate*. In the 1880s he took over the *Muskoka Herald* weekly paper established in 1878 by Fred Graffre, editor, and was its publisher until becoming sheriff. He married Miss Elizabeth Ann Oaten in 1884.

Several well-known residents of Bracebridge died during 1925, some of them having lived here from earliest pioneer years. William R. Archer, 78, died at the residence of his daughter, Mrs. George W. Boyer. He came in 1866 with his father, the Rev. Marmaduke Archer, Methodist Episcopal Missionary to Muskoka. He worked as a teen with Mr. Teviotdale and in 1873 married Jane Bryers. For 15 years they farmed near Stephens Bay, Lake Muskoka, then moved to a house on the Monck town line. He was employed continuously for 35 years with the J.D. Shier Lumber Company …

Mrs. Samuel Armstrong, the former Miss Emma Pratt, daughter of Josiah and Mrs. Pratt ... William Ball, 77, who came from England in 1873, bought a farm in Monck and married Miss Mary Elizabeth Stiles, with whom he had seven sons and three daughters. He was one of the earliest members of the Orange Lodge ... Mrs. Wesley W. Brooks, 48, the former Margaret Elizabeth Harper, born in Bracebridge ... Ernest Bruce, 49, son of Macaulay pioneers, died suddenly while at work ... Thomas Donally, 85, one of Windermere's pioneers and postmaster at Bardsville ...

Moses J. Dickie, 81, one of the first members of the Bracebridge Baptist Church. He came to Muskoka in 1871 and settled in McLean township, of which he later became Reeve prior to coming to Bracebridge in 1889 and commencing an insurance business ... John Faulkner, 93, came to Stephenson Township from Quebec in 1870 and lived at Parkersville and Falkenburg before moving to Bracebridge ...

Alfred Hunt, came from Sheffield in 1872. He worked in the mercantile business with Mr.Clerihue then with Mr. McPhee, and then in hardware with Mr. J.L. Fenn Sr. Mr. Hunt established the first bank in Bracebridge and carried on that business for 15 years. He served as reeve and mayor and was a leader in establishing the municipal power generating system and the Bracebridge waterworks. He was later clerk of District Court and deputy sheriff ...

Ewart Lount, 73, district magistrate of Muskoka. He came in 1868 with his father, Charles W. Lount, who was appointed stipendiary magistrate and registrar for Muskoka. He worked as a deputy in the registrar's office until he was made registrar, being engaged in this work for 54 years. His family residence was "The Grove" which was torn down in 1925 for the new high school building ...

Mrs. Sam Rusk, 70, daughter of James P. and Mrs. Rusk, who came to Bracebridge in 1879 ... Sidney Smith, 83, for whom the community of Port Sydney was named. He arrived in that vicinity in 1869, bought a sawmill built on the river by John McAlpine ... Mrs. Mary Tennant, 75, mother of George and Robert Tennant. She resided in Bracebridge since 1898.

## 1926

There were parliamentary elections in 1926 both for the House of Commons and Legislative Assembly, but in the Town of Bracebridge all elective offices were filled by acclamation. Water, Light and Power commissioners were George Tennant and J. Wellington Reid. On the school board were C. Spreadborough, Harry Boyer, Edward Hunt, George Fenn, T.N. Bird, Edward Rombourgh, and Dr. A.F. Bastedo. Monck Township reeve was James Glass, with councillors George Freemantle, Thomas Hammell, Jas. Fitzmaurice, and Wm. Gibbs. In Macaulay Township, the reeve was John Sloper, and the councillors Wm. Naismith, R. Zimmerman, Alex Cooper, and Fred Leeder. Muskoka Township reeve was W. H. Tincombe, and the councillors H.E. Beaumont, R. Stephens, C.E. Laycock, and S. Parke.

The election for the Parliament of Canada came in September following an interesting period in which Prime Minister Mackenzie King, in July, was forced to resign in the face of a vote of censure on his government in the House of Commons. Arthur Meighen, Conservative, was asked to form a government which in turn was defeated and an election was called.

Dr. Peter McGibbon received a majority of 3,320 votes over Liberal candidate Ben S. Johnson of Brechin in our riding of Muskoka-Northern Ontario. W.L. Mackenzie King again became Prime Minister with 119 seats to the Conservative's 91.

The outstanding issue in the Ontario provincial election held on December 1 was whether or not the sale of liquor would be placed under an Ontario Liquor Control Board.

George W. Ecclestone was again our Conservative candidate, opposed by the Rev. Fred Berner, who strongly favoured prohibition of the sale of liquor. Mr. Ecclestone was re-elected although it was noted that only 70 percent of the voters on the list turned out to vote. The normal amount was 75 percent but severe weather on election day was thought to have reduced the number.

One of the community's most prominent residents for over 30 years, Dr. J. Francis Williams, died this year. Dr. Williams had done outstanding work in reforestation. He planted a total of 56,000 red pine and spruce on his 65-acre farm in Oakley Township between 1923 and 1926.

*By the 1920s the lumber industry in Muskoka was in decline as the great stands of pine that had fed countless sawmills for more than half a century ran out. Many mills continued to operate on a more modest scale, processing both softwoods and hardwoods. The Tennant mill at Bracebridge was one of these, the last of several mills that had occupied the site just below the Hunt's Hill Bridge for several decades (behind what is now Northern Buildall). A conveyor known as a jackladder lifted logs from the river into the mill.* COURTESY OF BARBARA MCMURRAY

Dr. Williams, 68, graduated from McGill University in medicine in 1886, moved to Bracebridge in 1895, married Annie Bird of Barrie, and had one son who died in 1891. He served in the North West Rebellion and in World War I. In Bracebridge he was magistrate for several years. On the day of his funeral, flags were flown at half mast and funeral blinds drawn in downtown businesses.

Dr. Williams gave a scholarship in medicine at McGill and left an annual payment to the Bracebridge United Church. He also provided for an annual maintenance for the property which later became Annie Williams Memorial Park. His heirs planned to set up a trust fund to care for needy sufferers of cancer and tuberculosis being treated in their own homes in the district.

The merchants of Bracebridge arranged early closing of their stores from January to March but stayed open until 10 p.m. on Saturdays.

Bracebridge and Gravenhurst were, as always, rivals in hockey. In a match on January 4, 630 hockey fans paid admission. A Bracebridge hockey team won the district honours and moved on to the OHA semifinals, defeating Oshawa and Uxbridge but losing to Peterborough.

The ladies' hockey team had a very successful year ending with a defeat of Orillia 5-1, Kit Ecclestone being our star player. The Bracebridge intermediate team also won district honours and was guest for a game in Toronto to watch Irvine Bailey playing with the Peterborough senior team in the OHA championship.

Curling prizes, the Excelsior Cup and the Wasley-Ecclestone Cup, were won by the W.F. Wasley and E.W. Gaudrie rinks. The president was George Tennant.

A lacrosse league was revived with teams from Bracebridge, Gravenhurst, and Orillia. William C. Simms was president of the Bracebridge team, J.C. Kinsey secretary, and E.G. West treasurer. Our team consisted of J.B. Bastedo, Tom Foster, Harry Boyer, H. Parlett, I. Gavin, F. Bassett, Lorne Prentice, W. Anderson, "Bob" Ross, and C. Eddie.

Hammell Cup baseball games included teams from Bracebridge, Gravenhurst, Huntsville, Utterson, and MacTier. This cup was donated by W.J. Hammell who had been MP for Muskoka 1921-25.

Bass season opened June 16 with the legal limit now five, down from the eight of previous year. Mr. Alfred Warren caught a record 5-pound, 9-ounce smallmouth bass. Jack Hines caught a record 9-pound pickerel.

A lawn bowling league was once again organized on property adjacent to the Central School grounds.

Crowds at the Bracebridge Fall Fair were much smaller than the year before due to the heavy rains and late harvest. Horse racing was still the biggest attraction.

Charles E. Lount was appointed registrar of deeds and local master of titles, succeeding his father, Ewart Lount, who died in 1925.

With increasing motor traffic, those in public life were discussing the need for road improvement. Mayor Thomas and councillor Speers joined a delegation to the Premier's office to request widening and straightening of the trunk road between the Severn and North Bay. In Muskoka itself there was agitation for the construction of a lakeshore route to shorten the distance from Bracebridge to Milford Bay and Port Carling. There was no motor traffic outside of town and very little inside during the winter. Traffic opened between Bracebridge and Gravenhurst on April 23 and a car got through to Utterson April 27 even though we got another two inches of snow that day. Navigation did not open until May 7 with Captain C.W. Archer in the *Mildred* the first to reach Bracebridge. He was closely followed by the *Queen of the Isles* then the *Alporto* and the *Islander*. The summer was

*Another view of the extensive lumber yards at the Tennant mill, this from the east side of the river at the top of the falls.* COURTESY OF BARBARA MCMURRAY

wet and cool with a severe wind and rain storm on August 26 causing the *Sagamo* and *Medora* to stay overnight in Port Carling. In November the river was higher than normal spring flood level. Navigation closed December 1 with the *Queen of the Isles* the last boat out of Bracebridge Bay for the season. Lake Muskoka froze solid December 13.

Merchants had a good Christmas trade even though heavy rains kept some rural customers from their seasonal shopping.

The Bracebridge Business College continued in the upper floor of the Muskoka Herald building. L.A. Blayney was principal having succeeded Miss Williams.

G.W. Boyer was chairman of the library board, having retired after one year as mayor. The library had 5,837 books, 947 patrons, and a budget of $1,540.57.

A meeting of hotel and resort owners discussed how best to advertise Muskoka. Those present included Leslie Aiken, Windermere; Alfred Judd and Rex Snow, Judhaven; R.J. Stroud and Harry Sawyer, Milford Bay; A.K. Bickmore, Mortimer's Point; John Thomson and D'Alton Armstrong, Bracebridge; W.F. Wasley, Gravenhurst, as well as Mayor Thomas and councillor Speers.

Along the same lines, the Bracebridge Board of Trade, of which George W. Brooks was president, met to draw up ways to "boost Bracebridge."

Members of the Masonic Lodge AF & AM honoured Francis P. Warren, Past Master and 50 years a mason.

Joseph L. Caisse, who had resided on Victoria Street, purchased a residence on upper Manitoba Street occupied by C.S. Hare, formerly owned by George Brown.

Inspecting officer Col. William Rhoades, accompanied by Col. H.M. Hicks, district paymaster, was pleased with the proficiency of Northern Pioneers Company D and the condition of their records and stores at the militia inspection on March 12.

Rev. E. Edmund Seyzinger preached an eight-day mission at St. Thomas Anglican Church March 14-21. The church was packed all week.

Muskoka district school inspector George F. Rogers reported that Bracebridge High School "... was as fine as any in the Province. I know of no other town in the Province more worthy of commendation for the way it has taken hold of the high school problem than the Town of Bracebridge." Pupil-teacher ratio was 26:1.

George W. Ecclestone was granted permission to build a bridge between his store and the former Kinsey store which he had purchased.

The first annual commencement exercise was held at the high school December 8. Coldham Spreadborough gave a speech as board chairman and Margaret Spreadborough gave the valedictory address to a crowd which overflowed into the halls.

George S. Johnson, BA, principal of the high school, was appointed public school inspector for Muskoka after the sudden death of Mr. Rogers. Miss Priscilla V. McNeeley of Carleton Place was appointed the new principal.

There was a fire at the 4th Ward school in December. Miss Grant, the teacher, first noticed the smoke and got the children dressed and outside safely before the fire brigade arrived. It was decided to continue class in the Central School instead of rebuild.

At the first annual congregational meeting of the new United Church, Rev. Dr. Smith reported that the coming together of the two congregations had been completed in a most harmonious and satisfying way.

On June 18, Minett-Shields Ltd. turned out *Norwood III* for Mr. W.L. Clause of Pittsburgh and Norwood Lodge on Lake Joseph. Thirty-four feet long with a 5½-foot beam, she was a sporty model able to carry seven passengers and travel 39 m.p.h. She was designed and built by Mr. Minett of mahogany, with a stainless steel shaft.

Five other launches were nearing completion, including one for Mr. Houston Rawles of Bracker's Island, Lake Rosseau, and a sport runabout for Mr. Chauncy J. Hamlin of Buffalo. The industry was doing well with good prospects for the future. Minett-built boats had always been in high demand.

The newly reconstructed *Sagamo* was greatly improved with an observation cabin, staterooms, and larger stairways. She went into commission July 3.

Boys Scouts attended their annual camp on Strawberry Bay, Lake Muskoka. Tents were lent by Messrs. J.G. Golden, Dave Hodgson, and William Swanson.

Scoutmaster Parker kept the scouts busy building a variety of things including a bridge 18 feet long, 4 feet wide, and 5 feet high, which supported 12 scouts.

The Very Rev. Dean O'Leary was new Dean of the Deanery of the Peterborough Diocese.

The Rev. H. Good, graduate of McMaster University, came in October as minister to the Baptist Church.

William Wright, 72, former merchant in Huntsville, died in January. He had been member of parliament for Muskoka, elected as a Conservative and serving from 1904 until 1917.

Other deaths in 1926 included Gertrude Appleton, 42, dressmaker ... Mrs. James Clarke, who moved to Monsell, Macaulay, in 1891 ... Mrs. Alfred Cridiford, 55, postmistress of Fraserburg ... Mrs. M.J. Dickie, 77, of Bracebridge ... Mrs. Francis Fielding, the former Sarah Ann Jermyn of Draper. She moved to Bracebridge in 1910 ... Captain John Henry, 74, who served with the Muskoka Navigation Company for over 36 years both summer and winter. He came to Muskoka in 1868 ... Thomas Holliday, 91, one of the oldest residents of Muskoka. He came to Macaulay in 1870 where he farmed until 1909, moving then to Watt to live with his son and taking up bridge building ... Raymond Jackson, 77, one of earliest settlers in Muskoka township in 1878 ... Mark Kay, 59, was postmaster of Ufford and had been secretary of the Watt Municipal Telephone Association ... Joseph C. Lacombe, 78, born in Quebec City and came to Bracebridge in 1891 ... John G. McCracken, 46, of Uffington, bush foreman for the Standard Chemical Company ... Mrs. George Mills, lifelong member of the Methodist Church ... Archie Morrison, many years a trusted employee of the Power and Light Commission. He died of blood poisoning from a cut hand ... Captain John Rogers, 80, of Port Sandfield, a resident of Muskoka for over 60 years and famous for his maps of the Muskoka Lakes and of individual townships of Muskoka ... Mrs. Agnes Gertrude Sibbett, widow of George Sibbett, resident of Bracebridge since 1876 ... Mrs. Jane Speedie, 80, of Muskoka Falls ...

Byran W. Tillson, 66, who came to Bracebridge as a young man to start a tanning business, which was taken over by the Beardmore Tannery, later Muskoka Leather. He had a hardware business and later a successful poultry farm. Mr. Tillson was active in musical circles, being a splendid violinist, and was director of Knox Church choir, later of the St. Thomas choir, director of the Bracebridge Choral Society, and a band member ... William G. Trethewey, 60, former resident and member of the family for whom Trethewey Falls was named. He prospected in British Columbia, later finding a silver mine in Cobalt which yielded him $275,000 with little work. He had part interest in the Coniagas mine which he sold for $120,000 ... Mrs. Joseph Zimmerman, 86, a resident of Macaulay for 57 years, and a former school teacher and nurse.

In 1926 there were 61 births, 42 marriages, and 33 deaths in Bracebridge.

## 1927

Canada's population was 9,383,300, Bracebridge's assessment was $1,000,000, and Princess Elizabeth cut her first tooth April 21. Navigation started April 23 and ended mid-December with the *Islander* first and last steamship up the river. Bracebridge, with a huge bonfire, was part of a line of beacons all across the country celebrating Canada's Jubilee. Buildings were gaily decorated with pennants, streamers, and lighted arches. The Jubilee celebration and the Old Boys' and Old Girls' Reunion were successful beyond all expectation. People filled every stopping place; family and church reunions abounded; there was a splendid program of sporting events and a big pageant and music that filled the hours to overflowing. A historical pageant and baseball, football, and lacrosse matches abounded. People revelled in a square-dancing contest, step and clog dancing, tug of war, and baby contests. Winners of $5 gold pieces were Baby Hazel Watson, over six months, and Robert James, under six months. Miss Lorna Bates won the prettiest girl on the grounds. Horse races offered a purse of $300, won by "June Bride" of Bracebridge.

Mr. Cornie Reynolds was night constable (10:30 until daylight then replaced by Chief McConnell) at $60 a month. William McConnell was chief of police at $60 a month (he subsequently resigned in October after 24 years of keeping our streets free of vagrants). The Milford

*The view across Bracebridge Bay from the foot of the falls was quite different before a large quantity of rock was blasted from the steep hillside during the construction of what is now Ecclestone Drive. The breakwater was built in 1926 to divert currents from the steamboat wharf.* COURTESY OF BARBARA MCMURRAY

Bay to Bracebridge stage route had a new driver, Mr. Schomberg Mahon.

Bracebridge received a $3,000 Dominion government grant to reconstruct the breakwater, and awarded the contract to Andrew Ferguson of Gravenhurst. Taxi licences were set at $10 for the first vehicle and $5 for each additional, and bowling alleys were to pay $5 for each lane. The Board of Education asked for a budget of $32,000.

Average water consumption in Bracebridge was 40 gallons a day per person – 92,000 gallons a day total. The Water, Light and Power Commission staff said we needed a flow of at least 64 gallons a minute into the water reservoir. Development needed to be done on our pure water supply to connect the unused Peake springs to the Barron springs to give us a flow of 200 gallons a minute. The Commission sold its storehouse and 90-foot frontage on Manitoba Street to Earl Rosewarne who owned the adjoining garage. A new storehouse was to be erected at the old stone quarry on wharf hill (April).

A temporary power shortage in late August due to low water in the north branch of the river stopped factories. A hook-up to Ontario Hydro was to be made soon in case of other emergencies.

The first annual banquet of the Bracebridge-Toronto Association was held in Toronto March 3 with 279 guests. Harry Linney gave a history of the formation of the association.

Business changes saw the Princess Theatre moving picture show move to a new building on Queen's Hill.

John Thompson was having T.A. Hewitt do repairs and improvements on the old part of the Queen's Hotel. Mr. Bert Barnes had a machine in his plant that manufactured socks. He just had to package them at the end. Mr. William Addison contracted to redecorate the United church.

Dunn boat works kept five men employed in the winter and had many more orders. They turned out five rowboats and 30 canoes, besides many oars, paddles, etc. Northern Planing Mills Company was enlarging its plant and adding a second storey … Joseph Lazarra, owner of the old Dominion Hotel, erected a wall along the north side of the property, built a garage at the rear, and completely remodelled the interior … The Anglo-Canadian Company tannery employed over 100 men and was doing 500 hides per day. With some repairs and the installation of new equipment the capacity was expected to rise to 1,800 a day with 225 men employed … The barbershop owned by Fred Bradshaw was purchased by W.A. Shier of Windsor … The Dominion Café leased the store formerly occupied by George C. Crozier and remodelled the interior.

Rural telephone lines on the Bell system rose to a uniform rate of $1.65. Business phones went from $2.05 to $2.50 a month … Revenue for the post office since March 1926 for Bracebridge was $13,448.12, for Gravenhurst, $7,987.02, and Huntsville, $14,621.41. Rental on post boxes increased about $1. In 1926 postage was reduced from 3 cents to 2 cents a letter which led to a post office deficit of $3,820,000.

Sample prices at the W.C. Fryer store showed shirts at $1.50-$4.00, boys' all worsted hose at 75 cents; men's all wool fleece-lined underwear at $1.25 to $1.75. At Hutchison Bros. coffee was 60 cents a pound, granulated sugar $7.25 for 100 pounds, a bushel box of apples $2.00, old cheese 30 cents, seedless raisins 15 cents a pound, currants 18-20 cents, dried apricots 30 cents, cooking figs 11 cents, eggs 50 cents a dozen, tea 75-90 cents a pound, and veneer brick $18.00 a thousand.

The opening of the recently completed basement hall in St. Joseph's Church was celebrated with card parties of bridge, 500, and euchre. A hundred dollars in prizes was offered over five consecutive Monday nights. Dele-

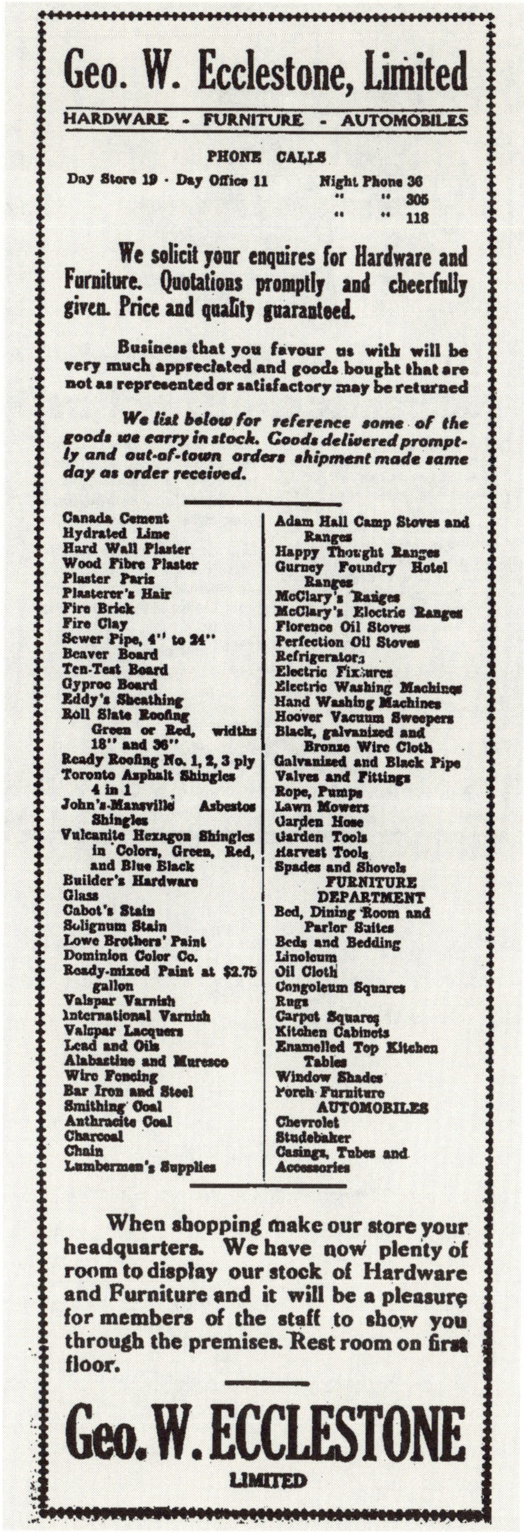

Geo. W. Ecclestone, Limited

HARDWARE - FURNITURE - AUTOMOBILES

PHONE CALLS

Day Store 19 · Day Office 11 Night Phone 36 " " 305 " " 118

We solicit your enquires for Hardware and Furniture. Quotations promptly and cheerfully given. Price and quality guaranteed.

Business that you favour us with will be very much appreciated and goods bought that are not as represented or satisfactory may be returned

*We list below for reference some of the goods we carry in stock. Goods delivered promptly and out-of-town orders shipment made same day as order received.*

Canada Cement
Hydrated Lime
Hard Wall Plaster
Wood Fibre Plaster
Plaster Paris
Plasterer's Hair
Fire Brick
Fire Clay
Sewer Pipe, 4" to 24"
Beaver Board
Ten-Test Board
Gyproc Board
Eddy's Sheathing
Roll Slate Roofing Green or Red, widths 18" and 36"
Ready Roofing No. 1, 2, 3 ply
Toronto Asphalt Shingles 4 in 1
John's-Mansville Asbestos Shingles
Vulcanite Hexagon Shingles in Colors, Green, Red, and Blue Black
Builder's Hardware
Glass
Cabot's Stain
Solignum Stain
Lowe Brothers' Paint
Dominion Color Co.
Ready-mixed Paint at $2.75 gallon
Valspar Varnish
International Varnish
Valspar Lacquers
Lead and Oils
Alabastine and Muresco
Wire Fencing
Bar Iron and Steel
Smithing Coal
Anthracite Coal
Charcoal
Chain
Lumbermen's Supplies
Adam Hall Camp Stoves and Ranges
Happy Thought Ranges
Gurney Foundry Hotel Ranges
McClary's Ranges
McClary's Electric Ranges
Florence Oil Stoves
Perfection Oil Stoves
Refrigerators
Electric Fixtures
Electric Washing Machines
Hand Washing Machines
Hoover Vacuum Sweepers
Black, galvanized and Bronze Wire Cloth
Galvanized and Black Pipe
Valves and Fittings
Rope, Pumps
Lawn Mowers
Garden Hose
Garden Tools
Harvest Tools
Spades and Shovels

FURNITURE DEPARTMENT

Bed, Dining Room and Parlor Suites
Beds and Bedding
Linoleum
Oil Cloth
Congoleum Squares
Rugs
Carpet Squares
Kitchen Cabinets
Enamelled Top Kitchen Tables
Window Shades
Porch Furniture

AUTOMOBILES

Chevrolet
Studebaker
Casings, Tubes and Accessories

When shopping make our store your headquarters. We have now plenty of room to display our stock of Hardware and Furniture and it will be a pleasure for members of the staff to show you through the premises. Rest room on first floor.

Geo. W. ECCLESTONE LIMITED

*Another 1927 local newspaper advertisement. On the roads of the era, a 90-day guarantee was perhaps all that was wise to offer.* COURTESY OF THE BRACEBRIDGE PUBLIC LIBRARY

gates from various Baptist churches in the Collingwood Association attended the February ordination of Pastor Henry Good. The Federation of Women's Boards observed an annual day of prayer at the Baptist church February 18. Rev. F.G. Sherring, pastor of St. Thomas Church, was off to England for a year, exchanging with Rev. A.G. Ford of Pensford, near Bristol.

Social activities for the year included shows by Kuba, "The Great Hypnotist and Mind Reader," "Old Time Ladies Aid Meeting" skit put on by United Church Ladies Aid, and *The Pill Bottle*, directed by Mrs. George Johnson for the Woman's Mission Circle, Baptist Church. The high school concert had Mr. Albert Steinburg, violinist, and Mrs. Broadmus Farma, accompanist, up from Toronto followed by folk dances and songs with scenes from the sleepwalking scene of *MacBeth*. The huge audience was crowded out into the halls. The Citizen's Band concert under the direction of Bandmaster George R. Simmons with 30 bandsmen, Clef Club, and orchestra was a success in every way. They even sold out seats in the hallway. The three-act comedy *The Adventures of Grandpa* put on by the young people of Knox Church under the direction of Mrs. C.W. Fryer played to a capacity crowd. Players included Mr. Lorne Prentis, Mr. Stanley Carr, Mr. A. Gerhart, Cecil Bruce, Miss A. Gerhart, Miss L. McConnell, Mrs. M.L. Watt, Mrs. W.H. Kinsey, and Miss Vera Thompson.

The Fraserburg and Purbrook Telephone Company box social raised $150.

The South Muskoka County Orange Lodge annual meeting held in Bracebridge showed a net increase of 34 members and considerable improvement in the financial condition of all lodges. Loyal Orange Lodge No. 218 had a special service at the Salvation Army barracks conducted by Captain Cornwaite.

The Boy Scouts put on a two-night demonstration of their skills under Scout Master Harry Parker and George Hooton.

The Bracebridge Black and White intermediate hockey team won the district championship. Over 200 enthusiastic fans accompanied the team to Gravenhurst for the last game which they won 8-4. The team lost the OHA semifinal to Newmarket. Russell M. Best was team president, Truman Clark treasurer, and Murt Dunn manager.

The Bracebridge hockey team retained the McGibbon Cup. Playing for Bracebridge were Doug Burton (goal), Kinsey and Walker (defence), Robinson at centre, and Doc Ryan and Archie McKay on the wings. Subs were Dunn and Greer. Irvine Bailey was doing well in the big professional hockey games with the St. Pats.

In curling, the Thomas Cup was retained by the Tennant rink. The curling club was reorganized in December with George Tennant as president, Fred Morris as vice, and Wilbert Richards as secretary-treasurer.

Baseball for the Hammell Cup was reorganized under

president C.S. Salmon and secretary J.E. Collins. Teams from Bracebridge, Gravenhurst, MacTier, Huntsville, and Utterson played games scheduled from June to August ... Six hundred attended the First Annual Muskoka Beach Regatta in August ... A.C. Salmon was president of the Bowling Club with G.W. Brooks as secretary-treasurer.

Deer hunting season was open from November 1 to 30 instead of the usual November 5 to 20. No Sunday hunting was instituted.

The Board of Trade annual meeting February 17 elected new president Wilbert Richards, vice president Will Towns, and secretary-treasurer D.T. Hodgson.

Jack Pawson of the Bank of Nova Scotia left for a post in Edmonton. The popular young man would be missed.

There was a great scarcity of houses in town with every place fit for habitation being occupied. D'Alton Armstrong purchased the large house, stable, and five lots on the river from the Muskoka Leather Company. Fred Higgins tore down his dwelling and planned to rebuild at the back of his lot, letting Dr. McGibbon buy the front part and extend his lawn. The Mahaffy property at Sandy Bay was sold to John G. Golden. Golden Beach, a Muskoka Lake subdivision, was first advertised in August, with Miss Lois Reid winning the prize for naming the endeavour.

At their annual meeting the 20 members of the Bracebridge Fire Company elected chief A.E. Ecclestone, 1st lieutenant Cornie Reynolds, 2nd lieutenant Oscar Simmons, and secretary-treasurer Clem Simmons. Others members were Bert Tibbett, George F. Gibson, Norman Simms, Allan Gardiner, Robert Banks, Fred Pickles, Gordon Black, Arthur Moon, and Alex Milne.

Fire in the upper part of the J.B. Bastedo residence caused the walls and floor to be soaked with tons of water. Most of roof has to be replaced. Fire completely destroyed W.J. Leece's garage and car. On one summer weekend the fire brigade responded to three chimney fires and two grass fires, one at Jubilee Park and one at Mrs. Tillson's egg farm. Fire destroyed an unoccupied house on River Road just beyond the Denniss Planing Factory. George Marshall, night agent, reported the fire. It was one of the oldest houses in town, first built by a member of the Tookey family and at the time of the fire owned by A.T. Wattie.

Firemen made a quick response but the fire at C.W. Fryer's clothing and gents furnishings store raced up the walls and beneath the floor of the Oddfellows Hall. Much of the stock including special stuff for Christmas was damaged.

The South Muskoka Agricultural Society annual meeting showed a paid-up membership of 112 with assets of $4,543.33 and liabilities of $111.25. The chairman was C. Spreadborough, and the vice-chairman A.J. Goltz.

Amendments to the Highway Safety Act included a 35 m.p.h. speed limit, compulsory lights on all vehicles, and special signs on the back of vehicles with four-wheel brakes.

The Muskoka Motor Club reported 718 cars registered in the Motor Park this year with over 2,000 people accommodated. Total receipts were $1,102.77. They took out a mortgage on the park.

So many people attended the high school commencement that it had to be held on two nights, December 7 and 8. Miss Ellen Hare was chosen valedictorian.

The Children's Aid Society report for the year ending October 31st, 1927, by superintendent W. D. Forrest indicated 75 applications for children; five children made wards of the society, and 120 complaints. The society made 135 investigations, 415 letters were written, 280 office visits made, and 6,508 miles travelled. There were 40 court cases and over 120 wards in the district. Work was secured for nine unemployed heads of the family and 11 children were adopted. The Children of Unmarried Parents Act had 30 cases.

Among the deaths this year were: Charles Henry Cox, 89, one of the oldest settlers of Muskoka Township, born at Rufford, England. He came to Canada in 1882, settled on a farm, then moved to River Road near Bracebridge. He was a builder, contractor, and master mechanic in making of scroll work and fancy wood trim ... Henry F Bickmore, Muskoka Township clerk for many years, living at Alport ... Jerold Gallagher, 82, well-known boat builder for Lake of Bays. He came to Bracebridge in 1876, engaging with Mr. George M. Black in boat building then moved to Dwight about 1910 to take up land and continue boat building … Mrs. Herman Goltz, 54, youngest daughter of Mr. and Mrs. Donald Mitchell, married in 1893, raised 13 children … Edward Kirk, came from England in 1865 with his parents Mr. and Mrs. John Kirk and eight children, married Miss Hannah Scholey … Jessie Sarah Mahaffy, 72, married William George Mahaffy and came to Bracebridge about 1887 … John McKay, one of our earliest settlers, died at the home of his daughter Mrs. William Inch of Beatrice … Mrs. Herbert Preston, 65, daughter of Mr. and Mrs. Charles Liddard who came here in 1864 … William H. Tinkiss, 89, one of the outstanding pioneers of Draper. He was present at the raising of the first sawmill in Matthiasville in 1871 … Amy Millicent Whitten, came to Bracebridge with her parents in 1883 and taught at Sebright and Bracebridge Public School. She took over book-keeping in her father's store.

## 1928

Bracebridge made great strides ahead this year getting a memorial hospital and paving many main streets. Council paid tribute to clerk A.C. Salmon who had 30 years on the job. Chief of police Cornie Reynolds retired in March to be replaced by Fred Sander for a salary of $100 a month.

The liquor store vote was taken in Bracebridge. "A dollar may be spent on booze rather than bread or boots" was the cry of those opposed. Over 100 voted for a government liquor store but they were opposed by two-thirds of voters, as many men were still in the lumber camps.

A cold winter made for good logging roads but ice was still on the lakes on April 19, followed by the highest floods in 40 years. The Denniss and J. D. Shier lumber mills were shut down due to high water, and the tannery ran light with water in the furnace rooms. Bird's Woollen Mill was closed. The Ecclestone & Bates, Bickmore, and Dickie boathouses were torn away, to be recovered near Beaumont's and secured to shore. About 200 logs belonging to George Tennant and Sydney Smith broke free and were dashed over the falls. Only great vigilance of men working night and day to clear the rubbish from the water wheels kept the light and power plant running. Fall was wet and cold enough to rot potatoes in the fields.

After much discussion about an appropriate soldier's memorial, Council decided upon a memorial hospital. By June, hospital project chairman Judge Mahaffy together with Red Cross representative Miss Willkinson approved of the Golden property for the hospital. The J.G. Golden home was secured on option at $6,500. The Ontario Red Cross would take over and run the hospital.

The Red Cross began operating hospitals in 1922 and now ran 24 on yearly agreements. Medical men of the town offered medical/surgical treatment to any returned men free of charge. Miss Fannie Arnot was to be the superintendent of nurses.

The hospital dedication service on November 11, 1928, was conducted by Rev. F.G. Sherring, assisted by Rev. Dr. Smith, Rev. Henry Good, Rev. William Farr, and Rev. Mr. Ellis. The Citizen's Band and massed choirs of the town sang *Oh God Our Help and Unto the Hills Do I Lift Up Mine Eyes*. A bronze memorial tablet, made by Messrs. Patterson and Heward, Toronto, inscribed with the 34 names of those killed in World War I, was unveiled by Dr. Peter McGibbon, MP. "In honour of those from Bracebridge and community who nobly died that freedom and right might live, that this hospital, with its memorial tablet is being dedicated."

The whole town worked together to raise money, necessary equipment and supplies for the new hospital. The

*Frank Arnott's house at the corner of Manitoba and MacDonald streets (now the site of the Kentucky Fried Chicken) was the first "hospital" in Bracebridge.* COURTESY OF THE TOWN OF BRACEBRIDGE

*For 36 years the Bracebridge Memorial Hospital occupied what had been the J.G. Golden home on Anne Street. In this picture, taken in the 1950s, an addition has been made to the front of the large brick house, providing space for among other facilities an elevator.* COURTESY OF BRENDA COX

Muskoka Falls Women's Institute Bazaar hosted by Mrs. R. Stephens raised $50. The United Church and Knox ladies held a shower for the new hospital for linens, blankets, and china. The Women's Patriotic League donated funds for a frigidaire system and electric range for the hospital (officers: Mrs. Kingsmill, Mrs. James Thompson, Mrs. T.N. Bird, and Miss Sibbett). A four-day canvass brought in $3,300, the Tag Day at the Fair $190, a benefit card party at St. Joseph's $45, plus there were many other business and private donations.

Fire chief A.E. Ecclestone and the fire brigade were kept busy with a number of serious fires. Dr. Bastedo's house burned February 21. The family saved just what they were wearing. Office records and furniture near windows were saved by neighbours. Although tons of water were used, the fire broke out again the next night. This house was one of earliest erected buildings in the community and was built by J.B. Browning of material supplied by the Gilman Wilson mill. Previous owners were Wm. Hanna, E.F. Stephenson, and Dr. Speers. Dr. Bastedo moved his office to the home of his brother beside the United Church. Mr. W.J. Leece's house on Monck flats, used to store flour, was destroyed in May. The interior and contents of the residence of Mrs. William Moore were destroyed. A fire damaged the roof of Milne's garage, the former Dufferin Hall.

The town fire team of greys were sold to William Richards of Macaulay.

The well known "Don Alton" delivery horse for Towns and Parlett dropped dead in his traces in Ward 4 in March.

The new Thomas Block had 64 feet of frontage on Manitoba Street and 60 feet of depth. It was built on solid rock. Chris Flynn blasted the rock close to the walls of existing stores. The only damage was one stone through the Thomas window across the street. Ausburn Hewitt

*River Street is an appropriate name for this road, under water in the spring freshet of 1928, highest since water-flow records were begun.* COURTESY OF THE BRACEBRIDGE PUBLIC LIBRARY

and Billy Lyren did stone and brick work while Ed Hunt did the wood work. Redmond Thomas had two rooms and a vault for his law office off Chancery Lane while the printing plant had the rest of that floor.

Mr. John Beaumont purchased the pool room business and stable trade, located in former Dominion Hotel, from Jos. Lazarra. Irvine Bailey was doing so well with the Toronto Maple Leafs that he purchased the service station of W.H. Kinsey. Fred Sibbery, Toronto, purchased two lots on Cedar Beach for a cottage

John Reid placed DeLaval milking machines on the farms of Dan McNaughtan and Wm. Brown. The Muskoka Foundry's M.P. McKay built a new stone crusher which could take six cubic yards an hour. With a 10-HP engine and a weight including elevator of five tons, it sold for $1,200. A new dye machine at Bird's Woollen Mills could take up to 2,500 pounds of wool at once.

Council approved sale of 18 feet of the library lot to J.H. Burton, who purchased the adjoining Neilson property to install a service station. Ed Hunt was to erect the garage.

A government survey party was marking out a proposed route of the highway through Muskoka, with a completion route through town around Kelvin Grove Park (Motor Park). William Lowe was in charge of building the new bridge over the south branch.

Miss Hattie Dickinson was once again appointed librarian at an annual salary of $650. The library loaned 15,000 books. Cash receipts were $1,377.68 and expenses $1,329.84. The library contained 5,774 volumes, 910 of them juvenile. The reading room was open 9:00-9:00.

In April C. Ralph Hagg of the Ontario Engineering Co., Fort Erie, was in town surveying and estimating the cost of paving Manitoba Street. A huge steam shovel started to work on upper Manitoba Street in August. A $35 offer from Richard Harper to sell part of his lot to widen Ontario Street at the turn of the hill was accepted.

The new pavement was officially opened November 4 at the intersection of Manitoba and Ontario streets by Mayor Thomas, the Honorable Mr. Finlayson, Minister of Lands and Forests, and G.W. Ecclestone, MPP. A banquet followed at the Queen's Hotel with a band, dancing, and bridge.

The Hon. W. Finlayson announced that the Ferguson Highway extending from Severn Bridge to Cochrane would be sign posted that year.

Three road camps were opened between Bracebridge and Gravenhurst to pave much of the Ferguson Highway. Local labour was preferred, and 250 men plus 40-50 teams were hired. Work was completed by July 1 with a 30-foot wide gravel surface midway between Utterson and Port Sydney ... An airplane crash at Beaumaris killed two and injured four.

The Board of Education stated that non-resident fees were to be paid the first of each month. They reopened the second room at Ward 4 school with Mr. B.R. Minns as principal. Miss Dunn resigned to go to northern Ontario and was replaced by Helen Fawcett.

Patricia Johnson, daughter of inspector George and Mrs. Johnson, came first in Ontario for general proficiency in honour matriculation course and won a $250 scholarship plus her tuition to McMaster University.

Lieutenant Colonel W.D. Forrest's Children's Aid Society report showed 72 applications for children, 11 children made wards, 99 investigations, and 6,056 miles travelled ... H.S. Dodgson, Muskoka Falls circuit pastor, released a sample schedule: Sunday services at 11 a.m. in

*By the 1920s, motor cars were becoming a more familiar sight on the main street of Bracebridge – during the summer, at least, when roads were passable. The Queen's Hotel, the post office with its clock tower, and the three-storey Bank of Nova Scotia (right) were an impressive grouping at this main downtown intersection.* COURTESY OF IAN TURNBULL

Ziska, 3:30 p.m. in Macaulay, and 7:30 p.m. at Muskoka Falls; Monday in Fraserburg church school at 4:30 p.m.; and Wednesday in the Trethewey Falls Hydro Camp.

The Bracebridge Black & White Intermediates won the district and came in second in the Ontario finals. Our team consisted of Greer in goal, Kinsley and Walker on defence, forwards Dunn, Robinson and McKay, and subs Ryan and Arbie. Bracebridge retained the McGibbon Cup. Irvine Bailey of the Toronto Maple Leafs was making a fine showing in professional hockey.

Ten men's curling teams competed for the Excelsior Life Cup presented to Muskoka Curling by Harry Linney. Don Reynolds' rink won (other members were Wm. Lowe, Chas. Penistone, and G. Tennant). The Thomas Trophy Cup given by B. Wasdell was won by the G.W. Boyer rink ... Ladies' bowling was active that summer.

There were many things to see and do such as the comedy *Safety First* put on by Knox Church Ladies Aid; a young people's dance in the high school with music by the Kelly orchestra, Toronto; and Bert Johnson, magician, illusionist, and ventriloquist at the high school. The annual Band Benefit Concert was held in the high school auditorium with 400 people attending. The excellent band program under the direction of bandmaster Simmons included Mr. J.G. Morrison with five drummer friends. A dance was held after the concert.

The Baptist girls' choir presented the cantata *Hiawatha's Childhood*. The United Church Ladies' Aid put on *The Dust of the Earth* in May. The Barnett Brothers Circus came to town in August with a parade and shows under a big tent. The Gravenhurst and Bracebridge combined choirs presented *The Holy City* in November.

Tourism was Canada's third place money maker

behind agriculture and forestry/lumbering. Harry Linney wrote, "Muskoka's future prosperity depends very largely on the holiday seeking public – need bigger summer businesses – increased demand for winter pleasure and holidays." To this end a film called *Regions of Romance* by Universal Films, consisting of Muskoka scenic pictures, was shown at Pantages Theatre, Toronto, for a weekend.

A.C. Ferguson of Gravenhurst was awarded a contract to build a revetment wall and install a sink with running water at the Motor Park. The Boy Scouts made bird houses for Memorial and Kelvin Grove parks.

There were 12,439 post offices in Canada in 1926 with 11,811 in towns and villages where the postmasters earned less than $2 a day and often supplied their own office. The Ziska post office was closed September 29. A daily Monck rural mail delivery commenced September 4, 1928, from Bracebridge town line to the McLeod farm on Lakeshore Road, along the side road to Cedar Beach, and out to the township hall. In Uffington, Herbert Allen, stage driver, was instructed to deliver mail. Sam Hawn was appointed to replace Harvey Buckler who had been postmaster for over 30 years. This created much dissatisfaction in the community.

The Fall Fair saw increased exhibits but cold decreased attendance. George Parrett won the field crop competition and Leslie Burns won potato field crops. The Tillson Egg Farm took 12 leghorn hens to Ottawa for Ontario egg-laying contest but the trip put the hens off. Agriculture in 1925 brought in $18,000; 1927 made $26,000; 1928 brought in $36,000. The Cooperative Company shipped 20 cars of sheep, hogs, and veal calves. John Hammell was secretary-treasurer and A.J. Goltz president.

The United Farmers of Ontario Annual District Convention was held in Bracebridge.

Deer hunting season returned to two weeks from one month. The Buck Horn Hunt Club at Pine Lake comprised Ed Price, John Philips, John Haight, Alex Milne, George S. Johnson, and William, Frank and Albert Fawell of Merriton. The Parletts also had a party at Pine Lake.

Mr. J. H. Elliott, issuer of licences, sold over 50 licences and 50 permits.

No prisoners were in the district jail over Christmas for the first time in 20 years.

Deaths included Rev. Canon James Boydell, 91, pastor to St. Thomas Anglican church 1885-1899, and one of the first to own a bicycle in Bracebridge. He frequently rode to various parts of the District and Toronto ... Ed Bailey, who came to Macaulay in 1873 ... Thomas Carr, 73, many years caretaker of the municipal building ... Mrs. Annie Dooley , 82, came as a young girl to settle in Macaulay near the falls ... Crispin Gibbs, 82, fell from a wagon and crushed his skull, came to Macaulay in 1878 ... Alex Hamilton, Muskoka road inspector, married Elizabeth Dollar about 1886 ... William Hare, 76, father of Walter and Will, killed in an auto accident ... Edward Wheaton Hay, 84, a Falkenburg merchant who moved there in 1898 ...

Robert Leishman, proprietor of the Albion Hotel until 1923. He came in 1880. His father built the first mill on the present site of the Albion Hotel. Fire destroyed it so he rebuilt the mill at Tennant's which worked until 1902 then was sold to the furniture factory ... Douglas Robinson, 10, son of Albert, drowned while trying to swim across the river at foot of the falls ... James Tribble, 73, worked in the Bracebridge electric light and power plant ... Elizabeth Veitch, 57, third daughter of Mr. and Mrs. Adam Veitch of Watt ... Gertrude Anne Williams (Bird), married Dr. Williams in 1889.

# 1929

This year will best be remembered by the serious train wreck near Falkenburg; the 12th of July Orange celebrations in Bracebridge; St. Joseph's 50th anniversary, and the decision to make a new highway approach to Bracebridge.

Ed Ball was appointed superintendent of power and water plants to succeed Wm. C. Simmons with a salary of $1,800 a year. The town set the mill rate at 51 mills. Street lights were put at the end of McMurray and paving was approved for Thomas, Main, Dominion, Quebec, and McMurray streets. Plans were approved for a new approach to Bracebridge via Kelvin Grove Park with a new steel bridge estimated to cost $100,000.

Town Council business included a bylaw to raise

$74,104.97 by 20-year debentures in $500 units at 5½ percent, a bylaw stating "No buildings may be erected without a building permit; no more gas pumps or tanks on the streets," a bylaw (521) to allow one mill on the dollar for the hospital, a bylaw (513) stating "Barbershops shall be closed 7 p.m. to 5 a.m. Monday, Tues, Thursday, and Friday, Wednesday 9 p.m. to 5 a.m., Sat 11 p.m. until noon Sunday." A petition was granted for drains on Quebec Street, and cluster lights were erected for the main section of Manitoba Street with ordinary lights at Memorial Park. The town assumed responsibility for indigent patients in urgent need of hospital care.

The Hospital Board consisted of chairman C.S. Hare with Henry J. Bird Jr., G.W. Boyer, Dr. Bastedo, Rev. Dean O'Leary, M.C. Newark, John Thomson, Captain L.R. Fraser, and Ensign Cornwaithe. The Red Cross met all expenses of running the hospital and collected fees from patients.

Mr. E. Wadsworth of Detroit made a $1,000 donation to the hospital for purchase of anaesthetic equipment and also bedside lamps. He also offered a one-month holiday at his Lake of Bays summer home to convalescent poor patients. A Victor x-ray machine was purchased in November. In total in 1930 the hospital saw 500 patients treated in 4,000 hospital days with 120 major operations, 25 births, 4 auto accidents, 4 fractured skulls, 12 ruptured appendix, and 2 strangulated hernias. It used 35 x-ray plates the first month the machine was installed.

The Board of Education comprised C. Spreadborough, chairman, and L.W. Anderson, G.W. Brooks, Ed Hunt, and George Fenn. A flu epidemic delayed public school opening by one week. The first cold snap, -35° in mid-January, assisted in quelling the flu. High school equipment was insured for $5,000. Roy Fraser of Hawkesbury was appointed assistant principal at the high school in place of J. Burrleigh Bastedo.

The high school presented *A Midsummer Night's Dream* along with the high school orchestra and vocal, violin, and piano solos. It was well attended. Commencement was held December 2 under the eye of Miss P.V. McNeeley, principal.

On February 19 a serious train accident occurred just north of Falkenburg at Moore's side road. A heavy freight train with 31 cars of pulpwood, lumber, and silver derailed, killing both the brakeman and fireman. The engineer was seriously injured and died a few days later. The coroner's inquest into the deaths found that although the train was inspected in North Bay, a broken arch bar or truck strap caused the accident. Inspectors could see the marks several miles back.

The annual meeting of the Board of Trade elected George F. Gibson as president to head a deputation to Toronto to support the new highway between Bracebridge and Port Carling.

Dominion Street was to be paved 30 feet wide with curb and gutters; other streets 20 feet wide with no curbs or gutters. Manitoba Street paving was $28,000 over estimate. The town accepted an offer from Shier Lumber to erect signs at the entrance to town. Bracebridge broadcast over CFRB Radio in May and June, sponsored by the Bird Woollen Mill, J.D. Shier Lumber, Minett-Shields, and Ace Bailey.

Spring was raw with below-normal temperatures. Lake Muskoka opened April 12. The earliest was in 1898 when the ice left March 31, the latest being May 8 in 1876. High water levels did considerable damage. Alvin Kaye of Scarborough drove the first car through to Bracebridge that spring.

The Mickle Company's log drive down the Muskoka River began late June.

The July 12 Orange celebration was a great success with over 6,000 visitors from 32 lodges, who arrived by special trains and steamers. A temporary bandstand was erected on the lawn of Mr. and Mrs. Towns.

President A.J. Goltz. of the South Muskoka Agricultural Society reported $309 in wet weather insurance and 108 members in good standing.

Royal Canadian Legion Branch 161 was formed with president Newark.

The Clef Club with president Mrs. W. Anderson, presented *The Violin Maker of Cremona*, *The Two Lunatics*, and the operetta *The Feast of the Little Lantern*, with proceeds to the hospital. Knox choir presented *Hearts and Blossoms* under the direction of Miss Viola Kirk. A dance given by Rayner Construction company with good music by Seavell's Orchestra from Orillia was well

*Constructed as part of the new highway access to Bracebridge, the Silver Bridge was the third spanning the falls (joining the CNR bridge and the Muskoka Road bridge). Its steel superstructure has long been gaily decorated with lights to provide a stunning night-time display crowning the falls.* COURTESY OF BARBARA MCMURRAY

attended; others watched or played bridge. Several thousand attended a street dance held August 22 with visitors from Bala, Port Carling, Huntsville, Gravenhurst, and Baysville. Speicher Brothers orchestra and tour band played both round and square dances.

The Ontario government seed-cleaning demonstration train travelled throughout Muskoka April 15-17.

Ken Hulme and Jack Forbes of Timmins skied through Bracebridge on their way to Toronto

The Ladies Bowling annual meeting elected Miss Lea Parlett president and Miss Margaret Bird secretary.

A Dominion Order-in-Council on March 4 declared all pleasure craft must show a licence and carry lights at night, a sound-signaling device, fire extinguishers, and life saving apparatus. Tax on all boats on lakes Muskoka, Rosseau, and Joseph and contributing waters was set at $1 for canoes and rowboats; up to 18 feet, $3.00; 18-26 feet, $4.00; 26-40 feet, $5.00; and over 40 feet, $8.00.

Irvine "Ace" Bailey won the Whiteman's Cup with the most goals scored in the NHL. He received a $100-watch plus $500 as the most valuable player. He was presented with a silver tea set from the men in town. Mr. Bailey married Gladys Rowne of Blind River on May 1.

Bracebridge's Black and White beat the airmen's hockey team at Camp Borden for the intermediate championship. Bracebridge had won eight straight games in the district. In goal, Greer; centre, Gerry Dunn; wings, McKay and Ryan; defence, Kinsey and Walker; subs, Dawkins and E. Dunn.

Ministerial changes included Rev. Alfred Eickenaar of McMaster University coming to the Baptist Church and Rev. A. Carmen of Hastings to the United Church. A Sunday School workers' conference was held in Bracebridge under the auspices of Muskoka Religious Educational Council at the Baptist and United churches. Principal speaker was J.J. Eaton, Toronto.

President H.C. Minett and the Muskoka Motor Club approved the installation of flush toilets, a refrigerator, and telephones in the park for $600. They raised daily fees from 50 cents to 75 cents a car and from $2 to $3 a week. Kelvin Grove Park had a new 7-foot by 14-foot building with running water put up by George Brooks under the direction of John Reid.

Sergeant Major White of RCR Toronto held eight weeks training for the Muskoka Northern Pioneers with classes in Bracebridge (20 from here), Huntsville, Powassan, and Sprucedale. Six hundred men from the Simcoe Foresters, Owen Sound Group, Northern Pioneers and Algonquin attended the brigade camp in Huntsville July 2-14.

The fire brigade had 30 calls in 1929, 15 serious fires, nine chimney fires, three grass fires, one roof put out by pails, and one barn burned down. Total insurance paid was $17,658.38. There were 12 meetings, and 42 hours were spent fighting fires. Average attendance at fires for the 20 members of fire brigade was 69 percent. The brigade budget totalled $673.12.

Dunn's boat works two-storey building was completely destroyed by fire on May 16. The whole winter's work of 40 rowboats and 30 canoes valued at $12,000 was lost. Only half were insured. Also destroyed by fire were the barn on Dr. Bastedo's property next to the public library, a shunter at Shier's lumber mill and the building that housed it, Mr. and Mrs. W.J. Whaley's dwelling, barn, and outbuildings in Monck, a house (including all household effects) occupied by Mrs. J. H. Brenn, and the Central School roof (not seriously damaged).

The Ross Business College opened a branch in Bracebridge in the Sibbett Block with Miss Gladys L. Philip, Toronto, in charge.

In August the Canadian Chautauqua offered 10 entertainments for 22 cents an adult and 10 cents a child, with plays, musicals, and speeches in Jubilee Park.

Work progressed rapidly on Ontario Hydro's Trethewey's Falls hydro dam with 2,300 HP for the Georgian Bay system. Work included a 30,000-volt transmission line. The Bala Electric Light Company station was transferred to the Hydro Electric Power Commission.

The 35-foot *Estelle IV* speedboat with three engines of 935 HP each, owned by Miss Betty Carstairs, was to compete in the Harmsworth International Trophy race on the Detroit River August 31. She was built on the Isle of Wright under the direction of Ditchburn boats but was tuned and tested at Gravenhurst.

Council accepted the Amiesite tender of $33,625.75 for paving. Thomas Street was paved 30 feet wide with a six-inch concrete base and a bituminous top. Jack Beatty was the first across the James Street viaduct gully.

Miss Lulu Golden won the Dominion Medal for the highest mark award by the Toronto Conservatory.

An earthquake at 6:30 August 12 woke people while the second tremor rattled windows and doors. The epicentre was in New York State.

G.W. Ecclestone announced a District Board of Commissioners for the old age pension, to begin at age 70 to a maximum of $20 a month for those with an income of $365 or less, no Indians. Sixty applied across the district for payments which began in November.

The Canadian Topographical Survey together with the Royal Canadian Air Force and Ontario Department of Surveys produced a coloured map of Muskoka showing roads, railways, and district and township boundaries.

H.C. Budd of Milford Bay was appointed returning officer for the October provincial election, but George W. Ecclestone, the Conservative nominee, was acclaimed MPP over W.E. Hutchison, the Prohibition Candidate.

The 55th anniversary of the Fall Fair was a splendid success with excellent weather and gate receipts which exceeded the previous year's total by almost $700.

The Milne garage was bricked and R. Craig sold the Albion Hotel to George Johnston of Clarksburg.

The 50th anniversary of St. Joseph's Church was held on a glorious June day. Father Brunelle of Penetang, Right Rev. Monsignor McColl of Peterborough, and Very Rev. Dean O'Leary led a parade of 600 men and boys with Bracebridge bands and 95 of the Dr. LaSalle Collegiate band.

Bandmaster George R. Simmons retired and was replaced by Mr. A. Morra of Toronto. The bandstand in Memorial Park was replaced by a larger structure to open in September with a first class concert including a cornet solo by Rocco Morra, euphonium solo by J.W. Reid, and Rev. William Farmer leading the prayer of dedication.

The annual report of Children's Aid showed 54 applications for children, 105 complaints, 111 investigations, and three children made wards. W.D. Forrest, superintendent, travelled 7,248 miles.

Curling president G.N. Ecclestone announced 11 rinks this year with Mr. Bernard Wasdell in charge of the ice.

Among the year's deceased were Mr. William Johnston, 71, who came to town shortly before the railway, and served as town assessor for several years ... Captain Edward McAlpine, 79, who for 25 years was master of the *Medora*, and completed 47 years with Muskoka Lakes Navigation Company in 1927 ... Miss Annie Hilda Beaumont, teacher at Beatrice and Alport, daughter of the late J.J. Beaumont ... Richard "Dick" Pawson, secretary to the fire company for many years and an avid hockey and lacrosse supporter ... Mrs. James Boyer, 88, mother of George Wilson Boyer, moved to Macaulay in 1868 ... William Charles Denniss, 82, who took up land on the 12th concession of Macaulay in 1874, and moved to town in 1923 ... Fanny Minett, 87, pioneer of Lake Rosseau and mother of the famous boat builder. She came to Muskoka in 1866, cleared land to farm, and opened her home to summer visitors ... Philip Leeder, 84, pioneer builder and carpenter ... John Keall, 89, of Monck. He came to Bracebridge in 1859 and helped John Bailey build the first barn in Town. He was a member of township council and director of the South Muskoka Agriculture Society for many years ... H.W. Shaw, 72, born in Bracebridge. He ran the mill with Mr. Perry at Wilson's Falls, then sold it to Messrs. Ford and Gillespie who sold to George Tennant ... William Simmons, superintendent of the water, light and power plant when first installed in 1895-98; in recent years he was inspector for driver's licences ... Rev. R.H. Reynolds, father of Cornier Reynolds, came in 1904 and had been a Free Methodist preacher for 25 years.

## 1930

Provincial and Dominion money poured into Muskoka in the form of road and bridge construction. The summer Dominion election saw the Honourable R.B. Bennett elected as Prime Minister of Canada with 137 seats out of a possible 243. Miss Agnes McPhail was the only woman to succeed at the polls in that election in July 1930. Dr. McGibbon, Conservative, beat the Liberal candidate Dr. MacDonald of Huntsville with a majority of 2,948. Celebrations lasted until the wee hours of the morning when a parade of autos came from Gravenhurst with horns and bells blaring. Election registrars for the town were Chas. Penistone, D.T. Hodgson, W.J.A. Brown, and R.H. Thompson. The Muskoka-Ontario riding had 146 polling places, 57 in northern Ontario County and 89 in Muskoka. There were 18,756 names on the list. Bracebridge had 1,417 voters. In all 16,503 votes were polled, 700 less than in 1926.

The municipal election held January 6 was the most keenly contested in many years with George F. Gibson winning the mayoralty race over Dr. Bastedo. The tax rate was set at 54 mills with a five percent discount if paid between June 1 and 15. Mr. R.H. Thompson, assessor, reported a total assessment of $1,055,751, up some $1,500 from 1929, while the population dropped 136.

The Board of Education consisted of Chairman George Fenn, J.H. Elliott, R.M. Best, T.N. Bird, and Wilbert Richards (replaced by George Jeffries). Miss Mary Jackson, a graduate of the University of Toronto, would teach Latin, English, and history, and be in charge of girls' physical culture classes in place of Miss M. Brown on staff at Bracebridge High School. Miss Hallett resigned to go to Haileybury.

The Board of Trade established a tourist bureau, managed by Major Lindsey, at the corner of Ontario and Manitoba streets. They also advertised tourism in Muskoka on their two-hour radio talk show, mentioning over 60 resorts. In the U.S. the Detroit-Muskoka Dinner Dance and the 2nd annual Bracebridge, Muskoka-Southern California Dance held in Los Angeles were most successful.

Bylaw 526, to expropriate land for the Ferguson Highway and to close part of Perry Street with a grade seven feet above the existing street level, was passed in May.

Department of Northern Development engineer, Kenneth Rose, started clearing the right of way for the new entrance to Bracebridge using local labour. The contract for bridges, retention walls, and roads was let to Messrs. Birmingham & Sons of Kingston. By August one span of new bridge had been placed and grading through the Motor Park was complete. A light railway had been laid along a portion of the road to enable the carrying of stone and other materials. There were still 10,000 rivets to put into the bridge, two coats of paint to put on the steel work, and cement floors to be laid.

With the thought in mind that "good roads will do more to bring people together for better citizenship," good progress was made surfacing the Bracebridge to Huntsville road. Stone was spread as far as Utterson and the tarria finish made for several miles. The Huntsville to Scotia Junction road was oiled. The Bracebridge to Dorset road was straightened and grades improved, and the Watt-Raymond-Rosseau Road also improved.Traffic officers appointed for the highways in Muskoka were Elmer Shepard and A.R. Clarke of Toronto.

Engineer Partridge of the Dominion Government Works Department inspected the Bracebridge wharf and proposed to build other district wharves as public works. Dredging of Coulter's and Jannette narrows to join Bala Lake [Bala Bay] with Lake Muskoka was completed.

The Hon. George S. Henry, Minister of Highways and acting Premiere, with R.M. Smith, deputy minister, and chief engineer C. H. Fullerton visited town in November as guests of Council at the Queen's Hotel. Council requested assistance to relieve our unemployment. They inspected the width of Manitoba Street, Tennant's and Ball's hills, and were appraised of the need for fill and a culvert at the hospital and for a new jail and residence. This visit was followed by a $13,500 cheque from the secretary of Ontario.

Commissions were established to improve hills, add fill at the hospital, and to widen Manitoba Street. Council agreed to have an open employment registry at the town clerk's office.A steam shovel was kept busy removing earth from streets to be paved. The soil was used to fill the hospital gully. Construction included paving 22½ feet wide on Nelson and Quebec streets, McMurray storm sewers on the north side to Rosemount and on the south side to Manitoba. A paving contract was awarded to Raynor Construction Co. for paving McMurray. A bylaw was passed to pave McMurray and Quebec streets, Nelson Street from John to Manitoba, and Buller Avenue from John to McMurray. The Town Hall was repainted for $126.13 by Mr. W.W. Adamson.

Other grants to Muskoka included, for Macaulay, $175 for road machinery, $1,400 for roads and a $300 direct grant; to Muskoka Township, $2,000 for roads and a $700 direct grant for a road to St. Elmo; to Draper, $150 for machinery and $1,750 for roads; and to Medora and Wood, $400 for an overseer and $10,250 for roads. The Dominion government paid 50 percent of the cost of relief in unorganized and one-third in organized municipalities. Men were paid $2.75 a day for a 10-hour day and $2.75 a day for a team working on the roads for a 10-hour day.

Prices included a 15-cent-a-pound reduction in the price of Red Rose tea, 60 cents for five yards of 36-inch flannelette, a house dress for 59 cents, overalls for $1.49 (on sale from $2.00), round steak 25 cents, roast 15-20 cents, corned beef 18 cents a pound; bananas 6½ cents a pound, oranges 25 to 75 cents a dozen. At the W. Towns Grocery, pitted dates were two pounds for 25 cents, white sugar 10 pounds for 55 cents, brown sugar 10 pounds for 53 cents. A six-hole Premium range with a large fire box for coal or wood sold for $45.00.

The field crop competition began in May for oats three acres or more and potatoes 7.5 acres, with cash prizes of $20, $15, $12, $10, $8, $6, and $4. Heavy rains and hail made for late seeding. John Hammell came in first in the South Muskoka oat crop competition followed by Alvin Goltz and C.H. Kaye.

The Fall Fair was a great success with field events, softball for girls and boys, auto races, team draws, horseshoe pitch, etc. Dan MacNaughtan's team won the heavy horse draw of 200 feet while Allan Keall's team won the light horse draw with 265 feet. At the championship school fair Miss Norma Hammond was best pupil, winning a gold watch. S.S. No. 3 Macaulay won a flag.

Ninety-three young men and women competed in the Muskoka-Parry Sound Royal Winter Fair Judging Contest to win one of the 20 four-day trips to the Royal. Miss Ethel Skinner, William J. White, and Eric C. Kaye won from Bracebridge.

His Lordship Justice Jeffrey, Court of Assizes, referred to the absence of crime in Muskoka in his address to Grand Jury in September.

*The year 1930 marked the closing of the Anglo-Canadian Leather Company tannery after 39 years of operation in Bracebridge. The tannery, on the south shore of the river below Bracebridge Bay, was served by a railway spur which continued on to the big J.D. Shier sawmill by the forks of the river.* COURTESY OF BRENDA COX

Mrs. John Thompson was the first president of the newly formed Woman's Auxiliary Red Cross Board of the Bracebridge Memorial Hospital. The Bracebridge branch of the Women's Institute was formed June 13 with Mrs. Wm. Grebhardt president.

Rev. Wm. Wallis was inducted into the pastorate of Knox Presbyterian Church with Rev. M.W. Heaslip of Penetanguishene presiding. A Mission was held at St. Joseph's by two Redemption Fathers in June. There was a Free Methodist Church camp meet with Pittsburgh evangelist Rev. R.B. Campbell complete with a community boarding tent. It cost $4 for the week and 25 cents for breakfast and lunch.

The United Church celebrated its 60th anniversary with speaker Rev. Frank Longford, secretary of the Board of Religious Education, and Rev. A. Carmen Hie conducted a historical review ... An interdenominational group met at the Baptist Church to form a Young People's Temperance Union led by Rev. E.A. Eikenaar. A meeting of citizens against opening of a government liquor store was held November 26.

A Cemetery Act was passed asking for legislation for permanent markers to be erected to identify graves. A work bee was held in Fraserburg to fix up the cemetery.

A free well-baby clinic started for the entire district, held once a week, providing free medical advice with doctors coming alternately.

Murt Dunn sold his confectionery and restaurant to the A.W. Hall family of Port Sandfield.

A fine summer produced a better than average tourist season, but too short, and it was followed by severe autumn storms, one of which blew down shade trees about town and broke electric lines in a dozen places. In mid-October a snow storm blocked the Bracebridge roads with 10 inches of heavy wet snow and over 25 inches just to the north. It was the worst snow storm in 58 years, according to Alf Thompson in Ridout. Precipitation from November 1929 to April 1930, as reported by John

Hollingworth, was 155 inches (12 feet 11 inches) total snowfall plus 8.52 inches of rain.

The Children's Aid Society had 47 applications for children, and 14 children were made wards (more than ever before). There were four complaints, 65,015 miles travelled, and 50 court appearances.

Alf Slater donated a silver cup to be awarded to the hockey champions of Muskoka District high schools.

Mr. and Mrs. Otto L. Carr celebrated their golden wedding anniversary on August 22. They had lived 38 years in Bracebridge.

The fish hatchery at Port Carling placed 1.5 million pickerel fry in Lake Muskoka, 750,000 in Lake Joseph, and 750,000 in Lake Rosseau.

A 500-pound bear was shot near Windermere by Mervin Longhurst, son of the Watt Township reeve.

Windermere electric lights were installed in most of the homes and public buildings in November.

Accidents during the year included the death of Phillip Gilbert, 47, crushed by a large galvanized culvert when the team bolted while working on the road crew. He left a wife and four children. James McKay, 53, was crushed by a log while working with Robert Wilson out beyond Baysville. He left his wife, the former Violet Mosey, and three children. Hundreds of men from all over the district attended his funeral held at St. Thomas' Anglican Church. Edward Nickason, 14, son of Mr. and Mrs. J.T. Nickason, Parkersville, broke his neck when a 40-foot by 60-foot barn crashed to the ground during a severe April storm.

Kenneth Kirkness, son of Mr. and Mrs. David Kirkness, drowned when he and Sherman Kirby tried to paddle across Lake Muskoka in heavy winds. They both made it to shore but Mr. Kirkness died when Mr. Kirby went for help. Clarence Peacock, 20, son of Mr. and Mrs. George Peacock, Macaulay, drowned in Lake Rosseau.

The hearse of W.H. Kinsey was destroyed on the way home from Huntsville when it collided with a car and burned. In January the Baysville mail stage team ran away while coming down Hunt's Hill. It turned south at the post office, thundered down Manitoba Street with the sleigh stage on its side, and started up the Ontario Street hill before it was stopped. Only light damage was done to the sleigh. On May 24 Mr. Crozier was driving down Manitoba Street in his buggy when he was struck by a car going in the same direction. His horse broke loose and ran away, being struck and killed by another car by the park.

The steamer *Newminko* sank near Chief Island in Lake Rosseau. A collision of the steamer *Medora* and the tug *Constance* at Muskoka Wharf injured Captain A.T. Corbett of Bracebridge. He was taken to the Toronto General Hospital with a badly fractured cheek bone.

In July, Minett-Shields built the 50-foot long; 13-foot beam cruiser *Lou* and shipped her to Orillia. She had a speed of 12 m.p.h. and could sleep seven. They also built a 55-foot, 400-HP cruiser for George Fulford of Brockville, which was written up in *Canadian Power Boating* as one of the most interesting boats of the year.

The Bracebridge Fire Department reported 21 fires, including 10 serious ones – a third fewer than in 1929.

Fire destroyed a large frame house on Shier Street in which Mr. and Mrs. Howard Matthew ran a boarding house. Mr. Matthew was badly burned when he went back into the flaming house to rescue their children. They had to jump into the snow from an upstairs window. Eli Richards' garage, including three trucks, a car, and supplies was destroyed. In July, the Shier Lumber Co. was struck by lightning and burned to the ground. It had been built 33 years previously by J.D. Shier, replacing the original mill which had also been destroyed by fire. Fire also totally destroyed the home of Thomas Mann, in Monck adjoining town. It had been purchased the previous fall from Aubrey White, and had been built by Jas. Prentiss. There was no insurance but most of the contents and the neighbours' houses were saved. In Port Carling the Duke Boat Storage Plant was destroyed by fire with an estimated loss of $50,000.

Canadian Chautauqua, which was to foster and develop Canadian ideals in music and colour right to our own homes, came to Jubilee Park with two plays, three talks, nine performances, a light opera festival, and the Garay Sisters. The largest crowd ever attended the closing performances – over 1,000 people.

A two-week Chetolah Fresh Air Camp was held for 80 children, 36 from Bracebridge, 36 from Huntsville, plus country children. Each child was given a bathing suit, towel, shoes, sweater, suit, soap, toothbrush, handkerchief, shampoo, brush, housecoat, dress or suit, and a suitcase to keep. Children were taught to swim, play basketball and volleyball, to march, do calisthenics, and be tidy, neat, and obedient. Miss Pepper was superintendent, assisted by Alan R. Fee.

The Christmas Cheer convener, Mrs. Thomas, and her committee consisting of two from each church, put together treats for 62 homes costing $253.19. The town team could not deliver all in one day so they hired two more teams and drivers. Mr. Hutchison supplied a barrel of apples, Mr. Parrett 13 bags of vegetables. The committee purchased potatoes and onions, a case of corn syrup, corn flakes, and tangerines, all at low cost from merchants.

Ed Ball and staff of the Water, Light & Power Commission decorated the bandstand with "Merry Christmas" in lights with a large star on top in Bracebridge's first attempt at a community Christmas tree. Dr. McGibbon headed the committee that organized such festivities as Santa Claus, the bugle band, combined church choirs, fireworks, and treats for each of the 1,200 children including pencil cases for the school-aged and rubber balls for preschoolers.

David Myers was elected to attend the Boy's Parliament between Christmas and the New Year.

Deaths during the year included Mr. J. Bailey, 90, who was among the first settlers to come to Muskoka. He lived in Bracebridge for more than 60 years and with his wife raised eight children. A carpenter and builder by trade, he built many of the buildings in early Bracebridge … Mr. M.A. Buckler, 73, former postmaster of Uffington for over 30 years … Peter A. Smith, manager of the Muskoka Leather Company. He was active in the Agricultural Society, a former councillor, and served as mayor for five years … Robert James Campbell, 63, father of Mrs. Wilbert Richards, born Muskoka Township. He had been a school trustee and served on township council … Mr. F. McKay, merchant in Dorset and reeve for many years … Mrs. William Ewing, resident of Monck for 59 years; she had six children … Robert Eddie, 94, owner of a brick-making business, married Miss Ada Walker in 1885, had nine children … Mrs. William Fraser, 63, nee Catherine Dixon, daughter of early Macaulay pioneers … Mrs. J. Ewart Lount, widow of deceased former registrar of Muskoka … Warren Bishop Moore, 57, married Miss Sibbett of the British Lion Hotel … Mrs. Edwin Pickles, 80, came to Bracebridge in 1902.

A.C. Salmon, registrar, reported 86 births, 37 marriages, and 45 deaths for 1930.

## 1931

The year 1931 was bad for fires in Bracebridge, in particular, the destruction of the skating rink and Knox Presbyterian Church.

In early January, the snowplow from Port Carling made it as far as Bracebridge, clearing a track 16 feet wide for the first time!

The Toronto *Globe* put on a truck service from Toronto to North Bay so the papers arrived by 7:30 a.m.

The Water, Light & Power Commission offered the Brobst Forestry Co. water at five cents per 1,000 gallons if the company supplied piping to town mains. A.E. Fawcett was in charge of installing town water in the United Church cemetery.

The Bird Woollen Mill was operating on a small scale and being kept in good repair. It formerly made heavy cloth for lumbering, but the mild winter, lack of bush work, and tariffs had depressed the market.

Council appointed A.E. Ecclestone fire chief for 1931 with a salary increase of $25. John Phillips was weed inspector, John Reid truant officer, and J.W. Reid was elected chairman of the Water, Light & Power Commission. John Carr, the Dominion public building caretaker, received a gold watch when he retired after 16 years.

The mill rate was set at 56: 29 for schools, 1 for the hospital, 11 for debentures, 1.25 for the library, 1 for the band, and 12.5 for general. The library was painted for $65. Council accepted one span of the old Severn bridge to be put over the railway rock cut on Queen Street for an estimated cost of $1,200. A government grant of $4,800 was received for a new wharf in Bracebridge Bay. The wharf house was moved and the road widened.

By August, lights on the new bridge and approach to town were up and the new sidewalks finished.

A bylaw was passed in Monck to raise $9,000 to improve the Falkenburg to Milford Bay road and complete River Road from Bracebridge to Golden Beach.

The Honourable William Finlayson, minister in charge of unemployment, visited Muskoka and Bracebridge in mid-October and stated that only those in need would be employed. A thousand men were to be employed on road improvements for Muskoka, from Dominion and provincial grants, in 40 camps. Several roads were widened to 24 feet and straightened: Gravenhurst to Bala and Foot's Bay, Bracebridge to Baysville, Dorset, and Minden, and Huntsville to Dwight and Dorset.

A fire, which started over the furnace, destroyed Knox Presbyterian Church on Sunday, January 25. The church had been dedicated December 17, 1876, on the site of the former Dickie house which was purchased in 1875 for $200. The original cost of the church was $3,000; it had been insured for $6,500. Rev. Dr. Wallis had just been inducted in April 1930.

The cornerstone of the new Knox Presbyterian Church was laid May 30 by Miss Nellie Thompson, the oldest member of the congregation. Church records, city and local news were placed in a receptacle and the stone drawn in place. The grey granite cornerstone was donated by Mr. Harry Boyer. Rt. Rev. Dr. Baird, moderator of the Presbyterian Church of Canada, spoke, as did Pastor Rev. Dr. Wallis. The opening and dedication of Knox Presbyterian Church was well attended on October 4 with the Rev. G.S. Lloyd, moderator of the Barrie Presbytery, Rev. Dr. Rochester of Toronto, and building chairman Captain Fraser present.

Work started September 14 on the United Church religious education addition. Dedicated in December, the addition had a 300-seat auditorium, stage, kitchen, boardroom, seven classrooms, and a gift piano from Leda Scovell. Mr. S.D. Boyer presented the granite for the new cornerstone which was laid on October 27 by the moderator of the United Church in Canada, Rev. Dr. Oliver. It also contained a time capsule.

The 25th anniversary of the ordination of Rev. Dean O'Leary of St. Joseph's was celebrated with a High Mass of Jubilee led by his brother, Rev. Joseph O'Leary of Saskatoon, and cousin, Rev. John O'Leary, Copper Cliff.

*A spectacular fire on January 25, 1931, gutted the Knox Presbyterian Church on McMurray Street. The church had been dedicated in 1876.* COURTESY OF THE TOWN OF BRACEBRIDGE

The Motor Park was filled to capacity for several nights in the summer. It now had two kitchens, bath houses, splendid lavatories, lights in the subway, and a telephone on the grounds, all kept clean by Mr. W.A. Campbell, caretaker.

The Legion employed returned men as they passed through Bracebridge and also gave $300 in local assistance. They held an annual meeting for all ex-servicemen in May and elected Rev. J.S. Smedley president, replacing M.C. Newark.

The Canadian Legion Field Day with $300 in prizes was held on Dominion Day in Jubilee Park for 25 cents

*Wiltown Lodge in 1931. The impressive 2½-storey wooden building was the home of William Towns and family.* COURTESY OF BILL TOWNS

admission. The 48th Highlanders Band of Toronto led a huge parade, and there was a baseball tournament with teams from Bracebridge, Gravenhurst, Port Carling, Milford Bay, Port Sydney, Huntsville, Mactier, and Orillia competing for the silver cup. There was highland and fancy dancing, and a street dance at night with the Hammond Brothers band for square dances and the orchestra of college boys from Western University, London, for round dances. Lieutenant Jones gave an aerial display of dives, rolls, and turns over Jubilee Park. Despite all the activities, attendance was only fair during the day due to temperatures of 100°F, but hundreds enjoyed the dances. It was a very hot summer with many days 95° and 100°.

One hundred men attended a plowing match held on the farm of Thomas Ball. It was decided to organize a Plowman Association with president H.L. Goltz, vice president Tom Ball, John Hammell, and Harry Buckler. The first Muskoka Plowing Match was held on October 3 with 16 competitors from Bracebridge, Galt, Burk's Falls, Powassan, and Vankoughnet.

The Bracebridge movie theatre reopened July 1 with equipment for talking pictures. Mr. Kirby now had two complete machines so pictures could continue without interruption. A nine-hole golf course opened on the G.A. McLeod property at the lake.

The 20-member fire brigade was granted a raise from $500 to $700, increased accident insurance, and new masks. Fire destroyed the three-storey building occupied by Mr. Mauro's billiard room. The building had been erected by Joseph Cooper about 1900 as a boarding house and later converted to The Lyceum moving picture house. A lumber storage building at Mr. W.J. Denniss' mill with both dressed and dry lumber went up in flames. The fire brigade valiantly saved three large gasoline tanks mounted on wooden supports thus preventing a greater eruption. There was no insurance. In July a similar fire burned an estimated 100,000 board feet of lumber in George Tennant's mill yard.

On June 7 a fire in the skating rink, built by John Dunn in 1901, was discovered by Mr. James Hardy of the Albion Hotel. The four-inch water mains were not enough to put the fire out. Firemen managed to attach some hoses to the six-inch mains on Manitoba Street and together with heavy rain managed to get control. Large pieces of burning shingles were blown across town as far as the public school. The reflection of the conflagration could be seen from Gravenhurst. It was a great loss for Mr. Dunn who had little insurance. All hockey equipment for teams was also lost. Police suspected arson. George Yearley had John Dunn & Sons construct a new 90-foot by 109-foot rink on the present arena site, with an ice surface 175 by 75 feet and seating for 1,000, and two sheets for curling. Additional land was purchased from Jos. N. Bird.

Arson was also suspected in the November fire in Mr. J.H. Burton's store on Manitoba Street. There was a considerable loss of stock. A fire in his residence on August 27 started in the garage when a car gas tank exploded. He lost a snowmobile and car.

A July 22 fire completely destroyed the home of Mr. Wm. McNabb, Monck. Neighbours saved the furniture and fought the flames but wells were soon emptied. The Queen's Hotel garage burned destroying five cars and one truck.

Fire destroyed 15 buildings including the Port Carling Boat Works in a huge fire October 28. It started in the basement of Hanna Co. store. The fire early on destroyed the electrical power so firemen lost use of their electric fire pumps. A bucket brigade worked until gasoline-powered water pumps could arrive from Bracebridge and Bala. All Muskoka sympathized.

*Road access to Bracebridge from the south had never been satisfactory due to the hilly terrain traversed by earlier routes. Construction of what is today Ecclestone Drive up around the southeastern flank of Bracebridge Bay provided a less tortuous and precipitous roadway capable of handling growing automobile traffic, and it avoided two railway crossings with limited visibility. In this picture the new road awaits only paving and additional fencing. At the base of the falls is the water-powered pumphouse for the railway water tank above.* COURTESY OF THE TOWN OF BRACEBRIDGE

Three people drowned in Muskoka during the year: Irwin Leeder, 15, at High Falls; Edward Lane, knocked off the *Sagamo* at Port Carling; and Gerald Gernakus, 16, in the south branch near Crozier's Falls.

The Board of Trade had two new buoys, one lit by gas, placed at the mouth of the river. They were built in town by Mr. B.Y. McBride under the direction of engineer Arthurs, Parry Sound.

The Hutchison Brothers completely remodelled their store. Brick veneer was put on Fenn, Anderson & Co., owned by Dr. J.W.B. Topp. Mr. A. Denniss opened a repair shop in the rear of the *Herald*, sharpening knives and scissors, building and fixing cabinets, and doing upholstery work. James Passmore reopened his butcher business in Chancery Lane.

By fall the Bird Mill had nearly its full staff working as a result of getting material for government programs and the change in tariffs.

Jim Thomson, local agent for car and truck licences, had sold over 1,000 already in the year. By November auto licences were paid on a cylinder basis instead of horsepower. Up to four cylinders the rate was $7 (up from $5); six-cylinder $12 (up from $6); and eight-cylinder $20.

With the closing of the tanneries and general depression in Bracebridge the population only dropped from 2,477 in 1930 to 2,435 in 1931. The decrease was in Wards 3 and 4.

Help, in the form of a good meal and some work, was available for unemployed at the stone cottage (town jail). Lists of unemployed men were to be completed by August 31 and wired to Mr. J.A. Ellis, secretary of the Unemployment Committee, Toronto. A real effort was being made to provide work for the coming winter. Bracebridge had 208 unemployed men registered, 112 of whom were married. Draper had 56, Monck 115, and Macaulay 100.

By mid-November 1,000 to 1,200 men were cut off

relief to save government money. The unemployment situation was becoming serious. Lumbering was gone.

The Legion annual meeting for all ex-servicemen saw Rev. J.S. Smedley elected president and Will Towns vice president.

The year 1930 was a record one for the Bracebridge Public Library, with 308 volumes added to the collection, and 845 borrowers.

Bracebridge Memorial Hospital installed special light signal systems, one for use by patients and one for emergency calls. Emergency lights for the operating room were devised and prepared by H.J. Bird and installed by Edward Ball with fixtures donated by Canadian General Electric. In August over 4,000 people crowded into Jubilee Park from all over the district for a street and band concert held to aid the hospital. George McKay of Dorset won the new Plymouth car and drove it home. Mr. Alb McKaye of Beaumaris and his brother donated an elevator and equipment to the hospital. November saw a petition for a new wing for the hospital. It was granted.

Bell Telephone removed poles from the business section and placed them behind the stores on the east side.

An estimated 5,000 people attended the Fall Fair, and in November the South Muskoka Agricultural Society purchased property formerly owned by John McWade. Forty-eight schools participated in a school fair parade and enjoyed contests such as mouth organ, vocal quartets, public address, first aid, and physical exercise.

It was an extremely dry summer, hay was short, and the crops poor. Muskoka statistics for 1930: 46,204 acres under cultivation, including wheat 480, oats 12,797; barley 992, peas 281, beans 15, rye 45, buckwheat 370, flax 7, mixed grains 654, corn 3,050, potatoes 986, turnips 324, sugar beets 4, sweet clover 34, alfalfa 81, carrots 30, and hay and clover. Muskoka ranked 15th out of 54 counties and districts on value per acre at $18.53. We had 2,917 horses, 15,242 cattle, 7,722 sheep, 6,117 swine, and 89,904 poultry.

Interesting visitors included three young men from Cobalt who stayed the night on their way skiing to Toronto on one long pair of skis with three sets of footholds ... The millionth Ford car to be made in Canada visited in May.

Bailey's Aces became both the Bracebridge Town League and district champions and had their picture in the Toronto *Telegram*. Irvine "Ace" Bailey gave a banquet for the team at the Queen's Hotel. The players were Walter Reynolds, Jack Everett, Frank Bailey, Joe Grozek, Lorne White, Spence Bickmore, Jack Elliott, Douglas Prentiss, Alvin Peacock, Clifford Davies, with coach Cornie Reynolds and trainer William Fraser. The Bracebridge High School hockey team won the Slater Cup. Bracebridge Juniors won the district.

One hundred participated in a carnival on the rink at Cedar Beach. Ten rinks of curling were organized by Pres. E.A. Whitten. The Palmer rink skipped by Charles Penistone won the Thomas Challenge Cup. Other sports were box lacrosse, lawn bowling, rugby, curling, and skating.

On December 22 Santa Claus and Jack Frost came to the Community Christmas Tree to give a present to each boy and girl. Heavy rain washed out the band and choirs but Mr. Yearley promised each free skating on opening day of the new rink.

Alvin Fry was elected to attend Ontario Boy's Parliament after a stiff race against Francis Rise of Huntsville.

Municipal politicians were all acclaimed before the new municipal election date of November 30.

Deaths included Captain William Bradshaw, 52, born in Bracebridge, became a captain of the *Cherokee* with the Muskoka Navigation Company in 1907 ... Christine Humphries, 77, came in 1879 ... John Reid, here over 50 years, built the Ward school and was also an auctioneer ... Mr. Spreadborough, 60, long-time employee of the hydro commission ... Mrs. Selena Mosey, 80, came in 1878 with James G. Hillman, who had a hardware business. After he died 1895 she married W. H. Mosey.

## 1932

The population of Canada according to the 1931 census was 10,353,778, an increase of 17.82 percent in 10 years. Muskoka's population was 18,278 with 8,255 in towns and villages. Per capita water consumption in Bracebridge during the previous year was 41 gallons.

The year started with green grass on the lawns. On

*By the 1930s cars outnumbered horses on Manitoba Street, and the road had been paved. This was not only the main street, but also, until the 1950s, the Ferguson Highway (Highway 11).* COURTESY OF THE TOWN OF BRACEBRIDGE

March 17 the snowplow made the trip from Huntsville to Severn – first time the road had been plowed that season.

The Hon. Wm. Finlayson, Northern Development, reported that the Ferguson Highway was built to develop tourism to help replace lumbering, that all but 40 miles were paved from Severn to North Bay, and that $711,028 had been spent in Muskoka in 1931 in the form of direct grants, bridges, and unemployment benefits.

Our new two-storey brick veneer hospital wing with 20 patient beds was completed. President Major Lyndon of the Hospital Board reported they now had 34 beds for adults and four for infants. There were four nurses with one supervisor, two orderlies, and one cook and a maid. The Red Cross received a cheque for $121.58 from the Women's Patriotic League, purchased a washing machine and cooking utensils for the hospital, and advertised for volunteers to mend and sew and to sew new clothes for the needy. It also received donations of 5 quilts, 24 pairs of socks, 4 suits, 10 layettes, and material for curtains for 20 windows.

Dr. Herbert A. Bruce, eminent Toronto surgeon, gave a $500 operating table with all the up-to-date attachments and electric heating to the hospital.

Mr. Tipper, agricultural representative, organized a boys' potato club for 12 to 20-year-olds. They could buy a 60-cent bag of certified Dorley, Russel, or New York potatoes to plant and keep records of their work. The purpose of this club was twofold: it was a worthwhile project, and it would introduce new varieties of potatoes into Muskoka.

The Game Protection Association, composed of people interested in the protection of game and fish, held its first meeting in January. The 40 people present elected Axiel Milne as president.

The Horticultural Society met with 90 members to elect Mrs. McGibbon chairman and Mrs. W. Galbraith vice chairman.

Vic Merithew and Ben Hewick, both 22, of St. Catharines, stopped on their way roller skating across Canada. They had travelled 1,190 miles covering about 45 miles a day.

Mr. George W. Ecclestone retired from the legislature after 16 years, to be replaced by S.H. Armstrong, who later died in office. Judge Mahaffy completed 20 years as District Judge.

Fire destroyed the dwelling of Mr. and Mrs. Lou Landon, Woodchester Ave., and all its contents. In April, an early morning fire broke out in the basement of the Muskoka Garage on Manitoba Street. Dense smoke ensued from a Cadillac car with considerable smoke in the Dodge showroom owned by D'Alton J. Armstrong. The fire broke out again and spread to the roof of Mr. Keeler's building which it practically destroyed.

In February, every seat in the new arena was sold and the standing room was full with 1,050 having paid admission to a carnival. A main drawing card was Ace Bailey and King Clancy of the Toronto Maple Leafs. There was a burlesque game of the clerks vs. firemen, an unemployed married men's race, and much more. Ace Bailey was the star of the Stanley Cup playoffs when the Toronto Maple Leafs beat the New York Rangers.

The Citizen's Band opened the box lacrosse meeting with a march followed by a recitation by Harry Ball, a Negro impersonation by Mr. Leslie Hart, and a piano piece by Mr. Jerome Mauro accompanied by his brother Norman. J.W. Reid was elected president and Geo. F. Gibson vice president, and it was decided to form a Tri-County League with teams from Bracebridge, Gravenhurst, Huntsville, Orillia, Barrie, Midland, and Camp Borden. On September 26, a game between Bracebridge and Gravenhurst drew 2,000 fans. Our valiant team consisted of Don and Ivan Gavin, W. Cudmore, Doug and L. Prentiss, C. Bruce, C. Woods, Ted Reid, C. Davis, Jack Foster, Tom Dankins, and Alvin Fry.

Despite the sports, concerts ,and contests, signs of the continuing difficult economic times were everywhere. Town Council gave their staff a 10 percent pay cut. Chief of police F.W. Sander now got $1,000 plus one uniform a year, but he was also to collect poll and dog taxes. Road overseer D. Kirkness got $80 a month, teamster A. Leishman $75 a month, and assessor R.H. Thompson $225 a year. The Board of Education cut teachers' salaries by 10 percent to take effect in the fall and decided not to open the Ward 4 school in September, which would cut one mill off the budget. Medora Township had 22 properties for sale for tax arrears, for $7.26 to $700-plus; Wood had 24 properties, McLean 18, Macaulay 18. However, taxes of $72.90 against Kelvin Grove Park were struck off by Town Council.

Some current prices were: eggs 15 cents a dozen, flannelette 10 cents a yard, broadcloth 15 cents, thread five for 29 cents, men's rubbers with leather tops $3.45, Mackinaw breeches $2.95, heavy wool socks 17 cents.

The town secured wood lots giving employment cutting wood needed for public buildings. A bylaw, aimed at peddlers, was passed prohibiting the retail sale of meat, vegetables, grain, hay, fruit, beverages, and small ware.

The library had never been so popular with 944 members, 238 volumes purchased, 5,791 books in the collection, and circulation of nearly 18,000. The reading room was wonderfully well patronized. The estate of John Walker donated 2,400 volumes.

The *Queen of the Isles* sank at the dock in about 20 feet of water in February, at the foot of Wellington Street.

A Highway Traffic Act amendment compelled motorcars to be equipped with lights that would illuminate the highway for a distance of 200 feet, and also cut the length of truck-trains from 65 to 50 feet.

The Township of Medora and Wood purchased Muskoka Lakes Telephone for $11,500. The lines ran from Bala to Port Carling and Juddhaven with two lines to Bracebridge from the central in Port Carling. Work commenced on the hydroelectric pole line from Bracebridge to Baysville and Dorset. The formal opening of the electric system in Baysville took place June 30 with Mr. Joseph Aldred, 82, their oldest resident, turning on the switch.

The Bird Woollen Mill installed an up-to-date sprinkler system attached to an eight-inch pipe. They were going back to doing custom work, that is, taking in farmer's wool and making cloth, blankets, and yarn.

Northern Planing Mills Ltd. had a new 90-foot-long sign on their roof painted by Rex Morris.

Bracebridge's leap year baby was the son of Mr. and Mrs. John W. MacDonald, born at Miss Stroud's nursing home ... In March profound sympathy was sent from every Muskoka family to the Lindberghs in response to the kidnapping of their baby.

The arts scene included *A Southern Cinderella*, a three-act comedy presented in Bracebridge and Gravenhurst by the United Church Ladies Aid with Mrs. E.G. Ellis as lead; an organ recital at Knox Presbyterian Church featuring Mr. C. Franklin Legge, organist of Westminster Central United Church, Toronto; a Canadian Art Show in the high school auditorium with Mr. Carl Shearer, Toronto, as lecturer to the exhibits and the works of Herbert S. Palmer. The three-act play *Crafty Grandpa*, choirs, dances and drills, gymnastics, and a trumpet solo by Ron McKay were all part of the high school commencement in November.

To raise funds the Boy Scouts made and sold bird houses. They also collected 23 dozen eggs on April 2, giving 10 dozen to the hospital and 11 dozen to needy families as their Easter good turn.

The patrol of Boy Scouts left for Toronto to take part in a British Empire Jamboree. Those going included Cecil Aulph, Harold Bates, Allan Hives, Edgar Willoughby, Will and Jack Kinsey, Hubert Jackson, and Wilbur Anderson.

Windows at St. Thomas' Church were dedicated to the late Bishop Thornloe, Bishop of Algoma 1897-1926, and unveiled by Mr. William Kirk.

The 37th Conference for the Eastern Ontario Free Methodist Church was held in town with 150 delegates. Mr. M.D. Shier was selected conference superintendent while Bishop G.W. Griffith, Los Angeles, opened the conference.

The Baptist Young People held a "Five Star Rally" Convention on September 5 with guests from Parry Sound, Burk's Falls, Huntsville, and Gravenhurst.

The official visit of Right Rev. Rocksborough R. Smith, Lord Bishop of Algoma to St. Thomas Church, took place in September.

The newly erected Roman Catholic Church at Norway Point was consecrated by His Lordship, Bishop O'Connor and the Very Reverend Dean O'Leary on August 19.

Mr. Greb of Windsor was a new teacher at the high school.

The Bracebridge Fall Fair committee with president Thomas Gray, 1st vice president John Hammell, and 2nd vice president Bert Buck, reported that entries were up 500 over previous years. They gave out $1,963.75 in prizes. Twelve local schools were represented in the children's parade. Miss Scovell's class won the prize for town schools. The farmers' horse race was won by Mr. James Watt; Dan McNaughtan's team won the heavy horse draw with 29 feet. In total there were 16 competitions including horseshoe pitching, athletic events, three ball games, etc. Twenty-seven schools took part in the school fair in Muskoka, one of 517 such fairs across Ontario. Young people who won a free trip to the Royal Winter Fair were Walter Taylor and Jewel Shier.

The annual plowing match was held at Tom Ball's farm on October 18 for the Echardt Trophy which was a silver tea service worth $50.

The Board of Trade announced that for July, August, and the first 10 days of September, 3,709 cars with 11,740 people stopped for information.

It was a very wet fall – too wet to harvest grain and root crops. H.L. Goltz won 4th prize in peas and 16th in barley at the Great Grain Show in Chicago.

The Bracebridge Hockey Club Executive hired hockey coach Mr. Bud Fisher for our local OHA teams. He had been a former goalie for the Grimsby Beach Kings before turning professional with Chicago in 1926.

Deaths included Frank Beaumont and his nephew, Jack, who drowned off the *Alporto* near Beaumaris ... Mrs. J.M. Bird, nee Miss Nellie A. Smith, who came here in 1898 ... Mrs. William Bower, came to Macaulay in 1862. Her husband (died 1902) helped chop out the road from Bracebridge to Falkenburg and did the first improvements on the Alport farm now owned by Beaumonts ... Harry Bowyer, 80, came in 1868 and established a marble business ... Mrs. George Bunting, 79, came in 1882 ... George Bunting, 80, died one month later ... Aboil Leishman, 64, 28-year member of the fire brigade, came with his father in 1878 ...Edward Pickles,

*The Waite's Bakery delivery sleigh, family home, and horse stable on Ontario Street, about 1933. The home was bricked over in 1942 with locally made brick.* COURTESY OF THE WAITE FAMILY COLLECTION

80, resident for 25 years ... John T. Shier, 57, came in 1897 as manager of J.D. Shier's Planing Factory, later in partnership with George Tennant ... Dr. J.W.B. Topp, 70, came in 1874 with his parents, practised dentistry for 45 years.

**1933** The Depression deepened. Macaulay ratepayers were informed that "owing to the financial condition of this Township we will not be able to supply relief assistance much longer ... single men will be put off the list. We deeply regret this move." On Hunt's Hill several houses were burgled with mostly food being taken. When spring came all gifts of clothing were discontinued. Seeds were supplied and people urged to plant gardens for their own vegetables. It was publicized that if caught driving a car no relief would be provided the following winter.

On the brighter side, Minett-Shields boat builders started back to work and hired several former employees, and the Bird Woollen Mill was paying 15 cents a pound for unwashed wool in good condition.

Social events during the year included *The Four Leaf Shamrock* presented at the Town Hall by St. Joseph's Church Dramatic Club in March, a three-church Young Peoples play *Fireside Hours*, and a series of discussions and fellowship. The Boy's Band, an auxiliary of the Citizen's Band under the instruction of Mr. John Morra, played *Let Mary Lou Do It* for the United Church Ladies Aid. Rabbi Eisendrath, former Toronto radio orator, spoke at the Trinity Men's Class. This was the 10th season of Monday night concerts by the Citizen's Band. Orillia and Bracebridge did several exchange band concerts. A fine concert was held at the United Church hall with the 26-piece Orillia Little Symphony Orchestra. The Dominion Festival Co. matinee and evening performance sponsored by the Clef Club included J. Franklin Cavery chalk drawings and the Paul Feddeson Artist Co. The Hockey Club cleared $67.45 on their minstrel show in December. The Horticultural Society's decidedly successful tulip show in the Town Hall and a peony show were held in June, with set-up by the Brobst Forestry Co.

The Dominion government purchased 200 acres to establish a landing field for airplanes at Reay as relief work. Highways proposed for improvement were Foot's Bay to Parry Sound, Huntsville-Dwight-Dorset, Bracebridge-Baysville-Norway Point, and the Watt Road from the Parry Sound highway to Windermere.

The road was gravelled and the new bridge over the rock cut completed (5th bridge for us) at cost of $912.90. Cutting, splitting, and handling wood for the wharf and schools cost $87.00. Repairing Tennant's hill cost $142.50. In total the town found relief for 109 men for 2,190 days for $4,500.

Relief work was agreed upon at one-third to be paid by provincial and one-third by Dominion governments to put water mains in Ontario Street. Dominion of Canada 1933 Refunding Loans were issued for two years at 3½ percent , six years at 4 percent.

Council set the tax rate at 52 mills: schools 23.7, library 1.17, band and hospital 1 each, debentures 12.5, general 12.88. Ratepayers could pay taxes in four instalments. The library continued to thrive, with circulation exceeding 1932 by over 1,000. Council decided on a curfew bell at 9:00 p.m. so that no children under 14 would be allowed on the streets alone.

The Board of Education chairman was G.W. Brooks, the secretary A.C. Salmon at $200 a year, and the truant officer Joseph Pelletier. Cups and saucers and several large coffee pots were purchased for Bracebridge High School. Mr. Donald Stirling was hired as vice principal at BHS.

John Keeler was named returning officer for Muskoka-Ontario when Mr. Rice resigned. The townships of Rama, Mara, Thorah, and Buck were added to the provincial Muskoka-Ontario riding.

Colonel, The Honourable W.H. Price, Attorney-General of Ontario, visited Bracebridge.

The South Muskoka Agricultural Society had 145 members. President Thomas Gray reported receipts of $2,469.77, expenditures of $1,974.50 in prizes with over 3,224 entries in the Fair.

Officers of the 19-member fire brigade were Chief A.E. Ecclestone, 1st Lieutenant Bert Tibbett, Captain of hook and ladder, Arthur Moore, and foreman of hose, Leslie Black.

In May Council decided to sell the fire horses and authorized purchase of a fire truck for $1,500. Teams for road work would be hired as needed. The town fire team had its final run July 3 to a roof fire at the residence of Reg Hines. C.W. Archer purchased the team and took it by barge to Browning Island.

The annual December Firemen's Ball was well attended and featured Elliot Porter and orchestra from Orillia, one of the finest dance bands in Ontario.

In July Bylaw 400 was passed "that all reels engines and vehicles of the Fire Department shall have the RIGHT OF WAY on the streets and highways of Bracebridge while proceeding to a fire or while answering a fire alarm. All vehicles should draw to the side of the street until the truck passes."

Separate fires destroyed two homes and two barns with the year's crop and various equipment. There were very bad bush fires near Bala with cinders falling as far as Gravenhurst.

A severe storm blew down trees and sent a lightning bolt that struck and killed Miss Monica Mahon, 17, daughter of Mr. and Mrs. S. Mahon, Port Carling.

The Hospital Board, with chairman, Mayor A.A. Lyndon, and secretary-treasurer J.A. Hutchinson, was given permission to erect a sign at the corner of Ann and Manitoba streets. Hospital liability was $5,000 for a new furnace. Four new private wards with bathrooms were installed in 1933. Mr. Carl Borntraeger, Pittsburgh, donated $1,000 to the hospital in memory of his brother, Henry.

Motorcar accidents were becoming much more common. In 1932, 8,733 men, women, and children were injured or killed on the highways. The most serious motor collision in Muskoka occurred just north of town, ending in one fatality and other driver being charged with manslaughter.

P.J. Marrin's horse ran away on Queen's Hill. It fell at the foot of the hill, broke its leg, and had to be shot.

A major spring tragedy involved the drowning deaths of two fine young men, Ernest Bland, 20, only son of Mr. and Mrs. Willie Bland, and Ronald McNaughtan, 19.

*Irvine "Ace" Bailey (1903-1992). A member of the Hockey Hall of Fame, he was a star forward with the Toronto Maple Leafs. In 1929 he won the Whiteman's Cup for the most goals in the NHL. He received a $100-watch plus $500 as the Most Valuable Player.* COURTESY OF THE BRACEBRIDGE SPORTS HALL OF FAME

second son of Mr. and Mrs. Peter McNaughtan. They were canoeing on the south branch of the Muskoka River just below the falls when they capsized in an eddy. Volunteers dragged the river with a great rake and teams on each side. One body was recovered quickly but the other took days to find. Thomas Seaton of Toronto drowned at Bala when his canoe upset. On July 31 Ther Lockheed, a young farmer in Muskoka Township, accidentally shot and killed himself while hunting porcupines.

Mr. G.W. Boyer was appointed collector of customs and excise to succeed superannuated Mr. R.A. Findlay (the first collector) at the year end. Collected were $26,102 in duties and $12,003 in excise ... Dr. E.G. Ellis moved his office and residence to north Manitoba Street, two doors north of Snider's Service Station.

The Department of Agriculture in Huntsville made seed grain available for the following prices: Alaska Oats 85 cents a bushel, barley 90 cents, Marquis wheat $1.10, Golden Vine peas $1.85, delivered to the nearest railway station.

Navigation opened April 29 with the *Waome* being the first steamer up river.

In a final tennis tournament Bracebridge beat Gravenhurst. Members were Messrs. W.W. Creswick, L.J. Stamp, Dr. Ryan, D.C. Thomas, Renard McKay, Elwood White, Gordon Taplen, and Esmond Scovell. The Tennis Club president was W.W. Creswick and the secretary Miss Arla McKay.

The Whitten rink won the season's curling. Fifty members in total enjoyed curling. The 30-year-old curling rink was torn down, as it had not been used for two years. The Ski Club had 48 members.

The Toronto Maple Leafs won the Stanley Cup and had a film made about them called *Hockey Champions*.

At the annual meeting of the OHA, hockey rules were revised to make overtime periods 10 minutes instead of 30. Also, any player fighting would receive an automatic one-game suspension. E.A. Walker was president of the Bracebridge Hockey Club.

On April 23 Rev. G.L. Lowe and Rev. Ben Wood were ordained at St. Thomas' Anglican Church by Lord Bishop of Algoma, Rt. Rev. Roxborough B. Smith.

The consecration of the Collegiate Church of St. John the Evangelist took place with clergy and a choir from Toronto under the direction of Mr. Healey Williams. Representatives from every Anglican order for men on the continent were in attendance. The conservatory was entirely built of Muskoka materials by Muskoka men. There was also a blessing of the Anglican Convent of Sisters of Ste. Margaret October 17 with Rt. Rev. Roxborough Smith. They purchased the residence of Miss L. Bickmore on Toronto Street hoping to start an orphanage. Mr. Cecil Yearley had the contract for remodelling.

A handsome communion table was presented to the Knox Church by Mrs. A.W. Wallis, wife of the late pastor. A Knox choir practice and social were held by organist Mr. B.R. Minns

One hundred and twenty-five representatives of Young People's Societies in Muskoka met for the formation of a Young People's Union for the district.

An open air service was held in Memorial Park by the local the Ministerial Association, with a farewell message by Adj. Watkin of the Salvation Army. Rev. A.C. Hie was president of the association, which also included Rev. A Eickenaar, Rev. P.W. MacInnis, and Rev. William Farmer.

Council Bylaw 585 was passed for the sale and transfer of certain property on Thomas and Main streets to Messrs. Frowe, Muskoka Trading Company.

A pasteurization plant was installed in the Dominion House by Ernest Taylor of Ashgrove Dairy. It consisted of a 400-quart tank heated to 100° for 30 minutes and then rapidly cooled by a two-ton ice-making machine; it could pasteurize 1,500 quarts a day. He would cover the routes of T.J. Ball, Harvey Gray, and E.E. Taylor.

The Ontario Retail Lumber Dealers met to discuss trade matters and the building outlook. Representatives came from Bracebridge, Gravenhurst, Huntsville, Parry Sound, Orillia, Sudbury, Toronto, and Midland.

In September, Miss Evelyn Gray and Mr. Stan Einarson represented Bracebridge at the Canadian National Exhibition as guests of the William Wrigley Company.

An unknown donor [G.W. Ecclestone] paid for a new roof on the bandstand.

Mr. Philip Thomas successfully completed the course at the Ontario College of Optometry.

A vote was held July 19, 1933, to ask "are you in

*The* Islander *and* Queen of the Isles *(left) at Bracebridge Wharf, 1932. The latter, a hardy little tug owned by Captain Levi Fraser, was nearing the end of her busy 39-year life on the Muskoka River and lakes. She had been originally put in service in 1885 by the Beardmore Tannery to tow scows of hemlock bark; Fraser purchased her in 1920 and used her to haul lumber. She was retired in 1934.* COURTESY OF THE BRACEBRIDGE PUBLIC LIBRARY

favour of the establishment of government liquor stores for the sale of liquor under the Liquor Control Act?" The result was a resounding "No."

The annual Children's Aid report indicated a very hard year for those trying to help the poor and needy. "There are so many that it is almost impossible to help all as much as we would have liked." There were 33 applications for children, nine children made wards, two sent to Industrial School, 11 new cases under the Children of Unmarried Parents Act, and 304 complaints – no work for the fathers to feed the children or buy them clothing for school.

The 50th anniversary of the Salvation Army in Bracebridge occurred November 19. Captain G. Wagner and Major A. Steele, District Commander from Orillia, conducted the meeting followed by music and lunch.

The 4th annual Community Christmas Tree was held December 15 with over 1,000 children each receiving candy, fruit, and a scribbler. The band played and choirs sang as Santa arrived on a sleigh with three reindeer to be given a civic welcome by Mayor Richards.

Bracebridge had 76 births, 36 marriages, and 48 deaths in 1933. The District of Muskoka total assessed population was 18,123. Bracebridge had 2,351; Huntsville 2,507, Gravenhurst 1,830, and Port Carling 508. Mayor Richards was acclaimed for his third term.

Deaths during the year included John Thomson, 76. He came in 1876, owned and operated a drugstore for many years, was mayor 1899-1901, served on Council and the Water, Light & Power Commission. He helped start the Mechanics Institute, sat on the school board, and was an enthusiastic supporter of cricket and lacrosse ... Mrs. Martha Beaumont, 90, wife of the late J.J. Beaumont, moved to Alport farm in 1888 ... Fred Cochrane, 66, station agent for many years and soloist cornetist in band ... John Cole, 74, 50-year resident and former town employee ... James L. Fenn Sr., came to town over 60 years earlier and contributed largely to building the Methodist Church and to the education and industrial life of the community ... George Foulkes, 85, came in 1867 ... Mrs. Thomas Lundy, 78, resident since 1894 ...George Mills, 79, settled in Macaulay in 1877 and worked on railway construction to help build the line through Bracebridge ... Joseph Musson, 75, came to start the linen mill and stayed ... Mrs. John Yeoman, 82, nee Mary Jane McNairney. She came in the 1860s, lived just off Gibbs Road, a member of the third family to settle here.

## 1934

Drought, wrestling, and relief were all part of our history this year.

At the inaugural Council meeting R.A. Findley was appointed assessor for $200. The old Cobb property on lots 20 and 21, concession 1 in Draper was purchased as a wood lot for municipal relief work. A.C. Salmon completed 35 years as town clerk, succeeding the late James Boyer. Later, Mr. Salmon was appointed sheriff for Muskoka District.

Council reported 37 men, women, and children on relief in town. Muskoka Mother's Allowance had 49 beneficiaries. The Children's Aid Society reported that many people were moving up from the city to take up old farms in the back part of the district, but with no rural experience. Statistics showed 37 applications for children, 14 wards placed out in homes, 80 wards visited, 18 new cases under the Unmarried Parent's Act, and six under the Adoptions Act with five more nearly completed.

Extremely cold winter weather limited water in the town reservoir. The Water, Light & Power Commission asked people to not let their taps drip. By spring, there was an acute water shortage. A dry summer marked by many bush fires followed. By August, Council met to pass a bylaw to issue $30,000 in debentures to bring in the Peake springs and a deputation went to Toronto to request the project be allowed as relief work. The estimated flow was 166 gallons a minute or an increase of 25 percent over the existing supply. By mid-November the project was completed at a cost of $9,000, the province paying 80 percent.

All of Ontario faced aridity but not as severe as Saskatchewan which was in its sixth year of terrible drought. A letter to the local paper asked for help. Brownish snow fell over Muskoka in December. Analyzed samples showed mica, feldspar, and quartz which scientists said came from dust storms in the southern states.

A deputation 50 strong from Muskoka went to see the Hon. Wm. Findleyson, Minister of Northern Development, requesting paving of the Lakeshore Highway (Gravenhurst-Bala-Port Carling-Bracebridge).

The stables behind the firehall were remodelled for the ladder wagon and equipment.

A plant was started on the British Lion property to make cement tile for street drainage. Relief work was overseen by the road and bridge committee.

The Red Cross Women's Auxiliary collected much clothing for the needy. Mr. Carl Borntraeger, Pittsburgh, donated $1,600 to hospital for a new x-ray machine in memory of his late son Carl. He had been a summer resident of Beaumaris for 30 years. The hospital advertised for vegetables, fruits, and other foods as it was very difficult to get cash to pay for supplies.

There were a great many untimely deaths during the year. The steamer *Waome* sank in a sudden gale on Lake Muskoka October 11. Captain Henshaw, Captain Thompson, and Mr. Coxon drowned. Fourteen were killed in auto accidents – two when a train hit their car at Falkenburg. The coroner's inquest emphasized an urgent need for a "wig-wag" to make Moore's crossing safer.

Orrie Lunan of Baysville sat on seven sticks of dynamite and exploded them after leaving a note for his friends. David Toll, a hydro worker, died by driving his Ford coupe off the wharf and into 20 feet of water at Shier's mill. Norman Ruttan was found guilty of the manslaughter of Gordon Weiser, 14, of Ryde Township.

Thomas Prentice died when struck on the head by a flying rock from a dynamite blast while working on the Bracebridge to Milford Bay road. He left his wife and 13 children.

Hector Goltz, 20, son of H.E. Goltz, drowned at Wasaga Beach while trying to rescue a young woman. Tony Middlebrook drowned in Muskoka Bay.

Joe Feeney and Neil Pannana were arrested in town by provincial constable L.H. Hardwick after kidnapping a North Bay taxi driver. Feeney was sentenced to four years in penitentiary with lashes.

Ace Bailey suffered a fractured skull in a December game at Boston. For several days it was nip and tuck as to whether or not he would live. Gradually, his strong

*A rapid increase in the number of automobiles during the 1920s and 1930s resulted in a new variety of business: the service station. Here is the Bracebridge Garage, beside the library (the present post office building occupies this site now). Note the old gravity-feed gas pumps.* COURTESY OF BRENDA COX

constitution pulled him through. A benefit game was arranged with an all-star team vs. the Toronto Maple Leafs in Toronto. Bracebridge fans were offered a special CNR rate of $2.50 return, Washago to Toronto. A bus to the Gardens from the station for 25 cents and $1.65 admission meant local fans could go for $5.00 including lunch. Alan Hutchinson and Harry G. Everett organized the trip. Our Citizen's Band and 125 fans made up part of the 15,000 fans who went to the game raising $23,000 for the benefit fund. The Maple Leafs offered Ace a three-year contract as assistant to Mr. Selke.

Ten teams competed locally in curling. Bracebridge retained the Excelsior Cup. Dr. Ryan was the new president. The 53-member Ski Club invited Mr. E. Loosli, a professional ski instructor from Switzerland, to address their meeting. Forty went on their first hike. The town roads and bridges committee directed Mr. D. Kirkness, the road overseer, to erect three slides suitable for bob-sleds and two small ski jumps. The Skating Club was active with president Mrs. Austin Fryer. The junior hockey team won the northern section of the Tri-County League. Our high school team won the Slater Cup.

The 70-member Tennis Club, under president W.W. Creswick, joined the Ontario North Tennis Association. They sponsored a dance in the high school gym with an eight-piece orchestra.

Wrestling was once again big in town and in Port Carling. Between 400 and 500 spectators packed into the arena to see Chief War Eagle, Freddie Kuffer (131-lb. champion of Sweden), Young Sampson of Dallas, the Black Panther (160 lb.), Sammy George of Texas (162 lb.), Leo Fishbough (168-lb. Champion of Ohio), and Jack Hagen (170 lb., of the U.S. Navy). Chief War Eagle defended his Junior Light Weight Champion of the World title against Howard Martin of Detroit in the Bracebridge arena in September.

Bracebridge Bowling had 11 teams competing. Ladies Bowling held a bridge tournament to raise funds for the club house and greens on McMurray.

Wilbert Richards helped organize the Tri-County

*In 1934 the town roads and bridges committee directed Mr. D. Kirkness, roads overseer, to erect three slides suitable for bobsleds, and two ski jumps. By 1935 the 109-member Ski Club was holding slalom, downhill skiing, and ski-jumping events on Gibbs' Farm just north of town.* COURTESY OF JUDITH RUAN

Lacrosse League with teams from Milford Bay, Huntsville, Barrie, Allandale, Camp Borden, Owen Sound, Orillia, and Alliston.

Deaths during the year included Francis P. Warne, 80, councillor and member of the library board for many years. A lawyer, he was avid in tennis and curling … Mrs. Alex Barron (Frances Cooper), 73, who came with her family in 1867 … James B. Brown, 76, father of Mrs. Dr. McGibbon. He worked in lumbering here since age 16, was appointed homestead inspector 1906-26, married Miss Annie Boyd in 1882, and raised four children … John Burbridge, 75, drove the stage to Gravenhurst before the railway came … James L. Fenn Jr., 64, worked in hardware business with his father (Fenn, Anderson & Co.), married Miss Lavina Killen in 1889 …George Foulkes, 84, came to town in 1867 … Rev. Henry S. Good, 32, died after an appendix operation. His first church was the Bracebridge Baptist in 1930 … John Killen, 71, pioneer of Ziska, married Miss Margaret Grant and raised eight children … Mrs. A.A. Mahaffy (nee Alice Rosalie Thomson), 63, married Arthur Mahaffy in 1891 … James McFadden, who came to work for Shier Lumber in 1888, married Miss Sadie Bovair in 1892 … William McNeice, 74, resident over 50 years, active in the Masonic and IOOF lodges … Charles Meakin, 63, painter and decorator, member of Citizen's Band … Mrs. Solon Meeks came to town in 1881, one of our first Salvation Army members … Mrs. Fred Sander Sr. (nee Miss Sarah Ellen Jones), 76, resident over 50 years, mother of the chief of police.

Port Sydney was incorporated as a Village with Reeve James Lumbers.

The Department of Agriculture suggested farmers clean their surplus grain and have it graded at once to get a better price. A shortage of seed grain after the previous year's poor weather made early ordering advisable. Price was $0.90 to $1.25 a bushel for oats and barley.

The South Muskoka Agricultural Society celebrated its 60th annual fall fair with an old-time exhibit for farming and household equipment. Exhibits, baseball and softball tournaments, a midway, huge parade, and an old time concert made this the best fair ever held.

At the CNE H.L. Goltz won 1st in oats and barley, Roy Goltz of Bardsville won 1st in wheat, Bert Buck 2nd in Barred Rock, and Arthur E. Cox 1st in white leghorns.

The Victoria-Haliburton Regiment from Lindsay held a three-day visit here. They were entertained with a boxing show at the arena, excursions on the lakes, a day of sports, street dancing, and band concerts. Evening music was provided by the Regimental Band.

The Muskoka Municipal Association appointed a committee to investigate the question of controlling the speed of motorboats in narrow channels.

The Monck Municipal Telephone System executive comprised chairman Thomas Wallace, Messrs. Geo. Freemantle and W.J. Fitzmaurice, and secretary-treasurer. J. Byron Kaye.

Mr. L.W. Anderson was in charge of the tourist bureau near the new bridge but the Chamber of Commerce decided to close it. It soon reopened, and was sponsored by the Bird Woollen Co. with Mr. Vernon Corbett operating it as a business venture. Over 4,000 cars stopped there in August.

H. Hughes Lessee opened the White Rose Service Station on the Ferguson Highway. D'Alton Armstrong was granted permission to place two gas tanks on Manitoba Street ... Miss Patricia Johnson was appointed librarian to succeed Miss Dickie.

The Free Methodist district meeting and Christian Worker's Convention was held at the United Church December 6-9 with Rev. R.L. Casement. People came from Orillia, Housey's Rapids, Wydale, Huntsville, and from across the district.

Our fife and drum band attended the 100th anniversary of the Orangemen held in Toronto.

A St. Thomas' Church organ and choral recital was held with the Gregorian Association of Canada. The choir leader was Dr. Healy Willen, organist at Church of Ste. Mary Magdalane, Toronto. Rev. Father Rose of the SSJE conducted the service, assisted by Rev. Douglas Brown, Guelph.

A United Church program of midsummer music with Miss Roxyna Phillips of Edmonton, contralto vocalist soloist, Miss Georgie Golden, violin, Lulu Golden, organ, and Mrs. Anderson, also organ, was splendid.

The hockey team raised $125 by sponsoring the Billy Pritchard troupe from Toronto in a street concert of hillbilly music. They erected a large platform at south end of the business district. Amplified sound made the round and square dancing great fun.

A bylaw passed for places of business to observe the weekly half holiday and close at 1:30. They could be open full time two weeks before Christmas and any week that had Friday a holiday – this in effect until the end of April.

The 50th anniversary of the Fraserburg United Church was celebrated on September 23 with Rev. A. Carmen Hie conducting the ceremony.

After October 14 all persons owning or harbouring a dog without a licence were to be hauled before the magistrate.

Candy and a wearable gift for almost 1,000 children were given out at the Community Christmas Tree.

Mayor Richards was acclaimed for his fourth term.

*"Ox cart and ancient vehicles" in the Transportation Parade, Old Home Week, 1939. "Ancient" is obviously a relative term! The year 1939 was Bracebridge's 50th anniversary of attaining town status, but the summer festivities celebrating the event must have been tempered by the ominous signs of war in Europe.* COURTESY OF VICKY BILLINGSLEY

# 1935–1944

## *Our 7th Decade: Battling Cancer, Battling Hitler*

LOCAL MERCHANTS maintained a vibrant business community in 1935, improving their premises, moving to more suitable locations, and advertising their fine wares. H.A. Rogers modestly solicited "a share of your esteemed grocery and confectionery trade," and offered White Rose wheat flakes for 25¢, sardines at 5¢, and chocolates for 20¢.

Mrs. E.J. Neal offered to exchange a four-year-old cow for chicks. Harry Linney sold Excelsior Life insurance coverage for $25 a month for life at 65, or a lump sum of $3,125, "if income isn't needed." S. Nasser advertised ladies' silk bloomers for 35¢ and ladies' corselettes for 79¢. Barber and bandmaster John Morra cut adult's hair for 25¢, singed hair for 15¢, and shaved men for 15¢.

On Manitoba Street, Andrew T. Waite announced that his electric bakery would make cracked wheat bread and hot cross buns for Easter … The McColl-Frontenac Co. leased land from the Bird Woollen Mill and built a service station. It also housed the Bird's Information Bureau to assist tourists … J.H. Elliott added to his store … W.J. Stuthers sold chickens and eggs near the old Free Methodist Church … Armstrong's Meat on Chancery Lane offered teams of mules, brown horses, and bay horses for sale … William Kingsmill left the Bank of Nova Scotia and was succeeded by Harry Wilson … The Bank of Canada opened and put a handsome new set of bank notes in circulation … Mr. and Mrs. H.A. Rogers sold their grocery store on Queen's Hill to William Snazel, proprietor of Ridley Cleaners … Mah Jack, proprietor of the Grand Café, took 23 weeks, 18 days by CNR liner to visit his sick wife in south China … Verne Corbett and Will Greer opened the Aragon Grill, in the former Pure Food Restaurant … Leonard Prowse opened a radio and hardware business next to Keeler's Restaurant, formerly occupied by Ridley Cleaners before that business moved to the former H.A. Rogers grocery store.

Mrs. G.J. Simmons purchased the grocery business of James Thompson run by Gerard Simmons … George Armstrong operated the butcher business of his brother Roy in Chancery Lane … Charles Penistone moved his shoe repair equipment to the former Gibson Shoe Store … Ted Corbett opened a dental mechanics business in the Herald Building and charged $10 for artificial teeth. Extra teeth were 25¢ each … Walter Reynolds successfully passed his exams at embalming school.

Thomas Johnson, Crown Attorney and Clerk of the Peace for the District of Muskoka, retired after 45 years. He had succeeded F. Adair. Mr. Clairmont took over from Mr. Johnson.

Bracebridge Baptists held their 50th anniversary services and the Men's Own Bible Class of the United Church celebrated its 25th anniversary. Knox Presbyterian Church observed 60 years of service.

The churches in Bracebridge at this time were: Bethel Tabernacle, Pentecostal, pastor, Rev. H.E. Taylor; Baptist, pastor, Rev. A. Eikenaar; United, minister, Rev. A. Carman Hie; Free Methodist, pastor, Rev. J.S. Smedley; Knox Presbyterian, minister, Rev. P.W. MacInnes; Salvation Army, Adjutant and Mrs. Ward.

Mayor Wilbert Richards was re-elected by acclamation. Fred Sander, chief constable, A.C. Salmon, clerk-treasurer, and Orma Peacock, assistant, were all re-appointed.

The town finalized its takeover of Kelvin Grove Park on Bracebridge Bay from the trustees and mortgagor Mr. Mungo Park McKay. The former tourist motor park became a public park for both locals and visitors.

The new tax rate was 52 mills, the same as 1934. Council agreed to rent the former Ward 4 school for $1 a month to L.E. Lavoe to establish a knitting factory. A new pumper for the fire truck was purchased for $954.

George W. Ecclestone, former MPP for Muskoka, who was defeated with the George S. Henry Conservative government the year before, was honoured at a retirement banquet. Young Conservatives of Bracebridge formed, with George Brooks as president and Dr. Fraser M. Greig as secretary-treasurer.

In the federal election, Stephen Furniss, Liberal, won by a landslide over Dr. Peter McGibbon, Conservative, H.E. Rice, Reconstruction Party, and Arthur Shipman CCF. Prime Minister R.B. Bennett was unseated.

Rene M. Caisse, RN, had refined a native remedy and was treating cancer patients in Toronto. She healed a patient of local skeptic, Dr. A.F. Bastedo. He was so impressed that he made a presentation to Council to have Miss Caisse open a clinic in Bracebridge. Armed with a petition, a delegation including Frank Kelly, MPP, Mayor W. Richards, councillor Herb Rawson, councillor David Hodgson, Mr. J.K. Shier, and Mr. A.W. Tingey met with the Minister of Health to encourage him to let Rene Caisse practise her treatments for cancer. The mayor and Council were very supportive and readily agreed to rent Miss Caisse space in the former British Lion Hotel on Dominion Street at one dollar a year. They even helped to furnish an office, reception room, dispensary, and five treatment rooms. In late August Miss Caisse opened her cancer clinic in Bracebridge.

Miss Margaret Bird of the Red Cross Women's Auxiliary thanked Miss Sibbett for providing a large sewing room in the Sibbett Block, Peter McNaughton for his donation of a stove, and Mrs. Thompson for a sewing machine to repair used clothing. Superintendent Miss F. Arnott moved to New Liskeard and was succeeded by Ms. Cunningham.

This year the ice was such that people could skate down the river and all over the lake. The Skating Club with Mr. Leslie Tennant, president, held its carnival in the arena, featuring music by the Bracebridge Citizen's Band smartly attired in Bird's red mackinaw coats.

The 109-member Ski Club events included slalom, downhill skiing, and ski jumping on Gibbs' farm. The president was Dr. Fraser Greig, the 1st vice president Mrs. Cowan, the secretary G. Leslie Tennant, and the treasurer Miss MacMillan.

The Bracebridge Hockey Club was grateful to the Bird Woollen Mill for its donation of stockings, and to Bernard Wadsell for team sweaters. The club sponsored a minstrel show of southern melodies and jokes. R.M. Best was the interluder between acts, and Mr. Gordon Sloan of Gravenhurst was pianist.

The dazzling Bracebridge Ladies Hockey Team won against the Preston Rivulettes in the Ladies Ontario Hockey Association sudden death final.

Leonard Ellis was president of the four-team Softball League. The Bracebridge Bowling Club president was E.G. West, with vice president Mrs. Thomas and secretary-treasurer D.T. Hodgson. In May, the Tennis Club held a dance to open its season. For the more athletic young men, wrestling was in full swing in July and August.

A concert at the United Church featured Mrs. W.L. Anderson at the organ, Georgie Golden on violin, with Lulu Golden and Laura Munday as sopranos.

Miss Gertrude Hawn directed the Anglican Young People's Association play *It Happened in June* at the Town Hall.

Local residents and tourists alike flocked to the lakes to enjoy the elegant cruise steamships. The steamship *Sagamo* provided a 100-Mile Cruise daily in the Muskoka Lakes, and offered an orchestra, dancing, staterooms, and community singing for $2.50 each. The RMS *Mildred* sailed under Captain C.W. Archer on Tuesdays and Saturdays from the Bracebridge wharf at 8:30 a.m. For a round trip costing $1, the guests travelled through four lakes and three rivers, stopping at Pinelands on Lake Joseph for dinner.

A crowd of 4,000 attended the fall fair which offered family entertainment including the "The Human Torch" in his "Dive of Death" 100 feet into a tank of fire.

Fraternal societies provided community compassion and offered members great opportunities for service. The Ladies Orange Benevolent Association, No. 777, chose officers: Mrs. William Traves, Mrs. William Crozier, Mrs. Gordon Cole, Miss Hazel Fullerton, Mrs. A. Hammond, Mrs. George Hammond, Mrs. William Wray, Mrs. Ed Kirkpatrick, Miss M. Fullerton, Mrs. T. Vincent Sr., Mrs. William Naismith, Mrs. F. Taplin, Mrs. J. Ornsby, Mrs. C. Crowder, and Mrs. William Cudmore.

Royal Scarlet Chapter officers for 1935 were Arthur E. Cox, David Gray, William Crozier, William Wray, Jos. Mussen, Elmer H. Forbes, Melbourne Anderson, Ernest L. DeLarge, William J. Butler, Bryson Vincent, Lemmel Godfrey, and Gordon Cole.

The First Bracebridge Troop of Boy Scouts was reorganized by E. Dollimore and T. Hooton.

An old-time tea and concert was given by the Loyal Orange Lodge and LOBA at the Orange Hall. Mr. G.W. Boyer was chairman and his son Robert J. Boyer sang *Mother Machree*.

The newly organized Muskoka Tourist Development Association (MTDA) elected Bracebridge members Wilbert Richards, H.G. Everett, J.K. Shier, and H.J. Bird Jr. The MTDA planned publicity for Muskoka costing $16,000 for radio advertising, newspaper publicity in the United States, distribution of booklets through government publicity departments, erection of signs, and the employment of a full-time secretary. The MTDA information bureau was opened June 3, south of Gravenhurst, by president A.H. Minett of Cleveland's House.

Meanwhile, the majority of inquiries to Mr. Corbett at the Bird's Information bureau were demanding to know the way to Callander, "where the quints are."

Nearly 4,000 two to four-year-old salmon and rainbow trout were dumped into Bracebridge Bay by the provincial game and fisheries department as an experiment.

At this time there was much discussion both federally and provincially to secure an area for a National Park along the Muskoka River from about High Falls north to Port Sydney.

Major Tudhope of the civil aviation department in Ottawa landed the first airplane at Reay Airport (Muskoka Airport) on August 23. The Trans-Canada Airlines plane was welcomed by manager W. Price.

The Canadian Automobile Chamber of Commerce reported 2,544 passenger cars and 396 commercial vehicles registered in Muskoka in 1934 ... Alex. J. Milne used his wrecker to pull a car out of the river at the Thomas Street bridge. The driver was wet but uninjured ... A car from Michigan rolled into the river from Bracebridge wharf while the driver was out watching the steamboats.

In March, heavy snow prompted the town to use its grader to clear ruts on the roads and make them convenient for trucks and sleighs. A mid-March heat wave brought pansies out in full at Mrs. B.Y. McBride's Manitoba Street home and Mr. and Mrs. M.P. McKay's tulips grew two inches in one day. The ice went out of the lake on April 25 and re-froze December 19. An earthquake was felt in Bracebridge at about 1:04 a.m. November 1, 1935, the most violent in Canada since 1874.

Jack McVittie built a log cottage on lakeshore property purchased from Herb Beaumont at the mouth of Alport Lake.

W.D. Forrest, superintendent of the Muskoka Children's Aid Society, reported that they had served 84 children. Thirty children under the Children of Unmarried Act were cared for and 15 homeless children were adopted.

Thirty soldiers of the 122nd Brigade D Company under the command of Lieutenant Lorne J. Stamp, and their bugle band, left for Huntsville for a week of manoeuvers.

Fire badly ravaged the Ontario Street home of Mr. and Mrs. L.J. Ellins, the summer home of George Tennant at Golden Beach (lightning), and the home of Dr. and Mrs. E.G. Ellis on Kimberley Avenue. A police alarm gong which could be heard all over town was installed in the fire tower to alert police by telephone.

The public library received 40 books from the Ontario Department of Education travelling library for a four-month period.

Deaths this year included Robert Henry Thompson, 69, came about 1896, served 22 years as town assessor ... Mrs. Elizabeth Moore, here since 1900 when she married William Sibbett, helped run the British Lion Hotel. He died and she later married Captain Moore who also predeceased her ... William J. Johnston, 84, came to Muskoka in 1863, was Port Carling's first postmaster ... Fred Macdonald, 23, his body found in his barn in Monck near the town line. He left a wife and young baby. Coroner E.G. Ellis investigated ... Mrs. Crispin Gibbs, 79, came to Wilson's Falls about 1885 ... William Gibbs, 60, married Miss Mary Ball in 1903, served on Council and the school board for Macaulay ... Mrs. George Spreadborough, 83 ... Mrs. Robert Patterson, 51, nee Lillian Fawcett ... Mr. Adamson, 85, decorator and painter ... Mr. William Kirkpatrick, moved in from Uffington about 1916 ... Mrs. A.T. Hewitt, nee Elizabeth, daughter of John Bailey ... Mr. William Holliday, 67, Macaulay carpenter, lumbermill owner until it burned in 1906 ... Mrs. Thomas Bowerman, 99, lived in the Queen's Hotel, a pioneer of the town, prominent with the Ladies' Aid of the Methodist Church, came to the area about 1870 ... Mrs. Daniel Olsen, 72, married in 1926, raised nine children, one of her four sons who went overseas was killed.

As part of the Andrew Carnegie centennial celebration a reproduction portrait of Mr. Carnegie was received by librarian Miss Patricia Johnson.

Miss Evelyn Davidson resigned from the Bracebridge High School and was replaced by Mr. W.R. Evanson.

The Canadian Legion arranged a May 6 celebration to recognize the jubilee of King George and Queen Mary to the throne. It was declared a public holiday with rockets, fire works, and a beacon fire on Ball's Hill.

Postmaster R.P. Perry received the Silver Jubilee Medal for being the oldest and longest serving employee of the Canadian post office.

Santa Claus attended the community Christmas tree in Memorial Park on December 23. He gave each girl and boy a gift of candies, popcorn, fruit, and a pair of stockings, and everyone sang carols.

## 1936

The town's flag was flown at half mast in honour of the death of HRH King George V on January 20. Radios were installed in three churches to receive the broadcast by the new King, Edward VIII.

Clerk-treasurer Alex C. Salmon was re-appointed at $812 a year, and assistant Miss Orma Peacock for $450. The weed inspector, John Phillips, was engaged for $25. Commissioner Reid was sworn in and George Tennant re-elected chairman of the Water, Light and Power Commission. Alex C. Salmon resigned in September and Wilbert Richards replaced him as clerk-treasurer. Edward J. Ball was superintendent.

Edward Hunt became chairman of the Board of Education, succeeding George. W. Brooks. A.C. Salmon was appointed secretary-treasurer for $180. Miss Katie Dinner resigned from the public school to be replaced by Kenneth Shier.

The triumph of the Muskoka Tourist Development Association's aggressive promotion of Muskoka meant an increase in business. Tourist resorts were busier,

*Motorists approaching the corner of Manitoba Street and Monck Road in 1936 would have to stop if they wanted to read all the destinations on this sign! The road leading away in this view, now District Road 4, was the main highway to Huntsville and beyond prior to the 1950s.* COURTESY OF REV. GEORGE JAMES

churches had larger congregations, telephone business expanded, and banks had more work due to the numbers of tourists.

To encourage winter tourism and sports, CNR offered one cent a mile round trip fares from Bracebridge to Toronto, Buffalo, Windsor, and Detroit. Trains for the winter season ran from Union Station to Huntsville in three-plus hours. It was formerly a five or six-hour trip.

Captain Levi R. Fraser of the Muskoka Municipal Association was appointed convener of a committee for a national park in Muskoka.

Dr. Fraser Greig opened offices in the Sibbett Block. The eastern side of Manitoba Street from the post office to Ecclestone and Bates was widened six feet. Hydrants and poles were removed. The fountain placed by WCTU in front of the post office 22 years previously was put on Thomas Street near the Muskoka Trading Company.

William F. Hammond added pasteurization equipment to his dairy in its new location next to Keiler's Restaurant, and the price of milk rose to 12 cents a quart.

Maher Shoes opened a branch store in the Burton Block with Harold Sloan as manager. Judge A.A. Mahaffy retired after 25 years as District Judge, and His Honour Judge E. Ainsley Wright was appointed to the job. William G. Gerhart retired as Crown lands agent and homesteads inspector, and Thomas Bruce took his place.

There were 27 box-holders on the rural delivery route No. 2 worked by Ivon Miles. Russell E. Salmon took over the McColl-Frontenac Red Indian (gas) Station from Fred Barker.

The Baptist Church built a two-storey schoolroom to accommodate a Sunday school classroom and a large assembly and banquet hall. The Glee Club gave a concert directed by Mrs. George Johnson. Rev. A.C. Hie left

*Rene Caisse opened her Bracebridge cancer clinic in 1935.* COURTESY OF THE BRACEBRIDGE PUBLIC LIBRARY

Bracebridge United Church and Rev. Archie L. Richards took his place.

Mrs. Hardwick's class produced "Vaudeville for 1936" on the new enlarged stage at the high school. Dancers included Evelyn Bates, Aileen Hines, Arla Jean Gavin, Patsy Parlett, Alma Peacock, and Norma Ecclestone. The St. Joseph's Church Dramatic Society presented *Blarney Street*, directed by Father Coffey and starring Joe Grozelle, Rita Caisse, Audrey Flynn, Louis Caisse, and others. The Clef Club arranged 11 events with Mrs. G.W. Skuce, president, Miss L. Scovell, 1st vice president, Miss C. Bird, secretary, and Miss L. Gerhart, treasurer. Poet Wilson MacDonald read at the high school.

A recital was given at the Cowley Fathers' Collegiate Church on a new Hammond electric organ. The Virginia Jubilee Singers, featuring music typical of the Negro people was presented by the United Church men's bible class, and Anglican Young People performed *Let's Get Married* at the Town Hall. The first summer concert of the Citizen's Band at Memorial Park introduced a new sousaphone. Openings for several instrument positions for boys were announced as well as plans to begin a girls' band.

The fire brigade arranged a big Labour Day program including a monster parade and hose-wagon race. Albert Ecclestone had been fire chief for over 30 years.

The *Herald* was behind in its printing schedule when the electric pot of the typesetting machine burned out.

Eva Duncan, 19, was burned to death in a July fire at Norma's Lunch in Port Carling. Smoke from bush fires around the Spence Lake and Draper area and from Northern Ontario darkened the skies in town.

Red Cross president Major Lyndon and vice president H.J. Bird announced plans to remodel the hospital and install an elevator as a memorial to the late Dr. Peter McGibbon.

A boys' and a girls' Juvenile Orange Lodge under W.G. Mary Vincent were begun in the Orange Hall. The Horticultural Society elected P.M. McKay president and W. Galbraith vice president. The Children's Aid Society had 240 members, with Dr. J.P. Davis as president. The 50th anniversary of the IOOF Bracebridge Lodge was held. The Dr. J. Francis Williams estate paid out $5,174 to those suffering TB or cancer.

The rustic little bridge leading from the powerhouse lawn to the side of the Bracebridge Falls was removed and replaced with a new concrete bridge. The highway bridge at the falls was painted and the water was lowered in the north branch of Muskoka River eight feet to repair the flumes at the powerhouse.

President Henry Longhurst of the Muskoka Municipal Association dealt with many issues including hospitalization for indigent patients, regulation of cattle running at large, and the attempt of the province to charge taxes for the land under water occupied by wharves and boathouses.

The finest ice carnival ever held in Muskoka was presented by the Granite Club of Toronto. Skaters included Eleanor Wilson, the 1935 Canadian Junior Champion.

The Muskoka Lakes Curling Third Annual Bonspiel was held in Bala with four rinks from Bracebridge competing. Geo. N. Ecclestone was president; Jack McVittie vice president, and A.S. Bates secretary-treasurer.

The Bracebridge Juniors hockey team wore new black-and-white sweaters made in the Lavoie Knitting factory, and beat the Gravenhurst Juniors to become the first

Muskoka hockey team to play in Toronto's Maple Leaf Gardens. Mayor Wilbert Richards declared the afternoon of February 27 a holiday so that as many as possible could motor to Toronto and see the game against the St. Michael's Buzzers.

Bracebridge was defeated 8-1, but the *Toronto Globe* said they played good hockey. The players were Freddy Goltz (goal), Clarence Kirkness and Sammy Nicholson (defence), Austin Hunt (centre), Harry Moore and Ralph Blanchard (wingers), and Bill Lynn, Clarence Fry, Ted Croucher, and Maurice McPherson (subs). The last two periods of the game were broadcast by Foster Hewitt on CKCL.

Earl C. Barnes' *Miss Moffat* won first prize at the CNE in the 50-75 HP motorboat speed races. *Marguerite V* won the world championship in the 225-cubic-inch hydroplane speed contest at the CNE with *Miss Quebec II* second. The first two boats were built by Minett-Shields.

The Muskoka Lakes Navigation Company turned 70 years old.

Local teamsters drew 14-inch-thick ice from the river in early January, but 31 inches of snow fell later in the month so that ladies had to wear ski-slacks to climb through the drifts to get downtown. This was followed by very hot, dry summer, with a caterpillar plague that defoliated trees throughout the area.

Another petition on behalf of Miss Rene Caisse and her cancer treatment was circulated, and as a result Sir Frederick Banting offered her an opportunity to work in his lab. Two cancer specialists came from New York City to examine her patients. Miss Caisse accepted the offer of a Chicago university to demonstrate her cancer treatment on patients and maintained the operation of her Bracebridge clinic.

Mayor and Mrs. W. Richards sold their Hiram Street residence to Mr. and Mrs. Robert Banks and moved into the McMurray Street home which they bought from Barnard Wadsell. Mrs. Wm. Barron sold her farm property near the Mission House on Hunt's Hill to the SSJE. Edward Hunt built the new home of Mr. and Mrs. Phillip Thomas on John Street. W.G. Gerhart purchased the Fenn residence on McMurray and sold his Woodchester Avenue house. Jack McVittie's stone house on John Street at the rear of St. Joseph's Church was completed. Capt. L.R. Fraser moved into his new house on Dill Street.

*These cars parked along Dominion Street have brought patients to the Rene Caisse cancer clinic.* COURTESY OF BRACEBRIDGE PUBLIC LIBRARY

The airport camp at Reay Airport was closed July 1 and the men assigned railway work. A four-passenger plane landed at the airport, en route to Callandar with George Weis from New York to photogram the Dionne family.

Roy Irwin's car was bounced into the Muskoka River from the rough road. Alvin Lawrence drove his motorcycle over the bank near the town wharf behind Brown's Boat Works. Young George Gascome and Stanley Candler were killed in a car roll-over on the Port Carling highway.

Jerry Dickie won $50 at the CNE in the grain class and Albert E. Ecclestone won about $30,000 in the Irish Sweepstakes.

Coroner E.G. Ellis inquired into death of Mrs. Celia Meredith at Bracebridge Memorial Hospital where she apparently died from carbolic acid poisoning. Arsenic poisoning was diagnosed in Harold Mortimer's death on August 6, the inquest jury deciding that he was poisoned by persons unknown.

The year took its toll of hardy pioneers and gentle residents of the area, such as Henry J. Bird Sr. He had spent 64 years in town and founded the Bird Woollen Mill, built the fine octagonal Woodchester Villa, and was a patron of town activities. He and Mrs. Bird, who passed away in 1912, raised three daughters and four sons.

Dr. Peter McGibbon, physician, soldier, legislator, and citizen died of pneumonia on October 10.

Other deaths this year included P.B. (Barney) Lequyer, 80, worked 46 years at Shier's lumber mill … Mrs. James Gibbon (Alice Maude Wilson) … Mrs. William (Elizabeth) McGregar, 79 … Thomas Robinson, 74, … John Yeoman Sr., 84 … Mrs. F.P. Warne (Susan Mulholland), 72 … Ray Reynolds, 46 … St. Elmo summer resident Hon. E.J. Davis … Mrs. Thomas (Mary) Winters, 83 … Thomas Gray, 67, colonization roads inspector … Mrs. Norma McCulley, wife of the chief of police … Chester H. Johnson, 71, the veterinary of Draper … Charles Edward Palmer, 59, tailor shop proprietor for nearly 40 years … William Naismith, 79, postmaster for many years in the area … Mrs. W.W. Anderson, 52.

## 1937

This year will probably be remembered as the "Year of the Tent Caterpillars." The infestation was so great that even trains had difficulty on the slopes as the tracks were slippery with caterpillars.

Henry J. Bird organized and supervised a campaign to rid Bracebridge of the caterpillars. He had several firms each supply one man for the work of burning the enormous numbers of caterpillars and tents. Residents in Monck were asked to destroy tent caterpillars on their property and township reeves had men working along road sides to destroy the voracious things.

The tax rate was set at 55 mills with the Board of Education getting 23.664, the library 1.154, and the band and the hospital each getting one mill. Debentures accounted for 12.595 mills, hospitalization and charity 3.863, relief (corporate share) 3.38, and general 9.34 less one mill government subsidy.

Police chief Fred Sander, assistant constable William Cudmore, road and bridges overseer David Kirkness, and assessor R.A. Findlay were installed for 1937. Mr. D.T. Hodgson was made chairman of the Mother's Allowance Board … A break-out took place at the District jail in the dungeon of the courthouse when bars were wrenched off a window. Night turnkey Dave Matheson, warden Reynolds, and night constable Cudmore chased the escaped prisoner.

This was a busy year for building and remodelling in Bracebridge.

Stop logs were placed in the slide at High Falls to allow more water over the falls.

Owner and builder George Yearley offered the arena for sale to the town as it was losing money, but Council granted him an assessment of $1,000 allowing him to afford to keep it.

"Bracebridge Muskoka" plates, to attach to licence plates, were available through the Board of Trade. Captain L.R. Fraser was re-elected president.

Church-sponsored events, volunteer organizations, social affairs, and a variety of entertainment filled the year's activity calendar. All churches took part in Universal Week of Prayer whereby parishioners attended a different church every night … The St. Joseph's Church Sunday School picnic was held at the farm of Mr. H.C. Minett, Lake Muskoka. The Baptist picnic was at Port Sydney, and the United Church parishioners picnicked at Gull Lake Park, Gravenhurst … The first inter-church Young People's debate for the T.J. Anderson shield had a large audience. The Baptist team of Misses Donalda Kirk and Arlene Black won over the Presbyterians Miss Leila Goltz and Mr. Ted Reid … In March, a Canadian Girls in Training group was formed at the Baptist Church, with Patricia Johnson as leader, Arlene Black president, Ellen McNaughton vice president, and Beulah Green secretary-treasurer … Rev. A.L. Richards, 54, United Church minister, died suddenly and was succeeded by Rev. R. Edis Fairbairn from Hamilton … Rev. R.L. Casement of the Free Methodist Church exchanged pulpits with Rev. N.F. Perry in Newmarket.

The Bracebridge Horticultural Society annual meeting elected Miss Jessie MacMillan as president … The Clef Club annual banquet was at the Queen's Hotel with toasts and skits … In April there was dancing at Muskoka Falls to Andrew's Orchestra and Baillie's Orchestra … In May, round and square dancing whirled at Falkenburg Hall, and the Northern Star Fife and Drum Band held a dance in the Orange Hall to raise funds for its band. The Bracebridge Horticultural Flower Show brightened June … The Muskoka Falls Merry Mixers met at home of Mrs. H. Speedie … The Strand Theatre held the first in a series of amateur nights in February. First prize ($5) was won by Misses Mina and Marie Pearson for singing with guitar accompaniment.

Accolades this year included the following: Mr. R.P. Perry was presented with a silver muffin dish for being oldest and longest serving postmaster at the Postmaster's Convention in Niagara ... 50th anniversary of Mr. and Mrs. Galbraith. He came as a surveyor about 1887 ... 50th anniversary of Mr. and Mrs. Thomas Wood ... Miss Audrey Wilson gave the valedictory address at the high school ... The Citizen's Band placed sixth at CNE competitions ... Fire chief Albert E. Ecclestone was honoured with an evening of cards, pool, and supper upon his completion of 40 years on the fire brigade ... The Cowley Fathers, Fathers and Brothers of Society of St. John the Evangelist, celebrated 10 years in Bracebridge ... The mayor hosted a reception for Muskoka pioneer Charles Bard's 100th birthday in November. He was out mowing his lawn in June ... Windermere cottager Albert E. Matthews became Ontario's Lieutenant-Governor.

The Rotary Club used the new banquet room at the Albion Hotel for the first time that month and arranged to keep their regalia there permanently. The Bracebridge Juvenile Orange Lodge initiated three young candidates spoken for by Miss Ruth Tinkiss.

Thirty-two lodges took part in the Orange Parade led by the Bracebridge Northern Star Fife and Drum band under Marshal Ausburn Hewitt. The celebrations included such things as softball tournaments, a Citizen's Band concert in Memorial Park, square dancing, round dancing, and a fife and drum contest (which Rosseau won). It was also a tag day for the Loyal True Blue Orphanage. Town merchants did a good business.

Tradesmen were busy building or remodelling houses, stores, and businesses. David Kirkness Jr. built a house on Hunt's Hill ... Swansons's Restaurant was converted to Thatcher's Studio of Photography ... Extensive renovations were done to the post office and customs house by Northern Planing Mills ... The Princess Theatre was remodelled in January and renamed the Strand Theatre by the new manager, Frank Giaschi. George Yearley had added forced air ventilation, a new screen, new seats, and a lobby ... Mr. Arthur W. Tingey, proprietor of the Albion Hotel, opened a new dining room ... Muskoka Trading Co. erected a new warehouse ... Fred Sander built a new livery stable on site of the old building which burned ... A new drinking fountain was installed at the post office ... Berofe's store was freshly decorated in black and silver ... The Rex Café was also decorated ... Mrs. J. Botting opened the Canary Tea Parlour and Cup Reading on Manitoba Street ... Fred Newton of Minett opened a coffee bar between Mayer's Shoe Store and Thatcher's Studio ... A new front was built on the Penistone Shoe Repair ... A 20-foot addition to the rear of the Ecclestone White Rose service station was erected ... Leonard Prowse of Beaumaris constructed a new home on McMurray and Norman Prowse built one on John Street.

The Colours of the 122nd Muskoka Overseas Battalion were rehung when handsome renovations were done to the courtroom in December.

The British American Oil Co. built a new station just north of the forks with river frontage for motor launches. Hunt's Hill on the Baysville Highway was banked on both sides by concrete walls, and the roadway was widened. E. Thatcher added new counters in his studio, and Penistone's Shoe Store (operated by Mr. Charles Penistone) moved to the premises occupied by the Ideal Shoe Repair. Geo. W. Ecclestone displayed the new Chevs in the window against a background of furniture and lamps.

The Watson Brick Company offered No. 1 red veneer brick at $16 plus six percent tax for a FOB truck at the yard. Inside brick per thousand was $14.00.

Several homes were destroyed by fire this year including that of Mr. and Mrs. Leslie Leeder on the Draper-Macaulay town line and Major and Mrs. A.A. Lyndon's at Wilson's Falls. Two sons of Mr. and Mrs. Gordon Mason died when their house burned down at Muskoka Falls. Nelson Stuthers' service truck burned outside his service station.

A public meeting, organized by Mayor McBride, was held to present speakers about the Rene Caisse cancer treatment. A petition with 14,000 signatures was taken to the Minister of Health at Queen's Park by Miss Caisse, MPP Frank Kelly, Mayor B.Y. McBride, and a large deputation of doctors, councillors, and others. Miss Caisse

also met with Sir Frederick Banting who showed great interest in her work. Two Americans, Dr. Emma Carson of Los Angeles and Dr. Richard Leonardo, visited the Rene Caisse cancer clinic in late summer and praised her work.

Five cases of infantile paralysis (polio) in town sparked major concern. The fall fair was cancelled and the schools were not opened until the end of September with lessons being mailed out to children.

The Bracebridge Hospital had a record 111 patients admitted in August with a total stay of 501 days and 107 operations.

The CNR offered a cent-a-mile weekend fare in January for the "Bracebridge Week Sports" which opened with a 32 teams in a curling bonspiel. Several hundred visitors enjoyed the skating carnival put on by a troupe of fancy skaters from Toronto's Granite Club and the University of Toronto Varsity Junior Hockeyists under the direction of Ace Bailey. Messrs. "Bud" Graham and Nelson Quarrington of the *Toronto Evening Telegram* were guests of the Bracebridge Board of Trade at the Queen's Hotel and gave the town great coverage in their paper. Jim Hunter was sent a Bird's coat and tam from the Board of Trade to thank him for promoting the carnival on CFRB.

In curling, 32 teams competed for the Ecclestone Cup with 30 competing for the Borntraeger Cup. The Bracebridge Juveniles won, in overtime, over Gravenhurst for the Ace Bailey Shield.

The Bracebridge Ski Club elected His Honour Judge Mahaffy president; vice president was George Tennant and secretary-treasurer Mr. W.G. Gerhart. The first moonlight ski hike had 23 skiers, and Mr. and Mrs. Gibbs served hotdogs and coffee in the clubhouse. Sam Stripp organized a Juvenile hockey league coached by Bill Snazel.

Lawn bowling commenced with club president Albert E. Ecclestone and secretary-treasurer D.T. Hodgson.

The first game of burro baseball in Bracebridge was held with Firemen vs. Businessmen. The Uptown softball team won the 1937 softball crest. Muskoka Kennels took five dogs to the Royal Winter Fair and all placed. Winners of the Plowing Match were Jewell Skinner, Melvin Hammel, and Charlie McNabb.

Verne D. Corbett took over the Muskoka Beach Inn after the death of W.H. Alderson and planned to operate it year round.

"The Northland" train commenced service between Toronto and Timmins and north with its air-conditioned sleeping cars.

The Coronation of His Most Gracious Majesty King George VI took place May 12, a public holiday.

The steamer *Mildred* struck a rock by Frank Island and sprung some seams. She had picked up 25 passengers at Cedar Beach wharf on her way to Bangor Lodge. She was pretty low in the water by the time she made Bangor, where several young men helped pump her out. No one was hurt but the cruise stopped there.

Mrs. John Thompson, president of the Red Cross, reported that 2,000 items were mended and furniture, linens, and Bird blankets were bought for the hospital. Mrs. Milton Shier donated rug materials and the T. Eaton Co. gave a large box of patches for quilts.

Deaths this year included: Peter Hutchison, founder of Hutchison Bros. Flags in town were flown and half mast to mark his passing … Commodore George Bailey, 95, had been continuously employed on steamboats for 61 years, and helped map out the lakes and mark the channels. He was first on the *Wenonah*, then captain of the *Nipissing* from her maiden voyage until she burned at Port Cockburn … Charles Milton Press, 97, had his 1st class stationary engineer's ticket and was an expert flour miller. He came in 1899 to take over the grist mill … Miss Emma Humphries, 63, daughter of the late James Humphries, a pioneer who opened "The House of Commerce" with Fred Merrill … Mrs. John Schafer, came in 1871, married William Ball in 1878, spent 41 years on the

*The interior of Hutchison Brothers, a large grocery store in downtown Bracebridge in the building now occupied by Richard's Fine Clothiers. Founder Peter Hutchison died in 1937.* COURTESY OF BRUCE MCPHAIL

Ball farm. He died in 1925 so she remarried ... Mrs. Norman Archer, nee Hilda Bouch, 24, died giving birth to a son ... Harry Coupland, 15, son of Mr. and Mrs. R.G. Coupland, drowned at Muskoka Falls ... Ken Shier, president of J.D. Shier Lumber ... Mr. John Irwin, 55, night clerk at the Albion Hotel, worked under Mr. Robert Craig and later under present proprietor, Mr. A.W. Tingey ... Mrs. Allan Fraser, 31, daughter of Mr. and Mrs. Alfred White but raised by grandparents Mr. and Mrs William Lowe, assistant in Dr. Ryan's office then on staff at Kirk and Son ... Captain William McCullen, 68, captain of the *Mink*, then mate on the *Cherokee* ... Mrs. John Davis, 59, daughter of the late Mr. and Mrs. Lundy Travis ... Lemeul Godfry, 72, came about 1891, married Miss Edith Cox ... Mrs. John Spencer, 83, 29 years in town ... Mr. Charles Forth, 87, came to Falkenburg in 1887, 28 years a sectionman for the Grand Trunk Railway, moved into town in 1909 ... Rev. Mr. Jacob Matthias, 65, lay preacher.

## 1938

On his 101st birthday, Charles Bard said that Muskoka was a healthy place. Municipal statistics of 1936 released included information that Bracebridge had 8½ people per acre, the highest density in Muskoka. The town covered 303 acres of land and had a population of 2,589.

The Bracebridge tax rate decreased by two mills to 53.

*Bryson D. Shields, co-founder of Minett-Shields Boat Works, ready to test the* Delta *at the factory on the south side of Bracebridge Bay, about 1938. He would show off the boats around the lakes to advertise and sell them.*
COURTESY OF BRENDA COX

Council agreed to oil unpaved streets. It also purchased a new snowplow and installed two new high-power lights on Chancery Lane. A bylaw was passed to tear down dilapidated buildings if they posed a fire danger.

The Dominion government spent $5,900 on the revetment wall at Hunt's Hill and the wharf at Bracebridge Bay. J.J. Thompson was in charge of the wharf while Captain L.R. Fraser was responsible for the retaining wall. The town had no trouble selling nearly $35,000 of debentures in the day of release for the Hunt's Hill work and Manitoba Street widening.

A.T. Tibbett objected to the proposed drain near Charles Street emptying into and polluting the river which would be cut as ice in the winter.

The west side of Manitoba Street was widened with the rock jutting from Chancery Lane blasted and the sidewalk laid on steel beams. The Bank of Nova Scotia basement, which extended over the sidewalk, was shortened and new walls put in.

J.H. Forbes of Glen Orchard told the Muskoka Municipal Association that colonization roads should be legalized.

The town bought a 2,500-cord woodlot from James Carson north of Gibbs' farm for $1,000. The road between the bridge and the town line on Toronto Street was paved. The wooden sidewalks from Ann and Hiram streets to the hospital were replaced by concrete.

Miss Patricia Johnson, BA, resigned from the Bracebridge Free Library to work at Newmarket Collegiate. Her sister Genevieve took over temporarily until Mrs. A.L. Richards, wife of late Rev. Archie Richards, was hired as librarian.

The power commission would no longer do private wiring and electric repairs, so customers had to seek local electricians. Bert Bock's Electrical Service instantly agreed to accept work as did Bridgman's Electrical Services.

His Worship Deputy Magistrate Redmond Thomas, KC, sat for the first time in Magistrate Court.

Entertainment in 1938 included local plays, musicals, and the latest motion pictures. The Baptist Girl's Glee Club gave a May concert. The Actor's Colony theatre performed in its fifth Muskoka season. The Philatea Club of Knox Church held a strawberry social on the Manitoba Street lawn of H.L. Goltz. The Bracebridge Fire Brigade sponsored a fine dance for the Muskoka Summer School teachers. The North Star Fife and Drum accompanied the Orange Parade up Manitoba to the Baptist Church.

Miss Louise Golden was elected president of the Clef Club. Boy Scout Tony Pierce was chosen to represent Muskoka and go to camp in Angus. The *Muskoka Herald* celebrated its 60th birthday. J.H. Elliott, jeweler, won $1,500 playing bingo.

William Gulston took over managership of the Maher

Shoe Store, having been transferred from Owen Sound ... E.L. Delarge remodelled his store in the IOOF building ... Rex Café added a neon sign and vitrolite plate glass windows ... Phil Stone's new store opened in the Wattie Block opposite the Dominion Hotel ... Ecclestone and Bates remodelled their plumbing showroom, the finest between Barrie and North Bay ... Hare Bros. Grocery was remodelled ... William Towns repainted his store ... Penistone's Shoe Store erected a large new awning ... Rocco Morro opened a photo studio and music store in the Queen's Hotel ... Mrs. J.M. Johnston and Emma moved from the Hamburg Bar to summer quarters at the Park Service Station ... Robert J. Sibbery built a larger kitchen and a dozen new rooms at his Bangor Lodge ... The A & P opened a self-service store on the west side of Manitoba. It sold oranges at 21¢ a dozen, sockeye salmon for 33¢, and Bokar coffee for 25¢ a pound ... You could buy a new Chev from Geo. W. Ecclestone for $820 ... Mr. George C. Marshall's funeral home on Manitoba Street got a handsome new brick front and nice lantern-style electric lights. He also built a chapel.

The public was invited to inspect Thomas Ball's new premises for his Lake Drive Dairy. They could watch the new pasteurization process which would be provincial law in December ... Allan Fraser became the distributor for Neilson's ice cream ... Drumkerry Cabins, owned by Mrs. Reynolds, added four new cabins.

Mr. S.R. Stevens, manager of the Bell Telephone office, announced a new battery method of operation. Telephone users could reach the operator merely by lifting the receiver, without the necessity of ringing by hand.

Fire destroyed the dance hall at Muskoka Falls and Loyal Lyntz's home burned to the ground in Matthiasville. Warren Hoover's barn at the bridge on the south branch of the Muskoka River was destroyed by lightning but the pigs and the chicks were saved. The Ontario Street home of Mr. and Mrs. Edward J. Ball was destroyed by fire that started in their Frigidaire. They rebuilt in November.

Health Minister Kirby tabled a bill to investigate cancer remedies but Rene Caisse closed her clinic refusing to reveal the nature of her cancer treatment Essiac or to submit it for testing. Yielding to her patients demands, she reopened, but risked the penalties of the new provincial cancer commission.

The province took over care of TB patients, assuming the $1.50 a day paid for the sanitarium care of patients. The Bracebridge budget was in deficit due to increase in tuberculosis. A British philanthropist promised an iron lung to every hospital in the British Empire.

The Dr. Peter McGibbon memorial additions to the Bracebridge Memorial Hospital were dedicated in September attended by Lieutenant Governor Albert Matthews.

William Kennedy was infected with Tularemia from skinning a rabbit.

Mr. and Mrs. Austin McCann celebrated their 50th wedding anniversary.

Postmaster Robert P. Perry was coolly dismissed by

*Interior (bottom) and exterior (top) of the Minett-Shields Boat Works, 1941.* COURTESY OF BRENDA COX the Dominion government after nearly 70 years service, "on account of his advanced age." Returned soldier and insurance man William C. Huckle was given the job. Stephen Furniss, MP, crossed swords with the Hon. Earl Rowe in the House of Commons over the cost of rural postal service. The post office at Muskoka Beach was closed with the area becoming RR1 Gravenhurst.

The Dominion government airport at Reay was put in readiness for Trans-Canada airliners. The Board of Trade received demand for a road from the Reay Airport and approved changing its name to Muskoka Airport

Miss Clara Goltz resigned from Bracebridge Public School and was replaced by Barbara Blair.

A committee was formed to arrange the town's 50th anniversary celebrations, consisting of G.L. Tennant, convener, L.R. Fraser, president of the Board of Trade, E.L. Burgess, William Towns, Harry Wilson, and George W. Boyer.

Citizens voted 798 to 510 in favour of government liquor sales in the municipal election.

Syd Bates and his team won the Ecclestone Cup in curling. Don Reynolds' team won the Duke Cup and Dr. Ryan's took the Borntraeger Cup. The new Curling Club executive comprised G.S. Robinson, president, Cecil Dickie, vice president, and A.S. Bates, secretary-treasurer … The Bracebridge Midgets hockey team won the Butler Cup in Baysville.

Over 40 participated in the first District Association Shooting Match held on April 21 in Bracebridge with teams from Minett, Port Carling, Gravenhurst, and Bracebridge. The District Shield was won by the Bracebridge team of George Brooks, Russell Salmon, Rev. J.S. Smedley, Dr. L.N. Ryan, and Don Reynolds. Muskoka Rifle Association match winners were F.R. Frailing's team and best score on the plank was claimed by F. Crozier

Two of Minett-Shield's boats competed in the Duke of York Trophy races in Torquay, England. *Miss Quebec III* ran second although it exceeded the fuel allowance, and engine trouble forced *Shadow II* out of the race. Sam Stripp left the arena due to ill health

The Skating Club hired D.C. Regimbal as their first professional figure skating instructor.

The Skeleton River was chosen by the Department of Lands and Forests as the site for a new fish hatchery and rearing ponds. Cost for the facility amounted to $50,000

To capitalize on increased tourism, a lengthy film of Muskoka Lakes was made by the Motion Pictures Branch of the Dominion Department of Trade and Commerce … A group of Muskoka hotelmen erected a large illuminated sign, "Enjoy Muskoka," at the Niagara Falls Peace Bridge … Gray Coach Lines handed out Muskoka travel literature … the Muskoka Tourist Development Association sponsored radio spots on CFRB and on WGR Buffalo … Bird's tourist information bureau was managed by Don Reynolds after Verne Corbett became manager of the Muskoka Beach Inn.

Cottage owners were warned by the *Globe and Mail* to clear roofs of nearly four feet of snow in March, but the sap was running on sunny days. Spring floods were the highest in 10 years, damaging boathouses and even carrying away Dunn's. It was warm in early November with pansies still blooming, and the winter carnival had to be postponed from December 7 because of poor ice conditions.

A reprieve was given after the previous year's terrible infestation of tent caterpillars. A parasite attacked them and there was no life in the tents spun this year.

Ice was so bad that Mr. Alfred Parrett, proceeding down Queen's Hill with his horse and laden sleigh, turned 180 degrees on the slippery road; the horse remained calm. Mr. Henry Speedie lost his team through the ice near Trethewey's Falls March 17.

Spreadborough's Hill was scene of three auto accidents within a few minutes with five people taken to the hospital.

A three-foot snake with short scaly legs was found on the Baysville Highway near the Pines. The monstrosity was thought to be from a freak show.

Pastor N.F. Perry of the Bracebridge Free Methodist Church was replaced by Rev. S.S. Bailey. Rev. A. Eikenaar was followed by returning Rev. Norman Dabbs at the Baptist Church. The Bracebridge Salvation Army Corps hosted the Salvation Army commissioner of Canada, Alaska, Newfoundland, and Bermuda.

The South Muskoka Agricultural Society celebrated

*The J.D. Shier Lumber Company float in the Industrial Parade, Old Home Week, 1939. Founded in the 1880s, the firm had been one of Muskoka's largest logging and sawmilling operations. For many years the mill at Bracebridge had sawn timber from the Hollow Lake region and Algonquin Park, the logs being floated down the waterways.* COURTESY OF VICKY BILLINGSLEY

64 years in August and its fall fair was well attended in glorious weather. J. Byron Kaye was elected president and H.B. Buckerfield vice president. Winners at the Muskoka Plowman's Match were Ernest Goltz, Roy Goltz, Norman Keall, Jack Ball, H. Blanchard, A. Morrow, and Bert Skinner.

Citizens were asked to take part in a Halloween masquerade sponsored by Board of Trade, public school, and Rotary.

The Loyal Orange Lodge No. 218, elected 1939 officers: Past Master, Bro. Herbert Rawson; Worshipful Master, Bro. Nicholas Wettlaufer; Deputy Master, Bro. J.C. Speck; Chaplain, Bro. Loosemoore, and Recording Secretary, Bro. Irvin Rutherford.

Deaths this year included: Mark Malloy, on his 84th birthday, an expert on estimating standing timber, expert scaler, married Miss Catherine Gillespie in 1911, lived in Dorset then moved to town in 1917 ... Frank Alcock, 78, an expert at breaking in oxen ... John Hector Dauphin, 79 ... Mrs. Walter (Josephine Scriven) Fowler, 66 ... Two-year-old David Jones of Oakley Township died after eating poisonous mushrooms ... William Weatherspoon, 81, active Salvation Army member ... Mrs. Arthur Wheatley, nee Harriett Crockford, 61 ... John Martin Patterson, 82 ... Mrs. B. Rosewarne, 78 ... Rev. Father Basil Kingsley, Bracebridge parish, died of pneumonia ... Mrs. George W. Ecclestone, 68, from injuries after a fall ... Mrs. John Thompson, first president of the Clef Club.

**1939** The Board of Trade re-elected president Captain L.R. Fraser and directors Alan Hutchison, Wilbert Richards, B.Y. McBride, E.W. Thatcher, Robert J. Boyer, Leslie Tennant, Harry Wilson, J.H. Elliott and D.C. Thomas.

Muskoka lumbering employed about 500 men in several camps. Joseph Lazzara found old Muskoka Lake steamboat schedules when he renovated the former Dominion Hotel billiard rooms. Joseph Ennis opened a grocery taking over from Simmon's grocery. The Joseph L. Caisse barber shop, the oldest business in town, celebrated 50 years.

Lawyer Redmond Thomas became editor of the *Bracebridge Gazette* and the *Muskoka Herald* quipped, "Doubtless he is the only K.C. in Canada to whack the editorial typewriter of a Canadian weekly."

The liquor store opened next to the Muskoka Garage, managed Mr. Reginald Hines and Mr. Murt Dunn, both of well-respected families. Mr. Jack Johnson ran the Brewers' Warehouse store on Main Street.

Mr. A.E. Fawcett announced that his Bracebridge Information Bureau would provide visitors with business and tourist information without commission or obligation.

Miss Mabel Campbell's Lingerie Shop opened across from the post office. There was a new front for Tom Pickles Barber Shop on Queen's Hill. Joseph Innis opened a grocery business and built a home on Robert Street. Riley's "properly pasteurized" milk and cream were for sale.

After a good deer-hunting season, William McConnell, "Muskoka's leading fur buyer" solicited raw fur, hides, wood, and deer skins.

In preparation for Christmas, merchants including grocers B.Y. McBride, Hutchison Bros., Hare Bros., and others tempted shoppers with candies, fruit and Christmas goodies. Anderson's Store presented fine clothes and Penistone's Shoe Store offered excellent shoes to go with them. The Whitten Co. Ltd. stocked toys and G.W. Ecclestone Ltd. offered handsome furniture and housewares.

*Miss Bracebridge (Ruth Dollimore) and Mayor B.Y. McBride wait beside the Catholic Church to take their position in the town's Old Home Week Parade in 1939.* COURTESY OF VICKY BILLINGSLEY

Mrs. Viviene Hardwick's dance recital presented Marion Dinner, Helen Jean Goltz, Yvette Hardwick, Douglas Rankin, Gwen Ball, Marion Rankin, Beverley Moore, Esther Holiday, Glenna Fraser, Betty Forest, Annie Thompson, Jean Anne Bowden, Pluma Corr, Bernice Goltz, Aileen Goltz, June Moore, Iona Hunt, Marie Hill, Mrs. Dwight Nelson, Grace Keall, Aubrey Goltz, Patricia Nelson, Evelyn Bates, Yvonne Hardwick, Georgia Giaschi, Helen Peake, Mary Cooper, Peggy Gibson, and Margaret Beckman.

Mr. Roy Fenwick adjudicated the singers and choirs taking part in the Third Annual Music Festival at the United Church. In November, Grades 7 and 8 of Bracebridge Public School presented *Pinocchio* in song, trained by principal B.R. Minns and music supervisor Oscar Kirk. Bracebridge United Church dedicated a memorial window to Mrs. H.R. Scovell in December.

The 1939 Council was comprised of Mayor McBride and councillors Dr. A.F. Bastedo, W.E. Hunt, E.A. Whitten, W. Hare, E.L. DeLarge, and Horace G. Parlett. Nicholas Wettlaufer was town foreman and David Kirkness his assistant. William Cudmore was appointed chief of police.

Oliver Johnson was paid $50 for his property so the highway south of the falls could be widened. The grading of the road south of the falls bridge was completed.

Council met in their new chambers at the Town Hall. The former Fire Department recreation room was partitioned off for offices for the town clerk and mayor. The stairway addition was built by Hewitt and Hunt with Ecclestone and Bates putting in a new heating plant.

A new turbine was installed at the powerhouse to replace the original turbine and produce 100 HP more electricity. The silver bridge over the Bracebridge falls was a blazing display of coloured lights in June. The powerhouse and gatehouse were also a myriad of coloured electric lights, thanks to superintendent Ed Ball's idea.

The Department of Highways promoted "Protection During Spring" and effective April 1 limited trucks to half loads and speeds to 20 mph. Horses were restricted to pulling loads of one ton or less.

At the request of the South Muskoka Agricultural Society a large building was erected at Jubilee Park to serve as an agricultural and community hall.

A fine celebration of the town's 50th jubilee took months of planning. A five-day celebration saw a monster parade, band music, and a historical pageant. Miss Ruth Dollimore was chosen as Miss Bracebridge and her sister Marjorie was named Miss Muskoka. Thomas Cooper and Mary Liddard-Strange returned to town, both first to be born in Bracebridge in 1863. Special excursion rates were arranged for trains for the homecoming traffic.

The new Bell Telephone building on Manitoba Street across from the park was built to house the amazing common battery operation service which went into effect in February. The mere lifting of the receiver signaled an operator that a connection was desired. Miss Ethel Lundie was in charge of the office.

In order to repair docks at Mary Lake in June, the water level dropped so much that the Bird Woollen Mill could not turn their turbine, and there were no street lights and reduced electricity to the residents.

Council changed a bylaw set at the turn of the century requiring stores to close at 6:00 p.m. to conform with Ontario statutes.

Mr. Isaac Brock Aulph received word that his services as clerk of the first Muskoka Division Court would end on September 1 after 21 years. The insurance man had been acting sheriff of Muskoka and Justice of the Peace. Mr. David T. Hodgson, motor licence issuer, was appointed clerk of Muskoka Division Court.

The Muskoka Municipal Association changed its name to the Muskoka District Council in October.

Mayor McBride was elected by acclamation for a fourth successive term. There had not been a mayoralty contest for 10 years, and there would be no voting this year as all candidates were acclaimed. W.A. Shier, barber, was elected to take the place of Mr. DeLarge.

Clarence Fry, a defenceman on Bracebridge Juniors hockey team, sustained a ruptured liver in a game with Orillia. A benefit game between Gravenhurst and Bracebridge was held for him.

In curling, Syd Bates' team won the Ecclestone Cup, Claude Duke's won the Borntraeger Cup, and Don

Reynolds' the Book Cup. The Bracebridge Curling Club thanked icemaker Bernard Wasdell for a good job and elected G.S. Robinson president, Cecil Dickie vice president, and S.A. Bates secretary-treasurer. The cherished Wasley-Ecclestone Cup was brought back to Bracebridge by A.S. Bates, W. Richards, and Don Reynolds and their teams.

The Ice Carnival was a brilliant winter event with the Toronto Granite Club again taking part.

The Bracebridge Rifle Club won the Borntraeger Indoor Trophy. Team one consisted of P. Bridgman, F. Campbell, and A. Cooper, with J.S. Smedley, F. Crozier, and W.K. Hare making up team two ... Mr. R. McElheren won the men's singles in the Muskoka Badminton League's third annual tournament ... Horse racing appeared as the Bracebridge Driving Club was revived after 15 years. President William Kingsmill sponsored equestrian events for the Homecoming ... Officers of the Ladies' Bowling Club were president Mrs. George S. Johnson, vice president Mrs. Sydney Bates, secretary, Mrs. M.P. McKay, and treasurer Miss Lena Parlett.

George Ecclestone III had an operation for tonsils. Later he heard about a friend having an operation for appendicitis and said, "Well, they might as well have taken my appendix out while they had me on the ironing-board."

Officials of the Ontario Cancer Commission visited the Rene Caisse Cancer Clinic in February and examined a number of patients. Miss Caisse appeared at the Cancer Commission sitting in Toronto along with a number of her patients.

A March fire in Milne's garage destroyed his records and his dog. The lighthouse and boathouse of Hon. Lieutenant Colonel J.R. Moodie was destroyed by fire at Lake Rosseau and Indian River with an estimated $8,000 loss.

Many people saw and nearly everyone heard the great TCA (Trans-Canada Airlines) plane which roared over the town in March. It was on its first flight on the overnight mail service to Vancouver.

Captain Harry Croucher's *Shamrock II* and Capt. L.R. Fraser's *Niska* were first steamers to arrive in Bracebridge this spring.

Two hundred Muskoka summer residents and former residents met in the Royal York Hotel, Toronto, to reminisce. They were welcomed by Miss Elsie Goltz, Miss Kay Tobin, Miss Anne McCulley, H. Fenn, and Fred Elliott.

The Red Cross Society paid off all but $1,000 on the mortgage principal of the hospital. Improvements at the hospital included a fire escape and a violet-ray machine for the x-ray room.

After months of local preparation, the visit of King George and Queen Elizabeth was omitted for Muskoka and local people had to travel to Bala, MacTier, or Washago to catch glimpses of the royal couple.

Trinity United Church choir of Gravenhurst took the service in Bracebridge United Church and Bracebridge performed a choralogue in Gravenhurst. Rev. Father Palmer was installed Superior of the Canadian congregation of the SSJE.

Thomas N. Bird retired after 21 years on the school board. Mr. C.W. Wright replaced William Evanson at the high school. Miss Evelyn A. Jewell replaced Miss Blair at the public school. Muskoka Summer School had 80 students from all over Ontario at its seventh session.

Wesley Hammond, 41, was shocked with 38,000 volts at the South Falls power plant. He suffered severe burns and a fractured skull. He later died of his injuries. A special nurse, Miss Titcombe, came from Baysville within an hour. In another terrible accident, a Cub airplane crashed into the Indian River at Port Carling, killing pilot Sidrel Hill, 21, of Gravenhurst. One of the first on the scene was Captain Wesley Hill, master of steamship *Ahmic*, who identified the body of his own son.

Robert Bird was badly cut in Toronto when a steam valve blew off a passing train in the Union Station yard and broke the window at his seat, cutting his face with glass.

Ragweed was considered a big problem and the Department of Agriculture suggested several different weed killer formulae. The Plowing Match was held at James Fitzmaurice's farm.

Maurice Fitzmaurice, 95, was cited as a real Muskoka pioneer living at his lakeshore property at Muskoka Lake. He helped to build the first house in Bracebridge and helped "log out" the first road in Monck.

Mr. Robert Dinsmore donated an arsenal of guns, grenades, and other pieces of Great War history to the town. A museum to display them was discussed before his death. The Loyal Orange Lodged elected Bro. N. Wettlaufer, J.C. Speck, and John Fox as officers.

An insidious feeling was invading the country and the Military District No. 2 Infantry and Machine Gun Association implored citizens and employers to encourage their young men to be given time off work to train with their nearest militia unit.

"The World is Still at Peace," wrote the editor, although acknowledging "that between the time of writing and the time this week's *Herald* reaches our readers much can happen in the tense international situation." Ex-servicemen James Russell, William Edward Reid, David Matheson, William Brazier, A.G. Connors, Bryson Vincent, Claude Mann, W. O'Brien, E. Strong, Syd Stewart, and William Wray, all of Bracebridge, and Wallace Toll of Vankoughnet, were sworn in August 29th by Magistrate Thomas to guard the South Falls power plant at Muskoka Falls.

Prime Minister Mackenzie King introduced the War Time Prices and Trade Board and in a speech, King George VI sought authority from Canadian Parliament for effective cooperation in this shadow of impending conflict.

Men took the Oath of Allegiance and were sworn for guard duty at the CNR bridges and the South Branch bridge: Harry Woodthorpe, H. Fraser, R. Givings, F.A. Reeves, H. Jarvis and L. Light. They were equipped with army issue and bayonets. All ex-servicemen were urged to register with Lewis Denis, the local registrar for the National Veteran's Survey. James Russell, E. Strong, and H. Kirkener were engaged as special constables.

On September 7, Governor General Lord Tweedsmuir announced that a state of war existed. Young men were enlisting. The voluntary registration of women opened in October headed by Mrs. Peter McGibbon, Mrs. W.L. Cowan, Mrs. George N. Ecclestone, and Mrs. G.W. Boyer. Aliens were asked to register at the post office and the Town Hall. The Muskoka Aerodrome was considered for use in the national and Empire landing fields plan.

Former Bracebridge Summer School principal Thornton Mustard and wife were victims of the *Athenia* torpedoing the first day of the war.

The Red Cross Society, one of the most important means whereby citizens of the town could aid in the war against Hitlerism and repression, was in action. Ward committees for fund raising were formed under captains Captain Fraser, Ward 1; W.W. Creswick, Ward 2; E.A. Whitten, Ward 3; and Jack Johnston, Ward 4. There was an urgent need for handmade, size 11 socks for the servicemen, and knitting instructions were published.

The Ontario government plan was undertaken to open private land for the benefit of relief and vacant lands were identified to be taken over. Any land within the town had to be plowed by the town, without remuneration, for the use of growing vegetables under the direction of the town foreman.

Mild weather in January caused poor ice conditions and disrupted hockey schedules, but in February the temperature dropped to -42°F, freezing wires and pumps, then rose 50 degrees by noon next day. Over 13 feet of snow was recorded during the winter. In September, two-inch hailstones broke windows and neon signs. On September 15 it was 89.4°F. An earthquake was felt at 7:00 a.m. October 19, shaking crockery and windows, and there was an eclipse of the moon on the night of October 19-20.

Deaths this year included: Captain George C. Parlett, 76, served many years with the Muskoka Navigation Company and then the Anglo-Canadian Leather Company. He was also a lumberman ... Mrs. Albert Tibbett, 57, of Ward 4 ... Miss Margaret Rain, a fount of historical knowledge and the longest resident in Muskoka's history She came with her family about 1855 ... Mrs. Thomas Bruce (Elizabeth Ann Gibson), 62, wife of the Crown lands agent ... John McNeil, 95, died after a fall ... Edward Grant, 77 ... Admiral John Denison, 85, of Denison's Island, Muskoka Lake ... John A. Ross, mechanic, one of the first employees at Muskoka Leather ... Mrs. William John Whaley, 82, of Muskoka Falls ... Mrs. George Parlett, died March 19 ... Hazel Lount, daughter of J. Ewart and F.R. Lount of "The Grove" ... Charles Peake, 82, had been in charge of stumping the show grounds of Jubilee Park ... Mrs. George Patterson

(Ethel Johnson) … Peter Grozelle, 59, had worked at tanneries and was sick for months … David Brown, 63, worked at J.D. Shier lumber factory … Walter Thompson, 8, drowned in the river behind Muskoka Falls School … Mrs. Phillip Lazzara (Sarah Battaglia), 83 … Mrs. Hugh Thompson (Florence Vanclief), 35, died of mercuric poisoning which she took instead of aspirin … George Yeoman, 84, had a remarkable collection of Indian arrowheads which he had found clearing … James Thomson, PhmB, 69, prominent in business and sports … Charles Bard, the "Grand Old Man," died at 101 … Mrs. Daniel McNaughtan, mother of Peter and others … Edmond Bard, another son of Charles.

## 1940

The terrible war affected everyone and everything in Bracebridge in 1940. Sporting events, musical concerts, and every type of entertainment continued to be held as best as possible, but with fund raising for war efforts the primary motivation.

In February, a patriotic skating party was held to benefit the British War Victims Relief Fund, and a benefit dance and card party was sponsored by the Clef Club. The Salvation Army War Service Campaign organized committees, and the Red Cross identified essential needs of the armed forces and encouraged the knitting of socks, undershirts, and scarves.

Canada's first War Bonds went on sale in January. The first group of young men to be recruited into the armed services included Kenneth Hare, Joseph Lazzara, Albert Wyman, Kenneth Vanclieaf, Earl Mooney, Roy Ketch, and Ernest B. Collins. By June there was a the long list of Muskoka boys who had enlisted.

At the opening of Muskoka Sessions Court, in May, Judge Wright appealed to all citizens to be vigilant concerning suspicious actions by possible enemy sympathizers or agents and report to police.

When Italy entered the war on the side of the German Reich, the Citizen's Band leader John Morra tendered his resignation, concerned over the town's feeling about his native land. His resignation was refused and band president J.W. Reid expressed their complete confidence in him as leader and also in his loyalty to the British Empire.

Weather conditions were no longer published by the airport which was under consideration as a major landing field for war efforts. Use of the airfield in the Empire Air Training Plan was determined to be not feasible because of the number of buildings that needed to be built on the property.

By mid-summer men up to 45 years of age were required to sign up for their country. A patriotic parade by hundreds of members of the Canadian Corps ex-serviceman marched on July 1 to a stimulating Drumhead Service.

Bracebridge went on Daylight Saving Time June 2 to September 1 as a war measure to save energy. Even though Bracebridge had its own power system, a return to Standard Time was required by the Dominion government although the town argued that it would not take power from outside sources.

To increase town security, the Civic Volunteer Guard was formed by ex-serviceman Thomas Pierce. Norman Prouse was named commissioner of a 100-member unit and soon four units were formed.

There was a request from Ontario's Premiere Hepburn for donations of rifles and shotguns for volunteer guards across the province.

British children were coming to Muskoka to live away from the horrors of the war. Tourist resorts and movie theatres put on events to raise funds for the Muskoka Children's Aid who were looking for homes for these displaced children.

Compulsory registration of every citizen in Canada was under way and Hugh Devereau of Bracebridge was named the assistant registrar for Muskoka-Ontario. Registry locations were set up in July for the convenience of summer visitors.

In July G.W. Boyer of Bracebridge and E.G. Rankin chaired a local campaign to promote war savings, and in September the Bracebridge Power, Water and Light Commission bought $5,000 worth of war bonds.

The Red Cross continued sending shipments of blankets, underwear, bandages, etc. to overseas servicemen, but they needed a larger budget and major fund raising took place to raise $3,000. The Red Cross offered directions for knitting two socks at once.

*This peaceful scene on Bracebridge Bay in 1940 contrasts sharply with the war raging in Europe. The* RMS *Segwun is moored at the wharf. Wartime restrictions on travel brought about a resurgence of steamboat excursions in Muskoka, temporarily reversing a decline brought about by automobiles and steadily improving roads.* COURTESY OF THE BRACEBRIDGE PUBLIC LIBRARY

The nation's nurses were registered for preparedness and over 40 men and women passed St. John's Ambulance courses in Bracebridge – just in case.

Army tanks, artillery, and armed infantry from Petawawa drove through town in preparation for War Games.

Several Nazi officers escaped from a prison camp "somewhere in Ontario" during the summer, and members of the Bracebridge Civil Guards spread a dragnet. Three hundred prisoners were moved to an eastern camp and northern prisoners were moved to the Muskoka camp for German prisoners in Gravenhurst.

Proclamation of conscription was published and Canada called its young men 21 to 24 years old for military training.

The E.J. Kirk property on Dominion Street, formerly occupied by Judge Mahaffy, was sold to Mr. A. Ursine of Toronto to be remodelled as a tourist lodge.

The new executive for the Board of Trade included E. W. Thatcher, president, George Hammond, vice president, and George Jeffries, secretary-treasurer. V.D. Corbett was asked to prepare a Muskoka tourist resort booklet for distribution.

J.H. Elliott's store was remodelled by Nelson Goltz …

The Whitten Co. took on the agency for Beatty Electrical appliances manufactured by Beatty Bros. of Fergus … Archie Morrow sold his spring maple syrup for $1.25 a gallon … Miss Edith Hare took over the ladies' ready-to-wear-business from Miss Ruby McCulley, earlier Miss Gurley's store … Mrs. W.C. Fryer offered Spirella Service (corsets) for ladies' figures in their own homes … Miss Permelia Caisse opened a lingerie and gift shop next to the Bank of Nova Scotia … A.T. Waite bought a truck to service resorts and more electric baking equipment … Dan Eaton, radio repairman, joined the RCAF … More than 675 telephone subscribers received new phone books … The famous Canadian tailor, Ed Provan, opened a store next to Ecclestone and Bates … Earle Rosewarne's Muskoka Garage joined two sections of the premises together to make one front … L.R. Fraser and Son were appointed authorized dealers of Chevrolet, Oldsmobile, and Chev trucks … The Toreador Restaurant operated by Charles Lazzara was transferred to Mrs. Holman Hunt when he left for the RCAF. She prepared a hot turkey sandwich, pie, and beverage for 25 cents as an opening special … In December, the Queen's Hotel closed. Since the death of Mrs. John Thompson, great nephews John and George ran it, but one joined the RCAF.

Bird's Information Bureau opened for the summer under Don Reynolds while Mr. R. Bell opened the Bracebridge Information Bureau representing resort owners.

The home of Frank Brodie in Ward 4 was destroyed by fire in January … Thatcher Studio and the E.W. Thatcher residence above were damaged by fire … The Harold White home owned by the Anglo-Canadian Leather Co. in Ward 4 was burned … Mrs. Johnston's house on Woodchester Avenue burned down as did Albert Kaye's home in Milford Bay … The Mortimer's Point post office in the home of George and Ted Mortimer burned in April.

Bracebridge Council raised the licence fee for slot machines from $100 to $400 for the first and $10 for subsequent machines. Players had to be over 18 and Sunday use was not allowed. The town's population was 2,529, a decrease of 20 since the previous year. The tax levy decreased 2½ mills to 50, after the Ontario subsidy.

In June, the Fire Brigade was talked out of quitting as a whole even though the Council could offer them no increase in grants … Under the Statute Labour Act, every male inhabitant between the ages of 21 and 66 was required to pay a Poll Tax of $5.00 to the chief of police William Cudmore … Oil was spread on the unpaved streets, and a new sign bylaw restricted erection of any signs without permission.

The Badminton Club wound up the season with winners Ron McKay and K. Jamieson … The Curling Club presented the Ontario Tankard Shields to the rinks of Russell Salmon and Dr. L.N. Ryan … The Softball Club elected Jos. Rose as president, Jack Ball captain of Uptown, Tom Dawkins of Hollow, Jim Taplin of Combines (wards 3 and 4), and E.L. DeLarge of Legion teams … Roller skating was a new Muskoka craze … A Junior C hockey team was entered in the OHA by Harold Frowe, club president, Earl Walker, vice president, and Vincent Kyle, secretary-treasurer.

Two RCAF planes crashed into Lake Muskoka, killing four airmen. One was found with is crew but the other was never recovered.

The Cancer Commission issued its long awaited report on alternative cancer remedies. It found that out of 18 treatment presenters at the hearing, only Miss Rene Caisse's Essiac evidenced any patient recovery.

The federal Mackenzie King government returned with a majority and local MP Stephen J. Furniss was returned to the "war parliament" with a 1,082-vote lead.

The Muskoka Lakes Navigation and Hotel Co. started its 75th year of service in April. Muskoka's first spring seed fair included an address on potatoes, and the organization of a boy's Potato Club.

Rev. J.S. and Mrs. Smedley were given a farewell from St. Thomas Anglican Church, and succeeded by Rev. R.K. Townbridge. The Baptist Church welcomed new minister Mr. W.A. Campbell.

The beautiful eight-bedroom nurses' residence near the hospital was opened by Lady Eaton in August. American summer residents and visitors donated 90 percent of the funds to build the residence. The iron lung arrived for the hospital from an English benefactor. Tourism was down in July but the August Civic Holiday weekend had heavy traffic.

Edward Hunt was re-elected chairman of the Board of

Education. The school fairs were suspended for 1940 in order to divert funds to war-time causes. The board arranged to have local dentists Dr. Shuttleworth and Dr. Ryan examine public school pupils and prepare reports for their parents.

At the CNE, Mr. H. Goltz won first for a group sheaf, oats, wheat and barley, with Roy Goltz second.

The Bracebridge Rotary Fair in aid of crippled children was held in conjunction with the South Muskoka Agricultural Society Fall Fair. People enjoyed the dancing and the entertainment. The fall fair committee elected 12 members according to the new Agricultural Act. Elected were H.B. Buckerfield, George Parrett, Charles Kaye, H.E. Beaumont, A.J. Goltz, George Boyer, H. Goltz, Tom Ball, Harvey Gray, Thomas Hammell, Richard Stephens, and Harvey Jackson. The ladies' committee re-elected consisted of Mrs. A. Goltz, Mrs. S. Smith, Mrs. J. Dickie, Mrs. D. Armstrong, Mrs. W. Denniss, Mrs. W. Huckle, and Miss Annie Parsons.

Clayton Gibbs built a home on the west side of Manitoba Street north of Milton Bailey's, and Mr. and Mrs. Ed Levesque built on Church Street.

In December, Mayor Ben McBride defeated E.L. DeLarge in the first mayoralty vote in 11 years. H.G. Parlett, Dr. A.F. Bastedo, Walter E. Hunt, A. Roy Shier, and A.T. Waite formed Town Council. A bylaw for extending the one-year term of office to two years was defeated 2-1.

Bracebridge was blasted with a blizzard on March 20, and the maple syrup was delayed, but the ice was out of the lake by May 2. A severe windstorm hit in early November and caused damage to buildings, poles, and wires.

Five planets, Mercury, Venus, Jupiter, Saturn, and Uranus, appeared all at one time during late winter and could be seen with the naked eye.

Deaths this year included George W. Ecclestone, after a lifetime of service as merchant and legislator. He served as mayor in 1912-13 and councillor 1906 and 1912-1916. Mr. Ecclestone was the Member of Provincial Parliament for Muskoka-Parry Sound for many years ... Mr. E.F. Stephenson, 90, founder of *Free Grant Gazette* in 1892, died in New Liskeard ... Mrs. Peter McGibbon died May 8 ... Mrs. John Dunn died in early May. Her husband owned and operated the skating rink across from the railway station and had a boat works at the wharf ... Thomas Cooper, first white child born here, in 1863 ... George F. Gibson, 61, died July 22. He was councillor from 1923 until 1935 except when he served as mayor in 1930-31 ... Harold Bolduc, 14, drowned near Wychwood Cabins, Port Sydney ... Mrs. Peter (Cora Gertrude Brooks) MacNaughton, died September 14.

## 1941

Bracebridge citizens wove war efforts into every fibre of their local activities. About $300 of war saving certificates and stamps were sold in a week, but more funds were needed. Every organization held fund-raising dances, bridge games, skating, and hockey games, whatever they could think of. So many groups were raising funds that Mayor McBride was hired as funds coordinator for War Services. Mrs. Nelson Goltz, secretary, assisted in the 1941 appeal.

Merchant business was affected by materials control and the War Exchange Conservation Act.

Dentist Dr. R.F. Shuttleworth closed his practice to join the Canadian Dental Corps ... Nurse Finlayson left the hospital to nurse at Camp Borden ... Optometrist Philip Thomas joined the RCAF ... The RCAF recruited in the Council chambers, and in May, the fully mechanized battery of the Seventh Army Field Regiment recruited in town.

Mr. Hugh Devereux wrote an open letter to politicians asking that local buildings be put to war use. The Anglo-Canadian Leather Co. building had been unused for 10 years, but was capable of making 500,000 pounds of sole leather a month. He claimed that the Queen's Hotel, empty since late 1940, could make a training school headquarters.

A sales organization for the 1941 Victory Loan was launched June 1 with an objective of $146,200, with George Ecclestone as chairman.

Hospital Day was observed in memory of Florence Nightingale and the VON met in an attempt to organize.

Floyd Tibbett was lost off the east coast of Nova Scotia, Sergeant Ivan Einarson of Clear Lake died in Singapore, and RCAF officer Andrew Stephen was killed in

*A parade led by motorcycle escorts and a band makes its way up Manitoba Street in 1939 as throngs of spectators line the sidewalks.* COURTESY OF BRENDA COX

England. Sergeant Gunner Percy V. Brazier was missing in air operations and had became a prisoner of war in Germany.

A German prisoner of war died in the Muskoka Internment Camp at Gravenhurst. Eighty prisoners of war attended, in full uniform, as the Nazi flag-draped coffin was buried in a local cemetery.

Minett-Shields and the Port Carling Boat Works built four 112-foot Fairmile anti-submarine patrol boats for the Canadian Navy. They did as much work as possible in their Muskoka plants, then shipped the pieces to their boat works in Honey Harbour for final assembly. Minett-Shields then built two mine sweepers.

The Canadian Auxiliary Territorial Services (CATS) was organized to train women to take over men's jobs.

A patriotic parade and drumhead service was led by Comrade William Brazier of the Legion.

The Wartime Prices and Trade Board was controlling food and clothing industry sales. Restrictions included no more sliced bread, double bread wrappers, or wrappers printed in more than one colour. Bakers and milkmen could make no special deliveries. Milk prices increased to 12 cents a quart and Canadian motorists were asked to cut gas consumption by 50 percent.

The manufacture of Canadian silk stockings, deemed non-essential, was banned. However, MacMillan Ladies' Wear Store had already received its first shipment of Canadian nylon hosiery, selling at a princely $1.65 a pair.

The third year of war started in September. Councillor Parlett was called to the RCAF where there were nine sets of Bracebridge brothers: Norman and Wilbur Archer, Buster and Percy Brazier, Bob and Jack Everett, Borden and Norman Lyndon, Carl and George Matthias, Willard and Don MacNaughtan, Don and Aubrey Shapter, and Tom and Ken Wotherspoon, about 60 locals in all. Over 80 were in the army. The Civil Guard drilled in the Armories.

Fund raising continued and Bracebridge was asked to raise $3,500 monthly or the equivalent of one Blitz buggy, a jeep-like vehicle for three men and a machine gun ... The first young ladies to be called to service were Mabel Patterson to the CWACS, and Ruth Quantz to the Canadian Women's Air Auxiliary Force ... There was no plowing match this year, as too many men were away.

Industries were faithfully doing their war work. The Muskoka Foundry built a complete sawmill for use in clearing Labrador's new air fields. The Bird Woollen Mill produced 30,000 army blankets, and 28,000 yards of khaki and air-force blue overcoating (for great coats), with more on order. They made about 20,000 pounds of yarn to be knitted into socks by Red Cross volunteers.

The J.D. Shier lumber company purchased the Gravenhurst Lumber Company from Charles Clark ... J.S. Bowden's service station on north Manitoba Street was taken over by P.J. Cole ... W.T. Ireland took over Ennis Grocery across from the public library ... Miss Valeen Slater completed 15 years in the office of Jerry Dickie and went to work with Minett-Shields when they received orders for warships ... Pinelands House was sold by judicial sale ... R.J. Sibbery enlarged Bangor Lodge with a dancing casino and tuck shop ... J.H. Elliott opened a watch and jewelry store in the former Rex Restaurant. He decided to sell only five cent to $1.00 items in his former premises. W.C. Denniss of the Denniss Planing Mill retired after 47 years, only to die a few days later at 72.

The Bird's Information Bureau was operated by the Muskoka Tourist Development Association and managed by Russell Salmon. The Bracebridge Information Bureau was operated by A.E. Fawcett.

A bylaw was passed to exempt photographers from the early closing in order to make them more accessible to the tourists ... The Queen's Hotel was taken over, on a rental basis, from the McLeod family ... Leslie Tennant bought the old British Lion Hotel from the town for an apartment building.

Captain Levi Fraser announced his retirement from steamboat work. Captain Lee completed 50 years on the Muskoka Lakes.

William Hammond sold his dairy to Robert Harrison, and joined the RCAF. Mrs. L. Johnson bought the George Olsen property at the corner of Manitoba and Ann streets for a lunchroom. W.A. Shier opened a huge barber shop in Nobel and Jack Brown managed Shier's Bracebridge shop in his absence.

The Philathea Club held its third birthday party at Mrs. G.S. Robinson's home, electing Mrs. Allan Fraser as president

Over 900 hundred people packed the arena for a patriotic skating carnival. The Knit Knuts Club actively knitted for servicemen, and the "18" knitting club displayed its work at a tea.

The Boy's Potato Club was led by president Robert Parrett, and a Boy's Swine Club was formed with the approval of the Department of Agriculture. The seed fair was held at the Town Hall this year. It was a success despite near impassable spring rural roads which prevented many exhibitors and visitors from getting there.

William Towns became District Deputy Grand Master of the Odd Fellows. They donated $400 to the *Evening Telegram*'s British War Victim's Fund after their annual summer cruise on the *Sagamo* and *Segwun*.

Exhibits at the fall fair included one of King George's horses from the royal stables in Britain, a display of London bomb photos loaned from the CNE, and a military demonstration.

Tom Ball was elected Curling Club president with Dr. Bastedo vice president. Local men took off for hunting clubs at Spring Lake, Moon River, and Pine Lake.

Fire damaged the following: Morley Beeler's tire repair shop and service station at the rear of Hammond's Dairy ... the Shier Street home of Arnold White which was owned by the Anglo-Canadian Leather Company ... Harry Boyer's home on Shier Avenue ... a second Anglo-Canadian Leather home Ward 4 in March ... the town's woodlot at High Falls. In July dry weather led to bush fires at Muskoka Falls and High Falls.

The road to the hospital was paved by the contractor who had paved Highway 11 below the falls. Wall bracket lights were installed on Queen's Hill.

Miss Joan Waite purchased a portion of land overlying a sheer drop of fifteen feet behind the family house and bake shop on Ontario Street for the princely sum of $10.

Council passed a bylaw in October to collect tax on new unassessed houses known as the Occupancy Tax.

Council was elected by acclamation but only after much canvassing were all the seats filled. The previous year's councillors Roy Shier, George Hammond, and A.T. Waite along with new councillors Thomas W. Pierce, J. Lawrence Frowe, and W.J. Ronald McKay filled the positions. Ernest A. Whitten defeated E.L. DeLarge for mayor by 150 votes. Outgoing Mayor McBride announced retirement from municipal service.

J.W. Reid was acclaimed for the Power, Water and Light Commission. Commission chairman George Tennant reported that a government report showed that the town water was bad, but it was water from Barron springs. Peake springs was pure, so an auxiliary pump was purchased to assure winter water.

Figures from the 1941 Census of Canada noted that Bracebridge had 2,435 residents. The town's assessment showed it as 2,401.

Council gave Miss Rene Caisse an extension to her lease of the old hotel for her cancer clinic at $5.00 a month. In late January, citing government interference, she finally closed it, thanking Bracebridge officials for their support.

A throng of ice cutters were working on the river by Charles Lount's house in late February. Albert Tibbett and Ernie Green, dealers in the summer commodity, cut 17-inch, blue-green blocks.

By summer, a $25 provincial bounty was offered on wolves. The bounty would be paid upon proof of the kill but the wolf skin would remain the property of the killer. In 1932 some 2,008 pelts had been collected but in the previous 11 months only 988 were reported.

Bracebridge residents traveled to Orillia for the new Unemployment Insurance.

Gerald and Inez Dunn survived a terrible car crash with a TTC streetcar in Toronto in March. She crawled out of the wreck and caught the next train home vowing not to return to Toronto. In June, E.L. DeLarge fell and broke his shoulder bone, the part where his arm was amputated due to earlier war injuries.

There were extra-large congregations at the World Day of Prayer services in March. Rev. Robert K. Trowbridge was rector of St. Thomas Anglican Church, Rev. S.S. Bailey was pastor of the Free Methodist Church, Rev. W.A. Campbell was minister of the Baptist Church, and Rev. C. Shapter was minister of the United Church.

Roy Fenwick returned to adjudicate the Muskoka Music Festival.

Carmen and Clayton Gibbs returned to their gold claims in Yukon for the summer.

Miss P. V. McNeeley resigned as high school principal to be succeeded by Don Stirling. W.C. Setherington, BSA, was engaged to replace Don Stirling.

Clarence Boyes and Alvin Hives received certificates in November from the "Red" Foster's Young Canada Club for reporting the location of an escaped prisoner from the Bracebridge jail. Delbert Peake was given the award for life-saving.

One hundred and twenty-five men of C Company, Grey and Simcoe Foresters from Camp Borden, marched into town as guests of the hockey team.

The Red Cross organized a collection of aluminum pots and such for the Aluminum Victory Dump. They also collected waste paper.

School students prepared a fine parade for the War Weapons Campaign. It included the Citizen's Band and speeches by Mayor McBride.

Two severe electrical storms struck in July doing major damage to trees, homes, and hydro equipment. March came in like a lion with a blinding snow storm.

Deaths this year included George Langford, 84, former

MPP, who built a house at the corner Ontario and Kimberley ... William C. Dennis, 72, a councillor of Bracebridge in 1910 and 1911 ... George A. Hines, 57, butcher and town councillor 1934 to 1936 ... Roy C. Armstrong, whose body was found in river in July. He had been missing since January ... Mungo Park McKay, 71, established the Muskoka Foundry. He gave the Motor Park the name Kelvin Grove Park ... I.B. Aulph, 81, was a councillor for the town from 1893 until 1902. He was clerk of the Muskoka Division Court for 21 years. The insurance man had been acting sheriff of Muskoka and Justice of the Peace. ... Mr. C.S. Hare, 61, former Royal Bank manager ... Harry Linney, newspaper columnist and one of Muskoka's greatest boosters. He travelled widely in the U.S. promoting Muskoka ... Eric Kaye, 28, killed at Nobel repairing hydro lines ... Isaac Matchett, 80 ... Basil Tobin, 29, of Tobin's Island, drowned in the Moon River ... Mrs. Will Towns ... Mr. Joseph Lazzara ... Captain Alfred Mortimer, 75, steamboat builder ... Hector Hammell, 20 ... Walter Spreadborough, 82.

## 1942

A state of war existed, and Bracebridge was involved down to its youngest citizen. Nearly every activity was impacted by the needs and challenges of the insidious war.

Rent control began in January and food restrictions and rations were tightening. Sugar was rationed to one pound per person per week, and restaurants were required to remove the sugar bowls from the tables. In July it was reduced to a pound per person per week with a coupon. Tea and coffee were rationed by coupon at one ounce of tea or four ounces of coffee a week.

News from servicemen came in letters such as from Norman Lyndon who wrote his parents in April telling that Sergeant Robert Everett had broken his leg in England during a parachute drop, and from LAC Nelson Boyes who chatted with King George and Queen Elizabeth during their visit to the YMCA in London. Other news was devastating. In January, Pilot Officer Roy Hines died in active service. Sergeant Melvin Hammell was reported missing in air operations in July. Sergeant Roy Ennis died in active duty in England and Flight Sergeant Haddo Bruce went missing over Germany. The Duke of Kent, the youngest brother of the King, was killed in an active service plane crash.

Flight Sergeant Aubrey Shapter escaped from a blazing plane which fell in the North Sea only to be killed as his father Rev. C.P. Shapter was conducting a memorial service for Floyd Tibbett, Roy Hines, Roy Ennis, Ivan Einarson and Haddo Bruce at his United Church. At Dieppe, Private William Grant, Royal Regiment, was missing, as was Private Thomas Armstrong of Baysville and Private Wilfred McDonald. Private Llewellyn Roberts was injured at Dieppe and Private W.G. French died handling a shotgun in Canada. The wife of Private Michael Boyer died after he left for war, and his 7-year-old daughter received word that her father was a prisoner of war at Dieppe. In November, Driver Frank Green of the Army Service Corps, formerly of Lake Drive Dairy, was killed in a blackout in England, and RCAF Pilot Officer William Laut, 21, was killed in action.

The Manpower Plebiscite vote was passed by all provinces except Quebec, giving the government the go-ahead signal to raise manpower by conscription for overseas service. At the end of May all unemployed men were required to register at the Employment and Claims Office of the Unemployment Insurance Commission.

Muskoka and Parry Sound were asked to raise $1,250,000 for Victory Loans, and Mr. B.Y. McBride was made chairman of the Bracebridge Victory Loan Committee.

Every church, social, sporting, and fraternal group held innovative events to raise funds for the many war relief needs. Captain L.R. Fraser headed up the War Finance Committee to amalgamate efforts of Victory Loan and War Savings campaigns. In May, the Bracebridge Red Cross began to raise $4,000 as their share of the Dominion campaign for $9,000,000 and the "18" knitting club raised money by baby sitting. The October Red Shield Drive got off to a slow start due to Captain Renick's poor health. The Victory Loan Committee fall objective was $185,000.

Salvage collection was coordinated by the town, Red Cross, Boy Scouts, and Rotary, and the Patriotic Salvage Committee called for paper, rags, fat and bones, bottles, cans, rubber, and magazines for troops. Conservation of materials and fuels forced grocers and retailers to reduce home delivery and Brewer's Retail restricted customers to one delivery a day. Only one automobile licence plate was issued this year, orange on black, and the old licence plates were turned over to one of several garages. Citizens were asked not to hoard goods beyond their needs as "cupboard quislings" (traitor to one's country) put stress on manufacturers. It was illegal to hoard scrap metal or unusable machinery, and unravelling old sweaters and re-knitting was recommended.

The RCAF took over the summer home of Mr. Frances Farwell at Milford Bay, which was fitted up as No. 1 Convalescent Home for 50 patients. The Canadian Women's Air Auxiliary Force was also there. Four Fairmile boats were launched in Georgian Bay in May and secondary school defence training was now compulsory.

By June, under the National Selective Service, no employer could hire anyone without the approval of a Selective Service Officer in an employment office of the Unemployment Insurance Commission. Later, manager William Towns established a local office where his clerk, Miss Betty Higgins, issued permits to those seeking employment. The Wartime Price Office and a Muskoka recruiting office opened in July.

It was the fourth year of war. Dr. F.M. Greig enlisted in the Royal Canadian Army Medical Corps and a platoon of Veterans' Guard was formed by Lieutenant Colonel K.A. Mahaffy, and Lieutenant Norman E. Prowse was put in charge. Women ages 20 to 24 were also required to register.

The Canadian Legion Cigarette Fund received proceeds of a Legion bingo and the admissions to a captured German propaganda film, *This is Blitz*, which was shown at the Town Hall. Retiring Legion president Comrade Lewis Dennis installed the new president Comrade W.C. Huckle, and1st vice president Comrade A.T. Waite. There were air raid precautions including disconnecting the gas supply in homes.

Robert J. Boyer of the *Muskoka Herald* left for the army in October, leaving his duties with Mrs. Boyer. Dr. R.E. Joyce of Port Carling took over Dr. Greig's practice. The price of coffee and tea was reduced 10 cents a pound by law, and milk had to be sold two cents a quart less. Further gasoline restrictions halted pleasure driving in October and soon bus travel was limited to 50-mile trips to save gas and rubber. The town clock tower was dark according to Canadian regulations. The Civil Guard was disbanded due to its inactivity.

Angus McKinnon Jr. bought the restaurant business of Mrs. H. Hunt. George Tennant's sawmill started operations, and Bert Tibbett bought William Towns' grocery. The contents of George Lee's restaurant were auctioned at J.G. Myers' store by E.L. DeLarge, auctioneer. In October, Northern Planing Mill and Shier's were working night and day. J.H. Elliott's Jewelry Store had closed but the stationery business was still operating. Parlett's Service Station, operated by Willard Draper since Mr. Parlett joined the RCAF, was closed indefinitely. John Morra moved his barber shop to the former Hines Butcher Shop and residence location. The Bracebridge Business Men's Club moved to new headquarters over the Hare Bros. store.

Rev. W. Argyle Campbell surprised the congregation of the Baptist Church in April by resigning at the morning service. The United Church choir gave a concert in May directed by G.W. Boyer, accompanied by Mrs. Anderson on the organ. Rev. Ellsworth Toll encouraged donations to the Red Cross. Salvation Army Captain Rennie was injured when his motorcycle crashed in Orillia. He and Mrs. Captain Baddley of Sudbury switched places. Rev. Father Roland F. Palmer, Superior of the SSJE, celebrated 25 years with the Anglican Church. Council voted down his request for permission to bring two Japanese men to work at the Mission House.

Mrs. and Rev. Peter W. McInnes left Knox Church for Durham in June. The president of the Ladies Aid of the United Church, Mrs. Albert Fawcett, resigned in October and Mrs. J.M. Johnston took over. Their anniversary supper was cancelled in view of the difficulty in procuring meat.

The Legion Hall was damaged by fire in January. The main lodge at Limberlost was destroyed by fire in February. Marilyn Denniss, 5, was burned to death in the barn of her great-uncle, councillor Richard Zimmerman of Macaulay. The Bell Telephone exchange alerted neigh-

*In this early 1940s scene, Fred Green and his team commence the long climb up the Wharf Road hill beside the powerhouse. Mr. Green was long a familiar sight in Bracebridge, carrying out a variety of chores. As late as the 1960s he was still clearing sidewalks for the town with a horse-drawn snowplow.* COURTESY OF VICKY BILLINGSLEY

bours about the fire as a public service. Within 10 days of the fall fair, the red barn for horses burned down.

George Tennant was chairman of the Bracebridge Power, Light and Water Commission again in 1942. Ladies were appointed to important positions for the first time: Mrs. R.K. Trowbridge to the Library Board, and Mrs. R.M. Best to the Board of Education.

A bylaw enabled retail stores to close at 10:30 Saturday nights during the winter, and stay open until 11:30 p.m. from July until September. The tax rate went up two mills to 52. Council approved the purchase of a new fire alarm system for the town in May, but permission to install the new metal machinery was refused by the Metal Control Board of Canada.

Council's hope that Bracebridge would be exempt from national power restrictions since it didn't buy from Ontario Hydro was abandoned. Manitoba Street was repaved up to the Monck road with the cost being shared with the Department of Municipal Affairs. The Department of Game and Fisheries restocked the north branch of the Muskoka River as requested by Council. Bad floods occurred in June when the McMurray Street drain plugged after heavy rain. The fire company's pump was needed to empty basements. Two long pieces of board lodged in a T-joint in the storm sewer drain were to blame for the flood.

Miss Norma Young injured her arm in a knitting machine at Bird's Mill. The Muskoka Curling Bonspiel was played on soft ice in February, and Wilbert Richards won the Duke Trophy and Russell Salmon won the Borntraeger Cup. Dr. W.G. Kenney, formerly with Dr. Bastedo, moved to Acton in February. Peter McNaughton Jr. designed a flag for the Alport School with a Union Jack, British lion, American eagle, and Russian bear.

The north door of the post office was closed because of ice from the roof of the tower.

Andrew Giaschi purchased Harry Rutherford's house on James Street. The former home of Mr. and Mrs. Leslie

*A spectacular display of lighting at Bracebridge Falls and the Silver Bridge. Note the "V" for Victory sign on the bridge in this 1942 photograph.* COURTESY OF THE WAITE FAMILY COLLECTION

Tennant was remodelled by Nelson Goltz. Miss Roxyna Phillips bought a house from William C. Denniss, formerly the J.L. Fenn residence.

The Agriculture Fair executive named George Parrett president and Jerry Dickie vice president ... The "18" Club held a tea at "The George" Apartments on Dominion Street for overseas war relief ... 50 attended the second annual meeting of the Muskoka Community Project where Mrs. C.K.S. MacDonald told of the "Skoka Crafts" table weaving loom ... A credit union was formed in May ... Alex C. Salmon was presented with a 50-year jewel for service with the IOOF ... Weldon Kilburn, prominent member of Toronto Conservatory of Music, conducted examinations of Bracebridge students in late June ... Dr. Edward G. Ellis reopened his office after a lengthy illness.

A RCAF bomber was damaged landing at the Muskoka Airport. Plans progressed for the opening of the Royal Norwegian Air Force training school by Crown Prince Olaf and Crown Princess Martha of Norway.

The first steamer up the river was Captain Harry Croucher's *Niska*. *Shamrock*, a sturdy tug also owned by Captain Croucher, was sold to Mr. John David Eaton of Toronto. Summer progressed with dances, movies, cottage visitors, and tourists.

Three days of draws, bugle bands, horses, and magician John Giordmaine highlighted the Rotary Fair in the arena. A horses-against-men drawing contest was great fun at the fall fair as were the softball games. The Plowing Match was held at Tom Ball's farm in October with winners Charlie McNabb, Norman Keall, and Ernie Keall ... The Boy Scouts had an Apple Day ... Citizens enjoyed watching Mabel Dadson riding her horse to town and tethering at the top of Chancery Lane to save gas and rubber ... Constable Cudmore arrested a "notorious defrauder" who was cheating soldier's relatives throughout southern Ontario.

Mr. John Lee grew a 16-pound turnip and Andy Clarke one of 14 pounds. Raspberries were picked in early November by Phyllis Mason in Ufford. George F. Armstrong closed his butcher shop for six weeks due to illness. Hunting season saw the departure of local men to the bush. The birth of George Wellington Reid was announced – a fifth generation Bracebridge resident.

A runaway Hammond Dairy horse crashed through a stout wooden picket fence between the Red Indian Service Station and the railway tracks. One hundred quarts of milk were lost but the driver and horse were fine.

Twenty men formed the Lions Club with officers including Vincent Kyle, president, George Hammond, vice president, C.R. Wright, secretary, and Gus Braida as treasurer.

Miss Irene Spence joined the public school staff in June and Mrs. Winnifred Fletcher the high school staff. Schools opened September 22 to allow many of 160 students to work on farms. Mr. William Setterington and Mrs. Fletcher taught defence training, and Mrs. Winnifred Fletcher took over Miss Farrellly's place in the English department. In November, Grade 2 teacher Miss Louise Gerhart resigned and was to be replaced by Miss Ethel Jeffries from Macaulay.

The Muskoka River opened March 21, and a big winter storm April 11 was gone in two days. A thick white frost June 15 affected a number of gardens. A heavy gale blew over Muskoka August 22 taking down power lines and trees with heavy winds and rain. An excellent view of an eclipse of the moon took place August 25. Eight inches of snow fell October 27; even the bell in the town clock was dulled by the heavy snow.

Some of the residents who passed away are recorded here: William McConnell, 78, 25 years chief of police ... Einar Einarson, 49, Vankoughnet lumberman ... Robert J. White, 77 ... Bennet Young McBride, 64, Muskoka Falls, former mayor and leader of most major organizations ... Mr. Newland Spreadborough, 63 ... Charles O. Shaw, 83, head of the Anglo-Canadian Leather Co. ... Captain W.A. Sibbett, 52.

## 1943

The impact of the war was keenly felt in town as families' loved ones made the supreme sacrifice. Canadians lived under the stress of restrictions on all facets of their existence. The service organizations made every effort to raise funds with a variety of activities for many causes.

Bracebridge "boys" and "girls" continued to enlist and in January, boys over 17 years old were enlisted for training with their parents' written consent. Single men were required to register in February and in May, 19-year-olds were asked to sign up. Graduate nurses had been required to register with Department of Labour in late winter.

Correspondence carried proud news such as when Flying Officer Tony Pierce won a DFC for service over the Alps in January. But throughout the year terrible news was received about the death and injuries of local servicemen. In February, Flight Sergeant Jack Sinclair Boyer was killed over Newfoundland and 21-year-old Sergeant Douglas Kaye died in England. RCAF officer Jack Fraser, 19, went missing after air operations in April, 23-year-old Flight Sergeant Keith Taylor was killed in action, and Sergeant Melvin T. Hammell was presumed dead. In July, RCAF Pilot Officer Jack Loucks, 19, lost his life in a plane crash in Canada and Sergeant Myrl Bunn was missing after air operations overseas.

As of August 1943, the Honour Roll of young servicemen was: RCAF, Jack Boyer, Haddo Bruce, Gilbert Boyer, Ivan Einarson, Roy Ennis, Robert Goodman, Melvin Hammell, Roy Hines, Douglas Kaye, William Laut, Jack Loucks, Aubrey Shapter, Keith Taylor, Floyd Tibbett; Ferry Command (Civilian), Glen McKay; Royal Canadian Army Service Corps, Frank J. Green; Royal Regiment of Canada, Wilfred McDonald; Royal Canadian Engineers, James Nichols. By September, flight officers Reg Coombs and Don Urquhart, and Sergeant Gordon Wright were missing overseas after air operations. Sergeant Lance Buttler of Port Carling, Flight Officer Reg Coombs, and Flight Sergeant Gordon Wright were reported as prisoners of war.

The federal government's National Selective Service announced early in the year that all men and women were required to seek employment only through that agency and employers must hire only through them. The first compulsory employment transfer order was enacted in May to assure that those employed in non-essential jobs would report to the Selective Service Office.

The RCAF Mobile Recruiting Unit was in town regularly to meet men and women at the Town Hall, and in September, Miss Alma Peacock and Mrs. T.W. Pierce were selected as RCAF recruiting representatives.

The Red Cross Society's contribution was enormous. In two months some 14,400 surgical emergency units were made by the Bracebridge Branch. Their next job was packing toilet articles for the women in the active services. A mobile blood donors unit held the first blood clinic in July.

Citizens endured food restrictions and rations. By the end of January, butter consumption was temporarily reduced to one-half pound each per week per person. Meatless days and meat rationing commenced in May. No meat could be served in restaurants, hotels, or institutions. About two pounds of meat per person per week was available with the coupon ration book. Fat and bone were salvaged to make glycerin for bullets and aircraft glue. The purchase of tea, coffee, sugar, butter, and meat was restricted. Preserves and sweet spread were rationed by coupon.

The Legion held a tag day to raise money to continue sending smokes to servicemen. A $1 donation would provide a soldier with 300 cigarettes. The Navy League asked for more than 150,000 ditty bags for the navy and merchant marine. The toiletries and goodies cost $3 to $5 each to fill.

The 1943 tax rate was set at 56 mills. Mr. John Johnson was appointed to the Power, Light and Water Commission in May for the balance of the late Mr. J.W. Reid's term of office. Chief constable William Cudmore proclaimed a curfew of 10:00 p.m. for children under 16 unless accompanied by parent or guardian. Council approved tag days for the Kinsmen Club's "Milk for Britain" fund and for the Navy League.

Mayor Ernest A. Whitten and councillors Roy Shier, Lawrence Frowe, Park McKay, W.J.A. Brown, Alan Hutchinson, and Earle Dunn were acclaimed to office for 1944. John M. Johnson was unanimously returned to the Power, Light and Water Commission, and other members were George Tennant, chairman, and E.A. Whitten. E.J. Ball was superintendent, and W.A. Richards secretary-treasurer.

Earle Rosewarne of Muskoka Garage bought the trucking business from Percy Hammell and Son in April. Lakeshore Transports, which had been owned by Allan Fraser for 12 years, was sold to Robert Meeks. Mr. Fraser continued to wholesale ice cream and milk. Pierce's Hairdressing Parlour moved to the next shop north of Thatcher's Studio.

Mrs. Irene Hunt purchased the Louise Shop from Mrs. Hugh McLaughlin (Edith Hare). Miss Marion Bird was in charge of the Bird's Information Bureau. The Muskoka Garage offered to sell wood and coal, when it was possible to secure it. Coal was in very short supply this winter. The Muskoka Trading Company built a grain elevator next to the Shell Oil Co. tanks at the railway. Dr. J.E. Bromley opened a medical office, with the approval of the Canadian Medical Procurement and Assignment Board, on Manitoba St. next to the A & P.

Rev. Robert Armstrong was called to the Knox Church … Capt. George Knox replaced Mrs. Captain R. Baddley at the Salvation Army … Rev. D.H. Easter became the new pastor at the Baptist Church. They had been without a pastor since May 1942.

The Loyal Orange Lodge 218 elected Worshipful Master John Fox, Deputy Master Edward McEwen, Chaplain William Wray, recording secretary N. Wettlaufer, secretary-treasurer George Hammond, 1st lecture Robert Meeks, 2nd lecture Harry Cole, and Marshall Dave Kirkness … The Lions Club received their charter at a gala occasion on January 21 with over 100 guests. The Lions re-appointed former officers, adding Alan Hives as treasurer, and operated a penny raffle run by Dr. E.G. Ellis and Lion F.W. Nettleton … The South Muskoka Agricultural Society elected C.H. Kaye as president, Harvey Gray first vice president, and Ernest Goltz second vice president … Miss Jessie MacMillan was re-elected president of the Bracebridge Horticultural Society with Mrs. G.H.O. Thomas vice president … The Clef Club held a banquet to recognize its 35 years of activity … R.M. Best was elected Rotary president … Miss Margaret Bird was re-elected a president of the Woman's Auxiliary of the Red Cross, ably assisted by Mrs. William Wray and Mrs. Cornie Reynolds as vice presidents … Major A.A. Lyndon was re-elected president of the Bracebridge Branch of the Red Cross … The Rotary Club marked its seventh anniversary in December. Its contribution to the community was proudly reported. The Rotary Club canvassed for $260,000 for Victory Bonds.

*During the war the Royal Norwegian Air Force had its headquarters beside Muskoka Airport – "Little Norway." Here a group of Norwegian women trainees stand at ease.* COURTESY OF BRENDA COX

The First Girl Guide Troop was formed by commissioner Mrs. George Hammell with Mrs. Chris Forth as president, Mrs. Willard Draper as secretary, and Mrs. Earl Walker as treasurer. At the May enrollment meeting, the captain was Miss Mae McCracken, assisted by Misses Eleanor Tennant, Evelyn Dickson, Phyllis Eaton, and Audrey Johnson.

Crown Prince Olav and Crown Princess Martha visited the Little Bergen airport, the new official headquarters of the Royal Norwegian Air Force (at the Muskoka airport in Muskoka Township). Later in the year, the Princess delighted shoppers when she and her three children bought shoes in Bracebridge.

New car markers (licence plates) were released with orange figures on a black plate, one plate per vehicle. Postal rates increased one cent making it necessary to use a four-cent stamp to mail a letter.

A District Seed Fair aimed to encourage better seed preparation in April.

Phil Hines caught a 25-pound, three-foot salmon trout in Lake Muskoka just as the summer season got under way with hotels opening and boat service beginning. Some well-known captains were Ralph Lee (*Sagamo*), A.T. Corbett (*Cherokee*), R.F. Leeder (*Segwun*), Wesley Hill (*Islander*), and H. Hatherly (*Ahmic*).

There were some unusual accidents. Jack McGeean, 17, fell off the gangplank and drowned at the dock just as the *Segwun* pulled away. Frank Avery, 28, drowned near Matthiasville when his car plunged into the river. Glen Coates, driving his Wood Specialty car, saved passenger Alfred Rivers from drowning. A runaway truck which had been parked at the library rolled down Queen's Hill and smashed a window in the Queen's Hotel. The *Ahmic* ran ashore in July after hitting a sunken buoy near Birch Island. The passengers were taken off in the life-boats and the RMS *Sagamo* and picked them up to continue on the 100-mile cruise.

Summer band concerts played as usual although the band was reduced in numbers – 12 members had enlisted: Phil Thomas, Albert Rutherford, Louis Caisse,

*Trainees at "Little Norway" take rifle practice.* COURTESY OF BRENDA COX

Stan Shier, Ted Reid, Bill Creswick, Harry Berofe, Harry Hewitt, Ken Bray, Bob Bird, Russ Reynolds, and Ron McKay. Harvey Kennedy was president. The junior band helped keep up the concerts.

Muskoka Garage exchanged its motors and mechanics for the festive appearance of the fifth Rotary Fair August 27-28, and drew record crowds. Over $1,000 was raised for charitable work at bingo, crown and anchor, horse racing, and lucky draws. Tommy Ball won the Lions Club outboard motorboat at the final bingo game of the season. The fall fair maintained its standard of excellence.

In October, the Rotary Club started its fifth Victory Loan Drive for $285,000. High school students competed in an ad-writing contest.

Wolves were heard out in the hills near the town line and sheep farmers George Harper, Fred Stuart, W.K. Kettle, H.E. Beaumont, B. Henry, and the Baker's and Spreadborough's farms reported 25 sheep killed by wolves or dogs in the preceding three weeks. A wolf pup was shot on Herbert Shire's farm and he claimed the $25 bounty for the 26-pound animal.

In spite of serious problems with transportation and other handicaps, the Muskoka District Tourist Development Association experienced the largest number of tourists in the history of the association.

The Lions and Rotary clubs developed an open-air ice rink in Jubilee Park for winter skating and hockey, headed by Rotarian Earle Rosewarne and Lion W.A. Shier.

Fire destroyed the Yearley arena skating and curling rink in January. The barn full of paper scrap on Quebec Street which had been used by the Patriotic Salvage Committee burned down in May. On November 22, the Thomas Block next to Chancery Lane was gutted in a spectacular blaze with damage estimated at $20,000.

In January, the Board of Education elected Edward S. Hunt chairman (his 24th year in this trusted position). George Jeffries, Milton Shier, and D.C. Thomas were returned as trustees and constable William Cudmore was re-appointed school attendance officer. High school principal Don Stirling enlisted in the RCAF and Cecil R. Wright was appointed acting principal. Michael Fife of Sudbury joined BHS in March after his honourable discharge from the army, and teacher William C. Setterington joined the Royal Canadian Navy. The schools started late in September, allowing students time to help with the work on the farms.

There was a big blizzard January 15 and Lazarra's barn behind the Whitten Co.'s store collapsed under the weight of snow, as did the roof of the Ecclestone warehouse behind the Armories. Muskoka shivered one night in February at -37°. Lake navigation opened later this year as the ice went out of the Muskoka Lakes April 29. The river flooded, with the wharf and River Street covered for days. An earthquake tremor was felt in March.

E.G. Rankin, Royal Bank manager, was transferred to near Ottawa.

Deaths this year included Charles E. Lount, 81, resident of Bracebridge for 73 years, registrar of lands … Robert G. Coupland, 54, mechanic, of Muskoka Falls … A.E. Fawcett, manager of the Bracebridge Information Bureau … James Henry, 45, killed by a tree he was felling … J. Wellington Reid, 62, accountant for Hutchison Bros. for 40 years … Dwight Nelson, electrocuted while working on a power line at Shier Lumber … William H. Shier, 63, vice president of Shier Lumber … James McBride of Muskoka Falls … Thomas M. Armstrong, a member of the Veterans' Guard … Charles S. McGaughey, 57, husband of Rene Caisse, died in North Bay.

**1944** Sons, brothers, husbands, and other loved ones were dying or being terribly injured continents away in the horrendous war and Bracebridge citizens, directly or indirectly, continued to support them as best they could. The monthly Red Cross blood clinics were bringing in 50 to over 100 pints of blood and every organization was raising war funds.

Reports showed pupils of Muskoka public schools purchased $3,365.66 worth of War Savings during the first four months of the 1944-45 term. In April, the public schools collected 12,390 pounds of salvage materials. Twenty-five school pupils entered a Victory Garden Competition sponsored by the Bracebridge Horticultural Society. Approximately 15,000 fruit baskets were collected. At Halloween, public school pupils collected for the Milk-for-Britain fund.

A Red Cross Reserve Nursing Unit was organized under the direction of Miss Beth Kirkpatrick, RN. Miss Margaret Bird was re-elected president of Red Women's Auxiliary.

A rehabilitation committee, headed by Harry Wilson, was established to prepare organizations to help re-establish returned men and women in civilian life.

Personal tragedy continued to strike the community as the news of Muskoka area men and women was made known: Flight Sergeant Ross Terry of Milford Bay, formerly reported missing, was known to be a prisoner of war. Private Harold Dixon of Port Carling was killed in action in Italy.

The Allies invaded Europe June 6 and D-Day was marked by prayer services throughout country. Local churches held joint services. The first Bracebridge boy to have made the supreme sacrifice in the Allied invasion of Europe was Sapper John Cecil Irvine who died as a result of injuries incurred on D-Day.

Those killed in action included Rifleman Herman Stock ... Private Harvey Walker ... Able Seaman Frederick Armstrong ... Rifleman Leslie McEachern ... Malcolm Stevenson, in Italy ... Stanley Bull, in France ... Cyril McQuillan, died from wounds ... John Roberts ... Albert Traves, in France ... Gerald Kingshott in Italy ... Corporal James Joselin, in France ... Private Rex Mann, in France ... Walter Cowan.

The list of injured included Leslie Stanhope, RCA. Recorded as missing were Bombardier Kitchener Hooton, Allan MacDonald, Don Shapter, James Speck (later believed to be a prisoner of war), and Corporal Alan Laut, later located as a prisoner of war.

Sergeant Mabel Patterson, Utterson, was awarded the British Empire Medal in the King's Birthday Honours; Flight Lieutenant Tony Pierce and Flight Officer Robert Pridday were awarded a Bar each to their Distinguished Flying Cross and given a civic welcome. Sergeant Clifford Tryon was awarded a Military Medal. Flight Officer Borden Lyndon earned a Distinguished Flying Cross.

Restrictions and rations continued. The 1944 motor vehicle permits included a windshield stamp that validated the use of the 1943 plate – a measure taken to conserve steel. The chartered banks of Canada published their role in "ration coupon banking." Grocers and others who accepted ration coupons from customers were deposited in the banking system with ultimate payment to the government. The brewing industry pleaded with customers to return empty beer bottles in their original containers, because new ones were very restricted. Distribution of ration book 4 took place in March and book 5 was available in October.

War pictures, sponsored by Legion, were shown at the Town Hall. Royal Norwegian Air Force planes raided town in a daylight bombing attack dropping thousands

*Although the war was far away, Norwegian air force planes based at Muskoka Airport roared overhead on training flights.* COURTESY OF BRENDA COX

of leaflets over the Memorial Park as part of the Sixth Loan campaign.

Military manoeuvers were presented at a band concert by visiting soldiers from Camp Borden followed by a street dance. A corn roast at Stephens' Bay sponsored by the Alport Neighbourly Club brought in $185 for the Red Cross. The Rotary Fair in Muskoka Garage brought in about $2,000 for war and community work.

The acclaimed Council was inaugurated in January. Mayor Ernest A. Whitten appointed councillor A.R. Shier acting mayor for the year. Council passed a bylaw requiring licences for local restaurants. In 1944 the tax rate was set at 53 mills, reduced by two.

Norman Prowse resigned as clerk of Monck Township and was named to the office of registrar of deeds and master of titles for the District of Muskoka, succeeding the late Charles E. Lount. Norman Willmott of Beaumaris replaced him.

George Jeffries was chosen chairman of the Board of Education at the inaugural meeting. The Muskoka District Council met and the constitution was re-drafted with W.J. Patterson of Stephenson chosen president.

E.W. Clairmont resigned as Crown attorney for Muskoka District and Lieutenant Colonel Kenneth A. Mahaffy was appointed. W.B. Elliott assumed duties as sheriff of Muskoka.

The former Denniss Mill, the property of the Northern Planing Mills, underwent extensive repairs. Mr. William Brazier was appointed by the Dominion government as caretaker of the post office building. He had been doing the work since the death of the former caretaker, Mr. Charles Grimwood.

Wilbert Richards looked after the John T. Andrews insurance business during the latter's illness. Edwin Senior opened for business in former Hartley Shoe Repair Shop.

Construction was under way on the local branch of Canada Wood Specialty Co. mill on the old Beardmore Tannery site. A cold storage plant was completed at Hammond's Dairy on the site of the former Beeler's Tire and Service Station. J.L. Bowie took over management of the Albion Hotel and Bigwin Inn celebrated its 25th anniversary.

On June 1 the Holiday House opened in Bracebridge. It was a transformation of the former Mahaffy house (Kirk house) at the south end of Dominion street, overlooking the falls and wharf. The new owners were Mrs. Wise and her daughter and son-in-law Mr. and Mrs. Allchin.

A memorial service for Ven. Archdeacon Frederick George Scott was held at St. Thomas Anglican Church and at the same service, an honour roll bearing the names of 73 members of the congregation on active service was dedicated ... Local women joined in a world-wide observance of a day of prayer February 25 ... Special services were held at the Free Methodist Church conducted by Bishop M.D. Ormston ... An honour roll was unveiled at Knox Presbyterian Church with Guides, Cubs, and the Legion taking part in a church parade ... Rev. B.A. Stutton preached his farewell sermon at the Free Methodist Church. Rev. C.R. Chatson was appointed to succeed him ... Bracebridge United Church observed its anniversary by paying off its mortgage on the church building. There was a mortgage-burning ceremony.

Crown Prince Olaf and Crown Princess Martha of Norway visited camp Little Norway at the conclusion of a brief holiday at Interlaken.

Dr. A.F. Bastedo was elected Rotary Club president ... John Fox was chosen Legion president ... Albert Hollingsworth was installed as Noble Grand and W.J.A. Brown was elected District Warden IOOF ... Dr. R.J. Dodds was chosen president of the Horticultural Society ... Mrs. W.C. Huckle was chosen president of the Women's Division of the Ontario Association of Agricultural Societies ... The Philathea Club celebrated its sixth birthday with a banquet ... The Clef Club celebrated its 36th anniversary ... The Oddfellows bingo raised $25 for the Knitting Club and their war work.

Premier George Drew addressed the Muskoka Tourist Development Association banquet at the Albion Hotel, promising to boost post-war tourist trade in Ontario. H.E. Rice was re-elected president with Mr. Tomlinson appointed executive secretary.

St. Joseph's dramatic Society presented entertaining comedy *Nora, Wake Up*.

A local unit of the Co-operative Commonwealth Federation (CCF) formed with John Johnston as local president. At their Aston Villa banquet G. Leslie Tennant was elected riding president.

G.U. Mills was chosen CCF federal candidate for Muskoka-Ontario. The Liberals choose George Panter, Gravenhurst, while the Conservatives opted for J.M. McDonnell.

Bob Everett gave a display of painting he did while in active service with the RCAF in England.

The school board hired Miss Irene Morgan to replace Mrs. Winnifred Fletcher on the high school staff. Campbell Kerr was also hired.

The Lions Club celebrated its first anniversary of charter night with a banquet and dance. Cecil Wright was the new Lions president.

The 70th fall fair in Bracebridge had 1,677 entries for competition and a military display by a company of soldiers from the Orillia Basic Training Camp. H.E. Beaumont won first place in field crop competition. Plans were announced for erection of new fair building.

Civilian deaths this year included ... Mrs. Ellen Fisher, 93 ... D'Alton Armstrong ... Mrs. I.B. Aulph ... William Galbraith ... James Young, 99, a Muskoka Township pioneer ... Mrs. Joseph Oliver ... Mrs. Alfred Parrett ... Mrs. Percy Hammell ... Mrs. Lillian Holliday ... George E. Brooks ... Mrs. Walter Reynolds ... Ernest Strong ... A.B. Bert Tibbett ... Harry Blackmore ... James C. Reid, manager of Bigwin Inn ... John E. Ramsay ... Mrs. Hugh Campbell, Muskoka Falls ... Mrs. Clarence McBride, Muskoka Falls ... Mrs. John G. Golden ... James S. Glass, Monck Township ... William McNeil, Muskoka Falls ... Mrs. Harold Bickmore.

*To cope with burgeoning post-war electricity demands, Bracebridge developed its last hydroelectric site in the late 1940s, at High Falls on the North Muskoka River. A concrete powerhouse and a dam were built into the northerly of the three cataracts making up the falls, with a control dam across the river above the road bridge. The latter connected the Baysville Highway with the High Falls Road until a dump truck went through it in the early 1950s during construction of the new Highway 11 crossing just upstream. Above photo taken 1948.* COURTESY OF DON CURRIE

# 1945–1954

## *Our 8th Decade: More Power for Post-War Growth*

BRACEBRIDGE BEGAN 1945, its 70th year of municipal organization, with Mayor A.E. Whitten and councillors J.A. Hutcheson, Lawrence Frowe, W.J.A. Brown, Roy Shier, George Hammond, and Dr. L.N. Ryan. In the outlying townships these men had been declared reeves: Dan MacNaughtan, Macaulay; George Freemantle, Monck; H.E. Beaumont, Muskoka; Wesley Morrow, Draper; and James Henderson, Oakley.

One of the issues this year was that of power shortages. This gave rise to the question of whether or not to develop a hydroelectric generating station at High Falls on the north branch of the Muskoka River. During the municipal elections in November the ratepayers gave their go-ahead with a 329-8 vote! Competition for hydroelectric sites was becoming fierce between Bracebridge, Huntsville, Gravenhurst, and Orillia.

It was noted that "all pistols and revolvers had to be re-registered with Chief Constable William Cudmore by July 1, 1945."

Just north of Bracebridge the ratepayers of Stephenson Township and Port Sydney met to vote on a proposed consolidated rural school, a scene that would play itself out in most Muskoka communities over the next two decades as the one room schools were ultimately phased out.

The work of the Society of St. John the Evangelist (SSJE) remained strong in the area. Sunday services were held at Port Sydney, Allensville, Martin's Siding, Port Cunnington, Ravenscliff, Melissa, Beatrice, Lancelot, Holy Cross (Taylor Line), St. Peter's (Rocksborough), Purbrook, Alport, Allan's Corners, and at the Mission House in Bracebridge. In February, Rev. J.W. Hawkes and Rev. R.F. Palmer of the SSJE officially dedicated the newly renovated St. Anna's House which had been the former Barron farmhouse on the eastern edge of town. It was at this time that it became the centre for the work of the Sisters of St. John the Divine who had come to replace the Sisters of St. Margaret who left in 1944. Members of these Anglican religious orders did much good work among the people of Muskoka during the difficult years of the Depression and the war.

The editor of the *Bracebridge Gazette* noted that the "ancient but not so venerable railway station" built in 1885-86 by the Northern and Pacific Junction Railway, might be replaced. It was hoped that the new structure would be "in keeping with the size and importance of the Muskoka County Town"; the project never came to fruition. It was to the railway station on Main Street that many soldiers, such as Percy Brazier, were returning. When he arrived in town on the Northland, hundreds of people gathered to greet him. He was the son of Mr. and Mrs. William Brazier, who had seven sons overseas during World War II. He had recently spent three and a half cruel years in a German prisoner-of-war camp.

The war effort was gradually winding down and the local papers gave weekly reports of those who had finally returned home. The students and staff of Bracebridge Public School participated in a Victory Program at the Town Hall, directed by Principal B.R. Minns. Hymns and prayers were sung and offered in the presence of local dignitaries and visiting parents. The school was commended for its outstanding war work which included the collecting of such things as milkweed pods (35 bags), licence plates, and 16,355 wooden baskets.

WE WILL REMEMBER THEM *The Cenotaph at Bracebridge*

*World War I*

John C. Allen
Timothy R. Allen
James Barrett
Harold B. Bates
Arthur H. Burridge
George C. Clarke
John E. Code
Stanley Dickie
Roy Foster
Edward Fradette
Percy Furlong
William Grimwood
Donald Jeffrey
Douglas Johnson
Ronald Kerr
Isadore Labrie
Harry Langmaid
Beart Leavett
William H. Lilky
Sydney E. Lount
Alex W. Mathieson
Elmer Mayes
Alfred Miller
Robert Moreland
Blain MacDonald
Samuel MacDonald
Rae Nelson Olsen
W. Claude Perry
James Pollock
James Robertson
Percy Robinson
Albert Rutherford
Charles Wormaid

*World War II*

T.M. Armstrong
Jack Boyer
Gilbert Boyer
Haddo Bruce
Stanley Bull
John Butler
Walter Cowan
Lemeul Davis
Allen Doley
Harold N. Dixon
Kenneth Earnshaw
Ivan Einarson
Roy Ennis
Jack Foster
Frank J. Green
Mel Hammell
James Hillman
Kenneth Hammond
Roy Hines
J.K. Hooton
J.C. Irvine
James Joselin
Douglas Kaye
Gerald Kingshott
Wm. Charles Laut
Jack Loucks
Rex C. Mann
Leslie MacEachern
Wilford McDonald
Glen McKay
James Nichols
Allen C. Olimer
John Roberts
Roy O. Rutter
Raymond Sander
Esmond Scovell
M.J. Stevenson
Aubrey Shapter
Donald Shapter
James Speck
L. Keith Taylor
Albert Traves
Floyd Tibbett
Ronald Thompson
Gordon Warnica

*Korean War*

Donald Bradshaw
Roy Elliott

Festive occasions were held too for the returning armed service personnel. One such gathering at Bracebridge High School concluded with the presentation of certificates of appreciation – 170 of them all artistically penned by public school teacher Miss Inez Ecclestone. Certainly the Remembrance Day service of 1945 had very significant meaning as the parade, under the auspices of Legion Branch No. 161, marched to the high school auditorium from the Red Indian Service Station then on to the hospital, where "Bus" Brazier placed the Ontario government wreath at the memorial tablet.

The names of the 44 local soldiers who gave their lives in the service of their country were remembered.

An unusual piece of Muskoka war history came to a close in mid-February when the Royal Norwegian Air Force at Camp Little Norway held an appreciation night for the training facility (as well as their holiday place at Interlaken in Sinclair Township near Huntsville) they had enjoyed at Reay since 1942. Their farewell to Canada came just five days before fire destroyed much of their beautiful log officers' mess. In the course of Little Norway's existence over 2,000 pilots, crew, and ground crew had been trained. This personnel was considered to be among the most effective of the Allied Air Command.

The Township of Oakley council purchased a half acre east of the Vankoughnet Orange Hall to honour the people of their township who had served in the war.

Elections were held in the spring of 1945 for both provincial and federal parliaments. Earlier in the year, the sitting MP for the Muskoka-Ontario riding, Stephen Furniss of Brechin, retired. His Liberal replacement, George Panter of Gravenhurst, was beaten by the Conservative candidate, J.M. Macdonnell, by 724 votes. This was the last federal election in which Muskoka-Ontario was an electoral district.

Provincially, the Conservatives candidate, Major Arthur Welsh of Sunderland, beat out the incumbent Liberal MPP, J. Frank Kelly of Huntsville, by 1,900 votes.

Although the restrictions of the war made travelling somewhat difficult, the Muskoka Tourist Development Association (MTDA) reported that Muskoka was still a popular spot for summer guests. For the first time since its inception the MTDA adopted a constitution with H.E. Rice of Huntsville as president and Wilbert Richards of Bracebridge as secretary-treasurer.

*V-E Day produced a spontaneous outpouring of joy after six long years of war.* COURTESY OF BRENDA COX

The Muskoka District Council, founded in 1920, was headed by Andrew Kellock, clerk of Huntsville.

Scoutmaster W.H. Thompson reported that the following boys had passed their Tenderfoot tests: Hugh Potts, Ken Black, Raymie Lee, Bob Parlett, Wes Finch, Brisant Oliver, and Len Kaye.

The remodelled stable that served as a clubhouse for lawn bowling and tennis was saved from destruction by fire by an alert member. This building was located beside the public school.

The home of Mr. Sol Bowers on the north side of Ontario Street in the "Hollow" was destroyed by fire. It was the last of "Sing Brown Row," a row of small frame houses built in the 1890s by businessman Singleton Brown.

Shoppers could purchase eggs for 41¢ a dozen, bread for 7¢ a loaf, and a pound of coffee for 43¢ at grocery stores in town such as the A & P, W.E. Baker, Hutchison Bros., Muskoka Trading, Hare Brothers, P.J. Marrin, and Mrs. D. McBride.

Herman Brooks purchased the butcher shop of Sam Armstrong in Chancery Lane. Ed Provan bought the original Orange Lodge building at the foot of Manitoba Street from R.M. Best, KC. Reverend Frank Nock was welcomed as the new minister at St. Thomas Anglican Church. Joan Waite and Glen Coates sang solos at his

*From the old swimming pool at Kelvin Grove Park, Edward Lynch and his children Mary Kelly and Bill gaze across Bracebridge Bay as a train steams over the bridge. Long before the creation of the extensive park around the bay, Bracebridge Falls was a scenic attraction for townspeople and visitors.* COURTESY OF MRS. MARY KELLY FENN

welcome in Browning Memorial Hall. One thousand telephone books were released in the area. Names with the most listings included Smith, Shier, Goltz, and Riley.

A popular series of articles about the "History of Muskoka" by Captain Levi Fraser began to appear in the *Bracebridge Gazette* starting April 1945.

Although now living in Barrie, Mary Liddard (now Mrs. Strange), the first white baby born in Bracebridge, was reported to have turned 82.

Musically, many events occurred during 1945. The Toronto Conservatory reported the achievements of many pupils, among them Bernice Shier, Daphne Wray, and Margaret Rosewarne who had successfully passed Grades 9, 8, and 6, respectively. The Bracebridge Choral Society was started with Miss Roxyna Phillips as conductor. Other officers were Mayor E.A. Whitten, president; Mr. D.C. Thomas, vice president; Miss Betty Higgins, secretary-treasurer; and Mrs. Alf Quemby, pianist.

With regret, the congregation of Knox Presbyterian Church accepted the resignation of Mr. B.R. Minns, organist since 1925 and principal of Bracebridge Public School.

In July, the Beaumaris Hotel, named after a famous resort in Wales, burned down. The fire started in the kitchen in the wee hours of the morning. Staff alerted all 200 guests and got them out safely. This resort had been built in 1871, the cornerstone being laid by Paul Dane, Tondern Island's original settler. The name Tondern was chosen because it was current in the news of the day about the Franco-Prussian War of 1870-71.

Captain Ralph Lee, who began his career with the Muskoka Lakes Navigation Company in 1889, retired in July. He had served as master of the *Sagamo* for more than 30 years.

A gold strike in Macaulay Township was reported by Frank Brown, a sawmill operator along the Kirk Line. The drilling was carried out by R.J. Gillmore of Kirkland Lake.

Bracebridge High School reported a record enrollment of 236 students.

Harvey Gray was elected president of the South Muskoka Agricultural Society. Five boys were also elected as junior directors to "encourage young people to take an interest in the work of the Society." These were Max Beaumont, John Kettle, Charlie Morrow, Melvin Goltz, and George Parrett Jr. The fall fair had over 4,000 people attend. The school parade winners for rural schools were Baysville, Milford Bay, Brandy Lake, and Uffington, while Miss Mae McCracken and Miss Edith Robinson's classes won for the town.

Deaths for this year included George Tennant, lumberman, resident of Bracebridge from 1887, figured largely in the town's progress, especially as a councillor and member of the Power, Light and Water Commission where he served for 31 years, 24 as chairman. In 1925 he established Northern Planing Mills on the site of the old furniture factory. He married Annie Phillips ... Roy MacCoubrey, 53, former Macaulay councillor and school section No. 1 trustee ... Salvation Army Major Thomas J. Meeks, 68, son of Muskoka Township pioneer Solon Meeks; he had entered full-time Salvation Army work at age 19 ... Reg Hines, manager of the LCBO ... Mary Jane Kaye of Monck ... Walter M. Lee, 84, pioneer of Draper, leaving his wife Margaret McConnell and sons John and Walter ... Mrs. E.R. Rutter, 81, came to Muskoka in 1876 with her parents Mr. and Mrs. William Stamp ... Sam G. Holditch, died in Orillia. He was a son of pioneer farmer and merchant William Holditch, who put the first powered boat on the Muskoka Lakes about 1864, it being worked by horses ... Seymour R.G. Penson, 94, illustrator of the noted *Guide Book and Atlas* published in 1879, died in Georgetown ... William Henry Inch, 87, who came with his family to Falkenburg about 1865 ... Orville Cooper, of Hamilton, whose grandfather James was the first whiteman to settle at North Falls ... Mrs. Sam Mereweather, 69, resident since 1893 and devout member of the First Baptist Church ... Henry Gohm, 67, pioneer fox farmer in Muskoka ... Hugh Campbell, 78, resident of Muskoka Falls. He had worked on many projects that helped in the development of Muskoka, such as bridges, the Bracebridge powerhouse, the South Falls log chute, dams, and the Northern and Pacific Junction Railway.

## 1946

A new mayor was elected in the person of Dr. A.F. Bastedo, a popular physician whose home and office were located beside the United Church. Joining him were experienced councillors W.J.A. Brown, Roy Shier, and Dr. L.N. Ryan, and newcomers Philip Thomas, Bert Bell, and Edgar Foreman. In the outlying townships the reeves remained the same as in 1945. The Muskoka District Council elected the mayor of Gravenhurst, Harold R. King, as president. District Council discussed such things as a district home for the aged, removal of suckers from the Muskoka Lakes, and more effective ways of dealing with tax arrears and tax sales.

The work of the churches continued to flourish 85 years after the first religious services were conducted in the tiny hamlet of North Falls. Early in the new year, several churches cooperated in a special week of prayer meetings, the speakers being members of the local clergy.

St. Thomas Anglican Church organized a Boy's Club with Jim Amm as president, Alf Goodfellow secretary, and George Ecclestone treasurer. The Salvation Army had Bill Clarke, the blind evangelist, as a guest speaker. Rev. R.H. Hamilton, son of a former minister at the old white frame church at the top of Free Methodist Hill, conducted revival services at the Free Methodist Church. The Holy Name Society at St. Joseph's Church held a popular social evening with speeches by Dean O'Leary, Morley Marrin, and Vincent Kyle. Rev. D.H. Easter of the First Baptist Church was chairman of the local chapter of the Upper Canada Bible Society. One of the newer church groups in town, the Pentecostal Assembly, was meeting in the former Holiness Movement Church on Ontario

Street. It being too cold for winter use, they were given free use of Browning Memorial Hall.

Fire claimed Canadian Keswick, a resort near Port Carling that catered to holidays with a Christian atmosphere. Originally named Ferndale House, it had been built by the Penson family in the 1880s.

The Orange Lodge celebrated the Battle of the Boyne July 12, with a church parade to the United Church led by the Northern Star Fife and Drum Band. Harry Cole was master, John Fox secretary, and George W. Boyer general chairman.

Even though the war was over, ration book 6 was issued by the Wartime Prices and Trade Board. Signs of less restrictive times were exemplified by Mr. Glen Coates' purchase of a new Pontiac, the first new post-war auto in Bracebridge, and the revival of the Board of Trade with Mr. W.N. Spearin, president. The Board of Trade, organized in 1899, was dormant during the war.

Some of the business changes in town: Walter Reynolds purchased the funeral business from George Marshall … Gravenhurst Machine Industries established a factory on the flats below the public school to manufacture cream separators and such … The Paisley Shops of Toronto had a store built at the corner of Manitoba and Dominion Streets … Manford Green purchased the ice delivery business of Mr. Tibbett … Herman Brooks' Appliance Shop in Chancery Lane opened a new record bar … E.M. Downey and Sons purchased Hammond's Dairy from Fred Lee … employment for women was offered by Bell Telephone and Rubberset – the latter offered free transportation to their Gravenhurst plant and music while the women worked. Men could hire on with Bell at 70 cents an hour to lay underground cable.

Miss Alma Peacock was president of the newly formed Business and Professional Women's Club who were told by a guest speaker "that women are the heartbeat and pulse of the world and men must learn to realize that business and professional women can express their opinions and be heard."

Mr. I. Yorke Murphy succeeded Mr. Harry Wilson as Bank of Nova Scotia manager. Mr. Murphy had some renovations done including the installation of new teller's cages.

During this year, Hutchison Brothers' store was selling roasting chickens for 47¢ a pound, and Remington Threesome electric razors were $[illegible]5.95 at the Thomas Company.

Dr. Fraser M. Greig, who had served overseas in the medical corps, returned to reopen his medical practice.

It was in 1946 that the war brides started to come to their new homes in Canada. Those coming to Bracebridge were welcomed in the local newspapers each week.

In recognition of those who gave their lives in World War II, as well as in thanksgiving for those who safely returned, the SSJE planned a war memorial to be hung on the east wall of its chapel. The large Christus Rex was sculpted in bronze by Emmanuel Hahn and was unveiled by Bishop Wright on Victoria Day. A replica of the crucifix was provided for each of the families whose names were on the memorial list. The original sculpture is now located in the small graveyard beside the former chapel.

As one would expect, the activities of the Royal Canadian Legion began to expand throughout the district. The Bracebridge branch, started by Mr. M.C. "Jack" Newark in 1929, helped institute the Bala branch in April and sent a bus load of members to the dedication of the Huntsville cenotaph in October. Since 1939 the former Fourth Ward school had been rented as a meeting place for the activities of Branch No. 161. Council decided to deed the building and property (which was originally the Primitive Methodist cemetery) to the Bracebridge Legion for permanent use. At that time the executive officers of the Legion were Henry Anderson, Bus Brazier, Phil Potts, and William Wray.

Curling had long been a popular winter pastime here, the first rink being opened in 1898. In later times the Curling Club used a rink that was operated in conjunction with the Yearley arena on James Street; however, both curlers and ice skating enthusiasts lost these facilities to fire in 1943. A fund-raising drive to amass $6,000 was begun in early 1946 by the Curling Club, whose executive members were Wilbert Richards, J.P. McVittie, and S.A. Bates. By year's end the new curling rink across from the burnt-out arena was open. It remained a familiar landmark until the club relocated to their present site off Liddard Street in the early 1970s.

In April, the ratepayers overwhelmingly approved a plan to build a new community centre as a war memorial on the site of the former privately owned Yearley arena. Mayor Bastedo made a personal donation of $1,000 to this project and by December the fund had grown to $20,000. Two other building projects in 1946 were additions to the high school for shop and home economics classes, and an addition at the hospital to house a maternity ward and a food service facility for the staff.

Some landmarks that were lost by fire were the large frame house on Wilson's Falls road that had been built by pioneer businessman John Teviotdale; George Weaver's house in Oakley Township, and Riverview Lodge (formerly Pulford House and Robertson Inn) in Baysville. As of February 15, the Muskoka jail, built by the government of John Sandfield MacDonald, was closed as it was considered to be a fire hazard. It had been the scene of two executions, those being Will Hammond in 1898 and George Cyr in 1922.

On the other hand, new things were happening around the area also. Mr. Gibbs, owner of Lilac Inn just north of town, added to his popular dance pavilion enough floor space to accommodate 20 more square dance sets ... Tanbark Hill by the high school was paved for the first time ... the Ontario Street entrance to Jubilee Park was closed in favour of a new entrance off Victoria Street ... Street signs were being put up in town and in the townships, and the familiar yellow-and-black Ontario Motor League directions signs were being placed at strategic corners to help motorists find their way along the rural routes.

On February 10, Mr. and Mrs. William N. Boyes of Vankoughnet saw a beautiful large butterfly. Albert Hollingworth of Beatrice reported the May weather with a high of 76° F, a low of 23°, and a scant 2.87 inches of rain. Dry conditions prevailed throughout most of the summer, ultimately causing power failure in town, forcing industries to close and appliances to be unplugged.

Agricultural news noted that Mr. H.B. Buckerfield received a diploma for meritorious service in poultry raising ... The 7th annual District Seed Fair held in the high school auditorium saw Roy Goltz of Monck as the top point winner, with other awards going to Clarence Canning, Walter Taylor, Harvey Gray, and George Parrett ... The fall fair was again a success, with Harvey Gray as president and Jerry Dickie as secretary-treasurer.

There was no lack of community activity. Under the leadership of Dr. R.J. Dodds, the Horticultural Society held its 14th annual meeting with much praise of the gardens at the falls and around the courthouse ... The 90-member IOOF Lodge No. 251 held its 60th anniversary celebration ... The Rotary Club sponsored a Youth Council with officers Keith Minns, Bernice Shier, Margaret Rosewarne, David Bishop, John Huckle, Eric Minns, Richard Giaschi, George Rombough, and Phil Potts, and in May held their second annual Rotary Show ... Miss Viola Kirk held her 20th piano recital ... The 47th annual meeting of the Woman's Institute took place in the Town Hall with Mrs. Ed Kirkpatrick the incoming president ... Mrs. Chris Forth and Mrs. McCulley took 23 girl guides to Ottawa where they met Lady Baden-Powell from whom local guide Shirley Elliott received her first class badge during the proceedings ... At High Falls Tourist Camp the Lions Club held their second grant fun festival on Dominion Day and all treats were free ... A CGIT class was started at Knox Presbyterian Church by Mrs. C. Brown and Mrs. F. Boake ... Wilson Boyer reorganized the ski club.

A successful inter-high school field day was held at the Fair Grounds involving Gravenhurst, Bracebridge, and Huntsville schools. The local first place winners were B. Ball, K. Sorenson, B. Amm, O. Hammond, M. Robinson, E. Minns, and Ken Ball. A newly organized West Muskoka Secondary Schools Athletic Association held its first annual meet at Port Carling with Mactier winning over the home team 145 to 67 points.

The 65th Teachers' Convention was held at Bracebridge with Eldon F. Gooding elected president by his colleagues. Mr. Gooding was transferred from principal of Bala Public and Continuation School to principal of the new Ontario Demonstration School at Utterson in 1947 (the V.K Greer Memorial School).

Chief A.E. Ecclestone was in his 50th year in the fire brigade. He became chief in 1906 ... Garbage collection was begun this year ... Lieutenant Colonel Welsh, MPP for Muskoka-Ontario, was appointed minister of the new department of Tourism and Recreation.

*Surrounding farms once provided milk to several dairies in Bracebridge, including Hammond's on Manitoba Street.* COURTESY OF SHIRLEY (LEE) LOTT

Captain Levi Fraser wrote a popular series of articles about the history of Muskoka which he made into a 152-page book selling for $2.

The local papers carried news accounts from many outlying communities such as Hekkla, Bent River, Purbrook, Reay, and others. Although social in nature, they revealed the visitation patterns of friends, relatives, and neighbours in a time when television had not yet interfered with people's free time.

With the addition of one more officer at the Bala OPP post (oldest in Muskoka) and one at Huntsville, there would now be a total of seven OPP officers serving Muskoka.

Deaths recorded in 1946 included W.S. Shaw, who had been manager of the new tannery (Shaw, Cassils and Co.) during the 1890s. He built the first generating station at Bracebridge Falls in 1892. He also donated the original bandstand to the town when it sat at the apex created by Manitoba and Dominion Streets. It was later moved to Memorial Park and was replaced in 1928 … Duncan Marshall, editor of the *Bracebridge Gazette* 1903-5; he had been responsible for changing the name from *The Free Grant Gazette and Muskoka, Parry Sound and Nipissing Advertiser* … Norman Prowse, clerk-treasurer of Monck from 1927 until 1944, when he became registrar of deeds for Muskoka … Master Mariner Albert F. Leeder, 78, died of a stroke. Son of Mr. and Mrs. Fred Leeder, he started work on the steamboats in 1884, married Lillian Jane Andrews of Draper, and became a pioneer resident in "The Hollow." Son Reg became commander of the *Sagamo* … Charles Wesley Archer, 64, of Browning Island, was a well-known ship owner and steamboat captain, his last steamer being the *Mildred* … John Schafer, 86, came to Falkenburg in 1866. He built a fine brick home on the east side of Highway 11 just north of town … J.N. Lamb, came to Bracebridge in 1907 and established the first permanent picture show, the Lyceum Theatre, on a site just north of Queen's Hill … John H. Jackson, 79, former employee of Ecclestone and Bates Hardware, previously an official in the old Bracebridge Brilliant Light Company which manufactured acetylene gas lights … R.M. Tipper, 59, agricultural representative since 1924, from a Stisted pioneer family … William J. Aikin, lifelong resident of town … Mrs. Walter Coulson, 74, Woodchester Avenue … Mrs. Frances Dashwood, 81, daughter of pioneer C.W. Liddard … Mrs. John Kirk, 94, nee Mary Jane Tookey … and many more.

## 1947

With no single opposing nominees, Mayor Bastedo, the councillors, the school board trustees, and the utilities commissioners all received acclamation.

In the townships, two new reeves appeared on the scene: Claude T. Boyes of Oakley and Clarence McBride of Draper. The Muskoka District Council elected reeve George E. Blair of Port Carling as president and retained J.H. Forbes as secretary-treasurer, a position he had ably filled since the old Muskoka Municipal Association was formed in 1920.

At a banquet held in the Albion Hotel in January, the Kinsmen Club of Bracebridge was organized with Gordon Dawkins as president. This Canadian service club made its debut in Hamilton in 1920. Special tribute was made to Wilfred Shier who got "the ball rolling" here in Bracebridge. Other charter members were Bill Dunn, George Matthias, Cecil Slater, Herb Carley, Phil Potts, Terry Haight, Harvey Hines, Burleigh Kirkpatrick, Cyril Minard, Jim MacNaughtan, Sam McEown, Otto McFadden, Ken McIvor, Doug Sieber, Roy Tennant, Bill Thompson, and Aubrey White.

*In 1947 Bracebridge Dairy took over Hammond's Dairy, and the following year still employed this horse-drawn delivery wagon, shown here with milkman Murray Anderson and "Queen."* COURTESY OF THE WAITE FAMILY COLLECTION

In the same month 30 candidates were initiated at the institution of Snow Queen Rebekah Lodge No. 332. Mrs. Alf Quemby was elected the Noble Grand. Other officers were Alice Pain, Mrs. Clayton Joslin, Mrs. G. Hooton, Mrs. Harold Campbell, Mrs. Ed Senior, and Mrs. Bruce Duncan.

Bill Towns Jr. was officially appointed registrar of deeds and Edgar Magee become collector of customs to succeed Ted Fenn who resigned due to ill health. Mrs. W.C. Fryer succeeded Mrs. J. Lake as the librarian. At the high school, Miss Nancy Hallett, Miss Ruth McCubbin, home economics, and Mr. Thomas Hopper, manual training, were hired. Gracia Hewitt, daughter of Mr. and Mrs. T. Ausborne Hewitt, was employed to work in the clerk's office.

Gordon Aiken, a gentleman who a decade later would become the Conservative MP for Parry Sound-Muskoka, joined R.M. Best, KC. Father Roland Palmer was feted farewell at St. Thomas' Anglican Church just prior to his leaving for Sorrento, BC, to establish a branch of the SSJE.

At the annual Red Cross meeting, George Hammond, president, T.M. Park McKay, secretary, and W.W. Creswick, treasurer. were all re-elected. Miss Conway, superintendent at the Bracebridge Memorial Hospital, reported there had been 1,155 admissions, 220 births, and 219 major operations in 1946.

In September work commenced on the new Community Centre. Service clubs and groups such as the Business and Professional Women's Club held special events to raise funds for this worthy cause. In August the BPWC held a two-day highly successful gay nineties garden party that brought thousands of people to town. Beginning with a Friday evening parade, events spilled over into Saturday when people donned costumes and enjoyed such things as music, fortune telling, and a great variety of contests. Popular among the younger set were the pony and cart rides provided by Miss Aria Dennis.

The Baptist Church was the scene of the 56th annual convention of the Women's Christian Temperance Union of Simcoe, Parry Sound, and Muskoka. Speaking and poster contests were won by Jean Bruce, Sheila Botting, Joan LeBarr, Glenna Fraser, and David Orr. The well-attended meetings were actively supported by many of the town's clergymen.

Other group presidents this year were Ernest Goltz, South Muskoka Agricultural Society; Gus Braida, Bracebridge Club; W.A. Shier, hockey club, of which Gordon Reid was coach; C.J. Dixon, master of Muskoka Lodge No. 360; Bob Harrison, master of LOL No. 218; and Robert Jefferies of the Royal Canadian Legion, the first veteran of World War II to hold that post. Councillor Philip Thomas was chairman of the Citizen's Band. This dedicated band of musicians under the baton of John Morra provided concerts in the bandshell regularly throughout the summer months, much to the delight of both local people and the tourists.

In March, a capacity crowd delighted in a presentation of the Choral Society, *Trial by Jury*, by Gilbert and Sullivan. Among the lead voices of this elaborate production were Robert J. Boyer, William E. Towns, Alma Peacock, and Rev. F.F. Nock, who played the "Great Judge". The following pupils took part in a June recital held by Mrs. Winnifred Anderson: Margaret Learoyd, Jacklyn McVittie, Bette Robins, Pam Shier, Vicki Boyer, Paul Shuttleworth, Robbie Shier, Terry Briese, Bonnie Bailey, Isabel Crozier, Brenda Best, Muriel Amm, Betty Penny, Sharon Rosewarne, Lois Crockford, Vera White, Joyce Hutchison, Marjorie Johnson, Alma Knowles, Reta Penney, Doreen Bastedo, Patsy Moor, Dorothy Richards, Betsy Rosewarne, and Bernice Shier.

A link with the past was severed with the tearing down of the Pentecostal Tabernacle next door to Buck's Electric Shop on the south side of Ontario Street. The building was originally occupied by Stephen Jarrit, a blacksmith. Later on, Brook Watson conducted a thriving cooperage business there. Upon his retirement, the Holiness Movement (Hornerite ) Church bought the old frame building, renovated and enlarged it, and used it as their meeting hall from the turn of the century until their congregation ceased to be viable. Some time in the 1920s the Pentecostal movement under the leadership of George Bombay and Rev. Lloyd Johnson began to use the building as their mission hall.

At the Holy Cross Church on the Taylor Line, Fathers Palmer and Garrod began a boys' league. At the initial meeting were Fred Goodman, Doug Cross, Lloyd Leeder, Syd Cross, Ron Murray, Ken Leeder, and Carl Goodman. Reluctantly, the congregation at the Baptist Church on Quebec Street had to say goodbye to their pastor R.D.H. Easter, who was called to Sudbury. Mr. Ernest Kirk presented a purse of money to the Easters as a farewell gift.

In 1947, Gray Coach ran three buses a day to Toronto, leaving from Muskoka Garage across from the public library. A round trip ticket cost $6.95 unless it was taken while the CNE was on, then the price dropped to $6.50 and included admission into the exhibition grounds – and then five trips were made daily, except Sunday. By way of comparison, a 100-mile cruise on the RMS *Sagamo* left the Bracebridge Wharf each day at 8:00 a.m. and cost $2.30, of which 30 cents was tax, and included a travelogue of the cruise and music on board under the direction of Charlie Musgrave.

There were many things happening in education, too. Inspector of Public Schools, George Johnson, announced that all of Muskoka (except Bent River and Ufford) was now set up in township school areas, the first county or district in Ontario to do this. Another feather in Muskoka's cap came with the September 2nd opening of the new public school in Stephenson Township built by the Ontario government as the model of a modern rural school. It was named V. K. Greer Memorial, in honour of the late provincial superintendent of elementary education. The Hon. George A. Drew, Premier of Ontario and Minister of Education, formally opened the school. The idea for such a building came from a visit he made to Iceland. The cost of the structure excluding equipment was $77,940.

The harvesting of the crystal crop from the river was enhanced with the purchase of a power saw by Manford Green that would easily buzz through ice 14 inches thick.

Lake Craft Boats on Wellington Street reported it had turned out its 100th outboard motorboat and was now making 22 craft a week. Milton Askin sold the North Garage to Ernest Colson and Jim Hillman. Hawn's Watch Repair Shop opened next to Buck's Electric, and the old frame Queen's Hotel closed to make way for an addition planned by its new owners, the Patterson brothers. G.R. (Bus) McCulley was hired as manager of Bracebridge Fridgid Lockers. Hazen Meeks announced he was now operating the British-American Oil Gas Station at the south end of town. Muskoka Garage became an authorized General Motors dealer. James and Jerome Mauro opened their new bowling alley beside Muskoka Trading. The Bell Telephone Company was installing new equipment to reduce the number of rural subscribers on existing party lines, and was hiring operators at a starting salary of $18.30 a week. Northern Planing Mills moved its offices into a new building nearer Manitoba Street. Haight's Bakery built a new bakery on Woodward Avenue and the former district jail was to be remodelled to become an OPP outpost.

In nearby Watt Township, the ratepayers voted 146 to 56 in favor of purchasing a power snowplow to replace their horse-drawn plows. At Matthiasville in Draper Township, the Town of Orillia was about to build a hydroelectric plant at an estimated cost of $878,000. The Bigwin Inn and Estate on the Lake of Bays was sold to the Vernon G. Cardy interests for $2 million, and Havington Inn, a fine summer hotel at Port Carling built in 1907 by W.K. Foreman, burned down.

A sample of river water taken at Kelvin Grove Park came back from the Ontario Department of Health with an "A" quality rating, dispelling the notion held by some tourists that Bracebridge was responsible for polluting Lake Muskoka. The fall fair was attended by at least 4,700 people in 1947.

A visit to town by Miss Margaret Stewart of Los Angeles, California, proved to be of historical interest to many local residents. Her father, Hiram James McDonald, was one of the earliest pioneers at North Falls, having been here even before the *Wenonah* made her maiden voyage to the hamlet in 1866. Mr. McDonald laid out most of what was uptown Bracebridge east of Manitoba Street. He named the streets after himself and female members of his family, Mary, Ida, Jane, Ann, and Margaret. The latter street was named for the visitor in question and it ran north of McDonald Street, east of and parallel to Hiram Street. In 1868, McDonald was made treasurer of the United Townships of Draper, Macaulay, Stephenson and Ryde, then he became a councillor in 1871, the year Macaulay became a township, and again was chosen to be councillor of the newly incorporated village of Bracebridge in 1875. Interestingly enough, no mention of him has been found after 1875.

Early in December, Bracebridge Council suspended chief of police William Cudmore and constable George H. Bishton, the only full-time officers on the town's police force. The suspensions were pending the clarification of a situation which arose in Algonquin Park, along with a policeman from Huntsville and a local OPP officer. Charges of shooting deer in the Park were laid against the officers in question and a trial ensued at Barry's Bay in Renfrew County, where the magistrate in charge reserved his decision and adjourned the case until early 1948.

The CNR gave the town its "water rights" at Bracebridge Falls, which the railway used to use to operate a waterwheel to pump water to its (now demolished) water tank beside the track.

Santa Claus was given a rousing welcome in early December by an immense crowd that gathered along the parade route that started at Holiday House, went out to Manitoba Street, over to the hospital, and then looped back to Memorial Park. This was the first Santa Claus parade the Business and Professional Women's Cub had sponsored and the committee consisting of Inez Ecclestone, Mrs. E. Allchin, Mrs. Alf Quemby, Phyllis Ecclestone, and Isobel Thomson were gratified at its success. At the park, Santa, with the help of his elves, distributed to each child a bag of candies, an orange, and a long candy cane. On the parade float that carried Santa, three young helpers attended the jolly white-bearded gift man; they were Gloria Giaschi, Bert Bell Jr., and Billy Quemby.

Deaths in 1947 included Judge Arthur A. Mahaffy, 87, former Muskoka District Judge and MPP. He came to

*A view north on Manitoba Street from the McColl-Frontenac service station (later the Texaco station, then Rombos Restaurant), circa 1950. A large sign on the Ontario Street wall of the building at left advertises the Bird Woollen Mill. The large vehicle in the centre of the street is a bus; in the original photograph "Muskoka Lakes Lines" is discernible on the sign above its windshield.* COURTESY OF BRENDA COX

town in 1887 to be associated with his brother's law practice ... Alex C. Salmon, 87, town clerk from 1889 to 1936 ... William Fish, 83, court constable for many years ... Mary Strange, the first white child born in Bracebridge, daughter of Charles William Liddard ... Alf Nye, 66, who came in 1909 to work for the Anglo-Canadian Leather Company ... William M. Ewing, 96, who came with his parents in 1865 ... Lambert Love, 93, founder of the Elgin House on Lake Joseph ... Edwin Charles Leef, 72, winter postmaster at the Clevelands House, first came in 1893 to teach at S.S. No. 6 Medora before taking over Stanley House ... Edward Austin, who came to Bardsville as a young child; his wife Millie Rawson predeceased him in 1920 ... George McCracken, 74, a highly esteemed citizen and member of LOL No. 218 and the Royal Black Knights preceptory No. 910 ... Wesley Doley, 28, who drowned on April 20 in Lake Muskoka ... Carl V. Saunders, 38, settled at High Falls in 1910, drowned along with his brother-in-law, Wesley, in Lake Muskoka, left his widow and five children ... Margaret Crockford, 40, of Purbrook, wife of Art who was in partnership with Seth Hillman, his brother-in-law, at the Down Town Garage on Thomas Street ... Shirley Wroe, 5, who was run over by a car at the fairgrounds during a softball game ... Mrs. Minnie Wise, 68, mother of Mrs. Ernest Allchin of the Holiday House ... June Ann Crockford, 17, in a single car accident at the Hoc Roc River corner ... Mrs. William K. Hare, 54, daughter of Mr. and Mrs. Thomas Hunt ... Adam Addington Veitch, 75, a pioneer of Watt Township ... F.W. Holt, 68, ex-reeve of Medora and Wood, where he was a Torrance businessman until moving into Bracebridge, where be became involved in many community organizations ... John S. Rusk, 66, proprietor of a tourist camp at the edge of town, son of Muskoka Township pioneer James Rusk ... Albina Allen (daughter of Mrs. and Mrs. Joseph Caisse Sr.), established a millinery business here with her sister, Permelia, which they owned until 1907 ... Sam Matthias, 84, son of Uffington area pioneers Mr. and Mrs. William Ira Matthias. He married Hettie Matthews in 1883 ... Gordon Dollar, 55, reeve of Ridout Township, dropped dead at work ...

Mrs. Sarah Crockford, 74, widow of Robert Crockford and daughter of Purbrook pioneers Mr. and Mrs. Thomas Colson ... Anne E. Snider, 76, widow of Frank Snider who operated a florist and market garden business in town ... Tom Pickles, 53, a highly popular barber in town who learned his trade with the late Joseph Caisse ... John H. Hollingworth, 73, a resident of Beatrice area since 1868 and whose family began official weather observations in 1876 ... Mrs. Rudolph Goltz, 74, of Bardsville, the former Emma Louise Klingbeil ... Mrs. Arthur Moore, 76, whose father Isaac Huber was a pioneer businessman in town and the first court clerk ... John W. Jerymn, supervisor for the building of the post office in Bracebridge ... Wilfred N. Creasor, 45, the well-liked treasurer of Watt Township ... Mrs. Hugh Fuller, 57, died suddenly at her home near the "Pinery" just east of town.

## 1948

Town clerk Wilbert Richards received nominations for the elected offices of the town on November 28, 1947, and once again no election was necessary. Only in Macaulay was the incumbent reeve challenged, but Dan MacNaughtan easily defeated his opponent, Ernest L. DeLarge.

The Muskoka District Council elected W.H. Muddiman, Monck, as their new president.

Watt Township gained a new clerk, Victor Creasor, replacing John Shea, who had held that position for more than 25 years. Norman Longhurst became the new treasurer following the death of Wilfred Creasor.

This was a year for several changes to the town police force. Early in the year Ray McCulley became chief of police and John O'Brien and George E. Elliott were hired as constables. In addition to one extra officer, arrangements were made to purchase a car for police force business. In June, Chief McCulley resigned, Mr. Elliott became chief, and John Harrington was added to the force. In July, Council released Chief Elliott and promoted Sergeant Harrington to chief and also hired Melvin Vincent. Mr. O'Brien resigned and was replaced by Allan V. Stevenson.

Alex J. Milne was made chief of the fire brigade with A.E. Ecclestone as honorary chief.

In late July, a contract was made with Wartime Housing Ltd. to build 35 approximately $6,600 four- and five-room homes on the Boake property near the hospital. Rental preference was given to veterans or their families with an option to buy after two years occupancy.

It was announced at the end of the year that the Canadian Red Cross would cease to operate the hospital and a local management team would have to be selected. The hospital executive consisted of M.P. McKay, T.A. Hewitt, Yorke Murphy, and W.W. Creswick. Members of the Board of Directors were Dr. Greig, George Hammond, Phil Thomas, George Ecclestone, Aubrey Shier, John McEown, and Alan Hutchinson.

Chief Harrington, with the cooperation of principal B.R. Minns, organized a traffic patrol of public school boys to provide safety for school children crossing at busy intersections. Team captains were George Brush, Paul Morra, Clayton Prettie, Arthur Gardiner, and Philip Murphy.

Glen Coates, Jack McVittie, Jack Johnson, Sid Bates, Mayor Bastedo, and Wilbert Richards of the Power, Water and Light Commission were given credit for their foresight in having the High Falls generating plant built to relieve power shortages in town. The 800-kilowatt facility became operational in December 1948.

The congregation of Bethel Tabernacle began to hold services in their new brick church which was dedicated by Rev. Norcross of Galt. The Rev and Mrs. L.H. Johnston were pastors.

Succeeding Rev. C.P. Shapter of the United Church was Rev. W.H. Burgess from Mount Albert. Rev. F.F. Nock of St. Thomas Anglican moved to Sudbury, to be replaced by Rev. Cyril Craymer of Bala.

Charter officers of the Kinettes included Ruth McCubbin, president, Myrna Ross, vice president, Shirley Shier, secretary, Eleanor Huffman, treasurer, Georgia Brooks, reporter, and Emma Dawkins, social

*A modern (1980s) aerial view of High Falls and the town's generating station. A public picnic grounds is a popular stopping place and provides splendid viewing opportunities.* COURTESY OF ONTARIO HYDRO

convener. The Kinettes donated $500 to the new Community Centre.

There was a revival in hockey interest due to the imminent opening of the new arena. The club met at W.A. Shier's home where 30 prospective players organized their new team named the Bracebridge Bears. The executive bought each player new pants at $12.50 a pair and coach Gordon Reid gave them a talk about staying in condition.

The ninth annual Seed Fair was held in the high school auditorium with a special Junior Judging Competition open to children between 12 and 21 … Three new development roads were announced by Arthur Welsh, MPP – one from Kahshe Lake to Housey's Rapids, one along the north shore of Lake of Bays, and the third north of Skeleton Lake … The post office announced that letters of up to one ounce would be sent airmail within Canada. Basic postage was four cents, special delivery an extra ten cents … Colonel Forrest resigned as superintendent of the Children's Aid Society, a position which he had held since the society started in 1918. He was succeeded by Russell Robinson.

The Norwood Theatre was built on the lawn of the former T.J. Anderson home just south of Memorial Park … Neil Haight left teaching in Gogama to become sales manager of Haight's Bakery … Myers Brothers opened their coal delivery business … James Kingshott took over the Master Feed Business of Tom J. Medley … Small Wears Baby Shoppe became Kay's Tot to Teen … Council decided to install parking meters on Manitoba and Dominion streets … Lorne's Marketeria announced its grand opening July 9 with such specials as bread at 10¢ a loaf, butter at 72¢, and Canadian old cheese at 46¢ a pound … James Maxwell, Toronto, replaced Angus McKinnon as manager of the Silverwood's Dairy plant … Gordon Reid, proprietor of Milford Manor and a former professional hockey player, was hired as manager of the new Community Centre.

Peter MacNaughtan completed his new store on Manitoba Street … Sutcliffe Motors, Manitoba Street north, became an authorized Chrysler, Plymouth, and Fargo dealer … Les Rosewarne of Bracebridge Garage announced the new English Ford cars at $1,530.

The Bell Telephone Company reported 920 telephones in use in 1948 compared with 550 in 1944. H.D. Husson, the local manager, said an average of 4,100 calls a day were made, requiring expansion of the Manitoba Street facility.

A school holiday was held on November 26 in honour of the birth of a son, Charles, to Princess Elizabeth and Prince Phillip.

Accidents included Robert Brooks, 56, fatally injured in Hekkla where he was at work on a skidway for Canada Wood Specialty Co. (his brother owned a business in Bracebridge) and Harvey Commandant, 27, in a boat explosion in Bala.

In the June provincial election, the Muskoka-Ontario riding re-elected Lieutenant Colonel The Hon. G. Arthur Welsh as Conservative MPP over Mayor J. Frank Kelly, Liberal, and Earl C. Mitchell, CCF. The government of George Greer was returned with a reduced majority, having lost many seats to the CCF.

Deaths this year included Robert P. Perry, 97, postmaster 1879-1938, came to Bracebridge in 1870 when his father and T.M. Myers purchased a saw and grist mill business. Robert E. Perry was our first post master 1870-1879 … John W. McNiece, 87, of Reay, came to Muskoka in 1874, worked for Mickle, Dyment and Son lumber company for 50 years … Alfred Fenn, 68, son of J.L. Fenn, a prominent businessman who built the Bracebridge Public School … Alfred E. Munday, 82, worked for the Gilmour Lumber Co. at the time when the tramway was being built near Dorset. In 1903 he purchased the Sheppard Grocery and Flour business which was where the Parkview Restaurant is now … L. Dennis, 78, settled with his parents Mr. and Mrs. John Dennis at Wood Lake in 1877. Later he ran a livery business on the site of what became the Down Town Garage … Margaret White, 80, wife of former police magistrate William J. White. She came to Muskoka in 1870 with her parents, Mr. and Mrs. James McBride … James Forsyth, 86 … Wesley Ellsworth, 83, had worked for J.D. Shier and Anglo-Canadian Leather but best known for his meticulous care of the town's parks … Herbert W. Slater, ran a tailoring business on the site where the MacNaughtan hardware store located … Saxon L. Moore, 82, lumberman and farmer, married Jessie Keall and raised eight children; his wife Jessie, 75, died later in the year … Lawrence Magee, 53, Muskoka Falls, served a drug apprenticeship with the late John Thompson and served with the 122nd Battalion … William Kingsmill, 73, who for 31 years beginning in 1904 was the manager of the Bank of Nova Scotia, succeeding C.C. Billings … Richard Dinner, 89, son of William Dinner who came to Monck in 1865 and was one of the earliest people to own an automobile … Samuel H. Christie, 90, former sewing machine and agricultural instrument rep … Mrs. J. Byron Kaye, 79, the former Charlotte Leith, daughter of Mr. and Mrs. David Leith who came in 1861 … Gordon Macdiarmid, 70, long-time member of the George W. Ecclestone Ltd. staff … Frank Bassett, 76, caretaker of many downtown businesses, admired for his sterling honesty … William Taylor, 82, son of pioneer Sam Taylor who settled near High Falls … Mrs. Neil McDonald, 73, daughter of pioneers Mr. and Mrs. Charles Liddard … George Peacock, 63.

## 1949

The official opening of the Bracebridge Memorial Community Centre took place on January 28 after long delays due to shortages of both workers and materials. This building was 112 by 250 feet with steel girders to carry the domed roof. The ice surface was 80 by 175 feet which was wider than called for by the OHA regulations. The John Inglis Co. installed the artificial ice equipment, which among other things included 38,000 feet of piping. Jack Thomson was in charge of the cement work and Nelson Goltz the carpentry. This magnificent structure was a credit to the town, made possible by whole-hearted cooperation of the entire community and an understanding council. This was the fifth skating rink in the history of Bracebridge.

Mr. J. Frank Kelly, past mayor of Huntsville, was elected president of the Muskoka District Council. Dr. Styles of Georgetown came to succeed Dr. John Murray as District Veterinarian. The members of the Veterinary Agricultural Committee for Muskoka were H.E. Beaumont, Emerson Farnsworth, Harvey Gray, and Nelson Hammell.

The BHS Seniors basketball team was the Georgian Bay COSSA Champions for 1949.

Ace Bailey, 47, a former NHL star, quit his coaching job with the University of Toronto Senior Hockey Club.

It had been six years since an intermediate hockey game had been played in town but that all ended in early

*The first hockey game in the new Bracebridge Memorial Community Centre commences February, 1949, between the intermediate Bears and the All Stars. Clarence Kirkness scored the first goal in the new arena.* COURTESY OF BRACEBRIDGE CULTURE AND RECREATION DEPARTMENT

February when the All Stars took on the Bracebridge Bears before the opening night crowd. Clarence Kirkness scored the first goal in the new arena on a pass from Archie Ball early in the game, but the All Stars finally won by a score of 13 to 12.

The Skating Club was reorganized with help from Joe Pope of London, Ontario, who agreed to instruct two classes a week. The executive positions were taken by D.C. Thomas, Robert Everett, and Mary Carleton. Over a thousand people attended the first Figure Skating Club carnival in the new arena. It began with a grand march and ended with a broomball game.

A tennis club was formed in May with Jack Huckle as president and Pamela Bird as secretary. Permission was granted by Mr. And Mrs. Brobst to use their court.

When the new motor licence plates went on sale at McBride's grocery store, it was noted that they were white with blue letters and numerals. Those sold here all began with the letter "U."

Milk prices rose from 17 to 18¢ a quart and 9 to 11¢ a pint in early January.

Postmaster Bill Huckle and his staff reported the greatest volume of mail ever had been processed over the Christmas 1948 season – 1,200 bags of parcels and 240,000 letters.

Miss Ethel Lundy, chief operator at the Bell Telephone Company for the past 18 years, moved to Oakville. The number of operators had increased from 6 to 19 while she was here.

Bell monthly rates were soon to be increased from $2.40 to $3.00 for a residence and $3.10 to $5.00 for a business.

As part of their newly formed business, Fowler Construction associates A. Fowler, Glen S. Coates, and Ralph V. Boothby announced the acquisition of a new ⅓-yard truck-mounted shovel … Noble Meeks announced the opening of his Radio Shop on Ontario Street … Muskoka farmers secured a Power Seed Cleaning Service, a portable machine drawn on a trailer from farm to farm. Mr. Lloyd Woods of Port Sydney was engaged as its first operator … James and Jerome Mauro announced the sale of the Bowling Academy to Cliff Davie of Orillia … McBride's grocery business was sold to Len Draper … New businesses openings during the spring were the Bracebridge Variety Store and the Cres-Mar Motel; meanwhile the White Rose service station was taken over by Rolf Weinert … .The wartime houses were officially opened on April 21 by acting mayor Roy Shier. The 25 modern homes on Aubrey Street were part of a grander plan of the Central Mortgage and Housing Corporation to provide 276,000 houses of this type across Canada. Mr. and Mrs. Al Lomas were the first to move in.

Mr. Gordon Aiken, of the law firm of Best and Aiken, moved to Gravenhurst to take over the law practice of Walter Clairmont.

The newly constituted Hospital Board began operating the 35-bed Memorial Hospital on January 1, the assets of which were estimated to be $200,000. Mrs. Alice Clark, who had been in charge of the former Red Cross Hospital for the past 10 months, was chosen to continue as superintendent. New daily rates at the hospital were set (reluctantly) at $4, $8, and $12 respectively for ward, private, and major operation recovery rooms

The Bracebridge Hospital Aid Society was formed to assist in the running of the hospital. Officers were Mrs. John Johnson, Mrs. T.A. Hewitt, and Miss Marjorie Johnson.

The new Huntsville Red Cross Hospital opened on May 17 with superintendent Miss Beth Kirkpatrick, RN, of Bracebridge.

Andrew Giaschi, manager of the new theatre, noted that the building would seat 615 people and was equipped with a curved screen to permit a direct view from any angle … The Queen's Hotel addition had space for two stores and boasted of steam heat, air conditioning, and additional plugs in the guest rooms … Hinds Manufacturing Company of Toronto leased a building in which to manufacture poultry-raising equipment … Mrs. Fred Boake purchased Len's Grocery … Louis Smoke Shop opened … Jack Atkinson took over the billiard parlors from Keith Gallinger, downstairs below the former Strand Theatre … The Grand Café at the foot of Chancery Lane changed ownership. Charlie Chin was serving regular meals anywhere from $0.45 to $1.00 … Brock Flumerfelt bought High Falls Cabins from Phil Potts … Muriel's Bake Shop opened at the corner of

*A "passenger view" of post-war downtown Bracebridge. It appears that the vehicle has a canoe on the roof. Many drugstores and restaurants advertise "sodas": obviously very popular then.* COURTESY OF VICKY BILLINGSLEY

Manitoba and Ann streets ... The Muskoka Lakes Navigation and Hotel Co. Ltd. was purchased by Muskoka Lakes Line Ltd., headed up by W. Eric Wasley; only the Royal Muskoka Hotel was not part of the deal.

The Choral Society presentation of Gilbert and Sullivan's *The Mikado* was a resounding success. The production was made possible by Mrs. L.W. Anderson, Mrs. D.C. Thomas, Tom Hooper, Guy Jackson, Mrs. G. Crichton, Mrs. Lorne Shier, and many members of a talented cast.

Bracebridge Public Library reported a total circulation of 15,056 books for 1948, based upon 7,358 books owned by the facility. In 1949 fluorescent lighting was installed.

Free chest x-rays were offered to all town residents over age 12.

At the 50th annual meeting of the South Muskoka Women's Institute, Mrs. V.S. Jobbins of Port Carling was returned as president.

A 36-foot cabin cruiser named the *Sarah Maud* exploded on Lake Muskoka leaving 12 of its 16 occupants severely injured, one of them dying later.

Two thousand and sixty regular and 407 junior entries assured another great Fall Fair in 1949. A team of horses owned by Highland Timber Products was judged the best on the grounds.

The six-man OPP were enjoying their new facilities built on the site of the old district jail.

The Board of Trade was reorganized and given the name Chamber of Commerce in keeping with the national organization. Leaders elected were W.N. Spearin, Harvey Berofe, D.C. Thomas, Glen Coates, Harold Frowe, Alvin Peacock, John Cockburn, and R.J. Boyer.

Rev. R.H. Armstrong left Knox Presbyterian Church after five years for Acton ... The Bracebridge Association of Church Schools was organized with L.W. Anderson as chairman and Captain Snider as secretary-treasurer. Other officers were Leda Scovell, Irwin Rutherford, Mrs. Clive Brown, Joan Waite, and Rev. S.M. Craymer ... The

Sunshine Credit Union meeting was held in the new Sunshine House of the Sisters of St. John the Divine. After the business, Father Morley acted as master of ceremonies for a musical program … Father John Hawkes resigned as the Superior at the SSJE to be replaced by Father Richard Morley … The Springdale Park Spiritual Association held its 12th anniversary … Mr. George W. Boyer retired as director of music at the United Church after 50 years of service … The Bible Society which originated locally in 1880 elected officers Rev. W.H. Burgess, president, Mrs. George A. Crozier, secretary, and Martin Johnson, treasurer.

The June Dominion election saw candidates Wilfred A. (Bucko) McDonald, Liberal, J.M. MacDonnell, Conservative, and Earle Taylor, CCF, running in the new Parry Sound-Muskoka riding. McDonald, of Sundridge, won. The Prime Minister of Canada, Louis St. Laurent, was returned to power with 193 seats.

Deaths this year included John Taylor, 75, son of Mr. and Mrs. Samuel Taylor … George Brown, died one day short of his 87th birthday, came to Bracebridge in 1871, was a contractor for the Sibbett Block. In 1889 he married Eliza Baker of Macaulay … Jane Sutherland, 100, the widow of James Sutherland Sr. She had come with her parents, Mr. And Mrs. Joseph Yeoman, to Falkenburg in the 1860s … Duncan McDonald, 85, who came to town in 1900 to work for the Shaw, Cassels Co. tannery. In 1909 he was appointed district jailer, a position he held until 1933 … George Jackson was a Macaulay Township councillor at the time of his death … Norman Kirkpatrick, moved to town in 1926 … Florence Annie Kaye, 93, widow of James Kaye … Thomas (Daddy) Moors, 75, one the district's best known and most loved Salvationists. He spent nearly 54 years in the service of his church … May Arnott, at the home of her sister Fanny (Mrs. Will K. Hare). She was the eldest daughter of James Arnott, one time the chief of police in town … Annie Maria Fenn Anderson, 84, came to Bracebridge in 1871 with her parents James and Emma Fenn … Wm. J.B. Smith of Baysville, a former McLean councillor and secretary-treasurer of the Lake of Bays and Haliburton Telephone Co. … Rev. R.K. Trowbridge, 48, a former pastor for five years at St. Thomas Anglican Church … Annie Veitch, 68, widow of Addington Veitch, at her son Cecil's home in Dee Bank … Samuel Taylor Jr., 85, dropped dead at the home of his son, Macaulay councillor Ted Taylor. He had come with his parents in 1869 to settle near High Falls. A family tradition of threshing was begun with Samuel Taylor Sr. that passed down through three generations … Henry J. Bird, 75, former councillor, mayor, and chairman of the Power, Light and Water Commission. Mr. Bird was president of the town's oldest industry, the Bird Woollen Mill, which had been established by his father in 1872. He was involved in many community organizations. In gasoline-powered transportation he was a local pioneer. He had the first motorboat in Bracebridge. To start the engine, a pan of gasoline outside the cylinder had to be ignited with a match! He was the first citizen in Bracebridge to drive a car in winter, and he was a charter member of the old Muskoka Motor Club … Marie Rose, 51, wife of Joseph Rose … Clara Peacock, 66, nee Forsyth … Jean MacMillan, one of the sisters who founded a millinery and ladies' wear business on the main street … Rev. Peter MacInnes, at Durham, a former pastor at Knox Presbyterian Church … Barbara Dunn, 12, daughter of Mr. and Mrs. Earl Dunn, stricken with polio … Mrs. Henry (Mabel) Anderson, 61 … Reeve H.E. Beaumont of Muskoka Township, died while on a trip to England with his daughter. Mr. Beaumont not only farmed but was a partner in a firm that ran two steamboats called the *Nymoca* and the *Alporto*, which were floating grocery and meat stores … Mrs. W.W. White, long-time resident of Dominion Street and whose late husband was a former undertaker here … Mrs. J.W. McNiece, 85, who settled at McLean's Corners in Draper in 1865. Her parents were Mr. and Mrs. Tom Galbraith … Patrick Connor, 62, long time sexton and caretaker of the cemetery for St. Joseph's Roman Catholic Church … Bernard Wasdell, 70, a butcher, then an ice maker at the new arena.

## 1950

The successful candidate in the 1950 mayoralty race was Dr. Laurie N. Ryan, DDS, a man who was born and educated in Bracebridge, and whose father, Richard W. Ryan, had served on council in

1896 and 1897. Dr. Ryan was a sports enthusiast who formerly had excelled at lacrosse and hockey, but now, due to the pressures of his dentistry work, was happy to play golf, hunt, and fish.

Late in 1949, the Muskoka Township council voted to name the road on the south bank of the Muskoka River, commencing at the south branch bridge, Beaumont Drive in honour of the late reeve, H.E. Beaumont.

At a well-attended joint meeting of the District Council and the Muskoka District School Trustees' Association in January, the advisability of establishing a health unit in the district was endorsed. A committee was appointed to make arrangements and draft a form of agreement to submit to the 28 municipalities involved. By July 1 the Muskoka Health Unit began to operate with Dr. Gordon Martin as health officer, Helen Etherington as supervisor of public health nurses, and Raymond F. Heath as sanitary inspector.

Town Council sought to secure mail boxes for the town and spent considerable time deciding where they should be located. Originally they requested five boxes but through the work of Bucko McDonald, MP, the number was increased to nine so that some surrounding township residents could also be served.

Following the resignation of Gordon Reid as manager of the Community Centre, Mr. J. Portland was hired to fill the position. He had a long record of amateur and professional sport behind him including 14 years in the NHL as a defenceman.

Only 196 of the 714 eligible voters turned out to vote on a bylaw to authorize the expenditure of $200,000 on water system improvements. Those who did take the time to vote were considered to have given their approval.

The Department of Highways was in the process of building a new highway diversion east of town. The Power, Water and Light Commission was duly concerned about the possible loss of water flow at the Barron spring as a result of the construction. Chairman Glen Coates announced that the department would reimburse the town for loss of and damage to the water supply. The commission decided to get legal advice as to whether or not the agreement covered any loss due to contamination through the use of road salt in the winter.

The Muskoka District Health Unit began offering its immunization program to the rural areas of the district, beginning at the Housey's Rapids school in Ryde Township.

In connection with the 25th anniversary of the United Church of Canada, five members of the local congregation were chosen to receive medals of merit for faithful service: George Boyer, R.A. Findlay, G.W. Skuce, E.L. Burgess, and T.J. Anderson.

Sixty years of services at the Anglican Church in Ilfracombe were recognized. The beautiful stone church was opened in 1887 but was preceded by a log building.

The Roman Catholic Church at MacTier was levelled by fire that was believed to have been started in a nearby rubbish pile. Three private homes were also destroyed at the same time.

Austin J. Thaxter of the Free Methodist Church was replaced by H.A. McLeod.

Rev. Vais was chosen as the new Knox Presbyterian minister. The annual turkey supper put on by the men at Knox Presbyterian proved popular again when they served over 300 people. Cost was $1.25 for adults and $0.75 for children

At Bethel Tabernacle, Rev. Johnston departed for Simcoe to be succeeded by Rev. Graydon Richards, who had been teaching at the Bible School in Toronto.

The pastor of the Baptist Church, Rev. W.E. Morrow, celebrated his 35th year in the ministry, which had begun in Bracebridge in 1915-20.

Mr. and Mrs. William Aitken of Windermere celebrated their 50th wedding anniversary on October 24 by laying the cornerstone of the new United Church in the village. They were assisted by Milton Goltz, superintendent of the project, and Clifford Smith, the stone mason.

After three years as president of the South Muskoka Agricultural Society, Ernest M. Goltz stepped down in favour of W.K. Kettle.

Many improvements had been made to the buildings and equipment at the fairgrounds and all reports, including the financial ones, appeared favourable. The directors were A.J Goltz, H.E. Buckerfield, Harvey Gray, G.W. Boyer, George Parrett, Rob Barron, E.M. Goltz, George Morrow, and Max Beaumont.

*In 1950 the Orillia Water, Light and Power Commission opened its 2,812-kW generating station at Matthiasville in Draper Township, now part of Bracebridge. The 269-metre-long power dam created a new lake on the South Muskoka River.* COURTESY OF ONTARIO HYDRO

A program of Gilbert and Sullivan operetta songs and other musical numbers was held under the auspices of the Choral Society to raise money for the flood victims around Winnipeg.

The South Muskoka District Women's Institute held its 49th annual meeting at the Women's Institute Hall in Falkenburg. A paper prepared by Mrs. Bailey was read by Mrs. Chris Forth noting the fact that the South Muskoka District WI was organized at Muskoka Falls in 1900 with Mrs. H. Speedie, Miss Lizzie Donnelly, and Miss Hollingworth as the main officers. In 1950 there were 16 branches and the work was progressing quite satisfactorily. Attention was drawn to the early work of the institute in procuring medical inspection of the schools in 1920.

T.J. Woods came from his winter home in Toronto to attend a regular meeting of Muskoka Lodge AF and AM No. 360 where he was honoured as the oldest member of the lodge in both age and membership. Among the many messages received was one from the Hon. Leslie Frost, Premier of Ontario.

A sketch club was organized to meet weekly with instructor Bob Everett, a local pharmacist and accomplished artist. Officers included Mrs. Ed Thatcher and Miss Norma Reid.

Ken Morris sold the Albion Hotel to James Stevenson of Toronto and Lauren Johnston of Midland. The latter was a son of the celebrated Canadian artist Franz Johnston ... Burt Smith Distributors opened, carrying paint, wallpaper, and floor coverings ... The Caisse Lingerie and Gift Shop was to become The Holiday Shop owned by Mr. L.H. Specht ... At Muskoka Electric, an Inglis ringer washer was selling for $129.95 during the April clearance sale ... Hammond's Taxi now had two-way FM telephones in their cars ... The Bracebridge Dairy Bar opened on July 25.

In October, fire destroyed the mill building of the Muskoka Canoe Co. on Monck Road. Alex MacIver said they would rebuild immediately. The fire that consumed the Muskoka Beach Inn dance pavilion and boat house lit up the entire countryside. Upwards of 30 boats were lost.

Lorne's Marketeria held a soap sale: giant sized Tide $0.62, Oxydol $0.72, Duz $0.70. The Holiday Shop expanded by purchasing the building formerly known as the Sea Captain's Chop. Due to increased costs, taxi fares increased to $0.35 a single fare and $0.50 for two to four passengers. The companies involved were Forresters, Hammonds, Kirkpatricks, Stevensons, Whites, Rosewarnes, Parks, Pattersons, and McKinnons.

The mill owned by Joe Olivero on Bardsville Road completely burned. Fire destroyed the home of Mr. and Mrs. Nelson Orr on Front Street. The blaze was discovered by Dr. E.G. Ellis who had gone to the home to visit a patient, thus avoiding a worse tragedy.

At a lengthy meeting of the Board of Education, the high school teachers requested the board establish a salary schedule. The idea was not well received, however, it was accounted for in the education budget of $76,944, $21,500 of which had to be raised by the local ratepayers. The high school principal, Mr. Wright, requested the establishment of a commercial course. Miss Mary Jackson would take a course to become its instructor.

A new 500-gallon GMC tank truck was ordered through Muskoka Garage for the fire department.

Hutchison brothers celebrated their 60th anniversary as food merchants in town.

*The teachers at Bracebridge High School, 1950-51.* Front (left to right): *Miss Hallet, Miss Jackson, Mr. Wright (principal), Miss Miller;* Back: *Miss Cunningham, Mr. Robertson, Mr. Jackson, Mr. Colmer, Mr. Doherty, Miss Carew. By the late 1960s the teaching staff would number more than 60.* COURTESY OF THE BRACEBRIDGE PUBLIC LIBRARY

In early May at least 190 men were working out of Dorset to fight the large bush fires raging in the area.

It was learned that Muskoka would be served by regular air transportation from Malton by Central Aircraft, a return fare costing $18.

A terrible infestation of forest tent caterpillars caused wholesale destruction of foliage, especially on maple and oak trees, in the district. Many camps and resorts contracted to have their properties sprayed from the air, but at $4.75 an acre it was much too expensive for any municipality to undertake.

Hotel Dorset was sold to the proprietors of the Albion Hotel in Bracebridge and was to be managed by Mrs. Franz Johnston and her daughter Wenawae Stevenson … Jack Winder of Baysville obtained 11 out of 12 firsts on his upper school departmental examinations … Bruce Findlay was placed in charge of Rubberset in Gravenhurst following Mr. Hewes' death … A St. John's Ambulance course was offered as a Civil Defence measure and was taught by A.J. Milne.

Exhibits at the fall fair were greatly increased but attendance was down due to wet weather … The first annual shooting match was held at Blanchard's field near Milford Bay sponsored by the Kinsmen Club of that village ... Mr. R. Creasor succeeded Mr. J.D. McNee as manager of the Skeleton Lake Fish Hatchery.

According to the latest government returns the following population figures applied to Muskoka's towns and villages: Gravenhurst 3,711, Huntsville 3,244, Bracebridge 2,717, Bala 358, Port Carling 490, Port Sydney 166, and Windermere 126. The Ontario Department of Lands and Forests established a permanent office in Huntsville with Mr. Rae Grimmell in charge. He would be in charge of reforestation projects throughout the district. A steel fire tower was to be built near the Wesley Morrow farm in Draper on property acquired in 1941 for that purpose.

The 17th annual Muskoka Lakes District Bonspiel, billed as the biggest curling event of the winter, got under way in town with 160 curlers who came to win the historic trophies and other outstanding prizes as well as to enjoy the competition. Only one of the coveted trophies remained in Bracebridge – the Book.

Among the many to thrill wrestling fans at the arena was Whipper Billy Watson, a former British Empire and World Champion. Artificial ice making equipment was installed in the curling rink.

Deaths this year included: Fober A. Findlay, 84, taught school at Fern Glen, Alport, and Rosseau. In the latter place he married Annie Meisenheimer then moved to town where he became the first local customs officer in 1911, a position he held until his retirement in 1933, when he became the town's assessor until 1945 ... Wesley Morrow, 76, the former reeve of Draper and son of a pioneer family at Muskoka Falls. He had spent his life farming and lumbering and took a keen interest in the affairs of his township as school trustee, councillor, and reeve ... Isabella Burbridge, 74, born at Bardsville, daughter of Mr. and Mrs. Joseph McCulley ... Thomas G. Patterson, 80, who spent his life in Stephenson Township as a blacksmith and garage operator ... George W.E. Patterson, 81, had been a resident of town since 1928 but had lived at Parkersville with his parents in his younger days ... Joshua L. Yeoman, 91, of the Falkenburg area, worked for 45 years with W.W. Kinsey in the undertaking business. He was one of the first embalmers in Ontario, having taken the course in Chicago. In 1882 he married Isabella Armstrong and they had 10 children ... Herbert J. Denniss, 80, died in Winnipeg. He was born in Draper but later lived in Macaulay. He and his brother, William, ran the Denniss Planing Mill for many years ... Mrs. L.R. Fraser, 74, wife of the well-known master mariner and historian, Captain Levi Fraser. May Jermyn was a daughter of William and Anne Magee of Northwood, Muskoka Township. She was a faithful member at St. Thomas Church ... William Dirby, 86, long-time resident of Monck. His first wife was Isabella Spencer and his second was Mabel Stroud ... Nellie Leishman, 70, daughter of a prominent lumberman whose sawmill stood where Northern Planing Mills is now located ...

Lemuel Scott, 69, married Emily Travers of Fraserburg. Four of their 12 children still lived in Bracebridge – Mrs. Ernie DeLarge, Mrs. H. Patterson, Lewis, and Ollie. He had been a member of the Independent Order of Foresters for 40 years ... Frederick R Bastedo, 80, of Baysville, leaving his wife, Jewel Mary Cronym, and four daughters, Annie Maynard, Myrtle Rykman, Edythe Tykman, and Lois Anderson ... Mrs. William Lowe, widow of the man who once served throughout Muskoka as the inspector of roads and bridges for the government ... Mrs. Mungo Park McKay Sr., 75, the youngest child of Mr. and Mrs. James Killen of Monck, taught for a time before her marriage in 1905 ... John L Galbraith, born at McLean's Corners in 1868 and worked for Mickle-Dyment Lumber Co. for 28 years ... Charles Walker Riley, came to the Milford Bay area at age 6 with his parents Charles and Emma Riley. At 21, he and his sister Mary purchased the Point Kaye post office and began a small resort known as Scarcliffe which was sold in 1943 ... Mrs. R.A. Green, 78, eldest daughter of Mr. and Mrs. Thomas Stephens of Muskoka Township ... Thomas Peacock, 67, of Falkenburg ...

John Greer, born in Ireland in 1861, came to Canada when he was 16 and settled at Raymond with his parents. After his marriage to Rosella Crouder, he moved to Skeleton Lake, then later to Bent River. He was a staunch Conservative and had been a member of the Orange Lodge for 72 years ... Henry J. Mortimer came to Medora Township in 1872 when he was 3 years old. His family was involved in the summer hotel business and he helped build their steamer the *Florence Main* ... Henry Warren, 78, first manager of the Dominion Bank when it opened in 1919 in the Queen's Hotel ... Tony Todoroff, 45, restaurateur, leaving his wife and four small children ... Alfred J. Slater, 67, businessman and star athlete prominent in hockey, basketball and lacrosse ... F.M. de la Fosse, 90, author of *English Bloods*, a story about pioneer Muskoka published under the pseudonym Roger Vardon ... Alexander (Sandy) Walker, 85, had served six terms on Council and was mayor in 1919 ... David Kirkness, former superintendent of roads and prominent in the Orange Lodge.

# 1951

Bracebridge entered its 76th year of municipal organization with mayor Dr. L.N. Ryan and councillors Walter Reynolds, Nelson Goltz, Alex MacIver, Dr. R.J. Dodds, B.B. Bell, and Harold Frowe.

In the townships of Macaulay, Monck, Muskoka , Draper, and Oakley, the reeves were Dan MacNaughtan, George Freemantle, Carl Laycox, Alf Ashley, and James Henderson. In September, Town Council decided to take over the town garbage collection using town men and equipment to do so. James Webb was appointed to manage the Bracebridge Memorial Community Centre.

Henry Longhurst of Windermere was elected president of the Muskoka District Council. The principal topic of

*Bracebridge High School Slater Cup champions in 1950.* Front row (left to right): *Ken Black, G. Ecclestone, Arthur Cox, D. Bruce, B. Bruce, L. Sawyer;* second row: *P. MacPherson, L. Vanclieaf, G.W. Colmer, B. Kelly, G. Bildson;* back row: *J. McCann, G. McDermot, L. Peterkin, J. Watt.* COURTESY OF VICKY BILLINGSLEY FROM THE R.J. BOYER COLLECTION

*Bracebridge Bears hockey team, 1951-52 finalists.* Front row (left to right): *Merv Robinson, Stu Reid, "Chub" Downey, Neil McKinnon, Normie Ball (mascot), Bruce Hook, "Dinty" Rowe, Fred Nichols, Ronnie Rowe.* Back row: *Bud Reid (stick boy), Gordon Reid (coach), Archie Ball, Johnny Thomson, Artie Dickson, "Stretch" Lawson, Harvey Hines (trainer), "Butch" Ecclestone, Verne Vanclieaf, "Bus" Brazier, Des Deslauriers, Ken Ross (manager), Jimmie Webb (arena manager).* COURTESY OF BRACEBRIDGE CULTURE AND RECREATION

discussion for the council this year was the caterpillar menace.

The Citizens' Band was granted the sum of $1,300 a year in place of a grant of one mill previously given. The band effectively lost $800 a year using this method, approved by a special bylaw vote. Gary Jackson was re-elected as Choral Society president; Roxyna Phillips and Winnifred Anderson were director and pianist.

At the 20th annual Horticultural Society meeting, Dr. R.J. Reynolds was again elected president. Membership was noted at 312. A special evening for confirming the Royal Scarlet Degree in the Orange Association was held at the United Church with Nick Wettlaufer acting as chairman. Mike Newell headed a discussion whereby a blood donor registry would be established at the hospital using, at first, members of the various local Lions clubs as a base group. An excellent evening of skating was described as "a refreshing lift" as over 700 figure skating fans enjoyed the performance put on by the pupils of Miss Mauvis Ferguson.

The Lions Club presented a "Pneolator" to the fire hall to be used as an automatic artificial respiration instrument. Sheriff W.B. Elliott was elected head of the Men's Club. Agnew Hammond of Jubilee LOBA No. 777 was made honorary member of the Ladies Grand Orange Lodge. Bert Taylor was elected head of the Lions Club. The Orangemen held their traditional Twelfth of July parade on a day that saw thousands of participants and spectators in town. The oldest man on parade was 91-year-old Thomas Woods from Toronto. Over 40 lodges took part with representatives from Baysville making an excellent showing.

A teen town council was formed with the help of the Rotary Club.

Charlie Ruttan, a sawmill operator from Stoneleigh, was elected Worshipful Master of the Orange Lodge. Les Rosewarne, a car dealership agent, was the Noble Grand of the IOOF, and Milton R. Askin was Master of the Masonic Lodge. Don Farnsworth, president of the Muskoka Crop Improvement Association, chaired a well-attended banquet at the Albion Hotel. Awards for the 100-bushel oat club were presented by agriculture representative Doug Tipper. Local winners were Edwin Longhurst, Ernest Goltz, Lloyd Seehaver, Ambrose Cook, James Dinner, W.D Taylor, George Parrett, Max Beaumont, and Charles Speicher.

As of January 27, Tom Dawkins announced that he had sold his grocery store business to G.F. Jacklin from Parry Sound. The Whitten company hardware store was purchased by George W Ecclestone Ltd. The Muskoka Canoe company expanded again to meet the growing demand for their product. John Olimer of Olimer Plumbing purchased the Prichard variety store business. It was managed by his three daughters, Maureen, Delores, and Lenore.

After a poll was taken, the merchants of town decided to change the half-day closing from 12:30 p.m. Thursday to 12:30 p.m. Wednesday instead.

Irwin J. Robson's mill at Vankoughnet burned. He purchased part of a farm owned by Ken Keith in Muskoka Township to set up a new mill. Six automated looms were installed at the Bird Woollen Mill. W.J.A. Brown announced the sale of his service station on Manitoba Street to Harry Knight and Neil Brodie. Bell Telephone sent out 28,400 new phone books which included all service numbers from Burk's Falls to Penetang. Pearse Manufacturing company, maker of pallets, opened in a portion of the Minett-Shields Boat Works. The Bracebridge Bowling Academy was purchased by Les Atkey of Gravenhurst.

One of the concerns of the District Council was the fluctuation in lake levels due to hydro dam controls which caused difficulties with fish spawning areas.

George Boyer was elected president of the Ontario Association of Agricultural Societies ... A team of bowlers for the Unemployment Insurance Office won the provincial championship for public employees. The team's members were Peggy O'Connell, Margaret Jackson, June Murphy, Clarence Kirkness, Harry Anderson, Merv Robinson, Ken Rutter, and Tom Stephenson ... Over 100 badminton players took part in the annual Muskoka Badminton Tournament with Douglas Smith in charge of the games. The doubles class was won by Kay Beers with Daisy Murphy and Jack Woodcock with Vern Payne ... 270,000 speckled trout were released in various lakes in the eastern part of the district ... free motion pictures were shown Tuesday evenings during July and August ... H.E. Rice, editor of the *Huntsville Forester*, retired after 52 years, the job going to his son, Paul ... The Springdale Park Lot Owner's Association held a successful sports day with horseshoe pitching as the highlight, according to Harold Locking, president ... The 1951 car licence plates were to be used again in 1952 to conserve steel. A sticker was placed on the windshield to make the licence legal ... Applications for Old Age Assistance between ages 65 and 70 were made available ... In September, the Dominion government proclaimed the Juvenile Delinquents Act to be in force in the District of Muskoka. Gordon Aiken was appointed judge ... Algonquin Park, which was set aside "for the benefit, advantage and enjoyment of the people of the province" in 1893, was once again enlarged ... Douglas Tipper was appointed as district agricultural representative succeeding Grant Mitchell. Mr. Tipper's father, Rowland, earlier held the position for over 22 years ... Roy Goltz and W.K. Kettle each won several prizes at the CNE in grain and sheep, respectively.

Bracebridge was one of many municipalities to proclaim a civic holiday for their residents to travel to North Bay to see HRH Princess Elizabeth and Prince Philip.

The November provincial election saw Arthur Welsh, Conservative MPP, returned to Queen's Park over Art Ferguson, Liberal, and Mrs. Earl Mitchell of Minett, the CCF candidate. The Frost government took 79 of the 90 seats.

The population of Muskoka was 24,353, an increase of about 2,500 since the 1941 census.

The cemetery board of St. Thomas' Anglican Church purchased property across from the existing cemetery ... Rev. Marshall V. Shields came as the new pastor at the Bethel Tabernacle ... The newly renovated and refurbished United Church was rededicated. The beautiful new chimes were heard throughout the town 20 minutes prior to the service ... The 67th anniversary of the Salvation Army in town was marked by the visit of the Earlscourt Boys' Band who did double duty by also parading with the church float in the Santa Claus parade.

Over 200 parishioners gathered at St. Joseph's Roman Catholic Church to honour the Very Rev. Dean O'Leary on the occasion of his 40 years as a parish priest. An address was read by W.J. Dinner in which he noted the starting of the Holy Name Society by Dean O'Leary. A presentation of $650 was made.

Thirty-four charter members formed the new Home and School Association at the high school with Mrs. William Fraser as president, Mrs. John Newark vice president, Mrs. Chris Forth secretary, and Mr. I.Y. Murphy treasurer … The School Board purchased 20 desks at $28.85 each and 20 chairs at $8.95 to accommodate instruction in typing which was to begin in September … After 25 years as school inspector, Mr. George S. Johnson retired to be succeeded by Gordon S. McIntrye … Music classes were started at the high school under Mr. Evans and at the public school under the direction of Mrs. Marj Quemby … The Gideons received approval to distribute New Testaments, first to Grades 5 to 8, then annually after that to Grade 5 students only.

Bracebridge deaths this year included Thomas Dowler, 94, at Barrie. His father established the match factory here near the corner of Victoria and Dill streets … Amanda Brice, 83, daughter of Mr. and Mrs. John McDonald, came to town in 1879 … J.H. Elliott, who came as a watchmaker and jeweler in 1900, established his own business, and married Florence Sibbett … Murt Dunn, 61, leading figure in sports, especially hockey, as player and coach, built the skating rink … Rev. Father Robert Hatherley Loosemore, 43, of the SSJE, came to the Society in 1933 and was pastor on the Uffington-Barkway circuit … Philip R. Marrin, 35, son of P.J. Marrin, died suddenly of a heart attack leaving his wife, Zita, and two small children. He was associated with his father's business P.J. Marrin and Sons … George Kirk, 91, married Catherine Ennis in 1904 … Guy Pritchard, 44, owner of a variety store business which he opened in 1949 in the Patterson Hotel … J. Wesley Botting, 71, came to town in 1913, won many prizes with his horses … Mrs. John Higgins, 89, came with her parents in 1873, married in 1883, and resided at Cloverdale Farm in Monck. She was the mother of Betty Reynolds … George Wettlaufer, 80, came to Muskoka about 1882. He farmed at Germania … George Ferrier, 83, a Beatrice town line farmer for over 55 years … Henry Creasor, 88, Watt … Albina Struthers, 86, oldest daughter of Macaulay settlers Mr. and Mrs. Joseph Zimmerman … Rev. St. George Mossom Boyd, 37, SSJE, came to the Mission House in 1940 … Ada Goodfellow, 88, came to cook at the Queen's Hotel … Charlotte Burton, 93, son of John Leishman who owned a mill where Tennant's later stood … Allen McCracken, 81, whose family came to Uffington in the 1880s. He was the father of teacher Miss McCracken … Wally Shier, 37, vice president of the J.D. Shier Company … Mrs. C.E. Mawdsley, a member of the pioneer Topp family, mother of Mrs. H.E. Beaumont … Captain Andrew Corbett, 80, a master mariner of the Muskoka Lakes and one time captain of the *Oriole* … Mrs. Jerry Dickie, daughter of the late Mr. and Mrs. George Spreadborough … Jack Fawcett, 30, stricken by polio and died. In 1949 he had purchased Ridley Cleaners with Doug Kirkness … Don Bradshaw, 22, casualty of the Korean War. His father Fred had been a barber in a shop now occupied by Thompson Barber Shop … Charles W. Dill, 91, a pioneer merchant for whom Dill Street was named … Major A.A. Lyndon, 79, who had spent 33 years in the army including service in the Boer War. He spent time in the Klondike gold rush in 1898 as a marshall for the Royal North West Mounted Police … Ernest H. Goltz, born in Monck in 1873, married Christina Hillman of Falkenburg in 1903. He was an excellent farmer … Frank Matthais, 59, lived on the eighth concession of Draper until 1927 when he moved into Matthiasville. In 1930 he gave the land to the SSJE upon which the church was built … T.J. Anderson, who had first worked in his uncle's general store here. He eventually entered the business world and ran the store for many years. In later years his son Wilbur took over … John Cope, former lock master at Port Carling.

## 1952

Friday, February 15 was declared a civic holiday of mourning for his late Majesty King George VI who had passed away 10 days earlier. A memorial service was held in the United Church with the town's ministers taking part.

*Post-war prosperity meant lots of cars, which here occupy every space along Manitoba Street, early 1950s. Perhaps this is a Saturday and everyone is in town shopping. At this point most stores are still located in the downtown core between Memorial Park and the falls. In the 1960s development would quickly spread north on Manitoba Street to Monck Road.* COURTESY OF THE TOWN OF BRACEBRIDGE

At the Muskoka District Council's semi-annual meeting, topics related to lands and forests, the Health Unit, sanitary inspection, and the Children's Aid Society were discussed. Carl Laycock was elected president, Jack Johnson vice president, and J.H. Forbes secretary-treasurer. Dr. C. Stewart succeeded Dr. William Stiles as district veterinarian.

Town Council completed negotiations with the Department of Highways for the exchange of the old dump site to a new site about 1,500 feet closer to Sharpe's Creek. The old site had been appropriated for the new Highway 11 bypass. Mr. Colan Cowan was appointed police constable for Bracebridge. Businesses and homes were given numbers according to a uniform measured number system.

Boake's Uptown Grocery was purchased by Don Smith of Walker's Point and later Gravenhurst, where he was a chainsaw agent. Mr. Smith planned to use the store as a sales and stock room. The grocery business, formerly run by Greers, Yeos, Bassetts, McBrides, Drapers and finally Boakes, was moved to Muriel's Bakery … H.J. Brooks and Sons was advertising eight-cubic-foot refrigerators at $299 … After 62 years in business, the grocery business of the Hutchison Brothers was sold to Lorne Hockridge … Garwood's Store was opened on a year-round basis by Roy Garwood who came here from Stratford … George Crichton sold his Essotane bottled gas business to Superior Propane … Waite's Bakery celebrated 25 years of business in town. Mr. A.T. Waite came in 1927 after buying the former W.J. Leece business. After six years in business he purchased the A.J. Wattie block in which daughter Joan managed the retail trade while her brothers, Calvin, Geoff, and Guy assisted their father with baking … A new laundry was established by Vic

Love of Elgin House. It was located beside the Lakecraft Plant in the industrial park along Wellington Street … The new Bracebridge A & P store was opened in the former theatre building on Queen's Hill with local man Ron Bombay as manager. This was the second time the company had started business here … Chester Grigg came to replace W.W. Creswick as manager at the Dominion Bank … MacNaughtan's Hardware extended the back section of their store … Bracebridge and Lake Drive dairies lowered the price of milk one cent on July 1 … Muskoka's first drive-in theatre opened for the summer on July 4, on Doe Lake Road … Lorne Hockridge opened his new store on the east side of Manitoba Street where Hutchison Bros. had been located … Nelson Goltz purchased the Parkview Restaurant from Mr. and Mrs. Tom Stephenson … In July, Rosebank Lodge near Baysville became a youth hostel.

The Rubberset company in Gravenhurst named Mr.Bruce Findlay as their new president. Gerry Dunn of Bala was elected a director of the Auditorium Owners and Operators' Association at the fourth annual meeting.

At the farm of Albert Pelissero, in Macaulay, an animal oddity was born to a Holstein cow, the face and neck being like a cow but the ears, legs, tail, and hoofs were characteristic of a deer.

Hawkins General Store in Utterson was destroyed by fire. The 50-year-old Royal Muskoka Hotel, built on an island in Lake Rosseau as a 175-room luxury resort, burned to the ground. Its first manager, Lucius Boomer, later built the Waldorf Astoria in New York City.

The Lions Club safety committee applied free "scotchlite" reflective tape to any bicycles that were brought to the arena. George Ferrier was in charge of the project. The Chamber of Commerce tourist booth began to operate out of Russ Salmon's service station with Ruth Tinkiss in charge. Highway 69 from Parry Sound to Sudbury was completed to a point four miles north of Britt.

Pioneer Days in Bracebridge included a parade, concerts, dances, bake sales, and an auction sale sponsored by the Business and Professional Women of the town. The Bracebridge School of Ballet under the direction of Mary Morgan held classes in the Orange Hall.

A span of the High Falls bridge was destroyed while a truck was crossing it. Two men escaped from the cab and reached shore safely.

The Bracebridge Fall Fair had a very large attendance and especially noted was the school fair work done by local students. Between 1,200 and 1,400 pupils marched in the school parade on Friday afternoon.

A mobile telephone centre was erected eight miles north of Bracebridge, which included the building of a 150-foot tower. It was located in Macaulay but close to its border with Stephenson Township.

Redmond Thomas, QC, became the district's full-time magistrate in November.

The officially designated approach to town from the south off the new highway bypass was to be the road from the Muskoka Falls turn via the "subway" (the CNR overpass near the present Scandura plant).

The South Muskoka Agricultural Society named Charles Morrow as president with first and second vice presidents Willard Draper and Robert B. Barron. The Chamber of Commerce became an incorporated body, authorizing it to operate within the town as well as in several surrounding townships. As of April 1, James Fairhurst of Windsor became manager and industrial commissioner to promote the town's business possibilities. In August, Mr. Fairhurst moved out west and was replaced by William G. Claridge. Mrs. Milton Shier was chosen president of the Red Cross Society. Milton Goltz was elected Worshipful Master of the Masonic Lodge. Aubrey Hawn was elected president of the Lions Club. Mr. Leslie Aitken was made an honorary life member of the Muskoka District Tourist Development Association. George Martin of Wigwassin was re-elected as president. Jubilee LOBA celebrated its 25th anniversary with a banquet and speakers at the United Church hall. Over 90 attended, including many Grand Lodge officers. Mrs. Birdie Huckle was elected the lady director of fairs at the annual meeting of District No. 11 agricultural societies. The Lions hosted over 1,000 at their huge Halloween party held at the Community Centre when over 4,000 prizes, toys, and novelties were "won" by the children at various game booths. The LOL 685 at Port Carling dedicated its new Orange Hall. With 49 members, the lodge was strong and ready to serve the community. Edmund

Senior was installed as Noble Grand for the IOOF and Mrs. Clayton Joslin became the Noble Grand of the Rebekahs. Ronald McKay became the Master of Muskoka Lodge AF and AM.

Henry Longhurst of Windermere replaced Rev. Craymer as president of the Children's Aid Society. There were 81 children in the society's care at that time.

Mrs. Olive Palmer (later the second Mrs. John Diefenbaker) addressed the high school Home and School Association on the importance of providing guidance classes for students. A large classroom to accommodate 30 students, as well as an apartment for the teacher, was opened on the Gibson Reserve.

An ambitious Empire Day program was held by the 42 students of Mr. Nelson's room at the public school. The pageant included 11 different songs and was very well received.

Rev. W.G. Julian was called to pastor the Bracebridge United Church. His wife Joy was already acquainted with Muskoka, being the daughter of Mr. and Mrs. George Hutcheson of Huntsville. Tribute was made on behalf of the Venerable Archdeacon Lindsell who had been in charge of the Port Carling-Port Sandfield parish for nearly 16 years. Rev. S.M. Craymer of St. Thomas Anglican Church since 1948, was called to a Port Arthur parish. He had served as president of the Children's Aid Society and had been involved in the Horticultural Society and the Hospital Board. The new rector was Rev. Alvin T Thomson from Port Arthur.

After its annual conference the Free Methodist Church received their new minister, the Rev. W.J. Daw. The Holy Name Society's annual dinner at St. Joseph's was attended by over 100 men. Proceedings were under the direction of Siegfried Paul (president), Frank McNabb, and Rev. Father Perdue. The Ontario Minister of Mines, Philip Kelly, addressed this gathering of Catholic laymen. Cherene Abbott of Clear Lake won the Dominion prize in the Sunday-school-by-mail competition.

At Kingston, the Bracebridge High School curling team placed third in a competition involving eight other teams. The skip was Don McVittie.

Our curling rink installed artificial ice-making equipment.

Many paid the admission price of $0.35 to see George Chenier, the North American snooker champion, when he played at Jack's Billiards.

The Hockey Greats of the past came for an exhibition game sponsored by the Bala service organizations. It was the first game of hockey to be televised in Canada.

Hockey was much on the minds of Bracebridge sports enthusiasts as they followed the hard-fought series between the Bears and the Minden Monarchs, which the local club won in the seventh game. After eliminating Camp Borden and Kingston in the play-downs, the Bears began the never-to-be-forgotten finals against Elmira. In one match, Elmira led the Bears by 4-0 until the last four minutes of play when in quick succession Bracebridge scored six goals. Ultimately they left the title at Elmira but won the heartfelt gratitude of their hometown fans. A teddy bear picnic in the high school gym was held to honour the team.

A ski tow was installed at Rainbow Ridge.

Deaths this year included Mr. S.J. Furniss, 79, member of Dominion parliament for the Muskoka-Ontario riding from 1935 to 1945 … George Barrett, a former town employee for many years … Robert Whaley, a blacksmith who came here from Ireland … Alex Skene, superintendent of the electric and water systems at the turn of the century. He went on to become a high official with the Hydro Electric Power Company … William Gerhart, 86, served as district Crown lands agent from 1924 … George A. Dickson, 80, came to Muskoka about 1881 and lived at Fraserburg. At one year of age he lost his ability to both hear and speak … Margaret McCracken, 68, daughter of Oakley residents Mr. and Mrs. William Landon. She married James McCracken of Uffington and raised two daughters, Mary and Lorna … Joseph Giaschi, 74, founder of a chain of theatres including the Norwood in Bracebridge and the Capitol in Huntsville and Port Colborne. He came to Huntsville in 1915 as a tannery worker for $1.75 a day … Donna Kirkpatrick Arnott, 19, died unexpectedly less than a year after her marriage to Keith Arnott … David Hodgson, 83, resident since the early 1890s and was division court clerk and issuer of motor licences … John Bain, 91, of the pioneer Muskoka Township family. They were members of the

*"Timmy" Allchin, owner of Holiday House. She was a wonderful organizer of community shows, and active in the Chamber of Commerce, Santa's Village, Business and Professional Women's Club, and the Santa Claus Parade.* COURTESY OF BRENDA COX

first Presbyterian Church when it existed in the old building on the Browning property near Lake Muskoka ... Jessie MacMillan, who came her as a young girl. Her brother, John, had a grocery store where the Grand Café later came to be at the foot of Chancery Lane. The family home was Braeside, facing Ontario Street and adjoining the courthouse grounds (now Michael Anne MacDonald's law office). Miss MacMillan later joined her sisters in business after they purchased the Perry Block. In 1949 the business was sold and became the Margaret Ellen Shop ... Mrs. James Thomson, whose brother-in-law, Jack, operated a drug store which later was purchased by G.W. Brooks ... Joshua Horner, 87, founder of the Red Chalk Fish and Game Club in Ridout Township in 1908, and was chief guide until 1939 ... Albert E. Robinson, 80, a scaler for J.D. Shier and other lumber companies ... George Mills, 75, son of Mr. and Mrs. Joseph Mills of Macaulay ... Robert E. Perry, 73, of Kirkland Lake. Son of postmaster R.P. Perry, he became the Canadian Express Company agent at the train station, then later went north ... Walter Taplin, 73, who spent 35 years as a lumber foreman in Draper ... Harriet Veitch Shea, 73, whose mother's people were United Empire Loyalists.

## 1953

This year, Ted Reid, Austin Hunt, Doug Wells, Nelson Goltz, Robert Jeffries, and Phillip Stone served as councillors along with Mayor Dr. L.N. Ryan. In the townships the only change in the reeves was in Draper where H.S. Wasson headed the council.

John Sloper, clerk-treasurer of Macaulay, missed his first council meeting in 39 years due to an unexpected stay in the hospital.

The salaries of the police officers were set at $2,600 for Chief John Harrington, $2,350 for Sergeant Rowland, and $2,200 for Constable Cowan. Works superintendent Nick Wettlaufer's salary was set at $2,350.

Reeve J. Johnston of Monck Township was named president of the Muskoka District Council, with Lloyd Parker of Windermere serving as vice president.

In view of a 125 percent increase in power consumption since 1946, the Town Council and the Power, Light and Water Commission discussed a plan to add to the High Falls power plant, which was approved by the ratepayers 185 to 26. The $247,000 cost was placed on a 20-year debenture.

The town band was reorganized under a citizen's committee to put it on a better financial basis. John Morra remained the conductor.

Council was approached by George N. Ferrier, president of the Lions Club, to form a recreation committee with a director.

In view of the fact that the 22nd Parliament of Canada was to be elected on August 10, the sitting member, W.K.

"Bucko" McDonald, Liberal, was to continue as that party's candidate. Opposing him on behalf of the Progressive Conservatives was a real estate agent and reeve of Burk's Falls, Stan Darling. The CCF named their candidate, Edward J Lawrence of Nipissing Junction. The Parry Sound-Muskoka riding fell in line with the rest of the country and returned W.K. McDonald for a further term to serve under Prime Minister Louis St. Laurent as part of the Liberal government. There were 80 polls in the district as a whole, with four each in Bracebridge and Draper, three in Macaulay, two in Oakley, and five each in Monck and Muskoka townships.

Five lives were lost in a head-on train crash at Southwood.

The latitude and longitude of Bracebridge were published as 45° 02' N and 79° 19' W.

According to the 1951 Dominion census, 2,736 children were attending Muskoka's public schools. It was noted that in the 6,860 homes in Muskoka, there were 6,175 radios, 3,890 telephones, 3,340 cars, 5,140 washing machines, and 2,450 vacuum cleaners. There were 365 Muskoka homes with none of these conveniences.

Edgar Magee, collector of customs and excise, moved to Oakville and was replaced by G.W. Robertson … Those involved in the Korean conflict were returning home … The Ontario Department of Health reported that on average, patient care cost $11.54 a day.

Trans-Canada Airlines service started on June 14 making daily stops on the Timmins-Toronto run. The first passenger was William Orr of the Sanatorium, who was flying to Ireland.

Full-colour portraits of Her Majesty the Queen were made available in various sizes and prices from the *Muskoka Herald* in honour of her coronation.

For the first time in 75 years there was no train service to steamers at Muskoka Wharf in Gravenhurst. Fourteen point four miles of a new section of Highway 11 between Muskoka Falls and Parkersville was opened in July.

The events of Coronation Day (June 2) in Bracebridge took place after the coronation service broadcast from London. They were as follows: Holy Communion at St. Thomas Anglican Church; Solemn High Mass at St. Joseph's; a children's parade with three bands, the Guides, Brownies, Scouts, Cubs, and Legion members; a community service of thanksgiving and dedication conducted by the Ministerial Association with music led by the Choral Society and a children's choir; Mayor Ryan planted a maple and an oak tree at Memorial Park; bell ringing from the United Church; a sports program at Jubilee Park conducted by the Kinsmen Club; a fireworks program provided by the town at Jubilee Park; and a coronation dance at the Legion Hall. Each elementary school child received a copper coin to commemorate the occasion, the inscription reading "Elizabeth II Regina Coronata MCMLIII." A Coronation Festival sponsored by the Business and Professional Women of town was held at the end of July emphasizing the various nationalities of Great Britain.

Italian and French workmen were working out of Falkenburg employed in raising and strengthening the CNR rail track from Bracebridge north.

Muskoka experienced a serious drought causing shortages of water in wells and creeks and the drying out of pasture fields. The *Islander*, one of the oldest steamers on the Muskoka Lakes, was purchased from the Navigation Company by Lloyd Readman of Gravenhurst.

Mr. G.W. Skuce and his wife left Bracebridge after his 33 years as station agent for the CNR.

The Rotary Club continued its financial support for the library at Bracebridge Public School.

For the first time on record the officers of the Lands and Forests failed to uncover any infractions of the game laws during the annual six-day deer hunting season. Over 3,000 cars and trucks were stopped for inspection.

The Bala Legion Hall was officially opened on November 20. Ted Wright became the new proprietor of Cleveland House at Minett, a pioneer resort that started with a log house in 1869.

William "Bus" Brazier succeeded Robert Jeffries as the Legion president. Bus was a popular veteran and a dependable member of the Bracebridge Bears hockey team.

The Muskoka Heritage Foundation was formed, its declared object being to "enable the people of Muskoka to achieve well-being while restoring and making constructive use of their natural resources."

*Memorial Park in the early 1950s; the silver maples planted in the early 1900s are now attaining considerable size. This band stand was first built without a roof.*
COURTESY OF BRENDA COX

Gordon Rosewarne purchased the land and buildings of Sutcliffe Motors on the east side of Manitoba Street between Ann and MacDonald Streets ... The law firm of Thomas and Thomas was purchased by Eric R. Marsden, a well-known criminal lawyer ... Bracebridge Dairy held a grand opening of their new dairy plant located right behind the Dairy Bar ... The Myers' business in the Hotel Patterson was taken over for offices by Bob Petry for the J.T. Andrews Insurance Agency ... The Ontario Hydro office moved temporarily into the Hotel Patterson then into its new office on Toronto Street ... The North Garage, operated by Hillman and Colson, became the dealership for Chrysler Corporation vehicles ... Mr. and Mrs. Doug Sieber purchased Kay's Tot-to-Teen ... Clara Robertson advertised machineless permanents at $4 in her Toronto Street hairdressing shop ... A new aluminum siding front was placed on the Liquor Store, located beside the Parkview Restaurant ... Wrixon's Smoke Shop opened at 22 Manitoba Street ... Tom Fisher opened his new flower shop on Manitoba Street just south of Ann Street ... The Byway Garage on the Port Carling Highway, a quarter mile from town, was opened to manufacture luggage trailers. William Little was the proprietor ... Nelson Forbes sold the Paisley Shop (now occupied by John deLang) to A.L. Carroll of Toronto ... Eight houses belonging to the Anglo-Canadian Leather company were sold by real estate agents C.L. Slater and Elmer Forbes ... Roy White moved his hairdressing business from the Thatcher Building to Ontario Street in a building formerly owned by Buck Electric ... Fred Lee opened his North End Grocery Store next to Harrington's Meat Market ... The Maher Shoe Store moved from its location next to Elliott's store into the former location of Lorne's Marketeria on the west side of Manitoba Street ... George W. Nutt opened a grocery store just north of town ... Neil Edwards and Aubrey Grimes built a half-mile track for stock car racing about one and a half miles north of town near Marge's Convalescent Home ... The Dominion Bank leased the Thatcher Building premises previously occupied by Maher's Shoes and White's Hairdressing ... The post office announced it would close on Saturday afternoon instead of Wednesday afternoon ... The Robinson Tire Service was sold to Herbert Lee.

Cale's Meat Market advertised boneless prime rib roasts at $0.65 a pound and bologna at $0.29.

Ten people, in an upstairs apartment, were awoke by the cry of a young child and saved from death when a fire started in the Silverwood's Dairy ice cream depot on the west side of Manitoba Street.

The coveted Canadian Professional Ski Instructor badge and standing was received by Stan Knowles, president of the local Rainbow Ski Club. Only two others out of a class of 40 received the CSI at a ceremony at Limberlost Lodge.

Irvine "Ace" Bailey, a Bracebridge boy who became an NHL star with the Toronto Maple Leafs, was obligated to leave the game in 1933 due to a near fatal injury. At that time his number, six, was retired, one of only two Maple Leaf numbers that had been retired. Bailey indicated he wanted the number renewed for 19-year-old rising hockey star, Eric Nesterenko.

Among the featured skaters in this year's Ice Review were Barbara Parrett, Anita Lindshow, Dianne Hammond, and Barbara Ward performing in a number called "Hot Canary."

Sirens screamed, horns blew, and victory shouts were prevalent as the Kin Kids hockey team coached by Russell "Chub" Downey won the OMHA Championship by defeating Orangeville. Members of the team were Bill

*Memorial Park in earlier days, with the original bandstand which was first located at the corner of Manitoba and McMurray streets. Fine old brick homes line Kimberley Avenue beyond – Scovell residence on the left, Thomas residence on the right. The spire of the Catholic Church on McMurray St. rises in behind.* COURTESY OF BRENDA COX

Sutcliffe, Guy Waite, Ray McDermott, Vern Hammond, P.J. Marrin, Boyd Ellis, Bert Bell, Hugh Sefton, Mel Cox, Allan Sander, Len Golding, Phil Clairmont, Ken Austin, Merv Clairmont, Bob Irwin, Ted Crozier, and Bob Lloyd.

Hardly had the excitement died down from this hockey success when the Bracebridge Bears brought home the OHA Intermediate B championship, defeating the Durham Huskies 10-3. Coached by Gordon Reid, the team players were Bruce Hook (goal), Merv Robinson, Darce Campbell, "Chub" Downey, Stu Reid (captain), "Dinty" Rowe, Ronnie Rowe, Freddy Nichols, Johnny Thomson, Art Cox, Bob Brown, Verne Vanclief, "Butch" Ecclestone, and "Bus" Brazier. The Bears had played 51 games that season for which total paid attendance at the arena for the home games was 35,635. It was noted that 80-year-old Mrs. John Rowe of Baysville was one of those faithful fans, two of her grandsons being on the team.

A Muskoka Council of Churches was formed at a meeting in Gravenhurst, to replace the South Muskoka Ministerial Association. The officers were Rev. Harry Martin, Bala United; Rev. Alvin Thomson, Bracebridge Anglican; Rev. Wayne Smith, Port Carling Presbyterian; and Rev. Grover Livingstone, Muskoka Hospital Chaplin. The object of the change was to include laymen in the work.

The United Church registered 340 members and the Presbyterian 147 ... Dr. Allen Knight, son of Mr. and Mrs. Fred Knight of Brackenrig, reported on his agricultural development work in Angola, West Africa. Allen had taught for three years at Clear lake in Oakley before going to Guelph to study agriculture ... The churches of town cooperated in a series of passion week services at Easter ... Rev. C.G. Vais, minister at Knox Presbyterian, completed his Doctor of Theology requirements through a Divinity School in Chicago ... Neil Haight, who had been at Gogama teaching, began at St. Augustine's Seminary to prepare for the priesthood ... Terry Best purchased the woodworking shop of the SSJE where church furnishing had been made ever since the war. Gerard Simmons and Tom Kennedy were retained as employees.

Deaths this year included George Penn, 91, married Eleanor Mortimer, moved to town about 1903, ran the Ecclestone and Bates office for many years … Elsie Ewens, RN, killed at a level crossing in the course of her Health Unit duties of visiting the Honey Harbour school … Frances Archer (nee Stewart), 74, widow of Captain C.W. Archer of Browning Island … Margaret (Kirkpatrick) Gibbs, who came to town in 1906 … G.W. "Billy" Wray, 81, came in 1874, was a prominent Orangeman in LOL No. 218 … Marshall Cathcart, 2-year-old son of Mr. and Mrs. Lyle Cathcart, drowned in the river … James G. Campbell, 81, of Muskoka Falls, had worked for the J.D. Shier Lumber Company for 35 years … Lance Corporal Roy Elliott, in Korea, son of Sheriff and Mrs. W.B. Elliott. He had enlisted in 1951 … Lucy Foulkes, 99, the town's oldest citizen at the time … Margaret (Wellerman) Scholey died unexpectedly at the hospital leaving husband Wilfred and three young sons … Thomas J. Hammell, former director of the South Muskoka Agricultural Society … Mrs. George Fish, 80, came to Bracebridge in 1897 … George Jeffries, came to town in 1923, active in community, church and lodge affairs, manager of Northern Planing Mills … William Bull, 87 … Mrs. Robert Watson, 88, daughter of Mr. and Mrs. William L. Fraser, pioneer residents of Fraserburg … Captain Ernest Taylor, brother of Walter, son of Mr. and Mrs. W.H. Taylor, early settlers in Muskoka Township … Mrs. Fred Mills Sr., 90 … Mrs. Allan Keall (nee Alberta Goltz), an active worker in the Women's Institute and fall fair committees … Cecil L. Slater, 43, died while having a cup of coffee. He established a real estate and insurance business here in 1942.

## 1954

Bracebridge was now at the end of its eighth decade as a municipality and no mayor had ever served more than five years successively. With the election of Nelson Goltz over Dr. Ryan for mayor in 1954, that pattern continued. Mr. Goltz became the 23rd gentleman to serve as the town's chief magistrate. Councillors were Robert Jeffries, Dr. R.J. Dodds, Lyle Cathcart, Edgar W. Reid, Austin Hunt, and Doug Wells. J.A. Fry was re-elected as the Power, Light, and Water Commission chairman, and Dr. R.F. Shuttleworth started his second term as Board of Education chairman.

In late November, Rodney White was appointed as constable to replace Reg Rowland who left for Saskatchewan. Monck Township passed a bylaw requiring building permits for new construction as well as renovations. The Power, Light and Water commission decided to install water meters in commercial premises around the town.

The public was invited to view the old 1880 public school to see for themselves the need for a new building. The ratepayers approved of the new school bylaw by a majority of 100.

Canada Packers acquired the former Anglo-Canadian Leather Company buildings with an aim to raise broiler chickens. The site had remained vacant for 23 years.

George W. Ecclestone advertised these items on sale: six-piece bedroom suite at $199, occasional chairs at $49.50, and sectional chesterfield four-piece suites at $139.

Unemployment was up nearly 400 over the previous year due to many reasons, including the closing of the Bird Woollen Mill and several lumber mills; as well, Ontario Hydro had laid off a number of employees. The Bird Woollen Mill was purchased by a group of Bracebridge citizens for $20,000.

Gordon Motor Sales was appointed Chevrolet-Oldsmobile dealer in town. Mr. Fred McCaskie of Peterborough moved to town to operate a specialized automobile service from the White Rose Gasoline Station at the south end. Cathcart's Garage became the dealer for International Harvester Trucks. Hoar Transport Co. of Toronto purchased the Hutchin's Transport Co., managed by Lorne Coulson here and in Gravenhurst.

The James Berofe general merchant business advertised its 41st anniversary of being in retail. Mr. Berofe was born in Russia, a land he decided to leave at an early age.

An 11½-acre property was purchased from Wilfred Scholey of Monck Township upon which Santa's Village would be built. The applicants for the charter were Roy

Garwood, Douglas Wells, Marion Allchin, Clarence Green, and Robert J. Boyer, who was later elected president. The authorized capital was $150,000 and the shares had a par value of $50. It was planned to open the village in 1955. Wilfred A. MacTavish of Toronto accepted the position as the first manager of Santa's Village.

The officers at Santa's Village for 1955 included Roy Garwood as president and Clarence Green as building superintendent. Bracebridge and Santa's Village received a great deal of publicity when Santa's first air-lift of toys was carried out. Over a hundred underprivileged girls and boys were brought to Malton Airport by the T. Eaton Company where Santa met them and distributed toys from his workshop to them. A TCA plane carried Santa and his group from Bracebridge to Malton.

Muskoka Pines, a business near the airport, was purchased by Earle Rosewarne from Frank Berry ... Robby's Snack Bar opened under the new management of June and Aubrey Hill ... William Golden joined the law firm of Best and Lee ... Birchwood Lodge, about two miles past the Bigwin Inn wharf, was sold to Mr. and Mrs. Perch Canivent of Toronto ... The Ross Coffee and Gift Shoppe opened in the building formerly occupied by the Carroll Antique Shop ... The Muskoka Canoe Company (Lakecraft) bought the Century Motors plant that had been operating out of the former Minett-Shields building on Shier Street. James Cridland, the sales manager, advertised a new 15-foot "Lakeshore" cedar boat for $345 ... Ted Rusk was appointed Regent Petroleum Products agent ... Dr. Hugh Smith opened his veterinary clinic at his home on Beaumont Drive ... Hazen Meeks sold his BA service station near Shier's bridge to Bert Cumberland ... Aubrey White of the Uptown Body Shop sold his equipment and stock to Leslie Rosewarne of Bracebridge Garage ... At Penistone's Shoe Store, Bobby Bauer hockey and skating outfits were being sold for $10.95 and up ... Dr. Irma Coyne opened her dental office in the former premises of Dr. Fraser Greig ... Lorne Shier's B.B. Auto and Sports Suppliers advertised the famous Dinky toys, made by Meccano of England, for $0.20 to $2.75.

The former Alexander Hamilton home at Fraserburg burned, but the box factory that operated there during the war was saved. The property was owned by Henry Nelson of Wheatley, Ontario ... Dr. Harold Lambert replaced Dr. G.K. Martin as the medical officer of health ... Dr. Fraser Greig, along with his new assistant, Dr. L.W. Black, moved his office from the Sibbett Block to 14 Kimberley Avenue ... Little Norway at Muskoka Airport was offered for sale by W.H. Doherty of Gravenhurst ... Clarence Sopher of Gravenhurst was contracted to carry mail between Washago and Parry Sound in place of the train baggage car system that had been in use.

Bill Marsh, 19, passed through the outskirts of town on the final leg of an 11,000-mile trek across Canada on horseback. His hometown was Kitchener. He was doing the journey on advice of his doctor to get more fresh air.

Bruce Duncan was one of 119 descendants of Mrs. J. MacLeod of Foot's Bay who helped celebrate her 100th birthday.

Dr. Edmund Bradwin, president of Frontier College, with which he was connected for 50 years, died at the age of 76. Teachers from this college had recently been in Falkenburg working with the CNR line improvement crew.

*Margaret Wyman working on the looms at the Bird Woollen Mill. The machinery was run by a complex system of shafts, belts, and pulleys connected to a water turbine developing several hundred horsepower from the falls.* COURTESY OF BRENDA COX

*The Bird Woollen Mill was established at Bracebridge Falls in 1872, three years before Bracebridge was incorporated as a village, and by the 1950s was the town's oldest operating industrial establishment. But in 1954 it closed after 82 years, a victim of changing technology, outdated equipment, and synthetic fabrics. The extent of the mill complex is evident in this aerial view; the main mill stood to the right of the railway track, while a large storage building (now the Bird Mill Mews) occupies the space between the railway and road bridges.* COURTESY OF THE TOWN OF BRACEBRIDGE

George Matthias and Al Lomas, among others, had their car windshields pitted with unusual white pin marks. Similar happenings had been reported in other sections of Canada and the U.S. during rainstorms but no solution could be established.

The old registry office built in 1868 at a cost of $800 was last used on May 6, when the transfer to the new office was completed. The new Canadian one-dollar bank notes began to appear in town, the new design showing Queen Elizabeth II.

Work on the Bowman Street (Entrance Drive) entrance to town was begun, taking the road beside the Muskoka Foundry building. Work on the new bridge at Severn Bridge was well under way and would eliminate another of the bottlenecks on Highway 11 into cottage country.

A cyclone swept across parts of Macaulay, levelling large trees near the homes of Charlie Ruttan and George Zimmerman.

Les Brown and his Band of Renown were scheduled to appear again at Gerry Dunn's Pavilion in Bala, and also Louis "Satchmo" Armstrong, the great jazz musician, who drew record crowds.

The Maplewood subdivision near Santa's Village was opened.

A summer hockey game sponsored by the Kinsmen Club between the Bracebridge Bears and the Junior All Stars drew a crowd of 1,800 spectators. The Bears won 6-3. One of the special features of this year's Fall Fair School Parade was the large number of bands, including the Citizens' Band, the Legion Pipe Band, the Baysville School Fife and Drum Band, and the Milford Bay School Trumpet Band.

More than 2,000 people took part in the second annual colour cavalcade at Gravenhurst, where Helen Johns was proclaimed Queen of the Leaves and Bruce St. John became Mr. Muskoka. The actual cavalcade route covered 75 miles amid the brilliant fall foliage.

The CBC Board of Governors recommended that Ralph Snelgrove of Barrie be allowed a licence to operate a television station in that town. It was hoped that the Muskoka area would be able to receive the signal clearly.

This was the year of Hurricane Hazel. She hit Toronto and area very hard, taking a high toll in lives. Muskoka got off comparatively lucky with only severe winds which knocked down trees and hydro lines, and substantial rainfall which caused extensive flooding.

Jim Stachan, 26, of Barrie, was hired as coach for the Bears' 1954-55 season. He had last played for Syracuse before an illness caused him to stop playing hockey. The first summer skating school attracted many hundreds of interested spectators and was considered a highly successful venture.

Fairview Lodge, owned by David R. Perrin of Port Sydney, burned down.

The South Muskoka Council of Churches elected Lieutenant Kenneth Evenden of the Bracebridge Salvation Army as its president. The main subject of discussion was the teaching of religion in the schools in rural Muskoka from Southwood to Hekkla. It was reported that everyone concerned was pleased with this effort by the local ministers. Rev. W.J.E. Dow of the Free Methodist Church was appointed the Youth for Christ director for the community. Passion Week services using the theme "The cross and Great Living" were held just prior to Easter. A fund to refurbish the 50-year-old Browning Memorial Hall was begun by the Anglican Church and proved very successful. Bethel Pentecostal Tabernacle held week-long evangelistic meetings with Rev. Clarence R. Aids of Huntsville, which included children's meetings every afternoon with "Jo Jo." Mr. W.C. Denniss Jr. was honoured at the Baptist Church for 40 years of faithful service as he was moving to Victoria, BC. Deacon Everett Doonan made a presentation of a new Bible. The new Salvation Army citadel on Ontario Street was officially opened by Colonel E. Wiseman, field secretary of the Salvation Army in Canada. Ernest Morgan was the contractor for the building. The local officers were Lieutenant Kenneth Evenden and his wife who shortly after this event were moved to serve in Toronto. Lieutenant David Hammond came as the new Salvation Army officer and soon announced his forthcoming marriage to Lieutenant Margaret McFarlane, ARCT. She sang at a benefit concert for hurricane relief. The Choral Society and Legion Band also took part. Lieutenant Hammond and his wife began a weekly radio series over CFOR in Orillia

Rev. and Mrs. W.J.C Daw of the Free Methodist Church were moved to Holt, and replacing them was Rev. George Sanders, a former missionary in Africa.

*Henry James Bird, 1842-1936, founder of the Bird Woollen Mill. He was one of Bracebridge's most prominent early citizens, and as a businessman and community leader helped advance the town in the late 19th and early 20th centuries. His woollen mill had a national reputation for its quality products.* FROM THE "PICTORIAL HISTORY OF WOODCHESTER VILLA"

Father Norman Thornton was elected Superior of the SSJE in October. He had entered the Order in 1934 and was serving the Clear Lake-Purbrook district at the time of his election. The refurbished Browning Memorial Hall was reopened and re-dedicated by Bishop Wright of Algoma (it is now a parking lot).

Willard Draper became the Agricultural Society president. Arthur Waite was elected president of the Men's Club.

History was made in the town's scouting movement when Queen Scout badges were awarded to Doug Hammond, Armand Hough, Don Elliot, and Ted Levecque.

Jerry Dickie, secretary-treasurer of the South Muskoka Agricultural Society, was honoured upon his retirement from the group after 38 years of service.

W.G. Claridge was relieved of his post as industrial commissioner due to financial difficulties within the Chamber of Commerce.

A pipe and drum band was re-formed at the Legion under the direction of Pipe Major William Hempkin. Members of the band were Drum Major Jack MacDonald, Pipe Sergeant Clarence Kirkness, Nicholas Wettlaufer, Elmer Gray, Douglas Kirkness, Frank Ormsby, Bob MacDonald, Milton Ruttan, Bob Jeffries, Carl Ball, Elwood Johnson, Louis Caisse, Art Dickson, Dalton Moon, Keith Snider, Charles Fish, and Harry Rutherford.

Mrs. Kettle received the coveted trillium brooch award from the Ontario Horticultural Association. Mrs. Allan Fraser was appointed division commissioner for the Girl Guides of Muskoka. Murray Lee won the Larry Minns Memorial Trophy when the Kin Kids were entertained at the Kinsmen Club's annual banquet (Larry Minns died of a brain tumour at age 10). The trophy was given for the most sportsmanlike conduct both on and off the ice. Aubrey Hill, Tom Mataija, Russ Gardiner, and Bruce Montgomery were among the new Kinsmen executive for 1954-55. The Lions Club elected Al Smith as president, Don Cale as secretary, Ray Heath as treasurer, Noel Stockton as lion tamer, and Ray Soleski as tail twister. School crossing lights were one of this club's main contributions in 1954.

Twenty-three lodges celebrated the Battle of the Boyne at Gravenhurst. The parade was led by County Marshall John Ruttan. The North Star Band of Bracebridge, Huntsville LOL 393, Three Mile Lake LOBA and Parry Sound JOL were among the prize winners.

The new Noble Grand at the Oddfellows Lodge was J.A. Oates, with Velma White filling the same roll for the Rebekahs. At a banquet at the Albion Hotel, the Muskoka Tourist Association chose George A. Martin as president. The County Orange Lodge elected Stanley G. Hay as county master. The lodge donated money for the hurricane relief and to the Orange Home at Richmond Hill.

The Kinettes made plans to hold a kindergarten in the

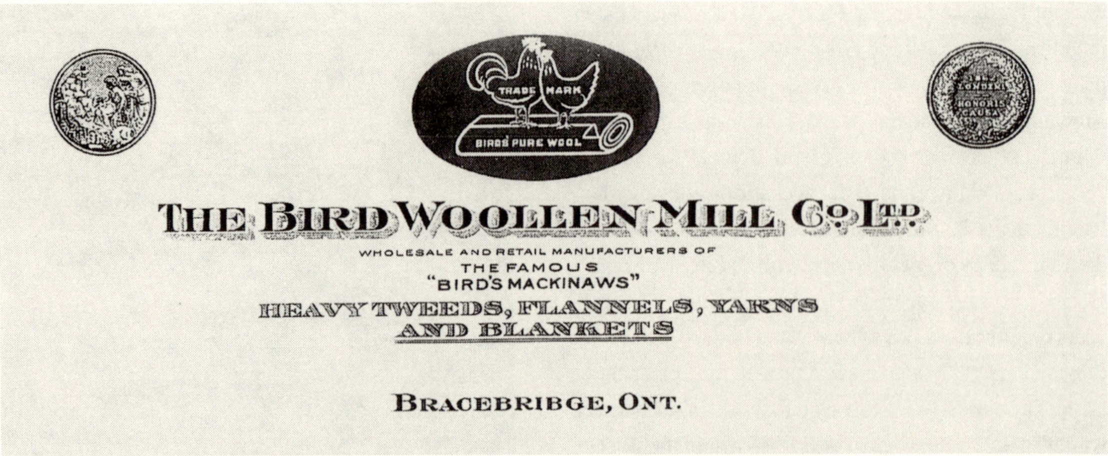

new Salvation Army hall Sunday school rooms and engaged Doris Lidstone as the teacher. LOBA 777 was honoured with a visit by their Grand Lodge officers. It was noted that Agnes Hammond had served as chaplain ever since the lodge opened 27 years previously. Bob Jeffries was installed as Legion president. Several Bracebridge ladies joined a newly organized Crystal Chapter Lodge in Gravenhurst headed up by Nettie Brockbank. The Masonic master was E.W. Reid. Charlie Ruttan was serving his last year as master of LOL 218.

Deaths this year included Edward J. Armstrong, chief of police about 1912 … Martin W. Johnson, son of the late Crown Attorney Thomas Johnson. He lived at "Shadynook" on John Street with his sister Marjorie and brother Gordon … Mrs. Oscar Simmons, who had lived her 52 years of married life in town. Her husband was employed at the Bird Woollen Mill for 60 years … Richard Harper, 91, the town's oldest inhabitant at this time, having come here in 1870 … Major Ada Cameron, daughter of Charles Liddard. She was a highly regarded Salvation Army officer … Philip S. Thomas, Phm.B, 77, last surviving brother of G.H.O. Thomas … Charles Saunders, whose brother Carl had drowned seven years earlier, drowned at Big Wind Lake leaving his wife, the former Hazel Buker, and two small children … A.E. Stephenson, son of the founder of the *Bracebridge Gazette*, died in New Liskeard … Salvatora Lazzara, widow of the late Joseph Lazzara, had lived here since about 1914 … Mrs. Sam McBride, 76, Draper Township …

Father Morley, SSJE, and Father Hanlon, a guest, both drowned in Lake of Bays. Father Morley had been Superior of the SSJE since 1949 and was returning after taking a student minister to his first summer mission … Mrs. Alfred Slater, daughter of pioneer Joseph Caisse Sr. … Ken Morris, former owner of the Albion Hotel, having purchased it from Ed Foreman … Robert Crockford, 63 … John G. Golden, 76, was involved in lumbering business … Earl Hall died in the gravel pit near the Kirk Line when the wall caved in and buried him under tons of gravel … Miss Violet Kirk, sister of businessman Reginald Kirk … Mrs. Alfred Mundy, nee Sarah Phillips, became a teacher at age 15 … Jo Anne Todoroff, 2, died in a fire that destroyed her parent's home on Ontario Street. Mr. and Mrs. Todoroff owned the Towne Grill and had three other children … Mrs. William Holden, 75, came to town about 1881 …Jack Vanclief, Baysville, a resident of Muskoka for 75 years. He was best known for the leather tops for rubber boots and moccasins, and the birch bark canoes, that he made … Many were saddened to learn of the death of Emilie, 20, one of the famous Dionne Quintuplets of Callander. Her sudden demise was due to an epileptic attack.

*During Bracebridge's 9th decade, perhaps the most significant of many elements of progress was the opening in 1963 of the new South Muskoka Memorial Hospital behind the small and out-dated Bracebridge Memorial Hospital on Ann Street. In the above aerial view, the old facility still stands in the lower right, with the nurse's residence between it and the new building. Visible along Aubrey Street at the top of the picture are several of the 1½-storey "war-time" houses built to ease the housing shortage created by returning veterans after World War II.* COURTESY OF THE BRACEBRIDGE PUBLIC LIBRARY

# 1955–1964

## *Our 9th Decade: New Hospital, School, and Town Hall*

THE YEAR 1955 will be remembered for the official opening of Santa's Village, the formation of the Recreational Committee, and the burning of Holiday House, among other things.

Town expenses included: Board of Education $45,000; Library Board $2,257.22; Hospital Board $2,345.34; garbage collection $3,500; arena expenses $ 5,000; police expenses $1,500; dog pound $200; and Recreation Committee $3,200. Frank Henry was appointed new office clerk at the Bracebridge Community Centre in charge of ticket sales and office routine.

An acute power shortage led citizens to vote 348-17 in favour of bylaw 985 to join the Ontario Hydro system. Bracebridge continued to operate its own three hydroelectric plants which under normal river flow conditions still provided most of the town's electrical needs.

One hundred seventy-five people were unemployed in town and William Towns Sr., manager of the unemployment insurance office, expressed concern over the high unemployment rate

Outgoing mail in a 10-day period measured 1,108,300 pieces, most of which went at the letter rate of two cents.

A round-trip bus fare to New York City was $30.00, a Sealy mattress cost $39.95 at Ecclestone's, and it cost seven cents to get a tie cleaned at Waggs. Dot's Tot to Teen Shop was selling anything in the window for a dollar. Cale's Meat Market had prime rib roasts at 65¢ a pound and at the Dominion Store one dozen eggs cost 39¢ and lean minced beef was 29¢ a pound. Muskoka Trading sold their eggs at 43¢ a dozen and Macintosh apples for $2.49 a bushel. Admission to the Bracebridge Bears Intermediate A hockey games cost from 60¢ to $1 for reserved seating, with general admission for 50¢ and children 25¢.

The hockey team "Champs" played the "Hopefuls" on January 19. The Champs roster included Ken Ross (manager), Stu Reid, Vern Vanclief, Johnny Thompson, Dint Rowe, Ronnie Rowe, Freddie Nichols, Merv Robinson, Darce Campbell, Chub Downey, with Bruce Hook as goaltender. The Hopefuls manager was Lyle Cathcart with goaltender Ken Austin.

Hockey school opened at the Community Centre.

The Bracebridge Legion held a "Smoker Party" which was actually a turkey dinner with 137 men present. Moving pictures were shown by Walter Reynolds, Lorne Hockridge, and Harry Anderson.

Bracebridge Memorial Hospital expenses were $97,635 with the nursing and radiology salaries at $41,970.

Scouts Doug Hammond and Arnold Hough were presented with their Grade B Cords by Scoutmaster Peter MacNaughtan. Peggy Crozier was presented with her Gold Cord at the mother-daughter banquet in the United Church hall.

The Salvation Army celebrated 70 years in Bracebridge.

Robert J. Boyer was chosen as Progressive Conservative candidate for the riding of Muskoka for the next provincial election. He won the nomination on the fourth ballot over Mr. Israel Ginsberg of Huntsville, Gordon Prowse of Beaumaris, Edward Wright of Cleveland's House, and Reeve Edwin Bonnell of Macaulay. In the provincial election, Mr. Boyer polled a majority of 550 votes over his nearest rival, Mrs. Wanda Miller, Liberal, who was followed by Mr. Watson.

The OPP had 18-foot patrol boats for the Muskoka Lakes this summer. Officers aboard enforced the criminal code, Liquor Control Act, and assisted the Fish and Game Department.

The investiture of Right Reverend M.J. O'Leary took place in St. Joseph's Church on June 7. Fifty-five priests from Peterborough Diocese and other places were present to witness the impressive ceremony conducted by Most Reverend B.I. Webster, Bishop of Peterborough. The bishop paid high tribute to Monsignor O'Leary for his almost 50 years of outstanding work in the dioceses.

Isabel Crozier was the valedictorian at the high school commencement exercises.

The Bracebridge Chamber of Commerce booth at the Sportsman's Show attracted much attention from people wanting to know more about Santa's Village. Bracebridge was getting many enquiries about hotels, motels, lodges, and cabins.

Rotarians marked their 20th birthday with an anniversary dinner at the United Church auditorium. Wives of the members prepared the food and supplied hilarious entertainment. Mrs. William Huckle led a sing-a-long with Mrs. Wilbert Richards accompanying on the piano.

The Bracebridge Memorial Hospital Board elected P.M.G. Thomas as chairman to succeed M. Park McKay who resigned after eight years. Others elected were Yorke Murphy, treasurer, and Milton C. Bailey, secretary.

The combined school choirs of S.S. No. 1 Macaulay and Baysville Public School was broadcast for 30 minutes on CFOR. Over 1,000 children marched in the mile-long Fall Fair Parade.

Macaulay Township Council held a benefit dance at Lilac Inn for Mr. and Mrs. William Naismith whose home had been destroyed by fire.

Tom Ball sold Lake Drive Dairy to Charles McNabb, Frank McNabb, and Ivan Keall.

Lofty Pines Restaurant, owned by Miss Dollie Brodie and her sister Mrs. Harry Knight, opened its doors to 200 hungry customers who were served delicious turkey dinners.

The Bell Telephone Co. experienced a record year in almost every way in 1955. Eighty-five telephones were added in town to bring the total to 1,395. With more telephones added, and more money spent on construction and employees, it was an overall benefit to Bracebridge. Bell Telephone manager Howard Guest announced that the Muskoka, Victoria and Haliburton Telephone Company was purchased by Bell Telephone, affecting some 50 customers east of Bracebridge, including Muskoka Falls, Uffington, and Vankoughnet.

Over 1,000 Grade One and Grade Two Muskoka children received their injection of Salk vaccine for polio immunization at the Health Unit for the first time.

A Recreational Committee was formed by Council and Mayor Nelson Goltz to coordinate all cultural, historical, physical, and social activities and services.

Salmon weighing seven to 15 pounds were being caught daily in the Muskoka River from the falls down to the mouth.

The Muskoka District Badminton Association held its annual tournament in town this year.

The Red Cross Drive met its target of $1,500.

Bracebridge voters made it very clear that they did not want alcohol being sold under any pretenses. They did not want to vie with Europe and the United States where consumption of liquor was not only easy but exceedingly comfortable. The questions on the ballot were: "Are you in favour of the sale of liquor under a dining lounge licence for consumption with meals on licensed premises?"; "Are you in favour of the sale of liquor under a lounge licence for consumption on licensed premises?" The first was rejected 748-656, and the second 758-651.

Santa's Village was officially opened by Premier Leslie Frost. The opening ceremonies included Gus Ryder and his Lakeshore Swimming Team. Life saving skills were demonstrated, and there was an exhibition of precision swimming by a group of young girls – brave souls, as the water temperature was a chilly 52°F. Marilyn Bell (the first woman to swim the English Channel) arrived after completing her three-mile swim from the forks of the river. And of course jolly old St. Nick was there too, in his traditional garb. When the speeches of welcome, congratulations, and good wishes were over, Marilyn Bell cut the holly-and-evergreen streamer, and Santa's Village was officially open. The village appointed a new manager, John E. Ricketts, who had been a director of the Walt Disney organization in the British Isles for 13 years.

James Bandell celebrated his 100th birthday while visiting his daughter, Mrs. Henry Hunt.

Mr. and Mrs. E.F. Doonan celebrated their Golden Wedding anniversary, as did Mr. and Mrs. Wm. Kirbyson.

Deaths this year included Charles Henry Bailey, 77. Born in Macaulay, he served with the 122nd Battalion during World War I, worked at Shier's mill, and was a crack lacrosse player and coach in 1906. He helped win the provincial championship in 1915-16. The fans were so proud of him they had a song to the tune of "Mr. Dooley."

*O Charlie Bailey, O Charlie Bailey*
*You're the greatest that Bracebridge ever grew.*
*O Charlie Bailey, O Charlie Bailey*
*We licked Toronto Junction five to two.*

Mr. Bailey's sons also went far in sports, Irvine "Ace" Bailey was one of the greatest stars with the Toronto Maple Leafs. Other deaths during the year included John Thomas Andrew, a prominent citizen of Bracebridge, councillor, charter member and past president of Rotary, charter member of the Bracebridge Men's Club, past master and past secretary of Muskoka Lodge AF and AM, and an elder for many years of the United Church ... Douglas Anderson, 14, son of Mr. and Mrs. William Anderson, who drowned in the river while canoeing with his 12-year-old brother Jackie. Jackie was rescued by Mrs. Howard High with her fishing pole ... Wayne Baker, 6-year-old son of Mr. and Mrs. Earl Baker, was attacked and mauled so badly by three wild dogs that he later died. It was believed that he tried to save his puppy from the pack ... Emanuel Nelson, son of Mr. and Mrs. E. Nelson of River Street, drowned in Mill Lake ... Reginald Boyes, 66, skilled boat builder at Minett-Shields ... Charles H. Kaye, 82 ... Mrs. George Tennant, nee Anna Ada Phillips, organist at the Methodist Church, gave piano lessons, died at her father's home, "The Pines"; she married in 1903 ... William O'Brien, 75, ... Mrs. Olive Newman, 86, pioneer of Macaulay ... sudden death of Earl Walker, who had a long hockey career in Bracebridge, married Lena McDonald ... Mrs. Albert Ecclestone, nee Flora Elizabeth Jermyn, died suddenly after a motor trip, leaving her husband and eight children ... Mrs. Gilbert Leeder, 55, nee Azilda Gibson ... Charles Kennedy, 76, came to town about 1880, married Ellen E. Leeder, daughter of Phillip Leeder, a pioneer family ... Mrs. Albert Goltz, 76, nee Henrietta Elizabeth Klingbeil, lived 41 years on Crescent Wood Farm in Monck, then Hill Crest Acres, and moved into town in 1947 ... Mrs. James Thomson, 81 daughter of Mr. and Mrs. David Cairns ... E.L. (Roy) Burgess, 77, Dominion and Ontario

*Nelson Goltz, who succeeded Clarence Green as manager of Santa's Village, drives the Candy Cane Express in 1963. That year Goltz introduced the* Kris Kringle *river boat.* COURTESY OF THE GOLTZ FAMILY COLLECTION

Land Surveyor, took over the business of William Galbraith in 1931. He retired in 1954 and sold the business to Fitzmaurice and Boyer ... Robert Watson, 80, came to town from Purbrook about 1915. He was a lumberman and 25-year member of the IOOF.

Ministers serving in Bracebridge this year included Rev. Alvin J. Thomson, St. Thomas' Anglican; Rev. W.E. Morrow, Baptist; Rev. C.G. Vais, Presbyterian; Rev. W.G. Julian, United; Rev. G.W.L. Sanders, Free Methodist; Rev. M.V. Shields, Bethel Pentecostal; and Lieutenant David Hammond, Salvation Army.

The SSJE held services at Collegiate Church, Bracebridge and Matthiasville, Holy Cross, Barkway, Beatrice, Clear Lake, Uffington, Falkenburg, and Vankoughnet.

A finely carved credence table, presented by Mrs. W.A. Kingsmill in memory of her husband, was dedicated at St. Thomas' Anglican church.

The 22-mile stretch of highway between Bracebridge and Severn Bridge known as "Death Row," where 16 people were killed in motor accidents in 1954, was set up with radar speed traps.

The *Newminko* supply boat, owned for many years by the Hanna Co., was destroyed by fire. The Bracebridge fire brigade attempted to save the boat but was unsuccessful.

Hon. Justice Moorhouse was staying at the Holiday House when fire broke out in the building. He wrote a letter to Mayor Goltz commending the efficiency of the telephone and fire-fighting service. Holiday House, a popular place for guests, banquets, and receptions, was gutted by the fire. The front part of the house, built of stone, had been one of the oldest buildings in Bracebridge. It was built by John Adair and sold to Judge Mahaffy.

During one week in early April our fire brigade fought 14 fires including one at the boathouse of Fred Mills in Beaumaris, 11 grass fires, and two chimney fires.

This year there were 226 births, four stillbirths, and 62 deaths. The town clerk no longer kept a record of marriages. The highest recorded temperature was 92°F in July, and the lowest -29 in December. Total precipitation was 25.66 inches of rain and 103.4 inches of snow.

## 1956

The Bracebridge Fire Company held its first annual meeting. The main concern was replacing firefighters who had moved away. The officers selected were A.J. Milne as chief, Ollie Scott as deputy chief, and Leslie Goodfellow and James MacNaughtan as captains. Don Pickles would drive the GMC truck and Cal Waite the Ford truck. James MacNaughtan was called on to be secretary-treasurer, and Harry Knight caretaker. During the meeting, the siren sounded for a call to Mr. and Mrs. Charles White's home on Toronto Street.

The Recreational Committee, with Walter Reynolds as chairman, had 115 children registered for their supervised playground.

An employee of The Maple Leaf Printing Co. in Toronto was robbed of the payroll she was carrying just as she was entering her place of employment. The thief ran to a parked car and made his escape. It came to the attention of Chief John Harrington that the felon might be staying at a rooming house in Bracebridge. Chief Harrington quickly apprehended the man and had him sent back to the city.

The Board of Education started building a new public school that was later called the Bracebridge Public School rather than Central School. The new Monck Public School was officially opened. Isabel Crozier was the valedictorian at the high school commencement exercises this fall.

Our school students joined together to form a parade that led to the fall fair, thus receiving a half holiday and free fair attendance. The parade was the largest and best in the province.

Max Beaumont was elected the new president of the South Muskoka Agricultural Society in place of Willard Draper.

Following an inept performance by the Bracebridge Bears, coach Mr. Strachan resigned to be replaced by Russell "Chub" Downey. Mr. Strachan stayed on as goaltender. The Bracebridge Bears improved and had Jim Strachan, Danny Poland, and Ronnie Rowe placed on the all-star teams of the Georgian Bay Hockey League.

John James O'Brien was found frozen beside his bed in his Macaulay home seven miles north of Bracebridge. He was found by his neighbours Stanley Titus and Denzil McLeod.

Heather Beers received her gold cord at the Girl Guide mother-and-daughter banquet held at the United Church hall.

Sharon Rosewarne and Bonnie Bailey obtained first place in piano duets under the age of 16 at the Kiwanis Festival of Music in Toronto. They played *The Children's March*.

Beverly Moore from the Bracebridge Figure Skating Club earned a spot in the Ice Escapades Show and left to train in California with the rest of the escapaders.

Santa's Village had a total of 207,468 visitors this year. The publicity received in all points of Canada and the United States was and would continue to be a distinct advantage to the whole area of Muskoka. Clarence H. Green, president of Santa's Village Ltd., agreed to assume the additional duties of manager.

A resolution was passed instructing H.J. Acres and Co. to proceed with their plans to order the equipment needed for the improvement of the Bracebridge Falls generating station.

Boats arrived for new OPP patrols of the lakes.

Work proceeded on Shier Street for the new entrance to town from Highway 11.

*Blithe Spirit* was presented for three nights at Town Hall. Howard Cable and other artists gave the first concert in the Women's Institute Hall at Bala. Araby Lockhart, a favourite of Muskoka theatre goers since her first appearance in *The Drunkard* in the first year of the Straw

Hat Company in 1948, appeared in her own revue show. A dinner meeting concluded the season's course of public speaking instruction.

Rt. Rev. J.L.W. McLean, DD, moderator of the Presbyterian Church in Canada, preached at Knox Church. Muskoka Anglican laymen held a service of witness at St. Thomas' Church. A public Vacation Bible School program was held. Rev. J.M. Patterson came as new minister of the Free Methodist Church. St. Thomas' Anglican Church celebrated the 60th anniversary of the opening of its building. Despite the foggy weather, many people attended. The highlight of the annual vestry meeting was "the burning of the mortgage" on the Browning Memorial Hall. Rector, Rev. A.J. Thomson presided.

Ontario highways minister James N. Allan toured several Muskoka roads with a view to future improvements.

Fitzmaurice and Boyer, surveyors, moved to their new offices formerly occupied by the *Bracebridge Gazette* printing office in the Thomas Block. Mr. Barry Kavanaugh, OLS, joined the firm to replace William J. MacLean who moved to Gananoque.

A horse-racing program was held at Jubilee Park.

The Bracebridge High School junior boy's basketball team won the COSSA finals against Barrie and Central Collegiate of Oshawa. The team consisted of Bill Purdy, Carl Blake, Malcolm Boyes, Larry Mayville, Armand Hough, John Goltz, Don Elliott, Elwood Patterson, Arthur Blake, and Neil Boyes. The coach was B.O. Dickson.

Bracebridge Scouts attended the World Jamboree at Niagara-on-the-Lake. Fred Finlay of Ottawa, the Canadian executive commissioner of the Boy Scout movement, attended the annual Muskoka-Parry Sound Scouter's Conference held at the Holiday House in October. The Rotary Club acquired the old Department of Public Works Building on Main Street (now part of Hiram), installed heating, laid a cement floor, and covered walls and ceiling to make a meeting place for the Scouts and Guides.

The Bracebridge Rotary Club celebrated its 20th anniversary. The gala was held at the Albion Hotel, where they were served filet mignon. Special guests included Bert Horton, district governor-elect. This year Rotary completed a $10,000 payment on the Community Centre. The combined Muskoka Rotary clubs sponsored a party for handicapped children at Santa's Village at Christmas. Over 30 children from all across the district enjoyed this special Christmas present.

The practices of Dr. F.M. Greig, Dr. Lyle Black, and Dr. Ferdinand Williamson merged to form the Greig Clinic in June.

Bracebridge became an Indian Village in appearance for the Colour Cavalcade. Instructions were printed about "How to make a totem pole." The Canadian Kodak Company issued 50,000 folders giving details of the event. The Festival was called "Tagwagi" – Ojibwa for Autumn.

Giovanni (John) Morra retired after 27 years as bandmaster. He had added much to the musical life of Bracebridge both as bandmaster and composer. He was awarded a watch for his outstanding service and long-time dedication. When he came in 1929 the band office was a room at the rear of the post office and the Citizen's Band was floundering. They played in the ancient wooden bandstand that leaned northeast and vibrated alarmingly to the tapping of the bandsmen's feet. He made order out of the cacophonous music and took on all and sundry engagements. They even played on moonlight trips to Bala aboard the *Mildred*. In 1932-33 the depression caused the band to fall on hard times and Mr. Morra was forced to set up his barbershop. In June of 1940, when Italy entered the war on the side of the Germans, Mr. Morra resigned because of his nationality. His resignation was refused and he continued as bandmaster for 18 more years. He was succeeded by Wilfred Manning.

The new student council at Bracebridge High School included president Jeanne Kennedy, vice president Neil Boyes, secretary Gail Langille, and treasurer Patricia Boham.

Stan Knowles, ski instructor of the Bracebridge Ski Club, graduated from ski instructor's school at St. Marguerite, Quebec as a Canadian Ski Instructor.

Midseason had more tourists than ever before with the continuing dry hot weather. The community was saddened by the drowning deaths of Mr. A.T. Clark, his daughter Elizabeth, 7, and Barbara Anne Steels, also 7, in

Lake Muskoka. Percy Beasley drowned at Milford Bay earlier in the season.

Deaths this year included Ray Matthias, 69, lumberman, married Millie Torrance in 1913 ... Mrs. J. Selwyn Rhodes, instrumental in establishing branches of the Red Cross in Milford Bay and Burk's Falls ... Alfred White, 79, farmer and bush worker ... Mrs. Stephen Magee, 84, one of the oldest inhabitants of Muskoka Falls, former postmistress and grocery business owner ... Mrs. Robert Forsyth, 83, the former Sarah Ann James, came to Muskoka with her parents in the 1870s, married in 1898 ... George Edgar Denniss, 82, who had worked with his brother William in a planing factory, married Alice Code in 1924 ... Thomas W. Bruce, 79, started lumbering at age 14, captain of the tug *Southwood*, builder, supervised the building of the power dam at High Falls, married Elizabeth Ann Gibson in 1939 ... Oscar Simmons, 50-year-employee of the Bird Woollen Mill and devoted fireman as member, deputy chief, and chief ... Harold Bailey, killed instantly in a car crash near Beaverton. He had been working for the Miller Paving Company ... Mrs. Daniel Ornsby (nee Anne Ellis of Reay), 78, resident for over 33 years ... Arthur T. Waite, resident of town for upwards of 30 years carrying on a bakery business and store. He served as a councillor, president of local Legion and Men's Club, and was an active member of St. Thomas' Anglican Church ... Cecil Mann, 59, son of the late Mr. and Mrs. Cecil Mann , married Miss Mable McBride in 1930.

The Lions Club took over arrangements for the Santa Claus Parade which included the Legion Pipe Band, the Baysville Fife and Drum Band, the Lone Ranger, Tagwagi, and many floats. It started up on McDonald Street. Part of the Christmas celebrations held at the Brace-

*The Bracebridge Central School originally built in 1881 on McMurray Street was architecturally more interesting than its 1957 replacement, but by the 1950s it was becoming too outdated to efficiently serve the burgeoning post-war generation. The new Bracebridge Public School was built beside it, then it was torn down.* COURTESY OF BRENDA COX

bridge United Church was a pageant entitled Christ for the World. Ninety children in total took part.

New records were set in field crops this year with the Willard Draper farm winning first in the 100 Bushel Oat Club award while George Parrett won first for silage corn. The average of 79.21 bushels an acre for oats was well above the provincial average.

## 1957

This was the year that the fire hall burned down.

The town assessor was William C. Knowles; engineers, Fitzmaurice and Boyer; fire chief, Alex J. Milne; weed inspector and pound keeper, Rod White; building inspector, Harry Rutherford Jr. Council raised the rate of pay for men employed by day to 90 cents an hour, and reduced the cigarette and tobacco licence from $15 to $10. The Town Hall auditorium got new seats for $4.00 each from the company demolishing Shea's Theatre in Toronto. Nelson A. Goltz was in charge of installation.

Water rates increased by 15 percent with a flat charge of $50 for connection. In April, a motion was passed to accept the principle of parking meters. Council purchased a new garbage truck from the City of Waterloo. Mayor Coates and Councillor Parlett made the deal and drove the truck up. The town sold the residence of Mr. and Mrs. Wm. Galbraith on Manitoba Street to Mr. and Mrs. Glen A. Parsons, Toronto, with the proceeds to go toward a cemetery.

Repairs were completed to the Bracebridge Falls generating plant and dam. The wooden crib dam was replaced by the much higher present concrete structure. It was a huge job with concrete being poured day and night The plant had been in continuous operation for over 50 years.

The new Ontario Fire College opened in Gravenhurst.

Fire Company officers for 1957 included Alex J. Milne, chief; Ollie Scott, deputy chief; James MacNaughtan and Les Goodfellow, captains; Don Pickles, driver of the GMC truck; Dint Rowe, driver of the Ford truck; Nels Kennedy, caretaker; James MacNaughtan, secretary-treasurer; and Les Goodfellow, chairman of entertainment. There were 19 men on the roll this year.

On April 1, 1957, the Motor Vehicle Fuel Tax Act came into effect, which charged 20¢ a gallon on fuel oil but not on gas or lamp oil.

The South Muskoka Agricultural Society had a successful year in 1956 with secretary-treasurer Mrs. Norvel Simmons, fair manager Ernest M. Goltz, and president Max Beaumont. They paid out $2,165.20 in prizes. Mrs. Allchin gave the town a $120 cheque as proceeds of the Pioneer Days Parade of Events.

All townships in the District of Muskoka were designated a supervised area for Brucellosis, meaning that all female calves and cows had to be vaccinated.

The Muskoka Cash Crop Association had been operating for two years with the objective to develop a cash crop with a high acre return.

Over 200 attended the Legion stag for Robert Burn's Day with the Legion Pipe Band. Master of ceremonies was Legion secretary Bob Jeffries.

The Red Cross Society raised $1,420 this year with president Mrs. Milton Shier and secretary-treasurer Mrs. Park McKay.

The Hospital Auxiliary reported total receipts $464.16 with 582 articles made, 265 mended. The president was Mrs. Jack Jackson.

The ACAF band under the direction of Lieutenant Clifford Hunt presented an enjoyable concert of light classical and popular music.

Mr. John Wilson McConnell established a $500,000 Foundation in memory of his parents. The interest of $25,000 a year was to be spent for charitable and educational purposes in the District of Muskoka. In May, scholarships and bursaries for Muskoka high schools of $500 each were announced for the student in each school with the highest standing in Grade 13, and up to four bursaries of $250 for each high school for study in Grade 13, at Ryerson, in nursing, business schools, or university. Officers for the trust were president Judge Douglas C. Thomas, vice president R.J. Boyer, and Jack Johnston.

The McConnells moved to Montreal in 1900 from management of St. Lawrence Sugar Refineries Ltd. to publisher of the *Montreal Star*, *Montreal Standard* and the *Family Herald Weekly*. John Wilson McConnell retired in 1954. Born near Bardsville on July 1, 1877, he was the youngest son of John and Margaret Ann (Wilson) McConnell, pioneers in Monck. John Sr. was a Monck Township councillor in 1873 and served three years as reeve.

Dr. William's Trust distributed $4,751.00 to 27 patients in Muskoka with a total paid out $130,217.

The Allensville post office closed after 86 years of service. Allan McNichol had been the first postmaster back in 1871

The Bracebridge High School boy's basketball team won the COSSA Senior B Championship for the first time. The team was comprised of Bob Bullen, Malcolm Boyes, Elwood Patterson, Neil Boyes, Arthur Blake, Dale Kennedy, and John Goltz, captain. George Murray was the coach. They played at Ryerson Institute in March to defeat Belleville, then Port Perry.

The annual commencement exercises at Bracebridge High School were the climax of Education Week. The principal was Mr. C.R. Wright and chairman of the Board of Education Mrs. K. Beers. The valedictorian this year was William McCormack.

Boy Scouts Gordon Atkins, Gordon Smith, Pat Boyer, Doug Slater, Don Caisse, and Barry Miners together with Neil Haight and Douglas Howard had a gruelling canoe trip. They paddled across Lake Muskoka to Bala, down the Moon River to Honey Harbour on Georgian Bay, and returned by truck.

Fred Buckman of the Bell Telephone staff in Bracebridge was transferred to Fort William. He had been in Bracebridge over 10 years, and was active with the School Board, Badminton Club, and Square Dance Club.

Mrs. Donald Morrison celebrated her 90th birthday on May 1. She had taught school at Monck and later Reay, and was a resident of Muskoka Township since her marriage in 1893

Clarence H. Green, president and general manager of Santa's Village Ltd., reported the purchase of a flat-bottomed boat with an inboard engine to offer rides at the village ... Town Council offered a $15 prize for the best design of a crest for the municipality.

George Matthias opened a new store, Matthias Furniture and Appliances, in premises formerly used by Bracebridge Radio and Furniture.

A benefit for Percy Medley raised $2,231 to help rebuild his home.

Girl Guides started to hold their meetings in the new hall on February 1. Miss Mary Hallett was named to the staff of the World Guide Camp to be held at Doe Lake in August to mark the 100th anniversary of birth of Lord Baden-Powell. Mrs. Charles Lazzara completed a three-year term as district commissioner. Heather Beers, a Sea Ranger, was Canada's representative at the International Guide Gathering in Cabana, Mexico.

The rink consisting of Dr. Smith, Bob Hopkins, and Allie Goltz came in second at Central Ontario Sportsmen's Bonspiel in Bracebridge. Mr. and Mrs. Jack Atkinson, Mrs. McFeeters, and Jim Mauro won first prize in the O'Keefe Mixed Bonspiel.

The Bracebridge Bears Hockey Club won the Intermediate B finals over Dundas 4-1. This was the second time

*The Town of Bracebridge logo in the late 1950s incorporated Santa Claus, in recognition of the popular new Santa's Village, and of course Bracebridge Falls which is also the basis of the current logo. The 45 refers to the latitude of Bracebridge (the 45th parallel passes through Muskoka Falls, 3 kilometres south of the old town boundary).* COURTESY OF THE TOWN OF BRACEBRIDGE

*Bracebridge Town Hall, 1881-1957.* COURTESY OF THE TOWN OF BRACEBRIDGE

Bracebridge has secured the provincial championship. We also won in 1953. A banquet was held, sponsored by Town Council and the Board of Education, to acknowledge success in senior boys (COSSA champions) and girls basketball.

Jubilee Park was plowed, levelled, and re-seeded, and the track made wider.

Wrestling returned to Bracebridge after a lapse of several years. In the Memorial Community Centre on August 9, Hard Boiled Haggerty, 255 pounds, met Ronnie Atchinson in the main event. Other bouts were between Baron Gattoni and Jack Lansky, and Johnny Barend and Art Neilson.

Dr. L.N. Ryan caught an 18-pound lake trout at the mouth of the river and Bus Brazier caught two 14-pound and one 10-pound trout. Smelt regulations were amended to allow use of a dip net up to six feet by six feet, up from three by three. People could obtain a Residents Licence to take Smelt for Personal Use for $1 and use a 6 by 30-foot seine net.

The minimum salary for elementary school teachers was set at $2,400 with a maximum of $3,800 for staff and $5,000 for a principal. The school tax levy was $49,340.82, up $ 3,840 from the previous year. Teachers engaged included Kenneth Black, H.R. Kerstake, Miss Diane S. Johnston, Austin R. Repath, and Miss Ann Neilson. Mr. George Young from Dundalk was hired to replace Mr. Cecil R. Wright as high school principal. Bracebridge High School registration was 414 this fall. The school won both the boys' and the girls' badminton tournaments in Parry Sound. Over 200 gathered to see the results of the Bracebridge-Rural Community Night School classes.

Douglas Wells was elected as new chairman for Memorial Community Centre. The resignation of Lorne Shier left room for Dick Hammond.

A 30-foot totem pole carved by Hydro workers and presented to the Chamber of Commerce was erected. The Chamber purchased three small totem poles as prizes for the best decorated store windows for the Cavalcade of Colour.

In 1948 the Children's Aid Society received $1,000 from Ontario Department of Public Welfare. In 1956 they got $5,033. Total payments to the municipality of Bracebridge were $13,165.

The annual Muskoka Farmer's Meeting and Seed Fair was sponsored by Muskoka Crop Improvements Association under president Harvey Gray. George Parrett won best display of oats. Roy Goltz of Falkenburg won 13 prizes including seven firsts.

Dr. Gordon Martin, our first district medical officer of health, left to work for the Department of Health and helped to produce the Salk vaccine against polio.

Wonder Construction Company built the new 128 by 146-foot, one-storey OPP station. The main building was of steel and concrete with a brick exterior backed by clay tile. It had a 20-year bonded roof and an oil-fired hot water boiler. It sat on six acres of land on the Highway 11 bypass. The police moved in on June 12.

Constable Tom Watt was a new addition to the Bracebridge OPP Detachment as Constable Larry Readman left for special duties on Lake Simcoe.

Tamarack Lodge, run by Dr. Fraser M. Greig and his sister Jean, was taken over by Mr. Rene Schubert and his wife Henny who used to manage the Old Mill Restaurant in Toronto. Mr. and Mrs. Norman Lyndon purchased the property on Ontario Street near Kimberley formerly owned by Miss Annie O'Hare and built a new house. The

Fountain Drive-In Theatre opened. The Ferrier Radio Shop moved from the corner of Manitoba and Ontario to larger quarters which had been the barbershop of the late Lloyd Peterkin.

The Toronto-Muskoka Air Service started June 20 with two flights each way. The flights took 90 minutes in a Beechcraft, a Lodestar, or a DC-3.

In 1956 library circulation was 20,540 with a total of 8,694 books. Miss Genevieve Johnston was named secretary as Mr. Jerry Dickie passed away.

A free chest x-ray unit was set up in Memorial Park sponsored by the Lions Club. Over 800 attended the Lions Club Bingo on August 3, which was called by Russ Salmon and Bus Brazier.

Forty-four children from Muskoka, North Bay, and Powassan were at the Rotary-sponsored crippled children's clinic held in the Bracebridge Memorial Hospital in May. Doctors from sick children's hospital and Bracebridge examined the children.

The Bracebridge Art Group elected Mrs. Gordon Prowse as president.

Harvey S. Bell retired as clerk of Division Court due to ill health and was succeeded by W.K. Hare.

There was a record number of visitors on the Civic Holiday weekend – so many, in fact, that Mrs. Tomlinson, in charge of Muskoka Tourist Association Information, reported that many people slept in their cars.

The Philathea Club of Knox Church held spring tea in

*In December 1957 a spectacular blaze destroyed the Bracebridge Town Hall, although a section at the back including the tower was salvageable, and incorporated into the replacement building.* COURTESY OF THE TOWN OF BRACEBRIDGE

the newly renovated Sunday School room. The Archbishop of Algoma, the Most Rev. W.L. Wright at St. Thomas' Anglican, confirmed 35. The United Church choir presented *The Holy City* under the direction of Mrs. Wilbur Anderson. The Baptist Ladies had their opening night of the Thursday Night Club at the home of Mrs. James MacNaughtan. President was Miss May Tibbett, vice president Miss A. MacGregor, secretary Mrs. Ellen Pickles, and treasurer Miss Genevieve Johnson. Rev. K. Guergis baptized nine children on Mother's Day at Knox Presbyterian Church.

A new electronic telephone device was now available that could answer your phone and take a message.

The Town Hall, housing the fire station, was completely destroyed by fire in a huge December blaze. Plans were made to build a new one as soon as possible. Nelson Goltz and his men were hired to clean up the debris.

Gas pipe lines were laid throughout Bracebridge and connected with the main line from Alberta. A public ceremony was held at Memorial Park to mark the start of work with Stuart Cameron, manager for Northern Ontario Natural Gas, as speaker.

Deaths this year included Jerry Dickie, a very active member of the South Muskoka Agricultural Society, the Library Board, and church. He served as deputy returning officer for many years. Nearly 70 years a resident of Bracebridge, he was born in Baysville ... Herman L. Goltz, 89, came to Monck Township with his parents in 1869, married Barbara Mitchell in 1893, and raised five sons and six daughters. He was a successful farmer whose products won many prizes in Toronto, Chicago, and England. He was a judge for the Department of Agriculture at fairs and field crops. He moved into town after his wife's death in 1927 ... Mr. Fred Hanna of Port Carling, member of one of oldest pioneering families, son of Mr. and Mrs. William Hanna who settled in Muskoka Falls then moved to Port Carling in 1888 to start a general store ... Mrs. George Kirkpatrick, 74, resident of Draper, the former Margaret Ketching, daughter of Mr. and Mrs. William Ketching. She was Uffington correspondent for many years ... Mrs. Charlotte LeQuyer, 94, came to Muskoka with her parents, John and Sharon Crockford, in about 1878, settled in and named Purbrook. John Crockford was the first postmaster there ... David J. Rankin, son of Mr. and Mrs. Alexander Rankin, pioneers in Macaulay, married Miss Mary Irene Dauphin ... Mrs. Herbert (Ida Jane) Slater, 84, born in Draper, married Herbert Woodly Slater in 1892. Her daughter was Mrs. Peter MacNaughtan ... Mrs. Thomas Lloyd, 71, eldest child of Mr. and Mrs. Patrick Sullivan. She spent her entire life in Bracebridge, married in 1913, had three children ... Miss Gertrude Sibbett ... Mrs. John Teasdale, came to town in 1941, active in the Salvation Army ... Mrs. Elizabeth L. White, 86, resident for 38 years, married Robert James White in 1890, moved to town in 1919, establishing a grocery business on Dill Street. Mr. White died in 1942; they had seven children ... Mrs. William (Mary Edith) Wray, 71, eldest daughter of Lieutenant Colonel and Mrs. Hennall. She came to Canada as a housekeeper at the Beaumaris Hotel. She was a partner with Mr. Wray in a plumbing business in town, married about 1927 ... Mrs. Thomas Dowler, in her 90s; her husband was on the public school staff 70 years earlier.

## 1958

Since the Town Hall was lost by fire in 1957, one of this year's major undertakings was the replacement of that facility. It was decided to rebuild on the former site and to include an auditorium. Exactly one year to the day after the destruction of the old Town Hall, a new, larger, and more conveniently arranged building was officially opened by the Minister of Municipal Affairs, the Hon. Mr. Warrender.

Mayor Glen Coates acknowledged many gifts from such organizations as the Business and Professional Women's Club, the Rotarians, the Lions, and the Orange Lodge. Tribute was paid to the late Mr. and Mrs. William Galbraith who left their residence as a bequest to the town. The proceeds from the sale of the property had been applied to the municipal auditorium.

Succeeding Clarence Watson of Watt as president of District Council was Jack Johnston. The council appointed a district assessor to help equalize the disparities regarding property values and taxation. The long-discussed idea of a District Home for the Aged became more hopeful. In the fall, a Board of Management was

*The falls during the spring freshet of 1957. This view was substantially altered later in the year with the construction of the present, much higher concrete dam lower down the falls, replacing the old wooden dam under the Silver Bridge. Bracebridge Falls drops a total of 16 metres (53 feet), the lower 10.7 metres (35 feet) of that being utilized by the generating station.* COURTESY OF IAN TURNBULL

appointed by the Lieutenant-Governor following a submission to the Minister of Public Welfare. Members of the board were Mayor Glen Coates of Bracebridge, councillor Herb Swift of Gravenhurst and Randolph Jupp of Huntsville, reeve Jack Johnston of Monck, and reeve Gordon Thompson of Franklin.

A new red station wagon was purchased for the use of fire chief A.J. Milne. It was equipped with a two-way radio and fire-fighting equipment. The burning of the home of Mr. and Mrs. Alex Irvine on the Taylor Line precipitated a plan whereby the Bracebridge Fire Department would cover some outlying areas.

There was a building boom in town in 1958 when a record of nearly $555,000 in building permits was issued by building inspector Harry Rutherford. Included were the post office, municipal building, a service station, and 11 dwellings besides many enlarged and renovated properties. Future prospects looked good with a high school addition, a new two-storey Bell Telephone building, and a new Dominion Store being announced.

In the second general federal election within a year, the results were overwhelmingly in favour of the Progressive Conservative government of John Diefenbaker. Gordon Aiken, MP, of Parry Sound-Muskoka was returned with a majority of more than 8,000 votes over Earl McDonald, Liberal, from Foot's Bay, and Hugh Bishop, CCF, from Gravenhurst. Both lost their $200 deposits as they received less than half of the total votes. Close to 75 percent of the voters turned out.

Ernest Jackson of Beaumaris was installed as Master of the Muskoka Lodge No. 360 during ceremonies conducted by Stan Einarson … Edith Hampson became Worthy Matron of the Order of the Eastern Star … Hannah Irvine became Worthy Mistress of LOBA No. 777 … Tom Hammond became Master of LOL No. 210 … Elmer Longhurst became president of the South Muskoka Agricultural Society … President Art Ferguson of the Children's Aid welcomed new director Mr. Dorington … Edward J. Ball became Rotary president … Mrs. Elymer McDermott was elected Women's Institute president. The WI offered beds, wheel chairs, walkers, and other aids free of charge for home use … Mary Herbert was the new Kinette Club president, and Jack Rowan president of the Kinsmen Club … Jack Burgess, manager of the Toronto-Dominion Bank, was elected president of the Chamber of Commerce.

Dr. William Craymer joined the Greig Clinic as did Dr. William Monk, general surgeon … The Gourmet Club held its 10th anniversary at the home of Mr. and Mrs. James Rankin … Ralph C. Mills, QC, became president of the Muskoka Lakes Association … Over 100 took part in the Orangemen's church parade led by the Welland County Fife and Drum Band … Bob Jeffries was elected president of the Legion. The Legion presented the hospital with two television sets, one each for the men's and women's wards … The Lions Club sponsored a performance of the North American Thrill Drivers in Jubilee Park … George Farrar of Guelph was appointed to act as director of both the Bracebridge Citizen's Band and the Gravenhurst Civic Band … Harry Lidstone, Ontario Hydro line foreman, received a $1,500 award for inventing tools for safe "hot-line" work … J. Willard Austin of Beatrice received an award for 15 years of service with the McColl-Frontenac Oil Company (Texaco). Besides his business interests with the garage and general store, Mr. Austin was an ardent supporter of the Beatrice hockey team and the IOOF lodge in town.

The Muskoka Health Unit extended its jurisdiction to the Town of Parry Sound. It was already working in the townships of Humphrey and Foley and the Village of Rosseau

An organizing meeting held for the Bracebridge Group of the Canadian Power Squadron saw the following officers elected: Commander D.A. Smith, Lieutenant Commander Harry Lidstone, First Lieutenant J.W. Lidstone, secretary L.M. Coutts, and treasurer W.H. Elliott. Charter night was June 20, 1958.

The Clef Club celebrated its 50th anniversary with a

*The Canadian Motor Lamp plant (now Meritor) commenced production on September 15, 1958. It was the first of several modern factories built near Bracebridge since World War II, differing from older industries not only in appearance but also in that they did not use local raw materials.* COURTESY OF THE TOWN OF BRACEBRIDGE

*This early 1890s view of Bracebridge Falls depicts one of the town's oldest industries, a 3½-storey water-powered grist mill. Built in 1864-65, it operated until it burned in 1909. As one of the few grist mills in Muskoka in the 1860s it was an important facility for local farmers and helped consolidate Bracebridge's position as a leading centre in the district.*
COURTESY OF THE TOWN OF BRACEBRIDGE

banquet at Holiday House. Charter member Eva (Bastedo) Reid and many former members turned out to help celebrate.

Judge D.C. Thomas, president of the McConnell Foundation, reported a successful first year of assisting district residents. Mrs. L.W. Anderson succeeded Catherine Bird as president.

Nine Scouts received their Queen Scout badges from district commissioner Norman Rosewarne. They were David MacNaughtan, Gordon Atkinson, John Blaney, George Reid, King Moore, Bill Beers, Roy Shier, Ted Dickie, and Barry Miners.

Mrs. R.J. (Patsy) Boyer, newly appointed Girl Guide commissioner for Bracebridge, presented lieutenant warrants to Caroline Kingsmill and Heather Beers. Margaret Askin and Catherine Todoroff each received the All-Round Cord, a new award to recognize Guides who had earned badges in a wide field of activities.

The Lions Club Air Cadets held their first parade. They began their basic training under Percy Good, a former member of the Royal Canadian Regiment.

A new Police Boy's Club was established in October and met in the Women's Institute building in Jubilee Park. The officers chosen were president Noel Stockton, vice president Murray Dauphin, treasurer Wilf Shier, and Doug Duff of the OPP. Directors were chief of police John Harrington, Sergeant Colan Cowan, Constable Joe Stevenson, and OPP officer Tony Jackson.

At the opening of the Court of Sessions, Judge Thomas received a chair from the Ontario Legislature Assembly previously used by the Muskoka members. The presentation was made by Robert J. Boyer, MPP, assisted by J. Frank Kelly of Huntsville, former MPP.

The new OPP building on Highway 11 was officially opened.

Construction began in May for the new post office building to be shared by the post office, customs, and employment services departments. The Department of Lands and Forests built a deputy chief ranger headquarters for the District of Muskoka at High Falls. The Rotary Club made an addition to the Boy Scout Hall on Main Street (now Hiram St.).

The gas pipeline construction from South River to Bracebridge brought 300 workers into town. Mayor Coates cut the ribbon at the official opening. The Ontario Fire College at Gravenhurst opened on August 22. Old "Rescue No. 1," our first fire truck, was given to the Fire Museum at the College. The Fountain Drive-In Theatre just west of town on Highway 118 was built. The J.D. Shier Lumber and Supply Ltd. built new offices and a showroom on Highway 532 (Ecclestone Drive) near the forks. Elizabeth Brodie had her Lofty Pines Restaurant converted into a convalescent home by Abe Dawson. Mrs. B.Y. McBride, issuer of motor vehicle licences since 1943, was succeeded by Russell Salmon. Danny Poland's Supertest Service Station was replaced by a new structure. His old building on the southwest corner of Willis and Manitoba was the former home of Charles Yeo. The plumbing and heating business of the late Jack Brooks was continued by his brothers Tom and Ian. Fred Moulton started an electrical contracting business. Ken Crockford opened a service station on Shier Street. In the former Jacklin grocery store, Robert Redfern of Toronto opened a recreation centre for arts, crafts, boxing, wrestling, and judo. The Toronto-Dominion bank installed night deposit equipment. The Canadian Motor Lamp Plant commenced production on September 12 with Ted Gervais superintendent of an initial staff of 15. Philip Kelly from Baysville started Muskoka Lakes Craft boat building company in the former Minett-Shields site on Bracebridge Bay. Joe Kolson took over the former Thompson's Barber Shop next to Cale's Meat Market.

Some 1,500 dozen eggs were destroyed in a fire at Ken Keith's Poultry Farm. Cale's Meat Market advertised hamburg steak for 35¢ a pound and loin chops at 65¢ a pound. Medley Motors advertised a 1958 Ford Fairlane with automatic transmission, radio, white walls, and many extras for $2,849.

Dale Hammond was voted Miss Bracebridge for the Cavalcade of Colour. Both the cavalcade and the Tagwagi Pow-wow were well attended. The fall fair was an even greater success than usual. One popular event was the "freckle contest" won by Nancy Findlaker, Jane Taplin, Rodney McFarlane, and Doug Saunders.

This year the first Auto and Home Show was held, which attracted thousands of people. Ray Soleski was master of ceremonies at the opening. Radio station CKAR ran a 48 hour marathon that raised over $7,500 for the Springhill, Nova Scotia, Relief Fund.

A week of prayer was held in January with Baptist, Free Methodist, Pentecostal, United, Presbyterian, Anglican, and Salvation Army churches participating. Rev. Gordon Black was inducted as rector of St. Thomas' Anglican Church. I. Yorke Murphy was elected recording secretary at the United Church to replace George W. Boyer who resigned after more than 50 years. Rev. Joseph Patterson left for Verona to be succeeded by Rev. F.N. Perry who had been here in 1937. Rev. John Hickey came as an assistant to Monsignor O'Leary at St. Joseph's Church. Rev. David Mitchell was transferred to St. Thomas' Anglican Church. Lieutenant William Kerr was transferred from Prescott to Bracebridge to lead the Salvation Army.

On January 21 the first annual 88-rink Muskoka International Mixed Bonspiel was officially opened and after five days of curling was deemed a significant success.

The golf course at Macaulay Centre opened on June 14. Officers of the new golf and country club were Ed Thatcher, Jack Burgess, Marion Black, Ed Leeder, John Stoughton, and George Freeland. This project was completed on the former Richards' farm known as The Elms.

Dr. H.J. Irwin was elected president of the Cricket Club. Harry Scott headed up the minor hockey executive along with W.A. Shier Sr. and Harry Davis.

The education grant structure was changed to meet the soaring school costs. School attendance now determined the grant rather than municipal population. Our board was eligible for just over $97,000. Mrs. Kay Beers was re-elected school board chairman. Neil Haight was named principal for Bracebridge Public School to replace B.R. Minns who passed away after 37 years there.

Deaths this year included Sam Bowyer, 71, son of the late Mr. and Mrs. Henry Bowyer, a member of the Lacrosse Club that had won the Junior Canadian Lacrosse Championship ... Hildred Joselin, 56, came in 1904, married Clayton Joselin who died in 1956. She was well known manager of the For-Get-Me-Not Shop at Santa's Village ... Sergeant Mafor Ward, 85, had served in the Boer War and in both World Wars, lived in Macaulay ... John Shea, 82, of Ufford, who served his township as clerk, assessor, and collector for 35 years ending in 1950 without ever missing a meeting ... Edward Fenn, last of the pioneer family that came early to Muskoka ... Warren Hoover, building contractor, died by his own hand ... Jack Brooks, a popular citizen and businessman was killed in an accident at his cottage ... Thomas N. Bird, son of pioneer Henry J. Bird ... Walter J. Lang, 67, died at his service station just outside of town on the Baysville Road ... Ernest A Whitten, 71, former mayor and businessman, active in community affairs and sports ... Rachel (Nicholson) Ryan, whose late husband started a photography business here in the late 1800s ... Bruce R. Minns, came to town about 1921, judge of the Muskoka Juvenile and Family Court and principal of Bracebridge Public School for 37 years ... Olive Hannah (Hooton) Inch, whose husband Bill was an operator at the Wilson's Falls power plant ... Emma (Huyunga) Fryer, librarian for 15 years ... Edward S. Hunt, 83, contractor, school board member for 45 years ... Henry Newark, 47, contractor ... Cora (Morton) Mahaffy, whose second marriage was to Judge A.A. Mahaffy. Her sister was Mrs. G.H.O. Thomas ... Robert S. Dollar, 88, born in Bracebridge ... Harold Hammond, 56, married Marjorie Peacock in 1927. He had been in the taxi business since 1944 ... William Misner, 67, a baker who assisted his daughter at Muriel's Bakery ... Milton Shier, 72, son of lumberman James D. Shier ... Herb Dyer, 70, former employee of the Watson Brick Yard and Bracebridge Water, Light and Power Commission ... Dr. Eva Fisher, 96, one of the first women medical doctors in Ontario, having graduated in 1893 ... Ethel Dodds, 77, an invalid, who came to town with her husband Dr. R.J. Dodds in 1942.

## 1959

Edgar W. (Ted) Reid of Northern Planing Mills was the 25th mayor of Bracebridge. All five of the surrounding reeves remained in office. Monck and Muskoka townships were entering their 90th years of incorporation. Draper and Oakley were at the 70-year milestone, and Macaulay at 87.

Fire chief Alex Milne, chief about 12 years, stepped down to be succeeded by Ollie Scott. Mr. Milne continued as District Coordinator of the five brigades. Others chosen as officers were Elton (Dint) Rowe, deputy; Harold Dawson and Bill Wyman, captains; Don Pickles and Nels Kennedy, truck drivers; Jerry Fox, secretary-treasurer, and Court Hay, social convener. Jim MacNaughtan, George Brooks, and Les Goodfellow were on standby.

Late in 1958, Council had accepted a preliminary report as to a proposed sanitary system. A total of 8.3 miles of sewer pipe, three lift stations, and a sewage treatment plant were agreed upon with the Ontario Water Resources Commission. The cost would be met by a user charges as well as four mills on the general tax rate.

On July 4, the Queen and Prince Philip arrived at Washago and motored to Gravenhurst where they enjoyed a concert at Gull Lake Park. The Royal Couple were in Canada to officially open the St. Lawrence Seaway.

It was announced on July 22 that the property known as "The Pines" would become the site for the new Muskoka Home for the Aged. The Province was expected to pay one-half the construction costs and three-quarters of the maintenance.

The fine residence at the corner of Woodward Avenue and Maple Street was purchased by Judge and Mrs. D.C. Thomas. Built originally by Henry Warren, it was owned by Henry B. Orde ... Phillip Laforce, the *Herald Gazette*'s Gibson Reserve correspondent, received an award for his outstanding column from the Ontario Weekly Newspapers Association ... The Muskoka Steamships Ltd., owned by M.C. Penhorwood, was sold to Jack Vincent and George Morrison of Gravenhurst, who planned to sell the *Segwun* and *Cherokee* and use the *Sagamo* as a floating marina. Steamship service on the Muskoka Lakes had ended in 1958 ... Alex (Sandy) Milne was appointed postmaster, succeeding William Huckle who retired after 21 years of service ... the Ontario Department of Transport issued the first *Driver's Handbook* ... the Driver Point Demerit System went into effect in April ... the first tile drainage demonstration day was held on the Muskoka Township farm of Walter Taylor ... Max

*Snapshots of the Bracebridge downtown business area from various eras are common. By the 1950s the old Queen's Hotel had been considerably renovated, becoming the Patterson Hotel (now the Al Beverly Decorating Centre) with no balconies and a much plainer facade.* COURTESY OF THE BRACEBRIDGE PUBLIC LIBRARY

Ginsberg, Gravenhurst, was named technician for the hospital's new pathology laboratory, working under Dr. Wright who was in charge of diagnostic services ... The fine old residence of Mrs. D'Alton Armstrong across from the Town Hall was destroyed by fire in early May. Originally the 90-year-old building was the office of the *Northern Advocate*, the first newspaper in the northern districts of Ontario, published from 1869 to 1875 ... Mr. Douglas A. Sieber was appointed to open a branch office of the Russell O. Reynolds C.P.A. Co. ... The bodies of two Huntsville taxi drivers, Francis Grosso, 29, and Bruce Spiers, 22, were found in the Dwight area, victims of robbery ... Dale Hammond, Miss Bracebridge 1958, crowned her successor Karen Love in the Cavalcade Queen Contest ... The Horseless Carriage Club toured through Muskoka ... Dr. H.L. Sargeant became director of a new Muskoka District Band.

The new federal building was opened September 29 by Gordon Aiken, MP. In 1864 the post office was first carried on in the Perry and Myers store. Later it moved to the original Orange Hall, then moved across the street to the site later occupied by Maureen's Ladies' Wear (Pelican Bay). After that building burned, mail was distributed from the Town Hall but returned to the former site when the new building was erected. In 1915 the Dominion Building at the corner of Manitoba and Thomas Streets was completed and was then used as a post office for the next 44 years ... About 4,000 chickens and 3,000 turkeys were destroyed in a fire in the former Anglo-Canadian tannery building. It was a serious loss for the Goodwin and West Co., according to plant manager John T. Daleman ... The public library was selected by the National Film Board as a site to store over 500 films and equipment ... The old post office was sold to John R. Burton of Burton Cliff Cabins on Lake Rosseau ... During the pre-Christmas period135,000 Christmas cards passed through the post office with over 2,000 bags of mail dispatched or received on trains.

James Armstrong of Huntsville was Muskoka-Parry Sound returning officer for the June 11 provincial election. The candidates were Robert J. Boyer, Progressive Conservative, member since 1955; Mrs. Wanda Miller, Liberal, and Charles E. Spencer for the CCF. There were 14,683 eligible voters, 72 percent of whom exercised their right to vote. Robert J. Boyer was re-elected taking 80 of the 98 polls in the district. The Hon. Leslie M. Frost thus began his 11th year as head of the Government of Ontario.

The LOL 218 chose Tom Hammond as its Master and LOBA 777 chose Hannah Irving as their Matron ... Henry Kirbyson was installed as Master of Muskoka Lodge No. 360, the ceremony being the first one performed in the new lodge room. Harry L. Martyn, Grand Master, dedicated the new Masonic Temple. The original lodge rooms, located in a building where St. Thomas' Church is now, rented for $31 a year ... Mrs. J. H. Learoyd was chosen president of the Muskoka Chapter of the Registered Nurses' Association ... Ted Boyer and Mrs. Roy Gillman headed up the IOOF and Rebekahs ... Alcoholics Anonymous began to hold regular meetings in the United Church hall ... Bracebridge Kinsmen sponsored the formation of a new club in Bracebridge with Doug Passmore as president ... Yorke Murphy was elected Rotary president ... The Dominion Store chain purchased the Orange Hall just north of the Dairy Bar, and the Orangemen built a new hall on Maple Street ... A new building was erected on the fair grounds ... In June the Muskoka Prospectors Club was formed with Al Bonnell as president. The club was formed under the Department of Mines and was one of only seven in the province ... The Bracebridge Lions Air Cadets had their first annual inspection ... Geoff Waite became Lions president ... Rev. George Menzies conducted the service of dedication of the Cenotaph under the auspices of District E of the Royal Canadian Legion.

Home Brick Ltd. under plant manager W.F. Hoggan winterized their plant and hoped to double their productivity of tile. John Watson had originally established the property, located just east of Highway 11 in Draper. Later, he was joined by Peter Hutchison. Albert Wyman operated the plant from 1908 until his death in 1934, then his sons Ted, Bill, and Albert operated it until the war. In 1943 and 1944 Ed Arnott operated the business, then it was sold to Stephen and Hughes who sold it back to the Wymans in 1947. In 1956 the Home Brick Company was organized ... Muskoka Lake Craft, Bracebridge, and Greavette Boats of Gravenhurst were well represented at the first Canadian Boat Show held in Toronto ... Harold Whyte was appointed area Ontario Rural Hydro manager ... The Margaret-Ellen Shop of Mrs. Sleeth was purchased by Mr. and Mrs. Thomas B. Johnson who renamed it Maureen's ... Shier's new Building Supply Centre was opened. The company had been reorganized in 1937. Aubrey Shier, president, and Roy Shier, vice president, were sons of the original owner, J.D. Shier ... Hammond's Transportation announced that all areas within one mile of the town limits would fall into the 50¢ taxi fare zone ... Adult haircuts cost $1.00, brush cuts $1.25, and children's haircuts 65¢ ... Miss Helen Reid opened the Band Box Beauty Salon next to the A & P ... Bell Telephone closed their offices at Bala, Port Carling, and Milford Bay and appointed collection agencies.

Education costs in Bracebridge were set at $215,635 of which $140,338 would be received in government grants. Fred Hammell, a native of Watt, replaced Gordon McIntyre, inspector of schools since 1951.

Rev. Stan Gibson replaced Rev. C.E. Fletcher as pastor at the Bethel Pentecostal Tabernacle ... Captain Bailey and Lieutenant Olstod were our new Salvation Army officers ... Rev. F.N. Perry retired from active ministry in the Free Methodist Church to be succeeded by Rev. W.R. Lohnes from Campbellford.

Sir Leslie Munro, New Zealand Ambassador to the U.S., opened the second annual Muskoka International Mixed Curling Bonspiel. Ed Thatcher, was chairman ... the Bracebridge Bears won the District Championship and went on to win the OHA Intermediate C Championship ... BHS captured all the main events at the COSSA Badminton Tournament. The team consisted of Patricia Ryan, Heather Beers, Arlene Weir, Reta Clarke, Doug Moon, Jim and Dan McKenzie, and Steve Black ... Bracebridge won the trophy over 151 entries in the first

District Badminton Tournament. Miss Diane Johnson was a triple winner … The resurrected Muskoka Cricket Club held a dinner with special guest Mr. George Boyer who played for Bracebridge at the turn of the century.

Deaths this year included Clive Brown, 65, a boat builder and repairer prominent in the First Baptist Church … Herman J. Brooks, 61, a popular businessman since 1945 when he established his electrical and appliance business … Captain Levi Fraser, 85, who began his steamboating career in 1893 and ran many well-known boats including the *Bigwin* on Lake of Bays … Margaret (Pooler) Fowler … John G. MacKinnon, 75, town councillor in 1955-56 … Mrs. G.H.O. Thomas, nee Evelyn Morton, who took a prominent and helpful part in church, society, and welfare activities in town … Mary (Desjardins) Dauphin, 90, who first came to Bracebridge with her husband in 1907 … John Sibbett (Tim) Elliott, 48, became an engineer in 1936, served overseas and was made a Member of the British Empire for his efforts building an airfield in Caen, France … Mrs. Arthur Green (nee Dickie), 80, moved to town from McLean in 1889 … Daniel Ornsby, 69 … May Isobel (Hodgins) Bird, who came to town as a teacher and married Thomas Bird in 1910 … Frank Bailey, 45, son of Carl and brother to "Ace" Bailey … Charles Ecclestone, 49, died suddenly, an avid sportsman and active in many community activities … Edward Arnott, 67 … Mel Arnott … Bill Adamson, 77, well-known painter and decorator … John Francis Fenn, 88 … Polidore "Polly" Jocques, 70, had been on championship lacrosse teams in 1901, 1906, 1909, 1912, and 1919 … Priscilla V. McNeeley, who came as principal of the high school in 1926 … Philip J. Marrin, 83, who came as a barber in Joseph Caisse's barbershop then started his own wholesale tobacco and magazine agency which grew into the present P.J. Marrin's wholesale business … "Johnny" O'Brien, 63, veteran of both World Wars and an active member of the Knox choir … William N. Boyes, an early merchant at Vankoughnet where he operated a general store from 1913 to 1942.

A tragic accident took the lives of the three daughters of Mr. and Mrs. Elwood Johnson when their car plunged into the river at the Hunt's Hill bridge. George Reid, present owner of Northern Buildall, a high school student at the time, rescued Mrs. Johnson. Despite many rescue attempts the girls were lost … Edgar Davis, 49, died as a result of an explosion of fumes aboard the *Peerless II* in the river at Bracebridge.

## 1960

The contract for the construction of the Muskoka District Home for the Aged was awarded to the Newman Brothers of St. Catharines. A sod-turning ceremony was held on Thursday, June 14, with H.E. Rice of Huntsville doing the honours.

Nelson Goltz was elected Board of Education chairman for 1960. Dr. Ellis resigned his trusteeship on the Board of Education after 24 years of service. The vacancy was filled by Lorne Purdy, who joined the board. Chief of police John Harrington was re-appointed truant officer. Arrangements to purchase heating oil for the two schools were made with Imperial Oil at $0.15 a gallon.

Mrs. Wanda Miller, mayor of Gravenhurst, was elected president of the Muskoka District Council for 1960.

The old narrow steel bridge connecting Thomas and Toronto Streets, erected in 1907, was replaced. The Cannington Construction Company of Sudbury won the contract for $154,025, 80 percent of which would be paid by the Department of Highways.

A long-term project to buy the boathouses on Bracebridge Bay and make the area into a park was announced. A planning board was set up comprising William Towns, George Brooks, Bob Petry, Don Boyer, Dr. Monk, councillor Bert Sugg, and mayor Ted Reid.

On behalf of the Town of Bracebridge, Nelson Goltz offered for sale 30 attractive lots east of Aubrey Street and north of Charles Street, on land above the CNR track. Woodland Drive gave entrance from Aubrey Street. Other street names were Hillcrest Avenue and Valley Lane (now Spruce Lane).

Wally Crouter of CFRB welcomed local people to visit the Bracebridge Curling Rink in mid-January where he was broadcasting his early morning show from 6:00 to 9:30 a.m. This was being done in conjunction with the International Mixed Bonspeil that had a record 112 rinks entered.

The first public performance of the newly formed Muskoka District Band took place in late February at the Port Carling Community Centre. Thirty players under the direction of Dr. L.H. Sargeant of Huntsville delighted the audience with classical and popular numbers.

Bracebridge was honoured by a visit from Mr. S.M. Burke, High Commissioner of Pakistan to Canada, who addressed the local Rotary Club and then visited local industries.

Under new ownership, the property once called Muskoka Beach Inn would now be known as Muskoka Sands Inn. The Muskoka Hospital at Gravenhurst closed and was purchased from the Department of Public Works for use by the Department of Health to house 300 patients from the Ontario Hospital School at Orillia.

The Muskoka Tourist Association opened an information office at Foot's Bay to complement the existing one at Gravenhurst. The Muskoka District Health Unit moved to the former Maxwell Company building on James Street, just across the street from its original location.

Over 5,000 attended the Auto and Home Show which was declared "the best yet."

Six Mile Lake Provincial Park, about six miles north of Port Severn, was fully staffed for the first time.

The Bracebridge Lumber Company Mill, owned by Anthony Forgione, was hit by lightning and burned.

A plan to form an Association for Retarded Children was announced in late December via the press. It was stated that these children needed specialized services currently not available in the ordinary day schools.

J.W. McConnell of Montreal arranged to enlarge the capital fund of the John McConnell and Margaret Ann Wilson McConnell Memorial Foundation by $100,000, bringing the four-year-old fund to a total of $650,000. The McConnell Memorial Foundation met and gave grants of well over $10,000 in total to district organizations such as the Children's Aid Society and the hospitals.

Bob Petry, president of the Chamber of Commerce, announced that the community bonfire of Christmas trees at Jubilee Park would be called off indefinitely due to the heavy and continuing snowfalls of early January.

Derry Taylor became the Worshipful Master of LOL 218 and was one of the many Orangemen in town who helped build the new Orange Hall on Maple Street during 1959. James Hardy and Wilbur Anderson donated and prepared a turkey dinner on behalf of the Royal Black Preceptory 910 at their annual meeting. Nicholas Wettlaufer conducted the installation of Ivet Brown as Worshipful Preceptor.

W.J.A. (Bert) Brown and Edward G. West of IOOF 251 each received their honourable veteran's jewels signifying 50 years membership in the lodge. Dr. R.J. Dodds began his 16th year as Horticultural Society president. Mr. Ernie Goltz announced that for the first time in its long history the Bracebridge Fall Fair would be held on a Friday and Saturday in an attempt to boost attendance.

Dianne Rimstead, formerly of Beatrice, was appointed as editor of *Eaton's News*, the staff news magazine of the T. Eaton Co. Ltd.

A branch of the Canadian Cancer Society was organized here and conducted a very successful spring fund-raising campaign. Later in the year, Mrs. L.A. Marriott became president.

Margaret Askin, daughter of Mr. and Mrs. Pat Askin, was presented as one of Ontario's latest Gold Cord winning Guides. The ceremony took place in St. Catharines where the first Guide Company in Canada had been formed 50 years earlier.

Miss Marion Bird was elected president of the Business and Professional Women's Club. Don Boyer became president of the Rotary Club. At the IOOF, William Gibbs was chosen Noble Grand. Louis J.J. Caisse was duly installed as Legion Branch 161 president.

The new Orange Hall on Maple Street was opened by the Deputy Grand Master of Ontario West, J. Elmer Wood of Orillia.

Members of the Muskoka zone of the Lions clubs prepared a Children's Aid Society Camp at Lake Stewart on land obtained from the CPR.

Roger Crozier, known as "Roger the Dodger," was chosen all-star goalie by the coaches of the Junior A series. He had a "hot" season with the St. Catharines Tee Pees.

Doug Smith, chairman of the Minor Hockey League, reported a 25 percent increase in registration over 1959 with 16 teams in four leagues. A new junior rural hockey

*The new Hunt's Hill bridge under construction in 1961, immediately downstream of the old, narrow steel bridge. Preceding the latter, a little further downstream, was an even smaller wooden bridge.* COURTESY OF MARILYN LONG

league came into being with four teams representing Bent River, Macaulay, Milford Bay, and Falkenburg.

Rev. Karam Guergis, minister of Knox Presbyterian church since August 1956, left for Thamesville near Chatham. After 16 years of service in Muskoka, the Sisters of St. John the Divine announced they had completed their work in Bracebridge. They sold the properly to Mrs. Ethel Flynn and returned to Willowdale. George Vais, a former student at BHS, was ordained as a Presbyterian minister. Rev. Clarence Roberts, a native of St. Thomas, accepted a call to the Baptist congregation on Quebec Street. In October, Rev. D. Clarke conducted a special service at the Bardsville Baptist Church (which met in the former one-room school house) recognizing the congregation as a full-fledged Fellowship Baptist Church. Norman Longhurst and Fred Moulton gave the history of the church (which later became Pinegrove Church) and its branch work in Macaulay.

Miss Dorothy E. Millar tendered her resignation from the staff of Bracebridge High School. Clare R. Prosser of Levack was named principal of the high school to replace George R Young. A piece of land was purchased from Silverwood's Dairy to add to the new high school athletic field. On April 27, Hon. John Robarts, Minister of Education, opened Macaulay Public School. J.H. Kennedy, assistant superintendent of education for Ontario, opened the two new rooms at Monck Public School, making it a five-room school.

Alex J. Milne retired as manager of the liquor store, a position he had held since 1945. He planned to expand his marine and grocery supply business at Wood Lake and also retain his position as fire coordinator for the district ... In April, Frank McGarry established a coin-operated automatic laundry in the building once occupied by the Dominion Bank and later Wrixon's Smoke Shop. On March 10, the Dominion Stores Limited opened their new market at 229 Manitoba Street with nearly 8,000 items in stock. Al Tracey, formerly of Whitby, was the local manager. David and Ronald Myers officially opened their renovated and enlarged hardware store, taking in the former Sig Paul Store as part of the business.

The change from manual to dial telephones took place at 3:00 a.m. on Sunday, May 15. All new telephone numbers were then preceded by MI5 in Bracebridge while in Milford Bay and Port Carling RO4 and RO5, respectively, were used. The phone books had to be totally revamped to coincide with the new system. The first dial call from Bracebridge was made by George W. Boyer to the Hon. Frank Bastedo, Lieutenant Governor of Saskatchewan. The Bell Telephone Company announced in December that toll-free calls were coming the next spring between Bracebridge, Gravenhurst, and Milford Bay.

Dr. Fraser M. Greig sold Tamarack Lodge to Charles E. Keene of London. Pine Point Service Station at the corner of Manitoba Street and Monck Road became the dealership of the air-cooled, rear-engined Volkswagen "beetle." Most businesses in town opted to stay open six days a week beginning in July. Russ Stevenson opened a paint supply store in the former R.J. White grocery store at the corner of Dill and Wellington. Reid's Sportswear store moved into the former Kirk Dry Goods store that had occupied the site since 1888.

W.J.A. "Bert" Brown sold his gasoline supply boat to Jack Ricard, an OPP officer from Newcastle.

The Moore Lumber and Builders Supplies of Falkenburg was destroyed by fire. This business was established by pioneer Matthias Moore. Efforts to extinguish the fire were severely hampered by at least 500 cars of curiosity seekers parked along the roadways.

Walter Reynolds built a new funeral home on the corner of Manitoba and Mary streets. Hammond's Transportation opened a new warehouse on the eastern edge of town beside Highway 118. Irvin J. Robson bought Muskoka Lake Craft Limited and intended to continue its production. Ted Rusk sold his Supertest Farm Agency to Joe Dinner. The Northern Construction Company's property in Ward 4 was sold to a steel fabricating company.

Deaths this year included Crown Attorney Kenneth A. Mahaffy, who had served in this position since 1945 upon

*The "old" Hunt's Hill bridge under construction in 1906.* COURTESY OF BRENDA COX

the retirement of Walter Clairmont … John Sloper, 81, of Macaulay Centre, who spent 25 years as township clerk-treasurer … Rev. William E. Morrow, minister of the First Baptist Church, who was about to retire after 45 years in the ministry … Edward G. West, who had come to Bracebridge as a watchmaker with the Thomas Company about 1910 … John Wilson, 76, who had worked at Northern Planing Mills for 30 years … Everard Doonan, 76, a former employee of the Denniss Planing Mill, J.D. Shier, and Moore Lumber and Supply … W.J.A. Brown, 71, former councillor. He had a gas and oil distribution business with a service station at Manitoba Street and Monck Road. He later operated the *Peerless II* on the Muskoka Lakes … Harry Read, 76, bailiff of the Bracebridge Division Court for 16 years … John A Longhurst, 77, third son of Ufford pioneer A.E. Longhurst, came from South Portage in 189[illegible] … Emma Elizabeth Roper, 90 … Mrs. Fred Elliott, had served as clerk of the township and secretary of the school board in Oakley … Isaiah Everitt, 85, who came to Macaulay about 1884 … Mrs. Ellen Everitt, 79, married to Isaiah for 55 years … Leonard Taylor, 86, son of Alport pioneers, father of Walter … Don McKinlay, 59, caretaker of the post office and for a short time clerk of Macaulay … William G. Gibbs, 84, 38-year employee of the railway and a citizen here since about 1905 … Mrs. William Tinkiss, 70, daughter of Mr. and Mrs. John Crozier of Draper … Leonard Larson, 84, who came to Muskoka in 1933 and started Riverview

*Obviously well-attended Mayday celebrations at the Bracebridge Memorial Arena about 1961– the children here are students from the old Alport School on Beaumont Drive.* COURTESY OF THE BRACEBRIDGE PUBLIC LIBRARY

Cabins ... Herbery Rawson, 73, of Beatrice, who from 1939 until 1950 operated a store and service station at the corner of the Parry Sound and Utterson roads ... Vernon Johnston, 35, an employee of Walter Finch and Sons ... Alexander F. Dickson, 78, a lifelong resident who began work at the Bird Woollen Mill as a young man and continued until the plant closed.

**1961** Master Wayne Douglas Short, 8 pounds 12 ounces, son of Mr. and Mrs. Gerald Short, was the first baby born. Mr. Short was the manager of the Silverwood's plant.

The 1961 tax rate was up three mills. Education was up $13,200 with the total tax levy being $225,429.30.

The town sewage contract was the big project for 1961. The new brick sewage pumping station between the CNR tracks and River Street was opened. Strings of coloured lights were hung across Manitoba Street for Christmas this year. Renovations were done on the breakwater at the Motor Park.

Nelson A. Goltz was re-elected chairman of the Bracebridge Board of Education. Other members included Dr. Irma Coyne, Robert Everett, Clarence Kirkness, Lorne Purdy, and Dr. William Craymer. The Bracebridge High School valedictory address was given by John Blaney at both the Junior and Senior commencements.

The Children's Aid Society held an official opening of their headquarters in Longhurst House on Kimberley Avenue.

Bell Telephone had a new manager. Bracebridge now had 2,066 telephones. Long distance charges between Bracebridge and Gravenhurst were eliminated in May.

Robert J. Sim succeeded Les Boucher as district municipal engineer. Mr. B.R. Morris was appointed new motor vehicle licence examiner in Bracebridge. His office was in Meeks' building on Ontario Street.

Mr. James Thwaites established an ambulance service.

The previous year had a record number of adoptions, according to Children's Aid director Robert Quinsey.

The nearly 60 employees at the Motor Lamp Company were on strike for three weeks.

The old house of Mr. and Mrs. Nelson Huntley, tailor, next to Muskoka Garage at the top of Queen's Hill, was torn down. Waite's Bakery was remodelled.

Bob Petry was the president of the Chamber of Commerce and in charge of the Muskoka Cavalcade of Colour. Mr. Reginald Kirk was guest of honour at the Chamber of Commerce annual meeting. He was presented with a painting by Robert Everett for 57 years continuous service with the chamber ... The Christian Businessmen's Committee of Muskoka met at the Albion Hotel as part of a world-wide organization.

Robert E. Saunders became the new director of the McConnell Memorial Foundation. Judge Thomas, chairman of the board, reported that the foundation had spent $189,452 ... In 1960 the Hospital Women's Auxiliary raised $529.25.

The 62-year-old Albion Hotel was purchased and remodeled by Clive Lennox.

Bracebridge Legion Branch 161 presented life memberships to Dr. L.N. Ryan and Earle Dunn, both of whom joined in 1925. Monsignor O'Leary celebrated 50 years at St. Joseph's Roman Catholic Church.

Mr. and Mrs. Eugene Mauro celebrated their 60th wedding anniversary, and Mr. and Mrs. Thomas Ball their 50th.

Mr. Lou Specht succeeded Mrs. Wanda Miller of Gravenhurst on the Muskoka District Council.

On April 18 the Bracebridge Baptist Church met to choose a name for their church. After lengthy discussions they choose "First Baptist" as they had been in the present building for over 75 years and they were the first Baptists here. In October, Rev. Clarence Roberts led the dedication for their fine new organ. Mrs. Thomas Pickles was organist. The two manual Hanrow organs had been purchased from Mr. and Mrs. Frank Gowland of Bala.

Roger Crozier was chosen All-Star Goalie for the second year in a row.

The annual Muskoka International Bonspiel had 112 rinks participating this year.

The Bracebridge Kinsmen hockey team won the OHA Championship over Watford in four games, the first provincial championship since the Bantams won in 1953. The team consisted of Jim Kennedy, Wayne Robinson, Don Coates, Ben Mann, Ike Pearson, Don Lidstone, Jim

Hickey, Sid Sarazin, Barry Miners, Mike Ovens, Ron Austin, Neil Thompson, Woody Lee, Whitey Travers, and Alan Kay, with Club Downey as coach.

Mr. Ed Thatcher was chairman to organize the Fifth Annual Tagwagi Golf Tournament. Jack North of Toronto won the Hawn's Jeweler's Trophy out of 130 golfers.

Darrell (Dee) Rowan, 7, son of Mr. and Mrs. John Rowan of Front Street, drowned in the river. His body was found two days after his disappearance just above Bass Rock. Ken Crockford, 43, and Mervin McDonald, 45, drowned at Pine Lake on a fishing trip. Mr. Crockford had the Imperial Oil Service Station on Shier Street.

Deaths this year included Mrs. Mary E. Stonehouse (nee Mary Elizabeth Taylor), 81, of Macaulay, married in 1902 and moved into Bracebridge in 1946 … Ted Rusk, 60, owned Riverview Cabins and was agent for Supertest Oil … Albert E. Ecclestone, 93, came here about 1896, married Miss Elizabeth Jermyn of Draper, formed a partnership with Arthur S. Bates to found Ecclestone & Bates. He served with the Bracebridge fire brigade for over 50 years, 30 of those as chief until he retired in 1946 … Mr. Eugene Mauro, 79, came about 1905 as a builder.

*Mr. and Mrs. Finlay Munro at the official opening of the new facilities at their Rainbow Ridge ski hill west of town.* COURTESY OF THE BRACEBRIDGE PUBLIC LIBRARY

**1962** Elliott's moved to the Sibbett Block (now the Factory Store) … The drug store business of George W. Brooks moved along Manitoba Street to between Geo. W. Ecclestone hardware and Thompson's barbershop … James Berofe's store, in business since 1913, closed … The Caisse building was sold to hairdresser Eleanor Van Hezewyk and husband Bert … Earle and Gordon Rosewarne opened the Esso Service Station at the corner of Willis and Manitoba streets across from their Gordon Motors dealership. In October, Gordon Motor Sales was appointed a General Motors dealer under the management of Mr. Frank Miller … Greavette Boats of Gravenhurst was sold to Heintzman Bros. with C. Herman Heintzman named president … Holiday House owners Mr. and Mrs. E.V. Allchin opened a new 10-room motel addition to the facilities with twin-basin bathrooms and TV in all rooms … The new dental clinic of Dr. Irma Coyne opened on Kimberley Avenue with Mrs. Roy (Jessie) Tennant as receptionist … The Thomas Company remodelled its store … Mr. and Mrs. Robert Patterson opened a new shoe store on Manitoba Street, formerly occupied by Louis Caisse … Bob Petry purchased the C.L. Slater Insurance business … The Parkview Restaurant was sold by David Johnson to Ken Moorhouse … Kenneth and Russell Downey, operators of Bracebridge Dairy for nearly 20 years, moved to Port Hope City Dairy and Ken sold his Charles Street (now Ann St.) house to Ernest Zentner … Mrs. Margaret Slater sold her house to Mr. and Mrs. Edward S. Sugg.

Trans-Canada Pipe Lines began building a $2,300,000.00 compressor station on Beaumont Drive.

James Stevenson was elected president of the Bracebridge Chamber of Commerce. Nelson A. Goltz was named as manager of Santa's Village in February succeeding Clarence Green. Plans included installation of a miniature passenger train and the building of "Kris Kringle's Show Boat." The boat was launched to great fanfare at the town dock in June.

J.D. Shier Lumber and Supply Ltd. completed 19 roof-trusses, 45 feet from eave to eave, that were the second largest ever built in Ontario … H.G. Everett, B.Phm., celebrated 50 years as a pharmacist, having succeeded Harry Bridgland and his father Dr. Samuel Bridgland in the same drug store. Robert E. Everett, B.Phm., returned to town to take over his father's drug store ... The Top Hat Restaurant, opened by owner John Koutis, replaced the burned-out Town Grill in the Lazzara Block.

Bracebridge Lumber, located along the north bank of the Muskoka River at the foot of Wellington Street, received orders for a half-million feet of lumber to make four-by-four vegetable crates for growers. About 21 personnel at the sawmill cut the winter supply of logs, some 600,000 board feet.

A two-storey structure at Finlay Munro's Rainbow Ridge Ski Chalet was constructed. Bethel Latex Products of Connecticut built an 8,000-square-foot plant one mile south of Bracebridge on Highway 532, formerly known as Lloyd's turkey farm, to manufacture rubber gloves. Ted Woodill purchased Northern Aviation at Boyd's Bay. In November, alterations and improvements were made to the Albion Hotel. A Canadian Tire Service Centre opened at Ann and Manitoba streets.

The official opening of the Muskoka District Home for the Aged, The Pines, took place January 4. The staff included Dr. Lyle Black, home physician, and John Biddle, superintendent. The auxiliary consisted of Mrs. Harrington, president; Mrs. Gordon Aiken, district volunteer visitor convener; and Mrs. L. Karner, convener, tuck shop. Glen G. Williams, secretary-treasurer of The Pines since 1958, retired in August. Arthur Cox was laboratory technician.

George Martin completed 16 years with the Muskoka Tourist Association and Edward Wright, proprietor of Clevelands House, became new head. I. Yorke Murphy, manager of the Bank of Nova Scotia since 1946, retired and Ralph E. Melvin, from Brampton, succeeded him. William Towns retired as manager of the National Employment Service after 20 years. He was replaced by Reg W. Law.

Charles Morrow was elected president and Lorne Hockridge vice president of the South Muskoka Agricultural Society Fall Fair. The Rotary Club elected Norman Rosewarne as president and H.E.S. Sugg as vice president, with Lou Specht as secretary. In May, Bracebridge Lions elected John Featherston president, George Mann 1st vice president, Harry Anderson 2nd vice president, and Bert Taylor as secretary, replacing Aub Hawn. The Loyal Orange Lodge had special music during the presentation of 50 Year Jewels to Brother Ausburn Hewitt and Brother Nicholas Wettlaufer. Mr. and Mrs. Frank Denniss and son Gary along with Miss Donna Pearson performed.

Louis J. Caisse made history in December when he was re-elected as president of the Bracebridge Branch of the Royal Canadian Legion for a third term. Past president Robert E. Jeffries had served more years but not continuously.

Three Muskoka lakes, Hines, Irvine, and Traves, were named in honour of Bracebridge "boys" who lost their lives in active war service in 1942 and 1944: Petty Officer Reginald Roy Hines, John Cecil Irvine, and Private Albert Traves ... The Bracebridge Lions' Club Squadron, No. 658, Royal Canadian Air Cadets took an actual training flight experience at Camp Borden.

J.J. Haight was appointed to the new position of provincial examiner of surveys for Muskoka and Parry Sound ... Pinegrove Baptist Church opened on Highway 118 at Pine Street in April ... A Children's Musicale by 850 public school pupils of central Muskoka directed by Mrs. Marge Patterson and accompanied by Mrs. Winifred Anderson was a delightful event.

The Muskoka District Health Unit distributed the new Sabin poliovirus live oral vaccine.

Gordon H. Aiken, Parry Sound-Muskoka's member of Parliament, was re-elected June 18 with a lead of 23,403 votes for Diefenbaker's Conservative Party.

The 1961 Census indicated a population of 2,970 for Bracebridge, 1,085 19 years of age or under.

The entire ceiling at St. Joseph's Roman Catholic Church fell away and crashed to the pews and floor during the night of July 27. It was discovered by the parish priest the Right Reverend Monsignor O'Leary.

Bracebridge voted for dining room licences in September, allowing for dining rooms to apply to serve liquor with meals, but men's beverage rooms were defeated.

The fall fair was again one of the best yet, the school children's parade being one of the best features. Lynda Matthias was chosen Miss Bracebridge and Queen of the Muskoka Cavalcade of Colour.

The Children's Aid Society funds committee included Mrs. K. Beers, Mrs. Earl (Jessie) Dunn, and Mrs. D. Gonneau of Bracebridge. Mrs. Munford Green, formerly Jean Gibbs, was honoured on her retirement from Bell Telephone after more than 32 years of service.

In November, Sterling Terry of Clear Lake located a RCAF rocket pod in Oakley Township, which had been dropped from an aircraft in January 1958.

John D.C. McBride of Muskoka Falls, reeve of Draper Township, was appointed Sheriff of Muskoka, succeeding W.B. Elliot who retired. Councillor Russell Crockford was appointed reeve for the balance of 1962.

Canadian Girls in Training held their annual Christmas vespers service with a 30-voice choir. Mrs. Glen Schroeder gave the meditation.

For Christmas, turkeys were 45 to 57¢ a pound, cranberries 29¢ a pound, and 2 pounds of red grapes 33¢.

Nelson A. Goltz was re-elected chairman of the Board of Education for 1962, and Noel Stockton vice-chairman. James R. Gray was appointed to the teaching staff of Bracebridge High School, to replace Miss McConkey who left in December. The little white Alport School on Beaumont Drive closed and $60,000 was approved to enlarge the Muskoka Central School on Muskoka Beach Road. Frank Miller was one of the popular teachers at the high school … Concern was raised about overcrowding of 530 students at Bracebridge Public School, built five years earlier to take 430. By July, teachers' rooms were converted for classes totaling 569 pupils. Construction of the high school addition was under way in July.

For the third year in succession, the goaltender for St. Catharines TeePees, Roger Crozier, was chosen for the "dream team" by area coaches. The Muskoka Trophy for curling was won by Ken Sander of Orillia, formerly of Bracebridge. The Bracebridge Trophy was won by Bruce Montgomery of Orangeville.

Douglas Smith, manager of the Community Centre, prepared for the Bracebridge Ice Revue featuring Barbara Wagner and Bob Paul, world champion pairs skaters. The Bracebridge Summer Skating School commenced July 2 under the direction of Paul Tattan, and all but one of the 39 students registered were from northern Ontario and other regions.

During May and June, the Bracebridge Golf and Country Club offered ladies' memberships and group memberships for $35.

In November, the Bracebridge Figure Skating Club re-elected Mrs. William Gibbs president, Mrs. Zeta Marrin first vice president, Mrs. Ralph Bustard second vice president, Mrs. Harry Lidstone secretary, and Douglas Smith treasurer. The Bracebridge Bears were planning to return to "big time" hockey and intended to import key players.

Mayor Edgar W. Reid welcomed Mr. Geoff Waite to Council at the opening session in January. Plans to pave Manitoba Street and to hook up new sewer customers were announced.

The entire new sewage disposal system and pumping station at the foot of Wellington Street was completed in January.

In March, Council purchased a year-round snow and street-work truck for $2,800 and would re-assume the garbage collection at the termination of the Hammond Transportation contract. The residential tax rate was raised five mills to 72 and the commercial tax rate to 79. The old Thomas Street bridge was removed for $1 and the salvage value of the steel. Removal of the concrete abutments was not included in the project. Gray Coach Lines re-routed their buses to avoid the work.

For the first time our town's population exceeded 3,000. Clerk-treasurer Wilbert Richards released new population figures showing an assessed count of 3,032.

Excavating the two-foot-thick concrete base and resurfacing Manitoba Street between Thomas Street and McDonald by Fowler Construction was completed ahead of schedule.

There was an urgent need to supplement the town's water supply. It was presently coming only from the Peake springs, and consultants were engaged in December to locate springs capable of producing an ideal 400 gallons per minute. The residents of Bracebridge suffered water restrictions when the springs could not supply the need because of continuous hot weather. The driest summer in years caused a fire amongst trees in Brobst Nursery. Conservation of water in every way possible was necessary. The power was closed off eight hours each night to build up the head of water at each plant.

*The new chalet and T-bar at Rainbow Ridge. Although it had a vertical drop of less than 60 metres, the proximity of the facility to town made it a popular spot for many years.* COURTESY OF THE BRACEBRIDGE PUBLIC LIBRARY

As of January 18, a total of 72.8 inches of snow had fallen. Two hired horses and a one-year-old truck plowed sidewalks and roads. In February, heavy snow collapsed the 350-foot roof of the vacant Muskoka Poultry Ltd. turkey barn.

Deaths included Mrs. B.Y. McBride, widow of former mayor ... Mrs. J.H. Elliott (nee Florence Mabel Sibbett). whose husband ran Elliott's in the Sibbett Block. She was busy with both the Clef Club and the Red Cross and had offered them space during the war ... Ms. William Pin, 93, took Free Land Grant at Purbrook about 85 years ago ... Frederick P. Bowyer, 71, son of former mayor H.S. Bowyer ... George S. Johnson, former public school inspector, born in 1884 ... George H. Flood, 63. of Dill Street ... Cecil Veitch, 61, died working his farm. He was a great builder and stone mason ... Joseph Ennis, 78, butcher, lived on Robert Street ... Mrs. Eugene Mauro died August 17 in her 80th year. She won prizes at the fall fair for needlework ... Frank Pickles, 74, a painter ... Aubrey R. Shier, 50, president of J.D. Shier Lumber and Supply ... W.J.M. Nichols, 27, died from charcoal burner fumes on his houseboat on the Muskoka River.

## 1963

The last meeting of the Bracebridge Memorial Hospital took place February 28 as the South Muskoka Memorial Hospital planned its new operation under administrator Frank Henry. Miss Elizabeth Fraser was appointed director of nursing, Arthur Woods building superintendent, Mrs. Margaret Waddington dietitian, and Keith MacInnes business manager. On October 20, the formal opening of the new South Muskoka Memorial Hospital took place. Mr. and Mrs. Walter Ruttan's son was the first baby born in the

*Bracebridge Memorial Hospital was established in 1928 in this fine old house. A subsequent addition altered the impressive front fascade.* COURTESY OF THE WILLIAM TOWNS COLLECTION

65-bed hospital, and Steven, the son of administrator Frank Henry was the first outpatient having cut his head on a sign post. The Kinettes began a campaign to raise $3,000 to furnish a children's ward at the new hospital. Local artist J.K. Partridge donated 12 fine paintings to decorate the walls.

Lots were offered for sale in new subdivisions, Mollmar Heights east on Richard Street, and Sunshine Village, east on Toronto Street.

The medical officer of health, Dr. W.H. (Bert) Cross, moved to the provincial department of health in Toronto in October and sold his house to Dr. and Mrs. O.R.J. Savijarvi.

Lack of water challenged the Bracebridge Water, Light and Power Commission as dry conditions caused problems in April. By August, the water shortage was very serious and the town reservoir dropped 54 inches. In a desperate move to stop the growing water shortage, plans were prepared to build a 60-foot-long dam in Macaulay Township.

Magistrate Redmond Thomas, QC, completed 25 years as District Magistrate of Muskoka in January ... Calvin Smith was chosen new master of the Muskoka Lodge ... Mrs. W.A. Shier was appointed new president of the Women's Hospital Auxiliary ... Father Roland Palmer was transferred back to the Canadian SSJE at Bracebridge ... the Grade One pupils of Miss Leda Scovell sang Easter music to residents of The Pines ... Robert E. Jeffries of the Canadian Legion was elected district deputy commander in April ... the Clef Club held its 55th birthday party ... Mrs. Marge Patterson's pupils gave a recital at the public school ... Dr. and Mrs. William Craymer purchased the J.H. Elliot estate property on Ontario Street.

Bracebridge residents were shocked when Dr. and Mrs. Bert Bastedo were killed when walking across a highway in Plainfield, Indiana, at the beginning of their annual holiday to California. Their contribution to the community was great, his last public act being the sod-turning at the new hospital.

Residents of Beaver Creek Correctional Camp made 100 penny banks for the Children's Aid Society to collect money for their work. The camp's unblemished record was spoiled in July when three persons escaped during two events.

Mel Goltz was a first student pilot of Northern Aviation at Boyd's Bay in May.

George Mann was installed as the president of the 1963-64 Bracebridge Lions Club.

Former Bracebridge fire chief and businessman Alex J. Milne, and wife Minnie, were honoured at their 50th wedding anniversary at the Wood Lake Cottagers' Association regatta August 1 by Bob Boyer, MPP.

Mrs. Charles Whaley, 54, wife of a Bracebridge blacksmith, drowned in 12 feet of water at the breakwater below Bracebridge Falls. Nancy Archer and her father, councillor Norman Archer, aided in the rescue of Max Smith when his boat exploded and burst into flames in the river in front their Beaumont Drive home.

Again, the fall fair was hailed as one of the best, and the parade judges had to view the various schools for the second time before they could award first to Mrs. Cowan's Grade One.

Robert J. Boyer was re-elected with a huge majority as member of the legislature for Muskoka.

Bracebridge Latex Products manufactured 64 dozen pair of cloth-lined rubber gloves a day at the new plant. The Skyway Restaurant was rebuilt to replace the business burned last October. Bangor Lodge constructed a $70,000 recreation centre during the winter.

Mrs. Timmy Allchin and Mrs. Marg Reid were elected to the Chamber of Commerce. Thomas Johnson, proprietor of Maureen's Ladies Wear, was elected president. The parking committee sponsored an evening of progressive entertainment, dinner, and dancing to raise funds for surfacing a downtown parking area.

The Wells Motel (now the Bellwood), built in 1950 by Mr. and Mrs. Douglas S. Wells, was sold to Mr. and Mrs. Onni Niskanen of Sault Ste. Marie. Holiday House planned a big season in the new "West Terrace," and the SSJE announced plans for a new building at the Mission House.

Alan Fry was appointed lessee of the British America Oil service station at 240 Shier Street and in June, Crockford's Esso Service Station was sold to Patterson Enterprises.

The CNR and the *Mildred* offered a package which included train fare to Bracebridge and a trip on the boat.

A $100,000, 16-unit apartment building was built on Morrison Street at Ball's Hill and Wellington Street, and a new medical suite was built for Dr. William Monk on Ann Street.

Wigwasson Lodge changed ownership after 32 years when Mr. and Mrs. George A. Martin sold to Martin Schill Jr. of Cleveland, Ohio, in late August. Phillip Murphy bought Matchett Bros. jewelry of Orillia in September, and G. Leslie Tennant sold The George Apartments on Dominion Street to E.P. Lee, QC, for his law offices.

The Bracebridge Falls bridge on Highway 532 was declared sound following two weeks of repairs.

*Construction under way for a new addition to Bracebridge High School, this wing containing the gymnasium and cafeteria (which will be on the side visible here, facing Tanbark Hill) as well as classrooms and shops. The 1958 addition is on the right, with the original building visible in behind.* COURTESY OF THE BRACEBRIDGE PUBLIC LIBRARY

The auditorium in the new high school addition was perfect to present "Tagwagi '63," a stage review about Muskoka happenings and personalities written by William Monk and others.

Miss Martha Jackson left the teaching staff of the public school, and new teachers Mrs. D. Snyder, Miss Pamela Shier, Miss Phyllis Brooks, Mrs. G. Waite and Mr. Robert Old (formerly principal at Muskoka Falls) were hired. Miss Mary McCracken, Miss Edith Robinson, and Miss Leda Scovell were honoured at their retirement. The new Composite School (high school) fall enrollment was 700, with 35 teachers.

Mr. and Mrs. George Matthias moved their furniture and appliance business to the former Elliott's 5¢ to $1 store building which they purchased.

The CNR announced the closure of the Bracebridge station each weekend from Saturday to Monday. The Albion Hotel starred singers Joyce Hahn, Tommy Common, and Shirley Harmer in early November.

Frank Miller bought the Bastedo residence on Dominion Street with plans to make apartments.

John Wilson McConnell, one of the great figures of his generation in Canada, died in November and was buried in Montreal. In memory of his parents, who were pioneers of Monck Township, he had established a philanthropic foundation for Muskoka families.

Corporal George Hankin of the Bracebridge OPP purchased the former Alport School in June to use as a year-round home.

The 1963 OHA intermediate season opened for the Bracebridge Bears in January, and the Richmond Hill rink won the Muskoka Trophy at the Sixth International Curling Mixed Bonspiel. Neil McKinnon's Rink won the 1963 Sportsmen's Bonspiel in March. Rainbow Ridge opened officially with a torchlight ski display staged by Stan Knowles, showing off the new T-bar. Jackie Wyman broke her shoulder in a tumble during the annual Bracebridge Figure Skating Club Ice Revue in February. Cathy MacNaughtan won the Junior Proficiency Cup at the club's annual competition, and Marion Prosser won the Senior cup. The High School junior soccer team coached by Ken Black won the Muskoka-Parry Sound championship and were Georgian Bay A semi-finalists in the fall.

Roger Crozier was a standout playing his first NHL game with the Detroit Red Wings on November 30, substituting for ailing Terry Sawchuk. On December 19 he had his first shutout, over the Boston Bruins in Detroit.

Deaths this year included Monsignor O'Leary who collapsed after his sermon in January and died at the altar, a parish priest for 52 years … Joseph C. Myers, 82, grocer for 30 years … Harold Alexander Hamilton, 20, killed in auto crash north of Gravenhurst … Dr. R. Melville Anderson, 68, a dentist … George Morrow, 80, had conducted a livery business … Mrs. William Towns, formerly a nurse … Charles Roy Yeoman, 72, many years at the Bird Woollen Mill … Mrs. Reginald Kirk (Hannah Tookey), organist and choir leader of Knox Church, and a piano teacher … Severiino Braida, 70, employed at J.D. Shier Lumber for 51 years since the age of 12 … Mrs. Alice McInroy, 83, lived in town 79 years … Roy Shier, 75, former president of J.D. Shier Lumber … Mrs. William Dinner, died July 4 at the age of 100 years … George Early, in his 74th year, drowned. He was a rural mail carrier along Beaumont Drive … Henry Michael Meakins, 48, died at his job at Fowler Construction … Albert Ernest Leeder, 59, died of heart problems after a career in sawmills … William Sinclair Peake, 18, killed in a motor accident … Percy Oliver Medley, in his 50th year. He was in the sand and gravel contracting business.

## 1964

Bracebridge was experiencing a building boom with the construction of the new hospital, the high school addition, Valley View apartments, the addition to the SSJE Mission House, and a four-room addition to the public school. The town got a new fire truck. Hometown boy Roger Crozier was picked as AHL Rookie of the Year.

Fire Chief Ollie Scott retired to be replaced by Harold B. Dawson, who first joined the brigade in 1957. Chief Dawson also became district coordinator for the Muskoka District Mutual Fire Aid Association. December was the worst month in many years for serious fires. The home of Mr. and Mrs. Gerry Hall, two miles south of Bracebridge, was completely destroyed by fire. The two trucks went out from town but had to alternate coming back for water. Firemen finally had to admit defeat and turned to protecting neighbouring houses. The Wellington Street home of Rudolph and Betty Mayhew was destroyed but two adjacent houses were saved. The third fire this month did much interior damage to the James Street home of Douglas and Sharon Ball. Lesser fires included a blaze started by hot foundry sand in hoppers at Muskoka Silicone Aggregates Ltd. four miles south of Bracebridge (here good-quality silicone was ground into fine powder and shipped to manufacturers of paint, cement block, terrazzo flooring, and the sandblasting industry). The volunteer fire brigade's quick action put out a fire in the Coin Laundry after an explosion blew out the front plate glass window. The new fire truck, purchased from C.E. Hickey and Sons Ltd., Hamilton, with a 145-inch wheel base and a 600-gallon water tank, arrived in May.

The Bracebridge Police Department got a pay raise.

Six hundred attended the official opening of the new wing of Bracebridge and Muskoka Lakes Secondary School on March 13. Architect Miles Allison of Barrie said it was the first split level school ever built. The food preparation course was unique in Ontario, with Mr. R.G. Hudswell as instructor. BMLSS had 774 students while BPS had 575 – up from the previous year. Regulation 210 closed the continuation school in Port Carling and the students were bussed to BMLSS. Kathy Ennis and Gail Melvin were Ontario Scholars this year.

Ken Black was named BMLSS vice principal. Lee Shea was appointed assistant principal at the public school. Mrs. Evelyn Cowe and Mrs. Marlene Waite resigned from the public school. A petition by nine Bracebridge establishments demanded that the BMLSS cafeteria discontinue serving meals to the public. The appeal went to Minister of Education who suggested the cafeteria charge more competitive prices.

Royal Canadian Legion Branch No. 161 celebrated the final payment on the cenotaph and the burning of the mortgage. The cenotaph was dedicated in August 1959 at a cost of $7,500.

G. Crawford was the new Royal Bank manager, succeeding Harry G. Merriman.

Norman Rosewarne's Muskoka Garage Ltd. opened its new addition. Matthias Furniture and Appliances opened in the former Elliott's store. The former Bastedo residence was now a four-plex apartment. It was purchased by Frank Miller from the estate and rebuilt by general contractor Charles Morrow. F. Courtney Hay Construction Company offered 25 fully serviced lots in the new Valley View subdivision between Monck Road and Wellington. Construction of a new Canadian Tire building was started on the corner of Manitoba and Ann by owner/builder Eddie O'Brien.

It was the 66th anniversary of the Bank of Nova Scotia. Formerly the Bank of Ottawa, it first opened a Bracebridge branch on June 2, 1898. Managers over the years were F.C. Mulkins 1898-1900; C.H. King 1900-02; C.C. Billings 1902-04; William Kingsmill 1904-35; Harry Wilson 1935-46; Yorke Murphy 1946 until he retired in 1962, then Ralph Melvin.

The South Muskoka Memorial Hospital chairman, George Beard, said that within one month the hospital was 70 percent occupied with an average stay of nine days. Frank Henry was administrator with a total staff of 100. Mr. Nelson Davis sent his 14th $1,000 cheque to the hospital. His first cheque was written in 1949. The Rubberset Employee's Fund gave SMMH $3,700.

Hawn's Jewelers gave out 200 engraved spoons at their grand reopening after seven weeks of renovation.

The *Miss Muskoka*, built at Wheatley near Windsor and owned by Muskoka Excursions Ltd., had her shakedown cruise from Foot's Bay to Gravenhurst. She travelled via Lake Erie, the Detroit and St. Clair rivers, and Lake Huron to Port Severn, then overland to Foot's Bay under command of Captain Tom Oake. She measured 70 feet long with a 24-foot beam, drew 4½ feet, and was propelled by two diesels of 540 HP.

The Munro's held their first "Beatles" dance in April at Rainbow Ridge, followed by six weekly Muskoka Folk Concerts plus two children's concerts. They received a dining lounge liquor licence and were the site of a photo shoot for the ski wear section of the Simpson-Sears catalogue. They also acquired a machine to make snow, and a kiddie rope tow.

The Tom Thumb miniature golf course opened at Santa's Village in July.

*"Mother Goose" was the hit of the 1964 Santa Claus Parade, and was one of the most ambitious floats in the parade's history. The driver had a small slit to see through; a guide up ahead on foot with a walkie-talkie provided manoeuvering instructions.* COURTESY OF MARILYN LONG

Village Forge Antiques, owned by Mrs. Henry Worsnip of Buttonville, opened in the old post office.

Medley Motors Ltd. won the contract to demolish the old hospital. They did so in just over six weeks. W.E. Towns was hospital board chairman. Bracebridge Dairy extended its plant and self-service area south 15 feet under proprietor Russell (Chub) Downey and contractor Bob Roper. The Banks Brothers TV and Appliances store was opened by Doug, Don, and Glen in the former Reid's Sportswear premises.

Bracebridge had a surfeit of ambulances, one run by Orvil Hammond, the other by James Thwaites of Muskoka Ambulance. Mr. Robert Rye, son of Mr. and Mrs. Thomas Rye of Chaffey, joined the law firm of E.P. Lee. Harold Dawson purchased the electrical contracting business from his father Abe. James Mauro, manager of the Brewer's Retail for 20 years, was transferred to Fort Erie.

In 1964 the commercial tax rate was set at 83 mills, and residential at 77 mills, a two-mill increase.

The Muskoka Foundry Ltd. property, two acres plus a 30,000-square-foot building in Ward 4, was sold to George W. Wilson. This property was part of Free Grant and Homesteads Act parcel to Augustus J. Alport, purchased by John Kean, sold to Robert E. Perry and Thomas M. Myers, then to the Muskoka District Agricultural Society for a fairgrounds. The society sold one-half acre to the Northern and Pacific Junction Railway Co. on April 30, 1886, and transferred title to the Village of Bracebridge. Subsequently, Samuel H. Armstrong purchased it and sold it to the Dominion Linen Mills Ltd., who erected a building. In 1914, after several ownership changes, it was purchased by Mungo Park McKay, F.M. Johnson, and John Robertson (later replaced by George Mahaffy) as the Muskoka Foundry. The foundry was previously located where Kelvin Grove Park is now.

A mortgage sale of Tamarack Lodge by Charles H. Thornton, auctioneer, was held.

The Society of St. John the Evangelist's enlarged mission house was consecrated by Archbishop W.L. Wright and Rev. Father Palmer, Father Superior. They named it the Larkin Wing after the late George Ross Larkin, a principal benefactor.

Mr. and Mrs. Arthur Leeder celebrated their 60th wedding anniversary. Arthur, son of the late Mr. and Mrs. Phillip Leeder, was a builder, construction supervisor of Bigwin Inn, and in charge of maintenance at the Anglo-Canadian Leather Company in Huntsville. Eleanor was the daughter of late Mr. and Mrs. Edward Bailey.

Muskoka had not been regarded as a farming area but in 1964 farm produce was valued at over a million dollars with 36,397 acres of land in crops.

The rapids on the north branch of the Muskoka River close to River Street formerly known as Halstead's Rapids were renamed Flynn's Rapids in honour of John Flynn, nearby home owner and government contractor for provincial dams and smaller bridges.

The new rock cut at Milford Bay on the Highway 118 bypass was the prettiest in Ontario with 40-foot walls of pink Precambrian granite gneiss formed some a billion years ago. Some 96,000 cubic feet of the rock was removed.

Carl Whittier, at Rainbow Ridge, won a new trophy given at the Manufacturer's Life Invitational Meet. He graduated first out of 26 pupils in the Canadian Ski Instructors All-In-One Ski School ... The rink consisting of Jack and Betty Atkinson and Bob and Helen Hopkins won the Rubberset Company's $3,500 gold broom in the International Bonspiel ... A splendid street parade led by the Legion Pipe Band, fire trucks, and a cavalcade of cars welcomed home Roger Crozier, rookie goaltender for the Detroit Red Wings. The organizers were Neil McKinnon, Chub Downey, and Roy Tennant ... Roger Crozier was introduced to parents and players at the Minor Hockey Trophy night ... The 12th International Hippodrome Circus drew 1,482 people, the largest crowd in 10 years. Minor Hockey cleared $375.

The Kinsmen sponsored a walking marathon from Bracebridge to Milford Bay and return. Stephen Pogue won the men's in three hours and 32 minutes. Mrs. E. Henderson did the course in her bare feet and still came in ladies' first. Of 23 entrants, 12 completed the course ... Doug Matthias came in seventh out of 40 in the Provincial Golf Tournament at Maple Downs.

The 70 present at the Chamber of Commerce annual meeting at Rainbow Ridge had cause to celebrate as the Chamber showed a surplus, the first in many years. The president was Tom Johnson, the vice president Frank Miller, and the treasurer William Towns.

Theatre arts included the Kinette Capers held at BPS with choral skits, a fashion show, pantomime, folk music, and poetry. BMLSS presented *Romeo and Juliette* and *The Old Lady Shows Her Medals*. The Straw Hat Players, the oldest continuously operating summer theatre in Ontario, offered plays in Port Carling and Britannia.

*As the home of Santa's Village, Bracebridge of course was always at the head of the line when it came time to schedule the jolly old gent for its parade. Here Santa (a.k.a. Russ Salmon) waves as the 1964 parade tails up James Street.* COURTESY OF MARILYN LONG

*The fire department's oldest truck still in use puts on a display at Bracebridge Bay in 1964, prior to its retirement. A new truck was purchased that year to join one bought in the 1950s.* COURTESY OF MARILYN LONG

Ralph and Louis Sutera, twin musicians and evangelists from Minnesota, conducted a week-long crusade in the Town Hall sponsored by Christian Businessmen's Club.

Knox Presbyterian Church was re-dedicated after renovations. The entire upstairs of the manse was renovated with tile floors and new ceilings. The church received a new asphalt roof, the lawn was regraded and seeded, and a new entrance built. J.J. Thomson did the carpentry, H.J. Brooks and Sons the electrical work, E.W. Holland and Sons the plumbing, J. Alan Wilson the painting, and Murray Ward the kitchen. A CGIT was started at the church.

St. Joseph's Roman Catholic Church laid their cornerstone using the same trowel as for the old corner stone laid June 8, 1879.

The South Muskoka School for the Retarded was held each morning at the United Church with teacher Mrs. Bert Olimer. The aim was improved coordination and concentration, following simple instructions, and recognition and awareness of objects and experiences.

George Rowling of Wharf Road saved the 4-year-old son of Mr. and Mrs. Duncan from drowning. Mr. Rowling saw the child slip off the icy edge and fall into the river. He immediately leapt into his rowboat and "rowed faster than he ever had in his life" across the bay to rescue the youngster.

A three-ton gravel truck broke through the ice into 132 feet of water just off Christmas Island in Lake Muskoka. William Pratt, 52, of Walker's Point was drowned and it took a few days to find his body. They had been hauling gravel for several days with two trucks.

A Toronto 7-year old fell from the dam while fishing and drowned despite the best efforts of Robert Fyke and Ronald Young who attempted rescue … Three young men died on the Severn River, including Percy Beatty, 25, son of Mr. and Mrs. George Beatty of Shier Street, when their motorboat took fire and exploded … Ivan Mills, 51, of

Macaulay, a councillor for 20 years, was killed in tragic car-truck crash one mile north of Bracebridge on Highway 532 (now District Road 4).

Deaths included Wesley Barton Elliott, 66, Sheriff of Muskoka 1944-1963, and also clerk of the Surrogate Court, local registrar of the Supreme Court of Canada, clerk of District Court, and District treasurer with over 40 years in the service of the provincial government ... Earle Claude Barnes, 62, boat builder, son of the late Charles Barnes who was manager of the Anglo-Canadian Leather Company for many years ... Edwin Bonnell, 74, former councillor and reeve of Macaulay 1944-52, and president of the Muskoka District Council and the hospital board ... Andy Giaschi, 64, came to Canada in 1914, built the Norwood Theatre in 1949, and raised the standard of movie entertainment in town to first-run pictures ... John Moore, 66, town employee for many years, having assumed the duties of Clifford Gibbs, died of a heart attack at work ... Monsignor O'Leary ... Dr. R.J. Dodds, came to Bracebridge as a chiropractor in 1937, and very active in the Horticultural Society ... Miss May E. Draper, 94, 30 years in the "Nut-shell" house in Ward 3 with Miss Cassels ... Anne Mabel Duke, 79, daughter of Mr. and Mrs. George H. Sutton, Indian River, in 1905 married Charles J. Duke who started Duke Boats in 1925 ... George Faith, 84, of Minett, then Bracebridge, was in the Imperial Cavalry in the South African War, later in India, joined the 122nd Battalion ... Elmer H. Forbes, 65, book-keeper at the Anglo-Canadian tannery, Anderson's store, and Bracebridge Lumber, in town since 1910 ...

Mrs. Edith Godfrey, 89, came to Muskoka Township with her parents Mr. and Mrs. Charles Henry Cox about 1883, attended Alport school, married Lemeuil Godfrey in 1896 ... Samuel Hawn, 88, son of Mr. and Mrs. Joseph Hawn, United Empire Loyalists, moved to Matthiasville as a small boy, was a mail courier, postmaster, and merchant, retired 1955 ... Jane Emily Sadler, 90 ... Edward Spreadborough, 90, operated a farm with his brother, Will, which was later sold to the Canadian Motor Lamp Company ... Mrs. B.W. Tillson (Daisy Hincks), 83, accompanied her brother Canon Francis H. Hincks to Bracebridge in 1910 when he became rector of St. Thomas' Anglican Church, married 1911, widowed 1926, then operated the Tillson Egg Farm ... Mrs. Charlotte Alice Waite, 94, came to Bracebridge about 1881.

Total snowfall to March 31 was 88.4 inches compared to 107.6 inches the year before.

*Spring runoff thunders past the ruins of the Bird Woollen Mill, March 1965. A century earlier, the power of the falls was being harnessed to saw lumber and mill flour for the frontier hamlet of Bracebridge.* COURTESY OF MARILYN LONG

# 1965–1974

## *Towards 100 Years: New Industries, New Boundaries*

THERE WERE 252 BIRTHS and 92 deaths in Bracebridge in 1965 ... Council passed the town's first Official Plan for development ... The town budget for the year consisted of expenditures of $359,988.49, revenues of $67,387.76, for a net tax levy of $292,600.73.

Wilbert A. Richards, the municipal clerk, was no longer secretary for the Board of Education, the board having formed its own administration. Mr. Richards was praised for his past faithful work as town clerk and as secretary-treasurer for the Board of Education and the Water, Light and Power Commission.

Bracebridge's Roger Crozier, goaltender for the Detroit Red Wings, was named by the Associated Press to the National Hockey League All-Star Team for the 1964-65 season.

Dr. George F. Buckley, MD, was welcomed as pathologist at South Muskoka Memorial Hospital.

Administration of the Retarded Children's School, opened in 1961, was taken over by the Bracebridge Retarded Children's Education Authority with Rev. D.A.C. Muir as chairman.

A metal safe that had been damaged by a sledgehammer and crowbar was found in the town dump by employees Leonard Goheen and Keith Snider. The owner was never found.

A week of prayer for Christian unity was held with the following clergy participating: Rev. John J. Hickey and Rev. Bernard F. Heffernan of the Roman Catholic Church; Rev. Canon R.F. Palmer and Rev. David N. Mitchell of the Anglican Church; Rev. Douglas Muir, United Church; Rev. J. Karl English, Presbyterian Church; and Rev. Clarence A. Roberts of the Baptist Church.

At the inaugural meeting of the Bracebridge Board of Education, Noel Stockton was elected chairman. Other members of the board were Wenawae Stevenson, Bob Petry, and E.S. (Ted) Boyer. School principals were Clare Prosser at the high school and Neil Haight at the public school. John Love of Glen Orchard was appointed as administrator of the two Bracebridge schools. Mr. Love was formerly secretary-treasurer of the Medora and Wood School Area Board. Bracebridge Public School had 579 registered students in September and BMLSS 1,369.

A piece of a fuselage of a Harvard Mark II World War II vintage aircraft was found in a dried-up swamp in Morrison Township. It could not be identified nor linked with the two planes reported missing from Camp Borden on December 13, 1940, which collided over Lake Muskoka near Browning Island. Only one of the four bodies was recovered.

Wilfred A. MacTavish, president of Santa's Village, advised that well over one million people had visited their facility in its nine years of operation.

Douglas Bruce, 9, suffered severe discomfort when his tongue touched the steel of the Toronto Street (Taylor Road) bridge railing on a bitter cold day. He was rescued by Clare Taplin and Mrs. Harry Knight.

Retiring fire chief Ollie Scott was honoured in a special ceremony for his 17 years of service to the Bracebridge Fire Department. He was succeeded by Harold B. Dawson.

Presidents this year included William Robertson, Bracebridge Horticultural Society; Charles Morrow, Bracebridge Agricultural Society; Mrs. W.C. Huckle, South Muskoka Association for Retarded Children, succeeding Dr. Irma Coyne; Allan G. Taylor, Kinsmen Club; Duane Miller (owner of Muskoka Laundry and Dry Cleaners), Lions Club; Rita Proulx, the St. Joseph's Catholic Woman's League, replacing Mrs. John Godin; Don Kennedy, Young Progressive Conservatives of Bracebridge, replacing Garnet Gervais; Lou Specht (news editor of the *Herald-Gazette*), Rotary Club, replacing Donald Hutton; and Ed Brazier, Royal Canadian Legion.

George Crichton retired as secretary-manager of the Muskoka Tourist Association and was replaced by Stephen Hay. John Biddle was re-elected secretary-treasurer of the Ontario Association of the Homes For the Aged. Principal C.R. Prosser of BMLSS was elected president of the Ontario Secondary School Headmaster's Council.

The Honourable Veteran's Jewel for 50 years membership with the Bracebridge Oddfellows Lodge was given to Herbert Jarvis, Alex Milne, and William Towns. Walter Trull of Draper Township was installed as Master of the Muskoka (Masonic) Lodge.

Elton (Dint) Rowe retired from the Bracebridge Fire Department after 10 years service.

The provincial government expanded the riding of Muskoka to include Baxter, Matchedash, and Tay townships along with the villages of Port McNicoll and Victoria Harbour, reported Robert J. Boyer, MPP for Muskoka and vice-chairman of Ontario Hydro. Mr. Boyer also announced the province's plan to create Arrowhead Park north of Huntsville and to build a two-storey addition to the Muskoka courthouse.

It was announced on February 15, 1965, that we had a new red and white maple leaf design flag of Canada. Getting the new Canadian flag approved was a very difficult task and heated debates took place in federal parliament and across the country. The provincial government announced plans to adopt its own flag, probably to be the Red Ensign.

Police Chief John Harrington retired from the town's police force on May 31. He had started his police career in Chatham in 1927 and moved to Bracebridge in 1948 to assume the job of chief constable. Council appointed Sergeant Colan Cowan as his successor. Constable Rod White was appointed sergeant and Nelson Kennedy was hired as a police constable. The chief's salary was set at $4,300 a year and the sergeant's at $3,900.

Council met with the Bracebridge Water, Light and Power Commission to discuss the shortage of the water supply feeding the town. It was pointed out that water consumption had increased by 50 percent between 1959 and 1964 and no further water was available from Peake's springs. James F. McLaren Ltd., engineers, presented a $1,032,000 plan to increase the capacity of the town water supply by running a transmission water main to Strawberry Point at Stephens' Bay on Muskoka Lake, a distance of 3.5 miles. Council asked the Ontario Municipal

Board for approval for the expenditure and were refused; however, through the efforts of Robert J. Boyer, MPP, the Department of Municipal Affairs offered to set aside $100,000 to assist the town in building the new water supply system. The plan for this expansion of the Bracebridge water supply was then approved.

Mr. and Mrs. Thomas Pierce retired from their hairdressing business on Manitoba Street. Patterson's Shoe Store purchased their building and moved in ... George and Jerry Brooks officially opened their new building called the Brodom Apartments ... John E. Jackson and Basil Coote opened their Bracebridge surveying office ... Wenawae's Gift Shop moved into the house at 172 Manitoba Street, previously occupied by Mr. E.T. Gervais ... Hilltop Style Centre, owned by Mr. and Mrs. Dan MacNaughtan, moved into 72 Manitoba Street ... Fred Moulton sold his electrical business to Harold B. Dawson ... Gordon Motor Sales appointed Allan Taylor as service manager. Mr. Taylor moved his business, Taylor Auto Electric, to Gordon Motor Sales with the appointment ... George South opened a chiropractic office ... Mr. and Mrs. Jack Johnston sold Aston Villa Resort to Henry J. Herbert ... William Stegelmeier opened his custom tailoring shop ... Gravenhurst Cable System installed cable television service ... Bob Pain purchased Dot's Tot to Teen Shop from Dot and Doug Sieber ... Norman Shill was appointed manager of the Toronto Dominion Bank, succeeding Robert W. Pack ... Les Rosewarne sold Bracebridge Garage to Seth Grimes and Son, and Lorne Purdy sold his drugstore business to Don Pollard ... Lawyer E.P. Lee announced that Allan Russell Black joined his law firm ... Bracebridge Latex Factory, makers of rubber gloves, closed due to staff difficulties ... Banks Bros. TV & Appliances, owned by Doug, Don, and Glen Banks, celebrated its first anniversary ... Ron Wilson, manager of Bracebridge Manufacturing, announced the building of an addition to their present structure, formerly the location of the Muskoka Foundry ... the official opening took place of the new Brewer's Retail store adjacent to the Dominion Store parking lot on Manitoba Street. Historically, this was were Mr. John Beal, first recorded resident of Bracebridge, homesteaded in 1859.

In response to a request made by Mr. Fred Hammell and Dr. William Monk from the Bracebridge Public Library Board, Council passed a resolution that a grant of $10,000 be made towards the renovations of the library as a Canada Centennial project.

Among the many deaths recorded this year were Jean Elizabeth Campbell, due to injuries received when struck by a car at the same time her husband Gordon was killed ... Dr. Ryan, DDS, former councillor, mayor, championship lacrosse player, and community supporter ... Louis Joseph L. Caisse, third generation barber in his family in Bracebridge ... Edward J. Ball, former superintendent of the Water, Light and Power Commission and town employee for 43 years ... William Henry Brazier, WWI veteran ... Dr. Roy H. Thomas ... Robert Patterson, owner of the Patterson Shoe Store on Manitoba Street ... Mrs. George Tibbel, mother of Mary McPherson ... Albert

*Bracebridge-born goaltender Roger Crozier made a spectacular debut with the Detroit Red Wings in the 1964-65 season, winning the Calder Trophy as NHL Rookie-of-the-Year. He later starred with the Buffalo Sabres.*
COURTESY OF BRACEBRIDGE CULTURE AND RECREATION

*"Okay, Gary, see if it'll start now!" In the spring of 1965 Bracebridge youngsters Gary and Barbara Long examine an old tractor on an abandoned farm north of town. Considerable land around Bracebridge was by Muskoka standards well suited for farming. Agriculture was a vital component of the local economy from the 1860s to the 1880s, and although its relative economic importance steadily declined after that, the farming community remained an integral element of the local social fabric for many more decades. A century after settlement began in the area, only a handful of the original farms survived, invariably those on the very best sites. The prominent outcrop of precambrian bedrock gneiss protruding in the background of this picture explains why many farmers gave up trying to make a living from tilling the "soil."* COURTESY OF MARILYN LONG

Alexander Fry ... Edith Florence Dunn ... Fred Anderson ... Richard Nye ... John Henry Hines ... Leslie Black ... Captain John Ariss, a skipper of the *Segwun* for 33 years ... Frederick Hind ... Walter Harper ... Mabel Florence Naismith ... Mrs. T. Wingate Topp ... Joanna Bennett ... Brian Joseph Haight ... Jessie (Mrs. George) Peacock ... Robert Ethbert Joyce, MD ... Sarah (Mrs. John) Kirkness ... Frank Lazzara ... Hugh William Lee ... John E. Leishman ... Jerome Mauro ... James Wesley Johnson, 81, having been in poor health for some time due to being gassed during service in World War I ... Mrs. Robert Taylor ... Alvin Tupper ... Elmer Emerson Smith.

Special guests at the 17th annual Bracebridge Skating Club Revue included Doug Leigh of the Toronto Cricket Club and Terry Fahlgren of North Bay. President Muriel Gibbs was credited with having one of the best skating carnivals ever.

Mrs. R.A.C. Wilson, RN, was appointed supervisor of nurses at the South Muskoka Memorial Hospital, replacing the retiring Elizabeth Fraser, RN.

Mrs. Thomas Marriott was granted the Decoration of Chivalry for her service to the cause of benevolence and good citizenship through her involvement with the Snow Queen Rebekah Lodge.

Toronto Street (now Taylor Road) was rebuilt and Highway 532 (now Ecclestone Drive) resurfaced.

Robert E. Jefferies was elected commander of District E of the Ontario Provincial Command of the Royal Canadian Legion ... Norman Miners Jr. was awarded the Bushman's Thong and Clark Hooton the Queen's Scout Certificate at the annual Boy Scout meeting.

Roger Crozier, goaltender for the Detroit Red Wings, was named to the NHL dream team for the 1964-65 season and won the Calder Memorial Trophy as the outstanding rookie of the year.

Alex Milne was recognized for his many years of hard work as district coordinator for the Muskoka District Fire Aid Association. His successor was Harold B. Dawson.

Aubrey Street residents celebrated the 10th anniversary of their annual fireworks display with Harry Lidstone and Norman Miners Sr. in charge. Duffy Fraser and Gerry Short contributed ice cream and popsicles for the children.

Bill Olimer of Bracebridge won three events at the International Fiddling Championships held in Pembroke, Ontario, and in the fiddling contest at the 72nd annual Coldwater Fair. Bill and Rudy Meeks also competed.

Art Dickson, former Bracebridge Bears hockey star, left Northern Planing Mill after 15 years to work for the Ontario Provincial Police.

Council applied to the Ontario Municipal Board for approval for the expenditure of $270,000 to build a new vocational wing at BMLSS, provided the provincial government contributed $102,000.

New officers of the Centennial Committee were Ted Gervais (chairman), Ron Harrison, Jackie Fenton, Basil Reid, John Biddle, Fred Hammell, Bill Quemby, Mrs. Chris Forth, Fred Klie, and Clara Robertson.

Fire destroyed the 65-year-old poultry exhibit building at Jubilee Park.

A cairn was erected at the High Falls Park to honour Aubrey White, formerly of Bracebridge, in recognition of his contribution to the development of Ontario. Mr. White had been the deputy minister of Lands, Forests and Mines from 1887 to 1915. Prior to that he had been Crown land agent for Muskoka and superintendent of Algonquin Park. Coming to Bracebridge as a teenager from Ireland, he worked at Alexander Bailey's store, the A.P. Dodge Lumber Co., which was harvesting white pine in Muskoka, and then with A.P. Cockburn where he became the captain of a steamboat on Muskoka Lake. After moving to Toronto to work with the government, he kept his cottage on Chief Island on Muskoka Lake, where he died on July 14, 1915. He was credited with having set up Ontario's forest fire protection system and was elected as Grand Master of the Masonic Lodge for Ontario.

The Rotary Fair again featured long-time favourite magician John Giordmaine. The second annual Muskoka Arts and Crafts show was held in Memorial Park.

Graduating BMLSS students David Mitchell, Sandra Burt, and Malcolm Stockton received Ontario Scholarships.

Muskoka District Veterinarian Hugh Smith was appointed acting director of the Regional Veterinarian Laboratory in Brighton. He was succeeded by Dr. S.A. Penzvalto.

Prime Minister Lester B. Pearson called a federal election for November 8, 1965. In Parry Sound-Muskoka, Gordon Aiken, the Conservative MP, was elected for a fifth term over Liberal Charles Barnett and New Democratic Hugh Bishop.

Harold A. Rogers, OBE, founder of the Association of Kinsmen Clubs in 1920, and his wife Elspeth attended the installation ceremonies of the Bracebridge Kinsmen and Kinette Clubs.

The Muskoka Cavalcade of Colour held their Tagwagi Show at the Bracebridge and Muskoka Lakes Secondary School auditorium. Carole Dinner was selected as Miss Bracebridge, succeeding Donna Mae Hillman. Miss Dinner would go on to become Miss Hidden Valley and Miss Muskoka, succeeding Peggy Ann Brown.

The body of a 5-year-old from Scarborough was found strangled in a cottage near Fraserburg. Constable Lyle Terry of the OPP investigated and a charge of capital murder was laid.

Over 6,000 attended the seventh annual Auto, Boat and Home Show at the Memorial Community Centre.

In a referendum, Sunday movies and Sunday sports were approved.

**1966** Tourism was changing from a resort-oriented clientele to a cottage owning one and was becoming a more significant economic engine for Muskoka, evidenced by more traffic congestion and restlessness in the merchant community as they changed to accommodate new shopping demands. The 1966 municipal budget required a tax levy of $305,670.94. Council purchased the street light system from the Bracebridge Water, Light and Power Commission at a cost of $8,173.35. The value of new buildings built from January 1 to October 30 was $1,893,675.

Council asked the Ontario Municipal Board to approve a debenture for $50,000 for an eight-room addition to the Bracebridge and Muskoka Lakes Secondary School vocational wing, itself only three years old, to accommodate a rapidly growing enrollment.

Kenneth C. Veitch of the Bank of Nova Scotia in Hamilton, born in Ufford, was appointed new deputy clerk for the Town of Bracebridge. He started April 1, 1966, and through the position of deputy clerk, then municipal clerk-administrator until his retirement in 1996, he did not miss a regular meeting of the Bracebridge Council. By his staff and many of the residents he was referred to as "Father Town."

The Bracebridge Lions Club donated $6,000 to the South Muskoka Memorial Hospital for the purchase of portable x-ray equipment.

Ron Jupp, Huntsville, was elected chairman of the Muskoka District Home for the Aged, replacing Jack Johnson.

The many deaths this year included Charles Thomas Peacock … Shadrach W.L. Kaye … William T. Ireland … Ernest Gibbs … Edith Jane (Mrs. Clark) Freeman, eldest daughter of pioneer Bracebridge postmaster Robert E. Perry … John Charles Hickey … Anne Lea Roberts and William Lea Roberts (husband and wife, both died on the same day) … Margaret Larrett and Herbert Larrett (husband and wife, died one day apart) … Mrs. Austin McCann … Harry Wilson … Ella May (Mrs. Ernest E.) Boyd … Alfred Edward Fry … John H. Willmott … Thomas Ernest McMurray … Bartley D. Campbell, MD … Emma Louise (Mrs. James) Lowe … Mrs. Francis Tough … Frederick Ricard Sr. … Francis Joseph McGarry … Mrs. Harry Bennett … James Harvey Anderson … Dr. Roy Huggard … Louis Stone, father of Phil Stone, owner of long-time business Stone's Men's Wear … Eliza (Mrs. Elijah) Veitch, grandmother of Kenneth C. Veitch … Louis Francis Fowler … Dr. E.G. Ellis … John Thomas George Fry … Robert Joseph Patterson … Adelaide Dora (Mrs. James Albert) Crockford … Lloyd Thomas (Shorty) Crozier … Charles L. Stark … Ellen May (Mrs. John) Nichols … Dr. Fraser McMurray Greig … Jessie (Mrs. Edward) Arnott … E. Walter Clairmont … Myrtle May Woodroffe … Thomas John Kerr … Henry Wesley McEown … Alexander Bedford Taylor … Constance Flora (Mrs. James R.) Elliott … Elizabeth (Mrs. John Francis) Fenn … Miss Barbara Gertrude Beaumont … Captain William D. Tinkiss … Ruth Elizabeth Thomas … Margaret Elaine Everett … Mrs. William Hammond … Edith May (Mrs. Arthur Thomas) Waite … Maxine (Mrs. Louis) Jacobs … Albert Nelson Patterson.

A dispute raged during the year between those merchants who wanted to close their retail businesses on Mondays and stay open all day Wednesdays, and those who wanted to continue to stay open Mondays and close half days on Wednesdays. The majority of stores decided to close on Mondays and stay open all day on Wednesdays, summer months excluded.

Keith's Market Garden was broken into and robbed for the third time and again two weeks later.

Direct distance dialing was introduced by Bell Canada at the Bracebridge exchange.

Accolades included: George W. Boyer, recognized for his many years of service to the United Church as Clerk of the Session ... The Hollingworth family, for their faithful work in keeping the official records of the weather for over 90 years, spanning four generations ... William Raaflaub, George W. Boyer, and Stan Darling (Burks Falls), all recognized for their long service to the Bracebridge Agricultural Society.

Allan G. Taylor was elected as Zone F, District 8 deputy governor for the Association of Kinsmen Clubs ... Elizabeth Fraser, retired director of nurses and Cordelia Willmott, retired head nurse of the maternity ward, were honoured by the South Muskoka Memorial Hospital medical staff for their long and dedicated service ...William Inch and William Fraser retired from the Bracebridge Water, Light and Power Commission after long service ... John Martin was appointed a new constable for the Bracebridge Police Department.

Muskoka District Council, under President Robert Pfrumpter, approved of a plan to do an area-wide local provincially authorized government survey.

Untimely deaths are always difficult to accept and Bracebridge had more than its share in 1966. John Robert Maki of the OPP was shot and killed by an inmate patient that he was escorting ... Harry Ashcroft, 14, of Etobicoke drowned in Bracebridge Bay ... Margaret Everett, 16, drowned in the Muskoka River ... John Hickey, 19, died after being hit by a car as he walked along Highway 11.

One of the oldest industrial buildings in town still standing, the Shier Building Centre Planning Mill, was destroyed by a managed fire by the Bracebridge fire brigade and the tallest town landmark, the 150-foot tower that stood behind the OPP station on the south side of Dominion Street, was lowered.

Train fare from Bracebridge to Toronto was advertised at $3.10 one way.

Redmond Thomas, QC, retired as Magistrate of Muskoka after 28 years and was replaced by Douglas George Bice.

Orvil Hammond of Hammond's Ambulance Service and James Thwaites of Muskoka Ambulance Service appeared before the municipal Council representing the Muskoka Ambulance Association and demanded that a subsidy be paid to them by Council in the amount of $1,088 ($544 each) or else they would withdraw their ambulance service from the residents of Bracebridge. Because Council had no idea it was going to be asked for a subsidy from these private companies, and because it had already set tax rates for the year, Council rejected the request. Following the termination date, ambulance service for Bracebridge residents was provided through the courtesy of Earle Rosewarne of Muskoka Garage, who made a station wagon available for ambulance calls, and councillor Norman Harkness, assisted by staff who served as attendants. Eventually Council agreed to pay a subsidy of $303.60 to the operators. A resolution was passed thanking Earle Rosewarne for his cooperation in providing the town with ambulance service when needed. The problem was finally resolved when the provincial government provided financial relief to ambulance operators.

John Christensen was elected chairman of the South Muskoka Memorial Hospital Board. Mrs. E.V. (Timmy) Allchin was elected president of the Chamber of Commerce, Lyle Cathcart president of the Lions Club, Sharon Crockford president of the Kinettes, Jerry Brooks president of Rotary, Ivan Beasley president of the Kinsman Club, and Leonard George was elected Master of the Muskoka (Masonic) Lodge.

Roger Crozier won the Conn Smythe Award as the most valuable player in the Stanley Cup Playoffs.

Doug Graham purchased Thatcher Studio from Ed and Laura Thatcher.

The 12th of July parade of the Loyal Orange Lodge was held in Bracebridge with 33 Lodges taking part.

*As baby-boomers hit Bracebridge Public School full force in the 1960s, classes bulged to as many as 40 students. Miss Mae McCracken, with four decades experience as a teacher, took it all in stride. This was 1967, centennial year; students were encouraged to dress in a historical theme, but the only one to do so was Nancy Cox (one of the co-authors of this book).* Front row (left to right): *Stephen Rowe, George Boyer, Bob Connor, Norman Miller, Marc Knowles, Ross Copeland, Rob Jones, Steven Watson;* Second row: *Barbara Webb, Heather Fraser, Laurie Suter, Lee Anne Poland, Wendy Etler, Janice Giaschi, Nancy Black, Jayne Smith, Loisanne Lee, Nancy Rosewarne;* Third row: *Nancy Cox, Laura Klie, Bonnie Kennedy, Cathy Thomas, Cathy Miles, Janice Learoyd, Melinda Cuthbert, Robin Specht, Valerie MacGregor, Lynn Traves, Karen Gray;* Back row: *Christopher Freeland, Lyle Habermehl, Don Sugg, Gary Long, Cathy Sugg, Jacquie Harper, Jerry Lawson, Greg Slatter, David Brooks, Guy Simmons.* COURTESY OF GARY LONG

The entire community was shocked and saddened when 10-year-old Kenneth Chisholm, only child of Mr. and Mrs. John Chisholm, and Charles Peacock, only son of Mr. and Mrs. Alvin Peacock, died in a tunnel cave-in in a gully along Charles Street.

Don Hollingworth, co-owner of Bracebridge Chainsaw and Marine, received serious head injuries while road testing a motorcycle. Council passed a resolution asking the Minister of Transport to require drivers of motorcycles to wear helmets.

The town was asked by the Bracebridge Merchants' Committee to demolish part of the abandoned Bird Woollen Mill, established in 1872, to create a downtown parking lot. Council agreed, and also sold the Bird Woollen Mill warehouse to H.J. Brooks and Sons for $3,000. The latter building, built in the 1918, now contains the Bird Mill Mews and Chamber of Commerce Visitor Centre.

Corning Glass Works of Canada started construction on a 130,000-square-foot manufacturing plant for making television picture tubes. Maurice G. Locklin was named as manager. At the announcement press conference, Mayor George A. Parlett, Robert J. Boyer, MPP, and Gordon Aiken, MP, all expressed a sincere welcome to Corning. At a meeting of town residents, 44 people signed a guarantee to assure the construction of 20 new homes that would be available for incoming Corning staff.

The pioneer building that housed the Women's Institute rest rooms and the office of Dr. E.G. Ellis on Manitoba Street was demolished for the construction of a parking lot. During the demolition, two 1874 newspapers were found in the walls.

The rifle range in the Armouries (part of the old post office, in 1999 owned by Robert Burton), was renovated into a coin laundry ... Wilbur Anderson closed his business, Anderson's Store (dry goods), and sold his building to Banks Bros. TV & Appliances ... Aston Fairways started construction on their new golf course ... Russell H. (Chub) Downey, president of Bracebridge Dairy, announced the purchase of Lake Drive Dairy. It had been owned at one time by Thomas Ball, who had sold it to Ivan Keall, Frank McNabb, and Charles McNabb in 1955. Bracebridge Dairy had been purchased by Mr. Downey and his brother, Kenneth, from Fred Lee in 1947 ... John Morra, owner of the Deluxe Barber Shop, 66 Manitoba Street, retired and sold his business to Ernest Chartrand.

Donald C. Kirkpatrick was appointed manager of the Canada Manpower office in Bracebridge.

Rev. Alfred J. Milligan was appointed minister of the First Baptist Church ... Bracebridge welcomed the Most Rev. Michael Ramsey, Archbishop of Canterbury, and Mrs. Ramsey. The guests toured the chapel and monastery of the Society of St. John the Evangelist ... Efforts were made to financially help "The Place," a controversial weekend dance and drop-in centre for teens under the aegis of the Society of St. John the Evangelist ... Knox Presbyterian Church celebrated its 100th anniversary. The minister in this year was Rev. J. Karl English ... Work began on the new St. Joseph Roman Catholic Church replacing the existing 87-year-old church building.

Although Bracebridge regularly experienced heavy weekend traffic on Highway 11, the longest line of stopped and slow-moving traffic ever seen occurred on the Labour Day weekend of 1966. Southbound traffic was at a standstill from Huntsville to Severn Bridge. The OPP were busy keeping the traffic moving, but it was not without its humour. Sergeant R.A.C. Wilson reported that one man jumped out of his stopped vehicle to get ice cream cones at a roadside store and instructed his wife to keep their place in the lineup. When he returned, the traffic had moved and his wife and vehicle were nowhere to be seen. The man went to the police office to report the problem and around midnight a phone call was received there from his wife, who was looking for him. She had driven all the way home to Toronto and had to return to Bracebridge that night to pick him up.

The reconstructed Vankoughnet development road through Draper Township was opened and work on the balance of the road through to Haliburton continued.

John Baker, Bracebridge's oldest citizen, celebrated his 100th birthday. Karen McCaskie was selected Miss Bracebridge for 1966.

Fifteen local citizens, led by Danny Poland, formed a committee to raise money to replace the 3.5 miles of refrigeration piping in the floor of the Bracebridge Memorial Community Centre. One of the fund raisers was watching the Grey Cup and a Boston Bruin hockey game starring Bobby Orr on the new technology of colour television.

A new law requiring vehicles travelling in both directions to stop when encountering school buses with their lights flashing was passed provincially.

The Children's Aid Society welcomed Peter Malton as its new social worker.

An auction sale was held at Bigwin Inn, at one time one of Muskoka's most prestigious holiday resorts.

Noel Stockton, Robert Petry, and Dr. Robert M. Drake were defeated in their attempt to get elected to the Board of Education. Elected were Dr. Lyle Black, Norman Rosewarne, Shirley Shier, and Robert J. McCrank. Gaye Anderson was named an Ontario Scholar.

Frank J. Henry and Guy B. Waite were re-elected to the Bracebridge Water, Light and Power Commission.

Election expenses in the amount of $105 were approved. Election staff consisted of Kenneth C. Veitch, Velma Flynn, Cecil W. Dickie, Sadie Crockford, and Jessie Dunn. Katherine Beers became the first woman to serve on Bracebridge municipal council. She was acclaimed along with Duane Miller and Norman A. Harkness. Carl Sander and James Stevenson retired.

The program for greeting the New Year and the 100th anniversary of the Confederation of Canada was advertised as a Centennial Parade on January 1, a New Year's Eve ringing of bells, and a reception on New Year's Day in the public school auditorium.

1967 The celebration of Canada's 100th anniversary of Confederation occupied much of this year's activities. Festivities abounded throughout the town. There were parades, fireworks, old fashioned costume contests, picnics, a homecoming week, Confederation caravans, Armed Services displays, and many other such events. All were well attended as the residents of the area were eager to celebrate their country's centennial.

H.E.S. (Bert) Sugg donated a Canadian flag to be flown from the flag pole in front of the town office and the Business and Professional Women's Club made a gift of a Centennial flag to the town.

The 1967 budget provided for expenditures of \$433,846.82 with revenues of \$80,000, resulting in a tax levy of \$353,846.82.

Leaders included John Evans, president of the BMLSS Student Council ... Frank Denniss, Master of Loyal Orange Lodge No. 218 ... Danny Culos, president of the Kinsmen for their 20th anniversary ... Lola Hart, president of the Kinette Club ... Mrs. John Newark, president of the Business and Professional Women's Club.

*The Bird Woollen Mill as it appeared in the 1870s. Henry Bird lived with his family on the top floor until he constructed Woodchester Villa in 1882.* COURTESY OF ARCHIVES OF ONTARIO ACC. 15963-23

The Bracebridge Lions Club celebrated its 25th anniversary and held their first steak barbecue in Annie Williams Park under the chairmanship of Phil Keppler.

Brad Jackson, son of Mr. and Mrs. Ernie Jackson, won the Southern Ontario Ski Zone D class race at the Oshawa Ski Club with Rip Pridday coming fourth.

The Bank of Montreal opened in the Reg Billingsley building on Manitoba Street ... George A. McLeod opened his accounting office at 187 Manitoba with Sharon Veitch as his assistant ... The Muskoka Real Estate Board was formed in this year ... Edgar Fraser took over Thompson's Barber Shop ... McEwan Industries started operations in Bracebridge to construct 50 newly designed potato harvesters ... Gordon Motor Sales celebrated moving into their new premises on Ball's Flats ... Dr. O.R.J. Savijarvi opened his dental clinic on Dominion Street ... Banks Bros. TV & Appliances moved into new premises ... The official opening of Ernie Colson's Supertest was held ... Mr. and Mrs. Henry Seto opened The New Haven restaurant at the former location of the Coach Light Restaurant ... Herbert Stewart purchased Garwood's Mens and Ladies Wear from Roy Garwood ... Parlett Transport moved to their new location on Highway 532 ...The Wells Motel was sold by Mr. and Mrs. Onni Niskanen to Garnet Gilbert and Morris Topping ... Ken Keith sold Keith's Market Garden to Raymond G. Lee, Murray I. Lee, and D. John Hartnett. The name of the business was changed to Top Valu Food Market ... Reynolds Funeral Home was sold by Walter Reynolds to Murray A. Dauphin ... The Thomas Block, built by the late G.H.O. Thomas in 1929, was sold to H.E.S. (Bert) Sugg ... Bracebridge Dairy was sold to Briars Dairy Ltd. ... A.E. Lepage Ltd., one of Canada's largest and oldest real estate firms, opened their regional office in town with Arthur Jennings as manager.

Crown attorney W. Alan Newell was elected president of the Muskoka Children's Aid Society ... E.S. (Ted) Boyer was elected chairman of the Board of Education ... L.T. (Bud) Walsh was appointed the new Canada Manpower manager ... Rev. J.H. Wilson was appointed pastor of Pinegrove Baptist Church.

Ice on Muskoka Lake was only four inches thick in mid-January but Mrs. E.A. Robinson, Milford Bay, official weather observer for the Department of Transport, advised that in the third week of January the temperature dropped from a high of 45°F to a low of -36°F. The snowfall for the winter of 1966-67 was 124.6 inches.

Clerk-treasurer Wibert Richards retired in June after 31 years in the position. He was clerk-treasurer from 1936 to 1967 following Alexander Salmon, 1898-1936, and James Boyer, 1875-1898. Mr. Richards had also served as councillor 1927-31 and mayor 1932-36. He was presented with a mantle clock at a retirement party in his honour. Mr. Kenneth C. Veitch, 27, was appointed as the fourth municipal clerk in Bracebridge's history, and the youngest. It was a position he would hold until retirement in 1996.

Deaths this year included Fred Sander, former livery stable operator, one of the first jitney service providers, and a former chief of police for Bracebridge ... Gordon Knowles ... Percy V. Brazier ... Thomas I. Fenn ... Mrs. Harry Dryland ... Joseph Nicholson ... John Golden ... William Edwin Dixon ... Joseph Fenn ... Reuben E. MacNaughtan ... Ineze Elizabeth Althea Dunn ... William Robert Peacock ... Violet Simpson (Mrs. Roy A.) Shier ... Frank Crozier, to name only a few.

The community was saddened by the Muskoka River drowning death of 2-year-old Dominic Malton, son of Mr. and Mrs. Peter Malton.

Hawn's Jewelers on Manitoba Street was the victim of a smash-and-grab robbery, losing 66 rings and 29 watches. On one weekend there was a rash of break-ins involving Bill Little's Texaco Service Station, The Golden Hour Jewelry Shop, and the Royal Canadian Legion. The Canadian Tire Store on Manitoba Street was broken into seven times between February and June.

The life of Peter Terry was saved by his brother Alex, (sons of Mr. and Mrs. Sterling Terry of Clear Lake), after Peter went through the ice on Big Wind Lake and having his snow machine fail when he tried to get home. Alex went looking for him and after a lengthy and difficult rescue got him to hospital.

The Mawdsley property along the Muskoka River on the east side of Wellington Street, purchased by Robert Mawdsley in 1880, was sold to Robmac Estates (Shier Lumber) for a housing development.

Two pioneer landmark buildings were destroyed in this year. First, the final chapter of the Bird Woollen Mill was written when the Bracebridge Fire Department set a controlled fire in the 95-year-old abandoned building to make way for a parking lot. Second, the stone jail behind the Town Hall, built by John Baker in 1904, was purchased by H.E.S. (Bert) Sugg and demolished to make a parking lot behind his legal office. In 1999, part of the jail's stone wall can be seen defining the side of the Sugg, Fitton & Taylor legal office parking lot along the side of Trader's Lane. Prior to the building of the stone jail, the "lock-up" was located in a corner of the basement of the Herald Building at the corner of Trader's Lane (now Robert J. Boyer Lane) and Dominion Street.

Jack Johnson, reeve of Monck Township, was elected chairman of the study committee for the Muskoka Local Government Review, and Donald Patterson was appointed by the Hon. J.W. Spooner, Minister of Munici-

*March 1965: within little more than a decade after it closed, the Bird Woollen Mill has become a ruin, roof collapsed, windows broken, masonry walls crumbling.*
COURTESY OF MARILYN LONG

pal Affairs for Ontario, as the research director. Several meetings were held throughout this year between the research director, the municipal councils of Muskoka, and other interested parties with respect to the future of local government in the district. The cost of the review was $80,000.

The clock purchased for the original Town Hall in 1880 was again placed in the municipal office. It and the council chamber chairs were the only items rescued from the Town Hall fire of December 12, 1957. The clock was restored and repaired by the late Dr. R.J. Dodds.

Don Hollingworth, recuperating at the Workmen's Compensation Hospital from a serious head injury resulting from a motorcycle accident, was again injured when he had to jump from a second-storey window because of a fire in the hospital.

Bob Spence was elected president of the Bracebridge Minor Hockey Association following E.S. (Ted) Boyer and A.M. (Tony) Jackson. Others on the executive were W.P. (Biff) Shier, Ken Shier, Douglas Duff, Elroy Terry, Elwood Kirkpatrick, Roy Tennant, Wayne Scott, and Donald Simmons.

The official opening of the Centennial project children's library addition to the library building was held with the following participating: Fred Hammell (chairman), Reg Kirk, Gordon Aiken, MP, Robert J. Boyer, MPP, Mayor George Parlett, Linda Sieber, Sharon Raeburn, and Margaret Mitchell.

Robert Spence was appointed a constable with the police department.

The Ontario Hydro Electric Commission unveiled a plaque at the Bracebridge powerhouse in honour of Bracebridge's contribution to electric power development in Ontario.

Jerry Brooks was elected president of the Rotary Club.

The Bracebridge town clock in the tower of the old post office building was restored as a centennial project by Dan MacNaughtan, public works foreman, the Bracebridge Chamber of Commerce, and the owner of the building, Mr. Bob Burton. The pleasant sound of the clock chiming the hour again was well received by those in the Manitoba Street downtown area.

Jessie Tenant and Ruth Marks, residents of Aubrey Street, appeared as a delegation before Council to complain about the children's playground that had been built by the Kinsmen Club on a vacant lot near their residences. Five other residents of Aubrey Street also appeared and made a presentation in support of keeping the playground in its present location. William Quemby and Danny Culos of the Kinsmen Club also attended the meeting. The playground was eventually removed, the property sold, and a senior citizens apartment building constructed thereon.

Basil Reid and Fred Hammell of the Centennial Committee appeared before Council and revealed a plan to construct a lighted fountain on a property owned by Reg Kirk at the corner of Manitoba Street and McMurray Street. Timmy (Mrs. Ernie) Allchin was instrumental in creating the plans for the fountain.

The following deaths were recorded: Sarah (Mrs. William) Kay ... Murray Secord ... Tom Mataija ... Nelson Huntley ... George Frederick Tibbell ... Arthur Leeder ... Roy Cowan ... Frederick Pickles ... Melvin Vincent ... Lillian White ... Harry Bird ... James Alfred Ewing ... Ada Jane (Mrs. Frank) Morris ... Elijah Veitch ... William Edward Bailey ... Fred J. Burridge ... Walter Smith ... Fenton Patterson ... Walter Finch ... Russel Kuhns ... Dr. Frederick Robert Shuttleworth ... Josephine Elizabeth (Mrs. George E.) Taylor ... Mary Caroline (Mrs. Robert) Pain ... Roy James Gilman.

His Excellency, the Most Rev. Benjamin Webster, Bishop of Peterborough, conducted the blessing for the new St. Joseph's Catholic Church. The first Mass had been celebrated previously, conducted by Rev. John Hickey. The First Baptist Church celebrated its 82nd anniversary.

Her Royal Highness Princess Alexandra and her husband, the Honourable Angus Ogilvie, landed at Muskoka Airport for a three-day Muskoka holiday.

Lee Merrill won the Miss Bracebridge title.

In the provincial election Robert J. Boyer won the Muskoka riding for the Progressive Conservative Party with 6,458 votes, compared to Lloyd Carstairs for the Liberal Party with 2,001 and Earl Heiber for the New Democratic Party with 1,959.

W.J. Wright, MD, chairman of the Centennial Committee, was awarded an Upjohn Post-Graduate Study Award at the annual meeting of the College of Family Practice.

The body of baby a few days old was found in the Draper garbage dump with a shoelace tied around its neck. In spite of an intensive search no trace of its parents or its murderer was ever found.

With Robert Jones as manager, Junior C hockey returned to Bracebridge with the Shier Lumber Kings.

Mayor George Parlett and H.W. Royl, president of Canada Foils Ltd., officially announced the company's intention to construct a 50,000-square-foot aluminum casting facility employing 50 to 60 people in Bracebridge.

Don Boyer and Austin Hunt were acclaimed to the Water, Light and Power Commission.

Shirley Shier, a trustee with the Bracebridge Board of Education, was elected as a director of the Ontario Urban and Rural School Trustees Association.

Mr. Fred Hammell, school inspector since 1959, was informed by the Department of Education that the English text book *Ideas into Words* which he co-authored had been approved for use in elementary schools.

E.S. (Ted) Boyer, Robert McCrank, and Ross Watt were acclaimed to the Board of Education. The premier of Ontario, John Robarts, advised the Board that they would be part of an integrated board within 13 months.

*On the slopes at Rainbow Ridge. The three men on the right are Don Coates, Syd Martin, and Ken Veitch.*
COURTESY OF KEN VEITCH

## 1968

It was a year of transition in local government as the town applied to annex parts of the surrounding townships to allow more growth. The Local Government Review moved slowly through a public process aimed at reorganizing the form of municipal government in Muskoka and the shape of its constituent municipalities.

The town budget was set at $460,663.39 for expenditures resulting in a net levy after revenues of $367,555.39. At the request of Monck Township, permission was granted for Monck Public School to connect to the Bracebridge sewer system.

It was in this year that the Town of Bracebridge started talking seriously about annexing parts of the surrounding townships in order to provide space for industrial and commercial expansion. It was obviously necessary because, while the Corning Glass Co. and Canada Foils Ltd. decided to build their manufacturing plants in Bracebridge, in fact they had to build in the surrounding townships close to the Bracebridge border because there was no space within the town boundaries to accommodate their needs. The Bracebridge Planning Board and the Board of Education had discussions with Town Council about the expansion of the boundaries and a resolution was passed by Council asking surveyors Fitzmaurice and Boyer to prepare a legal description of concessions 9 to 13 of Muskoka Township, those parts of Macaulay and Draper townships lying west of the present Highway 11 and south of the extension of the northern limits of the Town of Bracebridge, as well as lot 1, concession A and lots 1-3 on concessions 1 and 2 in Monck Township. It was later amended to include those sections of Monck lying west and south of Highway 118 to Lake Muskoka to the road allowance between conces-

*The original St. Joseph's Roman Catholic Church on McMurray Street was built in 1879; in 1966 it was replaced by the present structure – quite a contrast in design styles.* COURTESY OF MARILYN LONG

sions 4 and 5. Project Planning Associates were engaged to complete an annexation survey. The Township of Draper wrote the town authorizing the consultants to inspect their record and Corning Glass advised the town of their opposition to the annexation. Bylaw 1339 authorizing the annexation process was passed by the Council and the Ontario Municipal Board set the hearing for April 29, 1968. A decision on the application, however, was never made by the Board. In total, four hearing dates were set, each adjourned for minor reasons; the last one being to wait for the outcome of the Muskoka District Local Government Review.

Council passed a bylaw limiting the number of taxicabs allowed to operate in town to 10, on condition they provide 24-hour service, at the request of Bracebridge Taxi and Duff's Taxi.

Harold Dawson resigned from the position of fire chief in November. Mrs. Alick Cave was appointed Librarian succeeding Mrs. Sherman Tough.

Ken Black of the Bracebridge Recreation Committee convinced Council to establish a tennis court on the back parking lot of BMLSS. This was the first public court in Bracebridge. Another first for Bracebridge this year was the construction of the first townhouse development, located between Toronto Street (now Taylor Road) and Highway 118.

Margaret Mitchell, 17, daughter of Rev. and Mrs. David Mitchell, and Sandra Moore, daughter of Mr. and Mrs. Cecil G. Moore, were awarded Ontario Scholarships.

Council authorized the closing of a 10-foot-wide lane that led from Manitoba Street to the parking lot behind the Ecclestone Hardware building. This historic laneway had been used for the delivery of freight by horse and wagon and actually ran right through the middle of the hardware store.

Mr. W. Alan Newell received the designation of Queen's Counsel after having served as Crown Attorney since 1960, replacing the late Kenneth A. Mahaffy.

John B. Biddle was elected as Master of the Muskoka Masonic Lodge.

Flight Lieutenant Allan Lomas, CD, was awarded the Centennial Medal for distinguished service to the Canadian Armed Forces.

Mayor George Parlett, on behalf of the town, received a centennial plaque from the Ontario Centennial Committee in recognition of the contribution of community leaders to the 100 years of confederation. Reeve Jack Johnson of Monck Township and Mary McCracken received Centennial Medals.

E.S. (Ted) Boyer of Aubrey Street was re-elected chairman of the Bracebridge Board of Education in this, the last year of the Board's existence before becoming part of the new Muskoka District Board.

Robin Knowles, 14, daughter of Stan and Doris Knowles, won first place at the Southern Ontario Ski Zone D Class meet at Peterborough. She also came first for the girls and Rip Pridday came first for the boys in the slalom events at the Georgian Bay Secondary School Ski Meet held in Collingwood. The Bracebridge and Muskoka Lakes Secondary School boy's team came first and the girl's team came second out of 11 teams competing. Other competitors from BMLSS were Jane Jenkins, Kathy Carnall, Betty Ann Jackson, Larry Miller, Steven Boothby, and Brad Jackson … BMLSS captured the Muskoka-Parry Sound Junior Boys District basketball championship … The Bracebridge Bears Intermediate C hockey team eliminated Parry Sound and Powassan in the Ontario playoffs … Also this year the Rainbow Ridge Ski Team won the Rainbow Ridge-Toronto Summitt Martin Trophy Challenge Race.

Bracebridge-born hockey star Irvine "Ace" Bailey of the Toronto Maple Leafs restored the use of his number "6" for the use of Leaf player Ron Ellis. It had been retired after the near-fatal career-ending injury he received, inflicted by Boston's Eddie Shore.

The Knox Presbyterian Church made the final payment on the mortgage for their building renovations. James A. Thomson was appointed minister, a position he would hold with distinction for 28 years.

The Bank of Montreal installed a clock on a pedestal in front of their office on Manitoba Street, believed by manager Dwight Dillabough to be the first branch of their bank to have such an installation in Ontario.

Don Beacock was appointed constable for the Bracebridge Police Department. Doug Duff resigned from the Ontario Provincial Police and purchased the taxi, bus, and service station complex operated by Patterson Enterprises.

Miss Betty Brown, RN, was appointed director of nurses at the South Muskoka Memorial Hospital … Mrs. H. Boyer, president, and Pearl Beasley, secretary-treasurer, of the Bracebridge Women's Institute, held a campaign to purchase sick room equipment to be loaned out to residents of Muskoka for home use free of charge …

*In the 1960s Hammond's Ambulance was one of two competing ambulance services in Bracebridge. This International Travelall, depicted here in the 1961 Santa Claus Parade, is obviously a far cry from today's large vehicles with their sophisticated equipment.* COURTESY OF THE BRACEBRIDGE PUBLIC LIBRARY

Duane Miller succeeded Charles Morrow as president of the Bracebridge Agricultural Committee … Ray Fraser was elected Master of the Loyal Orange Lodge … Former councillor and mayor Edgar W. (Ted) Reid was elected president of the Ontario Retail Lumber Dealers Association … Doug Graham was elected president of the Lions Club, Paul Kirk of the Kinsmen Club, Ted Gervais of the Rotary Club, and Sharon Maguire of the Kinette Club. … Evelyn Bates was elected as D.D.G.M. for the Order of the Eastern Star … Debbie Fish was chosen Miss Bracebridge.

Vern Payne of Huntsville was elected president of the Muskoka District Council. The Hon. D'Arcy McKeough, Minister of Municipal Affairs, elevated Donald M. Patterson from research director to special commissioner for the Muskoka District Local Government Review and set a schedule to permit legislation in 1969 and adoption in 1970.

The Bracebridge Clef Club celebrated its 60th

anniversary Diamond Jubilee with 55 members, past and present, attending. A special tribute was paid to charter members still active, Margaret Catherine Bird, Mary Bird, and Eva Reid. Sandra Brooks, daughter of Tom and Florence Brooks, won a public speaking contest qualifying her for the provincial championship competition.

The community was shocked by the death of Douglas Matthias, 19, son of George and Dorothy Matthias. He was a brilliant student and a talented athlete.

The Gray Coach Bus Lines changed the location of their bus terminal from the Parkview Restaurant to Duff's Esso Service Station at 23 Shier Street (now the Woodchester parking lot).

The following deaths were recorded: Herbert Cecil Patterson ... Effie (Mrs. Joseph G.) Myers ... Eric Gordon Cole ... Eleanor (Mrs. Arthur) Leeder ... Douglas Matthias ... Julia Mary (Mrs. F.R.) Bastedo ... William James Johnston, inventor and developer of the "Disappearing Propeller" boat ... Sam Dickson ... Cornelius Reynolds ... Richard Watson ... William R. Johnston ... Jesse B. Biddle ... Arthur Dalton Moon, caretaker of the Bracebridge High School for 34 years ... Nellie Maude (Mrs. William) Allchin ... Samuel Holden ... Mrs. Ralph Lee ... Mrs. George Dawson ... Lois Audrey Flaherty ... Albert Tibbett ... Clara Elliott ... Charles Nelson McNeice ... Horace George Parlett ... Mrs. Thomas Boyer.

Myron Angus of Vankoughnet, a paint-by-mouth artist, put on a display of his incredible ability and talent for the Monck Public School students. Although he was born with no arms and only one leg, of which he had limited use, he became internationally recognized for his artwork.

Bernie Curtis, a conservation officer with the Department of Lands and Forests, had his life saved by his dog. While travelling on Skeleton Lake he fell through the ice. He managed to grab on to the tail of his dog who pulled him to safety. A man's best friend indeed!

William Deith, Douglas Potts, and James Rosewarne received their Queen's Scouts Certificates.

Frank Suter, manager of the Bracebridge Liquor Control Board store, was appointed district supervisor of the Central Muskoka District.

After 21 years in business, Mr. and Mrs. Stu Reid sold their clothing store, Reid's Sportswear, to Bruce McPhail ... Hammond's Transport officially opened their new facilities on Highway 532 (Ecclestone Drive) ... Sharon Taylor opened The Beauty Boutique ... Nicholas B. Roche, BA, LLB, joined the law firm of Lee & Black ... Russell (Chub) Downey and Kenneth Downey sold the Bracebridge Dairy Bar and Restaurant to John and Shirley Godin ... Harold and Pauline Dawson officially opened their new showroom for Dawson's Electric at 9 Monck Road.

Sergeant Douglas Hillman was appointed detachment commander for the Ontario Provincial Police in Bracebridge, replacing Sergeant Bud Soroka. Gordon David Kingshott was appointed constable with the OPP at Parry Sound.

Bracebridge police took into custody a car rented in Louisville, Kentucky, which had been left abandoned behind the Norwood Theatre. It was suspected to have been used by James Earl Ray, slayer of Rev. Martin Luther King.

William F. Golden sold his law practice in Huntsville to assume duties as judge of the Muskoka District juvenile and family court on a full-time basis ... Ed Stacey retired as the CNR agent in Bracebridge and was replaced by R.D. Burns ... John Baker, one of Bracebridge's oldest citizens, celebrated his 102nd birthday.

In the federal election, Gordon Aiken, Progressive Conservative candidate, won the Parry Sound-Muskoka riding with 12,045 votes compared to Gerald Taylor, Liberal, with 9,649 and Hugh Bishop, NDP, with 3,564.

Labour unrest: Local 257 of the International Association of Bridge, Structural and Ornamental Ironworkers, at Bracebridge Steel Fabricating, were on strike for seven weeks ... A strike and lock-out kept the Brewer's Retail Store closed for 26 days ... The postal workers were on strike for 22 days.

Hospital administrator Frank Henry successfully completed his Hospital Organization and Management studies from the University of Manitoba. Newman Bros. of St. Catharines were chosen to be General Contractors for the South Muskoka Memorial Hospital addition. Herbert Agnew Associates were the architects.

A resolution was passed by Council requiring every

THE CLEF CLUB

DIAMOND
ANNIVERSARY
BANQUET

1908–1968

*HOLIDAY HOUSE*
BRACEBRIDGE

*APRIL SIXTH*
NINETEEN HUNDRED AND SIXTY-EIGHT

new sewer connection to have a backwater valve installed due to the large number of basements being flooded by the sewers backing up. Council also required that all driveway culverts, up until now supplied free, be at the expense of the property owner.

School enrollment for this year was established at 864 for BMLSS and 698 at Bracebridge Public School. The Victoria Street School for the Retarded was officially opened.

Ontario Hydro honoured Harold Whyte, Roy Towns, and Jack McIntosh on their retirement from service after 40, 38, and 37 years respectively. As in other years, an incredible traffic jam occurred on the Sunday evening of Thanksgiving weekend when Highway 11 was stop-and go for 11 hours from Gravenhurst to the Utterson intersection.

In October Donald M. Patterson, commissioner of the District Local Government Review, presented his final draft for the reorganization of government in Muskoka. It incorporated 25 recommendations, including one for fewer and larger local municipalities and an indirectly elected District Council. Extensive public hearings were held throughout Muskoka on the recommendations.

A number of untimely and shocking deaths saddened the whole of the area of Bracebridge this year. Allan McNabb, Gary Keall, Kenneth Ball, and Garth (Butch) Brazier all drowned while crossing Gullfeather Lake on their way to their hunt camp at Spring Lake ... Brian John Cloke, son of Mr. and Mrs. John Cloke, drowned at High Falls during a walkathon put on by the students of the Macaulay Public School to raise money for the South Muskoka Memorial Hospital ... Jacqueline Ann Peake, 20, the bride of just over a month of Darwin Peake, died in a car accident on the Doe Lake Road ... The body of William C. Leigh, 56, of London, Ontario, was found in the Muskoka River by the OPP.

In the municipal election George Parlett was acclaimed as mayor and Katherine Beers resigned. Elected to Council were Norman A. Harkness, 806 votes; Duane Miller, 586; Geoffrey Waite, 530; beating out E.S. (Ted) Boyer. Those elected joined those whose term had not expired: A.T. Gervais, Frank McNabb, and Frank S. Miller. For the two Bracebridge seats on the reorganized Board of Education, Dr. W. Lyle Black was elected with 675 votes and Norman Rosewarne with 674, both beating out Shirley Gauley who received 517 votes. Norman Archer and Tom McNeice were acclaimed in Muskoka Township, joining reeve Cecil Shell and councillors Andrew Baston and Frederick Darvell. Frank Henry, 826 votes, and Guy Waite, 734 votes, were elected to the Bracebridge Water Light and Power Commission, defeating Gordon Parlett who received 255.

Allan (Buck) Rogers was presented with a long service and good conduct medal from deputy commissioner D.V. Whileley of the Ontario Provincial Police. Bruce Fraser was appointed to the position of district assessor and Ivan Beasley was bestowed with a life membership in the Bracebridge Kinsmen Club.

In response to a survey conducted in the community, the Ontario Housing Corporation submitted a report recommending that we build 16 low-income and 12 senior citizen rental units. Council agreed with the report and passed a resolution asking the O.H.C. to proceed.

The lowest recorded temperature for the year was -37°F, and the warmest 90°F.

**1969** Following the inaugural meeting of the newly formed Muskoka Board of Education, Joan Woodcock was elected chairman and Fred Hammell was appointed director of education. The board set up their administrative office in temporary quarters in the basement of the provincial courthouse on Dominion Street. As the former secretary to the Bracebridge Board of Education prior to its amalgamation with the Muskoka board, Wilbert Richards was commissioned to prepare a detailed history of Bracebridge schools. C.R. Prosser submitted his resignation as principal of the Bracebridge and Muskoka Lakes Secondary School to assume a position as superintendent of education with the Elgin County School Board, and Kenneth H. Black, BPHE, was appointed in his place with Donald E. Johnston, BSC, as vice principal. Although it had nothing to do with the local board, it was in this year that a walk-out by 80 students occurred at BMLSS in protest of the action of the Ministry of Education in extending the school year by 10 days.

The municipal budget was set at a tax levy of $438,999.84 including a school levy of $180,147.26 which was arbitrarily set by Council because the school board (now the Muskoka District Board of Education) was not able to present a budget until late in the year. It was eventually set at $5 million and most Muskoka municipalities expressed their concern with such an extravagant amount.

Mayor George A. Parlett, in his inaugural address, predicted that a district form of local government could be introduced this year.

A resolution was passed by Council requiring all utilities owning or installing facilities in Bracebridge to prepare maps of all present installations and that these be updated regularly. The chief of police was appointed the administrator of welfare. Armstrong Street was named in honour of Sam H. Armstrong, the first mayor when Bracebridge was elevated to the status of a town in 1889. Council was told that the province would be assuming responsibility for municipal assessment in the future.

George S. Brooks was elected Master of Muskoka Masonic Lodge. Myron Angus of Vankoughnet was chosen as a representative of North American artists to attend a world conference in Bombay. Leda Scovell was re-elected president of the United Church Women. Victoria Boyer was installed as president of the Toronto Conference of United Church Women. Father Bernard Heffernan left St. Joseph's Church in Bracebridge to take up duties with St. Michael's Parish in Cobourg. It was also this year that William Neville Cheeseman (Brother Neville) took his life vows of poverty, celibacy, and obedience with the Society of St. John the Evangelist at their monastery on the north side of Maple Street in Bracebridge.

Frank Spain was appointed Minister of the First Baptist Church.

The Windermere Lions Club, having received their charter in 1968, made their first presentation as a public service, a wheelchair to the Pines Home for the Aged. The presentation was made by President William Skinner and the secretary, William Veitch.

An advertisement was published advising that Hammond's Ambulance Service had been sold to the Ontario Hospital Services Commission, leaving Muskoka Ambulance as the only service provider in the area, through an arrangement for payment by the OHSC instead of a user pay system supplemented by municipal subsidy as demanded by the operators in the past.

The *Sagamo*, one of last big lake steamboats, was destroyed by fire while berthed at the Muskoka Bay Wharf in Gravenhurst.

Jerry Fox was appointed Bracebridge fire chief and district fire coordinator by Council, and district deputy fire chief by the Ontario fire marshal, replacing Harold B. Dawson.

The Bracebridge Memorial Community Centre celebrated its 25th anniversary. It was built at a cost of $280,000 to commemorate the 45 men from the area who lost their lives in World War II. The Royal Canadian Legion made a special presentation to band major John MacDonald in recognition of his 15 years in developing and building the Legion Pipe Band.

Following up on earlier successes, a talented young ski team of Bracebridge area youth, now training at the Curlew Ski Hill under head coach Stan Knowles, placed five skiers in the top 30 out of 140 entrants at Talisman

Ski Resort. They were Jamie Rosewarne, David McPherson, Kim Parlett, Ross Miller, and Norman Miller. At the Caledon Ski Club, Robin Knowles, 15, placed 2nd in Ladies 18 and under "C" Class 45-gate slalom, and 13-year-old Marc Knowles placed 2nd in boys 18 and under. Larry Miller finished in 5th place. In "D" Class Giant Slalom at Kitchener Chicopee Ski Club, Kim Parlett, David McPherson, and Jamie Rosewarne all finished in the top 10 out of 99 entrants.

In an heroic act , the life of Eva Keels, 73, was saved by former Royal Canadian Mounted Police officer Sergeant Ray Morris when he pulled her, unconscious, from her burning home on George Road.

The following deaths were recorded: Wilfred Andrew (Biff) Shier, operated a barber shop, developed Shier's Insurance, was a former councillor, charter member of the Bracebridge Kinsmen Club, and treasurer of the Bracebridge Minor Hockey Association for many years ... Viola (Mrs. George) Armstrong, one of the first telephone operators in Bracebridge ... Joseph A. Thatcher, architect of the Bracebridge municipal building, rebuilt in 1958 ... Martha Ethel (Mrs. Hubert) Rebman ... George Henry Hunt, well known as a fine horseman ... James Aubrey Longhurst ... Ilma Mabel (Mrs. Harold) Potts ... Chief Warrant Officer Norman Arthur Pierce, son of Mr. and Mrs. Thomas W. Pierce ...Thomas Harry Rutherford ... John Edward Dobbs ... Roland Walter Colson ... William Malcolm Naismith, and many others.

Ronald A. McNabb was elected president and chairman of the Board of Directors of the South Muskoka Memorial Hospital.

The Canadian Imperial Bank of Commerce opened its first branch in Bracebridge on a Manitoba Street property purchased from Mr. and Mrs. Bernard Wonfor, formerly owned by the pioneer family of Charles Bard.

Frank Miller sold his controlling interest in Gordon Motor Sales to Carl Sander.

An unfortunate automobile accident at High Falls Road and Highway 11 took the life of Harry Suffern of Watt Township.

Ken Black, principal of Bracebridge and Muskoka Lakes Secondary School, introduced a program for students geared to better prepare them for job searching after graduation. A stress guidance counselling program was also implemented.

The ice left Muskoka Lake on April 22, 1969.

Wiltown Lodge, at the corner of Toronto and Front Street (Taylor Road and Richard Street in 1999), was sold by William E. Towns to Mr. and Mrs. Gord Habermehl who developed it into apartments. This residence was built in 1870 for James Clerihue on land purchased from Joseph Cooper. It was sold later to Alfred Hunt, the entrepreneurial pioneer businessman and founder of Hunt's Bank, Bracebridge's first bank, and after whom the area on the east side of the river was locally named Hunt's Hill. The first telephone in Bracebridge connected Mr. Hunt's bank on Manitoba Street with his residence.

The rapidly expanding Senior Citizen's Club celebrated its first anniversary having been organized in 1968, although preliminary organizing procedures had taken place as a 1967 Centennial year project.

For the second year in a row the Ontario Provincial Police operated their marine patrol with special training for local detachment officers Tom Box, Bill Taylor, and Peter Alexander.

Determined to expand their municipal boundaries, Council passed a lengthy resolution requesting the Ontario Municipal Board to renew their application for annexation which the Board had arbitrarily set aside. Room for growth and financial needs were expressed.

Archer's Livery and Marina, owned by Wilbur Archer, son of founder Wes Archer, who developed the southeast tip of Browning Island, was relocated to the mainland beside the federal wharf at St. Elmo.

The Muskoka Pines Restaurant and Service Station owned by Muskoka Garage Ltd. and operated by Leo Quesnelle was destroyed by fire.

In the former Moore's Lumber Mill in Falkenburg a new gangnail roof truss plant was opened by Deco Lumber Products, owned by Irvin and Paul Robson.

The Bracebridge Public School hosted a very enjoyable visit by 52 grade 7 and 8 students from the Moosonee Public Schools.

Archie Rintoul was elected president of the Lions Club, Robert E. Jefferies as 2nd vice president of the Ontario Provincial Command of the Royal Canadian

Legion, and Sadie Campbell president of the Business & Professional Women's Club. Director of the Muskoka Children's Aid Society, Ruth Nicholson, became president of the Ontario Association of Children's Aid Societies, William Quemby president of the Kinsmen Club, and Sharon Veitch president of the Kinette Club. Carl Dawson was elected Noble Grand for the IOOF, Dr. Lyle Black president of the Rotary Club, and Evelyn Bates District Deputy Grand Matron for the Order of the Eastern Star with Norma Reid as Worthy Matron and Sydney Perry Worthy Patron. Thomas H. Salmon was elected president of the Bracebridge unit of the Cancer Society, and Elroy Terry president of Minor Hockey. Wilfred (Bucko) McDonald, one of Canada's premier hockey and lacrosse stars, was appointed hockey director of Bracebridge.

*Although the new South Muskoka Memorial Hospital had just opened a few years previously, by the late 1960s a large addition was necessary to meet increasing demand. Here administrator Frank Henry watches Miss Canada make her contribution to the work.* COURTESY OF THE BRACEBRIDGE PUBLIC LIBRARY

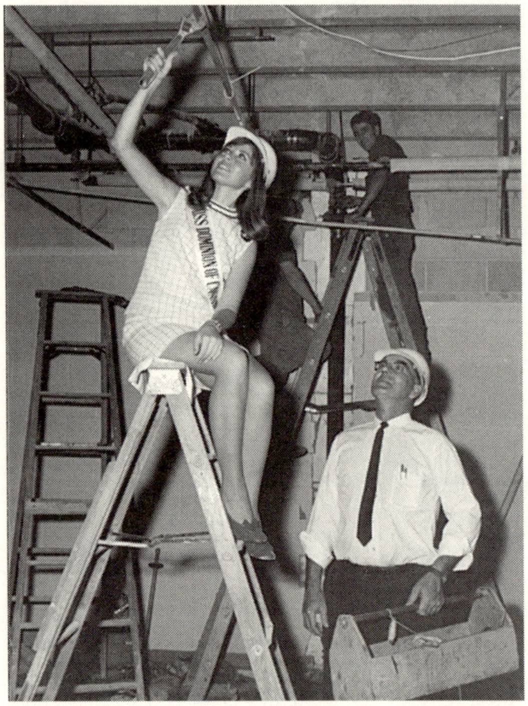

Tom Mataija was appointed secretary-treasurer and assistant administrator of the Pines Home for the Aged.

William B. Glennie accepted a two-year teaching position in South Africa.

Alfred J. Milligan retired from the ministry of the First Baptist Church.

All-Port Marina completed construction of their facility at Alport Bay and entered into a lease with Don Jones as operator.

The first modular home, called the Alcan Universal Home and built by Alcan Aluminum, was set in place on a lot on Pine Street and was purchased by Robert McCrank.

A committee headed by mayor George A. Parlett conducted a drive to raise money for a new building and equipment for a curling and golf club complex in Bracebridge. The success of their efforts resulted in an option to purchase the Lance Hardy farm on the north side of Liddard Street and plans developed for a six-sheet curling rink and an 18-hole golf course. Nick Roche, Jack D.C. McBride (treasurer), and Bob Merrill (secretary) also served on the committee. The result of the efforts of this committee was the formation of the South Muskoka Golf and Curling Club.

The T.J. Anderson & Sons store, formerly the Fenn & Anderson Co., closed out operations after 82 years and sold their Manitoba Street building to Banks Bros. TV & Appliances. The pioneer business had been owned by Lawrence Wilbur Anderson (an active sportsman, outdoorsman, and community worker) and was developed by his parents, Mr. and Mrs. T. James Anderson, who came to Bracebridge in 1871.

Mr. Kenneth C. Veitch successfully completed the Municipal Studies course at Queen's University, entitling him to use the letters AMCT.

The Water, Light and Power Commission and the Public Works Department entered into a contract with Northern Planing Mill to construct a garage and office facility on the south side of Baysville Road (now Taylor Road) near the water standpipe.

The Holiday House, owned by Mr. and Mrs. E.V.

Allchin (Ernie and Timmie), celebrated its 25th anniversary by hosting 400 guests at a garden party.

The Aluminum Company of Canada chose Bracebridge as the location for its new wire and cable production plant to commence operations in 1971. Fred Molland, Alcan's project engineer, stated that Bracebridge was chosen "because of the spirit of the community and the friendliness of the people."

Coincidentally, another division of the Aluminum Company of Canada announced the purchase of the Canada Foils Ltd. aluminum foil production plant in Bracebridge.

In response to a letter received from Brenda Cox suggesting that something should be done about the War Memorial Fountain that had been left unassembled in the Motor Park (now Kelvin Grove Park, part of Bracebridge Bay Park), Council gave her permission to restore it. It was relocated to the garden of Woodchester Villa, and it proposed to return it to Memorial Park for the year 2000.

In the continuing pursuit of gaining support for the Muskoka Local Government Review, the Honourable D'Arcy McKeough, Minister of Municipal Affairs, spoke to a packed house of municipal officials from across Muskoka at the Bracebridge Town Hall to explain the provincial government's view on regional government and to present the final report prepared by Mr. Patterson after extensive consultation with municipalities, groups, and individuals throughout Muskoka. The final report recommended that a two-tier system of government be created consisting of a regional level and six area municipalities and a three-year term for both councillors and school trustees. The Minister spent three days in Muskoka meeting with many groups and organizations including the District Council, who in 1966 had requested this review be conducted.

In view of the recommendations, Raymond Patchett of Vankoughnet organized a petition followed by a public meeting at the secondary school auditorium imploring that the existing boundaries of the 26 municipalities be maintained as part of the re-organization of local government in Muskoka. Roughly 500 people attended the meeting.

Bracebridge-born Rudy Meeks won the Ontario Open Fiddle Championship sponsored by the Orillia Lions Club.

The tourist operators of the Bracebridge Chamber of Commerce cooperated in constructing the first Local Accommodation Directory and installing it at the north end of Memorial Park. The directory served to advise the travelling public of places to stay in Bracebridge and the surrounding area (and is still in operation in 1999).

The Muskoka Falls United Church celebrated its centennial and it was noted that in 1860 Muskoka Falls was the first post office designated north of the Severn River.

As a matter of national interest, it was in 1969 that the first notification was received from the federal communications minister Eric Kierans of the federal government's intention to design a permanent public address postal coding system for Canada Post.

A charge of causing bodily harm by discharging a firearm was laid against Constable John Robert Martin of the Bracebridge Police Department. Council passed a resolution to engage legal counsel to defend against the action. In due course, the charge was reduced to one of assault causing bodily harm bringing a fine of $500.

Another "end of an era" occurred when the freight shed and waiting room at the federal wharf in Bracebridge Bay was demolished to make room for the construction of a parking lot as part of a wharf reconstruction project.

Imperial Oil Ltd. announced the appointment of Ross Veitch as their agent in Bracebridge following the retirement of Earle Rosewarne.

On September 14, 100 years of local newspaper service in Bracebridge was celebrated, the *Northern Advocate and General Advertiser for the Free Grant District of Muskoka, Parry Sound and Nipissing* having started in 1869.

The Bracebridge Fall Fair held its 102nd fall fair and Linda MacDonald, 17, daughter of Mr. and Mrs. James MacDonald, was selected as Miss Bracebridge and later as Miss Muskoka at the pageant during the Muskoka Cavalcade of Colour.

Robert J. Boyer, MPP, was appointed first vice-chairman of Ontario Hydro after having served as second vice-chairman since 1962.

A number of changes took place in the retail community this year. Robert Scott purchased the Muskoka Paint Centre on Manitoba Street from Frank Miller and Don Cale ... The Holiday Shop building on Manitoba Street was purchased by the Bank of Nova Scotia for expansion purposes ... Watt's Economy Drugs bought both the George W. Brooks Drugstore and the Anderson Barbershop building from George W. Ecclestone ... Anderson's Barbershop relocated to a shop in the Patterson Hotel building ... Howard Cable, famed band leader and musician, and his wife, Marie, bought the Paper & Party Shop and reopened it as the Square Pumpkin.

Donald E. Willis was appointed assessment commissioner for Muskoka, replacing Bruce J. Fraser.

Stuart Roland Young was appointed constable with the Bracebridge Police Department to replace John Robert Martin who accepted a position with the Water, Light and Power Commission.

The Bracebridge Kinsmen Club completed their three-year pledge to equip the South Muskoka Memorial Hospital physiotherapy department.

The whole of Muskoka became the focus of the news media during the kidnapping of Mary Nelles by six men from Toronto, all of whom later pleaded guilty to their charges. This largest search in the province's history ended when the victim was found unharmed on a deserted road in Foot's Bay west of Bracebridge. after a $200,000 ransom was paid by her husband and father.

The Toronto-Dominion Bank celebrated its 50th anniversary in Bracebridge ... Austin Hunt, former Bracebridge Bears hockey star and councillor, retired from the Water, Light and Power Commission.

The A & P Store announced its plan to build a new store in Bracebridge, and bought the buildings of Crozier, Bates, and Milligan at the southwest corner of Monck Road and Manitoba Street.

Russell Lackie retired from the Ontario Provincial Police after 32 years on the job and Allan (Duffy) Fraser retired from Neilsons as their regional distributor.

Mr. Nick Wettlaufer, a long-term and faithful employee of the municipality as road superintendent, presented a petition for the extension of the sewer system to service the residences on Holditch Street, which Council approved on a local improvement basis. Rene McGaughey (Rene Caisse) asked Council to define the sides of Hiram Street so that cars would stop cutting across the corner of her property at the southeast corner of Hiram and Liddard streets.

The Department of Energy and Resources Management requested the town cease burning at the town dump in Draper Township.

Council passed resolutions accepting the tenders for the construction of 12 senior citizen and 16 low income rental housing units.

## 1970

The town budget this year was set at $430,708. Council agreed to allow connections to their sewer system by residents of adjoining townships where they fronted on a line located on the town boundaries.

Due to the dramatic residential, industrial, and commercial growth, a new 900,000-gallon booster pumping station and reservoir was constructed on Highway 532 (Ecclestone Drive) across from Rockwell (Meritor) at a cost of $250,000, to supplement the new Stephens' Bay waterworks supply system. In just three years the growth of Bracebridge accelerated the schedule for expansion of the waterworks facilities ahead by 20 years.

Since the Water, Light and Power Commission office had been relocated to their new building on the south side of Baysville Road (Taylor Road), Council sold the former office located on Wharf Road to Morris G. Topping for his proposed use as a discount furniture store. Council approved a zoning change for Bracebridge Developments Ltd. to build an apartment building and townhouse units on the south side of Monck Road between Wellington and Morrison streets. The Community Centre Committee spent $35,000 on replacing the floor and refrigeration piping in the arena.

A list of requirements was assembled by Council to be met by developers of subdivisions, necessitated by accelerated residential growth.

At the request of H. E. S. (Bert) Sugg, Council passed a resolution approving, in principal, the formation of a Parks Board.

Representatives of the South Muskoka Association for the Mentally Retarded advised Council of their intention to establish a training centre for retarded adults.

The community was saddened by a number of accidental deaths. A tragic snowmobile accident took the life of Steven Hammond. Harry Knight was killed when he was struck by a limb from a tree that he was cutting. Hilda (Mrs. Charles) French died in an automobile accident.

Nelson William Ross Boyes of Vankoughnet was named Queen's Counsel. Harry Thomas Preston received his PhD in theoretical chemistry at McMaster University.

Gary Hillman of the Muskoka Sno 'n' Sports racing team had a good year on the snowmobile racing circuit, wining three first-place awards and a second in competitions at the MacTier Winter Carnival and the North Bay Winter Carnival.

A new assessment office was constructed on Pine Street by Gordon Habermehl Builders for Joyce Properties (Bracebridge) Limited ... Canada Foils held the official opening of its aluminum foil manufacturing plant ... Frank S. Miller and Ed Gould purchased Pinelands Lodge ... Michael Fitton, BA, LLB, joined the law firm of Sugg & Reid on Chancery Lane ... William Warren was appointed manager of the Royal Bank, replacing Archie Crawford ... The Canadian Imperial Bank of Commerce officially opened its new branch in Bracebridge with John Pickard as manager ... The engineering firm Totten Sims Hubicki Associates opened a Bracebridge office ... Gilbey Canada Ltd. announced the appointment of George A. Mann as their representative for northeastern Ontario ... the management of Skyways Restaurant and Service Station was transferred to Independent Motor Inns, Edgar (Max) Gaisford announced ... The Bank of Nova Scotia opened their expanded and renovated offices ... The Chamber of Commerce, after nearly having to surrender its charter due to a lack of interest from its members, was able to re-assemble an executive, led by Larry Giaschi as president ... The new A & P Store at the corner of Monck Road and Manitoba Street opened ... the South Muskoka Memorial Hospital opened its new addition, increasing the capacity of the facility to 96 beds. The Honourable Thomas L. Wells attended the opening and praised the hospital for its fine work in south Muskoka ... Frank S. Miller was elected president of the Muskoka Tourist Association and received a three-year appointment to the advisory committee to the Applied Arts Division of Georgian College in Barrie.

Ecclestone Hardware, in its 76th year of operation, held an official opening of its newly renovated and expanded store, making it the largest retail hardware and furniture business in Bracebridge. G.N. Ecclestone also celebrated his 50th year in the hardware business.

An era came to an end when the Falkenburg Station post office was closed after 107 years of operation. Also, the town "barn" (works garage) was torn down to create the library parking lot after the town public works department relocated to part of the new building constructed by the Bracebridge Water, Light and Power Commission.

Rev. Douglas Muir, minister at the United Church, moved to Thornbury United Church. He was replaced by Rev. Richard H. Moffat ... Rev. John J. Hickey was appointed parish priest of St. Mary's Church in Huntsville, and Rev. Herbert J. Fitzgerald was appointed as parish priest for St. Joseph's Church in his stead. The ever-expanding Pinegrove Baptist Church held a sod-turning for a new wing.

The *Peerless II*, a 21-ton boat which had supplied gas to businesses and residents on Muskoka Lake for 23 years, partly sank while moored to the Gulf bulk plant wharf on the Muskoka River near Shier's bridge. It was stopped from sinking completely by the quick action of firefighters Paul Hammond, Ron Tomlinson, and Bob Bobbette, who used portable pumps to keep it partially afloat until help arrived.

Presidents this year included Ruby Learoyd of the Bracebridge Senior Citizens Club, Phil Keppler of the Lions Club, Bruce Taylor of the Kinsmen Club, Carol Quemby of the Kinette Club, and Ray Savijarvi of the Rotary Club. Myron Beathune was installed as Master of the Masonic Lodge.

The members of the Bracebridge Legion elected Glen Allen as president, Percy Good as secretary, and Betty Terry as auxiliary president. This year the Legion celebrated its 40th anniversary of service. It started out as the Bracebridge Branch No. 161 Canadian Legion, British Empire Service League, with president M.C. Newark and Clarence S. Salmon, secretary.

Mary Jackson, BA, was honoured upon her retirement after 40 years as a teacher at Bracebridge and Muskoka Lakes Secondary School, and a "Mary Jackson Day" was held at the school. Norman A. Harkness of Muskoka Garage Ltd. was named Grand Master Salesman by General Motors for the fourth time in recognition of his automotive sales accomplishments. Alldyn Clark, a renowned Bracebridge photographer, was presented with an award for his photograph of a robin sitting on the edge of its nest feeding its young, taken in the backyard of his residence in Bracebridge.

Robert Spence resigned from the town police force.

After extensive reports, reviews, discussions and meetings, the Honourable D'Arcy McKeough, provincial minister of municipal affairs, announced the final provisions of the legislation for the formation of the District Municipality of Muskoka. The first reading of the legislation took place on May 7, 1970. The second reading before the legislature received unanimous support from the members of the Provincial Legislature, and the NDP Party leader, Donald C. MacDonald, was quoted as saying that all parties in Queen's Park were in favour of district government in Muskoka. The Act received Royal Assent on June 26, 1970.

The councils of 10 municipalities in Muskoka passed resolutions to hold referendums asking whether or not their voters were in favour of the implementation of district government. Those holding referendums were Bala, Brunel, Franklin, Macaulay, McLean, Port Sydney, Ridout, Stephenson, Stisted, and Monck. A total of 1,991 votes were cast with 1,820 voting against the implementation of district government for Muskoka and 171 in favour.

The Bracebridge Council decided not to present such a question to the voters, as did the balance of Muskoka municipalities.

The first chairman of the District Council, Bracebridge-born Milton Tibbett, mayor of Huntsville, was appointed by the Minister of Municipal Affairs, as were

*In 1964 the annual Muskoka Arts and Crafts show began modestly in Memorial Park, and continued there for a number of years until its popularity dictated a move to more spacious grounds at Annie Williams Memorial Park on the river. These pictures are from the 1966 (top) and 1971 (bottom) shows.* COURTESY OF MARILYN LONG the returning officers for the first election under the new Act; in the case of the new Area Municipality of Bracebridge, Kenneth C. Veitch.

The Association of Municipalities in Muskoka, known informally as the Muskoka District Council, having operated for nearly 50 years as a voluntary, problem-sharing and solving organization, was disbanded in view of the legislation introduced to form the District Municipality of Muskoka to come into effect on January 1, 1971.

The Muskoka River suffered the effects of two oil slicks due to the escape of contaminants from local operations.

The following deaths were recorded: George W. Boyer, president of Muskoka Publishing Co., ending a career of printing and publishing that started in 1903 ... Steve Thomas Hammond ... Henry Frederick Blanchard Knight ... Laura Anderson ... Pearl Olive (Mrs. Harry) Hitchen ... Mary Irene (Mrs. David) Rankin ... David DeCaire ... Edna Dorothy (Mrs. Robert) Everett ... Charles Samuel Close ... Amy Annie (Mrs. Reginald) Boyes ... Lottie Turner (Mrs. Douglas R.) Boyes ... Frank Wright ... Ivan Frank Thompson ... Joseph Flynn ... Lambert Elgin Love, whose parents started Elgin House resort ... Daniel Bowers ... Russell William Ernest (Butch) Jackson ... Hilda Rosetta (Mrs. Charles) French ... Mary Jane (Mrs. R. Wesley) Morrow ... Mary Ellen Langille ... Eva Jane Taplin ... Alexander Irvine ... George Beathune ... Mary Elizabeth Blair ... Alexander John Milne ... Peter Todoroff ... Bernard John Henry ... Ethel Irene Richards ... Gertrude E. (Mrs. William) Kingsmill, daughter of pioneers Dr. and Mrs. Samuel Bridgland ... Douglas J. Rankin ... Edith Sarah (Mrs. John) Sloper ... Leonard David Terry ... Mabel Gertrude (Mrs. David B.) White...William Albert (Bert) Shea ... Elizabeth Charlotte (Mrs. Peter) MacNaughtan...Milton Ross (Pat) Askin...Robert Herbert (Bobby) Walsh ... Marjorie Orr Taylor ... Earle Wayne McMurray ... Mae (Mrs. Herbert W.) Allen ... Agnes Florence (Mrs. William) Brazier ... Emily (Mrs. Albert) Pelissero ... Edmund Adam Darling ... William Russell Stevenson ... Ethel (Mrs. William) Terry ... Rita May (Mrs. R.F.) Shuttleworth ... John Baker (at 104 years of age) ... Frederick (Rick) Henderson ... Eric Armstrong, only grandson of pioneer Bracebridge businessman Samuel P. Armstrong ... Ronald Atkinson ... Hugh William McLaughlin ... James Vincent Dinner ... Brent G. Nelson ... Mary Elizabeth (Mrs. John Henry) Leshon ... Elizabeth Jane (Mrs. George) Jeffries ... J. Victor Hawkins ... Kent MacDonald ... Bernice H. (Mrs. Bert) Shea ... Gordon Emanuel Goodman.

The Highway 11 four-lane widening program was completed to north of Gravenhurst.

The Salvation Army started an annual soap-box derby which took place on the "Salvation Army Hill." It continued for several years and provided great entertainment and recreation for all.

Deborah Draper, Karen Longhurst, and Deanna Tryon were named Ontario Scholars.

The Centennial Fountain, built on property donated by Reg Kirk at the corner of McMurray and Manitoba streets, was completed and officially designated by Dr. W.J. Wright, chairman of the Centennial Committee, and Timmy Allchin, president of the Chamber of Commerce. Gaye Anderson received an award for suggesting the fountain in a contest held to receive ideas from the public on ways to celebrate Canada's Centennial.

Labour unrest included a rotating strike by postal workers, and strike by the Health Unit nurses that went on from May until August, and a wildcat strike at the Canada Foils Plant over claimed contract violations.

One-way traffic was imposed (later to be reversed) on parts of McMurray Street and Kimberley Avenue to alleviate traffic congestion. A new storage and public washroom building was completed in Annie Williams Memorial Recreation Park, and the committee administering the park asked Council if it would consider assuming the park on a lease basis in order for it to qualify for provincial grants. The South Falls Memorial Cemetery, a pioneer burial ground, was restored and recognized.

Dr. W. Lyle Black was elected chairman of the Board of Education. School registration in Bracebridge was 1,725 and the total registration for Muskoka 7,947, including 5,440 in elementary schools and 2,474 in secondary schools, the latter consisting of 978 in Bracebridge, 1,070 in Huntsville, and 426 in Gravenhurst.

Junior hockey returned this year when the Bracebridge

*Captain Ralph McPherson's* MV Mildred *offered sightseeing cruises from Bracebridge Bay down the Muskoka River and out into Lake Muskoka for many years. Originally steam powered, the vessel was previously owned and operated for the same purpose by Captain Wesley Archer.* COURTESY OF BRACEBRIDGE PUBLIC LIBRARY

Huskies Intermediate team decided to drop out of competition. The enthusiastic leadership of Danny Poland (coach) resulted in a new Junior C team executive consisting of Ken Smith, president, Joe Defabrizio, Bernie Black, Bill Morrison, Harold (Ding) Bell, Stan Montgomery, Roy Tennant, Bill Quemby, Alldyn Clark, Murray Ellis, Bruce Montgomery, Tom Robinson, Noel (Turk) Lees, Jim Smith, and Gary Martin.

Bucko MacDonald was hired by the recreation committee as hockey director for the minor hockey program.

Tommy Holiday, an ever-present fan at baseball games in Jubilee Park, was struck by a foul ball and had to undergo neurosurgery in a Toronto hospital. Nevertheless, he was back at the ballpark in short order, wearing a helmet and face mask for protection thereafter.

Bonnie Armstrong, daughter of Clifford and Esther Armstrong, was crowned Miss Bracebridge and went on at the Muskoka Cavalcade of Colour to win the title of Miss Muskoka.

In accordance with the provisions of the new District Municipality of Muskoka Act, a nomination meeting and municipal elections were held early in the fall so that a new Council for the amalgamated area municipality and member of the new District Council could familiarize themselves with their new duties. The election was held on October 5, 1970. In Bracebridge, George A. Parlett was elected mayor with 1,583 votes, defeating Frank S. Miller with 943. Councillors were Carl Sander, Norman A. Harkness, and Frank Henry in Bracebridge Ward (all acclaimed), Norman Archer (acclaimed) in Muskoka North Ward, Leo Robinson (acclaimed) in Monck South Ward, Dan MacNaughtan Sr. in Macaulay Ward (elected with 186 votes, defeating Charles Ruttan, 128, and Bob McCrank, 118), James D. Lang in Draper Ward (elected with 159 votes, defeating Alf Ashley, 155, and Emily Dworak, 87), and Neil Boyes in Oakley Ward (elected with 94 votes, defeating Keith Thompson, 92, and Bert Reid, 42).

The first meeting of the new Council was held on October 8 and from their own numbers elected Norman A. Harkness, Norman Archer, and James D. Lang to sit on the council for the District Municipality along with Mayor George A. Parlett.

At the last meeting of the old Council in Bracebridge (which became Bracebridge Ward of the Area Municipality of the Town of Bracebridge under the Muskoka Act), held on December 14, 1970, the following resolution was passed: "Moved by N.A. Harkness, seconded by Geoffrey Waite, that we do now adjourn this meeting as the last and final meeting of the Council of the Municipality of the Town of Bracebridge, the next Council meeting to be held in the Bracebridge Council Chambers will be comprised of the Mayor and Councillors of the new Bracebridge Area Municipality as called by His Worship the Mayor."

The inaugural meeting of the Council of the newly created District Municipality of Muskoka was held on Monday, October 19, 1970, in the auditorium of the Bracebridge Public School, with Ontario Lieutenant Governor the Honourable W. Ross MacDonald in attendance to administer the Oath of Office to the new Councillors.

Work commenced on a new building on Pine Street for an administrative centre for the district municipality.

Norman Rosewarne, Wilbur Archer, Melville Goltz, and Bev Thompson were elected to the Muskoka Board of Education (which had already been reorganized as a district-wide board two years earlier).

*Prior to the 1950s, the Muskoka Lakes Navigation Company's* SS Islander *regularly plied the Muskoka River up to Bracebridge. Here, downstream bound, she rounds Hairpin Bend about three kilometres below town. Logs bound for mills at Gravenhurst were a hazard modern boaters need not contend with. The logs would date this photograph as 1920s or earlier.* COURTESY OF NATIONAL ARCHIVES OF CANADA PA 32260

Frank Henry was appointed chairman of the Bracebridge Water, Light and Power Commission.

Stan Knowles of Bracebridge, along with Dr. Jack Langmaid, took top honours in the U.S. National Albacore Sailing Championship at Wynn Island in Chesapeake Bay, Virginia.

The Ontario Provincial Police prepared to assume policing duties in all of the Area Municipality of Bracebridge as of January 1, 1971, in accordance with the Muskoka Act.

The ice left Muskoka Lake on April 29. The highest temperature for the year was 41°F, and the lowest -31°.

## 1971

Alastair Watson was appointed municipal treasurer, William T. Quemby superintendent of roads and public utilities, James E. Kaye and Don Beacock as building inspectors, Colan Cowan and Rod White as bylaw enforcement officers, and Kenneth C. Veitch municipal clerk. Council decided to stop using the Motor Park for camping. Canadian National Railways advised Council that it was closing 90 railway stations across Ontario, including Bracebridge. Ontario Provincial Police took over police services on January 1 in accordance with the Muskoka Act.

At a party for the former town police officers they were all presented reclining chairs and were reassigned to other work with the town. In the townships or parts of townships that were now part of the new Area Municipality of Bracebridge (all of Macaulay, Draper, and Oakley townships, concessions 1, 2, and 3 of McLean Township, the Muskoka North Ward portion of Muskoka Township, and the Monck South portion of Monck Township) there was no change in policing because the OPP were already providing that service. Council took an option to purchase 80 acres in Monck South Ward from Gilbert Gibbs to be developed as a municipal cemetery. An option was also acquired on a parcel of property in lot 9, concession 3 of Macaulay Ward for the purpose of creating a municipal landfill site. The Department of Energy and Resources Management approved the new location.

Council hired Totten Sims Hubicki Associates to prepare plans to intercept the four major sewer lines that had been emptying into the Muskoka River, and direct them into the treatment system.

The district school board refused to take over the school guard crossing function. Council passed bylaws to create pedestrian crosswalks and the problem was resolved after much discussion and complaint.

The Charles Street (now part of Ann Street) railway crossing signals were approved to be installed. A fire protection survey and a study of the town's sewage treatment facilities were commenced. A bylaw was passed to require every connection to the town's water system to include a water consumption meter. Considering the demand for fire protection in the expanded area, Council authorized the purchase of a suitable truck and fire equipment to be used in the more remote areas.

Things were happening at the new District Municipality of Muskoka where Stewart J. Watts was appointed district engineer and Graham Power district planner. In order to meet the requirements of the Muskoka Act, District Council passed a bylaw to create a system of district-maintained roads between municipalities.

Ted Gervais retired as manager of Canadian Motor Lamp Co. Ltd. (now Meritor), and Joe Hauser was named plant manager of Canada Foils Ltd., replacing Drew Blacklock. John W. Shier joined the firm of Shier's Insurance and Real Estate, representing the third generation of the family to be part of that insurance company.

Aubrey Glass was elected president of the Muskoka Horse Association, James Stevenson president of the Georgian Bay Regional Development Council, and G. Wilson Boyer president of the Ontario Weekly Newspaper Association, and later director of the Canadian Community Newspaper Association.

Deaths this year included Charles Ernest Kaye … Cecil Daniel Nutt … Mrs. Oliver Johnston … Aileen Benjamin … Hannah Ethel (Mrs. H.E.) Beaumont … Norman Thompson … Leah Adams … Lucretia Maria (Mrs. John) Dobbs … Eliza (Mrs. Alfred) Dauphin … Elizabeth (Mrs. William) Inch … Elizabeth Ann (Mrs. Angus) Richards, one of the first babies born in Bracebridge (September 16, 1871) … James Albert (Kelly) Oates … William John Black … Robert Keith Burrows … William Kenneth Hare … Percival Ernest (Puss) Clark … Eliza Ellen (Mrs. Hiram) Medley … Isabella Blanchard, 100 years, eight months old) … Ina Marjorie (Mrs. W.L.) Cowan … Dorothy Louise (Mrs. Lionel) Davis … Margaret Ann Campbell … Thomas Leslie Wallace … John S. Schofield … Alice Eleanor Corrigan … W. Kenneth Kettle … Edmund Leveque … Amy (Mrs. Andrew I.) Corbett … William Percy Patterson … Arthur J. Somers … Mungo Park McKay … Florence A (Mrs. E. Ainslie) Wright … Cyril J. Boyes … Ethel (Mrs. Ernest) Leeder … George B. Moore … Iola Margaret (Mrs. Walter) Finch … William Charles Peake … James Berofe … Evelyn Mary (Mrs. Wilfred "Biff") Shier … Gladys May (Mrs. Clifford) Gibbs … Timothy Earl Rowe … John Henry Bird … Ethel Mary (Mrs. John) Booth … Bert Alexander Harbridge … Edith Rose (Mrs. George) Parrett … William Earl Patterson … Emily Elizabeth (Mrs. Thomas) Marriott.

The Governor General of Canada, the Right Honourable Roland Michener, and the Honourable James A.C. Auld, Ontario minister of tourism, visited Muskoka and participated in the winter carnival.

Bracebridge's population was stated to be 6,577 and the new addition put on the public school in 1970 was already filled to capacity.

In business, Matthias Furniture & Appliances on Manitoba Street was purchased by Allan Prowse and Hugh Sefton from George and Dorothy Matthias … Brian Robinson purchased the Bracebridge Coffee Service from Allan Prowse … Frank and Beth Anderson sold their wools and crafts business to Nan Munro … Wells Motel, at the corner of Manitoba and Ida streets (built in 1950 by Mr. and Mrs. Douglas Wells, among the creators and original shareholders of Santa's Village) was sold by Mr. and Mrs Morris Topping and Mr. and Mrs. Joe Gilbert to Benal and Helen Haight … Muskoka Containerized Services Ltd. commenced operations with Donald G. Coates as president, and was granted a contract by the town to place garbage containers in strategic locations in the outlying wards ... Canadian Oxygen Co. (Canox) opened their Bracebridge retail outlet on Wellington Street ... Currell's Books and Records, opened in 1970, relocated to the former original location of Everett's Drug Store ... MacNaughtan Hardware, started in 1946 by Peter MacNaughtan, expanded its store on the west side of Manitoba Street, on Queen's Hill, into an adjoining store and provided a back entrance onto Dominion Street. Charles Palmer, Merchant Tailor, was at one time located in MacNaughtan's building, and prior that, Henry Slater's Tailor Shop) ... Murray Lee, a partner with Raymie Lee in the Top Valu Food Market situated where the Riverside Inn now is, purchased Parkview Restaurant on Manitoba Street from Kenneth Moorhouse ... Hidden Valley Travel Service opened their Bracebridge office at 187 Manitoba Street, at the corner of Ann Street ... Jean Inglis started Inglis Secretarial Service, operating from her home at 14 Mary Street ... Orvil Hammond, president of Hammond's Transportation, and Paul Hammond divided their operations with Orvil retaining the bus operations and Paul taking over the trucking business to be called Muskoka Transport ... The Norwood Place Restaurant, featuring the only sidewalk cafe in town, was opened by Larry Giaschi ... Ron and Denise Wilson opened the Muskoka Hobby Shop ... The $7.5 million Alcan Wire and Cable plant was officially opened with 450 people in attendance, including the Honourable William G. Davis, Premier of Ontario, with Reinhard Zobrist as manager.

An official application was made for a credit union charter for Bracebridge signed by 25 interested persons, and the Patterson Hotel (formerly the pioneer Queen's Hotel) was purchased by Chris Yaneff and Walter Koturbash who planned to refurbish the premises ... The Top Valu Food Store was closed and the property sold to Harbridge Development Corp. of Etobicoke who revealed plans to develop an eight-store plaza (now Riverside Inn) and re-align the Beaumont Drive-Highway 532 (Ecclestone Drive) intersection, requiring the town to enter into an exchange of lands for road purposes ... Dr. George South completed construction of his new chiropractic clinic at 274 Manitoba Street, and the Fourth Season Ski Shop owned by Asgar and Mary Thrane opened ... Ross Veitch officially opened his new Esso Agency and Home Comfort Centre on Highway 118, one mile west of downtown ... John Brown opened his sporting goods store, the first sportsman centre in south Muskoka ... the Bracebridge Ski Club operated Rainbow Ridge ski hill with Paul and Sandra Miller contracting to operate the dining lounge.

Another era came to an end when trucks instead of the railway started bringing the mail to the area.

The Muskoka Snow 'n' Sports snowmobile racing team won 17 trophies at the Mactier Winter Carnival, with Allan Hillman winning the Molson's Golden Award. Other winners were Donna Medley, Ken Medley, and Gary Hillman.

The Bracebridge Midget hockey team won the Muskoka Championship for the first time in 20 years. The Bracebridge Bears Junior C team was eliminated

*In the 1960s and 1970s snowmobiling became an important winter recreational activity, but Muskoka residents had experimented with snowmobiles long before. This picture, c.1924, shows a machine owned by Jim Kaye of Milford Bay, often used to take people to the Bracebridge hospital. Later, two more wheels were added at the back, with tracks installed. A cab, heated by a wood stove, completed the "option package."* R.J. BOYER COLLECTION, COURTESY OF VICKY BILLINGSLEY

from the playoffs by Penetang. The Figure Skating Club won five medals in a Muskoka-Parry Sound competition.

Frank Denniss was elected Master of the South Muskoka County LOL, replacing Ray Fraser.

Frank S. Miller was elected provincial Conservative candidate, replacing Robert J. Boyer who retired after having served as Muskoka MPP for 16 years. Mr. Boyer also resigned from his position of vice-chairman of Ontario Hydro. Miller was elected in October defeating Ken Cargill (NDP) and Raymond Patchett (Liberal).

Due to a heavy snow load several buildings suffered structural damage, including the Shier Lumber building which collapsed under the weight.

John Biddle celebrated his 10th anniversary as superintendent and then administrator of the Pines Home for the Aged, having been appointed when it was opened in 1961. Coincidentally, he also resigned from the position in 1971.

Norman Miners Sr. retired as district commissioner for the Boy Scouts. Pearl Draper retired from the South Muskoka Memorial Hospital after 28 years of service.

Penny Stiver was elected resident of the Business and Professional Women's Club which celebrated its 25th anniversary, Robert E. Jeffries was elected 1st vice president of the Royal Canadian Legion Provincial Command, Gordon M. Smith as president of the Kinsmen Club, and Sharon Sharpe president of the Kinette Club.

The Meals on Wheels program was started this year with Margaret Newark as president, and the Big Brothers program became a reality and advertisements were placed for volunteers. Sidney Rosenblatt, 29, joined the staff of the Children's Aid Society and a retirement party was held for teachers Margaret Bailey, Mae McCracken, and Helen Thompson at Patterson-Kaye Lodge.

Bob Petry was elected president of the Rotary Club, and Fred Klie was appointed to the Water, Light and Power Commission to fill the vacancy created by the death of Donald F. Boyer. Frank Spain resigned as minister of the First Baptist Church.

Clerk-administrator Kenneth C. Veitch acquired grants to enable the town and volunteers to install floodlights on the baseball diamond in Jubilee Park, enabling night ball games to be played for the first time.

Led by teacher Colin Wilde, a group of art students from the Bracebridge Public School designed, carved, and painted a totem pole which was erected in front of the school.

Four students were named Ontario Scholars: William Deith, Larry Miller, Douglas Thomson, and Bruce Young.

Gregory W. Colmer, a very popular teacher at the high school for 26 years, retired. Scott N. Northmore, who later became a councillor and mayor, was appointed clerk of the first small claims court for the District of Muskoka.

Due to the severe congestion and traffic problems created by the success of the Muskoka Arts & Crafts Exhibition, its location was eventually changed from the Memorial Park to Annie Williams Memorial Park.

Rev. D.F. Sharpe resigned as pastor of the Free Methodist Church after seven years to move to Perth.

Sergeant Douglas Hillman, commander of the OPP detachment, was promoted to staff sergeant and Constable Jim Conners was transferred to Cochrane.

The Aubrey Street subdivision, opened in the spring of 1949 to accommodate World War II veterans and their families, held their first fireworks display, a tradition that would continue for several years.

School enrollment was 1,012 at BMLSS, 731 at Bracebridge Public, 230 at Macaulay, 178 at Monck, 200 at Muskoka Falls, 87 at Oakley, and 24 at Victoria Street.

On the 100th anniversary of the Federal Atmospheric Environment Service, Albert W. Hollingworth was presented with a plaque in recognition of his and his family's dedication in providing climatological observations. The reporting was started by John Hollingworth (Sr.) in 1876, continued by his son John Hollingworth (Jr.) and then by grandson Albert. Nowhere else in Canada was there such a record of one family providing this service for such a long time.

Manitoba Street was closed to traffic between Thomas Street (now Taylor Road) and Ontario Street for the town's first pedestrian mall. While it was looked upon by some with considerable reserve, it turned out to be a great success.

A special service held at the Muskoka Falls United

*Anyone who skated or attended hockey games at the Bracebridge arena will remember arena workers cleaning the ice with driveway snow scrapers, then pushing around the handcart to apply a fresh film of water. The new Zamboni-type machine considerably speeded up the process.* COURTESY OF BRACEBRIDGE PARKS AND RECREATION

Church unveiled a plaque commemorating the efforts of pioneers of the Muskoka Falls area.

Wilbert Richards, former clerk-treasurer of the town, was honoured by the Muskoka Tourist Association for his efforts in pioneering the association and as chairman of their inaugural meeting held in 1935.

Robert E. Everett was re-elected as chairman of Muskoka Arts & Crafts Association. W.A. (Bucko) MacDonald, director of Bracebridge Minor Hockey, was elected to the Lacrosse Hall of Fame. The high school junior girls volleyball team won the Muskoka-Parry Sound championship.

Sandra Cecilia Moore, daughter of Mr. and Mrs. Cecil Moore, received the Gold Medal for piano at the graduation ceremonies at the Royal Conservatory of Toronto Concert Hall. This was the first time in seven years this highest award in Canada had been won by an Ontario student.

The Ministry of Natural Resources officially designated 1,500 acres in Macaulay Ward just north of High Falls to be developed as a resource management area for public enjoyment.

On the same day in November that a petition was received by Town Council asking for sidewalks on Wellington Street, a child died after being struck by a car in that area.

Neil Haight resigned as principal of Bracebridge Public School to attend theological school ... In December, Gordon Aiken, MP, citing poor health, advised that he would not be a candidate in the next federal election.

*When the Bracebridge CNR station was closed in the early 1970s (it was later torn down), passenger trains still provided at least twice-daily service in both directions, but rarely did large crowds such as in this early photograph regularly congregate on the platform. Use of passenger trains declined rapidly after World War II as automobiles largely superceded them. Scheduled passenger train service ended in 1990.* COURTESY OF THE TOWN OF BRACEBRIDGE

The St. Thomas' Church, celebrating its 75th anniversary, recognized Mrs. Ernest A. Whitten for having served as their organist for 60 of those years.

**1972** The municipal Council opened its new sanitary landfill site in Macaulay Ward this year, with access off Kirk Line. It had received a great deal of negative reaction but proceeded based on the policy of the provincial authorities against open burning of garbage.

The contract with Bucko McDonald to act as hockey director was renewed, and the Red Wing Hockey School again operated in the arena during the summer. In the first move toward their own fire department, a fire pump was provided for the use of the residents of Oakley Ward. Council also initiated the first steps toward creating a separate cemetery board to administer the 23 cemeteries in the new area municipality. Ed Rowlands was appointed chairman of the new board along with the following members: Nick Roche, Louis Enrico, Dan MacNaughtan Sr., Walter Reynolds (secretary), Murray Dauphin, and Alf Ashley. Jack McLachlan was appointed municipal treasurer to take the place of Alastair Watson.

Although it would receive a great deal of revision as a result of many hearings before the Ontario Municipal Board, the first zoning bylaw (72-20) was passed to control the use of land in the new area municipality, eventually becoming Bylaw 73-60 upon completion. Irvin Robson of Deco Lumber initiated one of the first rezonings by applying to change the designation of the former Moore's Mill to accommodate a commercial building trades outlet.

Council made the important move of purchasing property to create the Eilean Gowan Island Park and to expand both Bowyer's and Kirby's Beach park areas. It also started discussion with the Ministry of the Environment to build a sewage treatment plant.

In an ongoing dispute that seemed to drag on for years, the property line location between the properties of W.J. Berry and A. Heics on Wood Lake was brought before Council. Council was continually being called on to settle petty arguments that erupted over use of the town road allowance that was located at the front of both properties.

A plan for the development of the new municipal cemetery was produced on land negotiated for the town by councillor James D. Lang in lot 5, concession A, Monck South Ward. Council also decided this year to build a 40 by 100-foot building for cold storage at the town/Water, Light and Power Commission garage site. This was changed in later years into a complete building and became the garage and offices for the town's, and later the district's, water and sewer department.

A presentation was made to Council to encourage more cooperation between the Parks Board, Recreation Committee, and the Community Centre Board, and to hire a recreation director.

The administration staff of the District Municipality of Muskoka moved into their new office on Pine Street, and the District Council held its first Council meeting in the new council chambers in March. At the official opening which took place later, the Honourable Ross Macdonald, Lieutenant Governor of Ontario, and over 40 members of the World War I 122nd Battalion participated in an impressive ceremony when the "Colours" of the Battalion were presented to district chairman Milton Tibbett for display in the new building.

The official opening of the completed development road (now Highway 118) between Highway 11 and Highway 35 in Carnarvon (Haliburton County) took place with district chairman Milton Tibbett and Haliburton County warden Malcolm McGillivray participating.

The Muskoka-Parry Sound Health Unit hired Dr. R.E. Stokes to take charge of the Mental Health Services Department.

Alan Peever, BA, was appointed principal of Bracebridge Public School. Helen Smith and Lorraine Hawn retired from teaching there after many years of service. J. Wimund Kirk retired as principal of Macaulay Public School.

The Bracebridge Memorial Community Centre moved into a new era of ice operations by purchasing a new Zamboni-type ice-flooding machine to replace the hand-pushed scrapers and flooding barrels. The Bracebridge Bears Junior C Hockey team defeated Powassan and Penetang to progress to the Ontario semifinals where they lost to Leamington in a series saddened by the death of four Leamington supporters in an airplane accident on their way back home from one of the games in Bracebridge. Doug Smith, former arena manager and building inspector for the town, was honoured by the Minor Hockey Association for his faithful work over the years in the hockey program from 1948 to 1972. He was known as "a friend to all players and the lowest paid baby-sitter in Town." Tommy Ball was also honoured for his lifetime dedication to town sports.

In other sports, Marc Knowles, 16, won the downhill event at the Southern Ski Zone B Division at Osler Bluffs, and the winner of the Ecclestone Trophy and Muskoka Champions in curling was a rink consisting of Dint Rowe, Gary Martin, Chris Ramshaw, and Rich Lynn.

The Kinsmen Club celebrated its 25th anniversary, as did the Snow Queen Rebekah Lodge. The Baysville Lions Club received its charter.

Patrick T. Freeburn was appointed manager of Ontario Hydro for the area. Vern Peake was elected president of the Agricultural Society, John Biddle president of the Muskoka Scottish Rite Club, and Stu Reid president of Rotary.

Jack Page retired from the position of manager of the Water, Light and Power Commission, which now only dealt with the town hydro service, and was replaced by Ernie Keall. Mrs. George S. Johnson retired and was honoured for her 48 years of service in church music with the First Baptist Church, and Nelson A. Goltz resigned as manager of Santa's Village and was replaced by Allan Lomas.

Sandy Milne retired as postmaster, having been preceded by William C. Huckle and Robert P. Perry, in that order, and was replaced by J.C. Elliott, who was then replaced by Earl J. Patterson.

The president of Fowler Construction Ltd., Glen S.

Coates, announced that Bruce S. Evans Ltd. of Agincourt had purchased an interest in the company. Mr. Coates would remain as president and general manager, and Ralph Boothby as superintendent of aggregate production, with a new officer, Kenneth Cummings, to be vice-president and engineer. Mr. Coates was elected president of the Ontario Road Builders Association. He was also appointed an honorary inspector general of the Supreme Council of the Ancient and Accepted Scottish Rite of Canada.

McDermott Holdings took over operation of the Patterson Hotel with Ronald Hawn as manager, and George A. Parlett announced the sale of Parlett Transport to Boyd Transport of Newmarket.

Buildings Trades Centre held the official opening of its new yard and showroom at Falkenburg, on the property formerly occupied by Moore Lumber.

Norman A. Harkness, head of sales for Muskoka Garage and town councillor, was notified that out of 26,000 GMC sales reps he was in the top 10 in sales and was again appointed as a member of GM's Grand Master Salesman Club.

John Newark celebrated 50 years in the boat fender business, and Watt's Economy Drugs opened its new store location beside the A & P Store on Manitoba Street (the Radio Shack today). The Industrial Mall on Armstrong Street at Wellington opened for tenants.

Rev. H.J. Fitzgerald was appointed monsignor having been chosen by Pope Paul VI as Honorary Chaplain to His Holiness the Pope.

An era ended in the closing of the Vankoughnet post office, and one started in Muskoka politics with Stan Darling of Burks Falls receiving the nomination as the Progressive Conservative candidate for the federal riding of Parry Sound-Muskoka. Another first occurred with Council passing a bylaw requiring all taxis operating in town to have fare meters.

The Central Food Mall opened in the former A & P Store on Queen's Hill on Manitoba Street, and Reynolds Funeral Home constructed an addition to the building at the corner of Manitoba and Mary streets. Angie's Delicatessen, Northern Custom Kitchens, Bavarian Bakery, Medical Centre Drugs (in the Wright Building on Manitoba Street owned by Barbara Whitaker), the Kentucky Fried Chicken outlet, and Bracebridge Bus and Truck, owned by Doug Nelson, all had their official openings during this year. Waite's Bakery put on an addition to accommodate a bake shop which previously had been part of the Waite's Coffee Shop on Manitoba Street. Dr. Morley Crockford announced his intention to open a dentistry practice in Bracebridge, it and Fraserburg being his hometown.

Deaths included E. Edson Veitch … Margaret Amelia (Mrs. W.C.) Campbell … John Giovanni Morra, barber and bandmaster for the Bracebridge Citizen's Band and a very popular citizen … Allan P. Tinkiss … Lawrence Ward … Norman Richard Leeder … Noble Meeks … Ina Doreen (Mrs. Percy) Brazier … Gordon Hayes … David H. Veitch … James Lucas (Mike) Fenn … Carey Johnson … Mrs. Jesse Lawrence … Sylvia Atkinson … Canon W.A. Hankinson … James Hannah … Margaret (Mrs. Alex) Cooper … Robert A. Howes … Adelina (Mrs. George) Reid … Bodo Alexander Nitzsche … John Henry Buker … Mrs. John McKeown … Burton F. Dawson … Henry McFadden … George S. Brooks … Thomas J. Ball … Ellen Spreadborough … Stewart Broad … Albert E. Gibbs … Herbert Thomas Hammond … Elizabeth (Mrs. Albert E.) Gibbs … Minnie Margurette (Mrs. Ernie) Holland … Grace Winnifred (Mrs. Harper) Atkinson … William C. Knowles … Ellen M. (Mrs. Charles) Lazzara … Wilfred G. Patterson … William Reginald Kirk, grandson of Mr. and Mrs. John Kirk, who came as pioneers to concessions 4 and 5 of Macaulay Township in 1864 and after whom the Kirk Line was named … Myrtle Janet (Mrs. Ernest A.) Whitten … Lyda Boyer … Albert H. Dixon … Gordon White.

The Kinsmen Club hosted the public fireworks display at Jubilee Park with Don Coates and John Davis in charge and Bob Spence as president of the club. Barbara Smith was president of the Kinette Club. Don Johnson was elected president of the Lions Club, and Inspector George Hankin of the Ontario Provincial Police was awarded a Queen's Commission by Lieutenant Governor W. Ross MacDonald.

Five people died in a car-truck accident at the intersection of Entrance Drive and Highway 11 (Cedar Lane now), and four died in a fiery car accident on Highway 11 just north of town.

Dr. William Monk, renowned surgeon and active participant in matters of artistic and literary interest in the community, was appointed to the Board of the Royal Ontario Museum, and Bracebridge-born Rudy Meeks won the Canadian old-time fiddling contest at Shelbourne.

Klaus Deger, Ina Berzins, Doris Zobrist, and Margaret Harper all qualified as Ontario Scholars.

TransCanada Pipelines carried out the major construction project of twinning the natural gas transmission line through Bracebridge. Aston Villa, a resort started by Mr. and Mrs. Jack Johnston after World War II, was sold by Mr. and Mrs. Henry Herbert to Grise Resorts.

Doug Smith was president of the Bracebridge Lacrosse Association. Carole Anne Flynn was selected Miss Bracebridge. The Watts baseball team won the Muskoka Fastball Championship. Henry Speedie celebrated his 100th birthday.

A $15-million hotel complex was proposed for the former Anglo-Canadian Leather Co. property, but although it was approved by Council to proceed, it never came to pass.

A federal election was held this year resulting in Stan Darling of the PC party getting elected with 14,558 votes over Allan Knapp, Liberal, with 8,988, and Ann Malton, NDP, with 7,076.

In municipal elections, George Parlett was re-elected mayor, defeating Nelson Goltz 1,754 votes to 950. In Bracebridge Ward, Norman Harkness (887 votes), Ralph Melvin (862), and Carl Sander (828) were elected, defeating Tom Reilly (374), Barry Hart (374), and Joe Defabrizio (161). Aubrey Glass was elected in Monck South Ward with 198 votes to Norman Keall's 137. In Macaulay Ward, Dan MacNaughtan Sr. was elected with 275 votes over Harold Dawson with 212. Draper Ward electors selected James D. Lang with 141 votes over Alf Ashley (97) and Bart Lydan (41). Elected by acclamation were Norman Archer in Muskoka North Ward and Neil Boyes in Oakley Ward.

For the Board of Education, Norman Rosewarne with 1,965 votes, Mel Goltz (1,580), Bev Thompson (1,551), and Wilbur Archer (1,537) were elected, defeating Garnet Tremblay (1,094) and Bart Goss (500).

Bill Currell was elected president of the Chamber of Commerce and Max Beaumont president of the Muskoka Soil and Crop Improvement Association.

## 1973

This was a year of further refinement of the new form of government as municipalities across Muskoka tried to make the best of what some thought was a system not as efficient as their own little operation, especially in the rural areas of the district. In the "indirect" election of district councillors, the Bracebridge Council choose Norman A. Harkness, Norman Archer, and James D. Lang to represent Bracebridge, along with Mayor George Parlett, on the District Council. Oakley Ward and the residents of the Vankoughnet area received the full support of the entire Bracebridge Council in their attempt to encourage the Muskoka District Board of Education to leave the Oakley Public School open instead of closing it as planned. Their hard work was rewarded and to the date of publication of this book the Oakley School is still part of the Muskoka school system.

The councillors' chairs which, along with the council table and town office clock were the only pieces of furniture saved from the Town Hall fire of 1957 (by Dr. Dodds, at the risk of his own safety), were re-covered and restored. The actual date of purchase of the chairs, still in use in 1999, is uncertain, but it is thought they were purchased before 1900, and perhaps as early as the building of the first Town Hall in 1881.

Council continued the program of buying the decrepit boathouses along Bracebridge Bay by passing a resolution to purchase the Shier Building Centre boathouse from the company's trustee in bankruptcy for $2,500.

In order to complete an agreement with Harbridge Developments in its construction of the Riverside Shopping Centre and relocation of Beaumont Drive away from the side of the Muskoka River, Council asked Captain Ralph McPherson to remove his residence and boathouse (in which he moored his cruise boat, the *Mildred*) from the road allowance along the river, upon which he had encroached for many years, so that the allowance could be closed and conveyed to the plaza owners. Attempts to negotiate with Mr. McPherson by the shopping centre owners were of no avail, although Council did agree to extend a sewer line to the residence in order to stop the pollution of the river, and eventually Council took legal action to have the building removed from the road allowance.

Council appointed a Centennial Committee to commence plans for the celebration of Bracebridge's 100th birthday which would take place in 1975. In addition to municipal clerk Kenneth C. Veitch, and other municipal councillors and staff, the committee consisted of Arla Rebman, Patsy Boyer, Sybil Jackson, Douglas Smith, Glen Coates, Peter Glazier, Tom Robinson, Al Taylor, Sean Kelly, and Gerald Murphy.

In response to a survey related to housing needs, Council passed a resolution requesting the Ontario Housing Authority to proceed with the building of 39 geared-to-income housing units. Council also passed a bylaw this year to require acquisition of a permit prior to erecting commercial signs.

Ralph Melvin retired as manager of the Bank of Nova Scotia and assumed duties in real estate sales with Peter G. Lush & Associates. Fred Davis was elected Master of Muskoka (Masonic ) Lodge, and Roy Gibbs as Master of the Loyal Orange Lodge.

Bev Thompson of Vankoughnet was elected chairman of the Muskoka Board of Education, and Marian Boothby chairman of the Algonquin Regional Library.

The Ontario Road Builders Association, headed by former mayor Glen S. Coates, voted to assist the Segwun Museum to complete the restoration of the *Segwun*, Canada's only remaining intact steamship.

The Bracebridge Curling Club members voted 96 to 8

*The Fall Fair Parade, in which public school students marched through town and down to the fair grounds, was a long-time tradition in Bracebridge. Dusty and possibly muddy streets were a drawback in the early days (this photograph on Queen's Hill is pre-1915), and marching in a straight line obviously was not a priority!* COURTESY OF BRENDA COX

to enter into an agreement with the South Muskoka Golf & Curling Club to transfer their assets and use the newly constructed curling facility. The Bracebridge Hawks, an Intermediate C team formed by players from the Industrial League, was organized and eliminated teams from Ganonoque, Elmvale, and Petrolia on their way to a provincial championship.

Tom Robinson was appointed arena manager by the municipality following the retirement of Doug Smith. Captain Al Lomas retired as commanding officer of the Lions Air Cadet Squadron.

Duane Miller was awarded a Certificate of Merit by the Department of Agriculture for his past service to agriculture. Robert E. Jefferies was elected president of the Ontario Command of the Royal Canadian Legion, while Pat Proulx was elected president of the Bracebridge Branch of the Legion. Robert J. Boyer was elected president of the Rotary Club, replacing Stu Reid.

Wayne Scott was elected president of Minor Hockey, replacing Carl Philips. and Betty Heath was chosen president of the Business and Professional Women's Club.

Achieving Ontario Scholar status this year were Jennifer Boyer, Ingrid Pawelke, and Daniel Hitchcock.

Stan and Marc Knowles won 4th place in the U.S. National Championship for Albacore racing.

Annie Bruce, owner of the Redmond Thomas house at the corner of Manitoba Street and Kimberley Avenue, advised that she was going to donate that building to the Bracebridge Cemetery Board with the request that it be sold and the proceeds used to build a memorial mortuary chapel at the new municipal cemetery, to be designated the Redmond Thomas Memorial Chapel.

W.J.R. McKay was elected District Deputy Grand Master of the Masonic Lodge, and Bob Quinlan, manager of the Hoar Transport depot, won a gold medal at the Canada Summer Games in Burnaby, BC, as one of the four members of the Ontario kayak team.

Kathy Hammond was chosen as Miss Bracebridge, and then as Miss Muskoka at the Cavalcade of Colour.

Murray Scarrow was welcomed as the new pastor of the Bethel Pentecostal Tabernacle, and J.L. Keeler of St. Joseph's Church resigned to take up duties as Parish Priest at Cardiff.

*By the 1970s, the children's fall fair parade had become quite elaborate, with students wearing costumes and some even riding horses. The event has since been discontinued.* COURTESY OF MARILYN LONG

In accordance with the announced restructuring of address data, the postal code for Bracebridge was designated to be POB 1CO.

Craig Stewart was appointed the examiner of surveys at the provincial registry and land titles office, replacing John J. Haigh. Joe Defabrizio was elected president of the Bracebridge Curling Club … Ralph Tippett, former chief ranger, was appointed by Leo Bernier, Minister of Natural Resources, as head of the Bracebridge District for the Ministry … Nick and Ruby Wettlaufer celebrated their 60th wedding anniversary.

After four years operating from the basement of the courthouse on Dominion Street, the administrative office of the Muskoka Board of Education relocated to a part of the District of Muskoka building on Pine Street. The Board also introduced a program into Muskoka schools encouraging the use of the metric system of weights and measures.

After many years of speculation about it, the Council this year seriously discussed the possibility of constructing a bridge over the Muskoka River to link Wellington and Stuart streets (Stuart Street eventually disappeared as the Beaumont Drive, District Road 4, and Ecclestone Drive alignments were rearranged). The bridge would be eventually located in the same area where in pioneer days a floating bridge consisting of barges tied end to end was located during the winter.

A significant improvement in highway service was set in motion when the Ministry of Transportation and Communications awarded a contract for the construction of a 6.76-mile section of Highway 11 to be four-laned from south of Muskoka Falls to High Falls Road, including a widened river crossing, and to be located on a new alignment to the east of the existing Highway 11 (which is now Cedar Lane).

The volunteer group dedicated to improving the arena, known as the Community Centre Improvement Committee, raised enough money to pay for the installation of safety glass above the end boards of the ice surface.

Rev. David N. Mitchell was honoured by being designated a Canon of St. Lukes Cathedral and of the Diocese of Algoma.

Forrest Jacobs, a renowned artist from the United States, completed his work on a mural 60 feet long by 9 feet high depicting the history of Bracebridge and Muskoka, to be mounted on the wall overlooking the IGA in the Riverside Shopping Centre. The mural would eventually become the property of the town through the courtesy of Dave Knappett of Maple Orchard Farms. It was added to as a 125th anniversary project with artist Mary Thrane.

Consistent with the accelerated growth of Bracebridge during this period, this year abounded with business activities. Simcoe Block (Muskoka) Ltd. announced their plan through the Ministry of Industry and Tourism to locate a plant in Bracebridge, and McEwan-Tougard expanded and moved their plant from Shier Street to District Road 4. Work commenced on a new factory building, also on District Road 4, for Cumberland Packaging.

In the downtown area, Lorne and Jean Hockridge closed Lorne's Marketeria in the Manitoba Street building which had previously been occupied by the Hutchison Bros. Grocery Store, and sold the building to McPhails of Muskoka which moved its clothing store there from the Reid Building on the opposite side of the street. Dr. Ray Savijarvi purchased the former Ecclestone and Bates Building on the east side of Manitoba Street and announced his intention to move his dentistry office there from his existing location on Dominion Street. The Patterson Bros. sold their bus garage on the north side of Ontario Street opposite the Waite's Bakery store to Waites, who renovated it for rental to retail businesses. The former Erma's Restaurant, adjacent to the south side of Chancery Lane, and an adjoining laundromat were purchased and renovation plans implemented.

Bob and Julie Scott relocated their Muskoka Paint Centre store from the south end of the west side of Manitoba Street, beside the former Myers' Hardware Store, to the Reid Building vacated by McPhails of Muskoka, where they expanded to include an art gallery. The Bracebridge Rent-All store opened for business at 79 Wellington Street, and Peter Corfe, artist, opened the Chancery Lane Shop.

Richard and Shirley Ryckman opened the Bracebridge Tire Service in the former Supertest Station at 216 Manitoba Street, and a group of businesses including Leah Pinaud Ladies Fashions, Sterling Trust, Riverside Shell Carwash, and Riverside IGA, all tenants of the Riverside Shopping Centre, had an official opening. Raymie Lee was appointed manager of both the centre and of the IGA. Everett's Pharmacy and Watt's Economy Drugs were bought by Harbridge Development Corp., owners of the Riverside Shopping Centre.

Rombo's Restaurant opened in the renovated Texaco Service Station at the intersection of Muskoka Road (now Entrance Drive), Manitoba Street, and Ontario Street (in front of Bird Mill Mews, the former warehouse for the Bird Woolen Mill). Work commenced on the Islander Motel on Baysville Road (Taylor Road) by Colin Shivers. Alpine Catering and Submarine Shop opened at 12 Thomas Street (now also part of Taylor Road).

The 66-year-old business of Tom Fisher, known as Fisher Florist, on the east side Manitoba Street in the second building south of the Ann Street, was closed and the building sold. The business had been started by his father, William R. Fisher. The Boathouse Boutique opened on Manitoba Street, the Albion Hotel was sold by

J. Andrukitus to John Pierre and Cor Spruyt, the Brodom Apartments were sold by H. J. Brooks & Sons to Robert Oaks, and John and Marette O'Brien sold their Canadian Tire franchise to Ron Doty.

The following deaths were noted: Alick Cave ... Holly Blair ... Jack Leon Howey ... Florence (Mrs. Walter) Hunt ... Russell G. Lackie ... Willard Pickles ... John D. Hassell ... Ethel May (Mrs. Oliver) Austin ... Orbery Kennedy ... Hattie (Mrs. Joseph) Oatley ... Eleanor Nell Fenn ... Roy Nelson ... Eva (Mrs. William) Bird ... Lillian Mary (Mrs. Gerald) Winnington-Ingram ... Ernest John Colson ... Florence (Mrs. William) McNabb ... the Honourable Frank Bastedo, a former Lieutenant Governor of Ontario and a son of Mr. and Mrs. David Edgar Bastedo, born in Bracebridge in 1886 ... Redmond Thomas, QC, former editor of the *Bracebridge Gazette*, magistrate, author of *Reminiscences* and other quality historical articles on Bracebridge and Muskoka, son of Mr. and Mrs. G.H.O. Thomas, pioneers of Bracebridge ... Elizabeth Beatrice (Mrs. William) Hawn ... Grant R. Smith ... Robert Pearcey ... Lillian Winnifred (Mrs. Arthur E.) Dick ... R. Douglas Thompson ... Jessie Evelyn (Mrs. Alva) Hetherington ... Carl E. Laycox ... Gertrude Eleanor (Mrs. Walter G.) Hare ... Margaret Bird ... Elma May (Mrs. Arthur V.) Dawson ... George N. Ecclestone, a business, municipal, and community leader who took over the hardware business of his father, George W. Ecclestone ... George E. Matthews ... Donald Kimberly Bray, player with the Bracebridge Bears Junior C hockey team) ... Alice Victoria (Mrs. Leonard A.) Taylor ... Jane Harriet (Mrs. W. Alvin) Cook ... Caroline (Mrs. James) Crowder ... Allan K. Lomas, general manager of Santa's Village ... Lloyd Clifford Conway ... Ethel Kirk ... Ruth Evelyn (Mrs. Joseph) Ennis ... Mary Odessa (Mrs. Henry James) Elliott ...Joseph Stevenson, former town police officer ... Ida (Mrs. Addison) Irwin ... Elgin Shea ... Nellie (Mrs. W.J.) Hammell ... Keith Dickson ... Shirley Agnes Flynn ... John Edward Lee ... Alexander Harrison ... Raymond F. Heath, Justice of the Peace ... Rosa Maria Cann-Rutland ... Sarah Gertrude (Mrs. George) Morrow ... Agnes Jane Hannah ... Eliza (Lila) (Mrs. Ernest) Kirk ... Leo F. Connaghan ... Eva Hutcheson ... Jessie Nicholson ... Harriet (Mrs. Robert) Meeks ... Thomas S. Stevenson ... C. Austin Fryer ... William J. Patterson, one of the founders of Patterson-Kaye Lodge ... Leonard Slater ... Thomas Sampson ... Marian "Timmy" (Mrs. Ernest) Allchin, owner-operator of the Holiday House in the building that was the home of the first District Judge, William C. Mahaffy, at the south end of Dominion Street (Inn at the Falls now).

H.E.S. Sugg was appointed a Queen's Council. Stan Darling, at the start of what would turn out to be a long term of service as MP for Parry Sound-Muskoka, made his first speech in the House of Commons.

Citing the reason as lack of available competent staff, Murray Lee, owner of the Parkview Restaurant, decided to close his business. The restaurant was originally a grocery business started by A.E. Mundy before the First World War and was changed to a restaurant during the war by John Keeler. It was subsequently owned by Tom Stephenson, Nelson Goltz, and Kenneth Moorehouse. Coincidentally, two other restaurants closed during the year: the Muskoka Restaurant and Waite's Coffee Shop.

An addition at the Monck Public School on Wellington Street was officially opened ... A fire at Allport Marina on Muskoka Lake destroyed 26 boats in storage.

A number of residential subdivisions were started this year. Work was commenced on the Andrea Drive, McNabb, and South Muskoka Golf & Curling Club subdivisions, and Harbridge Developments proposed a high-density residential development on a 60-acre parcel of land across from Canadian Motor Lamp (Meritor). This development was fraught with the problem of lack of capacity in the town's sewer treatment facility and prompted a lot of discussion and several proposals, but in the end the subdivision became one of an industrial-commercial nature, known as the Bracebridge Industrial Park. Pioneer lumberman Robert Dollar and community leader and solicitor E.P. Lee were honoured by having streets here named after them.

The Bracebridge population was announced to be 7,032, up from 6,841 the year before. The ice left Muskoka Lake on April 16 and special notation was made that this was the 21st anniversary of the first televised hockey game in Canada, which took place at the Bracebridge Arena on January 25, 1952. It was a game between teams consisting of NHL old-timers, sponsored by the Bala Lions Club. Gordon Sinclair, renowned broadcaster and CFRB radio personality, served as manager for both teams. The game was televised by the NBC network and broadcast only in the United States, there being no television stations in Canada at that time.

In a tragic accident, Hilary (Ray) Young of Gravenhurst, after serving as parade marshal at the Remembrance Day Parade in Bracebridge, died when his car left the road and plunged 80 feet into the South Falls gorge at Muskoka Falls. The car came to rest in the rapids where it happened to be noticed by workers in the area.

## 1974

Preparations and plans for Bracebridge's 100th anniversary in 1975 played a prominent role in this year's activities, along with a continuing list of new and expanding businesses.

Late in the year a contract was entered into with Canadian Swimming Pool Design Services Ltd. and Loaring Construction to proceed with the building of the Bracebridge Centennial Centre at a contract cost of $652,231. A major fund-raising project was undertaken, headed by Lloyd Flemming. The first organization to donate was the Loyal Orange Lodge which was celebrating its 100th anniversary in 1974.

An additional Centennial project took the form of repairs to the Bird Mill Pumphouse by Northern Buildall at a cost of $5,500.

The Centennial celebrations started on June 5 when a function was held in Memorial Park in recognition of the passing of a bylaw by Victoria County in response to a petition submitted by residents of the Bracebridge area in 1874 that gave birth to Bracebridge as a municipality. The marigold was designated as the Centennial flower with Mary Thrane designing the Centennial Crest.

In spite of a great number of protests, Council passed a bylaw prohibiting the discharge of firearms in the Monck South Ward between Highway 118 and the Muskoka River.

Council accepted, from Annie Bruce, the Redmond Thomas house at Kimberley Avenue and Manitoba Street. The Cemetery Board was to sell it and use the proceeds to build a memorial chapel in the new municipal cemetery in honour of Redmond Thomas.

Council continued with its expansion and development plans for Kirby's Beach Park and Bracebridge Bay Park by buying the Cecil W. Dickie cottage in the beach area and the Bracebridge Boatworks building on Wharf Road. In addition, Council hired Totten Sims Hubicki to prepare a master plan for Bracebridge Bay Park incorporating Kelvin Grove Park (the former Motor Park), Mill Street, and the federal government wharf, this under the leadership of William Quemby, town coordinator, and Kenneth C. Veitch, clerk-administrator.

As requested by Lionel Davis, president of the Senior Citizen Club, Council agreed to assist the club by contributing $1,500 to a proposed drop-in centre in the former A & P Store building on Queen's Hill.

The building of an interchange at Highway 11 and District roads 1 and 4 (Vankoughnet Road) was requested of the Ministry of Transportation and Communications, who responded in October by announcing plans to proceed with this construction … Council entered into a lease agreement with the executors of the Williams estate for Annie Williams Memorial Park.

Totten Sims Hubicki was authorized to proceed with engineering drawings for necessary alterations to the sewage system once a site was established; however the Ministry of the Environment did agree to permit the expansion of the sewer lagoons instead of building a treatment plant.

Tennis courts were built in Kelvin Grove Park in spite of Fowler Construction Ltd. encountering quicksand … Council bought the curling club building across from the arena for $35,000 and eventually tore it down to make room for a parking lot.

The public library, started by Mr. McGill (school principal), J.B. Browning, and Dr. Bridgland as the Mechanic's Institute in November 1874 with 225 volumes, celebrated its 100th anniversary.

The business community experienced more growth. Gordon Motor Sales expanded its building … Parkview Restaurant reopened after renovations and the acquisition of a new partner, George Evershed … John Brown's Sporting Goods merged with Emerson's Department

Store and relocated to the Riverside Shopping Centre with Eric Faulkner as manager ... Northern Ontario Foundry Ltd., a division of Ingenious Devices of Orillia, took over the former Muskoka Foundry building on Entrance Drive ... Maurice Fitzmaurice, OLS, moved his survey business (formerly Fitzmaurice & Boyer Surveyors) from 43 Ontario Street to 11 Thomas Street ... Rainbow Ridge was sold to Ottow Bertnik, owner of the Lobster Trap Restaurant in Toronto ... Jim and Mary Bradbury purchased Ridley Cleaners from Douglas Kirkness, who along with partner Jack Fawcett had bought the business from William C. Snazel shortly after World War II ... Fowler Construction Ltd. relocated their head office from Spencer Street to their asphalt plant near the Kirk Line ... Cathcart's Garage closed after 35 years of business and was sold to Doug Duff and Ron Hicks, who moved the business to the former Bracebridge Steel Fabricating building beside Shaw Street.

The Royal Bank of Canada announced its plan to construct a new branch building in the location of the former Muskoka Restaurant beside the lane (now Anderson Lane) to the rear parking lot ... In December, Andrea's Steak & Seafood House opened in the former Medley house at the corner of Manitoba Street and Monck Road ... Cavalcade Ford Mercury Sales commenced business ... Bucky Inglis started Arctic Sports from his home on Nichols Sideroad ... the official opening took place for Cumberland Packaging Ltd., a manufacturer of Sweet 'n' Low, with Art Ruttan as president ... Al Prowse, who bought Matthias Furniture from Mr. and Mrs. George Matthias in 1971, sold the building to Mr. and Mrs. Ross Ralph ... Rombo's Restaurant (now the site of the Bird Mill Mews Parkette) was sold by Chris Rombos to Timos Theodoropoulos ... construction on the 532 Industrial Mall started.

Jim Smith, manager of Bracebridge Chrysler-Plymouth, received the Moto-Ski Dealer of the Year award, chosen from 300 such outlets across Canada ... Whitney Construction opened a branch office in the Morley Crockford Building on Shier Street with Bob Jones as Manager (a different Bob Jones from the principals who purchased Shier Building Centre) ... Earl and Cecile

*The year 1974 marked the centenary of library service in Bracebridge. Although it had its origins in 1874, the Bracebridge Public Library did not occupy its present Carnegie building until 1908, at which time the collection numbered 3,808 books. This photograph was taken in 1939. The Uptown Garage is now a restaurant (the Old Station, appropriately).* COURTESY OF VICKY BILLINGSLEY

*A car on the road between Bracebridge and Gravenhurst in 1919. Little more than 50 years later, visitors from the south could reach town on a paved four-lane highway.*
COURTESY OF IAN TURNBULL

Bryant opened Bracebridge Optical and Hearing Aid Service at 97 Manitoba Street ... Max Smith of Modern Home Supply expanded by opening a warehouse on Ann Street across from his retail outlet, with John Smith as manager ... Mr. and Mrs. John Corfe sold the Chancery Lane Shop to Robert Edwards ... Thos. N. Shea Ltd. opened a real estate office on Dominion Street in the building previously occupied by lawyer R.A. Tweedie.

P.J. Marrin & Son officially opened their new building on Highway 118. This business was started by Philip J. Marrin in 1909 in a barber shop. It developed into a grocery store at 33 Manitoba Street, then changed to wholesale supplies in 1942, at which time it was the only such business on the Highway 11 corridor between Toronto and North Bay.

Jim and Jacqueline Niven purchased Holiday House (Inn at the Falls) from Ernest Allchin.

Following a reassessment of property values, Council took the unprecedented step of appealing the values placed on the factories of Corning Glass, Rockwell International, Alcan Wire & Cable, and Alcan Foils as being too low. Their taxes had been lowered by $100,000. Council succeeded in having the assessments adjusted, albeit in a minor way.

Residential subdivisions continued to grow and develop as planning processes and building permit applications abounded in the McNabb, Westvale Heights, South Muskoka Golf & Curling Club, Beacon Heights, Andrea Drive, Wilshier Estates, Brobst Forest, Clearview Estates, and the Ridge Lake Developments subdivisions.

The Bracebridge Ski Club leased the Rainbow Ridge Ski hills and lifts and operated them in a timely move considering that 4.5 feet of snow fell on Muskoka in a nine-day period in January.

The Bracebridge and Muskoka Lakes Secondary School ski team won the All-Ontario School Championship at a competition at Blue Mountain, Collingwood.

Bus Brazier, Bracebridge's own "Chief Musqua Ukee," a familiar figure in Bracebridge parades, celebrated his 25th anniversary working at the courthouse/registry office ... Roy White retired from his hairdressing business after 40 years of service ... James Patterson was appointed manager of the A&P Store ... Beverley Roberts was elected Master of the Muskoka (Masonic) Lodge ... Bertha Bell retired from the South Muskoka Memorial Hospital after 24 years of faithful service ... John Purchase was appointed district commissioner of Scouting for the Lake Muskoka District and Charles Morrow was elected president of the Agricultural Society.

Constable Bruce Kruger received a commendation and Certificate of Achievement for his part in saving the life of a 20-year-old man, the victim of a car accident.

Peter Terry escaped unhurt after his bulldozer slid into the Muskoka River above High Falls while working on bridge construction for the four-laning of Highway 11.

Frank Miller, MPP, was appointed Minister of Health in the cabinet of Premier William Davis.

Dr. F.F. Archdekin was elected president of the Muskoka Scottish Rite Club, replacing Bud Hampson. Nick Roche was elected president of the Lions Club and Joe Defabrizio zone chairman of the Lions Club organization. After 18 years of service on the executive, Ken Shier was honoured by the Minor Hockey Association. Wayne Scott was president of the association and Betty Lefler president of the Ladies Auxiliary.

*Highway 11 at Bracebridge as it appears today. There are many who would argue that Bracebridge is indeed the pot of gold at the end of the rainbow! Although the four-lane bypass was built in the 1970s, the Taylor Road interchange visible here was not added until later.* COURTESY OF LORRIE SZEKAT

The post office employees joined in with a national strike based on the union's opposition to the implementation of the new postal code system.

Work commenced this year on the new Pentecostal Church on Wellington Street.

The South Muskoka Golf & Curling Club opened its golf course with Ron Webb as head golf professional.

Bill Anderson, barber, informed the Ministry of Natural Resources about a pine tree in lot 5, concession 7 of Macaulay Ward (Yearley property, off the High Falls Road), that was the largest ever recorded in Ontario, being 141 feet tall.

Donald McVittie, born in Bracebridge, president of Arrowhead Motors in Huntsville, was elected president of the Automobile Dealers Association of Ontario ... Larry Giaschi was elected president of the Rotary Club, Betty Walker president of Meals-on-Wheels, and Don Coates and Joan Fish were elected presidents of the Kinsmen and Kinette Clubs, respectively.

Norman J. MacMillan, born in Bracebridge in 1909, grandson of pioneer Singleton Brown, retired as president and chairman of the Canadian National Railways and was appointed Companion of the Order of Canada.

In the federal election, Stan Darling, PC, won with 13,884 votes over Ted Leslie (Liberal) with 11,388 and Anne Malton for the NDP with 6,077.

The George Armstrong sawmill on Highway 11 north of Bracebridge was destroyed by fire ... Maher Shoe Store changed its name to Darling Shoes after Deering Gray sold the business to Ross Darling ... Jack McAnsh of Gordon Motor Sales was named a Grand Salesman by General Motors ... George Yearley of Lone Pine Esso received commendation from Imperial Oil of Canada for 50 years as one of its dealers.

The following deaths were recorded: Christopher Scott Burley ... Zaida E. Pashler ... Stewart S. Broad ... Thomas Sampson ... Benjamin Deith ... Pearl (Mrs. P.J.) Marrin Sr. ... Natasha Atkinson ... Percy Good ... Willard Speedie ... Ina (Mrs. Elmer) Philips ... Sarah Ellen (Mrs. A.J.) Popejoy ... Lillia May (Mrs. Dan) Goheen ... Bruce Duncan ... Elmer Phillips ... J. Arthur Fry ... David A. Danes ... Andrew Aiken ... Harold William Tingey ... Mrs. Ward Davison ... Amybel (Mrs. Norman) Rosewarne ... R. Stanley Vincent ... Wallace Matthews ... Allan James Keall ... John P. Currie ... John Dinner ... Peter Thomas Edward Cooper ... Odd Loreng Veset ... Ian Scott Nunn ... Whitney W. Kay ... John T. Greer ... Joseph Taylor ... Irene J. (Mrs. Alman V.) Loney ... Ernest Adamson ... Herman Davis ... Ruby Pearl Leonora (Mrs. C.H.) Kemp ... Mrs. Fred Bamford ... Roy Garwood ...

Wilbert A. Richards, former mayor, businessman, and municipal clerk, instrumental in organizing the Rotary Club, Muskoka Tourist Association, and the Muskoka Children's Aid Society ... Howard Pearson ... Walter Pashler ... Oliver H. Austin ... Mrs. Walter Leeder ... Charles Henry Taplin ... George Siberry ... Rocco Morra ... Henry Speedie ... Gertrude Rachel (Mrs. Richard F.) Taplin ... John J. Ball ... Gertrude (Mrs. Carl) Schultz ... William J. Ruttan ... Seigfreid A. Paul ... Abram Dawson ... Harvey Allan Kennedy ... Albert Pelissero ... Mrs. J.R. Bobbette ... Bertha (Mrs. Angus) McEachern ... Alma Victoria (Mrs. Howard) Jackson ... Peter Fitzmaurice ... Kathleen Anna (Mrs. Chris) Yaneff ... A.M. (Tony) Jackson ... Bryson L Vincent ... Stanley James Montgomery ... Pearl Kathleen (Mrs. L.N.) Ryan.

Eleven students from the Bracebridge and Muskoka Lakes Secondary School won Ontario Scholars status: John Plested, Debbie Black, Benjamin Deith, Sharon Morgan, Robert MacIntosh, Glenn Forrester, Clyde McDuff, Richard Booth, Michael Craymer, Randall Roberts, and Bernard Warren ... In spite of determined opposition, the Muskoka Board of Education banned smoking from its meetings, at that time a controversial decision.

The representatives elected for Bracebridge to the Board of Education were Norman Rosewarne, 2,238 votes, Wilbur Archer 1,632, Marilyn Rowe 1,621, and Bev Thompson 1,450.

Louise Wilson celebrated her 100th birthday at her home on Skeleton Lake, and Bill and Bea Raaflaub their 60th wedding anniversary ... Mrs. Claude Boyes was honoured by the congregation and friends of St. David's Presbyterian Church in Vankoughnet following her retirement as organist there for the past 42 years.

Darlene Slater was selected Miss Bracebridge, Sergeant Jerry Lynch retired from the Ontario Provincial Police after 35 years of service, and Bob Merrill was appointed manager of the South Muskoka Golf & Curling Club.

The Parkview Restaurant and St. Thomas' Anglican Church were damaged by a mysterious explosion.

Byron Shutt and Wayne Sander of the Bracebridge Bears Junior C hockey team received scholarships to play hockey at Bowling Green University in Ohio ... Ray Davis was elected president of the Chamber of Commerce.

Nancy Rosewarne earned a Gold Medal in dance in figure skating, the first skater from Bracebridge to have achieved the honour.

*Downtown Bracebridge, about 1973. Businesses change and storefronts get remodelled, but the general streetscape has changed remarkably little for several decades. Automobiles provide the quickest initial clue to the decade. If you've been watching the sequence of downtown scenes you'll have noticed that the unsightly tangle of overhead power and telephone lines had disappeared by the 1940s.* COURTESY OF THE TOWN OF BRACEBRIDGE

*One of the significant municipal projects in the first decade of Bracebridge's second century of incorporation was the creation of a system of parkland, walkways, and historical plaques surrounding the bay and the falls. The centennial of municipal incorporation in 1975 had sparked renewed interest in local heritage; the falls and the rivers had always been the defining natural features of the town. Here at the official opening of Bracebridge Bay Park in 1981 are (left to right) Mayor Jim Lang, Ontario Lieutenant Governor John B. Aird, Muskoka MPP Frank Miller, District of Muskoka Chairman Hugh Mackenzie, historian Robert J. Boyer, and the minister of the Baptist Church.* COURTESY OF THE TOWN OF BRACEBRIDGE

# 1975–1984

## *Our 2nd Century Begins: New Interest in Our Heritage*

THE YEAR 1975 was the centennial year of the incorporation of the municipality of Bracebridge. From a population of about 750 in 1875 Bracebridge has grown to 7,150. Chairman of the centennial celebrations was Peter Glazier.

A special Bracebridge Day celebration was held at Ontario Place, organized by Ruth Bell. Two thousand centennial coins, designed by Don Beacock and Susan Darrach, were minted and sold.

New events at the Muskoka Winter Carnival in Bracebridge included a polar bear dip, children's pet show, and a grin-and-win contest with a roving street camera. Tom Henderson entered the first polar bear dip and has been a contestant almost every year since.

James Lang was elected mayor for the first time, taking over from the retiring George Parlett. Frank Henry chaired the administrative committee, Aubrey Glass public works, and Ralph Melvin the planning committee.

The provincial government called for tenders for an overpass at Highway 11 and District Road 4 (Highway118) to Vankoughnet, a site of many accidents.

Computerized tax forms were done for the first time in the District on a newly purchased Century 50 computer.

Muskoka-Parry Sound Health Unit nurses went on strike for wage parity with hospital nurses and settled for close to their demands.

The Board of Education gave the elementary school teachers a 25 percent salary increase. Fred Hammell retired as director of education to be replaced by Cliff Whitfield.

Anne Malton, on ARC industries management, was appointed to the newly created position of district coordinator for mental retardation. Postmaster Earl Patterson retired at the end of the year after 22 years service with the post office.

District Judge D.C. Thomas was named general chairman of the current appeal of the South Muskoka Memorial Hospital with a goal of $250,000. Ivan Keall was elected chairman of the hospital board.

Peter Heath, Brian Jacques, and Malcolm Stockton were called to the bar of the Law Society of Upper Canada. Sean Kelly became a partner in the law firm of Lee, Roche and Kelly.

James Rosewarne, former pupil of Stan Knowles, received his Senior Pin in ski instruction. Vicki Billingsley, daughter of R.J. Boyer, now living in Inuvik, was elected to the National Board of the Consumers Association of Canada.

Dave Rankin raised $3,000 for cystic fibrosis research in a walk from Bracebridge to Toronto Sick Children's Hospital.

At the year's end, Seth Hillman and Arthur Crockford sold their Downtown Garage property to Jim Bradbury, thus ending their 40 years of continuous service in the garage business ... Former Bracebridge druggist Robert Everett had been widely praised for his paintings and was elected president of the Ontario Institute of Painters.

Jim Hillman was the new Worshipful Master of Muskoka Lodge 360.

The Presbyterian Church in Canada was celebrating 100 years as a national church. Knox Presbyterian Church in Bracebridge celebrated 100 years in its present location. Rev. James Thomson was named moderator and chaplain at the Centennial Assembly of the Presbyterian Church in Canada. The First Baptist Church in Bracebridge celebrated its 90th birthday.

The SSJE applied to offer half-way house services to ex-prisoners and parolees at its mission on Maple Street. The Right Reverend Frank Lock, former rector of St. Thomas' Anglican Church, became the 7th Bishop of Algoma.

The Latter Day Saints broke ground for their new church (1999 location of the Family, Youth and Child Services of Muskoka on Pine Street).

Students at BMLSS researched 50 years of school history in Bracebridge for their silver anniversary and produced a special, much larger *Spectrum* yearbook under the leadership of editor Norm Miller. The centennial year valedictorian was Cathy Thomas. Among the 54 graduating Grade 13 students were 11 Ontario Scholars: Brad Preboy, Teresa Churchill, Jacqueline Harper, Sandra Longhurst, Gary Long, Monica Proulx, David Royston, Gail Smith, Cathy Sugg, Cathy Thomas, and Allen Veitch.

Keith's Country Market near District Road 4 opposite Alcan Canada Foils was totally destroyed by fire. The main building of the sawmill of RMH Packaging on Highway 11 was also lost to fire.

Pauline Austin narrowly escaped injury when her car plunged in the Muskoka River at the forks. A school bus rolled over on District Road 12 but no injuries were sustained or charges laid. District chairman George Parlett was injured in a hunting accident on Georgian Bay.

The 1975 fall fair program honoured the Bracebridge centennial. Record crowds attended the RCMP Musical Ride, which had come to Muskoka for the first time and ended with a salute to Stan Darling, MP. Special exhibit trailers came from the Canadian Armed Forces and Borden Dairy. They brought Elsie the Borden Cow with her twins. Attendance was about 10,000.

In hockey, the Pee Wees, Bantams, Midgets, and Juveniles each won their OMHA Muskoka-Parry Sound District Championships. Both the Pee Wees and Juveniles also won the Georgian Bay round. Harold Wilson, formerly of Port Carling and still a summer resident, was named to the Sports Hall of Fame. He and his father built the Miss Canada series of speed boats and won a world championship with the *Miss Supertest*.

Loreen Passfield, marathon swimmer, set a record in a swim from Port Carling to Windermere, surpassing the one-year-old record of Cathy Nichols.

The long-time marina business of Wilbur Archer was sold to Reg and Ray Whitehead. The Corning Glass plant was slated to close in the fall.

For the centennial, several businesses announced how long they had been operating in town: P. J. Marrin Wholesalers 65 years; Elliott's 65 years; Thomas Company 94 years; Uptown Service Station beside the library since 1929; H.J. Brooks & Sons 30 years; MacNaughtan's

*In 1975, Lieutenant Governor Pauline McGibbon visited, and took part in honouring several Bracebridge women at a Dinner for Women in the Centennial Centre. She is seen here on the Town Hall steps with (left to right) councillors Ralph Melvin, Norman Archer, Frank Henry, Bruce McPhail, Emily Dworak, mayor Jim Lang, councillor Jim Boyes, clerk Ken Veitch, and Frank Miller, MPP. She returned in 1977 to visit Mrs. Charles McGaughey (Rene Caisse) and receive from her the Essiac cancer formula.* COURTESY OF THE TOWN OF BRACEBRIDGE

*In 1975 Bracebridge and Muskoka Lakes Secondary School celebrated its 50th anniversary. The huge multi-level complex, sprawling down the escarpment separating "uptown" from "The Hollow," attained this size in the 1960s and has had only modest additions since. The original Bracebridge High School constructed in 1925 is visible centre-top, with the Presbyterian Church beyond.* FROM BMLSS YEARBOOK "SPECTRUM '75"

Hardware 29 years; Shier Insurance 32 years; Muskoka Garage 55 years; Ecclestone's Hardware 81 years; Stone's Men's & Ladies' Wear 37 years; and Ridley Cleaners 40 years. The Muskoka Tourist Association entered its 41st year. It was the oldest tourist promotion organization for a particular district in Ontario.

Philip Murphy opened a jewelry store on Manitoba Street in the former location of P.J. Marrin. The Finishing Touch opened in the Matthias Furniture building. The official opening of the South Muskoka Golf and Curling Club was held in January, although curling had started in the building two months earlier.

Deaths this year included Wilfred Wesley Kirkpatrick 79, son of Draper pioneers ... Ted Wright, 73, former owner of Cleveland's House ... Ken Shier, 40, whose father had started Shier Insurance ... Father Thornton, 77, in his 39th year at the SSJE ... Fred Mills, 86, a Bracebridge boy who moved to Milford Bay. He was captain of the *Alporto* for many years ... Harold Bickmore, 78, son of Monck Township pioneers, raised on a farm along the Muskoka River ... Ernest Allchin, long-time proprietor of Holiday House along with his wife Timmy ... Minnie Brown, formerly Minnie Barron, 97 ... Mrs. Herb Hammond (nee Jessie Naismith), 78, of Falkenburg ... Mrs. William Harem (nee Fannie Arnott), 76. She was a long-time nurse and hospital worker and had attained the rank of captain in the army ... Catherine Bird, 89, of the Bracebridge pioneer Bird family.

## 1976

A relatively large number of business changes occurred in the town in 1976. There were some new buildings, some relocations, some purchases, and some closings.

Uniroyal acquired the Corning Glass property. Alcan Wire & Cable expanded its plant by about 25,000 square feet to make room for new production equipment. Ontario Belting opened in the Highway 532 Industrial Mall. The new OPP station on Highway 11 was completed and with it the police acquired a new mobile radar unit.

Town Council gave site plan approval for the construction of 65 condominium units on the 65-acre old tannery property on the north branch of the Muskoka River. The new senior citizen's complex on Alice Street became ready for occupancy.

Canadian Tire was planning to relocate to Ball's Flats. Dickie Insurance was purchased by Ken Rogers who continued to operate under his own name. The ARC Industries workshop on Wellington Street opened with 25 trainees and six staff. The Hotel Patterson underwent major renovations. The Petre Boutique opened on Manitoba Street in the building formerly occupied by the Boathouse Boutique. They stocked formal wear and bathing suits for women. Currell's Books & Records closed, to be replaced by the Herald-Gazette Shop selling books and office supplies. Ownership of the *Herald-Gazette* changed from R.J. Boyer to Hugh Mackenzie.

Closures included the Eaton's sales office and Lorne Shier's B.B. Auto & Sports Supplies. John deLang opened his hairdressing salon.

The Hollingworth family of Beatrice reached a milestone in February. Three generations of the family, John, John H., and Albert had been official weather observers for central Muskoka for 100 years.

After a long, much discussed controversy at District Council, clerk Glen Williams was made the District's first administrator while retaining his position as clerk.

Frank Miller, Ontario Minister of Health, was taken to Wellesley Hospital from Maple Leaf Gardens after suffering a heart attack during a game in which he was playing. He made a full recovery.

The Queen Street bridge was closed on the recommendation of an engineer. Two new cells to the Bracebridge lagoon were completed. They had become increasingly necessary with the growing population. The Vankoughnet Road overpass was officially opened.

Mrs. Barry Miners, formerly Phyllis Brooks, sent in the story of the *Miss Kingston*, a cruise ship in the Thousand Islands. She was built in Bracebridge in 1944 for the Royal Canadian Navy to be used in WWII, but she never saw active duty.

*Until 1925, the site of BMLSS was a large estate known as "The Grove," with this three-storey house, built originally by Thomas McMurray in the early 1870s, set amid expansive lawns on the hillside.* COURTESY OF BRENDA COX

There was a large number of ice sculptures at the winter carnival this year and also some women among the 12 polar bear swim participants.

Ken Hawthorn, Dan Mallett, and Roy Hull were chosen to compete in cross country ski events at the Ontario Winter Games in Sault Ste. Marie. Ken Hawthorn won a bronze medal in the relay ... In the 28th annual skating carnival over 200 skaters participated in "Fantasia." Sandae Raeburn won a gold medal in the Northern Ontario Section Figure Skating Championships.

The old Bracebridge Curling Club on James Street was torn down and the property turned into a much needed parking lot.

The BMLSS ski team were once again champions. They won the all Ontario slalom and giant slalom competitions. The school also produced another 11 Ontario Scholars this year.

The Bracebridge Public School Band played in the Lions International Parade in Quebec City.

The new OPP staff sargeant was Don Glass. Archie Buie became the new business administrator for the Muskoka-Parry Sound Health Unit. Bill Young was honoured for 25 years of service on the hospital board.

The new emergency services at South Muskoka Memorial Hospital were opened by Ivan Keall, president of the Board of Directors, and Judge Thomas.

In May, the scouts, cubs, guides, and brownies from Milford Bay planted 1,200 trees on Crown land up past High Falls and had a picnic lunch at nearby Duck Chutes.

The Muskoka Paint Centre & Art Gallery hosted a showing of recent paintings by Bob Everett who had been well received across the province. He was formerly a druggist on Manitoba Street.

The entire community was shocked to hear of the sudden tragic deaths of Richard Scriven, 21, and his brother Wesley, 20, in a snowmobile accident.

This was the year that recorded the death of Ethel Victoria Boyer, wife of the late George W. Boyer. The previous day she had been at her desk in the *Herald-Gazette* office, having just celebrated her 90th birthday 10 days earlier. Mrs. Boyer was the daughter of William and Jane Archer and granddaughter of Marmaduke Archer who came as a Methodist lay preacher in 1866. Most of her adult life was spent in the newspaper business. She left her sons Robert and Wilson, eight grandchildren, and several great-grandchildren.

Other deaths this year included Sydney Avery, 78, a well-known Muskoka man and son of a pioneer family. He had written *Reflections: Muskoka and Lake of Bays of Yesteryear* … Montague Mahaffy, 93, first District Judge … James Quigley, life-long athlete and supporter of athletics, did not recover from injuries suffered while working on Highway 11 … Brigadier General Charles Beresford Topp, 82, son of the late Dr. Topp … Fred Sander, 67, was in the printing business on Holditch Street … Muskoka's oldest citizen, Emma Gaisford, 104. Her son, Mac, operated the Skyways Restaurant … Ross Veitch, 43, a well-known Imperial Oil agent, took a sudden fatal heart attack at a Lions Club meeting … James Kingshott, 73, former lumberman and farmer, son of a Watt pioneer family … Roy White, 64, hairdresser in town for over 40 years … Edward Cooper, 75, of a Macaulay pioneer family, a farmer and township councillor … Roy Oaten, 91 … Mrs. Robert Ellis (Emma Jane), 98, lived in Baysville from age one … Paul Rimstead Sr., 71, came to Bracebridge from Beatrice in 1960 … Robert Barron, 89, lived on his father's farm with sister Annie until it was sold in 1965 … Bjarni (Barnie) Einarson, 87, son of Icelandic pioneers … Norman Donald, 93, of Bardsville … Bert Huggard, 86, last job was as a crossing guard until age 80.

Early in January the river was still wide open but it froze January 23 in the record low temperature of -38° F. In August, locals and cottagers alike were concerned with the huge drop in the Muskoka River level which according to a spokesperson "dropped almost six feet in one day." For eight days the level fluctuated several feet, considered to be caused in part by Bracebridge Hydro's continued usage during low water and in part by fluctuations in discharge from Mary Lake by the Ministry of Natural Resources.

A first and a special attraction to the fall fair was an approved competition by the Quarter Horse Association with 275 entries.

George Kay, son of Watt Township pioneers, celebrated his 100th birthday. He and Mrs. Kaye also celebrated their 60th wedding anniversary. They had lived for many years in Ufford before moving to a home on Ontario Street. David Leeder turned 90 years old, while Louise Wilson, formerly of Skeleton Lake, celebrated her 102nd birthday.

## 1977

Trans Canada Pipeline presented the Town of Bracebridge with a recreational park named after James W. Kerr, the company's chief executive officer and Lake Muskoka summer resident. This was the year that Town Council oversaw the restoration of the Bracebridge Bay area below the falls and its conversion into a park.

The first baby born in Bracebridge this year was Graeme Alistair, son of Mr. and Mrs. Christopher Mitchell of Baysville.

A campaign for the Bracebridge Memorial Community Centre Restoration Fund was started with R.J. Boyer as chairman, E.P. Lee as vice chairman, and James Perrin as campaign director.

The two Bracebridge bridges on District Road 4 were

*Teams in the International Run-a-bed contest at the 1975 Muskoka Winter Carnival race up Manitoba Street.* FROM THE BMLSS YEARBOOK "SPECTRUM '75"

opened after five weeks of repairs. Roads in the centre of town including Rosemount Boulevard were excavated and filled with sand before being repaved. The stoplight at Manitoba and Thomas streets became operational. South Monck Drive was given its name this year.

The contract for the 12-inch watermain and pumping station on Wellington Street was awarded to Codar Construction Co. Ltd., the second lowest bidder for $173,646, reported sewer and water superintendent Don Currie.

Council approved an increase in the number of volunteer firefighters from 21 to 23. Jerry Fox succeeded R. Whitehouse as fire chief. Fox was also coordinator of the Muskoka Mutual Fire Aid System.

In a provincial cabinet shuffle Premier Bill Davis made Frank Miller, Muskoka MPP, the new Minister of Natural Resources. Miller easily won his third term as MPP in the June 9 election over challenger Ken Cargill, NDP, and Mr. Fitzpatrick, Liberal. A poll was held at the hospital for the first time allowing 100-year-old George Kaye to vote.

This year saw the first five-year capital budget brought down for the District Municipality of Muskoka. George A. Parlett was re-elected District chairman.

District welfare officer Cecil Moore retired and the position was filled by Ian Turnbull. Jack McLachlan, town treasurer, retired after five years on the job to be replaced by Andy Nelan. All Muskoka road signs were converted to metric.

The cruise business operated by Captain McPherson closed its final chapter. He lost a court battle because of his location on Crown land. There was an auction to sell his artifacts and his boat the MS *Mildred*.

William Golden was appointed senior judge of Provincial Court (Family Division) for Muskoka, Durham, Northumberland, Victoria, Peterborough, and Haliburton … Mrs. Robert Boyer was made Honorary Fellow of Huntington University in Sudbury … Jerry Fox received the Queen's Jubilee Medal for service to the community. He served with the Bracebridge fire brigade for 23 years, the last nine as chief … The fire brigade purchased a new van to hold equipment such as uniforms, breathing

*From downtown Bracebridge, the Dominion Store (now the A & P) moved to upper Manitoba Street in the early 1960s, then to a new plaza on Ball's Flats in 1977 – a pattern followed by many other businesses. The ambitious Riverside Centre of the early 1970s, by the forks of the river, was the town's first shopping plaza. A commercial disappointment, it was converted to a hotel (Riverside Inn). On the other hand, Ball's Flats has seen explosive growth in retail development, as has the area along Ecclestone Drive south of town.* COURTESY OF THE TOWN OF BRACEBRIDGE

apparatus, saws, ropes, and shovels … Roy Goltz of Monck Township won a world championship in the open barley sheaf division at the Royal Agricultural Fair.

Merchants held their first Midnight Madness sale this summer. Stores on Manitoba Street opened from 10:00 p.m. until 2:00 a.m. in the most successful merchandising effort in the town's history.

The original location of the Building Trades Centre was on Shaw Street. Later a new building was erected on the former Moore's Mill property in Falkenburg. This greatly expanded the scope of the business and closed the town yard.

Northern Custom Steel of Bracebridge produced down draft wood stoves with manager Phil Keppler … R.J.'s Hairstyling for Men opened on Manitoba Street … Grant Kilpatrick, chiropractor, set up a new practice on Toronto Street … MacNaughtan Hardware moved a much expanded business into the old Dominion Store building … The old tannery buildings were demolished … 175 exhibitors took part in the 15th annual Muskoka Arts and Crafts Show.

Elves' Island opened at Santa's Village. Treasure Island had been converted into a children's play area with a snake tube crawl, a chimney slide, and a ball crawl. On July 25 Santa's Village set an all-time attendance record with 2,581 people through the gate, bookkeeper Jack Grant reported. Manager Ron Payne stated that people from 22 European countries had visited as well as people from the United Kingdom, Australia, New Zealand, Israel, India, Mexico, 14 states, and every province in Canada. Santa's Village was truly an international attraction.

Santa's Village adopted four children from other countries through the Foster Parents Plan with its Wishing Well money. On previous occasions the money had been given to various charities and to the Salvation Army.

Bracebridge Kinsmen and Kinettes celebrated their 30th anniversary as did the Snow Queen Rebekah Lodge

... Local scouts and cubs celebrated the 70th anniversary of scouting at their father and son banquet ... Nick Wettlaufer and Ted McEown were both honoured at a special dinner commemorating 65 years each in the Orange Lodge ... The SSJE celebrated 50 years of missionary work here ... Muskoka Lodge AF & AM celebrated its 100th anniversary. Worshipful Master was Ed Senior ... Peter Mitchell was re-elected president of the Agricultural Society ... Mrs. Keith McLeod was president of Bracebridge Red Cross ... Mrs. Isabel Greavette was installed as Worthy Matron of Lakeland Lodge, OES.

The first annual Dominion Day Regatta was sponsored by the Chamber of Commerce and Riverside Plaza. Hundreds of families crowded the government wharf and park to watch log rolling, canoe races, canoe tug of war, tennis, and swimming. Fred Johnson and Brad Sherman organized free dinner and prizes at the Riverside Centre afterwards.

Tom Mataija was appointed manager of the Bracebridge Farmers Soccer Club with president Gabe Tomassoni and coach Brian Campbell. The team played well and won a trophy for the "Most Sporting Team" by never receiving a caution from the referee all season.

The former Curling Club building on James Street was demolished and the land made into a parking lot. It had been erected with volunteer labour in 1946. In the early days curlers played on natural ice until power was supplied for artificial ice from the arena across the street.

After a slow beginning about 1972, the Bracebridge Tennis Club had over 300 members this year ... John Black won the trophy at the Christmas Ski Camp in Collingwood ... Ken Hawthorn placed well in cross-country ski races in Alberta and Alaska ... BMLSS captured the high school ski crown for Ontario for the fourth year in a row ... The Bracebridge Langlauf cross-country ski event had 500 participants; the 20-kilometre event produced a virtual tie for first place ... Michele Roy, 16, of Bracebridge was the first person to swim the 18-mile length of Lake Muskoka, in 12 hours ... Duane Miller entered his ponies in the Royal Winter Fair ... The Bracebridge Figure Skating Club sent representatives to an Invitational Tournament in London ... The Operation Challenge trophy which tested skill in navigation and seamanship between the Gravenhurst and the Bracebridge Power Squadrons was won by Bracebridge in 1977. Commander Denis Elliott accepted the trophy from Gravenhurst's Commander Jim Goodwin ... Fifty canoeists took part in the second annual Muskoka Shield canoe race down the Muskoka River ... The Garden Brothers Circus was in Bracebridge for its 40th anniversary edition.

Richanne Howard, 10, Julianne Howard, 13, and Marsha Cathcart, 15, participated in a three-and-a-quarter mile swimming race across Lake Couchiching. All three Bracebridge girls completed the gruelling swim against 21 other participants.

Stanley and Victoria (nee Tabor) Hill celebrated their 50th wedding anniversary, as did Mr. and Mrs. George Quinton.

Kathy Slemius, 20, of Gravenhurst was the Muskoka Winter Carnival Snow Queen. The Bracebridge segment of the carnival was adversely affected by the widespread snowstorm. Many competitors from outside the area could not make the trip. As a result, the dogsled races, snowmobile performance and motorcycle races were canceled. This meant attendance was down and income was below expectations.

*One of the early stores in Bracebridge, the District Exchange, established by John Teviotdale in 1868 on what is now the downtown portion of Manitoba Street. Quite a contrast with the Dominion a century later!*
COURTESY OF THE TOWN OF BRACEBRIDGE

Temperatures in January dropped to -40° causing breakage of town water mains and extra work and hardship for the town repair crews. Temperatures in December were in the -30° range.

James Kewlie and Ivan Watson, both BMLSS students, placed first in theory in the annual Chrysler Trouble Shooting Contest at Mississauga.

Edward Britton established a new weekly newspaper, the *Bracebridge Examiner*.

An escaped prisoner from Joyceville Penitentiary, James McGarth, 52, was shot to death by police. The coroner's jury took just 18 minutes to bring in the verdict of self-defence and clear Constables Bruce Kruger and Mark Murdock of any wrong-doing in the death. McGarth was using a shotgun in his bid to escape arrest. Coroner Fennell Archdekin observed that "the convict had died as he had lived – by violence."

Deaths this year included Ernest Goltz, 80, farmed just west of town. He served on Council and was a road superintendent, later worked for Fowler Construction and as the train engineer at Santa's Village. He was an avid curler ... Miss May Bird, 87, trained as a nurse in Toronto and practised her skills in World War I in Russia and Egypt, later joined the staff of the Muskoka Health Unit ... John C. Knowles, 82, raised in Ufford, joined the 122nd Muskoka Battalion and made Lieutenant Colonel in World War I. He was later elected to the Saskatchewan legislature ... Thomas Clarence McNiece, 84, often played the violin for square dances ... Mrs. William Patterson (nee Mabel Kaye ), 86, helped establish the Patterson-Kaye Lodge ... Joseph Bastedo, 78, became editor of the *Muskoka Herald* at age 17 during World War I because so many staff were overseas ... Doug Milligan, 57, best known as a dealer for BA then Gulf Oil at the Pine Point Service Station at the corner of Manitoba Street and Monck Road ... Earl Harper, 79, was in the radio repair business, served in the Veterans' Guard of Canada ... George Parrett, 85, farmer and former Muskoka Township councillor. He was a Bracebridge Fall Fair director and regular exhibitor as well as past president of the Agricultural Society ... William Huston, farmed all his life at Falkenburg and had excelled as a blacksmith, mechanic, and in maple syrup making.

## 1978

Gail Adams, who chaired the Bracebridge Winter Carnival was exceedingly pleased with the number of participants and the size of the crowds. The Snow Queen and Princess were Estelle Chaisson and Sharon Taylor. Seven men and women took part in the Polar Bear Dip.

Early in the year, Don Smith became the new editor of the *Herald-Gazette* ... George Parlett retired as District chairman to be succeeded by Hugh Mackenzie ... Sheriff Jack McBride retired ... Sybil Jackson was appointed new sheriff of Muskoka and was the first woman in Ontario to hold that office.

Rene Caisse was a member of a long-time Bracebridge family. Many years ago she had developed Essiac (Caisse spelled backwards). She strongly believed it to be a cancer treatment and claimed success with many patients. This year the Respirin Corporation was finally going to run clinical tests to ascertain its real value to cancer patients. Rene Caisse spent a lifetime in service to others. In August 600 people helped her to celebrate her 90th birthday at the Centennial Centre. In October she was named Woman of the Century. She died in December while testing of her beloved Essiac was still ongoing.

A large number of changes were occurring to Bracebridge businesses. A local group headed by Alex Clarke negotiated to buy Rainbow Ridge Ski Resort with plans for a large tourist resort. Another local group headed by Tom McNair bought Riverside Inn. There was an official opening for the new arena lobby. The work was completed thanks to the great efforts of the Kinsmen Club.

Midnight Madness was a huge success this year with large crowds shopping between 10:00 p.m. and midnight. ... Norman Rosewarne announced the sale of the buildings and land of the Muskoka Garage opposite the library ... A family business for 68 years, Elliott's 5¢ to $1 store was sold by Bill Elliott ... Ecclestone Hardware added another 10,000 square feet of floor space in a three-storey addition ... Rockwell International was awarded a General Motors contract and needed 30 more workers ... McDonald's opened their fast food restaurant in time to catch some of the summer business.

Legion president Bob Jeffries presided over the grand opening of the expansion of the Royal Canadian Legion

*The "Aubrey Street Boys" engaged in a favourite spring pastime: smelt fishing at the forks of the Muskoka River. Left to right, Ralph Young, Tom Robinson, Ken Veitch, "Turk" Lees.* COURTESY OF KEN VEITCH

building. It had at one time been the Ward 4 school and former teacher Inez Ecclestone cut the ribbon.

The *Wanda III*, a 94-foot steamship believed to be the largest private steam yacht in North America, was plying the Muskoka Lakes. Built in Toronto in 1915, she was first bought by Lady Eaton to travel from the train in Muskoka Bay to her cottage on Lake Rosseau. The boat has been restored over the last 12 years.

There were preliminary meetings for the purpose of creating a historical society. Wayland Drew was chairman with members of the executive being Ralph Melvin, Wendy Wilson, and Ted Currie. Their first project would be the restoration of the octagonal house built by Henry J. Bird almost 100 years earlier. The Rotary Club bought Woodchester Villa and was involved in the cost of restoration through to its completion.

The death occurred suddenly of Mrs. Robert Boyer, nee Patricia Johnson, at the age of 66. She moved to Bracebridge with her father when he came as principal of the public school. He later became public school inspector for many years. Patsy attended McMaster University and the Ontario College of Education. She was later appointed librarian and was acting editor of the *Muskoka Herald* for a time during World War II.

There were a number of significant birthday celebrations in the district. Mrs. Louisa Wilson, Muskoka's oldest citizen, at 104 years had along with her husband established Wilson's Lodge on Skeleton Lake. She died later this year ... Nick Wettlaufer turned 90 ... George Kaye turned 102 ... Mrs. William Kirbyson (Lena) of Ufford turned 96 ... Henry Longhurst of Windermere was 94 ... Ted Fitzmauice turned 89 ... William John Bunn celebrated his 90th birthday. It all goes to show that Muskoka was a healthy place to live.

The death occurred of Mrs. Sam Bowyer, 89, daughter of Mr. and Mrs. Harry Bowyer ... Ernie Patterson, 80, had opened the Downtown Garage, then with his brother, Fenton, bought the Uptown Service Station which they later sold to Ted Smith. The Pattersons then bought the Queen's Hotel and renamed it Hotel Patterson. Ernie bought and sold 1,300 acres north of High Falls, part of which became the Bracebridge Natural Resource Centre. For many years Ernie operated the school buses in the area ... Mrs. Peter Fitzmaurice, 85, nee Lillian Fleger, had taught school many years earlier ... Peter MacNaughtan, 87, had worked for J.L. Fenn Hardware, then Ecclestone Hardware, and then opened his own hardware business on the west side of Queen's Hill in 1946 ... John Harrington, 85, had been chief of police when the town had its own force, and before that he was a detective in Chatham ... Deering Gray, 68, Bracebridge merchant, had joined Maher Shoes Ltd. in 1938 and moved to Bracebridge in 1943 as manager of Maher's store on Manitoba Street.

*William Albert "Bus" Brazier died in 1979. He was best known for his role as "Chief Musqua Ukee" in which he participated in many parades and other community events. Here, in 1968, he poses with Miss Bracebridge, Debbie Fish.* COURTESY OF BETH GALBRAITH

Of importance to all of Muskoka was an Ontario Grant of $400,000 to complete the *Segwun* restoration. The Bracebridge Neighbourhood Improvement Program allotted $250,000 for Monck sewers.

At the fall fair there were 14 teams in men's horseshoe throwing and 18 men in the singles competition ... The Bracebridge Mercon novice team won the OMHA Championship ... Ken Hawthorn made the Canadian Junior Cross Country Ski team ... Ray Henderson won the provincial light heavy weight boxing title and took a bronze in the Canadian Championships ... Bracebridge Athlete of the Year was figure skater Sundae Raeburn ... The Cavalcade racing team of Wayne Lippert, driver, with John Rhines and Brad Smith as pit crew won a feature race at the Barrie Speedway.

## 1979

The New Year's baby was Michael Thomas, son of Mr. and Mrs. Thomas Sawyer of Ontario Street.

Council agreed to remove trees and add crushed rock to enlarge the parking lot behind our library. Fire chief Peter Mitchell sold the ¾-ton fire vehicle and replaced it with a 2,000-gallon tanker truck.

At the BMLSS Commencement, Jackie Vettorel was Salutorian while Marda Drew gave the Valedictorian address. Tim Rogers won six awards given out by school board chairman Barbara Brooks. Ken Black stepped down as principal to be succeeded by John Brownlee.

Forty-four students from Trois Riviere, Quebec, spent two weeks on an exchange with Bracebridge students.

Residents of the Pines Home for the Aged elected their own council for input into the running of the home. Administrator of The Pines was Tom Mataija while the newly elected council president was Reginald Coady.

Scott's of Muskoka opened on Manitoba Street ... Radio Shack opened ... Kimberley Place Restaurant opened in the former G.H.O. Thomas residence (The Thirsty Judge in 1999) ... Muskoka Publications merged with Argon Graphics to form Muskoka Graphics ... Staff at the Health Unit went on strike ... David Nairn was the new president of the Real Estate Board.

Muskoka District Council hired two planners to meet deadlines for the official plan.

Muskoka farmers reported excellent hay crops; however, the worst infestation of army worms since 1954 devastated many grain crops. Joe Dinner figured as much as two-thirds his grain was destroyed. Max Beaumont lost about 40 percent of his barley.

Dr. Patrick McTaggart-Cowan was awarded the Order of Canada from Governor-General Ed Schreyer. He was a Rhodes Scholar and has been the president of a university and director of the Meteorological Service. Dr. McTaggart-Cowan lived on a 200-acre farm on High Falls Road. In later years he was with the Science Council of Canada.

E.P. Lee, QC, was honoured with a road named E.P. Lee Drive ... Joan Coates, Kinettes president, presented Sheila Taylor with the Kinette of the Year award for 18 years perfect attendance ... Bill Towns, Muskoka registrar for 32 years, retired and was given a party at the Legion. Mr. Craig Stewart succeeded Mr. Towns as registrar ... Ted Crowder of Dudley Street was awarded Trucker of the Year by Broker No. 7 Club of Ontario. He hauled for Manitoulin Transport.

Russell and Rene Salmon celebrated their 50th wedding anniversary. They were known as Mr. and Mrs. Santa Claus to many people. Cliff and Winnie Murphy had lived together in married bliss for 50 years as well. Mr. and Mrs. Fred Lee also celebrated their 50th. He had owned the Red & White store. Bill Curran, Baysville resident and former Bracebridge sawmill owner, turned 100.

Thatcher Studio moved south two doors. They had been open since 1935 ... Lyle McIntrye's gallery of photographic arts opened in July ... Bracebridge Lumber, on the old Forgioni property on Santa's Village Road, moved to just north of Kirk Line ... Ken Heron was hired as the new supervisor of Muskoka and Family Services.

Jim Thwaites, operator of Muskoka Ambulance, purchased a $15,000 ambulance van, Number 607, which carried cots instead of stretchers for more comfort to patients being transferred. This type of van was developed by Government Services and was the first in Ontario.

Roy Gibbs and Kathy Tomlinson went to Scotland to play the bagpipes for the Royal Family.

Alvin Kaye donated a large quantity of antiques for use in the Bird House Museum (Woodchester Villa) project.

Deaths this year included James Raeburn, 66, owner of the Hind Manufacturing, died of a sudden heart attack ... William Albert "Bus" Brazier, 69, enjoyed hockey, curling, and as the colourful "Chief Musqua Ukee" led many parades throughout Muskoka. After serving in World War II, he was on staff at Northern Planing Mills , then caretaker at the courthouse ... William Greer, 78, carpenter ... Philip Hines, 69, had been with the Water, Light and Power Commission, was stricken with a sudden fatal heart attack ... Leila Cope, 92, Port Carling citizen and historian ... Albert Hollingworth, 72, official weather observer ... Edith Bassett, 98, had lived on James Street ... Gregory Colmer, 69, had been a high school teacher since 1945 ... David Leslie Leeder, 91, worked at farming, construction, as a cook on steamboats, and in logging ... Gordon Medley, 50, well known at Muskoka Pines Equipment ... Willard Austin, 86, had operated Austin's Service Station at Beatrice ... Elmer Cathcart, 82, an auditor in the Army Pay Corps in World War II and a teacher ... Joe Lang, 52, owned Bracebridge Propane and was a past commander of the Bracebridge Power Squadron.

Bracebridge skiers Liisa Savijarvi and Ken Hawthorn both won gold at the Ontario Ski Championships. Liisa trained later at Banff, Washington State, and Austria. She was named Bracebridge's Athlete of the Year. Ken won a berth on the Canadian cross-country ski team.

Suzie Azlett, a member of Canada's Alpine Ski Team from 1975 to 1977 and instructor at Rainbow Ridge, surprised the Women's Pro Racing Circuit with a first-place finish against over 60 others from Canada, the U.S., and Europe, at Hunter Mountains, New York.

Dr. David Kent entered the Labatt's Marathon in Toronto.

Michele Roy, an 18-year-old Bracebridge swimmer, swam the length of Lake Rosseau. She had swum Lake

Rosseau in 1978 and the 18 miles of Lake Muskoka in just under 12 hours in 1977.

A freak snowstorm in October caused downed trees, widespread power outages, and school closures. January snowfall was heavy with 82 inches.

Guy Jackson chaired the United Church Outreach committee which channelled money and activity to help sponsor the Vietnamese boat people. Treasurer Don Bisset reported that they had collected over $15,000 by the end of this year. The committee rented a house on Woodchester Avenue for a Vietnamese family of 58-year-old Nguyen, mother of sons Phat and Manh, 31. Manh had his wife, Pvyga, and their two sons with him. Dr. Morley Crockford also sponsored a Vietnamese family.

Trans Canada Pipelines replaced a section of their pipeline between Bracebridge and Gravenhurst.

## 1980

The phenomenally warm temperatures of January had everyone enjoying the freedom of no snow. The lack of snow combined with cold, sunny weather created ideal conditions for skating on Lake Muskoka. All was not fun for commerce, however, as the lack of snow had a detrimental effect on local hotels, motels, food, and novelty shops. All worries came to an end as snow finally fell on January 23.

Stan Darling, our Conservative MP, went on to win his fourth federal election, beating out Dennis Hay, NDP, and Ed Fisher, Liberal. A first for Bracebridge and for Muskoka was a "Candidates Meet the Press" debate on the community TV channel.

Bracebridge Town Council approved a resolution to set speed limits for boat traffic on the Muskoka River. All branches of the river were set at six miles an hour with exception that from Bracebridge Falls to Lake Muskoka the speed limit was 15 miles an hour.

A feasibility study was done to determine whether the library should remain in the historic Carnegie building or relocate to a new facility. The town had a survey done of the library property to legally identify and declare it an historical site.

A portion of the sidewalk on the Silver Bridge was replaced. The sidewalk which was hanging over the retaining wall was constructed in 1931. The District arranged for the reconstruction which was subsidized by the Ministry of Transportation.

George S. Yearley, who owned and operated Lone Pine Cabins and service station, passed away. Mr. Yearley was the son of pioneers of the Falkenburg section of Macaulay Township. He was responsible for the carpentry contract for the SSJE Mission House on Sadler Drive, and the nurses' residence at South Muskoka Memorial Hospital. Mr. Yearley erected an arena on James Street, which opened in 1932 but burned in the 1940s.

Sixteen-year-old Liisa Savijarvi won the Pontiac Cup for slalom skiing in Wakefield, Quebec. She continued to dominate the ladies giant slalom by coming in first at Winterpark, Colorado.

The Rotary Club officially turned over the keys of Woodchester Villa to Mayor Jim Lang. Renovations and restoration of the property including the Bird house, had been undertaken by the Rotary Club in 1977. Woodchester Villa, historic former home of the Bird family, was turned into a museum with an archive room. Ted Williams worked at restoring antique books. The town purchased an extra acre of land from the Bird estate for parking for the Woodchester Villa museum.

The *Herald-Gazette* was judged the best newspaper in its circulation category in the province. Robert J. Boyer, former publisher of the paper, also received the Gold Quill Award which recognized 50 years of distinguished service to the community newspaper profession.

The Uptown Garage officially closed after more than 47 years in operation as a Smith family-run business. It was one of Bracebridge's oldest service stations. It is now the site of the Old Station Restaurant.

Collair, commuter flight operators, suspended their commuter service after only four weeks. They had offered two daily flights to and from Toronto at $58 return.

The Deering Gray home on Dominion Street was torn down to make way for the new fire hall. For many years the residence was called the White Home. It was probable that the old residence was built about 1882, a few years after Mr. and Mrs. White arrived in 1876. This was when 94 property owners in the Village of Bracebridge appealed their assessment to the judge with Mr. W.W.

White being one of them. Mr. White predeceased his wife and after Mrs. White died the property changed hands. The late Deering Gray purchased the property from a Mrs. Wiggins in 1955. The demolition included everything except the foundation which was used for the new fire hall.

The ice went out in mid-April with flooding along the river. One cottage actually sank into the river.

Wharf Road was reconstructed as part of the beautification project at Bracebridge Bay Park. Town Council was confident the park would augment the town as a whole.

Official approval was given to the bylaw introducing separate mill rate figures for the wards within the municipality. According to the bylaw passed, the sum of $3,412,893 would be levied in respect of the year 1980.

The 100,000th land title since land registry opened in 1879 was processed in May. There are two land registry systems. By the old land registry system there was no guarantee of title. The land titles system was passed about 1925 and is guaranteed by the province. The original office was built in 1870 on the present site. Previous to that the first documents were registered in the old courthouse building. The existing building was built in 1955.

In October 1980, after years of restoration work, the RMS *Segwun* pulled slowly away from her moorings for a four-hour sea trial. The *Segwun* would once again cruise the Muskoka Lakes, for the first time since 1958.

The death of Captain Reginald Leeder broke what appeared to be the last living link with the captains of the great days of steamboating in Muskoka. Until 1958 he had been Captain of the RMS *Sagamo*. He was in his 85th year and had served as captain or in other capacities on all the steamers of the Muskoka Lakes in his lifetime. Captain Leeder was born in Bracebridge in 1895. He began his career in steamboating at the age of 15. He was seven years captain of the steamer *Islander*, then from 1938 to 1945 was captain of the *Segwun*, until he became captain of the *Sagamo*. He retired from his work in 1968. Captain Leeder had one dreadful experience when he and three others of the crew of the ill-fated *Waome* survived Muskoka's worst marine disaster. The four men swam with difficulty to a nearby island when the *Waome* was struck by an unusual autumn gale in October 1934 and sank.

Several historic documents relating to the founding of the Bracebridge Public Library were found while employees were doing some house cleaning. The documents included the original acceptance by the town of the Andrew Carnegie grant, with a résumé of the conditions on which the grant was made. There was also an agreement with the contractor, Henry Oscar Appleby, that listed minutest details of the specifications to which the building was constructed. The resolution, dated May 21, 1906, was signed on behalf of the town by R.M.H. Smith, mayor, and by town clerk Alexander Salmon. It accepted the donation of $10,000 by Andrew Carnegie and bound the town to certain conditions on which the grant was made. The town pledged itself to find and provide a site for the building, and also to provide $1,000 a year for its support, a generous provision at that date. The town undertook to maintain the library as a free library; however, that clause did not necessarily mean that there would be absolutely no cost to users. An accompanying letter from the Carnegie estate made it clear that such levies on the public as "fines" were to go toward the expenses.

The term "free library" was used as opposed to libraries run for commercial profit to which users paid a subscription, which was quite often considerable and limited the use of the "circulating libraries" to the rich.

In the thick bundle of papers found with the resolution, every sheet signed by contractor Henry Oscar Appleby, is a list of specifications for materials and labour for the building. The drawings from which the specifications were made have not been found, but they were made by G. Miller and Company of Toronto. The actual cost of the building was $6,993 and for this everything was of the best quality. The ornamental cut stonework at the front of the building is of first-quality Ohio stone, the cellar brick and the facing material first quality red brick. The find also included records of inspection done by officials of the inspections of Public Libraries Office, a branch of the Ministry of Education, in 1939 and 1943. The tone of the reports would seem to suggest that at the time the library held a more important place in the esteem and life of the town than it does now.

For the first time since the plant came into operation, a human error caused an oil spill from the Alcan Foil rolling mill into the Muskoka River. Alcan officials said that the spill, visible on the river as a thin film, and almost 100 percent edible oil, was also biodegradable. It would break down rapidly under contact with light micro-organisms. Strenuous clean up operations were put into place immediately after the oil was spotted. The Ministry of the Environment confirmed there was no cause for alarm.

Although many local residents were not aware of it, Muskoka was becoming known throughout the province for producing top-notch soccer players. Muskoka United finished the season proudly proclaiming no losses in their 18 games after more than 1,000 miles of travelling. Muskoka United was a member of the Newmarket and District Soccer Association, and of the 32 teams represented in the league, the only one to emerge from the season undefeated. They were most proud of winning the trophy "Most Sporting Team." Town Council decided that they would donate some funds to the team to defray travel costs. In light of their seasons results, it appears to have been a sound investment.

Terry Fox had captured the imagination and respect of all Canadians with his abundant display of courage, perseverance and dedication. Terry arrived in Muskoka in August of 1980. "I've run twelve miles today and I want to run eight more," he told a *Herald-Gazette* reporter. Not an overwhelming target except for one circumstance; the rain was sluicing down so hard the reporter and photographer were soaked. "I'm used to running in the rain, I did it all the time in Vancouver," was Terry's only comment. He ran at a slow pace, but with tremendous energy and concentration. The road sides were running with rain as Terry made his slow, purposeful way north along Highway 11. Muskokans raised a resounding $21,000 to support Terry's "Marathon of Hope" cancer campaign.

The Thomas Company, established in 1889, the longest established business in Bracebridge to have remained in the ownership of the same family, was sold to Paul and Doris Smellie. John Newark of Hiram Street decided to curtail his business in the boat fender industry. The business was instituted in 1922 and Mr. Newark was probably the only person who specialized in the rare craft.

A late evening fire gutted the Candle Shop (factory outlet). The building was originally the public utilities office. Fire also claimed one of the newer businesses on Manitoba Street when The Flower Basket went up in flames.

The Garden Cafe officially opened as did the new Rich Hill Candle Factory on Wharf Road.

The first Santa Claus parade in July was held. Huge crowds gathered to salute the 25th anniversary of Santa's Village.

## 1981

The community was saddened by the death of Russell M. Best, QC, of Bracebridge. The retirement from his law practice in 1980 brought to an end a legal career that extended over 60 years. Mr. Best began his law career in 1920, in Bracebridge. He was named King's Counsel in the 1930s. Soon after moving to Bracebridge, Mr. Best purchased the practice of the late George Mahaffy and occupied the same office in the Sibbet Block. His services as a lawyer soon became much in demand. Some years after he began his law practice, Mr. Best bought the property at the top of Chancery Lane, where a square frame building stood. This building had been previously used as a Chinese laundry. The old building was taken down and in the early 1930s Mr. Best had the brick building erected where he had since conducted his legal practice. Mr. Best served for a number of years on the Board of Education, and became chairman.

The worst commercial fire to hit Bracebridge in recent memory wiped out five businesses in the Thomas Block and almost claimed a sixth. The firewall that was installed separating the building from Thatcher Studio was said to be one of the main reasons that the fire was arrested before it travelled farther up the street.

About 1,500 cross-country skiers took the plunge and tried to ski in the frigid January temperatures. The thermometer was reading -38° C. Some skiers opted out of

*Contrast this modern view of Bracebridge Bay with that of an earlier era on the next page. A park and walkway system provides opportunities to enjoy both its scenery and learn of its fascinating past.* COURTESY OF GARY LONG

the race not wanting to risk the pains of frostbite. Hundreds of skiers did attempt the 12th Annual Muskoka Loppet. Ken Hawthorn, a native of Bracebridge, placed third in the gruelling 30-kilometre race. The Loppet was originated to draw attention to Muskoka as an ideal destination for cross-country skiing. In years to come it would be cancelled due to lack of snow.

Premier William Davis announced a March election in Ontario. Frank Miller, treasurer of Ontario and MPP for the Muskoka riding, won the seat over Ken McClellan, the Liberal candidate, Jim Maguire, NDP. Frank Miller won by the largest plurality in Muskoka's history and garnered more votes than both his opponents combined.

George William Hooton, a citizen widely known in Bracebridge and Muskoka, passed away. His family settled in Bracebridge when George was only four years old. He was a painter and a decorator. Mr. Hooton was a devoted member of St. Thomas' Anglican Church, where he had served as people's warden and later as rector's warden.

An unusually mild February had the pansies and crocuses in bloom enjoying the spring-like weather.

Bird's Mill pumphouse received some repair work to its foundation and the roof was painted. The old wooden water wheel pump was (and still is) in place. Public works suggested that application be made to have the pumphouse declared a historic landmark. It is one of the few remaining houses of its kind in Canada.

The Pines Home for the Aged received provincial and municipal support for a $2 million renovation and expansion program. The province and the District of Muskoka split funding for the project, which commenced in 1983. The first phase was an upgrading of the residential areas in need of improvement. The second phase was a planned enrichment of day programs for the seniors in the home as well as those who live in the community.

It was a whirlwind of paperwork as Rainbow Ridge Ski Resort changed hands. The resort was converted into a senior citizens' retirement home. Construction of Bracebridge Villa began immediately. The new purchaser, Ernie

Austin of Bracebridge, had been in the retirement business for 36 years, having been the former owner of Martin Manor in Gravenhurst.

Very sophisticated alterations cost about a quarter of a million dollars were undertaken to bring the Bracebridge courtroom up to the specifications of the Ministry of Government Services. The enlarged courtroom included as an impressive security measure, a plate glass dock. There was a new staircase at the back, with access both from the outside and from the courtroom to a new cell block. New interview rooms and a renovated and enlarged library were included, with new judge's chambers and washrooms. A new entrance off Dominion Street with a ramp for wheelchair access and complete renovation of the general office area was completed.

The death of Ernest Parnell Lee, QC, was mourned throughout the District. Mr. Lee came to Bracebridge in 1949, first joining the practice of Russell M. Best, QC, then beginning his own law firm, with offices in the historic residence at 25 Ontario Street, behind the courthouse. This is now the law firm of Michael Anne MacDonald. This house is believed to be the second-oldest home in Bracebridge, dating from the 1860s. Later, Mr. Lee purchased the apartment building at the corner of Dominion and Ontario streets, on the site of the former British Lion Hotel, now the firm of Lee, Roche and Kelly. He had the lower floors remodelled into offices but continued to use the old home on Ontario Street as his residence. He was the registrar of Algoma Diocese until he retired in 1975. Mr. Lee had been secretary of the Muskoka District Progressive Conservative Association and in 1956 became president, continuing in that office for 16 years. Mr. Lee assisted in the fundraising campaign for the new structure at the entrance to Bracebridge Memorial Arena, agreeing to take part because he believed in the importance of the arena building in the

*Bracebridge Bay had a more industrial character in early days. At the time of this view, circa World War I, it was still a harbour for steamboats engaged in freight and passenger trade, and many businesses had boathouses there. The* Islander *is docked at the wharf.* COURTESY OF THE ARCHIVES OF ONTARIO

lives of the young people of the town. He was involved in raising funds for the restoration of Woodchester Villa and joined in the organization of the Bracebridge Historical Society.

Reconstruction of Manitoba Street got under way. The first phase of the project replaced pavement and sidewalks from the Waite's Apartments (Manitoba and Ontario streets) to Thomas Street. After some trepidation and fear of loss of business, the merchants on Manitoba Street were satisfied that the work was being done.

Approximately 500 guests gathered at Woodchester to participate in the afternoon ceremonies to mark the official opening of Woodchester Villa and Museum. The Woodchester Villa was built by the Henry J. Bird family who came to Bracebridge in 1872. Woodchester Villa was built adjacent to the first church building in Bracebridge, which had been erected by the Presbyterians in the 1860s. It was used as a storage building by the Birds. It was torn down during the restoration and replaced by what is now the Chapel Gallery on the same site.

The official opening of Bracebridge Bay Park was attended by Honorable John B. Aird, Lieutenant Governor of Ontario.

Daniel MacNaughtan Sr. passed away. He was born in Bracebridge in 1903. His father was the buyer of leather hides for the Beardmore Tannery, Bracebridge. The family home was the northeast corner of Ontario and Milton streets. Daniel attended Monck No. 7 School. He had served as a councillor of Macaulay Township for four years, and then was 14 years reeve, being accorded acclamation for 12 of those. He retired from municipal work but returned to become a candidate in the fall of 1970 when the new Bracebridge Area Municipality was formed, and he was elected councillor for Macaulay Ward. His services were effective and much appreciated and he held the position for four years until his health did not permit him to continue.

Evelyn Sykes retired from her court reporting career that began in 1939. "I'm the longest serving court reporter that I know of," she said. "I did everything: inquests, police courts, District Court." The amount of court work had increased enormously during the more than 40 years since she began work. "In the summers we used to have the afternoons off: we'd go out and rent a canoe for 25 cents and have it for the whole afternoon."

*The Bird's Mill Pumping Station at upper Bracebridge Falls was designated a Canadian Waterworks Landmark by the American Waterworks Association. The plant was the town's first hydroelectric station and later water-pumping plant.* COURTESY OF GARY LONG

Water levels all over Muskoka rose to critical levels in the fall of 1981, washing away roads as little creeks came down in spate. The Bracebridge Bay wharf was under water and spectators enjoyed the sight of an impressive flow over the falls. A few historic signs were standing in water. The footbridge along the dam could be crossed by the adventurous – with their shoes and socks off and pant legs rolled up. The Ministry of Natural Resources blamed the widespread flooding was due to nearly two weeks of rainfall.

A new brick parkette was installed beside John DeLang Hairstyling, with steps for pedestrians to access Dominion Street from Manitoba, and new lamp standards with rods to hold hanging flower baskets.

*"A Bird's Eye View of Bracebridge" was the caption on the postcard version of this pre-1912 photograph. The double meaning would have been lost on anyone who didn't know the picture was taken from Henry Bird's Woodchester Villa. The Bird Woollen Mill can be seen in the lower left quadrant; the five-storey structure on the right was the short-lived furniture factory.* COURTESY OF BRENDA COX

A 250-pound black bear made an unannounced trip into Bracebridge, exciting some residents on Kimberley Avenue. The bear was cornered up a tree in a ravine above Bracebridge Bay Park. The Ministry of Natural Resources, unable to lure the bear down and into a special bear trap, eventually had to shoot the animal.

The town spent $2,000 on drainage work at the public library in an attempt to end flooding problems. Work crews had been called in after flooding caused extensive damage to the bottom floor of the library during the heavy rainstorms in the fall. On the outside of the building workers lifted the front steps and angled them so water will flow away from the building. A trench was dug and a storm drain was replaced along the side of the building. A concrete cap was also laid over the outside basement wall to prevent any water seepage.

The new fire hall was officially opened with Frank Miller, MPP, in attendance at the ceremony. In a presentation to the gathering he stressed the importance of municipal volunteer brigades across the province: "I'm impressed by the display of dedication, pride and spirit of the volunteer firefighters."

A new bill which could radically change Muskoka politics was passed by the provincial government. The bill, an act to amend the District Municipality of Muskoka Act, was passed by District Council in June of 1980. Once passed, the new bill meant that ratepayers could vote for District council members. In the past, District councillors were chosen by a vote in area council. In Bracebridge and Huntsville anyone would be allowed to run for District council. In other municipalities, voters would choose their District representatives according to the ward system.

A new walkway was installed down Chancery Lane. Along with new concrete, heating cables were installed underneath, to be kept on permanently during the winter to melt the snow and keep the pavement dry. The system was put in by the contractor when the lane was resurfaced. Specially designed heating cable, embedded in the concrete, was strung back and forth about four inches apart, and going from about three inches below the surface right down to the grate below. It would cost approximately $1,000 a year to heat. As thousands of people used the lane, the cost was worthwhile, as the whole purpose is one of safety.

A postal strike slowed down the mail. Nine members of the Canadian Postal Workers Union went out on a strike that lasted five weeks.

Princess Margaret visited Muskoka, spending three days at Temple Trees, the summer home of Lieutenant Governor John B. Aird on Lake Rosseau. Hundreds of plain-clothed and uniformed officers from the Royal Canadian Mounted Police and the Ontario Provincial Police kept the Princess and her daughter Lady Sarah under close guard.

The bandshell in Memorial Park had its roof replaced and new shingles put on ... John Street got new sewers and watermains ... The public library began to stay open on Saturdays to better serve the public ... Madge Kitching opened Madges Flower Nook on Manitoba Street ... The first Muskoka Home Show, held at Building Trades Centre, opened for the first time ... More than 250 people signed a petition to have an animal shelter in Muskoka ... The Student Employment Office had more than 60 positions to fill but couldn't find the students to fill them ... Sixteen-year-old Mike Hall caught a 39-inch pike at the mouth of the Muskoka River.

Interest rates reached a high of 18 to 21 percent, and yet people were still purchasing. A number of Bracebridge residents did join a huge convoy and headed to Ottawa to protest the federal government regarding the interest rate policy.

## 1982

The year came in with a bang. High winds and driving rain turned roads into slides. Packed snow turned to ice and school buses were unable to run. Warnings went out about the soft ice on the lakes, and the Ministry of Natural Resources advised people to stay off them.

Stan Darling's report from Ottawa stated that thousands of Canadians were struggling under the burdens of inflation, high interest rates, and unemployment.

Residents were concerned that they would lose the river crossing on the Macaulay-Stephenson town line, the boundary between the towns of Bracebridge and Huntsville. The Huntsville Council had already approved the replacement of the bridge which had served at that location for nearly 60 years. The steel bridge was much older than 60 years, since it formerly was the river crossing at the top of the falls in Bracebridge. It was constructed there in 1893 to replace the older wooden structure. The bridge was built at a cost of $2,400 of which the Ontario Crown lands department paid $2,000. In the early 1920s the Bracebridge Council decided to replace the structure with the bridge (called Bird's Bridge) and the steel bridge was sold by Bracebridge to the townships of Macaulay and Stephenson, who were now fighting to keep the bridge.

The Society of St. John the Evangelist decided to leave Bracebridge. The Anglican religious order, known to

*The view of Bracebridge today from the second-floor balcony of Woodchester Villa. The soaring white pines were little more than seedlings in the 1880s.* FROM "PICTORIAL HISTORY OF WOODCHESTER VILLA"

many as the "Cowley Fathers," intended to leave their Maple Street Mission House as soon as other arrangements could be made. The property that the Society had occupied since the late 1920s was sold. The Society came to Canada in 1928 from Cowley, near Oxford, England, to do mission work in the Muskoka area. Father Frere Kennedy explained that the Society's mission work increasingly took members out of Muskoka and that the order had declined numerically, making it difficult to run the premises, guest house, and printing business effec-

*Woodchester Villa, home to the Bird family for nine decades and now a museum, is one of the older houses in Bracebridge, and unique today as it was when built in 1882.* FROM "PICTORIAL HISTORY OF WOODCHESTER VILLA"

tively. There were also financial difficulties involved in operating the buildings and extensive renovations were needed.

In February 1982 Council accepted a tender by Braecon Ltd. for $118,942 to revamp the Town Hall, to provide a new council chamber and other office space. Originally, tenders were called for work to include the upstairs auditorium, but after four firms had tendered varying designs at figures ranging from $110,000 to $152,000, the auditorium work was deleted. Braecon was responsible for the first phase of the facelift: the general office area downstairs. Jim Boyes described the existing 24-year old building as "somewhat dysfunctional."

Special equipment was used to lower Bracebridge's historic town bell from the high tower above the municipal building. It was 60 years since the bell was on the ground. In 1922 the Bracebridge Council undertook to build the 60-foot-high tower, 12 feet square at the base and 10 feet square at the top. The tower was needed by the fire department for drying the canvas hoses. The hoses were attached to a square frame which was pulled up inside the tower. At the same time the Council had a stable building erected as an addition to the Town Hall, and there the town team, used to draw the fire-fighting equipment, and for work on town streets, was housed. It was in 1933 that Bracebridge had its first motor vehicle fire truck and the horses were sold. The town bell had formerly hung in a steeple on the northwestern part of the Town Hall roof. The bell was rung from inside the building. In 1922 the bell was lowered to the ground, then raised to the top of the new tower.

Under new arrangements after 1922, the bell continued to be used for fire alarms. Down the northeast corner of the tower a wire cable ran to the ground, and when pulled activated the clapper which struck the bell. At one time Bracebridge was divided into seven fire wards, and the instructions were to toll the number of the fire ward first, then quickly ring the alarm. Soon after World War II, in the time of Mayor L.R. "Pat" Ryan, the old fire bell system was abandoned in favour of a fire siren. The town bell, which was mounted and placed in front of the fire station, had been purchased by the town in 1893 for $183.50. It was bought from the McShane Bell Company of Baltimore. On the surface of the bell are the names of the Council for 1893. Starting in 1893 and continuing for many years, the town bell was rung each weekday at 7:00 a.m., 12 noon, 1:00 p.m., and 6:00 p.m., the times for beginning and leaving work. The time came, about 40 years previously, when the times were changed to 8:00 a.m., 12 noon, 1:00 p.m., and 5:00 p.m. It was, however, several years since the bell has been rung at all. In 1893 a curfew bylaw was passed requiring the bell to be rung at 8:00 p.m. between November 1 and April 30 and at 9:00 p.m. the rest of the year. All children under 14 were to be off the streets once the bell had rung, unless accompanied by a parent or guardian. At different times in succeeding years the curfew bell bylaw was re-enacted. In July 1983 the bell was moved to what was its third and possibly final home, in front of the new Bracebridge Fire Hall.

The proposed bridge connecting Wellington Street with District Road 4 would relieve a real bottleneck on Manitoba Street in the summer months, according to the mayor, Jim Lang. The bridge, which was scheduled to be completed by 1983, caused controversy in the past because of fears it would direct some traffic away from downtown Bracebridge. The mayor didn't feel that cottagers would bypass Bracebridge completely just because they would have easy access to Highway 118. "It's my feeling that the average cottager wants to get out to his cottage right off the bat. Then after all the unloading is finished, the family returns to Bracebridge to shop at their leisure." In a preliminary feasibility study on alternate routes through Bracebridge, completed two years before, it was noted that the average traffic levels on Manitoba Street in 1986 would range from 18,850 to 21,750 a day. The firm of E.E. Seegmiller of Kitchener were low bidders on the Wellington Street Bridge project. The full cost of three million was borne by a Ministry of Transportation development grant and surplus from the town's budget. The contract was a very complex document and work was stalled until the contract was signed.

Knox Presbyterian Church celebrated the 100th anniversary of the hiring its first minister, Rev. Allan Findlay. Dr. Findlay had already been serving the little congregation for seven years before it was able to extend a call to him. When he arrived in the community in 1875 the congregation numbered only 39 communicant members. The original call is still in the possession of the congregation and hangs framed on the wall in the church hall.

One of the best know citizens of Bracebridge, Alex Milne, passed away. He was the postmaster at Bracebridge for 13 years. He attended school in Bracebridge and was employed at the post office before becoming postmaster.

Another prominent Bracebridge resident died. James Stevenson had been a town councillor and president of the Chamber of Commerce. He had done much to advance Bracebridge as a business centre. He came to Bracebridge in 1950, having purchased the Albion Hotel property, which he sold in 1958, and began the operation of Wenawae's.

The *Lady Muskoka* cruise boat was sold by Captain Tom Oakes to Muskoka Cruise Lines Ltd. The 200-passenger vessel had operated out of Gravenhurst until the summer of 1982. Muskoka Cruise Lines moved the ship to the Riverside Inn where they operated cruises on a daily basis.

Fred "Bing" Crosby, a well-known figure in Bracebridge, passed away. His passing left thousands of friends to mourn. Most youngsters who rose through the ranks of minor hockey and baseball knew him. He was always there when needed, whether it was to tie up loose skates or mend a broken baseball glove. "Bing" probably gave away a fortune in his time to youngsters without money for pop, or for a taxi to get a young lad home. The sports community in Bracebridge greatly missed this good man.

Former Gravenhurst Mayor Allen Sander was elected District chairman when he defeated George Parlett by a 12 to 9 decision.

The helicopter landing pad behind South Muskoka Memorial Hospital got its finishing touches as eight amber approach lights were installed to show the perimeter of the landing area for the air ambulance.

An 80-foot stretch of Beaumont Drive slumped into the river. Residents living along the road started noticing slight settlement along existing crack lines. Public works filled the cracks with gravel every few days but the gentle slide continued. Eventually about three feet of the river bank was lost; stone fill was put in. Finally the big collapse came. A stretch about 80 feet long broke off, taking about one quarter of the travelled surface of the road with it. The fill had put extra weight on and the collapse was inevitable. Helen Parrett was first to find the slump and lucky not to have lost her car in the hole.

Historian Robert J. Boyer published the history of Woodchester Villa and the Henry Bird family. Three paintings dating from the 1880s were donated to Woodchester Villa and Museum by Mr. and Mrs. Alfred Schumann of Fairfax, Virginia. These were titled *South Falls*, *Camp on the River*, and *Bracebridge Bay*.

New additions to our town storefronts included Junetta's, operated by Isabel Milne, and Country Kitchen and Bath. A new structure added to the skyline as well: the building located beside the Crockford Building, beside what is now Browser's Paradise.

The official opening of the Muskoka Industrial Mall was held late in the fall of 1982.

## 1983

The proposed Wellington Street Bridge and resulting traffic bypass was one of the most contested developments in the 1980s. Gallons of midnight oil were burned while Bracebridge townspeople discussed the pros and cons of an alternate route to the Manitoba Street business section. The proposal had actually been in the book for decades, but it took the advent of the '80s to make final decisions and get the project under way. In February 1980, the *Herald-Gazette* led off with a story entitled "Proposed bypass makes some merchants edgy." That assertion would prove to be an understatement in the next three years, as persons from all professions joined in the fray. Another front page story said "Wellington Street Bridge likely choice," indicating crossings elsewhere on the Muskoka River were slowly being ruled out. It was at this time a young councillor named Ross Miller began to get vocal about his disagreement with the proposal. Miller was not a member of the public works committee, but asked to attend meetings as an observer to mount his campaign against the bridge. Local council went ahead and approved the proposal for a low

*Accompanied by a flotilla of motorboats and cheered on by thousands of spectators lining the shores of the bay, the* RMS Segwun *triumphantly returns to Bracebridge in 1982, for the first time since the 1950s. The event coincided with the centennial of Woodchester Villa, recently restored as a museum, making for a truly memorable day.* COURTESY OF MARILYN LONG

level bridge at Wellington Street, but that found opposition with those who wanted to see the RMS *Segwun* sail into Bracebridge Bay in future years. She wouldn't fit under a low level bridge and a high level one was going to cost too much. Group action opposing the bridge slowly picked up momentum as summer approached. By June 1980 the Bracebridge Horticultural Society and the Muskoka Steamship and Historical Society tried to negotiate with council, but to no avail. The *Segwun* required 55 feet of clearance to get under the bridge, and Council said the added cost could not be justified. The *Segwun* did make a trip to Bracebridge Bay two years later, but she would never make another. By the end of June a letter was received from the minister of transportation and communications, James Snow, giving provincial approval. It was stated the town would be responsible for building the bridge and District would take it over on completion. Of the total cost of construction, 90 percent would be provided by the province. In July a front page story appeared in the *Herald-Gazette* about the effect the new bridge could have on the Dominion Store mall and nearby land on Highway 118. Many people speculated that the area known as "Ball's Flats" would attract more commercial interest. The conflict became subdued for many months, but it was never forgotten.

In the fall of 1983, the first vehicles were allowed across the Wellington Street Bridge. There was an unofficial opening conducted by Bracebridge mayor Jim Lang.

For the first time in District history, committee meetings were opened up to the press and public

As a result of national policy decision, Canada Post decided to eliminate street letter box collection service. Residents in Bracebridge now have to deposit mail at the post office on Manitoba Street.

Block Parents came to Bracebridge. After 18 months of hard work, president Linda Kelly watched as constable Raye Harrington gave out the first Block Parent signs.

Nineteen-year-old Liisa Savijarvi placed third in the World Cup Ski races and first place in the Giant Slalom event at Collingwood. This was the first full year for Liisa in World Cup racing. She finished with the best time for her class in the Canadian Championships. Liisa went on to represent Canadian women skiers at the 1984 Winter Olympics in Sarajevo, Yugoslavia.

Bracebridge Public Library's expansion and renovation project got under way. Library Board chairman Bob Dolphin explained that plans were to make the outside look like an exact extension of the old Carnegie building. The restoration fund received a one-time grant of $11,000 from the McConnell Memorial Foundation and a $200,000 Wintario grant.

Strange and unexplained occurrences at Woodchester Villa prompted an investigation to try to determine whether the museum might be "haunted." A Bracebridge resident said she saw an apparition of a "tall, thin man in his early or mid-50s" about 10 years before when she was alone in the house. She requested anonymity because she did not conclusively subscribe to the existence of disembodied spirits. Bizarre as it may seem, Ted Williamson of the Bracebridge Historical Society delved into newspaper archives to try to identify an apparition allegedly contacted by tour guides using a Ouija board during the summer. The spirit identified itself as a relative of the Bird family, who built the octagonal house in 1882. The Bird family took exception to the publicity and stated that the house should be known for its historic richness and not as a "ghost house."

A small congregation gathered on Easter Sunday for the final solemn High Mass as the Society of Saint John the Evangelist started their move from Bracebridge to Hamilton. The service brought to an close 55 years of service in the community.

Former Bracebridge town councillor Ross Miller took over Bracebridge Auto Service on Manitoba Street and opened a new Chrysler-Plymouth dealership known as Muskoka Chrysler Sales.

To John Rutherford, music was not confined to classroom experience; the work of the band was an extension of the work of the classroom and a part of the life of the community. John Rutherford came to Bracebridge in 1969. Since then the band has played an important and popular part in the life of the town. Two concerts were held to honour the retiring music teacher.

The life of Jessie Iona Pepper came to its close. Mrs. Pepper was born in Bracebridge in 1898, a daughter of George Alfred and Mary Jane Hines. In 1905 her father built the handsome residence on Kimberley Avenue, which in later years was owned by the Rev. Thomas Dunlop and then by Mr. and Mrs. Russell Best, and it was there that Jessie Hines spent several years of her girlhood.

Not many towns can boast that they have the original water-powered pump, installed when the town went on watermains, still in operation. Bracebridge does. The big old Northey reciprocating-action pump, built in Toronto in 1894, was overhauled. Public Works superintendent Don Currie was the first to admit that she needed it. Both the pump and the handsome old building got an overhaul. "This was the only pumping station for the town," Currie said. "Now we have nine water pumping stations and eleven for sewage. I don't know of any municipality that has such old water-driven pumps." The building has a red brick one-storey facade under an attractive grey upper storey. At one time the operator had a home in the upper section. Earlier still, two operators kept a round-the-clock watch, in 12 hour shifts, on the machinery. The nighttime operator, who slept on a cot in a small loft, was so attuned to the sound of the pumps that he would wake instantly at a change in their tone. Now the pumps are automatically controlled from the powerhouse by the lower falls, though town employees check them twice a day. The flat roofed reservoir (on the opposite side of the road) has two sections, one of stone dating from 1894, the other built in the early 1920s. They hold 302,000 gallons of water brought by gravity from the fourteen wells at Barrons springs, near the old standpipe. "We never drain the reservoir," Currie said. "We just use the top four feet. The rest is for fire protection. On the occasion of the Thomas Company fire, at a rough estimate, one and a half million gallons of water were used. The fire hoses on that occasion did drain the reservoir, with water being pumped directly from the Muskoka booster station (opposite Meritor). The two historic pumps are there as back-up, and maybe for sentimental reasons. But the nineteenth century system that operates them is still in place."

Arthur and Sylvia Richardson bought The Holiday House on Dominion Street and did extensive renovations and renamed it Holiday House Inn. The Victorian house was originally built by John Adair. It was then sold to William C. Mahaffy, who was appointed Muskoka's first district judge in 1888. In the early years of the 20th century, the house remained a private residence, although it changed owners several times. In 1943 the property was converted to a hotel christened Holiday House with accommodation for 35 guests.

Deaths this year included Milton C. Bailey, 81, one of the sons of Charles and Charlotte Bailey. His father was an outstanding athlete and encouraged his sons and many other young men to live up to the principles of good sportsmanship. Milton Bailey attended the Bracebridge schools and then began an association of several years in the office of the Bird Woollen Mill. He was brother to "Ace" Bailey ... Harold Clarence Frowe, 79, went into business in 1933 as a merchant and was able to secure the property and buildings on Thomas Street where he established the Muskoka Trading Company. He served for some time as a town councillor. He helped families in many ways, often without the families being aware of who their benefactor was. This was part of his cheerful friendliness which made him one of Bracebridge's most popular men ... Edward (Ted) Fitzmaurice, 93, was the youngest and last survivor of 19 children born to Thomas Fitzmaurice and Anne Cooper McCarthy, original settlers of Muskoka. Before the war they sold lakeshore property to Mr. and Mrs. Jack J. Greig who built Tamwood Lodge. During the war the farm was sold and Ted

*Almost there! Each of the huge steel beams for the Wellington Street bridge arrived by truck.* COURTESY OF THE TOWN OF BRACEBRIDGE

worked for Fred Mills and Son for many years until he retired. Of local historical interest, Ted's mother Anne (Cooper) was a direct descendant of the Coopers who came to Muskoka in 1860 to build a road from South Falls (Muskoka Falls) to North Falls (Bracebridge). At North Falls were two log huts belonging to John Beal and David Leith. They built the first bridge across the falls in 1861. It was so well braced to withstand the spring floods that Ted and his mother always claimed that Bracebridge got its name from this well-built bridge. The Coopers got 300 acres of Bracebridge proper, one lot of which was on both sides of the falls. They built a tavern, ran a saw mill, a grocery business, and Anne's father became a councillor. They built the first log house north of the falls. Ted's father, Thomas, arrived in Monck in August of 1861.

July 1983 saw the opening of the first public fully licensed patio on Bracebridge's main street. Stiliano's (now The Thirsty Judge) on Kimberley Avenue was the only one around at this time other than the private golf club. Outdoor drinking was a long-time tradition in Europe but a fairly recent phenomenon in Canada. After all, it wasn't so many years since the windows of "beverage rooms" were covered over lest the public be horrified by the appalling sight of people having a beer. Other restaurant owners could be expected to follow suit.

In a cabinet shuffle, Muskoka's MPP, Frank Miller, left the job of treasurer of Ontario to become minister of trade and commerce. Miller had tabled five budgets in the legislature – a long time for anyone to be treasurer. Miller held the portfolio through one of the toughest economic periods in Ontario's history and was credited with creating policies for recovery and maintaining the province's high international credit rating.

Members of the town staff did an excellent job of planting and maintaining the flowers and shrubs around the Cenotaph in Memorial Park. A unique above-ground sprinkler system was installed.

All the indicators in a newly released Economic Overview showed Bracebridge as having a stronger and more diverse economy than any of its neighbours. The labour force here grew 56.3 percent between 1971 and 1981, compared with an average growth of 36.6 percent among the other five municipalities. In fact our labour force expansion was 23 percent higher than the provincial average. Population trends also showed Bracebridge in the lead. Between 1976 and 1981 the town's population grew 7.5 percent. The average growth in other Muskoka municipalities was only 2.6 percent. Georgian Bay Township actually registered a net loss of 2.4 percent.

Bracebridge Villa officially opened its new west wing. Local contractors began work on the addition in June. The opening of the new wing marked a step forward in the provision of care to seniors.

It started to snow in the afternoon of December 21 and continued almost unabated until Christmas Eve. By that time the Muskoka Airport weather station staff had recorded a fall of 69.4 centimetres. The snow was blown in by brisk south and southeasterly winds, gusting up to 52 kilometres an hour. By December 26 we had a total accumulation of 74 centimetres. When final snowfall measurements were taken at the end of the month the amount of snow easily beat previous records for the end of December which stood at 71 centimetres.

## 1984

This was a year of great change to the Bracebridge landscape. The value of building permits increased by 46 percent over 1983. The addition to the Bracebridge Public Library was completed. The old Supertest service station at the corner of Manitoba and Willis streets was demolished to make way for the new Becker's convenience store. The golden arches arrived in Bracebridge with the opening of McDonalds on March 4 and by lunch time cars were lined up 20 deep at the drive-through. By the end of the day 960 Big Macs had been served. A new chapel of The Church of Jesus Christ of Latter-Day Saints at the corner of Muskoka Road 42 and Taylor Road was constructed. The former location on Pine Street became the new offices of the Muskoka Family and Children's Services. The Pines held the official opening of their addition.

The Ontario Ministry of Housing gave final approval for the new 12-unit non-profit housing complex to be built on Liddard Street as part of a 51-unit complex. A seven-unit condominium comprising Phase 2 of the Riverwoods Development created by Bruce Evans on

Southbank Drive and the 16-unit Falls View townhouse complex beside Kelvin Grove Park on the former site of the Building Trades Centre, were approved.

Additions included a new showroom at the Greavette Fox GM dealership, a second storey to the Modern Home Supply store on Ann Street, the conversion of the former Hinds Manufacturing Plant on Woodland Drive into five apartments, and the renovation of the house north of the post office by Larry Giaschi, into apartments at the rear and main street office space at the front.

New businesses were Shards 'n' Shavings, featuring local Muskoka handicrafts; Muskoka Insurance Brokers in the Heritage Investment/Chelsea Real Estate business block; Dr. Kenneth R. Hawthorn's office with Dr. Kimberly G. Parlett at 48 Ann Street; and Deborah Golledge's new Chiropractic Clinic. The Wandlyn Hotel chain of Fredericton, New Brunswick, acquired the Riverside Inn. The Muskoka Riverside Inn had been turned into a first-class hotel in 1979 by several local businessmen after having originally been built as a shopping plaza ... Ray Coulson took over the Minnow Man from John Cooper ... The Patterson Hotel was foreclosed on and sold to Arron Edwards ... A & P announced their purchase of the Pine Point service station at the corner of Manitoba Street and Monck Road.

The most notable local business failure was when McEwan-Tougard was placed into receivership. The company, which manufactured waste handling equipment, garbage containers, garbage trucks, and trash compactors, had as recently as 1981 employed 28 people but had only four employees at the time of the shutdown.

The new sewage treatment plant came on stream in February. It was capable of processing 700,000 gallons a day. Construction of a $300,000 sewage line and pumping station commenced in January along District Road 4 to extend out to the 532 Industrial Mall.

The official opening of the Wellington Street bridge took place June 29, when ceremonies attended by Lieutenant Governor John B. Aird, the Honourable James Snow, the Honourable Frank Miller, and federal MP Stan Darling took place.

Following a three-year battle by local ratepayers in the Balsam Chutes and Bonnie Lake Road area, the town line bridge over the North Branch of the Muskoka River on Stephenson Road 1 was reopened in August after being restored and brought up to safety standards.

After considerable debate the town, acting on behalf of the Bracebridge Agricultural Society purchased for $55,000 a 32-acre site along Highway 11 at the corner of Fraserburg Road to be the new home of the Bracebridge Fall Fair. The new Muskoka Pioneer Power Association immediately expressed its wish to cooperate in developing the site.

The first Muskoka International Air Show was held. Among the flying acts were three World War I aircraft, including a twin of the Fokker D-7 triplane flown by Germany's famous Red Baron.

Councillors gave themselves a 10 percent pay raise, bringing their annual remuneration to $5,830 and the mayor's to $9,900.

A major forum on acid rain was hosted by the District's Acid Rain Committee.

The Muskoka Festival celebrated its 50th anniversary of producing theatre in Muskoka.

In late December, District Council passed a resolution to create the new Muskoka Tourism and Marketing Agency (MTMA) to begin operation in the new year, after which the old MTA, first organized in 1935, would be dissolved.

Total Muskoka enrollment was counted in September as 4,232 elementary students and 2,291 secondary, with the local numbers being 519 at Bracebridge Public School, 309 at Monck Public, and 947 at BMLSS. In December Murray Green was elected chairman of the Muskoka Board of Education, replacing the outgoing Edith Nichols. Long-term trustee Marilyn Rowe was president of the Ontario Public School Trustees Association.

Labour unrest was widespread: 127 unionized employees of Alcan Wire and Cable went on strike for two months ... 56 unionized employees at the District were on strike for six weeks ... a one-week strike occurred at the Rockwell plant ... there was a very real threat of a teacher's strike.

Some presidents this year were: Allen Taylor, Bracebridge Rotary Club; Derek McNeil, Kinsmen Club; Dick

*Construction under way on the addition to the Bracebridge Public Library; this is the room that houses the adult circulating collection.* COURTESY OF THE TOWN OF BRACEBRIDGE

Ellis, Lions Club; Ted Currie, Historical Society; and Allan Wilson, Legion. The Rotary Club presented *Finian's Rainbow*, the 1947 humorous musical fantasy. with its famous song hits by E.Y. Harburg such as *How Are Things in Glocca Morra*. In June, the recently restored Woodchester Villa was recognized by the province as an historic site with the erection of a plaque by the Ontario Heritage Foundation. The Historical Society sponsored their first annual three-day Antique Show and Sale.

The Bracebridge Senior Citizens Club spearheaded by their president Earl Baker and building chairman Nelson Goltz had the former Armstrong residence on Dominion Street demolished, and erected a 30 by 70-foot building.

At the South Muskoka Memorial Hospital, a solarium was added to the end of the north wing at a cost of $300,000. Also included was a new entrance road off Liddard Street, 32 new parking spaces, improved access ramps, as well as some additional beds. However, hospital administrator Frank Henry had to announce a $100,000 operating deficit at year's end. Chairmanship of the Hospital Board passed during the year from Peter Johnston to Marvyn Couse.

At a civic reception in Memorial Park the Salvation Army celebrated its 100th anniversary of service in the Town of Bracebridge. They had established a corps in Bracebridge only six years after its inception in London, England, by William Booth in 1878. The Salvation Army purchased four lots between Toronto and Richard Streets where they planned to erect a new building to replace their 30-year-old building on Ontario Street.

The big athletic story of the year was the showing of local native, 20-year-old Liisa Savijarvi in February at the 1984 Winter Olympics held at Sarajevo, Yugoslavia. Liisa, a four-year veteran of the Canadian National Ski Team, placed 9th in the giant slalom and earned an 18th place finish in the downhill event. She also placed fourth in the giant slalom in the World Cup at St. Jurveau, France, and after returning from Sarajevo to Stoneham, Quebec, she won the gold medal in the Canadian women's giant slalom championship. Her 17-year-old sister, Amy, a former Canadian juvenile champion from 1982, was named in May to the National Development Team, the grooming ground for the National Ski Team.

The Muskoka Shield canoe race held on the Musquash and Gibson rivers was won by two Bracebridge professionals, dentist Ken Hawthorn and land surveyor John Hiley in the MC1 racing class.

In the September, voters in the federal election chose from the same three candidates as in the previous two elections: Burk's Falls realtor Stan Darling, 73, Conservative MP since 1972; Parry Sound school teacher Ed Fisher, Liberal; and Gravenhurst factory worker Dennis Hay, New Democrat. Darling coasted to easy re-election while the Conservatives took 211 seats to the Liberal's 40 and the NDP's 30.

Dr. Robert McClure, former moderator of the United Church of Canada, was guest speaker for anniversary services at Bracebridge United Church. In July, Lady Patience Baden-Powell, chief commissioner for the Girl Guides in the United Kingdom, visited Bracebridge. On September 15, the Bracebridge Royal Canadian Legion Branch assisted with guard duty during the first ever Papal visit to Canada when Pope John Paul II conducted an open-air mass at the Martyr's Shrine. The Cellar Singers, a 40-voice choir founded in Bracebridge in 1968 under the direction of Dr. William Monk, was invited to perform at the Martyr's Shrine Church for the arrival of the Pope.

On September 26, hundreds of supporters from Bracebridge turned out to greet Steve Fonyo, the one-legged runner from British Columbia as he passed along Highway 11 on his cross-Canada journey to raise funds for cancer research.

Orvil Hammond celebrated the 40th anniversary of the creation of Hammond Transportation ... Shier's Insurance celebrated 40 years of serving Muskoka ... Norm Shill retired after 44 years with the Toronto Dominion Bank, the last 19 years as manager of the Bracebridge branch.

The government of Ontario, represented by the Honourable Frank Miller, honoured six Bracebridge area citizens with the presentation of the Ontario Bicentennial Medal, awarded in recognition of services to their communities. The local recipients were Robert J. Boyer, Orvil Hammond, Bill Robertson, Mrs. Kay Beers, Mrs. Vi Ferguson, and Mrs. Eva Orr.

Some well-known area residents who passed away during the year included the following: Long time Bracebridge Hydro employee William John Inch, 84, became powerhouse operator at Wilson's Falls, a position he held for 39 years ... Mrs. John E. Dawkins, nee Florence Mills, instrumental in founding the women's auxiliary of the Red Cross Society in Bracebridge and a life member of the Salvation Army ... local tradesman Ernie Holland, 75, began his plumbing and heating business in 1947 ... Mrs. Bruce R. Minns, 85, daughter of T. James Anderson and Annie Fenn. Her father was the founder of the Fenn, Anderson & Co. Ltd. whose business had continued for 82 years until 1966 when their building on the main street was sold to the Banks Brothers ... Henry Kirbyson, 78, of Ufford, married Freda Nichol in 1933 ... William P. Anderson, 80, came to Bracebridge in the 1920s as a builder before opening a barber shop which he operated for 20 years during the 1950s and 1960s on Queen's Hill. A skilled oil painter, many of his canvases hang in Bracebridge homes ... Local businessman William S. Little, 79, Draper Township. A councillor and reeve, he moved into town in 1955 and established the By-Way Garage and Auto Wreckers; later he ran the Texaco service station until it was converted into Rombo's Restaurant ... Fred Ricard, 79, a long-time member of the town's fire department .... The town was shocked at the sudden death of Keith Peacock at age 38. He was an ardent supporter of local hockey, having managed both the Juvenile Bears and the Junior C Bears ... John Newark, 81, had lived in the same house on Hiram Street for the past 75 years where he had operated a boat fender manufacturing business for 56 years ...

Archie Ball, 65, a son of Thomas and Isabella. He was best remembered as a star of the Bracebridge Bears Intermediate Hockey team during the late 1940s and early 1950s ... Grenville W. Martin, 48, owner of the Bracebridge Lumber Co. on the Kirk Line, which he just purchased seven months previously. He was killed in a light plane crash near Malton. He had assembled one of the largest hardwood operations in North America with mills throughout Ontario ... Seth Hillman, 76, partner of Arthur Crockford in the Downtown Garage from 1936 till the 1970s ... Lorne R. Hockridge, 67, purchased the historic Hutchison Brothers Grocery in the early 1950s which he operated as Lorne's Marketeria. He was remembered for his horses which he exhibited at many fall fairs ... Mrs. Thomas Flynn, 70, nee Velma Agnes Lloyd, had worked on the town's office staff for 24 years ... Finlay Munro, 79, developed and operated the Rainbow Ridge ski resort.

*At the end of its 12th decade of incorporation, Bracebridge reached a milestone: 100 years of municipal operation of hydroelectric generating stations. The familiar stone powerhouse at the foot of the falls began lighting the community in 1902, but in 1894 the town had acquired its first hydro plant, at the upper falls.* COURTESY OF GARY LONG

# 1985–1994

## *Growth, Recession, and a Century of Electric Power*

THE YEAR 1985 was a good one for Bracebridge. We gained a non-profit housing project, a Senior Citizens Centre, a shelter for battered women, an animal shelter, and a new land titles office. Our library was reopened after extensive renovations and there was an addition to the hospital.

Our local MPP, Frank Stuart Miller, became leader of the Conservative party and the 19th premier of Ontario, albeit for a short time.

The winter carnival showed much "Muskoka spirit" with broomball, dancing, log sawing, suspended doughnuts, a highly competitive bed race, a volleyball challenge in loose snow, and of course the ever more popular "polar bear" swim.

The Bracebridge Midget hockey team won the All Ontario Finals against Seaforth.

The Kinsmen Club donated $5,000 toward an ice-cleaning machine for the arena. The total cost was $30,000.

The value of building permits issued in 1984 was up $3.5 million from the 1983 permits. Building inspector Ben Einarson said the increase was due to commercial structures including the new Greavette-Fox Motor Sales building, the Big Top Department Store, the Bracebridge non-profit housing project, the Senior Citizens Centre, the Children's Aid Society, and major renovations to South Muskoka Memorial Hospital. The new land registry office that was to be built behind the courthouse on Dominion Street in 1985, was also included in the figures because the permits were issued in 1984.

Muskoka acquired a crisis shelter for battered women with the Ministry of Community and Social Services paying all of the capital and 80 percent of the operating costs. District Council voted unanimously to contribute the other 20 percent of the operating

*The impressive Bracebridge Public Library at the top of Queen's Hill was opened in 1908. Those familiar with the building prior to the creation of the children's library in the basement in 1967 will remember the big wooden staircase that spiralled down to the lower level through a balustraded stairwell just inside the front entrance.*

COURTESY OF THE BRACEBRIDGE PUBLIC LIBRARY

costs. A house was leased in Bracebridge and contributions of money and furnishings literally poured in from local organizations and individuals. On November 13, the 10-bed shelter opened its doors and continues to be run the Muskoka Women's Advocacy Group under the direction of Joy McCormack.

The District of Muskoka took over sludge and hauling.

The new district land registry office was officially opened on November 25. It cost $1 million. The old registry office, built in 1955, was torn down to provide for 22 parking spaces. The registrar in 1985 was Craig Stewart.

St. Thomas' Anglican Church, built in 1896, underwent structural renovations of up to $150,000. The church had been built on the site of a brick yard. The underground supports had subsided causing cracks inside the church early on but no action had been taken until 1985. This is the third Anglican Church in Bracebridge. The first church was a log structure out near the cemetery. In 1872 a square white wooden church was built and then the 1896 modified gothic brick building that we see today.

Muskoka's oldest continuously publishing newspaper changed ownership in March of 1985, the new owners being Don Smith and a group of local business people including the *Herald-Gazette* publisher, Raymond Lee. The deal included the purchase of the *Huntsville Herald*, the *Muskoka Sun* and the *Near North Sun*. Robert Boyer continued as associate editor of the *Herald-Gazette* and editor of the *Muskoka Sun*.

In mid-March, a roads department crew cut up the former steamship *Cherokee* at Kirby's Beach, which had become its final resting place. It was cut down to the waterline before a backhoe removed the ice in front of the hull and two tow trucks and bulldozers pulled the it up on shore where workers finished cutting up the hull.

Don Currie, water and sewage supervisor, reported water levels were low in order to clean up the Bird's Mill Pumping Station and to replace a short section at Wilson's Falls.

A boat went over Balsam Chutes, drowning Mr. and Mrs. Nyakas and their five-year-old son.

Deaths this year included Mrs. Leslie Hart (nee Leola Nelson), 76, worked on the staff of Bell Telephone. She married Leslie Hart and helped run Hart's and Flowers greenhouses on River Road ... Mrs. Cornie Reynolds (nee Ethel Elizabeth Dixon), 94. She was born at Housey's Rapids and moved to Bracebridge in 1901. She worked at the Bird Woollen Mill until she married Cornelius Reynolds in 1932 ... William Lyle Black, respected physician and citizen. He and Norman Rosewarne formed the first Wolf Cub Pack in Bracebridge. He was resident physician at The Pines where a plaque was dedicated in his honour. Dr. Black served as a town councillor and as a Muskoka Board of Education trustee and chairman. He was active in Rotary, and the Muskoka Progressive Conservative Party ... Mrs. Constance Ecclestone, 91, wife of George N. Ecclestone, former owner of Ecclestone's Hardware. Constance was the last surviving family member of Robert P. Perry, postmaster of the town who had succeeded his father, Robert E. Perry, the first postmaster ... Mrs. Elymer McDermott (nee Alice Aileen Hurst), 75, married in Port Carling in 1931, moved to Bracebridge in 1943. She was active in the United Church, Women's Institute, and the Seniors' Centre ... Mrs. George Hammond (nee Edna Lillian Leeder), 81, married in 1922 ... Bruce Sword, 71, had a welding business in Beatrice ... Mrs. Viola Alexander (nee Viola Ellen Rutter), born in Draper in 1907 ... Mrs. Jack Atkinson, 70, a fine teacher and avid curler ... Agnes Ann Gibson, 99, came with her father when he supervised the installation of the Dominion Linen Mills and stayed ... John Naismith, 64, stonemason ...

Evan Luker, 9, son of Arthur and Pat Luker of Fraserburg Road. Evan was riding in a car that was hit while crossing Highway 11 at the Fraserburg Road level crossing. This was the second death in three months at the intersection. The son of a high-profile athletics teacher at BMLSS, Evan took after his father. He was active in gymnastics and soccer but especially enjoyed cross-country running. Each year in the fall, the Evan Luker Run is held with children from the Bracebridge elementary schools participating at different grade levels of cross-country running competition. There is not a child in any Bracebridge school that doesn't know the name Evan Luker. An outcry from town citizens produced a petition campaign to the Ministry of Transportation of Ontario to request an overpass be built.

Lawyer Thomas Wood was appointed Queen's Counsel for his interest in law, local history, and music. He lives and works at 47 Quebec Street in the former home of postmaster Perry. Mrs. Rita Dinner was awarded the Bicentennial Medal for her quiet, selfless efforts helping those in need. Bracebridge's Uniroyal earned an award in recognition of 600,000 accident-free hours. This was their only belting plant in Canada.

Michele De La Plante was Valedictorian at the BMLSS commencement. Best Girl award went to Bev Hammond, and Harry Vanderreen won the Best Boy award.

Greg Waite, 15, won two gold and two silver medals at the provincial level of the Special Olympics in swimming.

*The two-storey library addition at the rear was designed to convey in both form and materials the character of the original Carnegie building.* COURTESY OF GARY LONG

Jane Loftus joined Gravenhurst Cable System's Cable 10 in July. The company had been operating since 1963.

Allan M. Howell returned to be the new president of The Church of Jesus Christ of Latter Day Saints. He succeeded Mr. Grant Barrick.

Wandlyn Inn, the former Muskoka Riverside Inn, changed their quiet piano bar into a mix of country and rock 'n' roll.

A pilot project to recycle glass, metal refuse, and newspaper products began May 3 with the former Cathcart building as the central depository. Muskoka Containerized Services agreed to provide containers at discount rates.

The Bracebridge Block Parents started with 40 members and reported almost 300 active members in 1984.

A 28-day lock-out at the beer stores across Ontario ended March 25. The local Ontario Secondary School Teachers' Federation went on strike, with 150 teachers peacefully picketing outside the Muskoka Board of Education offices. The strike was settled with a five percent pay increase in one year and a four percent increase in the second year of the contract.

Nurses at The Pines received a 30 percent pay raise to give them parity with the hospital nurses.

Taxi fares increased from 13 to 15 cents per one-tenth mile. The minimum fare rose to $2.

*Frank Miller with two of his most ardent supporters, Brenda and Nancy Cox. The popular Bracebridge businessman had become Muskoka's MPP in 1972, served as a cabinet minister in the Davis government, and became premier in 1985.* COURTESY OF BRENDA COX

The Silver Bridge was closed from mid-April until June for necessary rehabilitation works and new expansion joints. Traffic lights were put up at the corner of Wellington Street and Highway 118.

A & P purchased the local Dominion Store. Meadow Heights Estates, a new $14-million, four-phase subdivision started construction in May with Fowler Construction making the roads. Santa's Village underwent a million-dollar renovation.

The Coalition on Acid Rain held meetings in Bracebridge to raise awareness of their concerns.

The Carlsberg team and wagon took part in the fifth annual Muskoka Home Show at Building Trades Centre.

On May 24 Lieutenant Governor John B. Aird cut the ribbon to officially reopen the newly restored and extended Carnegie Public Library. Chairman of the Library Board was Bob Dolphin. The librarian was Nancy Jones, who shortly thereafter left for Woodstock.

On May 31, Bracebridge mobilized to help in the Barrie area after a tornado disaster. All active police personnel were called in and dispatched to the Barrie detachment. Ontario Hydro had 11 staff and four trucks at the scene rebuilding lines and restoring service to the devastated area. Muskoka Ambulance offered help and were called in to give emergency coverage to the Orillia area, from which every available ambulance had been drawn to the scene of the disaster. Local churches and service clubs offered collections and donations to the disaster relief.

In June, the Ontario Humane Society constructed the first animal shelter in the area, under the direction of president Merle Matthews. The local branch raised $28,000 for real estate, site preparation, and initial operations. The portable building was given by the OHS head office and relocated from Mississauga. At present, the building is still located at Cedar Lane and Entrance Drive and serves as an office, clinic, and animal shelter.

On June 21 the new Senior Citizens Centre was officially opened on Dominion Street. President Earl Baker of the Senior Citizens Club and Olive Goddard cut the ribbon in front of a huge crowd of well wishers. The new 51-unit non-profit housing complex for seniors was managed by Pete Glazier. Senior citizens' pensions were de-indexed this year.

In the Seniors' Bonspiel, 16 rinks participated from Bracebridge, Huntsville, Gravenhurst, and Orillia for the John Scott Memorial Trophy.

Rotary Citizen of the Year for 1985 was Nelson Goltz. Mr. Goltz was former mayor, and chairman of the school board when the vocational wing of BMLSS was opened. Of Nelson's many other contributions to the well being of Bracebridge, the most recent was his superintendence of the building of the new Senior Citizens Centre.

Rotary produced *Mame* with Coray Schroder, Doug Skilliter, and Earl Ingleson.

In July the Bracebridge Fire Department received a new fire truck. The new $110,000 Pierre-Thibault truck featured a 1,200-gallon water capacity with a foam tank for spreading foam on gas and oil fires.

There was an explosion and fire at the Canox building in the new industrial mall. The home of Dan Currie on Bonnie Lake Road burned down. On October 9 at 6:00 p.m. the National Fire Drill was held.

Five local businessmen applied to the CRTC for a licence for a 50,000-watt radio station to operate in South Muskoka, from a tower on the Fraserburg Road. Doug Nelson, Don McVittie, Russell Black, Murray Dauphin, and Joe Duchesne hoped to establish an FM station in simultaneous broadcasting with Huntsville's CFBK-AM on both the AM and FM frequencies, with complete FM programming in five years.

In October the rumble of more than two dozen big motorcycles turned more than a few heads in Bracebridge. This was the Muskoka Motorcycle Club cruising slowly through town on a tour of Muskoka to collect toys. Vice president Ken Wettlaufer said that each bike rider was required to strap a toy of some kind to the back of his or her machine. The toys were donated to radio station CFBK in Huntsville for their annual drive for Christmas toys. These toys were then donated to agencies in the district for distribution to needy families.

The ice went out April 25 and flood levels surpassed the 1980-81 levels. On July 4 we had a record high temperature of 28°C. The temperature dropped to a record low (for that date) of 10 degrees that afternoon. We had 194.6 centimetres (6.4 feet) of snow in December which broke the 1942 record of 181.4. On December 31 there was 94 centimetres on the ground.

## 1986

In 1986 the assessed property value in Bracebridge was $315,852,362, an increase of 2.4 percent over 1985. A noise bylaw was passed which prohibited the use of loudspeakers or electronic sound-enhancing devices. It also forbid the use of horns, bells, gongs, and whistles, and forbid barking dogs. Fines up to $1,000 for the first offence were laid out. The bylaw officer was Colan Cowan.

In response to taxi companies' request, Council cut the number of taxi permits from 18 to 12. Dial-a-bus, which had been operating for eight years, stopped running.

Water and sewage superintendent Don Currie reported $25,000 was required for repairs to deteriorated equipment, worn parts,and a badly designed electrical system, which had plagued the sewage treatment plant since it was installed.

Muskoka Houseboat Rentals caused the Muskoka Lakes Association to lobby for a bylaw to prohibit the renting of houseboats on the Muskoka Lakes, and Bracebridge complied.

Bracebridge IOOF Lodge No. 251 celebrated its 100th birthday.

Rockwell International laid off 49 workers and plant manager Jerry Moroz said there was no relief in sight. At Scandura, 58 employees formed a union affiliated with the United Steel Workers.

The Board of Education had a 10.5 percent increase in its budget. Principal Dan Patterson at BMLSS reported it would cost $65,000 to replace the PA system.

In February, Sylvia and Arthur Richardson were forced into receivership of Holiday House. They had spent more than $260,000 on renovations when they purchased the business in 1983. Although they felt they had finally reached a point to see the business break even, the Richardsons just didn't have another penny to spend. The receivers asked them to stay on as managers until the new owners Peter and Jan Rickard completed the purchase.

Muskoka Transport displayed the Muskoka logo on its trailers with the caption "Muskoka, The Greatest Lakes."

Dave Murphy, son of jeweler P.D. Murphy, was the new owner of Maureen's.

Liisa Savijarvi, 23, helped the Canadian National Women's Ski Team achieve its best showing in four years. Her performance in the World Cup competition, in Furano, Japan. ranked her fifth in the world in downhill and tenth in overall combined downhill-slalom points standings.

Our Atoms hockey team won the zone championship.

The public health nurses went on rotating strikes until they were locked out.

A 50-year-old Lockheed L-10A landed at Muskoka Airport as part of Air Canada's 50th birthday celebration. Many townspeople enjoyed touring the aircraft.

A chapter of the Association for Children With Learning Abilities was formed.

The town was given quite a scare at the beginning of March when it was told by the Ministry of the Environment that one of the four springs that supplied drinking water to the town was slightly contaminated by a cancer-causing agent called tetrachloraethylene. The source of contamination was never found and the problem still exists. The contaminated source, Peake's springs, was measured at having two to five parts per billion of the agent. The MOE stated that a level of eight to ten parts was safe. In October, the MOE announced that Barron's springs was contaminated with the organic chemical associated with leaded gasoline. After re-examining the possibilities, Council could only relate it to a spill of 4,000 gallons of gasoline approximately 10 years earlier in the same vicinity. The result was the provision of chemically treated lake water instead of spring water.

Bracebridge Produce on the Baysville Road, managed by Doug Snelgrove, was consumed in a huge blaze that brought all 20 volunteer firemen out. Estimated damage was $85,000. Our fire brigade assisted the Milford Bay brigade with a fire at the home of Aston Villa manager Fred and Shonnie Grise. A fire at the home of Joseph Wyman on Hugh Campbell Drive injured the four residents as they escaped through windows. A benefit dance held by the Legion raised $500 for the family.

Vankoughnet got its own fire brigade this year, as it took the town firefighters 30 to 45 minutes to get out there. Bracebridge gave the new brigade our refurnished 1974 fire pumper.

After the recent extensive renovation, the library's roof leaked. Mr. Bob Dolphin arranged with the architect and contractor to have it fixed ... Anne Marie Darling was hired as the new Bracebridge librarian.

Salvage crews had to rescue the 140-tonne *Lady Muskoka* from where she had sunk in the Port Carling locks while stored there for the winter.

Julie Coates, 17, was crowned the 1986 Snow Queen by outgoing Queen Cara Helde. Snow Princesses were Lisa Fowle and Terri Mitchell.

Magna International purchased 800 acres at the west corner of District Road 4 and Muskoka Beach Road. Magna's intention was to build a huge car-part company with 150 employees, a technical training centre for students in robotics, computers, and tool and die, and a $20-million investment for the area.

In May, an OMB hearing passed the building of a second retail project – a 30,000-square-foot Loblaws grocery store, even though the plan was opposed by the A & P Company, owner of two existing grocery stores in Bracebridge. The store was to open opposite the Dominion Plaza in the spring of 1987.

In May, the Muskoka Non-profit Housing Authority was granted 25 low-income rental housing units by the Ministry of Municipal Affairs and Housing to be located behind the McDonald's restaurant.

At their Change of Officers Night in June, the Rotary Club of Bracebridge awarded Viola Ferguson and Leda Scovell Citizens of the Year. Miss Scovell had been a great supporter and volunteer member of the United Church as well as a grade one teacher at Bracebridge Public School, having taught several generations of children. Vi Ferguson was also a strong volunteer worker and member of St. Joseph's Roman Catholic Church. She had provided volunteer work for the Senior Citizen's Club and the Pines Centre for Seniors and was well known for her fundraising teas. The Rotary musical was *Camelot*, starring Stuart Barnett, Elaine Heron, and Dan Brooks.

The Rebekah Lodge honoured Mrs. Alice Pain with a 60-year pin and Mrs. Marge Patterson with a 50-year pin.

Dr. Bill Coleman was presented Lion of the Year by incoming president Jack McKinzey and outgoing president Bruce Kruger.

Flo Rebman won the Bronze Quill Award from the Canadian Community Newspaper Association. A Jessie I. Pepper Room was opened at SMMH in memory of her devoted work for the hospital auxiliary.

Greg Waite received the Jim Quigley Memorial Trophy as athlete of the year. Greg qualified to compete in swimming events in the national Special Olympics in Calgary.

Bill Calvert, chief administrative officer for the District, resigned to go to Hamilton-Wentworth. He returned to his old job a month later.

John Shier purchased the Bob Petry Insurance Service, established in 1953.

Cliff Dawson was elected president and Bruce Crawford secretary at the second annual Pioneer Power meeting.

Muskoka sheriff Sybil Jackson resigned in September. Miss Jackson was the first woman to hold the post of sheriff in Ontario and in 1986 was the only woman holding both the sheriff and local registrar's titles at once.

The Muskoka Board of Education removed the playground equipment from Bracebridge Public School, believing it was unsafe for children to use. This spurred on the development of an in-depth inspection of all public schools in the District and by December the majority of the schools were deemed unfit for young children. A seven-member panel cited a need for better lighting, smoke detectors, wheelchair access, cleaner washrooms, and better storage of chemicals. Bracebridge lost its playground completely, mainly because the play equipment was made by volunteers – parents of the children. The Board was concerned about insurance liability.

A retired naval commander, Donovan Arnaud, attempted to convert the former SSJE Mission House into an interdenominational private school called Vanguard Academy. However, Arnaud failed to raise the requisite funds of over $700,000 and the scheme fell through. In December, Braceport Ltd., owners of the property, created 32 lots with the Mission House building redeveloped as two houses. The company preserved the cemetery but the chapel was eventually renovated into a home.

Deaths in 1986 included Thomas Ewart Hammond, 59, heavy equipment operator, married Ella Atkinson in 1946 ... Harry Rutherford, 80, member of the Royal Canadian Legion Pipe Band and St. Thomas' choir ... Martin Boothby, 43, of Dwight, died after falling off his roof while shovelling snow ... Miss Annie Barron, 96, active in the Agricultural Society, Women's Institute, and the United Church. She was an avid gardener ... Jack Cloak, commissionaire at the Ontario Fire College and later well-known security guard at the South Muskoka Memorial Hospital ... Mr. William Henry Vanclief, 75, of Baysville ... Milton L. Davis, 51, employed at Building Trades, goal judge for the Bracebridge Bears ... Mrs. Lucy Bromley, 97, a former RN ... George Roy Potts, 81, inspector for the Ontario Workmen's Compensation Board until his retirement in 1969 ... Wallace Rowe, 53, salesman for Wonder Bread, avid curler, gardener, hunter, and fisherman. He took great pride in the achievements of his wife, Marilyn ...Edgar W. Thatcher, 79, founder of Thatcher Studio, active with the Board of Trade, charter member of Lions Club in 1945 and one of the founders of the first Bracebridge Golf Club and of Santa's Village ... Ronnie Rowe, whose name with his brother's, Alton (Dint) Rowe, was known for their years together on the Bracebridge Bears OHA Intermediate B team which won the Ontario championship in 1953 and 1957 ... Dalton E. Moon, 72, a painter by trade ... Mrs. John P. McVittie (nee Audrey Norma Slater), 79 ... Mr. Thomas H.V. Salmon, 79, taught at Allensville and Bardsville, married Winnifred Goltz in 1929. After she died he married Elaine Brooks in 1963. Mr. Salmon was secretary of the Masonic Lodge No. 360 1970-79 and secretary of the Muskoka Scottish Rite Club for many years. He was active in the Senior Citizens Club, Red Cross Society, and was superintendent of the St. Thomas' Anglican Church Sunday school ... Dave Ellis, Brackenrig, well-known golf pro. He was the assistant pro at Bracebridge Golf and Country Club 1959-62. In 1963, he became assistant pro at Muskoka Lakes Golf and Country Club, becoming pro in 1972. The Muskoka Lakes Golf and Country Club honours his memory with the Dave Ellis Pro-Am Golf Tournament, held each year to raise money for the local charities and the South Muskoka Memorial Hospital ... Mrs. Elsie (Cox) Speck, 91, born in Muskoka Township and raised by her grandparents, Mr. and Mrs. Charles Henry Speck. Mrs. Speck was a 50-

*Amy and Liisa Savijarvi made Muskoka a household word in the skiing world.* COURTESY OF JOSIE SAVIJARVI

year member of the Ladies' Orange Benevolent Association, a charter member and president of the Royal Canadian Legion Ladies' Auxiliary, and a proud member of the Order of the Eastern Star.

Total snowfall this winter was just under 12 feet.

**1987** At the beginning of January Ken Black of Bracebridge hadn't officially announced that he would run on the Liberal platform in the election to be held in September, but it was rumoured that he was going to be in the race. He was still a superintendent of education for the Muskoka Board of Education and would eventually retire to carry on a political career under David Peterson's government. Black made his decision to run on January 30. He had supported Tory Frank Miller through most of Miller's provincial politics, but in interviews said he felt it was time to return to the Black family's traditional support of the Liberal party saying, "I've always been a Liberal philosophically." He won the Muskoka-Georgian Bay Liberal nomination in March against three other candidates: Paul Hayden, Huntsville; John Moreau, Penetanguishene; and Nancy Pratt, Bracebridge. Family ties became stronger in April when it was announced that his son Greg had won the position of vice president in charge of communications for the Ontario Liberal Party.

Premier David Peterson visited Muskoka in July while NDP leader Bob Rae vacationed in Baysville. By the time the election was called on July 31, Premier Peterson was immediately in Bracebridge with a band of Liberals, old and new.

On election day, Black swept every poll in the new larger riding area that included Georgian Bay. The Conservative Party hold on Muskoka had been broken. Muskoka had always set the tone for the rest of the province at election time and this was no exception. The province had a sweep of Liberals over Tory Ontario.

In January, James and Margaret Vettorel of McMurray Street were presented with medals authorized by Pope John Paul II for devoted service to the Roman Catholic Church. The Peterborough Diocese Bishop James Doyle conducted a Mass and the presentation to the Vettorels. He said that the honours are rare and he has had few occasions to confer them throughout the Diocese, this being the first in Bracebridge. Also in the Fall of 1987, Harold Dawson of St. Joseph's Catholic Church received a brief audience with Pope John Paul at Vatican City and was served Mass by the Holy Pontiff in the Pope's private chapel. And in November, special services were held to celebrate the official opening of Monsignor Michael O'Leary Separate School in Bracebridge.

In March, Liisa Savijarvi continued to show off her skiing capabilities by placing first at the Canadian Women's Downhill Ski Championships in British Columbia. In addition to winning the downhill, she came second in giant slalom and third in the super giant slalom. However, the rest of the season would plague Liisa with illness and a major knee injury that required surgery and left her out of the 1988 Winter Olympics in Calgary.

At the same time, Trent Andison, son of John and Mary Andison, also suffered a knee injury but went on to play for the Ontario hockey team at the Canada Winter Games. The Ontario team came home with a silver medal after playing the championship round against Quebec. Although the final score was 6-5, Trent managed to score two goals and assist on another. During the school season, Trent played for the St. Mary's Junior B Lincolns and was approached by several American universities to further his education. He attended Cornell University, was drafted by the San Jose Sharks, but decided to play professional hockey in England for a few years. Trent now lives in Bradford.

An early indicator of summer came on the week of March 18 when the ice left the Muskoka River. Canoeists were out taking advantage of the balmy weather by that weekend. The summer turned out to be one of the hottest in decades. The week of July 12 was the hottest in 23 years. Local residents found their wells going dry in mid-July and by August the town's Public Works department was supplying dozens of homeowners with water from taps located around town. Many didn't get water back in their wells until October.

In April, Judge Stanton Hogg administered the oaths of office to Muskoka's new sheriff, Lynn Wagner.

Alcan of Canada's outlook in Bracebridge looked strong in April as Al Taylor, manager of the Alcan Foils plant, announced a $2.2-million expansion to add new equipment and 4,400 square feet of new space to the existing facility on Keith Road. That was the last good news at the foil plant, though business was continuing in good shape at the Wire and Cable Plant. But labour relations were deteriorating at Foils. The contract with the union in the plant expired on April 12 and three days later the workers walked off in an illegal wildcat walkout. By September 17 Alcan Rolled Products vice president Fred Durdan made the much-feared announcement, that the plant would be shut down for good. It threw 135 men out on the street including the plant manager. Their total payroll was estimated at $3 million. The closing was hard not only on the workers, but also on a number of small businesses that relied on Alcan for a large part of their income. Muskoka Transport estimated their loss of business at around $1 million. Barry Brown, owner of Bracebridge and Commercial Distributing, lost $100,000 worth of income for his pallet-making business.

Also in April, the University of Waterloo held their annual national testing finals in physics, mathematics, and chemistry. In physics, five students from BMLSS placed in the top 10 percent of 6,000 candidates, and Lori Fitch and Doug Coote had outstanding achievements. In mathematics, three students, Bruce Murphy, Chris Jean-Marie, and Andrew Boyes were awarded certificates of distinction with combined marks placing BMLSS second out of 18 schools entered. In chemistry, Chris Jean-Marie ranked in the top four percent and Bruce Murphy in the top six percent in the country.

In May, lawyer Tom Wood was elected to the prestigious governing body of the Law Society of Upper Canada. Mr. Wood was one of 39 lawyers from outside Metro Toronto running for the 20 benchers positions in the Society. Benchers handle the administration of the Society, the organization that grants Legal Aid, receives complaints about lawyers, disciplines lawyers found to have performed wrongly, conducts lawyers' bar admission courses and exams, and handles the financing and operation of legal libraries across the province. Terms for benchers run for four years.

*Seth Hillman and Art Crockford operated the Downtown Garage on Thomas Street (now Taylor Road) for 42 years. Being interested in hunting, the two brothers-in-law also sold ammunition and repaired guns. Locals would congregate at the garage for conversation on such topics as local politics, hunting, fishing, the weather – even cars! Seth passed away in 1984, Art in 1987.* COURTESY OF BRENDA COX

Also in May, Dave Veitch was the recipient of the Jim Quigley Award – Bracebridge's Athlete of the Year. Veitch was a goaltender with the Bracebridge Ready Mix Midgets and was instrumental in helping his team reach the All-Ontario finals.

Tuesday, July 3 was the night the small twister hit Bracebridge. Like a giant blender, it whirled across the north edge of town, scooping up a wooded area beside St. Thomas' Anglican cemetery. It knocked trees through several homes. The force of the twister smashed several vehicles. It took about a week to clean up the damage done by the storm, but even by 1999 remnants remain next to the cemetery and along the Muskoka River banks.

In July, after a long career as district court judge (supernumerary), Judge Douglas Cameron Thomas

*With its rising mist, moulded ice forms, and stark contrast between black water and white snow, Bracebridge Falls is as splendid in winter as in any other season. Picture taken in the 1960s.* COURTESY OF MARILYN LONG

retired. A dinner in his honour was held at Holiday House (Inn at the Falls) with his wife Arla in attendance.

Evelyn Finlayson, a top ballet instructor from Toronto, opened a school of dance in Bracebridge, beginning in St. Joseph's Catholic Church, then moving to the Monck School House on Highway 118, and later to the upstairs of The Granary (formerly the Muskoka Trading Company) on Taylor Road. Evelyn studied at Ryerson Canadian College of Dance and received high accolades. She later joined the acclaimed Les Ballets Jazz de Montreal before bringing her talents to Bracebridge.

In November, Raymond (Raymie) Lee was honoured as Citizen of the Year for his active role in numerous community activities, including president of the Muskoka Red Cross, president of the Rotary Club, president of the Kinsmen Club, and involvement in minor hockey.

Early in the year, Bracebridge Council elected to send out a survey to all the town's retail businesses to see how many wanted Sunday shopping hours allowed. The survey showed that very few of the retailers down Manitoba Street were interested in opening on Sundays or, for that matter, on Boxing Day or other statutory holidays. Many of them grouped together, fearing that extended shopping hours would give some merchants an unfair competitive edge and eventually force all stores to open on Sundays. A minority of retailers, though, did call for extra shopping hours. In mid-March, Bracebridge Council began easing towards more liberal shopping hours, allowing art galleries to stay open on Sundays and holidays. However, by Boxing Day, Council passed a bylaw allowing stores to open on December 26, but another motion to allow Sunday shopping was defeated.

Noted deaths included Bob Jefferies, who passed away at age 67. Bob attended school in Bracebridge and was employed at Northern Planing until he enlisted in World War II with the Royal Canadian Navy, patrolling the North Atlantic on two different destroyers and an Algerine-type vessel. Upon returning home in 1945 he became employed with the municipal police department until he returned to work at Northern Planing in 1949. At that time he also became a town councillor, holding that office until 1954. He was for five years president of the local Royal Canadian Legion Branch and then became the zone commander, later district commander of District E, and then third vice president of the Ontario Provincial Command, advancing to second and first vice president. In May, 1973, he was unanimously elected president of the Provincial Command. He also was a member of the Dominion council of the Legion, travelling across Canada. Locally he was responsible for the organization of the Bracebridge Legion Pipe Band and he took pleasure in leading the band as they participated in events across the province.

Mr. William Spreadborough died at age 96, having been born and raised in Bracebridge. The family had previously resided at Parry Sound before returning to farmland they had located just south of Bracebridge in Draper Township. William and his elder brother, Edwin, for many years operated the farm until the Canadian Motor Lamp Co. (now Meritor) purchased most of the acreage. Mr. Spreadborough served as president of the Agricultural Society for several terms.

William Robertson passed away April 19 at age 80. He and his wife Clara bought the Forrester Farm in 1937 and worked it for nine years. In 1945 he and his family moved back into Bracebridge where Mr. Robertson was employed with Muskoka Trading Co. (now site of the Muskoka Cottage Brewery) for 30 years until his retirement in 1974. Mr. Robertson was a member of Knox Presbyterian Church for 50 years, 26 of those as an elder, and served as a trustee and a member of the board of managers. He was a member of Bracebridge Lodge, IOOF, being past Grand of the lodge. He was a strong supporter of the Senior Citizens Club, being past president, and was a member of the Agricultural Society. Outstanding in his service to the community, Bill worked for the Bracebridge Horticultural Society of which he had been president. For many years he had assisted in the work of planting and caring for the town flower beds, an important contribution to the attractive appearance of the town. Town Council recognized his work by recommending Mr. Robertson to receive the Ontario Bicentennial Medal in 1984.

Austin Hunt passed away May 10. He was best remembered for his participation in sports, especially hockey, having played with the Bracebridge Juniors in the 1930s. He served with the Royal Canadian Air Force in World War II. Soon after the war, Austin played forward with the Bracebridge Bears Intermediate OHA team which won provincial championship honours. He was a member of the Water, Light and Power Commission and later served as a town councillor. He had been a member of the Bracebridge Fire Department. For many years until his retirement, Mr. Hunt was a member of the sales staff of the Ecclestone Hardware store.

In May, Paul Rimstead passed away at age 52. Paul had lived on a farm at Beatrice and attended Monck No. 7 school and later Bracebridge High School. He was well known as a columnist for the *Toronto Sun*, writing a column in which he often wrote about his Muskoka background and mentioned many of his friends. He started his career with the *Orillia Packet and Times*, *Kingston Whig-Standard*, *Toronto Globe & Mail*, the former *Evening Telegram*, the *Toronto Star* and finally the *Toronto Sun*. He was the author of two books, one of which was accepted for publication just before his death.

W. Fred Hammell passed away on May 28 at the age of 74. Mr. Hammell held an outstanding place in Muskoka as the first director of education for the district. He attended township schools and then Bracebridge High School. After teachers college, his first school was in Aspdin, then he became principal of the continuation school in Port Loring. He served during World War II in the Royal Canadian Air Force. After the war he returned to Queen's University to obtain his BA and then was granted a degree in Pedagogy from University of Toronto. As school inspector in Norfolk County he published on mathematics and other subjects. Mr. Hammell was transferred by the Department of Education to succeed Gordon McIntyre as school inspector in south Muskoka. When the Muskoka District Board of Education was established in 1969, the Board selected Fred to be the director of education. He was chairman of the Bracebridge Library Board when as a town centennial project space was opened in the library for a children's department. He was also active with the group that established the Victoria Street School, at first with its own sponsoring organization and then as part of the district school administration. Fred was also a valued member of the Rotary club of Bracebridge. During his retirement he wrote articles about rural life for the *Muskoka Sun*.

Arthur Bates died September 9 and the age of 70. He attended local public and high schools and then joined his father to learn the trade of plumbing in the Ecclestone and Bates Plumbing and Heating firm and continued to run the business after his father's death in 1968. Mr. Bates played on the Bracebridge Junior hockey team. He was a member of the Bracebridge Citizen's Band and the Bracebridge Curling Club. He was a past Noble Grand of the Bracebridge Odd Fellows Lodge, a charter member of Snow Queen Rebekah Lodge IOOF, member of the Muskoka Lodge, AF & AM, and an associate member of the Royal Canadian Legion, Central Muskoka Branch.

W.J. (Jack) Page passed away on November 8 at age 80. Mr. Page contributed to the Bracebridge community through his work as the superintendent of the Bracebridge Water, Light and Power Commission from 1955 to 1972. He came to Bracebridge in 1955 to succeed the late Edward Ball at which time the town depended on three town-owned generating stations to supply Bracebridge with electricity. The three plants continue to be used in addition to substantial supplies from the Ontario Hydro system. Another development of importance for which Jack was responsible was the increase in municipal water supply that had depended on two springs. A standpipe was erected in the Hunt's Hill section to supplement the reservoir capacity. Then in 1967 a pipeline was built from Strawberry Point (now decommissioned), Lake Muskoka, more than doubling the town's water supply and requiring additional reservoir capacity. This was a key factor in the industrial development of Bracebridge. Mr. Page knew his work thoroughly; the conclusions he reached as to the needs of the town's utilities systems were of value in the forming of municipal policy and practice. He was a former elder in the United Church, a Mason, and a member of the Rotary Club of Bracebridge.

Finally, Douglas Kirkness died on November 20 at the age of 68. He attended local schools and early in World War II enlisted in the Royal Canadian Air Force, holding the rank of Flying Officer. After the war he and Jack Fawcett formed a partnership to purchase Ridley Cleaners from the original owner, William Snazel. After Mr. Fawcett's death, Doug continued the business for 25 years until he became ill. Doug was a member of the Central Muskoka Branch of the Royal Canadian Legion, serving as an executive member and as secretary-treasurer. He was a piper in the Legion Pipe Band when it was first organized. He was also a member of the Bracebridge Lodge 251, IOOF, and a devoted member of the Knox Presbyterian Church. He also served as a club executive of the OHA in Bracebridge.

**1988** In January, Liisa Savijarvi carried the Olympic torch just north of Bracebridge on Highway 11 on its way to the Calgary Olympics. Although able to run with the torch, her knee, shattered in a fall in 1987, was not strong enough to allow her to compete at the Olympics.

Also in January, Susan Mitchell, a 16-year-old BMLSS student suffering from cancer, was awarded the Ontario Junior Citizen of the Year from Lieutenant Governor Lincoln Alexander. She also received a rare Special Distinction Medal from the Ontario Secondary School Teachers Federation. This seldom-awarded honour had never been presented to a student before. An active athlete, school prefect, and president of Students Against Drunk Drivers, Susan was diagnosed with a brain tumour two years earlier. Her condition became inoperable. However, Susan was able to talk about her operation and how it had affected her life. Alexander spoke of Mitchell as providing a role model for her fellow students, describing her as a leader because of the positive attitude she had kept through all her trials. Susan succumbed to her two-year battle with cancer by Easter.

Premier David Peterson forced Council to deal with the Sunday shopping issue again early in 1988. The councillors decided to petition the premier, asking the province not to relinquish control over Sunday and statutory holiday retail shopping activities.

*The Bracebridge Public School Band on a "march-a-thon" in 1976 to raise funds for a band trip. The band was begun by teacher Leo Peltomaki, who was its leader until his retirement in 1988.* COURTESY OF MARILYN LONG

In February, a lot levy system was proposed as a way to cover the costs of new development in Muskoka, with the lot levy systems of some area municipalities being scrapped.

In February, the Bracebridge Blades Novice Precision Team won silver at the Northern Ontario sectional championships to qualify for the Canadian precision title race in Toronto.

In March, Judge William Golden of the Muskoka Family and Juvenile Division court announced his retirement from the bench, effective April 7. For several years, Judge Golden carried a heavy workload, presiding at courts in Bracebridge and the Simcoe County area.

In May, Stan Knowles, of Knowles Plumbing, was inducted into the Canadian Ski Instructors' Alliance Hall of Fame. Mr. Knowles, a ski instructor and coach for 40 years, had the only family in Canada with three Level 4 certified instructors as family members. Stan first started skiing in 1933, serving in the Canadian Army Ski Troops in 1944 and 1945. In 1960 Stan began working on ski hills in the Muskoka area, starting as director of skiing at Rainbow Ridge, then moving to Curlew Ski Hill in Huntsville where he coached Liisa Savijarvi in her early days of skiing. Stan then became director at Hidden Valley Ski Resort in Huntsville. He served part time from 1966 to 1968 as the assistant coach to the National Alpine Ski team. In the 70s, his skills began to attract international demand and Stan worked part time as a ski instructor in Colorado, Italy, and France.

The 1988 Jim Quigley Athlete of the Year was Rob Barrett. Rob was on the BMLSS Nordic Ski Team where he won the Georgian Bay championship. At the Ontario

*Memorial Park today and yesteryear from the corner of Manitoba Street and Kimberley Avenue, looking south. Dirt streets, often muddy, meant that for the convenience of pedestrians, sidewalks crossed the road.* COURTESY OF GARY LONG (TOP) AND IAN TURNBULL (BOTTOM)

championship, Rob came third in one race and won gold in the relay. Rob went on to compete in the Canadian Junior Nationals in British Columbia, where he placed in the top half of his division.

In May, Leo Peltomaki, the founder of the Bracebridge Public School Band, officially retired as teacher and bandleader. At the last band performance of the year, former students interrupted the concert to play tribute to their former band conductor. The band, originally supported by the Bracebridge Lions Club, is best known for its role as a marching band in the town's Santa Claus parades as well as in parades all over Ontario.

In July, long-time resident and former owner of Muskoka Garage (now known as the Crockford Building), Les Rosewarne, received a rare life membership award from the Rotary Club of Bracebridge.

Also in July, District Crown Attorney W. Alan Newell retired after 27 years. He was appointed Muskoka's fourth Crown attorney on March 1, 1961. Judge Stanton Hogg and Judge D.C. Thomas considered Mr. Newell one of the finest Crown attorneys they had known and one of the best in Ontario. Mr. Newell's successor was Kenneth Anthony.

A Hollywood movie moved into Bracebridge in September when a production company filmed the *Welcome Home* in and around Bracebridge. Movie stars Kris Kristofferson, Jo Beth Williams, and Sam Waterston were frequently seen on Manitoba Street during filming.

Cliff Whitfield resigned after 13 years as the director of education for the Muskoka Board of Education in September, effective February 1989. His reason for leaving was stated as "the education in Muskoka can benefit from the infusion of new and different talents." He and his wife Pat later moved to British Columbia to enjoy full retirement.

Thomas Wood, QC, who began practising law in March 1974, was appointed judge of the Family Division for Muskoka and Simcoe by the Ontario attorney general, succeeding Judge William Golden. Because of his new appointment, Wood gave up his association with his law firm, and resigned as federal prosecutor and as bencher of the Law Society of Upper Canada. His home court would be the Muskoka District courthouse in Bracebridge.

In the 1988 municipal elections Jim Lang again held his seat as mayor. His town councillors were Norm Harkness, Heather Coupland, George Brodie, Scott Northmore, and Katie McCann. District councillors were Jim Boyes, Aubrey Glass, and Pat Malone, the school trustees Gayle Barnett, Ken Silcox, Marilyn Rowe, LouAnne Miller. The Separate School trustee was Peter Bradley.

In November the federal election saw 77-year old Progressive Conservative Stan Darling elected for his sixth term to represent Parry Sound-Muskoka as its member of parliament in Ottawa, under the re-elected Mulroney government. He became the oldest serving parliamentarian.

The Rotary Club of Bracebridge awarded its Citizen of the Year for 1988 to Elaine Young, in honour of her efforts organizing Addiction Outreach in Muskoka.

District's official plan was passed in November after much controversy. In December, the start of a new District Council saw Bracebridge-born Allan Sander elected as District chairman for an unprecedented third term. The 22 newly elected District councillors met to decide who would lead them through the next three years. Sander narrowly won on the second round of voting, defeating Bernard Reynolds of Huntsville 12 to 10.

On December 3, 1988, Herb Stewart closed the door at Garwood's Men's and Ladies' Wear (now Marty's Coffee House) ending another chapter in the local history book. Garwood's was established by Mr. Garwood and was later bought by Herb Stewart in the 1960s. The spiral staircase, still in the store today, came from the drug store owned by Dr. Sam Bridgland on the opposite side of Manitoba Street when his medical clinic was on the second floor (now Smellies Stationary).

A historic residence was torn down at the corner of Ida and James streets to make way for the James Street Retirement Home, modelled after Windermere House. On December 8 the proposal was outlined to Council to build a three-storey retirement home to accommodate 46 residents. The demolished home was built more than 100 years earlier by the Orville Arnold family. Mr. Arnold was one of Bracebridge's leading lawyers. Arnold Wattie, a former mayor of Bracebridge, John Golden, Phil Stone, as well as Mr. and Mrs. Russ Salmon, also owned the house over the years. Prior to its demise it was known as the Inglis Apartments, owned by "Bucky" Inglis.

The following deaths to remember in 1988 included Norman Lyndon, who passed away on March 27 at age 68. Norm was the younger son of Major Alfred and Elinor Lyndon who made their home in Bracebridge when Norm was four years old. Norm attended public and high school in Bracebridge and enlisted in the Royal Canadian Air Force in 1940, training as a wireless operator and gunner in Montreal. Later in the year he graduated with the rank of sergeant and went overseas to Britain. Norm flew operations over Germany with the No. 78 Squadron and No. 405 Squadron. In 1942 he received his commission as pilot officer. Norm experienced many dangerous missions overseas including being shot down. He earned his pilot's wings by the end of the war, rising to the rank of flight lieutenant, and was transferred to the reserves in peacetime. Norm attended University of Toronto in forestry but devoted himself to surveying, articling with the late E.L. Burgess and successfully completing his Ontario Land Surveyors examination in 1953. Over 35 years in surveying, Norm enjoyed his work in this part of the province. His skilled work was essential to the opening up and improving property in Muskoka.

Philip Stone died on March 27 at 74. Mr. and Mrs. Stone moved to Bracebridge in 1938 and purchased the dry goods business formerly operated by Simon Nasser, opening the business known as Stone's Mens and Ladies Wear at the south end of Manitoba Street. Phil served the municipality for a number of years as a town councillor and was a director of Santa's Village. He was a life member of the Bracebridge Odd Fellows Lodge, No. 251, and a life member of Mount Sinai Masonic Lodge, Toronto. For 20 years he had been a member of the board of the Men's Club of Beth Tzedec Synagogue, Toronto.

Doug Smith passed away on May 13 at the age of 80. Doug was one of the town's best known and most popular citizens, a prominent figure in recreation management as manager of the Bracebridge Memorial Community Centre. Doug was born in Monck Township to the Smith family renowned for their expertise in stone work. Doug continued in this field for some years under the employment of George Yearley of Falkenburg. He was involved with the construction of the former SSJE Mission House. Doug was chairman of the Bracebridge Memorial Community Centre when in 1958 Ken Black resigned as the centre's manager. Doug was encouraged by Council to accept the position, which he did. Mr. Smith brought new attractions to the arena and gave strong support to the organizations that relied on the community centre for their programs. He was a major figure in the Bracebridge Figure Skating Club and aided the Lions Air Cadets Squadron by arranging for their accommodation. Doug was also instrumental in starting the annual Red Cross swimming instruction for elementary school children. He was president of the Intermediate hockey club, the Bracebridge Bears hockey team, and actively encouraged the building up of the minor hockey league. For this Doug was made a life member in the Minor Hockey Association. Mr. Smith was also active with the committees in the United Church.

T. Alvin Peacock died June 24 at the age of 76. Born in Bracebridge, Alvin lived for a time at the McLeod farm on Lake Muskoka, the present site of Bangor Lodge. After attending local schools, Alvin became the Metropolitan Life Insurance agent in Bracebridge, continuing until he enlisted in the Canadian Army in World War II. He then served in the Royal Canadian Ordnance Corps overseas, returning home to continue his insurance business. Mr. Peacock was a member of Central Muskoka Branch of the Legion and an active member in St. Thomas' Anglican Church, having just donated the carpeting in the newly renovated church in memory of his wife, Bette.

Ted Reid died on July 17 at age 75. Ted was descended from two well-known Muskoka pioneer families, the Killens and the Kirks. After attending the Bracebridge schools, he was engaged in insurance, then was with T.J. Anderson and Sons store just before World War II. In 1941 he married Phyllis Tennant of the Tennant lumbermill family. Ted served in the Canadian Army and served with the 10th Battery, 2nd Field Regiment, in the UK, Sicily, Italy, France, and Belgium. Upon returning home, he was with the Shell Oil Company for five years, then joined the staff of Northern Planing Mills, of which he became sales manager until his retirement. He was elected to the town council in 1953, heading the poll with a record number of votes. He served six years, first as chairman of welfare, then of public works, and later of finance and as acting mayor. With the retirement of Glen Coates as mayor, Mr. Reid was elected to the position by acclamation and served from 1959 to 1962.

Ted was a member of Masonic Lodge and was Worshipful Master in 1954, later serving for several years as lodge treasurer. He was member of the United Church, the Royal Canadian Legion, director of Santa's Village Ltd., director of the Ontario Housing Corporation, and, in his youth, a member of the Bracebridge Citizen's Band. Ted was president of the Ontario Retail Lumber Dealers Association in 1968. He had been an outstanding athlete in local hockey and lacrosse and enjoyed curling in his senior years.

## 1989

In 1984 streams of people began flooding into Bracebridge. By 1989 their presence was felt more than ever. In 1989 the Muskoka population grew by seven percent, one percent higher than the year before and three percent higher than the four-percent-increase in 1987. Bob List, District planner, said that most of the people who had suddenly decided to move to Muskoka were former summer visitors who thought it was better here than in the city. The result was higher-priced housing, crowded schools and hospitals, overtaxed sewage and water plants, and an increase demand on social assistance programs.

Elementary schools saw a four-percent increase in enrollment, with a two-percent increase at the secondary level. The total enrollment in Muskoka was 7,617. The situation was so bad that there were 54 portables at Muskoka schools. Monck Public had as many classrooms outside as in the school.

In 1989 the hospital was forced to house some patients in hallways because of increased demand.

Ken Black, MPP, noted that a two-percent financial growth rate was expected in 1990 across the province. One reason was the high interest rate, another the high value of the Canadian dollar which hurt tourism and manufacturing. He indicated that if the dollar were around 75 to 80 cents U.S. the situation would be better.

In February another recreation director resigned from the town's parks and recreation department, after two years. Ron Richards had accepted a position in Port Colbourne. He was the third program director in Bracebridge in five years.

Also in February, a fire swept through the maintenance garage of Muskoka Containerized Services, owned by Don Coates. The fire left a trail of destruction but Mr. Coates said he had many calls of assistance. It would be necessary to rent trucks in order to fulfill their customer commitments, but otherwise it would be pretty much business as usual. Bracebridge firefighters fought the fire for close to five hours to bring it under control. The fire started around 12:10 a.m. on one of the coldest nights in weeks. Firefighters tried in vain to save the 9,000-square-foot building and seven trucks stored inside. An initial estimate of the damage amounted to $1.4 million.

In March the Town of Bracebridge entered into an agreement to purchase with Donald Moore for the former SSJE chapel. The town was responsible for rezoning. The chapel, known as Collegiate Church, had been a religious landmark in Bracebridge since its consecration in September 1933. Part of the purchase agreement called for the retention of the chapel cross, a famous sculpture of Christus Rex by the late Emanuel Hahn, which was consecrated as a war memorial following World War II and placed on the exterior east wall of the church. The cross was removed and placed in the small cemetery, which would be maintained in perpetuity.

The newly formed rowing club announced that it had acquired a 64-foot shell from the Argonaut Rowing Club in Toronto, allowing the Muskoka Rowing Club to proceed with its first season. The club used the old stone building at Bracebridge Bay Park as its original clubhouse. The first chairman of the 16-member executive was Art Luker.

*The Bracebridge United Church building turned a century old in 1989, having been built as the Methodist Church in 1889. This is how it looked in its early years, complete with drive sheds in behind.* COURTESY OF VICKY BILLINGSLEY FROM THE R.J. BOYER COLLECTION

Rod Hare, a BMLSS graduate and former high school wrestling champion, testified at the Mr. Justice Charles Dubin Inquiry into drug abuse among athletes. Hare charged that a cynical failure to provide funds for athletes unless they won medals was at the heart of the steroid problem. At the time, Hare was vice president of the Ontario Amateur Wrestling Association.

In April, amateur theater groups raised concerns about their most-used venue being no longer available. The Town Hall auditorium was converted into office space to accommodate the Development Services Department and the Building Inspection Division.

Prime Minister Brian Mulroney appointed Patrick Boyer, son of Robert J. Boyer, to the position of parliamentary secretary to external affairs minister Joe Clark. Patrick was member of the federal riding of Etobicoke-Lakeshore, having been elected in 1984. He practised law in Toronto with the firm of Fraser Beatty.

In May, 10-year-old Keri Wills became the youngest recipient of the Jim Quigley Athlete of the Year Award. Keri was a skater with the Bracebridge Figure Skating Club under the coaching direction of Marilyn Leigh. She won numerous medals during the year, including a gold at Northern Ontario Sectionals. She was chosen to represent the Near North Region as a guest skater with world champion Brian Orser at North Bay. The youngest athlete to win the Jim Quigley Award before Keri was another skater, Sundae Raeburn, who was 11.

In July, Ted Drenth opened Bracebridge's newest grocery store, Mr. Grocer (now Your Independent Grocer) on Highway 118 across from the A & P Plaza.

The Rotary Club of Bracebridge, in conjunction with the Bracebridge Agricultural Society and the Town of Bracebridge, announced that they would build a $500,000 youth centre and multi-purpose building. The building was to be built on two lots owned by the town and used by the Agricultural Society at fair time. The building would be home to the Cubs, Scouts, Guides, and Brownie packs, as well as other youth-related organizations.

July saw the town's first heart transplant recipient. Mark Conway, recovering well from his heart transplant performed at Western Hospital in Toronto. Mark had been operated on 12 years prior and had been given heart bypass surgery. He suffered a series of heart attacks that required a heart transplant. A donor organ from the Ottawa area was received and the operation successfully completed.

On September 22, Mariette and Greg Hammond

*A present-day view up Manitoba Street. Comparison with the photograph on the next page shows many of the same buildings still standing.* COURTESY OF GARY LONG

became the proud parents of Muskoka's first ever triplets. The combined weight of all three boys was just shy of 20 pounds and all were healthy. Greg is the son of Orvil and Fran Hammond of Bracebridge.

In November, the Bracebridge Bucks softball team finished their season with two great wins. The Bucks were able to repeat as All-Ontario champions and also win the Bulova Watch Tournament at the CNE in Toronto. In the Bulova Watch Tournament, the team beat the second-seeded Senior A Ontario team and the Senior B division silver medallists.

Colin MacDougald received the Rotary Club's Citizen of the Year Award for 1989. Colin, who retired from the post office, was recognized for his outstanding community service including regular visits to hospital patients.

Opal MacDonald died on February 1 at the age of 67. She was best remembered for her devoted work for Central Muskoka Branch 161 of the Royal Canadian Legion of which she was the first woman member. She held most of the offices of the branch and was the first woman president, holding that position for five years.

Mary McCracken died February 20 at age 95. Minnie, as she was known, was born in Uffington and after schooling at the Uffington Public School, attended Bracebridge High School where she boarded, there being no school transportation in those days. Prior to attending North Bay Normal School, Minnie taught for a year at the Brackenrig School. To reach the school from her home in Uffington was a day's journey by stage, steamboat, and horse and buggy. It was from the two-room school in Utterson that both Minnie and Bruce Minns came to the Central School, as Bracebridge Public School was then known. Mr. Minns taught entrance class and was also the principal, and Minnie taught what was then called junior fourth, now grade seven. Since her death many former students recalled her with gratitude and affection. Upon retirement in 1963, Minnie travelled widely. In 1975, she received the Bracebridge Centennial Medal for her contribution to education in the town and was given the award by Lieutenant-Governor Pauline McGibbon. As well, in 1975, to mark the 60th anniversary of the federation of Women Teachers of Ontario, Minnie received a citation honouring her years of teaching. At her funeral Rev. David Stephens stated that a close friend remarked that to have known Mary McCracken was to have had a glimpse of all that was best and highest in life.

On August 21, Bishop Frank Nock died at age 73. Bishop Nock had been the rector of St. Thomas' Anglican Church from 1945 to 1948. He and his wife were popular in the community, being remembered for their part in Bracebridge Choral Society productions of Gilbert and Sullivan operas, in which Rev. Nock sang the leading tenor roles. After leaving Bracebridge they kept up their acquaintance with friends, which was strongly renewed when he was elected Bishop of the Diocese in 1975.

On September 5, John Biddle died in his 80th year. John would be best remembered for his musical abilities, especially as a tenor soloist in earlier radio programs, and as a church soloist and concert artist in Toronto and many parts of Ontario. In Bracebridge, John became the first superintendent (later changed to administrator) of The Pines Home for Seniors. John studied at the Toronto Conservatory of Music before going to New York City to study under Ferrari Fontana, a soloist with the Metropolitan Opera Company in New York and the Chicago Opera Company. It was there that John met Lydia Bodrug-Berezowska, a talented soprano who was also studying with Fontana. They married in 1937. Mr. Biddle, who was also a gifted pianist, received an offer from the Canadian Broadcasting Corporation to host his own

*A century ago the view up Manitoba Street was in some ways similar and in others very different. The dark blobs in the street behind the hay wagon are evidence of the prevailing method of locomotion; these would be scooped up quickly to fertilize local gardens. The three-storey building with balconies on the right is the Dominion Hotel, one of several large downtown hotels of the time. It was long ago converted into a business block.* COURTESY OF BRENDA COX

radio show out of Toronto sponsored by the Lipton Tea Co. In 1957, the Biddles moved to Bracebridge to operate the Albion Hotel, which they purchased from Wenawae and Jim Stevenson. In 1961 the Albion was sold to Cline Lennox and John was appointed superintendent of The Pines. In 1971, Mr. Biddle was appointed interim administrator by the Ontario Department of Public Welfare and left The Pines to travel to other senior citizen homes to overcome management problems. John was music director at the Bracebridge United Church for 10 years and a member of Knox Presbyterian Church choir. He was a life member of the Victoria Lodge AF & AM in Toronto, and affiliated with Muskoka Lodge, being Worshipful Master in 1968. He was also a member of the Royal Arch Degree in Parry sound, and the Muskoka Shrine Club. He was a member of the Rotary Club of Bracebridge, serving as president in 1978, and a past president of the South Muskoka Association for the Mentally Retarded.

On November 14 Maureen Johnson passed away at the age of 67. She served in World War II with the Women's Auxiliary Air Force in England and Ireland and for a year following the war in Egypt. She met and married Tom Johnson in Ireland. In 1959 they moved to Bracebridge to purchase the Margaret Ellen Shop, which was renamed Maureen's (now Pelican Bay). She operated the business until 1986 when David Murphy purchased the well-known business and retained the name.

On December 5, Canon David Mitchell passed away at age 73. He had been the rector of St. Thomas' Anglican Church for almost 25 years. In 1959 he began his long association with Bracebridge as the rector, a period of advance in the work of the parish. He was editor of *The Algoma Anglican* from 1961 to 1972. In the last few years of this rectorship, he was asked to take on additional work in mission churches round Muskoka. He enjoyed the best of relations with churches of other denominations and was always pleased in his ministry in Bracebridge to promote ecumenical services and events.

## 1990

At the beginning of the year the main concern was the soaring numbers of welfare cases. Carol Garvey, District director of social services, noted that it was not unusual for Muskoka's social assistance caseload to rise in the winter. However, in the preceding three months the caseload had increased 55 percent over previous years. Garvey speculated that publicity about Muskoka's rapid growth may have influenced people to move here. But many did not consider the reality of winter layoffs. However, by June the welfare caseloads had not decreased even with seasonal jobs.

On February 3, Carol and Russell Lindup of Bracebridge won $1,043,930.60 in the Lotto 649. Carol, a regular lottery ticket buyer, purchased the winning ticket at Muskoka Drug Mart on Manitoba Street.

The ongoing saga of Magna International and a parcel of land south of Bracebridge went on all year, starting with Magna selling over 810 acres of land to a development company. Magna only retained 30 acres but continued to indicate that they would be building. However, in March, the *Globe and Mail*'s "Report on Business" indicated that Magna would report massive writedowns. The story said that the company was reeling under slow sales in the auto market. Then there were questions about the severance of the land, with councillor Katie McCann indicating that there should be provisions in the severance agreement for Magna to dedicate some of the land for parkland. As well, it was felt that an agreement between the District and Magna should be terminated, which would have allowed Magna a reduction in the charges for sewer service. By October, the development company was proposing a golf course, cluster housing, and commercial and industrial development. The Bracebridge land development committee was obviously skeptical about the proposal, their main concern being its financial stability. As well, town planner Peter Niece noted that most of the land was not approved for development. The town's urban boundaries would need to be expanded and an official plan amendment would be required. As of 1999, the property remained undeveloped, although preparatory work had commenced on the commercial and golf course aspects.

In March Rob Barrett earned himself a spot on the National Junior cross-country ski team after an excellent showing at the Canadian Junior Cross-Country Ski Championships at Camp Fortune, Quebec. Barrett had two skiing goals for 1989-90: to place in the top five at the national competition, and to earn a national medal. He was able to accomplish both.

After almost 100 years of selling hardware in Bracebridge as Ecclestone's Hardware, the store on Manitoba Street began a new era as Sutherland Interiors. Company president John Sutherland bought the store from George Ecclestone in the 1970s and continued to run it as a hardware and furniture store until 1990 when he converted the store into up-scale furnishings by La-Z-Boy.

On March 12, Rev. Father James Conrad of St. Joseph's Catholic Church presented His Holiness Pope John Paul II with the Jamot Medal. He made the presentation to the Holy Father after the concelebrated Mass in the private chapel of the Vatican, Italy. The medal was created to honour the first Bishop of Peterborough who was also the first pastor of St. Joseph's. The Pope was told of the medal's history and expressed his gratitude and appreciation in receiving it.

On March 20, Bracebridge education trustee Marilyn Rowe was presented with a 15-year service pin. She was first elected in 1974. She had served as president of the OPSTA in 1984, chairperson of OSTC in 1987, and Board chairperson 1987-88.

Tammi-Lynn Taylor, a 17-year-old BMLSS student and member of the Muskoka Limberettes gymnastic club (coached by Vivian Wright) became Canada's top B-level gymnast. Taylor won the Canadian championship, leading her provincial teammates to first place in the team competition. She placed first out of a field of 34 competitors with a score of 36.7 out of 40. This victory also allowed Tammi-Lynn to win the 1990 Jim Quigley Athlete of the Year Award. The award committee's decision was unanimous.

In April, the Muskoka-Parry Sound Health Unit announced that a new medical officer of health would be in place by July. Dr. Harold Robinson retired on June 30, 1990, and was replaced by Dr. Walter Ewing.

Also in April, the town negotiated with Brian and Dave Hough to bring a Junior B hockey team to Bracebridge. Called the Muskoka Bears, the team would replace the fallen Bracebridge Bears Junior C team. The town's approval would allow the Houghs to apply to the Ontario Hockey Association to allow the franchise. The team would be in place for the 1990 season.

Douglas Parrett, formerly of Bracebridge and son of Robert and Helen Parrett, was ordained an Anglican priest. His first parish was Bonne Bayworth in Rocky Harbour, Newfoundland.

In September, the Toronto-Dominion Bank relocated to 205 Manitoba Street, next to MacNaughtan's Hardware store, on the site of what had been the second Brewer's Retail store. The T-D would move after starting banking in the downtown core of the town at the present location of Rainy Day Projects and, prior to that, CC Pant Shop. The manager, Carson Wells, noted that the building would be state-of-the-art with a complex computer system including an automatic teller machine.

In May, Mr. G. Leslie Tennant received a special award from the town for his dedicated service as secretary-treasurer of Annie Williams Memorial Park since 1965, when he was appointed by the Rotary Club. Mayor Jim Lang made the plaque presentation on behalf of the people of Bracebridge for 25 years of personal service.

The 90 jobs at Muskoka Transport in Bracebridge and Barrie were in jeopardy if new trucking restrictions were not implemented in Ontario. Muskoka Transport president Paul Hammond said that truckers across the province were in peril so long as the federal and provincial governments failed to protect them. Truckers from the U.S. had been taking jobs from Ontario truckers since deregulation was imposed in 1988. The small family-run carriers had been struggling to survive for the last six months. As of 1999, Muskoka Transport was still thriving with the Hammond family in command.

In September, Macaulay Tree House Day Nursery opened its doors at the corner of Cedar Lane and The Granite Bluff, to 53 preschool children. A grant of $875,000 to cover 100 percent of the initial cost was obtained from the Ontario Ministry of Community and Social Services. Although the grant was usually 80 percent, MPP Ken Black helped demonstrate the need for a full funding based on local economic statistics. Once up and running, the nursery became self-funding as a non-profit organization. Cathy Insley was the school's first board of directors president.

*Jessie Dunn, life member of the Muskoka Children's Aid Society, celebrated her 80th birthday in 1990 with Ken Black, MPP, and Ken Heron, executive director of the society. She died in 1995. The CAS has a memorial award presented annually to one who personifies the vibrancy, humour, selflessness, and dedication that marked Jessie Dunn's life.* COURTESY OF THE CAS

In June, Don Coates, president of Muskoka Containerized Services, became the Ontario Waste Management Association president, being elected by a body of 260 members. Coates had been a member of the association, which dealt with environmental protection through proper waste management, for 10 years. For the prior two years he was the vice president.

In July, the province allowed grocery shopping on Sunday. Initially, only the A & P Store stayed open in Bracebridge. It wasn't long before other stores followed suit.

If the late Herman Brooks were alive today, it would be hard for him to contain the pride he would feel in the accomplishments of his two grandsons. Alex and David Brooks carried on the family tradition that was built on vision and hard work. In 1945, after working for Ecclestone's Hardware for many years, Herman Brooks opened his own furniture and appliance business in a small store on Chancery Lane (presently The Bistro). H.J. Brooks and Sons prospered and together with his two sons, George and Jerry, Herman built a much larger store on Manitoba Street with two floors of display space (presently The Mighty Dollar). By 1990, the grandsons owned three stores in Bracebridge, Huntsville, and Orillia under the Leon's franchise, and the foundation for a new store was already under way at the corner of Robert Dollar and Ecclestone Drive in Bracebridge. The new store, opened in December 1990, contained 20,000 square feet of floor space on one level.

In July, three physicians opened the Bracebridge Medical Centre at 28 Manitoba Street (formerly Darling Shoes), having renovated the facade in keeping with the contemporary 1800s vintage building. The doctors offered 24-hour service, seven days a week. However, South Muskoka Memorial Hospital's chief of staff, Dr. Mike Krawetz, was not convinced a walk-in medical clinic was needed in Bracebridge. In fact, he felt that a fully equipped medical clinic would have a negative effect on the hospital's finances.

In August, the Bracebridge Public Library put its automated system into effect. The system saves time, using a library bar code with a scanning wand to sign out books. As well, card catalogue drawers were replaced with computer terminals for public use.

In September, the first "super mailboxes" were set up around Bracebridge. Bracebridge was the first town in Muskoka to get them. The boxes are located within relative walking distance of homes to allow postal service without going to the post office. The community mailboxes also meant the issuing of new postal codes for many town residents.

September saw the opening of The Cedarbrook Christian School, originally starting at the Pinegrove Baptist Church. Forty-seven students were enrolled in the school in its first year. A permanent building was constructed on Cedar lane where the Bracebridge Animal Hospital was formerly located (now the home of Georgian College). It opened in November.

Also in September, Muskoka-Georgian Bay saw another precedent-setting political upset when the Ontario New Democratic Party candidate, Dan Waters, defeated the Progressive Conservative candidate Marilyn Rowe and the incumbent, Liberal Ken Black, in the provincial election. The NDP had a landslide victory across the province. The end result showed that people had lost confidence in the government of the day and a change was necessary. Waters was born in Barrie but settled with his family on North Bohemian Island when he was three. He attended Windermere Public and Monck Public. He went to BMLSS and Gravenhurst High School. He eventually was employed with Alcan Wire and Cable as a forklift operator.

On February 15, Dr. Philip Thomas passed away at the age of 78. Bracebridge had always been his home and there was no one who had served any longer period in the business and professional life of the town. His career as a Doctor of Optometry began in the 1930s and continued to 1990 with the more recent association with Dr. David Cox, his great-nephew. Philip was the second son of George Henry Oakwood Thomas and was born at the family home at the corner of Kimberley Avenue, Nelson Street, and Manitoba Street. For many years his optometry practice was located in the Thomas Co. building on Manitoba Street and the north corner of Chancery Lane. Philip served the municipality as a member of the Board of Education and then as a town councillor. For several years he was a member of the board of the Bracebridge Memorial Hospital, and a member of the board of Muskoka Health Unit (now the Muskoka-Parry Sound Health Unit) both during its inception and later. In 1936 he was a charter member of the Rotary Club of Bracebridge and was its last surviving charter member. In St. Thomas' Anglican Church he served as People's Warden and then as Rector's Warden. He was a long-time member of the clarinet section of the Bracebridge Citizen's Band and later the Muskoka District Concert Band. He was also a member of the Bracebridge Choral Society. Philip was remembered as a avid golfer and skier. He was a member for many years at Muskoka Lakes Golf and Country Club and later South Muskoka Curling and Golf Club. Mr. Thomas had requested an uplifting funeral concluding with *When the Saints Go Marching In* played on trumpet by Gravenhurst's Hugh Clairmont.

On February 1, Clifford W. Parrett passed away at age 87. Mr. Parrett was a farmer and market gardener, following his father in this work at the Parrett property west of Wellington Street, with the family home at the corner of Ewing and Dill streets. He was the son of Alfred Parrett, a Muskoka pioneer who first settled in Stisted Township before moving to Bracebridge. Mr. Parrett was a member of the Senior Citizens Club and was especially active in the building of the Seniors Centre. He had been an annual exhibitor at the Bracebridge Fall Fair and a member of the Agricultural Society. For over 20 years he was judge of the vegetable and flower section of the Junior Fair (a trophy is given in his memory to the youth who received the highest points in these two categories). He was an active member of the Bracebridge Curling Club, serving on the executive and as president. He had been a councillor of Muskoka Township and a member of the board of managers for Knox Presbyterian Church. He also was a member of Muskoka Lodge AF & AM.

On March 6 Ellis Smith (Smitty) died suddenly at age 61. Mr. Smith had been a partner in the firm of Dawson-Smith-Baker Electric. He was active in the Lions Club of Bracebridge for 15 years and was the club's first vice president at the time of his death.

On May 3, Mrs. Eileen Parsons died at the age of 68. The Parsons family lived in Bracebridge 10 years, occupying the residence once the home of Mr. William Galbraith on Manitoba Street (this home is now contains apartments that are accessed from McMurray Street, and is hidden behind a commercial store front presently occupied by My Book Store). Although the family moved to Toronto, they maintained their Muskoka ties through their summer home, first on McVittie Island and then at Port Carling. Eileen was a graduate of the Pasadena Playhouse, the California School for Theatre, and taught voice production, speech and drama, and makeup at the Royal Conservatory of Music in Toronto. She also taught at the Royal Conservatory Opera School and held classes for the Canadian Opera Company in its earlier years. She was director of the New Play Society and was managing director of her own summer theatre, the Niagara Playhouse, a forerunner of the Shaw festival, at Niagara-on-the-Lake. While living in Bracebridge, she continued to teach in Toronto. In 1962 and 1963 she directed Tagwagi shows for the Bracebridge Business and Professional Women's Club; such shows were formerly popular performances staged during the Muskoka Cavalcade of Colour each autumn. Mrs. Parsons was also skilled in interior decorating and gave her time to decorate the council chamber and Town Hall when the Bracebridge municipal building was newly constructed in 1958.

For many years Dick Hammond was among the best-known men associated with the construction industry in Bracebridge and all who remember him recall his competency as a stonemason and builder. He passed away on July 22 at the age of 84. As a young man he learned the skills of stonemasonry working with William Smith of Falkenburg. He later began his own business. In addition to stonemasonry, Mr. Hammond was a builder, being the general contractor for the remodelling on the United Church in 1951.

Levi Nutt passed away at age 97 on September 12. Mr. Nutt may be said to have typified the undaunted pioneer spirit, that characterized the early development of Muskoka. The hardships of his boyhood days were evident in his going to work at the age of 12 in logging camps to help support his family. Few years were spent in school. He settled a farm in Raymond and was a skilled blacksmith. As well, he worked for many years for the Department of Highways. Mr. and Mrs. Nutt moved to Bracebridge in 1966. Many stories of Levi's experiences of older times were written by the late Fred Hammell and were published in the *Muskoka Sun*.

Mrs. Elaine Salmon passed away on October 21 at the age of 79. Married in Toronto following World War I to Herman Brooks, she came to Bracebridge in 1922. With the assistance of his wife, Herman opened his own furniture business immediately after World War II. Mrs. Salmon enjoyed choir work and other church activities in the First Baptist Church. For some years she sang in the choir of the Bracebridge United Church and following her marriage to Tom Salmon, enjoyed choir work at St. Thomas' Anglican. Mrs. Salmon was also remembered for singing with the Bracebridge Choral Society and took a leading part in the choral group at the Senior Citizens Centre. Mrs. Salmon was an active member in the Bracebridge Business and Professional Women's Club.

## 1991

The year started and ended with Jack McVittie. In January, John Phillips McVittie was named the Rotary Club Citizen of the Year. The immediate reason for this recognition was the announcement that McVittie had donated 200 acres of land in the interior of Eilean Gowan Island in Lake Muskoka as a nature reserve, under special arrangements for its management and maintenance. However, the presentation was not just for that. His family home had been where the Pines Centre for Seniors now sits. The land had been given to the board of management for the home at a "most favourable price." He also contributed substantially to its construction. After J.P. completed his education, he worked for some time in mining and prospecting in northern Ontario. In the late 1940s he became a member of the Bracebridge Water, Light and Power Commission at the time it built the High Falls generating station and changed the delivery of electricity from two phase to three phase. He was also very active in reforestation, having planted many acres of fir timber across Muskoka. He was a member of the Bracebridge Curling Club and, along with George Parlett, purchased the Hardy farm at the north end of Bracebridge and incorporated what is now South Muskoka Curling and Golf Club.

Having received the Citizen of the Year Award at the beginning of the year, Mr. McVittie passed away on December 22, just two days shy of his 85th birthday.

In January a fire at the CC Pant Shop caused $300,000 damage. The building, on Manitoba Street next to the Bank of Nova Scotia (now the Little Moose bakery) had once been Campbell's Yard Goods owned by Sadie Campbell. Although the owners of the building indicated they would renovate, the building was eventually torn down and is presently a vacant lot.

Another new medical officer of health started at the Muskoka-Parry Sound Health Unit in May after the resignation of Dr. Walter Ewing. Dr. Nancy Cameron took up the position.

Local gymnastics sensation Kerry Richardson, competing with the Ontario provincial team at the Interprovincial Cup Gymnastics Meet, picked up a silver medal on bars, made it to the finals in the vault event, and helped her team win a gold medal in the overall standings. This came on the heels of her exceptional showing at the Ontario Winter Games when she helped the Northern Region team place third overall.

Athlete of the Year was awarded to Heather Medley who received the award at the Bracebridge Centennial Centre on May 14. Medley was a BMLSS student who was involved in many activities such as track and field, badminton, tennis, and basketball.

After many delays and problems, the Rotary Club of Bracebridge held opening ceremonies for the new Rotary Youth Centre in June. A large number of people turned out to watch the official ribbon-cutting conducted by members of the Scout and Guide troops who would use the hall. The new building replaced the old Scout Hall, now a parking lot on Main Street (part of Hiram Street today), that had served the needs of scouting in Bracebridge since 1956. "The new building represents the kind of service and community spirit that will enhance the town," noted Rotary president George Irvine. The Rotary Club held its first luncheon in the new structure on June 7 and would continue its weekly meetings there.

At the same time, the town officially inked a 20-year agreement with the Bracebridge Agricultural Society and the Muskoka Pioneer Power Association to give them the right to build facilities for annual events at the new fairgrounds (named the James D. Lang Activity Park) on Fraserburg Road. The town would build a track for horse shows and dirt bike races on the property.

Also in June, the BMLSS Dixieland Band brought home a silver medal from the National Stage Band Festival in Vancouver, BC. The band, under the direction of music teacher Warren Brownlee, competed against 9,000 other students from across Canada.

As of July 21 retail businesses of all kinds could open their doors for business on Sunday. District Council passed bylaw 91-66, permitting Sunday shopping in Muskoka from Victoria Day to Thanksgiving and also on Boxing Day.

In July it was announced that a new adult competitive precision skating team would commence in the fall. The team applied to Parks and Recreation for ice time starting in September. The group also became an arm's length sponsored group of the Bracebridge Figure Skating Club. Formation of the team arose from several meetings of the Port Carling Vintage Blue Team, it being decided that two levels of precision skating could thrive in Muskoka. The team became known as the Muskoka Blades and at one point was ranked fifth in Canada in adult precision (now known as synchronized) skating.

Norm Woods captured the North American power boat racing championships for the second year in a row. Woods received an award for the best performance of any power boat racer at the meet held in Quebec. The flawless race was won in his boat named *The Gambler*.

In August, concern about the Muskoka welfare caseload loomed again. It was expected to jump by an additional 300 people by year's end, surpassing the previous record set in the 20-year history of the department.

Also in August, a proposal to renovate the Bird's Woollen Mill warehouse on the Albo's property (at the corner of Manitoba Street and Entrance Drive at the Silver Bridge) was considered for the new home of the Bracebridge Chamber of Commerce. Councillor Aubrey Glass invited architects to make presentations on the feasibility of using the building, which had been owned by the town and used for storage. Being located on the river beside the falls, it would provide a superb lookout with proper design. The decision was made in favour of this proposal and the Chamber of Commerce, a café, and a charming art gallery soon took up leases.

In September, Monck Public School officially opened the doors of the new multi-million-dollar expansion. The additional featured a new gymnasium and increased office and classroom space. However, even with the new addition, portable classrooms still remained on the grounds.

For several months, it had been privately suggested that the only way a second ice surface could be afforded in this town was through user fundraising rather than from the tax base. It was suggested by mayor Jim Lang that a recreational capital foundation be developed for the raising of funds for many recreational capital projects.

After months of meetings, petitions, studies, and debates, the District of Muskoka would enter into the Ministry of Natural Resources subsidized aerial spray program against the gypsy moths. Muskoka suffered a total of 287,000 acres of defoliated forests, accounting for one third of all gypsy moth defoliation in Ontario in 1991, far exceeding the next closest region.

Before the end of October, Wayland Drew received an Honorary Doctor of Letters degree from Trent University and the Lieutenant Governor's award from the Conservation Council of Ontario. The award was designed to recognize outstanding achievements in conserving and protecting the natural environment. The Doctorate recognized Drew's contributions as an author and essayist for 12 books and numerous essays, mostly on environmental issues.

The third major blaze in a year on Bracebridge's main street raised questions about the safety of the aging buildings along Manitoba Street. The Banks Electronics building on the south-east corner of Anderson Lane and Manitoba Street, destroyed by a disastrous fire in October, was among the oldest commercial buildings in Bracebridge. The building had survived a number of serious downtown fires through the town's history, including the blaze of December 1908 which burned all the properties north of it on the east side of Manitoba Street. The building was erected for Topp & Anderson Dry Goods and was the Anderson store until purchased by Don and Doug Banks (Banks Bros. TV).

Marsha Wates was honoured with the Solicitor General's Award for Crime Prevention at a ceremony held at the Muskoka Sands Inn. Wates had been involved in community crime prevention since 1981 and had been actively involved with community policing committees in both Bracebridge and Gravenhurst. She chaired the Bracebridge Community Policing Committee and was involved in the newly formed Neighbourhood Watch Program.

In November, an historic mystery was uncovered from the waters of the Muskoka River. Workers installing trunk main lines discovered a propeller in such good condition that it still turned on its bearings. Digging though the history of steam in Bracebridge revealed the most likely source as a small but prestigious tugboat called *Queen of the Isles*. Built in 1885 in Orillia, the ship changed owners several times over the years, was employed for a while as a tug for the Beardmore Tannery (located not far from the spot the propeller was recovered). While owned by the tannery, a larger propeller was fitted on the boat and the old prop may simply have been discarded in the river. Residents who once lived along the banks of the Muskoka River at Captain Levi Fraser's boathouse recalled that the *Queen of the Isles* lay in berth for a number of years and may simply have rotted away there. Another story may be that it was the propeller of the *Oriole*, built in 1886 in Toronto. She capsized in 1904 in the location of the find. Its narrow lines made the it slightly unstable under heavy loads, and in the spring of 1904 it was carrying an exceptionally heavy load when it capsized. The *Oriole* drifted almost a mile downstream before it ran aground a second time. Later it was repaired at the Muskoka Wharf. The town water and sewer crew cleaned up the prop to put on public display in Kelvin Grove Park.

In December, the 1992 agricultural executive was picked. The members were Jerry Fox, Steve Harper, Ken Milroy, Cecile Beaudry, and Irene Thompson.

Thirty-two years after he first started helping his dad with the dairy herd, Don Goltz quit the milk business, selling off 34 head of dairy cattle to a farm in Newcastle. With Goltz's retirement from the dairy business there remained only three dairy herds in Muskoka. In the early days, when Don Goltz was getting started, there were 64 milk producers in the district.

In December, Frank Miller, former MPP for Muskoka and premier of Ontario, became the fifth chairman of the District Municipality of Muskoka, defeating Allen Sander by one vote from the District councillors. Sander was seeking his fourth term as chairman. Miller noted that overlapping of duties between the District and the area municipalities was one of his main concerns, indicating that government could no longer afford to increase its budgets while the rest of the taxpayers were simply struggling to hold jobs.

As well, Jim Lang was re-elected as the 29th mayor of Bracebridge since the village became a town in 1889. Mayor Lang was about to begin his 18th year in office – the longest seated mayor in the town's history. Prior to Jim, George Parlett held the title for 12 years before retir-

*The Bracebridge Town Hall constructed in 1958 retained the tower which survived the 1957 fire that destroyed the old Town Hall. The exterior remains largely unaltered despite extensive interior renovations.* COURTESY OF GARY LONG

ing from the job to successfully seek the office of District chairman. Bracebridge Council included Heather Coupland, Jim Boyes, Jim Lang, George Brodie, Katie McCann, Scott Northmore, Dave Heatherington, Dan Brooks, and Bill Glennie.

David Myers, in his 77th year, died on January 6. With his brother Ronald, he had been in business in Bracebridge for 26 years in Myers Bros. Hardware. They retired 15 years prior and closed the business. They had started the business with a coal yard near the CNR station (now a parking lot on near Taylor Road on Hiram Street) then opened a CIL agency in part of the Patterson Hotel (presently Al Beverley Decorating). Before long they opened their hardware business in the building on the west side of Manitoba Street downtown, where years previously their father had owned a grocery store. In his student years at Bracebridge High School, David played the saxophone in the school orchestra. He was elected as Muskoka member of the Ontario Older Boys Parliament. In his university years at the University of Toronto, he worked summers as a purser on the RMS *Segwun*. Mr. Myers worked for 11 years as an accountant in Toronto before returning home to set up business with his brother. He was an active and devoted member of the Bracebridge United Church, where he served as secretary of the Sunday School.

Norman B. Miners Sr. would long be remembered for the devoted active leadership which he gave over many years to the Boy Scout movement in this community and the wider district. Mr. Miners passed away on January 21 at the age of 77. He was a Cub, Scout, and Rover leader, then a district commissioner.

Charles French died February 8 in his 80th year. When Mr. French came to Bracebridge in 1929 he worked on the Ewing and Lovatt farms and those of James Carson and Sam Holden. For some time Ernest DeLarge, who operated a store and auction headquarters in downtown Bracebridge, employed him. During World War II, Charles was employed with the Minett-Shields Boat Works on Bracebridge Bay in the production of Fairmile ships and other craft for the Royal Canadian Navy, his work taking him occasionally to Montreal. He continued with the boat works after the war, helping create mahogany pleasure craft still popular as vintage boats today. Mr. French was the first locally to go into the refrigeration business, working on his own and for 15 years for Ecclestone's Hardware. When Ecclestone's sold their appliance business to his son, Jim French, he joined as a partner in the firm known as French's Appliances.

The name of Wilfred "Bucko" McDonald will live on in Parry Sound-Muskoka as a doughty sports hero, a strong contender in team games, a former parliamentary representative, and treasured by a legion of friends. He passed away on July 19 in his 80th year. In his youth he played lacrosse and only took up hockey in his 20s, becoming a strong defenceman. In 1934 he signed a professional contract in the National Hockey League with the Detroit Red Wings, playing with the team when they won the Stanley Cup in 1936 and 1937. He was sold to the Toronto Maple Leafs who won the championship in 1942, the same year Bucko was chosen on the second NHL all-star team. He was traded to the New York Rangers in 1944. His last season was 1944-45. Returning to his home town of Sundridge, he was elected to the House of Commons as the federal member for Parry Sound-Muskoka on the Liberal ticket and served from 1945 to 1957. Bucko built up a championship team in Sundridge called the Sundridge Beavers OHA Intermediate team. In 1949 Bucko brought the team to Bracebridge to use the artificial ice at the new Bracebridge Memorial Arena. In 1971, as a hockey instructor, he changed his attention to Bracebridge and became coach-in-chief of all minor hockey in the town. He also coached the intermediate team known as Bucko McDonald's Bracebridge Huskies and continued his association with Bracebridge for many years.

*Ethel Bennett at the piano in 1974. She and her sister, Gladys, enlivened the Bracebridge cultural scene for more than 30 years.* COURTESY OF MARILYN LONG

The town was saddened by the unexpected death of Colan Cowan on July 30 at the age of 62. Mr. Cowan joined the Bracebridge police force in 1952 when the late John Harrington was chief. Colan was a constable on the force, then became chief of police, a position he held until policing work was reorganized in 1970 with the introduction of District government, the OPP taking over the responsibilities. Colan then became the chief bylaw officer for the town. Mr. Cowan was an active member of the Bracebridge Fire Department and a former member of the Orange Lodge.

The death of Miss Mae MacCracken occurred on October 29 at the age of 85. With her family, Mae moved to Bracebridge when she was 4 years old. She started school at the Fourth Ward School (now the Legion Hall) and continued her education in Bracebridge, then entered North Bay Normal School in 1925 to become a teacher. Mae's first school was at Falkenburg, then McLean's Corner's in Draper, and then Severn Bridge. In 1934 she joined the staff of what was then called the Central School in Bracebridge. There she taught several generations of young children until her retirement in 1971. Many students remember her for her story-telling, usually a continuous tale from year to year. In addition to her teaching duties, Mae found time to be a leader in the local Girl Guide movement, as well as being active as a leader in the Canadian Girls in Training in Bracebridge.

At age 93 Miss Ethel Bennett passed away on November 14. Miss Bennett grew up in Calgary and during World War I she worked with the Red Cross and assisted in concerts given to welcome returned soldiers. She was fond of sports, excelling in tennis. After her family moved to Toronto, Ethel entered federal government service, working for the taxation department until her retirement. She also obtained her ATCM degree from the Royal Conservatory of Music. After both she and her sister, Gladys, had retired, they moved to Bracebridge and acquired their home at 118 Shier Street. With retirement came travel, which they did frequently, to far off places not fashionable nor easily accessible at the time – such places as Russia, Japan, Nepal, Africa, Thailand, Indonesia, Greece, South America, and New Zealand. From these travels, the Bennetts began presenting public lectures describing their many trips abroad. Ethel was also heard as pianist in special recitals and of much pleasure to their audiences. She and John Reynolds co-operated in giving musical programs, with John playing the church organ.

On December 1, Mrs. Ivy Bates passed away at the age of 101, having lived all her life in Bracebridge. She was born in Bracebridge and attended school here, and for some years operated a very successful millinery business in the downtown Manitoba Street business section. Mrs. Bates was a charter member and life member of Lake Land Chapter No. 245 Order of the Eastern Star, and a member of the Bracebridge United Church. She was a member of the Lawn Bowling Club in former years, enjoyed ice skating, and was a great outdoor sports enthusiast. The Bates home on the southeast corner of Manitoba and McDonald streets and is now occupied by her daughter Evelyn.

## 1992

Bankruptcies rose 10 percent this year. Elgin House went bankrupt with a $4-million mortgage taken on by Manual Life. Windermere House went into receivership. River's Edge Estates owed $121,000 in realty taxes but was involved in a battle between Keith Sammitt and Louis Goldenburg, London entrepreneurs, and Carl Strand's claim to the site through Budjerator Landing Inc.

There was a major reconstruction of Bracebridge Hydro's generating station and reservoir at Wilson's Falls, and new sluiceways were installed ... Council purchased a rig for cleaning snow from the sidewalks ... the 1922-23 town bell tower was repaired ... After three motors at the sewage treatment plant and two pumps at the water-pumping station were damaged by lightning, the public works committee purchased fail-safe devices that cut power to machines before damage could occur.

The new Canadian Tire Store, on the south side of Highway 118, opened in April with Ron Doty as owner. The business had opened in 1962 in the building of Dr. Wright. Subsequently it moved to the Economy Fair location, then up the street to the Gordon Motors building, and in 1976 to its first location on Ball's Flats. The store employed about 62 staff with a 14-bay service department, warehouse, and outdoor garden centre.

Bob Sieber, owner of KKJ Graphix, opened the Factory Outlet. This was the first factory outlet owned by the manufacturer on Manitoba Street ... Bert French, contractor, won a contract to build a laboratory on Ellesmere Island. The lab's purpose was to study the ozone layer ... the Bracebridge Radio Controlled Speedway offered races every Sunday at the Muskoka Falls General Store ... The Bracebridge School of Ballet celebrated its fifth birthday ... Jack Naulls opened Muskoka Auto Sales and Leasing on Robert Dollar Drive ... The former Muskoka Garage was sold to Toronto Design and Construction Company ... ARC Industries closed ... Larry Giaschi purchased the former Building Trades property ... Thatcher Studio held a closing out sale. Doug Graham had been in the business for 43 years. Thatcher's was moved from Haileybury to Bracebridge 58 years earlier ... Junette's Ladies' clothing store, run by Isabelle and Howard Milne, also closed. They had been in business since 1980 and were ready to retire ... South Muskoka Memorial Hospital installed electronic parking meters on its parking lots. You could get in free but had to pay $1 to get your car back out. ...Banks Electronic Warehouse had

*In recent years structures and equipment have been upgraded at the Wilson's Falls generating station. Here the plant is under construction in 1910, on the site of the old Norwood Mills sawmill.* COURTESY OF BRENDA COX

a grand opening at 35 Manitoba Street ... Bell Telephone completed $11.9 million worth of upgrades in Muskoka, bringing in digital switching equipment ... Karen Kusnierczk was hired as audiologist for the Health Unit ... The Chamber of Commerce moved into the Garwood building with president Steve Audett and secretary James Saunders ... Bruce Kruger, commander of the Bracebridge Detachment of the OPP, was promoted to acting inspector of the field coordination branch in Orillia. He was succeed by Staff Sergeant Terry Kidd.

Muskoka Trading ended its sixth decade. The Trading Company was 40 years old when Betty and Donald Speck took over in 1975. In 1989 they moved the store to Ecclestone Drive but a robbery in December of 1991 was a blow from which they never quite recovered.

Santa's Village underwent a $2.1-million expansion with four new attractions for older teens. Phil Murphy explained the need for attractions such as a batting cage, miniature golf, a go-cart track. and a roller blade trail.

The Rockwell plant received a Quality of Excellence Award from the Chrysler Company for a consistently high standard in manufacturing.

The Bracebridge Recreational Capital Fund Foundation recognized Norm Harkness at a fund-raiser that netted $6,600 from some 250 people. The foundation was established in 1991 by mayor Jim Lang to receive donations for recreational, historical, cultural, and environmental improvements to the town.

Dr. William Monk retired after 34 years to be succeeded by Dr. James Campbell from St. Michael's Hospital and his wife, Dr. Rebecca Campbell, an anesthetist.

Bracebridge Jehovah's Witness quickly built their new church in June.

Darcy Brown had the job of tearing down the Anglican Church's Browning Hall to make way for a parking lot. Many of the old fixtures were re-used in the new St. Thomas' addition. Mr. Brown recycled most of the remainder.

This year was the 125th anniversary of the Bracebridge Fall Fair ... The Lions Club celebrated their 50th anniversary with a dinner and dance at the Centennial Centre. The club, with president Leo Peltomaki, moved into their new club house on the Fraserburg Road in the fall. The Manna Food Bank was displaced due to the demolition of Browning Hall so the Lions Club graciously offered their hospitality in the new club house ... Art in the Park celebrated its 30th anniversary ... 120 athletes attended the fifth annual Special Olympics sponsored by the Bracebridge Kinsmen and Ontario Special Olympics ... A record 191 players participated in the 30th annual Tagwagi Tournament at the Muskoka Golf and Country Club. The 1993 event was sold out before this year's tournament ended. The committee in charge consisted of Phil Keppler, Nick Roche, Dave Norsworthy, Geoff Marritt, J. Bert Reid, Herb Stewart, Bob Jones, Greg Mann, Sean Kelly, Patti Pearson, Jacquie Mann, and Jennifer Webb, with strong support from over 20 local businesses and companies.

Council invited all former town and township councillors and mayors to celebrate Canada's 125th anniversary at Kerr Park. Mayor Jim Lang presented each with token gifts ... J. Patrick Boyer, MP for Etobicoke, was named Queen's Counsel for his contribution in writing six books on election law published between 1981 and 1988 ... Fred and Ellen Quinton celebrated their 50th wedding anniversary as did Art and Dorothy Morrow.

Through the Muskoka Heritage Foundation $30,000 was awarded for phase one of the first major archeology survey in Muskoka. The coordinator was Ron Reid.

Antonia Goldthorp received her All Around Cord ... Ken Miller organized the East Muskoka District Trees for Canada. Beavers, Cubs, and Scouts planted 3,000 trees ... A trails plan was unveiled by author Katie McCann which mapped the existing trails and indicated future ones. A hiking trails bylaw was passed giving the town authority to maintain and control the trails.

The Bracebridge Bears took four games out of six over the Metro Toronto Hockey League. Brian Hough was named coach of the year for the second year. Rookie of the year went to Francois Charlebois. Top defenceman was Michael Rusk, and Corbie Kent most gentlemanly player. Jim Ensom, Corbie Kent, and Michael Rusk were all drafted to the OHL.

Muskoka Containerized Services won the Outstanding Recycling Program Operation Operator of the Year award from the Recycling Council of Ontario. MCS president Don Coates began recycling in the 1970s with the blue box program starting in 1988.

All five BMLSS bands brought home medals in the Muskoka-Georgian Bay Music Fest. The Dixieland Band received a gold medal, the stage and concert bands each received silver, with bronze going to the jazz group and the brass quintet.

A BMLSS student, Leif Loberg, won the Canada-wide Science Fair, getting a $5,000 trip to Israel. The BMLSS Midget Junior track team won the OFSSA championship. Allison Durocher, Elissa Healey, Corby Kent, Lindsey Mathews, and James Daves took the gold, silver, and bronze medals. Best All Round Student awards were won by Kelly Creasor and Kailey Mathews. Two hundred and thirty students graduated from BMLSS this year. Ryley Webb was chosen Athlete of the Year to win the Jim Quigley Memorial Award. Miss Webb won the first Canadian Junior Golf Championship for Optimist Clubs in Canada at a tournament in Kitchener.

The Muskoka Blades took fifth place in the Canadian Precision Skating ... Steve Morrison won the 40-kilometre Muskoka Mountain Bike Tour against 198 other participants ... The new hardball diamond at Kerr Park was completed, "close to major league size."

Director of education David Story was replaced by acting director Wayne Weaver under puzzling circumstances. Board of Education chair Marilyn Rowe refused to comment on the change. Mr. Story became an administration consultant but no duties were assigned to him.

Brennan Webb, 17, entered the U.S. Junior Championship after qualifying in Rochester, New York shooting 73-74 over 36 holes to win the golf tournament by six strokes. He was awarded the U.S. Golf Association gold medallion. He also qualified in the Ontario Men's Amateur Team, the Ontario Junior Championship, and the World Optimist Finals in San Diego.

The *Lady Muskoka* was sold by Herb Smith, general manager of Muskoka Tours (a cooperative with Aston Resort Hotel, Santa's Village, Pinelands, and the Muskoka Festival). Her new, private owners were Al and Bonnie McLellan who brought the 200-passenger vessel from Elgin House. Tom Brown has been Captain of the *Lady Muskoka* for10 years and Kirsten Joch for six.

Concerts in the park were sponsored by Bracebridge Arts Council and the Business Improvement District.

A benefit dance raised close to $10,000 for Michael Howden, son of Brian and Jan, who suffered a serious head injury in a snowmobile accident on Wellington Street.

The Arts Council and the Muskoka Rowing Club

teamed up for "River Reflections" marking the heritage of the Muskoka River and its meaning to Bracebridge. Rowing demonstrations and the Couchiching Songs and Dances Group provided some of the entertainment.

The Muskoka Rowing Club erected its new boathouse with the help of $12,333 of provincial grant money. Enrollment was at 40 members in this fourth year of operation ... The 30th annual Muskoka Arts & Crafts Show took place ... The Pioneer Power Show was a success with music provided by the Music Making Mums.

The old coal chutes under the Manitoba Street sidewalk were filled in because the support beams were getting too old to safely support the sidewalks. There used to be a coal chutes with a metal lid in front of each store.

Crime was rampant this year. The community was shocked by the shooting death of two young men and the wounding of OPP constable Scott Couse in Barrie. Jonathan Wesley Young, 19, was shot to death near Bracebridge with his childhood friend, Santo Michelin of Etobicoke. Three men faced charges of double homicide and the wounding of Constable Couse.

A Gravenhurst man was charged with the stabbing death of Mark David Dobson, 25, of Bracebridge.

Deaths this year included Mona Darling, 75, beloved wife of Stan Darling, MP. They were married in 1940 and had lived in Burk's Falls for 52 years. Prime Minister Brian Mulroney and wife stopped in to give their condolences ... Irvine "Ace" Bailey ... Mrs. Henry Hunt, 92, daughter of Mr. and Mrs. James Sandall, pioneers of Muskoka Falls ... Leonard Avery, 100, born in Dorset ... Margaret May Henry, 92, daughter of Alex and Catherine Cowan of Ufford, married James J. Henry in 1921 ... Douglas Dugdale, 67, died at the Muskoka Golf & Country Club, had been a RAF pilot, then director of materials for Litton Systems Canada Ltd. ... Paul Everett Kneeshaw, 51, was shot to death in his home. He owned the Bracebridge Bingo Hall as well as one in Orillia and another in Sturgeon Falls ... Dr. Morley Crockford, 67, returned to Bracebridge in 1974, married Donna Black in 1987 ... Jim Kaye, 75, building inspector, Monck councillor for 14 years and reeve for two years ... Wimund Kirk, 85, principal of Macaulay School 1946 to 1972, Macaulay Township clerk 1957-61 and councillor 1968-70 ... Alfred George Jarvis, served with Royal Canadian Navy, was dog catcher for many years ... Alice (Ecclestone) Jackson ... Allan Slater, 44, general contractor ... Daniel Charles Curry, 66, came to live on Bonnie Lake Road in the early 1940s, married Edna May Hubbard in 1963, worked in lumber camps, then maintenance and handy man for the Bonnie Lake Campgrounds ... Miss Anne Bruce, 84, former deputy sheriff, active in the community including Meals on Wheels ... Alma Peacock, born in Falkenburg, daughter of Thomas and Emma (Forsyth) Peacock, on the staff of the Thomas Co. and the *Bracebridge Gazette*, took over her father's insurance business and ran it for 25 years until she sold it to K.W. Rogers Insurance Brokers ... William Irvin Botting, 72, worked for Peter MacNaughtan Hardware for 20 years, ran Botting's Ice.

A & P cashier Janis Washington was credited with using CPR to save the life of a two-year-old in the store. She was aided by an unidentified woman.

Gary Bernarde and Graydon Smith with Muskoka FM 101 raised $1,000 in food and about $2,000 in donations in a 52-hour radio marathon.

Bracebridge owned 416 acres of park land.

The year 1992 was very wet. A September storm uprooted trees and downed power lines all over south Muskoka. Winds to 85 kilometres an hour and rain falling at one inch an hour left 1,500 customers without power over night and caused numerous accidents. There were floods at the mouth of the river. September alone had 253 millimetres of rain – the average is 102. Winter came early with 16.6 centimetres of snow on October 18.

## 1993

On January 15 the Rotary Club of Bracebridge selected William and Helen Towns as Citizens of the Year. This year was the first time that two people were chosen for their exemplary commitment as volunteers in the community. Mr. and Mrs. Towns had been hard workers and supporters of the South Muskoka Memorial Hospital for many years. Bill sat on the board and Helen was president and a member of the Hospital Auxiliary.

In February, there were many happy faces when Muskoka-Georgian Bay MPP Dan Waters announced the province would contribute $7.7 million towards an $18-million water treatment plant to be built in Bracebridge at Strawberry Bay (Kirby's Beach Road). The money would be added to $6 million from the province that had been sitting in a security account. The town would have to pay $4.3 million through reserves, development charges, and tax increases.

The Bird's Mill warehouse proposal was still on the table in 1993. Steve Rhys of Moorhead Associates showed the outline plans to include the building with a parkette out front at the corner of Manitoba Street and Muskoka Road. An action committee was formed to address its role in the Moorhead plan that would also include the renovation of the downtown core. The project on the mill got delayed further when confusion arose over the terms of the tender and the high bids.

In March the Willard family lost their home on Gordon Street (now Santa's Village Road) to fire. A chimney fire caused by an overheated wood stove ravaged the house.

A number of top Bracebridge athletes took part in the Ontario Winter Games in Cornwall. Participants included Heather Medley and Karen Clarke in badminton and Kerry Richardson in gymnastics. Kerry took a bronze medal for individual overall and a gold medal for the Northern Regional team combined score. The blizzard of 1993 hit Cornwall and many athletes were forced to stay over, billeted at the homes of local athletes.

In April, Frank Miller asked District staff and councillors to cut an additional $120,000 from the budget in order to achieve a zero percent increase in the mill rate. Miller managed to persuade members to look for ways to squeeze more out of their already tight budgets.

On May 12 Brennan Webb was named Jim Quigley Athlete of the Year for 1992. The top golfer also played on the BMLSS senior boys basketball team.

In May, Bracebridge Council decided not to remove parking meters from Manitoba Street, to the disgust of the BIA. The decision was slipped through at a special meeting of Council. Councillor Jim Boyes, chair of the administration and finance committee, supported the decision of Council in this matter. However, he was shocked to find that the BIA board members wanted him removed from his post as council representative because of his lack of support on the parking meters issue. Mr. Boyes advised Council that he would step down as the representative and a resolution was passed to do this.

*Chancery Lane has added interest to downtown Bracebridge ever since it was built to provide direct pedestrian access between Manitoba Street and the Town Hall on Dominion. This is a 1999 photograph.* COURTESY OF GARY LONG

After a long and illustrious career as federal MP for Muskoka-Parry Sound, Stan Darling, 81, announced he would not run in the fall federal election. Stan had been the riding representative since 1971.

In June, BMLSS graduate Nicole Wray paid a visit to Bracebridge to perform at the annual Bracebridge School of Ballet recital. She was preparing for her second season as a member of the Toronto Argonaut Sun-dancers squad, which performed at the CFL team's home games.

In July, a storm that hit Muskoka cost Ontario Hydro $500,000 to repair the damage done. During the storm

*Another present-day scene in the "old" business district. The movement of many businesses to north Manitoba Street and the plazas on Ball's Flats and Ecclestone Drive in the last 30 or 40 years has created a challenge of maintaining a viable commercial area in the historic downtown. Street beautification and proximity to Bracebridge Falls and its surrounding parkland are points in its favour.* COURTESY OF GARY LONG

winds reached speeds of 100 miles an hour, which downed trees and power lines, leaving parts of the area without power.

Four Muskoka Aquatic Club swimmers took part in the Canada Games Swimming Trials in Etobicoke. Megan Sullivan, Ali Sullivan, Marcie Horton, and Sarah Burke all qualified to race at the highly competitive meet.

On July 14 Bracebridge track athlete James Dawes participated in the Canadian National Junior Track Championships held in Sherbrooke, Quebec. James qualified for two events and came in sixth overall. At the same time, the South Muskoka Golf Team won the Ontario Rolex Pro Junior Championship. The team was comprised of Ryley, Brennan, and Ron Webb.

Ontario Premier Bob Rae came to Bracebridge on July 16 to announce a $960,000 grant to Interval House, to increase services for battered women and children. The facility would expand to accommodate 15 beds. Premier Rae also toured the Rockwell plant (now Meritor) to tell them how important the auto industry was to Ontario. A later visit to the Rotary Youth centre wasn't as pleasant because several protesters met him outside the building.

In July, Bracebridge-born hockey great Irvine "Ace" Bailey was honoured in the new Hockey Hall of Fame in Toronto. An entire wall of the hall was devoted to the incident that ended his playing career.

In September, a retirement party was held for Wayne Weaver, a Muskoka Board of Education superintendent who worked for the board for 11 years.

Also in September, it was announced that boaters would have to pay a user fee at the Port Carling navigational locks, beginning in 1994. It would cost $5 to $22 to lock through, depending on the size of the boat.

In October, Liberal Andy Mitchell won the Parry

Sound-Muskoka riding in the federal election, which saw the Liberal Party win a majority government. Reform Party candidate Jim Newman was second, Progressive Conservative candidate Terry Clarke third, and NDP candidate Shirley Davy fourth.

Muskoka Board of Education chair Marilyn Rowe again announced she would step down at the end of her two-year term as chair in December, but that she would stay on as a trustee for Bracebridge.

In November, there was a big controversy over the switching from the first Saturday in December to the first Sunday in December for the Bracebridge Santa Claus parade. The change caught members of the Bracebridge Economic Development Committee by surprise.

On November 17 former Beaver Creek Institution convict Philippe Clement was handed two life sentences for his brutal attack on a woman in her Winhara Drive home in September 1992. Clement said he was sorry for his actions but also blamed the correctional system.

In November, Muskoka Board of Education trustee Bill Grimmett advocated cutting the number of trustees from 16 to 7. That could save over $150,000 a year.

On January 24, Robert Parrett passed away at age 67. Bob went to Bracebridge schools and after working for the late Tommy Ball at Lake Drive Dairy and the Mills family farms at Beaumaris, he returned home to help his father on their Beaumont Drive dairy farm. Bob and his wife Helen sold their herd in 1981 and concentrated on gardening, being known for their "Parrett's Corn." He was involved in beekeeping, belonging to the Beekeeper's Association. He was a member of the Bracebridge Agricultural Society and other agricultural associations.

Milton Tibbett died on February 1 at the age of 80. Born in Bracebridge, Mr. Tibbett was known throughout Muskoka as the first chairman of the newly incorporated District Municipality of Muskoka 1970-74. He worked as manager for the Bracebridge Dominion Store for many years and then moved to Huntsville to work for Muskoka Wood Manufacturing Limited. After serving in the Royal Canadian Air Force during World War II, he returned to Huntsville to start his own refrigeration business. After serving on council Mr. Tibbett became the mayor of Huntsville in 1963.

On March 10, Charles Whaley died at age 92. He was a lifelong Bracebridge resident remembered for the blacksmith business begun by his father and continued by him. He was a bass player in the Bracebridge Citizen's Band and devoted member of Knox Presbyterian Church. He lived on James Street, his lot backing onto his father's blacksmith business on Manitoba Street, opposite the Memorial Park, part of which is now the Bell Telephone building. The business was moved more easterly towards the residence. In his senior years, Mr. Whaley became the first tenant of the seniors apartments on Alice Street.

On March 18 prominent Muskoka and Bracebridge-area reporter Lou Specht passed away at the age of 73. Lou served in World War II in the Royal Canadian Air Force, then with his wife Jean came to Bracebridge in 1951. They became involved in the Holiday Shop, a ladies' wear business run by Jean's mother Isobel MacAskill. Lou became a regular member of the *Herald-Gazette* staff in 1961. After a short term writing for the the *Bracebridge Examiner*, Mr. Specht returned to the *Herald-Gazette.* In 1989, the Ontario Community Newspaper Association awarded him the Silver Quill Award for 25 years of community service in the newspaper industry. Lou was also a town councillor in the 1950s, and prior to that was president of the Chamber of Commerce. He was president of the Rotary Club in 1965 and chairman of the Muskoka Cavalcade of Colour Committee. He was a member of the Legion and an honourary member of the Lions club and the Air Cadets. He was a member of the board of director for Santa's Village Limited, working for most of his time on the board as secretary.

Mrs. Edna Brooks passed away on March 20 at age 96. She was the wife of the late George W. Brooks, who had purchased the local pharmacy of John Thomson just after World War I. Mrs. Brooks was an active member in many ladies' associations, including the women's work of the United Church.

Mrs. Emily Fraser passed away on April 22 at the age of 86. She was born in Gravenhurst but came to work for R.M. Best, QC, as a legal secretary in 1938. She had given valuable service to such organizations as the Cancer Society, the Girl Guides of Canada, and the United Church women. Emily was from Muskoka pioneers, her

*The Bird Woollen Mill warehouse, the only surviving part of the Bird mill complex, has been transformed into an attractive Mews.* COURTESY OF GARY LONG

great-grandfather Alexander Bailey having set up a trading post on the Muskoka River, then in the early 1860s opened a general store on the Muskoka Road south of the Bracebridge Falls. He became the first postmaster and also set up the first sawmill in this vicinity. Her grandfather worked on the first steamships, obtained his master's papers, and was captain of several of the Muskoka Lakes steamboats, and then for several years was commodore of the Muskoka Lakes Navigation and Hotel Company's fleet of steamers. It was Captain Bailey who fashioned many of the wooden sculptures that were placed on top of the wheelhouses of the early steamboats. Her late husband's father was also a captain (Levi Fraser) who operated a tugboat service on the Muskoka Lakes.

On June 16 Paul Robson, 58, former owner of Building Trades Centre, died after falling from a ladder at his summer cottage in Milford Bay.

## 1994

In January, plans for a major commercial/retail project were unveiled at a town development services committee meeting. The land north of Monck Public School was targeted as the spot for a super store. By March Wal-Mart stores had been confirmed as a prospective tenant for the proposed development, having 109,000 square feet of retail space. By the end of March, Town Council passed a rezoning and official plan amendment for the big-box store just north of the school. The matter went to the OMB, which did not find in favour of Wal-Mart.

On January 19 a $1.5-million fire, which started in the attic, destroyed the 30-unit seniors apartment building on Alice Street, and left all residents homeless on one of the coldest nights of the year (-40°).

In February, long-time firefighter Murray Ellis retired from the Bracebridge Volunteer Fire Department after 33 years of serving residents. Murray had opened his own appliance business on Manitoba Street after working most of his career for French's Appliances, locating directly across the street.

On March 2 South Muskoka Memorial Hospital administrator Frank Lovelock announced his early retirement after 27 years with the hospital. Lovelock said he was not pressured into it following a survey that criticized the hospital's leadership.

On March 16, the Rotary Club named Dave Whiteside Citizen of the Year. His creative and innovative methods of teaching had pushed students to reach for their greatest potential.

In March, the Bracebridge Blades Novice, Junior, and Muskoka Blades Adult Precision teams swept the Northern Ontario Sectional, bringing home six golds. In April, the Muskoka Blades adult team took silver at the Precision National Championships, ranking them second in Canada. The Bracebridge Blades Juniors and Novices both took silver in the national competition.

East Tennessee State University won the Southern Conference golf title with Brennan Webb on the team. Brennan is the son of Ron and Jennifer Webb, Ron being the golf pro at the South Muskoka Curling and Golf Club. Kerry Richardson continued to win with a gold medal at the Elite Ontario Gymnastics Championships.

In April it was announced that McLaren Press was $3 million in debt, according to a bankruptcy notice. Secured creditors were owed $2.055 million and unsecured creditors $2.85 million. A trustee appointed by McLaren Press said that assets would be sold to the highest bidder. Price Waterhouse Ltd. was the Toronto firm working on behalf of the unsecured creditors.

On May 4, the Bracebridge Centennial Centre Pool was closed down when swimmers felt electrical shocks while learning water rescue techniques on the deck. The pool would be closed for much of the summer to repair the recurrent shock problem and complete other needed work. While closed, a new pool deck was installed as well as a new soundproof ceiling. Summer swimming lessons were held at Bowyer's Beach, having been held at the pool since 1975. Prior to that, swimming lessons were held at Kirby's Beach.

By the end of May, another culture and recreation director left, Richard Morwald moving to Welland. In June, Bracebridge parks and recreation head, Tom Robinson, was relieved of some of his duties due to health. He eventually took full disability and retirement. By the end of September, Leo Broere was appointed the new Bracebridge parks and recreation director.

On June 22, James Dawes was honoured as Bracebridge Athlete of the Year at the Recreation Capital Fund Foundation dinner. James showed his form in long jump at many track meets during the year, winning gold at the Ontario Provincial Indoor Championships in February. At the same dinner, 11 members of the community were also honoured for their service in making Bracebridge a better community. They were George Parlett, Bob Boyer, Mel Rowan, Jean Specht, Max Beaumont, Evelyn Bates, Phil Keppler, Marita Elliot, Judge William Golden, Tom Ball, and Lyle Cathcart.

Mike Fountain ended an excellent season of hockey after being called up to the Vancouver Canucks for the playoffs, in which they reached the finals. Fountain did not dress but practised with the team every day.

In July, after 21 years as mayor of Bracebridge, Jim Lang announced that he would not seek re-election. Instead he opted to run for District of Muskoka chairman. Unfortunately, in December he lost the chairmanship race to former Gravenhurst Mayor Gord Adams.

Also in July, Nat Faulkner came up with two big wins on the same weekend. He took the Guelph/Niagara-on-the-Lake triathlon and the Kids of Steel Ontario Championships, making him one of the top distance triathletes in North America.

In August, Ms. Leslie Talbot became the Bracebridge Chamber of Commerce's new general manager when Gordon Olsen moved to Utah to return to school.

*In the early 1970s, from this viewpoint, you would have seen a two-lane highway surrounded largely by fields and pastures. Now, "Ball's Flats" is a busy commercial district with several plazas and many of the businesses one would formerly have found in the old downtown. The space requirements of many modern retailers, both for indoor display and parking, virtually dictated expansion to formerly rural areas adjacent to town.* COURTESY OF GARY LONG

Melissa Fielding was among the province's top equestrian riders, placing third overall in the Ontario Training Championships.

In October, former Catholic priest Father Timothy O'Connor pleaded guilty and was sentenced to six months in jail for two counts of sexual interference.

On November 16, former District solicitor Russ Black became Bracebridge's new mayor, campaigning on a platform to simplify Muskoka government. Mary Jane Philp, Linda Matthews, and Sidney Rosenblatt became trustees for the Muskoka Board of Education.

And in November, Kerri Wills won gold at the Northern Ontario Sectional Skating Championships in Thunder Bay. She qualified to go onto the Divisional Championships on her way to the Nationals. That made Kerri Bracebridge's top singles figure skater ever. No other skater from the Bracebridge Figure Skating Club has ever gone to divisionals.

Robert Emerson Everett passed away on February 21 at the age of 74. Bob was a prominent artist who would be remembered for the excellence of his portrayal in oil paintings of the outstanding scenery of Muskoka District and Algonquin Park. He can well be called the Dean of Muskoka artists. He attended Bracebridge schools, finding his talent for art early in his life. He joined the Royal Canadian Air Force during World War II, rising to the rank of Flight Sergeant Navigator. Bob flew Hampden bombers, and after crashing during active service, was permanently discharged due to injuries received. He graduated from University of Toronto College of Pharmacy and returned home to practise in partnership with his father, Harry G. Everett. The store was located where Smellies Stationary is presently located on Manitoba Street.

Bob's love for painting continued throughout his life, his subjects being mainly autumn and winter scenes of Muskoka. He was a member of the Ontario Institute of Painters and became its president in 1975. In 1986, he was elected as an associate member of the Pastel Society of America, and a full member of the Pastel Society of Canada. His paintings have been displayed at the Eaton's Gallery and the Art Gallery of Ontario in Toronto, amongst others. Many of his works now reside in the homes and corporate headquarters of the wealthy and famous in Canada, Unites States, and Europe.

Miss Katherine (Kay) Ross died after a one-day illness at the age of 91 on March 12. She graduated from the University of Manitoba at a time when women were considered bold to attend higher institutes of learning. Her vocation as secretary took her to England, where she was a secretary to a general in the British War Department. After World War II, Kay returned to Canada and in the late 1940s she and her parents moved to Muskoka. Kay worked for the Shier Lumber Company, then in 1951 began her long association with Milford Manor, Lake Muskoka, and the family of Gordon Reid. For many years Miss Ross was a volunteer at South Muskoka Memorial Hospital, and with Meal of Wheels. As well, she was a great worker for the Bracebridge library and the Literacy Society.

Sherman Tough contributed much to Ontario mining development. He died March 22 at the age of 83. Sherman graduated from Haileybury School of Mines as a practical mining engineer. He worked as a prospector and as an underground miner and surveyor in the Kirkland Lake area before moving with his new wife, Agnes, to North Carolina, in search of gold. Many people remember Agnes Tough as the firm but likeable school librarian at BMLSS. During World War II Sherman worked on the airframe design of the Lancaster bomber. After the war, the Tough family returned to Sherman's father's log home on the Muskoka River. This allowed Sherman to commute to Toronto in an endeavour to raise capital for digs in northern Ontario. Sherman was not a company man, nor could he resist the lure of the Precambrian Shield where his father and uncles Robert, John, and Thomas had first discovered what would become the Tough-Oakes mine. In 1990 Sherman was recognized by his peers, and was made an honorary life member of the Prospectors and Developers Association of Canada, of which he had been a director for many years.

Al Bonnell was 81 when he died on May 1. He was the son of former reeve of Macaulay, Ed Bonnell. In 1951 the Bonnells jointly purchased Bonnie Lake (at the time known as Mud Lake). The lake's name was changed to Bonnie Lake, this being Ed's name for his wife. Al moved to Bonnie Lake in 1941. During the war, Al joined the Royal Canadian Navy. Retiring from the war to Bracebridge, he worked at Harrington's Meat Market, Santa's Village, and Cale's Meat Market. He joined the LCBO in Bracebridge and retired in 1969. Before and during retirement, Al received great enjoyment from teaching and participating in dancing.

Maggie Ringling's accomplishments in the community were cut short by her death on July 1 at the age of 53. Ms. Ringling worked with the United Church as a supporter of the recent building campaign and on the hiring committee. She was involved with the Children's Services Advisory Group and the Muskoka Women's Advisory Group. She was directly involved with the establishing of Muskoka Family Focus, Macaulay Tree House Day Nursery, and Interval House. She received her BA at Glendon College, York University, and taught at Seneca College and Georgian College before coming to Muskoka when she was hired to work as the director of the Children's Services Advisory Group.

Mrs. Audrey Hammell, widow of the late Fred Hammell, passed away on July 20 in her 82nd year. She was born and lived in Bracebridge at the family home in the fourth ward. After her high school years, Audrey worked for the Benham family in Beaumaris. During her years in Port Loring with Fred, Fred authored school textbooks and Audrey illustrated them. Her artistic interests flourished under the tutelage of Bob Everett and William Anderson. Audrey was a founding member of Muskoka Arts and Crafts, through which she displayed her oils and other artworks for sale.

On November 12 Gordon Reid passed away at the age

*In the 1990s a large condominium complex was built on the level land between Ecclestone Drive and the North Muskoka River below Bracebridge Bay. A century earlier, one of the town's major industries for nearly 40 years, the Anglo-Canadian Leather Company tannery, located here. In the photo below, circa 1960, several tannery building still stand; the largest one, 100 feet by 400 feet, was built in 1910. They were demolished in 1977. Cathcart's Garage stands lower centre; the house to the left of it is now Ecclestone Cycle.* COURTESY OF THE TOWN OF BRACEBRIDGE

of 84. His passing had brought to the memory of many friends the leadership Mr. Reid took in the immediate postwar years in popularizing hockey as Bracebridge's leading sports organization and as well in organizing a recreation program based at Bracebridge Memorial Community Centre, of which he was the first manager. Gordon had been the proprietor of Milford Manor on Lake Muskoka at Milford Bay, which he bought in 1943 under the former name of Cedar Wild Hotel. In his early days, Gordon had played professional hockey in the American Hockey League for nine years. When the Reids came to town, Bracebridge was without a hockey and skating rink, the building owned by the late George Yearley having been destroyed by fire in 1943. With World War II drawing to a close, townspeople wanted a revival of their intermediate hockey team and persuaded Gordon to coach the team, which became the championship Bracebridge Bears. Bracebridge Memorial Community Centre also became the war memorial for the town. In the summer of 1948, construction had lagged and in order to have the building finished and in operation, Town Council cancelled the remaining principal contract and turned the work over to Gordon Reid as superintendent and manager of the centre. Mr. Reid at once assembled a group of workers, being assisted by John Thompson and Nelson Goltz, and the Community Centre on James Street officially opened in February, 1949. Reserved seats numbered 2,200 and yet attendance was much greater when

*In a farsighted move that would reap big dividends, Bracebridge in 1894 became the pioneer in municipal hydroelectric system operation when it bought the small hydro plant constructed by W.S. Shaw two years earlier at the top of Bracebridge Falls. The plant straddled and drew its water supply from the Bird Woollen Mill head race, utilizing about five metres of drop at the upper falls. Subsequently, the town built the powerhouse at the lower falls in 1902, another at Wilson's Falls in 1910, and the High Falls station in 1948. These three hydro plants still operate today. They have a total installed capacity of 2,000 kW and can produce more than 15,000,000 kW-hours of electrical energy annually. The photograph shows the original powerhouse in the early 1900s; it was used exclusively as a water-pumping station after a second generator was added at lower falls powerhouse in 1906.* COURTESY OF THE TOWN OF BRACEBRIDGE

the Sundridge Beavers, coached by Bucko MacDonald, came to town. Mr. Reid was also a member for some years of the Bracebridge Rotary Club.

Almost all of the long and active life of Mrs. Gladys Parlett was spent in Bracebridge and when she passed away on November 15 at the age of 96, friends noted that her death marked the ending of a time that connected life and activities in the town from the beginning of the century through until today. She came to Bracebridge as a baby in 1900 when her father (Alexander Salmon) was appointed town clerk, an office he would hold for 36 years. Gladys attended the schools of Bracebridge and she married Horace Parlett in 1922, making their home on Kimberley Avenue (presently owned by Larry Giaschi, two homes down from the corner of Rene Caisse Lane and Kimberley Avenue). Mr. Parlett had an active business in town and served as a councillor at one time. Mrs. Parlett had taken an active part in the United Church and other community organizations. In later years, she enjoyed attending the Senior Citizens Club when there were card games, especially if her brother Russ Salmon was her partner.

Canon McCausland died on December 17 at the age of 86. He had been one of the most prominent and active members of the Society of St. John the Evangelist at their Bracebridge Mission House. For a number of years he was the Father Superior of the fathers and brothers of the local Canadian congregation, also known as the Cowley Fathers. In the dozen or more years since his retirement, Father McCausland came occasionally to Muskoka. He was present at the services of deconsecration of the SSJE Church and later was preacher at a service at St. Thomas' Anglican Church when a window honouring the work of the Cowley Fathers was dedicated.

*Bracebridge today is one of only about a dozen municipalities in Ontario that still own and operate hydroelectric stations.* COURTESY OF GARY LONG

*Waterfalls have always been an essential part of Bracebridge, both as a source of power and as a scenic focal point bringing enjoyment to townspeople and visitors. In the late 1990s, a committee of volunteers under councillor Edith Nichols inaugurated a spring Festival of the Falls to take advantage of the splendid cataracts as a rallying point for a weekend of festivities in an otherwise slow tourist season. Guided tours of various falls within the municipality included Wilson's Falls, shown above from a vantage point few witness it from. Hard to believe this wild scene is barely 2 kilometres from downtown!* COURTESY OF GARY LONG

# 1995–1999

## *Towards the Millennium: Wild Weather, Scenic Falls*

THE YEAR 1995 will be remembered for its weather. After 1994 was declared one of the mildest on record, the first few weeks of 1995 brought record snowfalls to the district with accumulations of up to 84.6 centimetres. Then the rains came and between January 11 and 16 we had 37 millimetres. This had a detrimental effect on tourism, as the lakes were not safe for snowmobiling, ice fishing, or skating.

Spring was hot and dry, and by June there was a total fire ban across the northern half of the province, including Muskoka. The fire ban remained in effect until late August when light rains fell, to be followed by heavy downpours in the autumn. However, before the rains came, central Ontario was hit by one of the fiercest storms ever recorded in the area. It was midnight on July 15. A massive storm front developed over Lake Huron and pressed itself onto the coast of Georgian Bay around 1:30 a.m. There was a tremendous light show for about a half hour before the rain and wind hit. The storm didn't last much more than 15 minutes, but it left a stunned and demolished Muskoka in its wake. According to weather trackers, lightning hit the ground 3,569 times in Muskoka and Parry Sound. At least three tornadoes accompanied the storm as it swept through the district at 120 kilometres an hour. In all, 75,000 homes were left without power and it took weeks to clean up and restore electricity to them all. Fortunately there were no serious injuries reported after the storm, but the rampage caused tens of millions of dollars in damage.

The rains of late summer and early fall put water levels at the flood mark. The Big East river in Huntsville came over its banks. Although the MNR worked feverishly to drain the water out of the system, the rains kept coming. From the first day of November, the rain turned to snow. By the end of the month, Muskoka had received three times its normal dose of snow for the period – an estimated 120 centimetres over the 30 days. This established a new record for the month, but it was only the beginning.

December 10 was a day most Bracebridge residents won't forget. Snow was falling so thickly that visibility was lost after 40 or 50 feet. It continued for hours on end. Muskoka Airport reported 104 centimetres of snow – nearly 3½ feet from that one storm. It closed highways for hours, forcing a state of emergency. Local snowmobilers were recruited to help police rescue stranded motorists on the highways. Emergency shelters were set up in the community halls of both Gravenhurst and Bracebridge. Snow plow operators worked steadily for 24 hours to try and clean up after the storm.

On a happier note, Baby Simon, the first baby born in 1995 at South Muskoka Memorial Hospital, arrived on January 1 to proud parents Judy and Doug Dunford.

Mary McPherson, 80 years old, was one of the last persons who knew and worked with Rene Caisse at her cancer clinic on Dominion Street. In a ceremony held at the town office in early January, she turned over the recipe for the herbal remedy used by Rene Caisse for more than half a century as a treatment for cancer and other common ailments. The recipe is as follows: 6½ cups of burdock root (cut), 1 pound of sheep sorrel herb (cut) and ground in blender, ¼ pound of slippery elm bark (powdered), and 1 ounce of Turkish rhubarb root (powdered). Mix together thoroughly and store in a glass jar in a dry cupboard. Use 1 ounce of the herb mixture to 4 cups water. Boil hard for 10 minutes, then turn off heat but leave sitting on warm element; keep cover on pot. Let sit over night. In the morning, heat steaming hot and let settle a few minutes, then strain into hot, sterilized bottles. Cap while hot and set to cool. Store in a dark cupboard. Must be refrigerated when opened.

The year 1995 was one of celebrations. In February, the Pine Cone Treadlers, a group of weavers founded by Keitha Boyer, celebrated 10 years together, with an exhibition at the Chapel Gallery ... MPP Dan Waters was on hand to open the new shelter for women called Interval House. The shelter had been in existence for 10 years, but had outgrown its old facilities on James Street. The new location on Mary Street had more beds and space to provide counselling ... A May celebration was held to mark the 50th anniversary of the end of World War II. The event was called High Hopes, with parades, dancing, and music ... There were 30,000 people at Muskoka Airport to see the display of vintage aircraft in honour of VE-Day. Among those craft present were a Cornell trainer, two Harvard MK IV's – one of which was owned by Ross Watt of Bracebridge – and a Yale NA-64 ... Muskoka Tourism celebrated the opening of its new office in May. The $600,000-facility at Kilworthy on Highway 11 would be staffed year-round, and on evenings and weekends. It would also serve as a rest stop for weary travellers, providing picnic facilities and toilets.

The Bracebridge Capital Fund Foundation held a roast for Roger Crozier, the former NHL goaltender, to raise funds for a second ice surface. Roasters included Danny Poland, Jack Huckle, Wally Schwartz, Jeff (Hutch) Hutchison, and Paul Savage. The auction included items donated by local business as well as sports memorabilia, such as Don Cherry's autographed Russian hockey stick as featured on Hockey Night in Canada. There were also sticks, used in games, from Kris King of the Winnipeg Jets, Paul Coffey of the Detroit Red Wings, and Mike Gartner of the Toronto Maple Leafs.

In a press release at the Inn at the Falls, Roger Crozier announced the formation of the Roger C. Crozier Foundation to help provide young people the opportunity to succeed. The first recipient was Camp Oochigeas on Lake Rosseau, for children battling cancer. A "New Year's Eve in August" which raised funds for the foundation had a surprise when Charles Cawley from the United States MBNA America Bank flew in and donated $250,000. Unfortunately, the year ended with some sad news about Roger Crozier. In November, he was diagnosed with prostate cancer.

The Town of Bracebridge celebrated the opening of the new water treatment plant at Kirby's Beach. The facility cost $11 million and had been under construction since August 1993. The building was a two-storey, 43,000-square-foot structure capable of sucking up more than one million gallons of water a day out of Lake Muskoka. It was also the end of an era as the District took over the responsibility of the town's water and sewer department.

Santa's Village turned 40 this year and celebrations were held throughout the summer months. The Summer Festival Parade held on July 29 drew thousands of people. There were over 50 entries, one of the most popular being the steam calliope.

Alcan Cable celebrated 25 years in Bracebridge on September 10. The plant employed 185 full-time workers with a payroll of $9.2 million. The plant produced copper and aluminum wiring for both local and international markets.

The Simcoe County Roman Catholic School Board celebrated the opening of its first high school in Muskoka in September. The new facility, called St. Dominic Secondary School, was located at the 532 Industrial Plaza. Because of the lack of gymnasium facilities, the board worked out a plan whereby the students could use the gym at Monsignor O'Leary Elementary School, as well as some of the town facilities such as Kerr Park and the Centennial Centre.

October saw the sod-turning ceremony for the new medium security prison adjacent to the Beaver Creek facility.

Over the course of the year the Town of Bracebridge saw many changes. Bracebridge planner Peter Niece resigned effective February 8, to return to southern Ontario to head up a new planning department with the Essex County Board of Education. He had been with the town for eight years. Ruth Smith was appointed to replace Mr. Niece. Trish Conley, a graduate of Conestoga College's recreation leadership program, was hired as the new program coordinator for culture and recreation. She would be working primarily on programs for pre-school children and teens.

Deputy mayor Scott Northmore retired from his 22-year career at the Bracebridge courthouse. Mr. Northmore began his career as clerk and bailiff of the small claims court and eventually became deputy sheriff for the judicial district of Muskoka. Friends and colleagues paid tribute to his career in June.

In July, service awards were presented to many town employees. Volunteer firefighter Jerry Fox received an award for 40 years service. He also received an exemplary service medal from Governor General, Romeo Leblanc.

*This steam calliope was one of the most popular entries in the Summer Festival Parade, one of many events held to coincide with the 40th anniversary of Santa's Village. The calliope also appeared in the 1975 Centennial Parade. Santa's Village was established on the Muskoka River by local businessmen in 1955.*
COURTESY OF MARGARET WILSON

Fire chief Peter Mitchell and Robyn Gibbs of the water and sewer department also received Governor General Awards. Mr. Mitchell and Mr. Gibbs received rings for service of 35 years and 25 years, respectively. Fifteen-year pins went to Susan Cockburn, property maintenance department; Crystal Smith, assistant treasurer; Brian MacFarlane, culture and recreation; and Wayne Johnson and Rick Conway, firefighters. Ten-year pins went to Keith Taverner, roads; Neil Johnson, water and sewer; Carolyn Vincent, library; Donald Terry, firefighter; and Ruth Smith, planning department.

In August, the town hired Robin Walker, 27, to fill the position of planning technician which became vacant when Deanna Howarth was promoted to assistant planner. Rob was also president of the Canadian Association of Certified Planning Technicians.

The end of August saw the end of an era for the Bracebridge when town clerk Ken Veitch, 55, announced his retirement effective January 5, 1996. Ken was appointed clerk-treasurer on June 1, 1967, to succeed Wilbert Richards. In all his years in this position, Ken did not miss one Council meeting.

In sports there were several outstanding achievements this year ... Keri Wells was the first skater in the Bracebridge Club history to pass all CFSA Gold tests ... Chris Tolton of Bracebridge was awarded an NCAA scholarship, and would play first base with the Maryland Terrapins ... Ryley Webb of the South Muskoka Golf and Curling Club won another junior provincial championship in Peterborough.

The Bracebridge Blades earned a gold medal at the Challenge Cup in Newmarket and went on to win gold at the Northern Ontario Sectional Invitational held in North Bay. In Calgary at the Canadian Championships for the Challenge Cup, the juniors won the silver medal. The adult team qualified for the Gold Cup, placing sixth out of nine teams.

Nat Faulkner and Elissa Healey were named BMLSS athletes of the year. Nat was an excellent triathlete known for Nordic skiing, mountain bike racing, and track. He was presented with the Jim Quigley Memorial Award at the Roger Crozier celebrity roast. At the end of August, Nat won the Canadian Cycling Championship and went to Austria on a Rotary Exchange. Elissa Healey was best known for her accomplishments on the track.

The BMLSS rowers won gold and silver at the regional competition in London. Then in the final competition held at Kirby's Beach, our teams cleaned up, taking the gold in all six races. They competed against teams from Barrie, Durham, and Midland.

Bracebridge and Muskoka lost a number of notable citizens over the year, some of whom were Jessie Dunn, 85, volunteered 30 years of service at South Muskoka Memorial Hospital and more than 40 years with Muskoka Family and Children's Services. She also worked with the Red Cross, Boy Scouts, and Girl Guides ... Lorne T. Shier, a long-time member of the Curling Club and a member of the Bracebridge Memorial Community Centre Board. He had opened Bracebridge Auto and Sports Supplies after World War II, from which he retired in 1972 ... John Black Aird, former lieutenant-governor of Ontario, had been a summer resident on Lake Muskoka at his cottage, Temple Trees, for many years. He had a collection of antique boats which was well known to enthusiasts.

The Town of Bracebridge welcomed retired Major-General Lewis MacKenzie and his family who decided to settle here. They moved into an historic home in the north end of town. MacKenzie was taking up a new career as an author and international affairs consultant. MacKenzie, who was appointed commander of the United Nations Protection Forces in the former Yugoslavia in 1992, had retired after more than 30 years in the Canadian Armed Forces. His wife's family lived in the area and this prompted their move here.

## 1996

In many ways, the events and significant occurrences of 1996 reinforced the fact that Bracebridge is indeed the Heart of Muskoka.

The community was saddened with the death of Roger Crozier in January at the age of 53. Throughout his stellar career as a goaltender in the National Hockey League, playing for the Detroit Red Wings, Buffalo Sabres, and Washington Capitols, Roger was known for his skillful and fearless netminding. He was the only NHL player ever to be awarded the prestigious Conn Smyth Trophy, given to the playoff's most valuable player, as a member of the losing team.

Following his NHL tenure, Roger launched a very successful career as a senior project manager with the MBNA Bank, one of the world's largest issuers of credit cards. Roger supervised development of many of the bank's building projects, including the spectacular corporate headquarters in Wilmington, Delaware. This beautiful structure, built with a significant Canadian content of architectural pre-cast concrete panels produced by Pre-Con Industries of Brampton Ontario, was named the Bracebridge Building.

The MBNA Bank, which held Roger in very high esteem for his management skills and affable personality, later financed the Bracebridge Sports Hall of Fame, installed in the Bracebridge Memorial Arena. In 1998, the bank forged closer ties with the town through an affinity credit card agreement, whereby a portion of proceeds from a special credit card program would flow to the Bracebridge Recreation Capital Fund Foundation to support its objectives of community betterment.

Proving that Mother Nature is in charge, the weather in 1996 held some surprises. Town forces were unable to install the innovative floating snowmobile bridge at the Trans Canada Pipeline crossing of the Muskoka River, due to difficult ice conditions. In a cooperative effort, the town worked with the Muskoka Sno Bombers Snowmobile Club to create an ice bridge across the river to facilitate a safe crossing for snowmobilers.

In January popular town clerk-administrator Ken Veitch retired after 30 years of distinguished and dedicated service to the Town. During his years at the administrative helm, Ken was a major player in the organization of the District of Muskoka in the early 1970s, which brought several outlying townships into the Town of Bracebridge. Many significant advances occurred during Ken's tenure, including the magnificent transformation of the Bracebridge Bay area into a lovely and popular parks and trails system. The former warehouse of Henry Bird's woollen mill was acquired by the town and developed into a striking centrepiece of the falls and Silver Bridge area. The Bird Mill Mews is home to the Chamber of Commerce, which operates a very active visitor information office on behalf of the town, as well as a café and art gallery. Ken was instrumental in implementing development of the town's recreational trails network, an increasingly popular feature for residents and visitors. Ken's vision and commitment and his numerous accomplishments truly reinforced his nickname, "Father Town."

In February, Murray Clarke began his duties as Ken's replacement. Murray came to town after spending 12 years as clerk-administrator with the Township of Erin in Wellington County. Remarking on the move to Bracebridge, Murray noted that being in Muskoka was something of a professional homecoming for him, since he began his career with the Township of Georgian Bay in 1980 following graduation from Seneca College.

The previous month, Stan Darling, who served as member of federal parliament representing Parry Sound-Muskoka for over 30 years, published his memoirs, *The Darling Diaries*. Mr. Darling appeared at Scotts of Muskoka on Manitoba Street for a special signing to promote the book, which entertained and offered interesting insights into his political career.

*Fastball pitcher Mike Crawford of Bracebridge has made a name for himself in the 1990s. He won the leading pitcher award in the World Championship of Fastball, played for the Waterloo Twins when they won the Canadian Men's Championship, and in 1999 led the Bracebridge Legion team to the Eastern Canadian Intermediate B championship.* COURTESY OF KEN VEITCH

On the local government front, the year was marked by innovation, change, and challenge. Continuing its leadership in solid waste diversion initiatives, in partnership with the District and Muskoka Containerized Services, the town embarked on a pilot solid waste co-collection program. This groundbreaking measure included one of the first organic compostible materials curbside pick-up in Canada. In tandem with the comprehensive blue box recycling services and regular solid waste collection, the pilot was so successful that it was soon incorporated into the regular program and expanded across urban Bracebridge.

Muskoka Containerized Services, based in Bracebridge, had long been recognized as a leader in the solid waste industry and had been awarded national and international accolades for its progressive approach to waste diversion and recycling.

Throughout the year the on-again, off-again issue of local government reform continued to be debated at the District of Muskoka council table. Proposals which did not succeed included reducing the size of District Council from 22 to 16 and eliminating the six area mayors from District Council.

In town, a suggestion that Draper and Oakley Wards be joined, with elimination of one member of Council, was also rejected.

In February, Town Council embarked on a path, not without difficulties and challenges, to ultimately expand the service area of the Bracebridge Hydro Electric Commission into territory then under the authority of Ontario Hydro.

Town Council and staff continued to work diligently toward implementation of a comprehensive civic addressing system, an important step toward achieving 911 emergency response service for the town and across Muskoka. The addressing project, which involved naming and renaming several roads and streets, was very well received by the public, not only for its association with 911 service, but in establishing a very clear and accurate system to facilitate giving directions to property, particularly in rural areas, waterfront lands, and islands. As time progressed, residents and visitors, delivery services, and emergency service providers all came to rely on the familiar reflective property number signs sprouting up along the roads.

Local government continued to be challenged by massive reductions to transfer support payments by the provincial government. Many subsidy programs were eliminated altogether. In January, the District of Muskoka faced a $1.75-million cut in provincial funding. Later in the year, clerk-administrator Murray Clarke described a $250,000 provincial transfer reduction as "good news." Clarke indicated that the town had anticipated an even greater hit from the province, an indication of just how much the fiscal relationship between the province and local government had changed in recent years.

During 1996, work began on the first-ever Town of Bracebridge official plan. Under the leadership of councillor Al Taylor, along with Ruth Smith, the director of development services, the project was a collaborative effort among the town, the District of Muskoka, and a special ad-hoc steering committee. Serving on the committee were mayor Russ Black, councillors Al Taylor, Edith Nichols, Barry Young, George Brodie, Heather Coupland, and Scott Northmore. Others on the committee were Michael Michalski, Greg Mannion, Wayne Moore, and Tom Smith. These individuals were volunteers who generously contributed their energy and time to this important project. Rounding out the committee were clerk-administrator Murray Clarke, planning staff Rob Walker and Deanna Howarth, as well as Judi Brouse of the District of Muskoka planning department.

Following a process characterized by extensive public and stakeholder consultation, the project was successfully completed in September 1997 with formal adoption of the official plan. It is significant to note that the plan was ultimately approved by the District of Muskoka with no objections or referrals to the Ontario Municipal Board.

An article in the February 14 issue of the Bracebridge *Herald-Gazette* noted the arrival of a Hollywood film crew at Windermere House on Lake Rosseau to film scenes for the adventure movie, *The Long Kiss Goodnight*. Directed by Renie Harlin, the film starred Geena Davis and Samuel L. Jackson. Noting the move to the new location, Pinelands Resort owner Bruce Reville said, "And I think it ends with the hotel burning down," a chilling portent of what was to befall Windermere House.

On February 27, a spectacular fire destroyed the historic lodge, often referred to as the "Lady of the Lake." The tragic fire attracted international attention, including offers of financial assistance from well-known film stars who frequently visited the resort. Ontario fire marshal's investigators concluded the cause was difficult to determine, possibly a result of high intensity lighting used by the film crew, or by the hotel's own old wiring. Three years later the parent companies of the film production unit paid a settlement of an undisclosed sum. In March, Bill Wakefield, an owner, vowed that "the Lady will rise again" – in this case a happier prediction which came true.

During 1996 the former Muskoka Trading building in downtown Bracebridge on Taylor Road was gradually transformed into "The Granary" by businessman George Snider. Ultimately the lovingly restored feed and grain mill came to house a florist, the Muskoka Heritage Society, a realtor, an office supply firm, a consulting engineering office, a dance studio, and Lakes of Muskoka Cottage Brewery.

In February 1996, Gary McMullen and Kirk Evans, lifelong friends, announced the creation of the brewery and the launch of Muskoka Cream Ale. The success of the brewery is a shining example of how a vision can be achieved through sheer grit and determination, along with a good dose of savvy business know-how and solid research.

Bracebridge knows how to have fun, and how to mix this love of fun with celebrations of the community's heritage and values. In 1996 the Bracebridge Winter Carnival, held in the second week of February, was another solid success.

In January it was announced that the fabled Mariposa Folk Festival would be held in beautiful Annie Williams Park on the Muskoka River, on July 10. Deputy mayor Scott Northmore gave full credit for the coup to the town's director of culture and recreation, Leo Broere, as well as a group of enthusiastic and highly motivated community volunteers. Considered a success, the granddaddy (or grandmommy) of Canadian folk festivals featured headliner English blues legend Long John Baldry.

The Probus Club of Bracebridge No. 69 received its charter on September 11 under Arthur Richardson, Murray Griggs, and Ken Cumming.

Deaths this year included Harold Wilson, 84. Mr. Wilson was a Muskoka motorboat racing legend who, piloting his *Miss Canada III*, snatched the President's Gold Cup from the U.S.A. in 1939. Aboard the *Miss Canada IV*, Wilson set an unofficial North American water speed record in 1948 at 139 miles an hour.

During 1996 there was a major shakeup on the local newspaper scene. The *Herald-Gazette* ceased publication when its owner, Muskoka Publications Ltd., went bankrupt. The company also published papers in Gravenhurst and Huntsville, as well as the district weekly the *Muskoka Advance* and the *Muskoka Sun* in the summer. Edward Britton, publisher of the Bracebridge *Examiner*, Gravenhurst *Banner*, *The Muskokan*, and *The Weekender*, acquired the assets and retained the *Muskoka Sun* and *The Advance*. Several former Muskoka Publications employees banded together to start *The Times*, which as of 1999 publishes an on-line paper and the quarterly magazine *Vintage Muskoka* under Brad Hammond.

Bracebridge and sports are synonymous terms. Indoor, outdoor, on turf, on water, on snow, in the gym, or on the trails, sporting activities of all kinds continue to flourish and thrive in our town. In January the Metro Junior A Hockey League held the first ever league all-star game to be held outside of Toronto. Played in the Bracebridge Memorial Arena, the exciting game resulted in the East prevailing over the West 11-10, with three minutes and 57 seconds remaining in the overtime period.

In March, in the Memorial Arena, the Canadian National Hockey Team played the Czech national team to a 4-4 draw in a fast-paced and highly charged match ... Josh Faulkner, who played for the Bracebridge Bears Metro Junior A team, was awarded the Jim Quigley Memorial Trophy as Bracebridge's athlete of the year. In June Josh was drafted by the Peterborough Petes of the Ontario Hockey League ... Muskoka, including Bracebridge, is increasingly becoming known as a golf mecca. Riley Webb won Ontario and American tournaments for junior girls and chose to attend the University of New Mexico, which provided her with a full golf scholarship. In 1996 Riley was ranked the number one junior golfer in Ontario and 18th in the world ... In August, motorcyclist John Kehoe held a firm grip on top at the Canadian National Speedway championship.

The year 1996 drew to a close with the Festival of Lights and the annual Kinsmen Santa Claus parade.

*In 1997 Evelyn Brown became the first Director of Education for the newly formed Trillium Lakelands Board of Education.* COURTESY OF GARY DENNISS

**1997** Major changes this year included voting by mail in the November municipal elections and the start up of the 911 service in Muskoka.

On December 17, 1997, 911 became a reality for Muskoka. It had been five years of hard work with many obstacles overcome. The ceremony took place at the District office where District chairman Gord Adams symbolically "plugged" in the system. The Muskoka Falls Public School was on hand to sing at the ceremony. The cost of having the 911 service would be 32 cents a household each month – not much for having the peace of mind that comes with it.

There were both federal and municipal elections this year. In the June federal election, MP Andy Mitchell won the Parry Sound-Muskoka riding with 42 percent of the vote. He beat out Tory Lewis MacKenzie, who had 27 percent, and Reform candidate Peter Spadzinski, who had 26 percent.

The November municipal election was another first for Muskoka. This was the first year that alternative methods of voting were allowed. Bracebridge tried a "vote by mail" system which went like this. Beginning the week of October 20, electors received their "vote by mail" kits. Inside was a letter of explanation, a voter declaration form, a ballot, an inner ballot envelope, and a yellow postage-paid envelope. The voter completed the ballot and then inserted it into the inner ballot envelope, completed the voter declaration, and placed the form and sealed inner ballot envelope in the yellow envelope. It could then be mailed or dropped off at the municipal office. The deadline for the receipt of ballots was November 10, 1997, at 8:00 p.m. To ensure that ballots were received on time, they had to be mailed by November 3 at the latest.

Everything seemed to go off without a hitch and a new Bracebridge council was elected: Mayor Scott Northmore defeated former District councillor John Shier. Acclaimed were Al Taylor in Bracebridge Ward and Barry Young in Macaulay Ward. Elected were Jerry Fox in Draper, Barb McMurray in Oakley, and Edith Nichols in Muskoka-Monck. Bill Glennie, Heather Coupland, and John Kelly won seats on District Council. There was a 43 percent voter "turnout," up over the previous figures of 36 percent for the municipal election in 1994.

The year began on a sad note as tragedy struck the Cormack family. William Robert Cormack was killed when an out-of-control vehicle hit him head on. Icy roads were to blame. Mr. Cormack's daughters were also injured in the accident. Another tragedy later in the month, also due to bad weather, took the life of Trevor Schmidt of Bala. The head-on collision also landed eight people in hospital. In April, an all-terrain vehicle accident took the life of Christopher Blakely, 19, of Bracebridge

Fires took their toll on property and lives in 1997. In February, an estimated $250,000 damage was done to the chapel of the new medium security prison north of Gravenhurst. The fire rendered the chapel unsalvageable, but did not affect the opening of the new facility. In March, a fire caused $35,000 to $40,000 damage to the former Pentecostal Church on Ontario Street. The building was owned by Western Larch, a Woodbridge company. The cause of the blaze was believed to be a defective electrical heater used to heat the enclosed porch.

In May, a spectacular blaze ripped through the North-

*Bracebridge-based Muskoka Transport began an initiative to promote Muskoka across the continent with large Muskoka "rolling billboards" on the sides of some of its trailers. Standing in front of one with a Bracebridge theme are Paul Hammond of Muskoka Transport, councillors Edith Nichols, Al Taylor, and Jerry Fox, with clerk Murray Clarke and mayor Scott Northmore.* COURTESY OF THE TOWN OF BRACEBRIDGE

ern Buildall building on Entrance Drive, a Bracebridge landmark since 1925 when George Reid's grandfather established the Northern Planing Mills. Since then, the building had undergone several name changes. The first call came between 4:30 and 5:00 p.m., but when firefighters arrived, the building was fully engulfed in flames. The owners, George and Alana Reid, could do nothing but stand and watch. Train traffic on the CNR had to be halted for several hours. Damage was estimated at in excess of $500,000, but could have been much worse had it not been for the efforts of the Bracebridge Fire Department. The small cottage-like structure on the property was not damaged and served as a temporary office.

In November, at approximately 5:15 a.m., OPP were called to a fire at a Queen Street home. Two people had escaped the blaze, but Jamie Dunlop went back into the house to save his girlfriend, Michelle Mueller, and perished along with her and friend Mark Woodruff. All three worked at the Meritor Plant on Ecclestone Drive. Their co-workers were stunned by the news and out of respect, the flag flew at half mast.

Just one week before Christmas, fire destroyed the Pegg home. There were two units in the house where John and Ingrid Pegg and Jennifer and John Pegg resided. The call came into the 911 service at 1:45 p.m., just two hours after the service had been activated.

In the new year, the Muskoka Board of Education learned that it would be amalgamated with the Haliburton and Victoria County boards of education, this is in a move by the provincial government to reduce the existing 129 boards of education down to 66 new district boards. There would also be a reduction in the number of trustees from 1,900 to about 700. In the fall, Evelyn Brown was appointed acting director of the new school board.

In other school news, an alternative school year was offered at Bracebridge and Gravenhurst Public Schools this year. There were 70 students who began classes at Bracebridge Public School in August, instead of September. There were three groups: primary (grades 1-3); junior (grades 4-6); and intermediate (grades 7 and 8). The students got a two-week break at Thanksgiving and two weeks at March break. They also got the same Christmas holidays as the regular school year students. It was felt that students retain what they learn better with shorter breaks in between.

*Skateboarder Jason Wyda demonstrating his skills. The popularity of this activity prompted construction of a skateboard park near the Rotary Youth Centre in Jubilee Park.* COURTESY OF IAN FRANKS

Teachers in Muskoka joined a province-wide illegal strike on October 27. The strike which lasted two weeks, disrupted classrooms, and caused mixed feelings in the community.

Those we said good-bye to in 1997 included Leda Scovell, 93. She moved to Bracebridge when she was an infant and lived in her home on Kimberley Avenue until 1989, when she moved to The Pines. She attended both public and high schools in Bracebridge. Following Normal School, she returned to Bracebridge to teach Grade One. She retired in 1963 after 40 years of teaching. She donated a piano for the new addition to the United Church in 1931. Miss Scovell was an active member of the community. In 1986, the Rotary Club made her Citizen of the Year ... Her father, Holland Rockwell Scovell, was inspector of public schools until his death in 1923 ... Kirk Evans, 28, co-owner of the Lakes of Muskoka Cottage Brewery. Hundreds of friends and relatives gathered to pay their respects at a memorial service held at the Bracebridge Centennial Centre. Kirk was involved in an early morning car accident in August, 1996, and had been in hospital ever since. He appeared to be doing well, when he contracted a flu virus. The whole community was saddened by his death ... Rene Lacroix, 47, died of a massive heart attack. He had been a barber on Manitoba Street since 1970. He was known for his sense of humour and a zest for life. His daughter carried on his business.

Bracebridge had some lucky people in 1997. Beatrice Dunn, a South Muskoka Memorial Hospital worker, was the first ever Encore $250,000 grand prize winner for Super 7. She purchased her ticket at Armstrong's Variety on Manitoba Street. The business received $1,000 for selling a winning ticket. Betty Fleger won $1,088,043.10 in Lotto 649. She retired after 30 years at Rockwell.

Some interesting events took place this year. The Bracebridge Kinsmen celebrated their 50th anniversary with a gala dinner and dance. There were over 100 guests, including some prominent past Kinsmen: long-time former mayor Jim Lang, Don Coates, Bruce McPhail, and

John Shier. The 11-member Kinsmen Club was responsible for putting on one of the best Santa Claus Parades ever and also for the fantastic fireworks display on July 1.

The BMLSS Student Parliament volunteered at the 6th Special Olympics held in Collingwood in February. This was an international event with over 2,000 athletes from 90 countries. There were 500 coaches, 2,000 friends and family, and over 3,000 volunteers at this year's Olympics. The students from BMLSS helped at the alpine skiing event. They donated their time to travel for training and orientation and paid their own board. Thanks to many donations from the community, as well as the students' own efforts at fund-raising, they were able to have the experience of a lifetime.

Councillor Heather Coupland prodded Town Council to make plans for the 125th anniversary of the village of Bracebridge in the year 2000. Don Coates was appointed chairman and Ken Veitch vice-chairman of a committee to plan for this celebration. This book you are reading is a direct outcome of that step.

The Rotary Club of Bracebridge honoured Jerry Fox, 58, as Citizen of the Year. Jerry has been a fan of the fall fair for many years and was instrumental in moving its location. He had recently retired from Northern Buildall, after 37 years. He had been a member of the Bracebridge Fire Department for 42 years. Paul Hammond presented the award to Jerry.

Evelyn Finlayson, artistic director of Bracebridge School of Ballet, was awarded the Enrico Cecchetti Diploma by the chairman of the Canadian Cecchetti Ballet Society. She was one of only 12 people in Canada to pass the gruelling exam and hold this degree covering Cecchetti's life work.

On June 7, Ontario premier Mike Harris was on hand to officially reopen Windermere House. The new Windermere House was constructed around the original historic stonework. The exterior design was as faithful to the original as current building code and materials permitted. The inside was replicated to the best of the design team's ability. The dignitaries arrived by steamer as they would have when the grand lady first opened. There was a formal ribbon-cutting ceremony on the original stone verandah. During the evening a gala event was held.

In August, the Strawberry Point Lookout Trail was opened to the public. The trail is just over a kilometre long and leads to one of the most scenic lookouts over Lake Muskoka. This trail would not have happened had it not been for all the hundreds of volunteer hours of many dedicated people.

October 1 marked the beginning of a five-year contract between the District and Extendicare for the management of The Pines Long Term Care facility in Bracebridge.

Muskoka Lakes Cottage Brewery won the prestigious People's Choice gold medal award for its Muskoka Cream Ale at the Great Canadian Brewing Festival held in Guelph. There were 20 breweries competing in the three-day event. The gold medal that they won the year before was a thrill, but the Peoples Choice award was even more rewarding.

This year saw the first annual Santa Lights Up Bracebridge Contest. Prizes were donated by both Bracebridge Hydro and Ontario Hydro, and several local businesses. The winners in the residential category were the Nickles at 206 Maple Street, the Kirks on Purbrook Road, the Bolands at 25 Wellington Street, the Leeders at 75 Glendale Road, the Takacs at 15 Ridge Valley Drive, and the Coulters on Coulters Lane. Sweet Cremes won the commercial-retail division while James Street Place won for institutions.

Bracebridge had many promising young athletes, too many to mention them all, so here is just a sampling. In January, the BMLSS badminton players competed in the Georgian Bay District Badminton Association Junior Championship in Midland. The came home bringing the gold and silver. Kate Wood won two gold medals, Amy Schroter and Sean Willis won the U16 mixed, Jake Einarson took the silver in the U20 singles, and Jon Waterman and Jake Einarson took the silver in the U20 doubles … Kendra Medley, 19, who skated with the Bracebridge Blades Precision team for 10 years, was now skating with the Burlington Ice Image senior team. Kendra was also a singles skater. The Burlington team represented the western section of Canada at the Canadian championship in Halifax … Also in skating news, Miranda Hall, 19, became a member of the Black Ice senior precision skating team while studying at York University. The 27-mem-

*Leading the town into the new millennium, the 1998-2000 Bracebridge Council and senior administrative staff. Left to right: clerk-administrator Murray Clarke, councillors John Kelly, Edith Nichols, Jerry Fox, and Barry Young, Mayor Scott Northmore, councillors Barbara McMurray, Allen G. Taylor, and Bill Glennie, treasurer Andy Nelan, and councillor Heather Coupland (in front of Mr. Glennie).* COURTESY OF THE TOWN OF BRACEBRIDGE

ber team won the senior gold medal at the National Precision Championships in Halifax. This event qualified the team to attend the World Challenge Cup in Turku Finland in early April, where they also won the gold medal. Then back at home, Miranda was awarded the Jim Quigley Award as the 1997 Bracebridge Athlete of the Year … Michelle Mellow, an accomplished rower who competed in the 1996 Olympics in Atlanta, spoke to students at the BMLSS athletics awards. Mike Bridle and Jenn Faulkner were presented with the senior athlete-of-the-year awards, while Ben Serwaczek and Kelly Slater won for juniors.

Kris King, a 31-year-old Bracebridge native, signed a four-year contract with the Toronto Maple Leafs. The year before he played left wing for the Phoenix Coyotes (formerly the Winnipeg Jets). He began his hockey career in Gravenhurst minor hockey, then Gravenhurst Junior C. He played his first NHL game on December 27, 1987, with Detroit. Not only was he a good hockey player but he did charitable work too, winning the 1995-96 King Clancy Award. Kris and his wife, Paula, now lived in Peterborough with their three children … Bracebridge bade a fond farewell to the Muskoka Bears, a Metro Toronto Junior A team based out of the Bracebridge Arena this year.

1998 The year began with El Nino making its presence felt with unusually warm temperatures, causing unsafe lake conditions. The mild weather wreaked havoc on winter activities, such as snowmobiling, skating, and skiing. Then in the second week of January the "Big Ice Storm" hit eastern Ontario and Quebec and northern parts of the United States. Although Muskoka did not suffer the effects of the storm, our communities pulled together to send help. Four OPP officers, Ray Dawson, Shawn Campbell, Dave Moffatt, and Larry Butterfield, went to help with security, traffic control, and the transporting of food and supplies to those without electricity. The Bracebridge and Gravenhurst Rotarians filled a tractor trailer with donations of blankets, wood, nonperishable food items, and generators. The trailer was sent to Drummondville, Quebec, where some people were without electricity for weeks.

By early April, the North Branch of the Muskoka River, along with the Black River, flooded their banks causing minor road washouts. The volume of water was just what the 1st Annual Festival of the Falls needed to show visitors how spectacular the falls really are. The festival that took place on May 2 was a great success. Buses took visitors to view some of the area waterfalls as well as displays and entertainment.

After the flood waters receded, the dry spell came. A total fire ban for the area was imposed by the District of Muskoka fire chiefs from mid-April to mid-May following a rash of careless brush fires. Then Mother Nature unleashed her fury on Muskoka on May 31, when a major storm hit Bracebridge, downing huge trees, knocking out power, and flooding streets. Cable service was disrupted and Moose 100-FM was knocked off the air. Fortunately, there were no injuries.

In June there was a water problem of another sort when a water main at the corner of Ontario and Manitoba streets burst at 5:30 p.m. Monday, June 15, flooding the intersection. It turned out to be an eight-inch main with cast iron leaded joints that had been installed about 60 years earlier. The water had to be turned off while District employees worked all night to make the repairs.

Bracebridge lost many citizens this past year. The town was in shock when they learned of the death of John Shier at age 47. Mr. Shier had a heart attack while at home. John served on Town and District Council 1994-1997. He had just recently been appointed to a three-year term as a member of the Bracebridge Hydro Commission. In 1975 he joined Shier's Insurance, a company that had been founded by his grandfather. He was a great asset to the business community and would be sadly missed.

Ernie Keall, 77, was a long-time Bracebridge Hydro manager. He grew up on a dairy farm where the Covered Bridge subdivision is now. He began as a powerhouse operator in the early 1950s. He had just delivered a speech at a retirement party when he suffered a heart attack.

Robert "R.J." Shortreed, 57, of R.J. Hairstyling, had suffered a closed head injury while doing carpentry work at his winter home in Costa Rica on March 12. He became unconscious and remained in Costa Rica until April 26, when he was stable enough to be moved to London Ontario's Health Science Centre. His family hoped he would be moving to Bracebridge to convalesce, but he took a turn for the worse and never regained consciousness ... G. Wilson Boyer, 81, a past publisher of the *Herald-Gazette* and later, after moving to Fort Erie in 1973, worked for the Fort Erie *Times Review*. He was instrumental in establishing the *Muskoka Sun*. Mr. Boyer was an avid curler and he loved music. While in Bracebridge he was an active member of the Rotary Club and served a year as president of the Lions Club ... The town was in shock to hear of the tragic death of Sarah Leeder at age 16. Sarah died of an allergic reaction to peanuts. Sarah was a graduate of Macaulay Public School and had just finished Grade 9 at BMLSS and was enjoying her summer job ... Wayland Drew, 65, a retired BMLSS school teacher and author, best known for *Halfway Man*, *Wabeno Feast*, and *Superior:The Haunted Shore*. Wayland was a founder of the Bracebridge Historical Society and the Woodchester Villa and Museum.

The youth of Bracebridge are tomorrow's future and with these fine examples, Bracebridge will be in good hands. Courtney Doran, 19, a student at BMLSS, played for the North York Aeros women's hockey team. She travelled back and forth to Toronto, playing a total 130 games in the season. The Aeros won the All-Ontario Provincial Championship for women 21 years and under. ... Ryley Webb, a former Bracebridge Athlete of the Year, continued her success as a golfer. Ryley was attending the University of New Mexico where she continued to maintain her academic standing as well. The New Mexico team placed 4th in the Western Athletic Conference Championships, while Ryley placed 2nd in the individual title race. She was also named the Western Athletic Conference Freshman of the Year. Later in the season Ryley placed 6th in the individual race in the NCAA Championship ... Kristy Mulligan and Bryan Oates set new records at the 8th annual Cardinal Carter Track Classic held in Etobicoke. There were 2,700 athletes from 142 Ontario schools participating in this event. Kristy Mulligan's record of 11:27.9 for the Junior Girls 3,000 metres beat Ryley Webb's record set in 1994 ... Bryan Oates' junior boys 800-metre record of 2:04.1 broke the old record held by Greg Broadworth and Ken Hawthorn. Later in the year, Kristy was given the award for best junior female athlete of the year. Andrew Mackay was given the award for best junior male. The senior awards went to Justin Faulkner and Tracey McNabb. These awards are given to individuals involved in two or more sports, who attend practice regularly, are team players, and encouraging to others, in addition to their own personal achievements. Bryan Oates was awarded the Jim Quigley Award at a ceremony held at the Town Hall, for his achievements on the cross-country running and track teams.

Miranda Hall, a former Bracebridge Blades Precision Skating Team member, who now skated for the Black Ice Precision Team, won gold at the Canadian Championships and then silver at the World Challenge Cup in France on Easter weekend ... Leanne Stewart received the Muriel Gibbs Triple Gold Achievement Award. She was the second member of the Bracebridge Figure Skating Club to achieve gold in free skate, dance, and level 1 skills.

The BMLSS Dixie Land Band won gold at the Collingwood music festival in March, earning them a spot at the National MusicFest in Vancouver, BC, in May, where they also won gold. Band members were Stacey Combdon, Heather Graham, Frazer Pritchard, Joe Manuge, Theo Tzavedas, Chris Smid, Sean Willis, Tracy O'Donnell.

In March, David Reid, owner of the Albion Hotel, discovered some old topographical maps of the site dating back to 1852. They were original Geological Survey of Canada maps of the rivers of Muskoka drawn by Alexander Murray, Esq., under the direction of Sir William E. Logan. There was also a link to a recreational backwoods trip taken by an Oshawa crew detailed in an October 4, 1865, *Toronto Globe*. The crew of four is known to have included the reeve of Oshawa, D.F. Burk, and native guide Charles Jacobs of Rama. An account of their expedition is given in the book *Muskoka and Haliburton*, as well as Alexander Murray's report of his expeditions.

This year marked the 100th anniversary of curling in Bracebridge. The first curling rink was built in 1898 and since then there had been three other locations. The present rink celebrated its 25th anniversary this year.

On Tuesday, April 14, the South Muskoka Memorial Hospital opened Phase I of its expansion and renovation. Phase I included a new CCU (Chronic Care Unit) providing more space for the CCU beds and equipment. Patients were moved in once the new equipment arrived. On hand to help cut the ribbon celebrating the opening was Bill Grimmett. Not only was the project completed on time, but also on budget. Phase II of the project will see a new emergency room.

Also in April, the Town of Bracebridge and the Bracebridge Public Library made a deal to establish and operate a branch at the new Medium Security Prison, Fenbrook. Fenbrook would pay $11,000 in management fees and there would be an additional 35 hours of work available to library staff. As well, library patrons would have access to 10,000 new books and the town collection would be available to prisoners.

In other library news, the Bracebridge Public Library received grants to purchase computer software and hired a student to teach the public how to use the software and the Internet. Heather Arsenault, a University of Waterloo computer/math student, also informed the business community about the risks of the Y2K millennium bug. The library had four computers for public use.

The Town of Bracebridge launched its website, made possible with a grant from the federal ministry of industry. The site was designed by Karl Tellman of Wannaweb. The address is www.town.bracebridge.on.ca. The site has information about the town with links to the library, Rene Caisse and Essiac, and other interesting topics.

Muskoka went on the road. Muskoka Transport now had twenty 53-foot tractor-trailers with eye-catching images of Muskoka displayed on the sides. These trailers travel the roads throughout the eastern U.S. from Maine to Texas and all points in between. This exciting initiative was the brainchild of Paul Hammond, owner of Muskoka Transport. Partners in this project included the federal

*In spring, High Falls always puts on an awesome display as the North Muskoka roars over a cliff surrounded by majestic white pines. It is one of the star attractions in the Festival of the Falls.* COURTESY OF GARY LONG

government, province of Ontario, area municipalities of the District of Muskoka, but would not have been possible without the generous support from Alpine Graphics, the 3M Company, and Molson Brewery.

A fire at the Wellington Street Plaza caused major smoke and water damage to all 10 units. Damage was estimated at one million dollars. The units at the north end suffered from the effects of the fire the most. The Ontario fire marshall's office and the Muskoka crime unit investigated the fire, which was started by vandals. The grand reopening of the plaza was held on October 24, only five months after the fire.

Another grand reopening took place August 21-23 at Northern Buildall, after more than a year of hard work. It, too, had been destroyed by fire. The old building contained 6,500 square feet of heated and 1,500 square feet of unheated space, while the new building had 10,000 square feet of heated space. The staff remained at 23 with a couple of changes through retirement.

The 4th Annual Air Show was held in May. The weekend began at a hangar party on the Friday night with a dance featuring the Legends of Rock & Roll. This year saw the return of the Snowbirds, Canada's premier flying acrobatic team. Other acts included Bill Carter in his Pitts S2B bi-plane, Walt Addison Linscott in his Russian Black Magic, Canadian Harvards, and the Hamilton Sport Jumpers. The show was a great success with actual attendance figures between 20,000 and 25,000.

The new, state-of-the-art medium security prison, Fenbrook, opened its doors to its first group of inmates in August. At full capacity it will house approximately 400 prisoners. One building houses a library, a school program, and a gym where inmates will be able to get their Grade 10 equivalency and attend workshops. The buildings were equipped with heat sensors to control the climate, thus saving money. There was also a hospital with operating rooms, dentists, doctors, and nurses. The new facility would employ 249 people, many of them local.

In November, Bracebridge officially welcomed the Crown Group of Companies. The Michigan-based company built its first Canadian Crown facility, a plastic-finishing plant across from Scandura. It was expected to employ approximately 50 workers.

Some more of Bracebridge's finest: Bruce Evans was chosen the Rotary Club's Citizen of the Year for 1998. Mr. Evans was the chairman and CEO of Evanco Corporation. The companies under the Evanco umbrella employed over 600 people in Muskoka. Mr. Evans was also the head of the South Muskoka Memorial Hospital fund-raising campaign ... John Gray received the Medal of Bravery for saving the life of Sarah Falkanger in April 1996. Sarah was five years old when she fell into the fast-flowing waters of the Muskoka River. Mr. Gray risked his own life to jump into the icy waters to save her. He received his award from Governor General, Romeo LeBlanc, in a ceremony held in Ottawa ... Judge Douglas Bice retired after 32 years of serving on the bench.

And to end the year, the town celebrated with its 5th Annual Festival of the Lights on Friday, November 27. Santa arrived around 6:00 p.m. and the ceremonies began. There were fireworks, the lighting of the silver bridge, and the parade up the main street to Memorial Park. Bracebridge also had its 2nd annual Light Up Bracebridge contest and of course the annual Santa Claus Parade put together by the Kinsmen.

*The fire department put its water cannon to good use fighting this major blaze at the Muskoka Containerized Services recycling plant.* COURTESY OF DON COATES

## 1999

The shoe, in this case the snowshoe, was on the other foot as Muskokans watched in amusement as Toronto was paralyzed for several days by a major snowfall. While Bracebridge did experience significant snowfall activity over a sustained period, by working long days round the clock, town crews were able to keep our roadways clear. Noting that the public works department was prepared for major snowfall events, town engineer Ron Walton remarked, "Sometimes snow doesn't fall at a convenient time either." He was very likely thinking back to December 1995!

The heavy snows didn't throw a blanket over retail sales. Ron Doty, owner of the Canadian Tire, and George MacNaughtan, owner of MacNaughtan's Home Hardware, both reported that stocks of snowblowers had completely sold out.

Paul Shaughnessy of the Muskoka Snow Region (MSR) cautioned that the snow cover resulted in poor ice conditions on area lakes and waterways; the MSR and the Ontario Provincial Police warned snowmobilers to stay off lakes and rivers.

"Once in a blue moon" may suggest infrequency, but in January and again in March the night sky lit up with two full moons in each of those months.

In January, Jan and Peter Rickard announced the sale of the Inn at the Falls to Deborah Prychidny and Leonard Alksnis. In 11 years of working long hours each day, the Rickards transformed the former Holiday House into a world class inn. Featuring a spectacular view over Bracebridge Bay, the falls, and the Silver Bridge, the operation expanded to include former private homes along the entire block of Dominion Street up to Ontario Street.

At the Riverside Inn, owners Brenda and Don McGillis celebrated the grand opening of the new indoor pool and fitness centre facility. Joining in were mayor Scott Northmore, deputy mayor Al Taylor, councillors Bill Glennie and Edith Nichols, as well as town CAO Murray Clarke. Also participating were Ken Veitch and Bob Dolphin of the town's economic development committee. Brenda and Don were justifiably proud of this addition to the Inn, which had evolved into a destination, much more than simply a hotel.

Buoyed by the official registration of the Bracebridge

section of the Trans Canada Trail, the town's parkland and trails committee, under the leadership of Dr. David Kent, embarked on a major campaign to raise funds and attract volunteers for trails development. Frank Denniss, 91, a lifelong resident of the Springdale Park area of town, was celebrated as the first donor to the trails fund. Mr. Denniss, who recalled walking to high school and crossing Wilson's Falls on a log boom, said he thought recreational trails were a great idea. From the number of inquiries about our trails system and the increasing use by residents and visitors, clearly many agreed with Mr. Denniss.

Ron Walton was managing the process to construct the new sections of the trail, including the installation of a bridge at High Falls. Town Council also agreed to include Bracebridge in the Relay 2000 event. The relay will be an active, mobile celebration designed to mark the official opening of the Trans Canada Trail. Water will be drawn simultaneously from the three oceans bordering Canada, and from April to September some 2,000 carriers will transport this water along the trail to the National Capital Region. On September 9, 2000, the water will be poured ceremoniously into a newly created Trans Canada Trail Fountain, which will operate in perpetuity as a symbol of our collective achievement. The relay event will be held in Bracebridge in early August, 2000.

*In the 1920s and earlier, fire-fighting equipment was a bit more primitive – a fire wagon pulled by a team of horses. The team was engaged in road work when not responding to blazes.* COURTESY OF IAN TURNBULL

The annual Bracebridge Winter Carnival, held in the second week of February was once again a rousing success. Under the leadership of Linda Boon, who appears to have an inexhaustible store of energy, the carnival was a big hit with residents and visitors to town.

On February 27 a King Air B100 aircraft crashed in a bush area just off Hugh Campbell Drive, only 200 metres from a nearby residence. The pilot and his 14-year-old son were both transported to Toronto hospitals after being taken to South Muskoka Memorial Hospital. Bracebridge firefighters attended at the scene to assist with removal of the plane's two occupants.

In February Russ Hogg retired after 27 years as general manager of the Bracebridge Hydro Electric Commission. At a reception held in his honour, Russ explained his plan to continue in his retirement to concentrate on poles and lines, from his fishing boat! Chris Litschko took over the general manager's post, moving to town from the Dunnville Hydro Commission.

The town's building department released 1998 permit activity data showing that the $17.9-million construction value total was up in excess of $3 million over 1997. Deputy mayor Al Taylor, chair of the development services committee, expressed optimism that the 1998 values would be exceeded this year. First quarter statistics released in early April suggest that councillor Taylor's prediction might be realized.

The second annual Bracebridge Festival of the Falls was held April 30 and May 1 and 2 under clear skies and unseasonably warm, actually hot, temperatures. Led by councillor Edith Nichols, an expanded group of volunteers put together a creative and entertaining program. The Waterwalker Film Festival of the Canadian Recreational Canoeing Association kicked off the event and its

*At the opening ceremony of the Second Annual Festival of the Falls, councillor Al Taylor, portraying an old-fashioned "Town Father," greets "voyageur" Murray Clarke.*
COURTESY OF THE TOWN OF BRACEBRIDGE

popularity was evident with a sell-out crowd filling the auditorium of the high school. The film program was hosted by canoeing legend Kirk Wipper and featured a lyrical and compelling slide and spoken work presentation by renowned outdoorsman Hap Wilson and his partner Stephanie Ackroyd. Deputy mayor Allen Taylor, resplendent in his period suit and top hat, hosted the opening ceremony held at the historic hydro generating station at the foot of Bracebridge Falls. On Saturday evening the Festival held an old-time street dance on Manitoba Street, the first street dance in Bracebridge's downtown core since 1945. The central theme of the Festival is a celebration of Bracebridge's 22 waterfalls, more than any other municipality in Canada, or so we claim!

Deaths up to July 1999 included Mr. Lloyd Edward (Ted) Crozier, 61, son of late Lloyd Crozier and Mildred Austin. He lived all of his life in Bracebridge working as a plumber and builder ... Myra Victoria Oates, nee Johnston, 92, wife of the late Joseph (Kelly) Oats ... Norah Elizabeth Hoad, nee Finlay, 85 ... William Herbert Smith, 81, born in Falkenburg, the youngest of five children of the late Mr. and Mrs. William and Grace (Glass) Smith, married Joan Love in 1942. He was married 56 years and had three sons. Mr. Smith was very active in the community with some 20 years with Meals On Wheels, Manna Food Bank, and the Chamber of Commerce ... Kenneth Henry Devitt, 59, electrician ... Mrs. Anna Hunt, sister of Rev. M. Joseph Lynch of River Street and sister of the late Monsignor O'Leary ... Mavis Julia Jackson at The Pines, wife of the late George W. Jackson, sister of former premier Frank Miller.

During the spring, the Crown Group launched a campaign to recruit personnel for the new automotive finishing plant located on District Road 118 across from Scandura Industries. The 55,000-square-foot facility was a joint venture with Algonquin Automotive, a strong presence in the Muskoka industrial community. Production at the plant was slated to begin in late summer.

This major new investment in Bracebridge was contingent on extension of trunk sewer service to the site. Town officials were confident that this important infrastructure expansion would spark additional interest and attract new investment in the municipality.

In June, the District of Muskoka was putting the finishing touches on the reconstruction of Manitoba Street from Taylor Road to McDonald Street. The project, costing nearly one million dollars, amounts to a roadway and sidewalk facelift along that section of the town's main street. During the same period, crews were completing reconstruction of Quebec Street from Dominion Street right in front of Town Hall, to McMurray Street at the high school.

Effective April 1, the service area of the Bracebridge Hydro Electric Commission expanded to take in 3,200 customers formerly serviced by Ontario Hydro, thereby completing a process begun three years previously. The price tag to acquire Ontario Hydro assets within the expansion area totalled $6.2 million.

During April and early May, unusually warm weather combined with minimal rainfall to create very low water levels in area lakes and rivers. The dry conditions prompted District of Muskoka fire chiefs to impose a total ban on outside burning. The Bracebridge Hydro Electric Commission noted that the low flows in the Muskoka River could present a problem for the system's hydro generating stations. On the positive side, there were little or no spring flood conditions along the district's waterways.

In late April Ontario premier Mike Harris announced that a provincial election would be held on June 3. On election eve, the premier, along with Ernie Eves, the Tory candidate for the newly configured riding of Parry Sound-Muskoka, led an old-fashioned rally for supporters in the Bracebridge Centennial Centre. The event was marred by the arrest of five persons who participated in a large protest outside the meeting hall. No charges were laid. The Harris Progressive Conservatives swept back into power with a majority government. Ernie Eves won handily in the local contest.

During the campaign Bracebridge received wonderful news. The province finally approved a grant in excess of $8 million toward renovation and expansion of South Muskoka Memorial Hospital. Along with the revenue from the Hospital Foundation's remarkable fund-raising campaign and a commitment from the District of Muskoka, the project was expected to proceed later in 1999. During a groundbreaking ceremony on the grounds of the hospital District of Muskoka chair Gord Adams noted that some might regard the provincial announcement during an election campaign with cynicism. His response was, "Who cares, we're getting the money!"

Bracebridge is the heart of Muskoka and our hospital is the heart of our town.

Following a fun-filled campaign to seek public input on a name and artwork for a label, in May the Lakes of Muskoka Cottage Brewery launched a new product called Muskoka Steam Beer. Based on the only brewing method indigenous to North America, the new product was an instant hit, a companion for the successful Muskoka Cream Ale introduced in 1996. Owners Bo and Gary McMullen generously volunteered to donate a portion of sales revenues from the new beer to the 125th anniversary program of Bracebridge and to the 100th birthday celebration of the Town of Huntsville.

On May 18 a devastating fire swept through the recycling plant owned by Muskoka Containerized Services.

*Celebrating 25-plus years of service in June 1999 are (left to right) Sidney Rosenblatt, Terry Handy, Ivy Joynt, Morris Hudasek, Val Welcher, Mary Soucie, and Gary Handy.* COURTESY OF DONNA BENSON

*The champs! The Bracebridge Legion Fastball Team outscored the opposition 16-2 in five games to take the Eastern Canadian Intermediate B Fastpitch title.* Front row (left to right): *Mike Crawford, Bill Leonard, Randy Carr, Ted Conway, Ryan Boyes;* second row: *Brian Harrington, Grant Patterson, Bill Michel, Trevor Murphy, Mike Kupsch, Tony Peacock;* third row: *Colin Newell, Mike Tzekas, Clint Boland, Ken Veitch, Dan Beaudry, David McLaughlin, and Shawn Lee.* COURTESY OF KEN VEITCH

The 5,500-square-foot building and its contents were a total loss. The Bracebridge Fire Department, assisted by neighbouring fire brigades, fought the spectacular blaze using over 1.5 million gallons of water. Don Coates, vice president of MCS, assured the community that recycling collection service would continue with no interruptions.

Meritor announced a $1.5-million expansion of their Bracebridge factory … At a Council meeting held on June 9, Chuck Schwartz of the Home Depot announced that the giant household products retailer had committed to establish a store in Bracebridge. The location, a 35-acre parcel at Taylor Road and Highway 11, would require full planning approvals, including an official plan amendment and rezoning. Town Council and staff anticipate the project would generate significant interest from residents and the existing retail community.

Council approved the purchance of an Emergency Response and Fireboat in partnership with the Tri Island and Browning Island Cottager's Association (Lake Muskoka).

Grace and Lew Ringham celebrated their 50th wedding anniversary in October, as did Morris and Phyllis Topping.

A Wayland Drew Award was presented to avid birder Bob Burton for his work with the Muskoka Naturalists and his great achievement of getting the bluebird off the endangered species list. The award was also presented to David Leeder for his environmental efforts at BMLSS and for being co-founder of the Envirothon Club … Saying she was honoured and shocked, 18-year-old BMLSS graduate Brittany Mathers was named the recipient of the Jim Quigley Memorial Trophy as Bracebridge's Athlete of the Year. Active in basketball and track and field, Brittany would attend Queen's University in the fall to study physical education. Her goal was to establish a career as a sports therapist.

In August, the provincial government announced it intented to continue the local government reform initiative begun during the previous term. The minister of municipal affairs issued a directive to compel four regions to develop recommendations by November to reduce the size and cost of municipal government, while the District of Muskoka was among a second group targeted for reform. It is anticipated that this reform agenda will stimulate debate and dialogue across Muskoka and involve all stakeholders, our residents, ratepayers, elected representative, and municipal staff. The process is expected to include an examination of the existing system, and the development of a range of options and recommendations to improve the delivery of municipal programs and services. The desired outcome is to reinforce the tradition of excellence in Muskoka local governance.

On September 12, the Bracebridge Legion men's fastball team won the eight-team Eastern Canadian Intermediate B Fastpitch Championship in North River, Nova Scotia. Mike Crawford pitched a no-hitter in one game and was named the tournament's Most Valuable Pitcher. Trevor Murphy had the highest batting average. Town Council hosted a reception at Kerr Park on October 3 to honour the team's fine achievement.

As 1999 advances, planning for the town's 125th anniversary in 2000 accelerates. Projects include the book you are holding, a commemorative coin, a special Canada Post stamp, gala ball, homecoming, collector's calendar, parades, and a special fireworks show, Mayor's levee, a historical mural, a theatrical production, anniversary quilt, a private label wine, a historical homes plaque project, special garden, and many other activities and events.

Along with Muskoka Arts and Crafts, the town has committed to create a sculpture garden on the grounds of the Bird Mill Mews. Significantly, Council elected to mark the anniversary by committing $150,000 toward the expansion and renovation of the South Muskoka Memorial Hospital.

The first official function of the anniversary committee took place in the Council chamber on June 5, to recognize the passing of Victoria County bylaw Number 162 on June 5, 1874. That bylaw established the original Village of Bracebridge effective January 1, 1875. On hand to join in the celebration was Victoria County warden John Macklem and his wife, Darleen.

As we approach the year 2000, Bracebridge looks to the next Millennium with optimism and hope. With the rich heritage of its past, and a bright future ahead, the Heart of Muskoka will continue to beat steadily and with undiminished vigour.

*At the inaugural meeting of the Bracebridge Centennial Council, January 8, 1975, George A. Parlett (right) hands over the gavel to mayor-elect James Lang. Retiring as mayor at the end of 1974, Parlett had served in the position for 12 years – more than any other person up until that time. Lang then held the position for next 20 years.* COURTESY OF THE TOWN OF BRACEBRIDGE

# MUNICIPAL POLITICIANS

## *Bracebridge Reeves, Mayors, and Councillors*

*Reeves*

Robert E. Perry 1875-76
J.W. Dill 1877-78/81-83
John Smith 1879-80
Alfred Hunt 1884-85
James P. Humphries 1886
William Kirk 1887
S.H. Armstrong 1888-89

*Mayors*

S.H. Armstrong *1889-90, 1907-10*
Walter W. Kinsey *1891*
James Dollar *1892*
Alfred Hunt *1893-95*
Singleton Brown *1896-98*
John Thomson *1899-1901*
James D. Shier *1902-03*
Peter A. Smith *1904-6, 1914-15, 1922*
P. Hutchison *1911*
G.W. Ecclestone *1912-13*
G.H.O. Thomas *1916-17, 1926-29*
Alex Walker *1918*
Jos. G. Myers *1919*
A. Wattie *1920-21*
Henry J. Bird Jr. *1923-24*
G.W. Boyer *1925*
Geo. Gibson *1930-31*
Wilbert Richards *1932-36*
B. McBride *1937-41*
E.A. Whitten *1942-45*
Dr. A.F. Bastedo *1946-49*
Dr. L.N. Ryan *1950-53*
Nelson A. Goltz *1954-55*
Glen S. Coates *1956-58*
E.W. Reid *1959-62*
George A. Parlett *1963-74*
James D. Lang *1975-94*
A. Russ Black *1995-98*
Scott Northmore *1998-2000*

*Bracebridge Council*

*1875*
Robert E. Perry *reeve*
H.J. McDonald
Joseph Cooper
James Clerihue
John Smith

*1876*
Robert E. Perry *reeve*
John Smith
Jacob W. Dill
Joseph Cooper
James Clerihue
John Topp

*1877*
Jacob W. Dill *reeve*
John Smith
R.Whipp
Alfred Hunt

*1878*
Jacob W. Dill *reeve*
John Smith
Joseph Cooper
T.M.Bowerman
Henry J. Bird

*1879*
John Smith *reeve*
E.F. Stephenson
James Langdon
Joseph Cooper

*1880*
John Smith *reeve*
T.M. Bowerman
Alexander Later
James Langdon
Joseph Cooper
R.H. Browning

*1881*
J.W. Dill *reeve*
George J. Beattie
Thomas Myers
Joseph Cooper
R.M. Browning

*1882*
J.W. Dill *reeve*
Alfred Hunt
Thomas Myers
Joseph Cooper
R.M. Browning

*1883*
J.W. Dill *reeve*
T. Bowerman
John Haw
S. Armstrong
R.M. Browning

*1884*
Alfred Hunt *reeve*
J.P. Humphries
S.H. Armstrong
Richard Swain
John Leishman

*1885*
Alfred Hunt *reeve*
J.P. Humphries
S.H. Armstrong
T. Bowerman
John Leishman

*1886*
J.P. Humphries *reeve*
Wm. Simmons
John Leishman
John Dollar
Richard Swain

*1887*
William Kirk *reeve*
Richard Swain
John Leishman
S. Armstrong
Singleton Brown

*1888*
S.H. Armstrong *reeve*
Singleton Brown
John Leishman
T.M. Bowerman
Walter W. Kinsey

*1889*
S.H. Armstrong *reeve*
Walter W. Kinsey
William Sibbett
Richard Swain
Henry L. Bowyer

*1889*
*(Town of Bracebridge)*
S.H. Armstrong *mayor*
John C. Wells
George H. Fuller
William Sibbett
Alfred Hunt
Henry L. Bowyer
Richard Swain (*died, replaced by* T. Collinson)

*1890*
S.H. Armstrong *mayor*
Alfred Hunt
Thomas Collinson
James Dollar
William Sibbett
Henry L. Bowyer
Josiah Pratt

*1891*
Walter W. Kinsey *mayor*
H.L. Bowyer
Alfred Hunt
Joseph Cooper
Frederick Merrill
William Sibbett
Charles W. Diggle
Josiah Pratt
James D. Shier (*June*)
John Reid

*1892*
James Dollar *mayor*
Josiah Pratt
John W.B. Topp
Moses Dickie
Joseph Cooper
James D. Shier
John Reid
William Webster
Alfred Hunt
Thomas Perry

*1893*
Alfred Hunt *mayor*
Josiah Pratt
David Daniels
Moses Dickie
Joseph Cooper
James D. Shier
George R. Firth
Isaac B. Aulph

*1894*
Alfred Hunt *mayor*
David Daniels
Moses Dickie
Joseph Cooper
James D. Shier
George R. Firth
Isaac B. Aulph
William Webster
Wm. Simmons
Henry Bowyer
Singleton Brown

*1895*
Alfred Hunt *mayor*
William Ross
Moses Dickie
James H. Copeland
Angus McLeod
Josiah Pratt
Isaac B. Aulph
Wm. Simmons
Henry Bowyer
Singleton Brown
Thomas Hunt
John Leishman

*1896*
Singleton Brown *mayor*
Alfred Hunt
J.D. Shier
James Calvert
Wm. Webster
James L. Fenn
A.A. Mahaffy
Isaac Aulph
Richard W. Ryan
Henry Bowyer

*1897*
Singleton Brown *mayor*
William Sibbett
Alfred Hunt
James Copeland
Henry Bowyer
Isaac Aulph
R.W. Ryan
J.D. Shier
Thomas Hunt
Robert Ford

*1898*
Singleton Brown *mayor*
William Sibbett
Alfred Hunt
Isaac Aulph
J.D. Shier
Thomas Hunt
John Thomson
Wm. Simmons
John Bailey
Robert Howard

*1899*
John Thomson *mayor*
Peter Hutchison
J.D. Shier
I.B. Aulph
Angus McLeod
John Bailey
William Fraser

*1900*
John Thomson *mayor*
Peter Hutchison
Peter Smith
I.B. Aulph
A. McLeod
J.D. Shier
John M. McMillan

*1901*
John Thomson *mayor*
I.B. Aulph
H.J. Bird
P. Hutchison
H. Bowyer
A. McLeod
J.M. McMillan

*1902*
James. D. Shier *mayor*
John Thomson
A. McLeod
O.M. Arnold
G.H.O. Thomas
I.B. Aulph
H. Bowyer

*1903*
J.D. Shier *mayor*
G.H.O. Thomas
John Thomson
P. Hutchison
H.J. Bird
H. Bowyer
Peter A. Smith

*1904*
Peter A. Smith *mayor*
G.H.O. Thomas
T.J. Anderson
H.J. Bird
Daniel S. Sweetman
J.D. Shier
Thomas Hunt

*1905*
Peter Smith *mayor*
I.B. Aulph
H. Bowyer
S. Armstrong
J. McMillan
J. Thomson
D.S. Sweetman

*1906*
Peter Smith *mayor*
John Thomson
Geo. W. Ecclestone
G.H.O. Thomas
S.H. Armstrong
H.J. Bird
Fred Sander

*1907*
S.H. Armstrong *mayor*
A.E. Mundy
P.Hutchison
H.O. Appleby
H.J. Bird
R.H. Thompson
F. Sander

*1908*
S.H. Armstrong *mayor*
John Thomson
T.J. Anderson
T.J. Woods
P.A. Smith
R.H. Thompson
G.H.O. Thomas

*1909*
S.H. Armstrong *mayor*
Wm. McNeice
T. Anderson
H.S. Bowyer
P.A. Smith
R.H. Thompson
Thos. E. Godson

*1910*
S.H. Armstrong *mayor*
P.A. Smith
P. Hutchison
Thos. Godson
J. Whitten
H. Bowyer
Wm. C. Denniss

*1911*
P. Hutchison *mayor*
Geo. Thomas
Thos. Godson
James Whitten
W.S. Ferguson
W. J. Kirk
W.C. Denniss

*1912*
Geo. W. Ecclestone *mayor*
Geo. Tennant
James Whitten
W.J. Kirk
R.A. Lawson
Alex Walker
J. Myers

*1913*
G.W. Ecclestone *mayor*
Geo. Tennant
J. Whitten
J.G. Myers
W.J. Kirk
Joseph Caisse
Alex Walker

*1914*
Peter A. Smith *mayor*
G.W. Ecclestone
Geo. H.O. Thomas
Geo. Tennant, W.L.P.
JohnThomson
George Parlett
William Lowe

*1915*
Peter A. Smith *mayor*
G.H.O. Thomas
Wm. Lowe
G.W. Ecclestone
Geo. Parlett
Alex Walker

*1916*
G.H.O. Thomas *mayor*
Ross
A. Walker
A. Wattie
Elliot
F. Warne
P.P. Campbell

*1917*
G.H.O. Thomas *mayor*
Ross
A. Walker
A. Wattie
Elliott
F. Warne
Peter Campbell

*1918*
Alex Walker *mayor*
A. Wattie
Morris
Ross
Albert E. Fawcett
Joseph G. Myers
F. Warne

*1919*
Jos. G. Myers *mayor*
Ross
A.E. Fawcett
Morris
Higgins
A. Wattie
F. Warne

*1920*
A. Wattie *mayor*
Higgins
A.E. Fawcett
D. Hodgson
F. Warne
A. Walker
G.W. Boyer

*1921*
A. Wattie *mayor*
Higgins
A.E. Fawcett
D. Hodgson
F.P. Warne
A. Walker
G.W. Boyer

*1922*
Peter A. Smith *mayor*
D. Hodgson
J. Reid
A.E. Fawcett
G. Gibson
Geo. Boyer
F.P. Warne

*1923*
Henry J. Bird Jr. *mayor*
J.W. Reid
Geo. Gibson
D. Hodgson
G.W. Boyer
F.P. Warne
A.E. Fawcett

*1924*
Henry J. Bird Jr. *mayor*
J.W. Reid
Geo. Gibson
G.W. Boyer
A.E. Fawcett
Chas. Bailey
D. Hodgson

*1925*
G.W. Boyer *mayor*
Chas. Bailey
A. Gavin
Geo. Gibson
J. Reid
Edward Speers
D. Hodgson
G.H.O. Thomas

*G.H.O. Thomas served on Bracebridge Council for 15 years, 6 of them as mayor.* COURTESY OF BRENDA COX

*1926*
G.H.O. Thomas *mayor*
Chas. Bailey
A. Gavin
Geo. Gibson
J.K. Shier
Ed Speers
D. Hodgson

*1927*
G.H.O. Thomas *mayor*
George Marshall
A. Gavin
Geo. Gibson
J. K. Shicr
W. Richards
D. Hodgson

*1928*
G.H.O. Thomas *mayor*
George Marshall
A. Gavin
Geo. Gibson
J.K. Shier
W. Richards
D. Hodgson

*1929*
G.H.O. Thomas *mayor*
G.Marshall
J.H. Burton
Geo. Gibson
Dr. A.F. Bastedo
W. Richards
D. Hodgson

*1930*
Geo. Gibson *mayor*
Elwood Foster
T.A. Hewitt
D. Hodgson
G. Marshall
W. Richards
Wm. Towns

*1931*
Geo. Gibson *mayor*
A.F. Bastedo
T.A. Hewitt
D.T. Hodgson
G.C. Marshall
W. Richards
Wm. Towns

*1932*
Wilbert Richards *mayor*
A.F. Bastedo
Geo. Gibson
D.T. Hodgson
T.A. Hewitt
L.H. Simmons
Herbert Rawson

*1933*
Wilbert Richards *mayor*
A.F. Bastedo
Geo. Gibson
D.T. Hodgson
T.A. Hewitt
Lyndon
Herbert Rawson

*1934*
Wilbert Richards *mayor*
A.F. Bastedo
Geo. Gibson
D.T. Hodgson
Hines
R.A. Whaley
Herbert Rawson

*1935*
Wilbert Richards *mayor*
A.F. Bastedo
Geo. Gibson
D.T. Hodgson
Hines
R.A. Whaley

*1936*
Wilbert Richards *mayor*
A.F. Bastedo
Eccelstone
W. Hare
B. McBride
Hines
Hutchinson

*1937*
B. McBride *mayor*
A.F. Bastedo
Ecclestone
W.E. Hunt
E.A. Whitten
W.K. Hare
Hutchinson

*1938*
B. McBride *mayor*
A.F. Bastedo
Ecclestone
W.E. Hunt
E.A. Whitten
W. Hare
DeLarge

*1939*
B. McBride *mayor*
A.F. Bastedo
H.G. Parlett
W.E. Hunt
E.A. Whitten
W. Hare
DeLarge

*1940*
B. McBride *mayor*
A.F. Bastedo
H.G. Parlett
W.E. Hunt
E.A. Whitten
W.K. Hare
W.A. Shier

*1941*
B. McBride *mayor*
A.F. Bastedo
H.G. Parlett
W.E. Hunt
W.A. Shier
Waite
Hammond

*1942*
E.A. Whitten *mayor*
W.A. Shier
Pierce
J.R. Frowe
M.P. McKay
Hammond
Waite

*1943*
E.A. Whitten *mayor*
A.R. Shier
Pierce
J.R. Frowe
M.P. McKay
Hammond
Waite

*1944*
E.A. Whitten *mayor*
A.R. Shier
J.A. Hutchinson
J.R. Frowe
M.P. McKay
Earl Dunn
W.J.A. Brown

*1945*
E.A. Whitten *mayor*
A.R. Shier
J.A. Hutchinson
J.R. Frowe
Dr. L.N. Ryan
G.H. Hammond
W.J.A. Brown

*1946*
Dr. A.F. Bastedo *mayor*
P.M.G. Thomas
W.J.A. Brown
R.E. Foreman
Dr. L.N. Ryan
B.B. Bell
A.R. Shier

*1947*
Dr. A.F. Bastedo *mayor*
P.M.G. Thomas
W.J.A. Brown
W.B. Paterson
Dr. L.N. Ryan
Bert Bell
A.R. Shier

1948
Dr. A.F. Bastedo *mayor*
P.M.G. Thomas
W.J.A. Brown
R.E. Foreman
Dr. L.N. Ryan
Bert Bell
A.R. Shier

1949
Dr. A.F. Bastedo *mayor*
P.M.G. Thomas
W.J.A. Brown
William B. Paterson
Dr. L.N. Ryan
Bert Bell
A.R. Shier

*1950*
Dr. L.N. Ryan *mayor*
P.M.G. Thomas
N.A. Goltz
W.B. Paterson
A. MacIver
Bert Bell
W.L. Reynolds

*1951*
Dr. L.N. Ryan *mayor*
H.C. Frowe
A MacIver
W.L. Reynolds
Dr. R.J. Dodds
Bert Bell

*1952*
Dr. L.N. Ryan *mayor*
N.A. Goltz
H.C. Frowe
R.E. Jeffries
Phillip Stone
Dr. R.J. Dodds
Bert B. Bell

*1953*
Dr. L.N. Ryan *mayor*
A. Hunt
R.E. Jeffries
Phillip Stone
E. Reid
D.S. Wells
N.A. Goltz

*1954*
Nelson A. Goltz *mayor*
N. Lyle Cathcart
Dr. R.J. Dodds
R.E. Jeffries
Austin Hunt
E.W. Reid
D.S. Wells

*1955*
Nelson A. Goltz *mayor*
Lyle Cathcart
Dr. R.J. Dodds
R.E. Jeffries
J.G. MacKinnon
E.W. Reid
D.S. Wells

*1956*
Glen S. Coates *mayor*
Lyle Cathcart
Dr. R.J. Dodds
Wm. Raaflaub
E.W. Reid
D.S. Wells
J.G. MacKinnon

*1957*
Glen S. Coates *mayor*
Lyle Cathcart
D.S. Wells
Wm. Raaflaub
K.E Downey
H.E.S. Sugg

*1958*
Glen S. Coates *mayor*
Lyle Cathcart
Wm. Raaflaub
Geo. Parlett
H.E.S. Sugg

*1959*
E.W. Reid *mayor*
L. Cathcart
H.E.S. Sugg
L.H. Specht
Dr. R.J. Dodds
Wm. Raaflaub
George Parlett

*1960*
E.W. Reid *mayor*
L. Cathcart
H.E.S. Sugg
L.H. Specht
Wm. Raaflaub
George Parlett
Dr. L. Black

*1961*
E.W. Reid *mayor*
Dr. R.J. Dodds
H.E.S. Sugg
L. Specht
Wm. Raaflaub
George Parlett

*1962*
E.W. Reid *mayor*
Dr. W.L. Black
H.E.S. Sugg
L. Specht
Dr. R.J. Dodds
Wm. Raaflaub
Geoff Waite

*1963*
George A. Parlett *mayor*
Lorne Purdy
Carl Sander
James Stevenson
Dr. L. Black
Geoff Waite

*1964*
George A. Parlett *mayor*
Lorne Purdy
Carl Sander
J. Stevenson
Lyle Cathcart
Geoff Waite
Wm. Raaflaub

*1965*
George A. Parlett *mayor*
Wm. Raaflaub
Norman Harkness
J. Stevenson
Geoff Waite
Lyle Cathcart
Carl Sander

*1966*
George A. Parlett *mayor*
S.J. Coad
N. Harkness
J. Stevenson
Geoff Waite
Lyle Cathcart
Carl Sander

*1967*
George A. Parlett *mayor*
S. Coad
N. Harkness
Geoff Waite
Duane Miller
Frank McNabb
Mrs. Kay Beers

*1968*
George A. Parlett *mayor*
Ted Gervais
N. Harkness
Duane Miller
F. McNabb
Kay Beers
Frank Miller

*1969*
George A. Parlett *mayor*
Ted Gervais
Norman Harkness
Duane Miller
Frank McNabb
Geoff Waite
Frank Miller

*1970*
George A. Parlett *mayor*
Carl Sander
Norman Harkness
Duane Miller
Frank McNabb
Geoff Waite
Frank Miller

*1971-72*
George A. Parlett *mayor*
Norm Harkness
Frank Henry
Carl Sander
James Lang
Dan MacNaughtan
Leo Robinson
Norman Archer
Neil Boyes

*1973-74*
George A. Parlett *mayor*
Norm Harkness
Norman Archer
Neil Boyes
Ralph Melvin
Carl Sander
James Lang
Dan MacNaughtan Sr.
Aubrey Glass

*1975-76*
James D. Lang *mayor*
R.E. Melvin
Frank J. Henry
J. Archie Rintoul
Aubrey Glass
Bruce McPhail
Jim Boyes
Norm Archer
Emily Dworak

*1977-78*
James D. Lang *mayor*
Harold Dawson
Ralph Melvin
Carl Sander
Norman Archer
Aubrey Glass
William Lefler
Russell Crockford
James Boyes

*1979-80*
James D. Lang *mayor*
D.R. MacNaughtan Jr.
Ralph Melvin
Frank Henry
Ross Miller
R. Crockford
Norm Archer
Wm. Lefleur
H. Dawson
James Boyes

*1981-82*
James D. Lang *mayor*
D.R. MacNaughtan
Peter J. Bird
R.E. Melvin
George Hankin
Ross Miller
Harold Dawson
R. Crockford
James Boyes

*1983-85*
James D. Lang *mayor*
R.E. Melvin
Aubrey Glass
J.H. Boyes
D. MacNaughtan
G. Hankin
Wayne Lippert
Patricia Malone
R.M. Conway

*1986-88*
James D. Lang *mayor*
R.E. Melvin
Aubrey Glass
J.H. Boyes
George Brodie
N.Harkness
Nancy Pratt
Katie McCann
Patricia Malone

*1989-91*
James D. Lang *mayor*
Norm Harkness
Aubrey Glass
Pat Malone
James Boyes
George Brodie
Katie McCann
Heather Coupland
Scott Northmore

*1992-94*
James D. Lang *mayor*
J.H. Boyes
George Brodie
Dan Brooks
H. Coupland
Bill Glennie
Dave Hetherington
Katie McCann
Scott Northmore

*1995-97*
A. Russ Black *mayor*
Scott N. Northmore
George Brodie
John Shier
H. Coupland
Barbara McMurray
Edith J. Nichols
Allen G. Taylor
Barry Young

*1998-2000*
Scott Northmore *mayor*
Heather Coupland
Bill Glennie
John Kelly
Allen G. Taylor
Edith J. Nichols
Barry Young
Jerry Fox
Barbara McMurray

*Town Clerks*

James Boyer 1875-1899
Alexander Salmon 1899-1936
Wilbert Richards 1936-67
Kenneth Veitch 1967-96
Murray Clarke 1996-

# BIBLIOGRAPHY

*The list below includes sources containing information about Bracebridge and the history of Muskoka affecting the town. Additional material may be found in the Muskoka Collection and vertical files at the Bracebridge Public Library – for instance, copies of numerous articles that have appeared in local newspapers and other publications.*

Boyer, E. Victoria. *Memories of Bracebridge: A Pictorial History of Some of the Homes of Early Business-Men in the Bracebridge Community...* Bracebridge: Herald-Gazette Press, 1975

Boyer, George W. *Early Days in Muskoka*. Bracebridge: Herald-Gazette Press, 1970.

Boyer, Robert J. *Early Exploration and Surveying of Muskoka District*. Bracebridge: Herald-Gazette Press, 1979.

——. *Fifty Years of Service Above Self in Our Town: Rotary Club of Bracebridge.* Bracebridge: Muskoka Publications Ltd., 1986.

——. *A Good Town Grew Here*. Bracebridge: Herald-Gazette Press, 1975.

——. *One Hundred Years: Bracebridge United Church*. Bracebridge: Herald-Gazette Press, 1961.

——. *Pictorial History of Woodchester Villa*. Bracebridge Historical Society, 1982.

——. *Power from Water*. Bracebridge Hydro Commission, 1994.

*Bracebridge Horticultural Society History 1932-82*. Bracebridge, 1982.

Conway, Abbott. *A History of Beardmore and Company Limited and Anglo Canadian Leather Company Limited*. Canada Packers Inc., 1990.

*Robert J. Boyer, author of* A Good Town Grew Here *and several other books. A former newspaper editor and publisher, and Muskoka's MPP 1955-71, he is descended from Bracebridge pioneer families and has meticulously chronicled many aspects of Bracebridge and Muskoka history.* R.J. BOYER COLLECTION


Conwell, James. *Muskoka and Her People*. Toronto, 1933.

Denniss, Gary. *A Brief History of Churches in Muskoka*. Bracebridge, 1997.

——. *A Brief History of the Schools in Muskoka*. Bracebridge: Herald-Gazette Press, 1972.

——. *Free Methodist Hill: A Centennial History 1879-1979*.

——. *Macaulay Township in Days Gone By*. Bracebridge: Herald-Gazette Press, 1970.

Duke, A.H., and W.M Gray. *The Boatbuilders of Muskoka*. Toronto: W.M. Gray & Co., 1985.

Fraser, L.R. *History of Muskoka*. Bracebridge, 1946.

Hamilton, W.E., John Rogers, and Seymour Penson. *Guidebook and Atlas of Muskoka and Parry Sound Districts*. Toronto, 1879.

Long, Gary. *This River the Muskoka*. Erin: Boston Mills Press, 1989.

McFarland, Mary. *Bracebridge and Muskoka Lakes Secondary School*: Bracebridge: Herald-Gazette Press, 1975.

McMurray, Thomas. *The Free Grant Lands of Canada, from Practical Experience of Bush Farming in the Free Grant Districts of Muskoka and Parry Sound*. Bracebridge, 1871.

Murray, Florence B., ed. *Muskoka and Haliburton, 1615-1875: A Collection of Documents*. Toronto: Champlain Society; University of Toronto Press, 1963.

Petry, Bob. *Bracebridge: An Early Settlement in Muskoka*. Bracebridge, 1999.

Pryke, Susan. *Explore Muskoka*. Erin: Boston Mills Press, 1987. Revised edition 1999.

——. *Explore Muskoka Lakes*. Erin: Boston Mills Press, 1990.

Scott, Harley E. *Tales of Muskoka Steamboats*. Bracebridge: Herald-Gazette Press, 1969.

Scovell, Beatrice. *The Muskoka Story*. [c.1980]

Smith, Gail. "Bird's Woollen Mill." In *An Introduction to the History of Muskoka*. Muskoka Board of Education, 1975.

Tatley, Richard. *The Steamboat Era in the Muskokas*. Vols. 1 & 2. Erin: Boston Mills Press, 1983, 1984.

Thomas, G.H.O. *Bracebridge in 1884*. Bracebridge, 1934.

Thomas, Redmond. *Reminiscences, Bracebridge, Muskoka*. Bracebridge: Herald-Gazette Press, 1969.

Thomson, Rev. James A. *A Brief Pictorial History of Knox Presbyterian Church, Bracebridge*. Bracebridge, 1975.

# INDEX

*The index comprises two sections, the General Index, and beginning on page 376, the Index of Family Names, each separately alphabetized. Every effort has been made to include all family names encountered in the text; any omissions are inadvertent. In the General Index, many headings are listed as italicized sub-entries under general categories such as churches, education, sports, etc.,which are in* SMALL CAPS. *The category* TOWN *includes many items relating to municipal matters.*

## GENERAL INDEX

## INDEX OF FAMILY NAMES

*A view of Bracebridge Bay in the early 1900s when the steamboat wharf was still near the outlet, at the foot of Dill Street. The large wooden building in the background is the water-powered gristmill, originally constructed in the 1860s with traditional millstones to grind grain from pioneer farms. In the 1890s modern roller-mill machinery replaced the stones, allowing for volume production of the pure white flour increasingly favoured by consumers. Access was via Mill Street on the east side of the falls (now a walking trail). The mill burned in 1909. On the hilltop directly above the right end of the mill is Woodchester Villa.* COURTESY OF THE BRACEBRIDGE PUBLIC LIBRARY

*J.D. Shier built this state-of-the-art steam sawmill in 1898 on the south branch of the Muskoka River, by the forks, replacing his earlier mill which burned. Shier had acquired vast pine timber limits in the headwaters of the river east of Lake of Bays. By 1900 he was logging in Algonquin Park and floating his logs more than 130 kilometres down to Bracebridge. The new mill was one of the largest in Muskoka. Sawn lumber was shipped out by rail – a 1-kilometre spur ran from the main line down the ravine between Shier and Young streets. The diamond-shaped window was a common functional adornment on otherwise utilitarian mill buildings of the era.* COURTESY OF THE TOWN OF BRACEBRIDGE

*An aerial view of downtown Bracebridge and the falls about 1960, at the mid-point of the time period covered in* A Good Town Continues. *At the time this area was still the physical and commercial heart of the town, and the Bird Woollen Mill (right), closed but still standing, provided a tangible link to one of the early industries that harnessed the power of the falls and helped spur early growth. Although this core is no longer the dominant business area that it was once, it still defines Bracebridge in the minds of many who grew up in town.* COURTESY OF THE TOWN OF BRACEBRIDGE